| **Conditional Proof (CP)** | **Indirect Proof (IP)** |
|---|---|

|  |  |
|---|---|
| /∴ q ⊃ r | /∴ q |
| ┌→ p | ┌→ p |
| │  q    CP, /∴ r | │  ~ q    IP |
| │  • | │  • |
| │  • | │  • |
| │  • | │  • |
| └  r | └  r • ~ r |
| /∴ q ⊃ r | /∴  q |

where (1) the conclusion of an argument is either a hypothetical or logically equivalent to a hypothetical, and (2) if '$\beta$' is an individual variable appearing at 'q' then it cannot appear free in an assumption within whose scope '$\Phi\beta$' lies.

where 'r • ~ r' represents any contradiction.

✔ KU-573-458

# TRUTH TREE RULES

### Truth-Functional Logic

~ ~ p ✓
|
p

**Denied Negation (DN)**

~ (p • q) ✓
╱╲
~ p    ~ q

**Denied Conjunction (DC)**

p • q ✓
|
p
q

**Conjunction (C)**

p ≡ q ✓
╱╲
p    ~ p
q    ~ q

**Material Equivalence (ME)**

p ∨ q ✓
╱╲
p    q

**Inclusive Disjunction (ID)**

~ (p ∨ q) ✓
|
~ p
~ q

**Denied Inclusive Disjunction (DID)**

p △ q ✓
╱╲
p      q
~ q    ~ p

**Exclusive Disjunction (ED)**

~ (p △ q) ✓
╱╲
p    ~ p
q    ~ q

**Denied Exclusive Disjunction (DED)**

p ⊃ q ✓
╱╲
~ p    q

**Material Implication (MI)**

~ (p ⊃ q) ✓
|
p
~ p

**Denied Material Implication (DMI)**

~ (p ≡ q) ✓
╱╲
p      q
~ q    ~ p

**Denied Material Equivalence (DME)**

# LOGIC AND RATIONAL THOUGHT

**Frank R. Harrison, III**

*University of Georgia*

**WEST PUBLISHING COMPANY**
*St. Paul      New York      Los Angeles      San Francisco*

UNIVERSITY OF BRISTOL
Department of Philosophy

9 Woodland Road
Bristol
BS8 1TB

Copyediting and Text Design: Custom Editorial Productions, Inc.
Cover Design: Paul Konsterlie
Cover Art: *Cosmos and Maroon,* Lamar Dodd. Reprinted with permission.

COPYRIGHT © 1992    By WEST PUBLISHING COMPANY
                    50 W. Kellogg Boulevard
                    P.O. Box 64526
                    St. Paul, MN 55164-0526

All rights reserved

Printed in the United States of America

99  98  97  96  95  94  93  92          8  7  6  5  4  3  2  1  0

**Library of Congress Cataloging-in-Publication Data**

Harrison, Frank R., 1935–

    Logic and rational thought / Frank R. Harrison, III.
      p.    cm.
    Includes index.
    ISBN 0-314-66814-4
    1.  Logic.   2.  Critical thinking.   I.  Title
  BC108.H237   1992
160—dc20                                                        90-20087
                                                                CIP

*In profound appreciation,*
Logic and Rational Thought
*is dedicated to*
*my mother*
*Annye Mae Blackwelder Harrison*
*and my father*
*Frank Russell Harrison, Jr.*

A Chinese Sage of the distant past was once asked by his disciples what he would do first if he were given power to set right the affairs of the country. He answered: "I should certainly see to it that language is used correctly." The disciples looked perplexed. "Surely," they said, "this is a trivial matter. Why should you deem it to be important?" And the master replied: "If language is not used correctly, then what is said is not what is meant; if what is said is not what is meant, then what ought to be done remains undone; if this remains undone, morals and art will be corrupted; if morals and art are corrupted, justice will go astray; if justice goes astray, then people will stand about in helpless confusion."

—*Confucius*

# CONTENTS

# PREFACE FOR THE TEACHER

Logic and rational thought are among the most important subjects that can be taught and taken in any educational environment. The information learned and skills mastered are necessary for anything beyond rote memorization, robot-like applications of manual tasks, and expressions of merely personal beliefs. Organizing information, understanding issues, making judgements, providing evidence, and drawing conclusions require using logic and rational thought. The question is not whether logic and rational thought are to be used in any of these activities, but how well or poorly are they used. And insofar as being able to make judgments, provide evidence, understand issues, organize information, and draw conclusions are necessary ingredients in leading a happy and productive life, logic and rational thought have an essential bearing on the possible happiness and productivity of any individual.

## EXAMPLES, EXERCISES, AND SOFTWARE

Since the study of logic and rational thought is as much the mastery of skills as it is the understanding of principles, there are over 2500 examples and exercises in this book providing opportunities for the student to "do" logic and rational thinking. Answers for odd numbered exercises are found at the back of the text. Even more exercises are provided with the version of the software package, *The LogicWorks*, customized by me for *Logic and Rational Thought*. Further exercises for each chapter of the book, not found in the text or *The LogicWorks*, are provided by Eric Kraemer. These can be used in various ways—to create tests, for instance. Also accompanying the book is a teacher's manual, *Solutions and Suggestions* which contains answers to all of the even numbered exercises in the text. Continuing to remind the student of the universal scope of logic and rational thought, the examples and exercises in each of these teaching aids draw upon a wide range of topics—acid rock to quantum mechanics; social problems to art history; the stock market to religion.

*The LogicWorks* is powerful software that can be of enormous help to both you and the student. Many of the exercises in *Logic and Rational Thought* are found in this program. Thus you can assign the student to work these exercises on the computer. When a mistake is made, the program aids the student in discovering the correct answer. Student work can be graded and the grades recorded for you. You are also informed of how much time the student spent at the computer in working the assigned exercises. The program even allows you to create your own exercises and quizzes to be done by the student outside of the classroom. Work at the computer frees class time for other topics that you might wish to discuss.

Great flexibility is provided in the various types of exercises found in *Logic and Rational Thought*. In Chapters 2–12 you will discover several groups of exercises at the end of a section. Using one or more of these groups, you can stress purely formal aspects of the study of logic, the application of logic to language and the skills needed in translation into logical notation, or a combination. Characteristically the exercises found in any group in the book are ordered from easiest to most difficult. In a typical group of fifteen exercises, the first five are "easy," the next five are "moderate," and the last five are "difficult."

A number of exercises ask the students to provide their own opinions about different topics, to justify their opinions, and to share this work with their classmates. These sorts of exercises give you an opportunity to guide the thinking of students as they create their own arguments, definitions, and the like. Even in larger classes the students can be encouraged to interact with one another outside of the classroom or lecture hall to work with available software, while you assign creative work at the computer with the interacting program, *The LogicWorks*.

## STRATEGIES

Learning logic can be compared with learning games such as backgammon or football. One advantage of this comparison is that it can help students overcome fears of anything that looks "different," and especially if it reminds them of mathematics. Another advantage is that this comparison provides a natural introduction of the notion of *strategy* or *heuristic* into the teaching of logic and rational thought. Throughout *Logic and Rational Thought* strategies are introduced to guide students in the appropriate application of the rules they learn. Often students, when presented with a set of rules to apply in different exercises, have little grasp of when or how to use these rules. These students are almost certain to become frustrated and do poorly. Students typically find a set of strategies very useful to guide their applications of rules in concrete situations. No one set of game strategies ever *guarantees* success in every situation. The strategies in this book are only guides for doing things appropriately. You can develop and introduce more, and different, ones. While insight is always required at some level or another, and it is this insight that separates truly superior "players" from others, nonetheless properly constructed strategies will help a poor "player" become better, and perhaps even good.

## FOOTNOTES AND NEW TERMS

You will find useful footnotes throughout this book. Frequently these relate to the topic being discussed in the text to other topics. These footnotes provide you with opportunities to explore new subjects while reminding students that they are learning a subject and acquiring skills that go far beyond the boundaries of one course offered in a particular department.

When new terms are introduced, they are set off on a page and immediately defined. Such terms are always accompanied by illustrative examples. At the end of the chapter there is a list in which these new terms are again set forth with their definitions. The "Review of New Terms" provides a convenient place for the student to examine the more fundamental points of a chapter before studying the chapter and in reviewing it. There is some duplication of new terms in a few chapters so that different chapters can be used and others omitted without loss of essential information.

## ORGANIZATION

You, the teacher, are by far the most important factor for students in coming to learn and practice logic and rational thought. A lively and well-versed teacher can turn the most unlikely students into avid learners, who enjoy and excel in what they do. But even the best teachers can use aids in their important work. *Logic and Rational Thought* is offered as a tool to help you teach logic and rational thought better within a wide range of academic environments and pedagogical goals.

*Logic and Rational Thought* is written with an eye to flexibility in constructing various one term courses in contemporary logic, traditional logic, and logic and fallacies. Following are some general *suggestions* concerning how such courses might be constructed. These are *general* suggestions because each teacher has different needs influenced by personal interests, departmental assignments, the institution in which a course is taught, and the students expected to take that course. Here are several "flow charts," each indicating a possible course developed using *Logic and Rational Thought.* You will, no doubt, think of more.

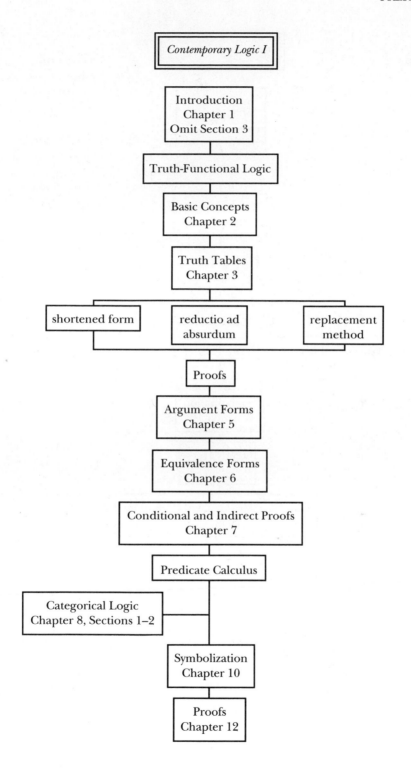

*Contemporary Logic I*

Introduction
Chapter 1
Omit Section 3

Truth-Functional Logic

Basic Concepts
Chapter 2

Truth Tables
Chapter 3

shortened form

reductio ad
absurdum

replacement
method

Proofs

Argument Forms
Chapter 5

Equivalence Forms
Chapter 6

Conditional and Indirect Proofs
Chapter 7

Predicate Calculus

Categorical Logic
Chapter 8, Sections 1–2

Symbolization
Chapter 10

Proofs
Chapter 12

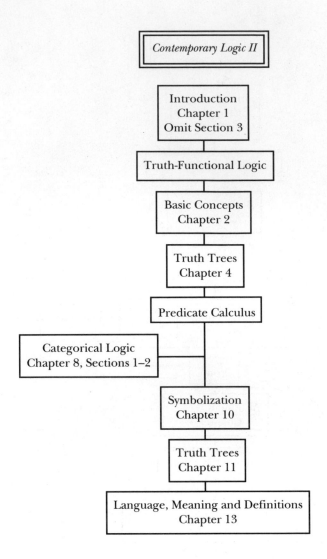

Contemporary Logic II

Introduction
Chapter 1
Omit Section 3

Truth-Functional Logic

Basic Concepts
Chapter 2

Truth Trees
Chapter 4

Predicate Calculus

Categorical Logic
Chapter 8, Sections 1–2

Symbolization
Chapter 10

Truth Trees
Chapter 11

Language, Meaning and Definitions
Chapter 13

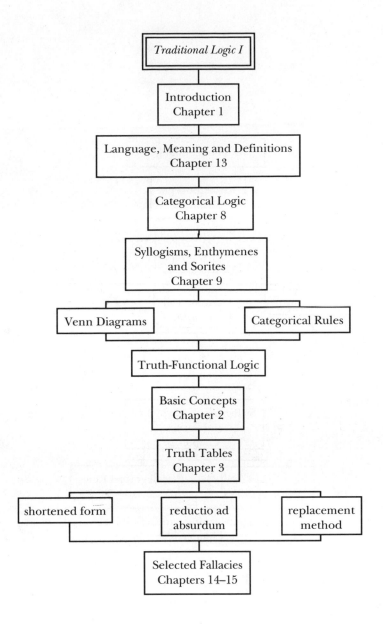

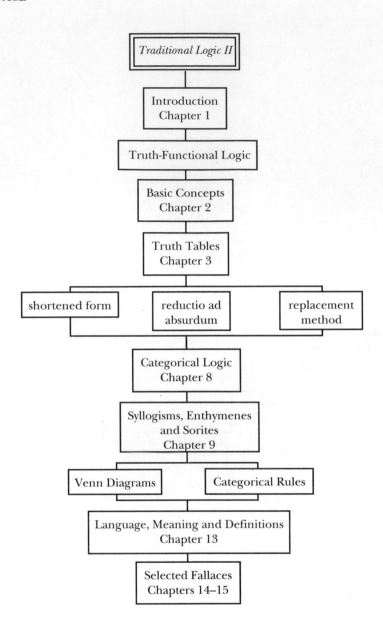

*Traditional Logic II*

Introduction
Chapter 1

Truth-Functional Logic

Basic Concepts
Chapter 2

Truth Tables
Chapter 3

| shortened form | reductio ad absurdum | replacement method |

Categorical Logic
Chapter 8

Syllogisms, Enthymenes
and Sorites
Chapter 9

| Venn Diagrams | Categorical Rules |

Language, Meaning and Definitions
Chapter 13

Selected Fallaces
Chapters 14–15

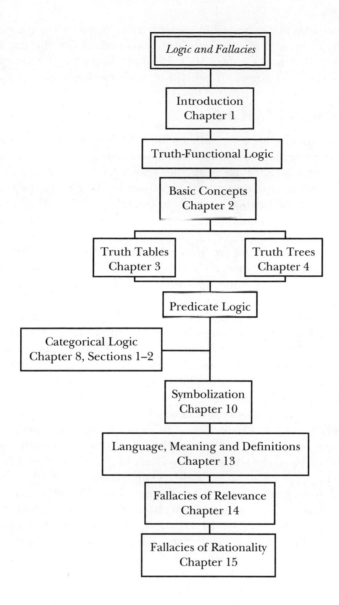

Chapter 1 introduces general issues common to contemporary logic, traditional logic, and rational thought while also preparing the student for more specific topics found in *Logic and Rational Thought*. Chapter 2 develops truth-functional operators by examining how the correct use of many English expressions indicates them. In doing so, the chapter stresses skills helpful in the careful reading and writing of English. Various linguistic weaknesses become apparent when students attempt to symbolize even simple statements. So studying Chapter 2 and working through its many exercises helps students to master better the uses of English. And it is precisely this mastery that is demanded in moving from English into the notation of logic required in Chapter 2. Similar considerations underscore the importance of Chapter 8, Sections 1–2, and Chapter 10. Achieving a higher level of linguistic proficiency is one of the chief goals and benefits of studying this book.

## CONTEMPORARY LOGIC

A course in contemporary logic typically includes both truth-functional and predicate logic. Having presented Chapters 1 and 2, you can decide which of the following chapters, 2–7 or 10–12, to use in further constructing a course in contemporary logic. In presenting truth-functional logic, you might wish to use truth tables, truth trees, or natural deduction methods to establish validity. *Logic and Rational Thought* provides abundant materials for any of these approaches, or combinations of them.

If a *truth table* approach is taken, after Chapters 1 and 2 move to Chapter 3. There you will find the shortened form truth table method, the *reductio ad absurdum*, and the replacement method. It is not likely that all three methods will be introduced to students, although each is preferable to the others in some situations. If you prefer using *truth trees*, then move to Chapter 4. Truth tree rules are more easily grasped by the student who has learned the rules governing the logical operators introduced in Chapter 2. Chapter 11 presents truth trees for predicate logic, so you can move directly from Chapter 4 to Chapters 10 and 11. Before going to Chapters 10 and 11, however, you might find it helpful to introduce the student to Chapter 8, Sections 1–2.

Using a *natural deduction* approach instead of truth tables or truth trees, you can go from Chapters 1 and 2 to Chapters 5–7. In these chapters, argument forms and equivalence forms are introduced separately. The rules are introduced in small groups of two or three so the student is less likely to be overwhelmed by a mass of rules to learn and apply all at once. Students can master a relatively small area of information and skills, transporting this to the next level of complexity.

Having presented truth functional logic, a course in contemporary logic can begin predicate logic with Chapter 10. Whether you wish to use truth trees or natural deduction in developing predicate logic, Chapter 10 is important. One of the typical problems students have in learning predicate logic is moving from English into logical notation. Chapter 10 addresses this problem in a step by step procedure, going from simple examples to complex ones. Once more, before moving to Chapter 10, you could introduce Chapter 8, Sections 1–2.

Categorical logic can be a useful pedagogical tool in introducing predicate logic. This is one reason why Chapters 8 and 9 follow truth-functional logic and precede predicate logic, unlike the ordering of books following a more historical development of logic. Even in a course devoted to contemporary logic, you might find parts of Chapters 8 and 9 useful in helping students to master translation, develop a comprehension of the internal relations of non-compound statements, and visualize these relations through uses of Venn diagrams. However, Chapter 12 is developed independently of Chapters 8 and 9, as is Chapter 11. You do not need to cover the material in Chapters 8 and 9 to introduce predicate logic.

# TRADITIONAL LOGIC

You might wish to present a more traditional course in logic instead of stressing only contemporary logic. Typically studied in such courses are categorical logic and truth-functional logic. Here Chapter 1 is important as a springboard for the students. In many traditional logic courses, categorical logic is introduced before truth-functional logic. If you wish to follow this path, Chapters 8 and 9 can be taken up after Chapter 1. Notice that Chapter 9 permits you to develop categorical logic in terms of Venn diagrams or rules of syllogistic validity.

Beginning with truth-functional logic is another way of developing a course in traditional logic. Following this path, students are introduced to relations that can hold between statements, along with the notion of a proof, before they are introduced to the concept of classes and the relations that can hold between them. If this procedure is adopted, you can first develop truth-functional logic in terms of truth tables, truth trees, or natural deduction. Then, you would introduce Chapters 8 and 9. The student now appreciates how categorical logic can deal with validity and invalidity in ways beyond the scope of truth-functional logic.

Having worked through truth-functional and categorical logic students can then be presented the themes in Chapter 13; namely, language and definitions. In many logic books, the topic of *language* is introduced before more specific subjects are discussed. *Logic and Rational Thought* breaks with this tradition. Here the view is adopted that students profit more from general discussions of language *after* they have been introduced to formal structure and the conditions under which statements count as true or false. The topic of definitions, developed in Chapter 13, also appears better discussed after students have mastered the notions of *premises*, *conclusions*, and *arguments*. After all, definitions can appear in arguments under the guise of analytic statements or they can be used to clarify important words appearing in premises or conclusions. On the other hand, Chapter 13 is written so that it can be taken up immediately after Chapter 1 if you wish. This would be a more conventional approach to teaching traditional logic.

# LOGIC AND FALLACIES

A third type of course for which *Logic and Rational Thought* is appropriate combines a study of logic and fallacies to create courses in rational thought. There are almost as many opinions of what such a course should contain as there are people teaching them. Nonetheless, today there are global problems raising the need for courses in rational thought. These problems also suggest the content of such courses. For instance, instructors in most disciplines complain that students often cannot read with sufficient comprehension. As an example, they well might not grasp the difference between saying 'If interest rates fall, then the stock market will stabilize', 'The stock market will stabilize only if interest rates fall', and 'Interest rates fall if and only if the stock market stabilizes'. Students would realize that each of these claims is "talking about" interest rates falling and the stock market stabilizing. Yet many students would not understand what relation is suggested to hold between interest rates and the stock market by each claim.

It is repeatedly said that students do not comprehend how sentences are related to one another in descriptions, explanations, and arguments. Given various true statements, students, for example, cannot draw conclusions from those statements or draw wrong ones without being able to grasp why they are wrong. Another complaint is that students frequently are not able to analyze critically what is being presented to them as theses, hypotheses, beliefs, and the like. Courses in rational thought are offered to provide some help in surmounting these, and similar, shortcomings.

Addressing such problems, you might begin with Chapters 1 and 2. Then, selections from Chapters 3 or 4 would be appropriate, followed by selections from Chapters 8 and 9. Both truth tables and truth trees offer visual illustrations of what is going on in a truth-functional argument relating premises to conclusions. Venn diagrams are equally as successful in picturing relations in categorical logic. Moving to Chapter 13, students are introduced to other functions of language necessary to grasp if one is to think rationally. Finally, in Chapters 14 and 15 students are made aware of numerous fallacies, other than formal ones, that typically occur, often unnoticed, in arguments.

## MY INDEBTEDNESS AND APPRECIATION

Many people have been involved in the evolution of *Logic and Rational Thought*. Students at the University of Georgia who have used various sections of manuscript, helped catch errors, made suggestions for improvements, and the like, are legion. Then there are the various readers and reviewers to whom West Publishing Company sent the manuscript at different stages of its development. In particular my sincere thanks goes to Waldo Asp, Normandale Community College; Richard Behling, University of Wisconsin–Eau Claire; Sherry Blum, University of Texas; Henry Carrier, Brevard Community College; Henry Folse, Loyola University; Thomas Foster, Ball State University; Steve Giambrone, University of Southwest Louisiana, James Gould, University of South Florida; Craig Harrison, San Francisco State University; Ronald Houts, California State University–Los Angeles; Hugh Hunt, Kennesaw State College; Fred Johnson, Colorado State University; Charles Kielkopf, Ohio State University; Eric Kraemer, University of Wisconsin–LaCrosse; Jarrett Leplin, University of North Carolina–Greensboro; John Meixner, Central Michigan University; John Nolt, University of Tennessee– Knoxville; David O'Connor, Seton Hall University; Dennis Packard, Brigham Young Univerisity; John Peterson, University of Rhode Island; Robert Redmon, Virginia Commonwealth University; Michael Scanlon, Oregon State University; James Stuart, Bowling Green State University; and Arnold Wilson, University College–University of Cincinatti. The comments of these people were insightful, often profound, and always welcomed.

More particularly, Dr. Tim Lytle of Mississippi State University, Dr. Larry Mayhew of Western Kentucky University, and Dr. John Presto of Winthrop College have all used large parts of this book in their classrooms. These teachers have also made useful suggestions. Special thanks must also go to Mary Goeller Daniel Wyatt, Esq. who took time from her busy law practice and family to read, proof, and comment on *Logic and Rational Thought*. Messrs. Tim Lytle and Karl Haden, former graduate assistants, were untiring in their suggestions for improvement in, and use of, the manuscript. Mr. Steve Martin was my graduate assistant and right-hand man while Chapters 14 and 15 were in the final stage of completion. His was a valuable contribution, especially to the success of the exercises in these chapters. Mr. Mike Thompson, a student and friend, has been of immense help in keeping my software and hardware together. Not only do bugs live in software, monsters inhabit machines.

I wish to thank Mr. Frank Scarpace, president of Image Processing Software, Inc., Madison, Wisconsin, for his fine product, "TURBOFONTS," the software I used in typing all logical notation in the book manuscript and *Solutions and Suggestions.* Also the voice at the other end of the hotline at Image Processing Software, Mr. Michael Thompson, was always most pleasant and helpful.

A truly outstanding artist of our era, Lamar Dodd, offered me one of his paintings, *Cosmos and Maroon,* to use for the cover of this book. I deeply appreciate this extremely kind and generous gesture from my long-time colleague and friend. The noted photographer, Robert Nix, supplied for the printer the transparency of Professor Dodd's painting. Professor Nix also receives my sincere thanks.

Peter Marshall, Executive Editor, and Jane Bacon, Developmental Editor, of West Publishing Company have been supportive, understanding, and unbelievably helpful at every turn in the writing of this book. They are dedicated professionals and genuinely caring human beings in a world where it is difficult to be both. The copyeditor, Catherine Skintik, was insightful and unerring in her painstaking work. I am very appreciative of her efforts.

My wife, Dottie, however, must surely deserve the most understanding and appreciation of all. For she had to live with me during the entire process of writing, rewriting, editing, and on-and-on. It was not easy for Dottie to come home from her job of directing a computer center and hear constantly about logic, fallacies, and rational thinking. I am eternally in her debt—indeed, a happy obligation—for many things. Surely supporting me while writing this book is one of them. And this is to say nothing of the proof-reading, editing, and computer work she did helping me prepare the manuscript.

There are, no doubt, errors still remaining in this book in spite of all the help given me. These are my responsibility. It is a fearful business to write a book, send it out into the world, and realize that there, on a page in front of me, may be a mistake not seen! I hope that you and your students are charitable of such errors, and that you will write to point them out so that they can be corrected in future editions of *Logic and Rational Thought.*

Frank R. Harrison, III
Department of Philosophy
University of Georgia
Athens, Georgia    30602

# LOGIC AND
# RATIONAL THOUGHT

# 1

# STARTING OUT

## 1. WHY BOTHER WITH RATIONAL THOUGHT?

Everyone has beliefs, some of which they assert as statements. Many of these statements are true:

> There are important changes occurring in eastern Europe.
>
> Environmental issues are becoming politically more sensitive.
>
> Murder is the illegal and intentional taking of a human life by another human being.

And others of them are false:

> A person always needs to lie and be deceitful to be successful.
>
> *AIDS* is carried by bacteria through the air.
>
> The only purpose of an education is job training.

Any statement is either true or false, but not both. Commands and questions are neither true nor false. It makes no sense to say that 'Go to your class!' or 'Where do you keep you car keys?' is true or is false. While every statement is either true or false, it might not be known whether a particular statement is true or not. No one knows whether 'There is life similar to human life somewhere in the Universe other than Earth' is true or not. Even so, a *statement* is

**a linguistic entity that is either true or false, but not both.**

A person can take three postures toward any statement. She can accept it as true, reject it as false, or suspend accepting either the truth or falsity of the statement. Of course, the immediate question for a person is which of these stances is appropri-

1

ate. While people usually assert what they believe to be true, there is a great difference between believing that a statement is true and it being true. Because a statement can be true or false when the opposite is believed, it is often appropriate and important to demand reasons for substantiating a claim that a statement is true or is false. It is important, among other reasons, because beliefs expressed in statements often, for good or bad, motivate and guide human actions.

The more important the actions that acceptance of a particular statement might motivate, the more vital it is to require good reasons for accepting that statement as true or as false. If one is going to act in a situation involving abortion, it is important to have some reasons, other than mere belief, for accepting 'Abortion is always morally wrong' or 'Abortion is morally permissable'. For instance, someone could suggest 'Abortion is murder' as a reason for accepting 'Abortion is always morally wrong'. But is this a good reason? What reasons might be offered for accepting 'Abortion is murder'? Imagine this:

> Certainly murder is the unlawful and intentional taking of the life of one human being by another human. And abortion is the intentional taking of the life of a fetus by a human being. Further, a fetus is an unborn, but living, human being.

These claims are presented as reasons for accepting the statement, 'Abortion is murder'. Again one can ask are they good reasons?* A statement is no more justified than the reasons given to support it.

It is in every person's best interest to act as well as possible. To act well, a person needs to determine which action-guiding statements are true, or likely to be true, and which false, or likely to be false. For it seems reasonable to suppose that a person who is acting in accordance with true statements, and not false ones believed to be true, is more likely to reach acceptable goals. Acceptable results are not guaranteed, but they are more likely. Similarly, acting in accordance with false statements believed to be true does not guarantee an unacceptable outcome. However, it seems reasonable to suppose that unacceptable results are more likely to occur.

A fundamental purpose of this book is to introduce and develop techniques connected with analyzing reasons given in the support of statements and how such reasons are related to the statements they are supposed to support. *Rational thought* is, in part,

> **to analyze reasons given for different statements and to determine how these reasons are related in justifying and/or understanding other statements.**

No one is born with the skills necessary for rational thinking. They must be learned and developed through constant practice. There are compelling reasons to do this.

---

* What sorts of reasons are being offered here for accepting 'Abortion is murder'? For instance, is it a factual assertion to say that murder is the unlawful and intentional taking of the life of one human being by another human? Or is this some sort of definition of 'murder'? Is each claim in the above example a definition? If so, can a series of definitions serve as reasons for accepting a claim that might lead to, or even elude, action?

Some of these reasons involve expectations that rational thinking will likely increase the abilities to understand better what is being said, to express oneself more clearly, to distinguish between justified and unjustified beliefs, to see how statements can be related in various ways, and to guard against being duped by those who would attempt to persuade someone to do what is not in his own best interests. Equally important is the ability to protect oneself against self-deception, wishful thinking, and avoidable ignorance. To increase the likelihood of living well, a person ought to demand and seek what is true, both from others and from himself. In those cases where it is unlikely that one will or can find the truth, at least one can look for what is rationally acceptable to help avoid error. The ability to think rationally is helpful in finding the truth and what is rationally acceptable, and in avoiding error.

### EXERCISES

#### Group A:

Do you suppose it is reasonable to assume that acting in accordance with true statements increases the likelihood of, but does not guarantee that, a person will reach desired goals and avoid unpleasant situations? Support your answer.

#### Group B:

List several statements you have heard that you believe require justifying. Possible examples are 'America no longer needs a strong national defense', 'More tax dollars ought to go to student support rather than to welfare programs', 'The primary purpose of going to college is to prepare for a job and not to obtain an education', and 'Everyone should be tolerant of different life styles'. Of those statements you mention, with which do you agree or disagree? Why?

## 2.  LOGIC AND ARGUMENTS

To the extent that rational thinking involves giving reasons for some statement, reasoning can be expressed in arguments. An *argument* is

> **a series of statements some of which, the premises, are offered as providing reasons for another statement, the conclusion.**

Here 'argument' does not mean *disagreeing* or *fighting*, but rather *providing reasons for* some statement. Any statement used in an argument to provide a reason for some other statement is a *premise*. Every argument has at least one premise, although there are often more. The collection of all the premises in an argument, even if there is only one, is the *premise set* of that argument. The premise set allegedly provides the grounds on which some statement is adequately justified.* The *conclusion* is that statement for which reasons are offered. Every argument has one, and only one, conclusion.

---

* This comment becomes one of the major themes of the last three chapters of this book.

Some arguments are good ones and some are not. In rational thinking, a person needs to be able to distinguish between good and bad arguments.

> **Logic is the study of criteria determining good and bad arguments and the practice of applying these criteria to specific arguments.**

Logic, an essential part of rational thought, is both a study and an activity. There are rules and techniques to be learned. But for these to be effective, they must be correctly applied in particular situations. Both the rules and techniques, and their correct applications, are part of logic.

It can be difficult to identify the conclusion and the premises in an argument. Consider this example:

(1)   The *Colts* win if the *Rams* lose. The *Rams* lose. The *Colts* win.

As (1) stands, it has neither a conclusion nor any premises. It is merely a collection of statements. To signify premises and conclusions, different indicator words can be used. The following words, for instance, might be used to indicate premises:

(2)
a) as
b) because
c) due to
d) follows from
e) for
f) on account of
g) since

Conclusions might also have indicator words. Some of them are:

(3)
a) accordingly
b) as a result
c) consequently
d) hence
e) it follows
f) so
g) subsequently
h) therefore
i) thus
j) wherefore

In other cases, the context in which an argument is presented can provide clues to help identify the conclusion and premises. Using a conclusion indicator word makes it possible to express example (1) as an argument:

(4)   The *Colts* win, if the *Rams* lose. The *Rams* lose. Therefore, the *Colts* win.

Suppose someone says 'No one ought to do illegal drugs' and is challenged to provide reasons for this remark. This argument might be presented:

> **(5)** The great majority of illegal drugs are dangerous to a person's health. Indeed, using illegal drugs is often fatal. Now, no one ought to do anything dangerous, or fatal, to his health. Therefore, no one ought to do illegal drugs.

The word 'therefore' indicates the conclusion, 'no one ought to do illegal drugs'. The remaining statements are premises put forth as reasons to support the conclusion.

The premises and conclusion of an argument can be ordered in different ways. The conclusion, for emphasis, might be stated before the premises. Indicator words can still be used to distinguish the conclusion from the premises. Here is a rewording of (5):

> **(6)** No one ought to do illegal drugs. This is evident for the following reasons. No one ought to do anything dangerous, or fatal, to his health. The great majority of illegal drugs are dangerous to a person's health. Indeed, using illegal drugs is often fatal.

In this example it is not a word, but 'This is evident for the following reasons' that is used to indicate the premises.

Notice that a different premise set could be offered to support 'no one ought to do illegal drugs'. Someone could argue like this:

**(7)** Anyone who does illegal drugs puts himself in great danger of being arrested, paying heavy fines, and ruining many chances he might have for a career. But no one ought to do anything that puts himself in any of these dangers. Therefore, no one ought to do illegal drugs.

Both (5) and (7) present a series of premises to provide reasons to sustain the conclusion. And while both arguments have the same conclusion, different reasons are furnished to support it. A conclusion can be supported in a variety of ways, some of which might be successful while others are not.

In assessing a passage containing an argument, always begin by extracting that argument and putting it into **standard argument form**.\* To do this, write down in a series all the explicitly asserted premises and the conclusion of the argument. Do not write down anything from the passage that is not a premise or the conclusion. Many passages containing arguments include background information, irrelevant opinions, asides, and other comments that are neither premises nor the conclusion. Write down the premises first and the conclusion last, marking off the conclusion with a conclusion indicator word. It is helpful to name each premise and the conclusion. Then they can be cited more easily in discussion. Numerals can be used as convenient names.

---

\* The topics of standard form, argument reconstruction, and the Principle of Charity introduced in this section are discussed further in Chapter 14.

Here is a passage containing an argument. This passage needs to be put into standard form so that its argument can be more easily seen and analyzed:

(8)  Everybody seems to be screaming for more personal freedom. A burning desire for freedom is the propelling force of the holy quest of the twentieth century. The cry for freedom is found everywhere. Nonetheless, many people are not truly free. Why? Because many people are not disciplined. They don't even understand the importance of discipline. They refuse to be disciplined by someone or to discipline themselves. But look at those relatively few people who are great athletes, businesspersons, entertainers, or diplomats. All of them are truly free because they have discipline. A person is truly free only if she is disciplined. Those people who will not bend to discipline cannot be truly free. Merely screaming for freedom from cradle to grave will not make anyone free. So, I say, many people are not truly free.

A good number of background comments in this passage sets an emotional tone for its argument. However, the passage is about personal freedom, who does and does not have it, and why. The major thesis, or conclusion, the author offers is 'Many people are not truly free'. This statement is presented in both the fourth and last sentence of the passage. What evidence is given to support this conclusion? (8) contains two premises; namely, 'A person is truly free only if she is disciplined' and 'Many people are not disciplined'. Given these statements, (8) can be put into standard form like this:

(9)

    1) A person is truly free only if she is disciplined.

    2) Many people are not disciplined.

    3) So, many people are not truly free.

After putting an argument into standard form, one might see that some premises or the conclusion has not been explicitly stated. In carefully constructed arguments, neither missing premises nor missing conclusions can be tolerated. This is because any implicitly understood remark always increases the probability of *misunderstanding*. It is impossible, of course, to assert everything relevant to understanding a particular argument. Some background agreement between the presenter and the receiver of the argument must be assumed as part of the context of the argument. But the presenter needs to make explicit whatever material is essential for the receiver to assess clearly an argument in a specific context.

Consider this argument:

(10) I'm not going to classes today because I've a fever of at least 101°.

First, put (10) into standard form. The conclusion is 'I'm not going to classes today' and the premise is 'I've a fever of at least 101°'. These statements can be represented in this way:

(11)

    1) I've a fever of at least 101°.

       **(2)**  So, I'm not going to classes today.

The premise of (11) does not supply adequate reasons for accepting the conclusion. There is a gap between the evidence presented and the conclusion. This gap can be identified by asking, 'What is the relation, for the presenter of this argument, between having a fever of at least 101° and not going to class?' A premise relating these concepts needs to be supplied by providing an ***argument reconstruction***:

> An ***argument reconstruction*** **is an argument put into standard form and any missing premise or conclusion explicitly stated.**

What can reasonably be supplied for the missing premise of (11)? One candidate is 'When I've a fever of at least 101°, then I don't go to classes'. Assuming this premise, (11) can be presented as a complete argument:

    **(12)**

        **1)**  I've a fever of at least 101°.

        **2)**  When I've a fever of at least 101°, then I don't go to classes.

        **3)**  So, I'm not going to classes today.

    Often when it is necessary to reconstruct an argument, the presenter is not available to answer questions and provide clarification. The receiver simply has to do the best he can. However, be as fair as possible to the argument. To help maintain a sense of fairness, follow the ***Principle of Charity***. This principle demands that the receiver of the argument put himself in the position of the presenter. In interpreting the argument, the receiver supplies any missing premises or conclusion. But he must do so in keeping with the views of the presenter and the context of the argument. Nonetheless, the receiver must minimize substituting his views for those of the presenter. If an argument is presented by a known socialist, it would not be in keeping with the Principle of Charity to introduce assumed premises favorable to a capitalist.

    The Principle of Charity demands that an argument be understood in a way making it as free from error as possible given what is known of the presenter and the context of the argument. Nonetheless, the primary purpose of reconstructing an argument is to clarify it, not to turn a bad argument into a good one. It might be that a reconstructed argument is still a bad one. Following the Principle of Charity tends to produce the strongest form of a completed argument that would be acceptable to the presenter. Remember, the purpose of reconstruction is to achieve maximum clarity of an argument. Once this clarity is achieved, it is then usually easier to see errors in the argument if, of course, there are any.

    Following is an example stressing that the primary purpose of reconstruction is to clarify and not to turn a bad argument into a good one.

    **(13)**  Because homosexual activities aren't normal they ought not to
            be condoned.

This argument can be put into standard form like this:

      **(14)**

        **1)**  Homosexual activities aren't normal.

(2) Thus, such activities ought not to be condoned.

There is a gap between *not being normal* and *not being condoned*.

What premises might be supplied for (13) in keeping with the argument? Here is a possible candidate:

(15)

1) Homosexual activities aren't normal.

2) Whatever is not normal ought not to be condoned. [added premise]

3) Thus, such activities ought not to be condoned.

The added premise, while completing the argument, does not turn it into a good one. The word 'normal' in the new premise can be understood in several distinct ways. Nor does the context in which it is used indicate which meaning is intended. This ambiguity could flaw the argument. For instance, while many things and activities are not statistically normal, they are socially and morally acceptable. Having an IQ of at least 120 and being a college student is statistically abnormal, but generally "condoned." There are far more people who are not college students with an IQ of at least 120 than who are. 'Normal' cannot successfully be used in its statistical sense and still function as part of the reasons for supporting the conclusion of (13). Yet, if 'normal', appearing in the second premise, is used in the sense of 'morally acceptable', then the argument verges on being circular to the extent that condoning something involves accepting it. Nonetheless, by reconstructing (13), difficulties in it are now more readily apparent in (15).

---

## EXERCISES

Put the following arguments into standard form. If there appear to be any missing premises or conclusions, suggest what they might be. In doing this, follow the Principle of Charity. There might be several different premises that could serve equally well to support the conclusion. Hence, do not look for the *right* answer. Rather, look for a *reasonable* one.

1. Because the *Razorbacks* will win only if they play well, they will win on account of their playing well.

2. The Russian government is obviously corrupt. After all, it is totally atheistic.

3. Abortion is always morally wrong for the simple reason that murder is always morally wrong.

4. Since it has been found that men wearing glasses are perceived to be not only more intelligent but also more affluent than men who don't, young businessmen should wear glasses in order to impress their superiors.

5. *HTLV-3* is now chiefly contracted through drug use. This finding is based on a recent study of known carriers of the retrovirus, showing 53% to be needle users.

6. Amy's degree will provide her with specialized training in specific job skills, but not with broad views and general cultural appreciation. After all, she is majoring in accounting.

7. "This place fits the definition of a sweatshop perfectly," the safety inspector said. "Look at the exit! You can't get out. The windows are all sealed, too."

8. The recent fall of the dollar and collapse of the stock market could've been predicted. Every time there is excessive greed, corruption, and a general loss of the old virtues of this Republic, the dollar falls and the market collapses.

9. On account of the drop in the dollar against both the yen and mark, coupled with a slow decrease in the national deficit, it follows that inflation can be expected to rise substantially over the next several years.

10. To pass analytic chemistry, a person has to work very hard and be well prepared. Consequently, Dottie has to work very hard and be well prepared.

11. People with low levels of adrenalin may be more susceptible to alcoholism. In a controlled study, volunteers with a family history of alcoholics, and a control group who didn't have alcoholics in their families, were given stress tests and then measured for the amount of adrenalin injected into their bloodstream.

12. Since the probability is very high that anyone with the retrovirus *HTLV-3* will develop *AIDS*, Chuck will probably develop *AIDS* because he contracted *HTLV-3* during a blood transfusion two years ago.

13. According to the American automotive industry, the Japanese are lagging behind in auto safety. This is substantiated by the number of people who have died in Toyotas—more than in any other automobile in the United States.

14. Pollsters recently concluded that the national economy, as a whole, is better now than it was four years ago. This finding is based on a recent poll of fifty American families. The poll showed that the majority of them have a higher income than they did four years ago.

15. What must be concluded from the evidence at hand? It is clearly the case that if there is less premarital sex among college students, there is less need for abortions within that group. It's equally obvious that premarital sex will continue within that group at its current rate or only a little less owing to the fear of sexually transmitted diseases.

## 3. ARGUMENTS, EXPLANATIONS, DESCRIPTIONS, AND RHETORIC

An important skill in rational thinking is the ability to distinguish among passages used as arguments, explanations, descriptions, and rhetoric. Admittedly, these uses can overlap. For instance, in some cases it is difficult to determine whether a passage contains an argument or an explanation. Arguments can be used in rhetorical ways, and sometimes, as in the sciences, explanations can be used as arguments. Nonetheless, in rational thinking a person needs to distinguish between these as clearly as possible. The reason for this is that different criteria of success and failure apply to arguments, explanations, descriptions, and rhetoric.

Arguments should be distinguished from *explanations* even though both can be used to provide reasons for something. However, explanations tend to answer the questions 'Why?' or 'How?'. Explanations tend to say *why something* is the case or *how something* is the case. In addressing 'Why?' and 'How?', explanations stress *understanding*. In contrast, arguments are used in trying to give evidence for accepting or rejecting a statement as true or for something being the case. Arguments, therefore, emphasize *evidence*.

There are various types of explanations. For instance, some scientists, such as physicists and chemists, tend to offer causal or physical explanations. Here is an example. Several people are looking at a frozen pond, and one says,

(1)   The water froze because the temperature went below 0°C.

No attempt is made to provide evidence for the truth of the statement 'The water froze'. Rather, citing the fact that the temperature went below 0°C gives a causal explanation of *why* the water froze. If everyone in a particular situation agrees that something is the case, then they do not seek reasons supplying evidence that it is the case. Rather, they look for explanations of why or how it is the case.

Psychologists and sociologists also recognize motives, purposes, and goals as explanatory. This can be seen in (2):

(2)   She took the job paying less money because she wanted the security it offered.

*Why* did she take the lower-paying job? She took it because she viewed the job as helping to fulfill her goal of security. Notice that the word 'because' is used in different ways. It can be used to indicate a premise in an argument or, as in (1) and (2), to indicate an explanation. In legal situations, it is common to explain the actions of an individual by citing motives:

(3)   Mr. Ambicioso has a classic reason for killing his uncle. Ambicioso, who is greatly in debt, is the sole beneficiary of his uncle's multimillion dollar estate.

Sometimes a person wants to understand *how* something happens or is going to happen. Explanations can be given in these situations. Here is a simple example:

(4)   He plans to murder her by putting arsenic in her drink.

(4) answers the question, 'How is he going to murder her?' Here in a single claim both *why* and *how* are addressed:

(5)   Since Mary is deeply concerned with environmental pollution, she is going to campaign for greater preservation measures to save the national forests.

Mary's deep concern for the environment explains *why* she is going to campaign. Her campaign explains *how* she intends to help preserve the environment.

Does the following contain an argument or an explanation?

(6)   You won't be able to hear the concert too well tonight. The acoustics in the building are terrible.

Without some specific context, some longer conversation or passage in which this example can be placed, no one can say whether (6) is an argument or an explanation. Is the presenter giving reasons to support the statement, 'You won't be able to hear the concert too well tonight', or is he explaining why? In an example such as (6), it is best separately to interpret it critically as an argument and then as an explanation. This process will make more obvious any mistakes in reasoning.

Neither arguments nor explanations should be confused with *descriptions* although descriptions are often woven in and around arguments and explanations.

Descriptions purport to say *what* is the case. They do not provide evidence or causes for anything. Consider this passage:

**(7)** It is one of those lazy summer days in the deep south. A day when the sun streams through the tall pines while the rain gently falls on their long needles. Mosquitos, big as horseflies, love this type of weather as any self-respecting porch sitter knows.

No evidence is presented in (7) to support a conclusion. No reasons are provided to suggest why something is the case. Rather, the passage relates the properties or characteristics of something. The day has the properties of being a summer one and a lazy one. The mosquitos have the property of being as big as horseflies.

Consider the following situation in which description, explanation, and argument are interwoven:

**(8)** Father McElroy is a Roman Catholic priest. It is Lent, a traditional time to talk about fundamental theological issues. So, Father McElroy is developing several arguments to support the claim that God exists. On the third Sunday in Lent, his argument is this:

> There is no object, man-made or natural, that doesn't have a cause. That this is so is evident both from our own personal everyday experiences and our knowledge of that larger world which science is continually revealing to us. But, if everything in order to exist and be what it is has a cause, then there must be a first cause which is its own cause and caused by nothing else. If there were not this first cause, nothing would exist since everything must be caused by something. This first cause is, in part, what we understand God to be. So, God exists.

To describe McElroy as a Roman Catholic priest or to explain why he is presenting this argument by pointing to the traditions of Lent in no way counts for or against the argument he gives to support the conclusion, 'God exists'. To accept or dismiss the argument simply because McElroy is a priest or because of his motives is to ignore whether the premises succeed or fail to provide support for the conclusion.

Arguments should not be confused with *rhetoric*. The primary purpose of rhetoric is to persuade. From the viewpoint of rational thinking, the primary purpose of an argument is to provide evidence for a conclusion. These purposes are distinct and can be at cross-purposes. Arguments can be used to persuade individuals to accept statements that are neither true nor in their own best interests. The purposes of arguments and persuasion need not be at odds. Arguments can be used to persuade someone to accept some statement that is both true and in his best interest. Of course, supplying support for a statement being true, or very likely true, might not be sufficient to persuade someone to act in accordance with that statement.

Humans often need more than arguments to persuade them to do what is in their own best interests. A diabetic can accept this argument:

**(9)** Ice cream is not healthy for a diabetic. A diabetic ought not to eat what is unhealthy for her. I am a diabetic. It follows that I ought not to eat ice cream.

And a tobacco user can accept this one:

> **(10)**  Tobacco is a cancer-producing agent. No one ought to use can-
> cer-producing agents. Accordingly, I ought not to use tobacco.

Acceptance of these arguments might not provide enough motivation to avoid eating ice cream or using tobacco products. Yet the individual who is shown through arguments what statements are true, or probably true, is more apt to act in accordance with those statements. And this is one psychological connection between arguments and persuasion. On the other hand, the individual who is simply told, or commanded, to do something said to be in his best interest is less likely to be motivated to do it.

While arguments are used to provide evidence for some statement, nonetheless they are *conditional* in two ways.* *First*, the relation holding between the premises and the conclusion is conditional. In justifying a conclusion, grounds for supporting it as true are provided by the premise set. The conclusion is supported on the condition that the premises are true. *IF* the premises are true, *THEN* these are reasons for the conclusion's being true. Suppose that someone argued in this way:

> **(11)**  The number of poor in this country will decrease under a Republican administration. The evidence for this is found in the policy of the Republican Party to lower both corporate and capital gains taxes. If these taxes are lowered, more money will be invested in industrial growth. Such growth will create more jobs for the unemployed.

*IF* the premises are true, *THEN* they provide support for the truth of the conclusion. If this conditional relation does not hold, an argument fails to supply reasons for accepting the conclusion.

*Second*, arguments are conditional in that the premises themselves are *assumed* to be true when they might not be. Indeed, all the premises of a particular argument might not be accepted by everyone. Typically a Democrat would deny at least one premise in (11). She might say that the money saved from lower corporate and capital gains taxes will not be returned to the industry to create new jobs. Rather, it will go to the stockholders or be invested in building automated factories that eliminate even more jobs. In that case, grounds could be demanded for those premises not accepted by everyone. So, a premise in one argument might be the conclusion of another. The presenter of (11) now needs to supply evidence to support his premises. Such demands often create arguments nested in other arguments. Reasons for accepting premises vary widely. Firsthand experiences and observations, commonly held opinions, key terms defined in certain ways, and the views of authorities are examples.[1] Even so, if there is to be an argument, the demand for evidence cannot go on forever. Eventually there must be premises that are accepted if only tentatively for the sake of getting started.

Notice that if a particular argument does not justify its conclusion, it does not follow that no argument can. It *might* be the case that some statement cannot be

---

* Of these two ways in which arguments are conditional, the first is treated in Chapters 2 through 12, and the second in Chapters 13 through 15.

† These are further important topics of the last three chapters of this book.

justified by any argument. This, however, is itself a claim standing in need of support. The longer and harder one tries to justify a particular statement and fails, the more likely there might not be good reasons to uphold that statement. If the statement being considered is not thought very important or interesting, probably little time and effort will be spent in trying to provide evidence for it. Nonetheless, if the statement is not justified, that does not show it is unjustifiable. Imagine someone asserting this:

(12)   Obviously there is no God such as is claimed to exist in the Judeo-Christian-Islamic traditions. If there were such a God, there would by now be a proof of His existence. But no such proof exists.

Suppose that as of today no proof *does* exist for the existence of God. From this fact, it does not follow that no proof *could* exist for His existence. The statement, 'No proof could exist for the existence of God', is itself a statement standing in need of supporting evidence.

## EXERCISES

### Group A:

Which of the following are descriptions, explanations, or arguments? Give reasons to support your answers. Note that some of these exercises might be interpreted in more than one way. And some might contain a combination of descriptions, explanations, and arguments. Put any example you declare to be an argument into standard form, reconstructing it if there are missing premises or conclusion.

1. I said, "I can't come over tonight." After all, I won't study if I come over, but I have to study to pass my MIS test tomorrow.

2. R. Gene Simmons, Sr., killed sixteen people in late December 1987. Fourteen of them were relatives.

3. It is not known why Mr. Simmons killed these people, but he appears to have been afraid of them. He is reported to have said, "I've gotten everybody who wanted to hurt me."

4. If it's true that I'm determined to do well in this assignment, I ought to study. Assuming I ought to study, I can't go out tonight. I'm determined to do well in this assignment. Hence, I can't go out tonight.

5. Why am I going to hear *U2* tonight? Because I'll no doubt enjoy the concert since I've liked all the other *U2* concerts I've heard.

6. Steve did well on his exams because he is naturally intelligent while having a great desire to achieve his goals.

7. Because of her bout with childhood polio, Jane is very uncoordinated in many physical activities.

8. Since Louis said he'd be here today or tomorrow and he hasn't come today, he'll be here tomorrow.

9. Suzy killed her boyfriend because he continually abused her both physically and psychologically.

10. I just heard the weather report. It said that tomorrow there's going to be heavy snow or rain. Classes are called off whenever there's heavy snow, and I'm not going to classes through hard rain. Anyway, tomorrow is Friday. So, what do I need to tell you about my going to classes tomorrow!?

11. When two objects of unequal weight are dropped simultaneously from the same height, both being in a vacuum near the surface of the earth, they strike a surface at the same moment as a result of gravitational force.

12. The stock market has been doing poorly owing to the national deficit, the falling dollar, and fear of inflation.

13. Because all communists are obviously evil people, it follows that Mikhail Gorbachev is evil since he is a communist.

14. Newtonian mechanics isn't a satisfactory explanatory physics because it can neither explain phenomena at the level of subatomic "particles" nor at great astronomical distances. But surely these phenomena cannot be ignored by any satisfactory system of physical explanation.

15. The math class had over forty students in it and was taught by a grad assistant who could hardly speak English. Surprisingly enough, I enjoyed the class.

**Group B:**

From different magazines and newspapers, find several examples of descriptions, explanations, arguments, and rhetoric. Give reasons why you classify your examples as descriptions, explanations, arguments, or rhetoric.

**Group C:**

Imagine some event, such as humans landing on the moon. Describe that event, then explain it, and finally give an argument supplying reasons for accepting the claim that the event occurred.

---

## 4.   DEDUCTION AND INDUCTION

Study this argument:

(1)   Either San Diego is the capital of California or Sacramento is. But San Diego isn't the capital of California. So, it must follow that Sacramento is.

In (1), two premises are presented in support of a conclusion. In analyzing any argument, one can always ask just how strongly does the truth of the premises support the truth of the concluion. The occurrence of 'must' in the conclusion indicates that the premises of (1) are taken to support the conclusion very strongly indeed.

The relation suggested to hold between the premises and conclusion of (1) is as strong as this relation can be. If all the premises are true, then the conclusion must also be true. (1) is an example of an argument that is ***deductively valid***:

> **An argument is *deductively valid* if and only if, when all the premises are true, the conclusion must also be true.**

Another way to characterize *deductive validity* is this:

> **An argument is *deductively valid* if and only if, when someone accepts all the premises as true and rejects the conclusion as false, that person has contradicted herself.**

A person ***contradicts*** herself if and only if she accepts two or more statements that in conjunction cannot possibly be true.

(1) displays a particular logical form or pattern. That the conclusion of (1) must be true, assuming the truth of the premises, is guaranteed solely by this logical form. Let squares and circles represent different spaces in which any statement can be expressed. Whatever statement is expressed in one square must be expressed in every square. The same restriction is placed on any statement expressed in a circle. The logical form of (1) can be pictured like this:

**(2)**

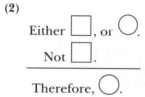

Any argument displaying this logical form is deductively valid no matter what statements are represented by the squares and circles.

Here is another deductively valid argument displaying the logical form shown in (2):

> **(3)**   Either George Bush is a Democrat or Edward Kennedy is a Republican. George Bush isn't a Democrat. Therefore, Edward Kennedy is a Republican.

If 'George Bush is a Democrat' is written in every square in (2) and 'Edward Kennedy is a Republican' in every circle, then one can literally see that (3) displays the same pattern as (2). (3) is a deductively valid argument because it displays a logical form guaranteeing that if all the premises of any argument displaying this logical form are true, then the conclusion of that argument must also be true.

That (1) and (3) are deductively valid does not depend on any content of their statements. (1) is about cities and state capitals while (3) refers to membership in political parties. It is their common logical form that guarantees not only their deductive validity, but the deductive validity of any other argument having this form. A telling difference between (1) and (3) lies in the truth of their premises. All of the premises of (1) are true. This is not the case in (3). While (3) is deductively valid, only (1) is ***sound***:

> **An argument interpreted deductively is *sound* when and only when it is both valid and all of its premises are true.**

Here is an argument that is ***deductively invalid***:

**(4)**   If Martha is going to land a good job after graduation, she'll have to have a high GPA. She certainly has a high GPA. So, Martha will necessarily land a good job after graduation.

> **An argument is *deductively invalid* if and only if, when all the premises are true, then the conclusion might not be true.**

This is to say:

> **An argument is *deductively invalid* if and only if, when someone accepts all the premises as true and rejects the conclusion as false, that person has not contradicted himself.**

Using squares and circles, the logical form of (4) can be pictured in this way:

**(5)**

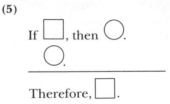

No argument having this form is deductively valid. The truth of the premises does not guarantee the truth of the conclusion. The conclusion of an argument displaying this logical form could be either true or false no matter what the truth or falsity of the premises are.

Here is an argument having the form seen in (5):

**(6)**   If Robert Dole is the United States President, then he is at least 35 years old. Moreover, Dole is at least 35 years old. Therefore, he is the United States President.

Both premises in (6) are true. Nonetheless, the conclusion is false. The truth of the premises does not guarantee the truth of the conclusion. Since this form does not guarantee that the conclusion of an argument must be true if all the premises are, any argument having this form is deductively invalid. Hence, (4) and (6) are deductively invalid.

An argument displaying the logical form of (5) *might* have a true conclusion. Further, all of the premises of the argument might be true. Here is an example:

**(7)**   If the Russians are reducing their military forces in eastern Europe, the United States is in a better position to spend tax dollars on domestic problems. The United States is in a better position to spend tax dollars on domestic problems. Subsequently, it is certain that the Russians are reducing their military forces in eastern Europe.

Each of the premises in (7), as well as the conclusion, is true. Nonetheless, because the statements in (7) have the form seen in (5), the truth of the premises does not guarantee the truth of the conclusion. So, (7), like (6), is deductively invalid.

An argument might be interpreted deductively or inductively. When an argument is viewed as supplying reasons bearing on the *likelihood* that its conclusion is true, it is being interpreted as an *inductive argument*. Inductive arguments are neither valid nor invalid but rather strong or weak. An argument interpreted inductively is ***strong***

> **if and only if the truth of the premises provides a high probability that the conclusion is also true.**

An argument interpreted inductively that is not strong is ***weak***. Notice that the distinction between *inductively strong* and *inductively weak*, unlike between *deductively valid* and *deductively invalid*, is a relative one. Whereas an argument interpreted deductively is either valid or invalid (but never both), there are degrees of inductive strength and weakness.

If an argument is interpreted as deductively invalid, it still might be inductively strong. The next paragraph gives an example of a deductively invalid argument. This argument does not guarantee, because of its logical form, the truth of the conclusion assuming the truth of its premises. However, assuming the truth of the premises does supply strong reasons for accepting the conclusion as very probably true.

Several independent testing agencies run extensive tests on different toothpastes in connection with the reduction of cavities. People using these products are compared to a group who use toothpaste with no cavity-preventing agent in it. Those persons using brand 'Z' toothpaste, having a cavity-preventing agent, develop fewer cavities over a period of five years than any of the other control groups. Someone now argues:

**(8)** It has been established that brand 'Z' tooth-paste prevents more cavities for more people than any other brand of toothpaste currently on the market. I'm going to use brand 'Z'. Consequently, probably brand 'Z' will prevent more cavities for me, too.

The truth of the premises does not guarantee that the conclusion is true. But the premises do strongly support the likelihood of the conclusion being true. Whether the conclusion is actually true or not could be established by the presenter of the argument's buying brand 'Z' toothpaste, using it over a period of time, and noting the increase in cavities before and after using brand 'Z'.

An argument could be deductively invalid and inductively weak:

**(9)** Either I'm going to lose my car because I can't pay my loans or I'll win the lottery. I'm not able to pay any of my loans with only my present assets. Knowing this, I've bought several lotto tickets for the lottery. And I really believe that I'm going to win the big one this time. So, I'm not going to lose my car.

Even if all the premises of (9) were true, they would not guarantee the truth of the conclusion. The argument is deductively invalid. But neither is (9) a strong inductive argument. There is no evidence given, other than strong belief, that any of the purchased lotto tickets is going to be a winner. While someone might strongly believe that he will win the big one, believing that he will win is hardly evidence to substantiate that he will, in fact, win.

Considerations needed to establish conclusively the conclusion of an argument interpreted inductively include, but go beyond, those that are actually presented in the premises given to support the conclusion. Because of this, arguments used inductively often make predictions about future events. These arguments become important in attempts to use past experiences to judge the probability of future events. Not all arguments interpreted inductively make predictions, however. Here is an example that does not:

> **(10)**   The majority of eighteenth century southern Americans were
> conservative in their political leanings. My great great great
> grandfather was an eighteenth century southern American. So,
> it is likely that he was conservative in his political leanings.

Do not confuse an argument used inductively that makes a prediction about events yet to occur with one having a conclusion such that evidence yet to be discovered tends to confirm or disconfirm that conclusion.

Notice that 'probably' appears in the conclusion of (8) and 'likely' in (10). Each of these words is used as an indicator word suggesting that (8) and (10) are to be interpreted inductively. Some words used to indicate that an argument is to be interpreted inductively are these:

> **(11)**
> **a)** likely
> **b)** might
> **c)** perhaps
> **d)** possible
> **e)** probable

**The supposed relative strength of the argument can be suggested by indicator words. The following suggest that a very strong inductive argument is being presented:**

> **(12)**
> **a)** extremely likely
> **b)** most possible
> **c)** highly probable

**Other indicator words are used to suggest less strong inductive arguments:**

> **(13)**
> **a)** somewhat likely
> **b)** moderately possible
> **c)** fairly probable

On the other hand, here are some words that can be used to indicate that an argument is to be interpreted deductively:

> **(14)**
> **a)** absolutely
> **b)** certainly
> **c)** doubtlessly

**d)** surely

**e)** without doubt

**Such indicator words might not be used. Then the receiver of an argument has to rely on the context of the argument to supply clues indicating whether it is to be interpreted deductively or not.**

## EXERCISES

Here is an assignment to test your logical intuition. You might wish to jot down your answers and at the end of the course review what you have written. Of the following arguments, which do you suppose are deductively valid? deductively invalid? Of those that you believe are deductively invalid, which do you think are inductively strong? Why?

1. Whoever works hard does well. Accordingly, if Russell works hard, he does well.

2. Some people are corrupt and some are politicians. So, some politicians are corrupt.

3. A heavy snow is likely this winter. You can tell by looking at the fuzz on the woolly worms.

4. I'm going to the movies. After all I've the money and nothing else to do. And whenever I can afford it and don't have anything else to do, I go to the movies.

5. People from Middle Eastern countries are probably all corrupt. I've personally known several and all of them expect a favor whenever they do anything for you.

6. Anyone who is well prepared for the race, even though he might not come in first, will make a good showing. Steve is well prepared. Accordingly, he'll make a good showing.

7. There is going to be world peace. This is obvious for the following reasons. If there is going to be world peace, then numbers of conventional weapons will be reduced. But numbers of conventional weapons are being reduced.

8. If there is going to be social justice, then individual income will be redistributed through federal taxation. Individual income is being redistributed through federal taxation. Therefore, there is going to be social justice.

9. Annye Mae was in her office or was at the bank. Assuming she was at the bank, she was making a payroll deposit. Annye Mae was not in her office when I called. So, I can only conclude that she was at the bank making a payroll deposit.

10. It's rather obvious that the stock market hasn't been steady lately. It's equally obvious that unless the market is steady, it's going to drop considerably. As a result, it's certainly the case that the stock market is going to drop considerably.

11. Yes, Mary is possibly taking analytic chemistry next term. She told me that she is going to take either sophomore English or analytic chemistry, and perhaps even both. She also said that she had to take the English course. But I also know that she's a chemistry major.

12. People with low levels of adrenalin may be more susceptible to alcoholism. In a controlled study, volunteers with a family history of alcoholics, and a control group who didn't have alcoholics in their families, were given stress tests and then measured for the amount of adrenalin injected into their bloodstream. Those with low levels had more alcoholics in their families than those with higher levels.

13. The United States government will lift its blockade against Iraq only if Iraq leaves Kuwait and releases hostages. If Iraq leaves Kuwait and releases hostages, the United States government will then negotiate frozen Kuwaitian assets. Consequently, assuming the United States government will lift its blockade against Iraq, the United States government will then negotiate frozen Kuwaitian assets.

14. I conclude that the Republican party will probably win the next presidential election. This claim is supported by a national poll representing 15% of the voting population taken in all parts of the country, both urban and agrarian, and randomly drawn from all socio-economic classes. Further, most economic indicators point to a continuation of a Republican administration.

15. The United States is very likely to suffer significantly from lack of economic, industrial, and political leadership within the next decade. Look at the evidence. According to the majority of studies, there is little interest on the part of students in science, theoretical or applied. Students are, in large part, not concerned with learning foreign languages. Nor do they wish to spend their time in grasping the subtleties of creative thought by taking courses in English, history, and philosophy. Primarily they are interested in business, law, and the "quick buck."

## 5.    SOME FINAL OBSERVATIONS

Language can be viewed as a complicated tool having many uses. In using language, assertions are made, questions asked, commands issued, prayers raised, emotions expressed, definitions proposed, and rules and principles set forth. Language can be used poorly. Definitions can be confused with factual assertions. Is 'A whale is a mammal that lives in the ocean' a definition of 'whale' or a statement about whales? Statements can be formulated in ways making their content dangerously vague, ambiguous or generally misleading. What does one understand about Lisa's financial situation from this statement: 'All of Lisa's bills are under a hundred dollars'. Sometimes the context of a claim is ignored or not clearly grasped. 'He went over to his house only to find her' is an example. A lack of perspective can generate problems in grasping how a claim is being used and what is to be understood by it. Frequently, the person making a claim is as confused as the person hearing it. These sorts of bad uses of language will infect any argument in which they are found, casting doubt on the worth of that argument. Problems of this sort are discussed in the last three chapters of this book. The remainder of the book focuses on formal properties of statements and arguments interpreted deductively.

In emphasizing these formal properties, the focus of study is directed primarily toward statements. Statements have various formal properties that remain constant no matter what they are about or how they are linguistically expressed. Chapter 2 begins by focusing on the formal properties of a certain type of statement known as *truth-functional statements*. For instance, each of the following is a truth-functional statement. While each is grammatically different and has a different content, each has the same formal structure.

(1)    New York City is the largest city on the East Coast while Los Angeles is the largest on the West Coast.

(2)  J. S. Bach composed during the baroque period of music but W. A. Mozart writes in the contemporary period.

(3)  Earth has nine moons even though most planets have many more than nine.

The logical form of each of these can be suggested by this picture:

(4)

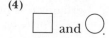 and .

In (1) the square represents 'New York City is the largest city on the East Coast' and the circle 'Los Angeles is the largest city on the West Coast'. Reading (2), the square stands for 'J. S. Bach composed during the baroque period of music' and the circle for 'W. A. Mozart writes in the contemporary period'. For (3) the square pictures 'Earth has nine moons' and the circle 'most planets have many more than nine moons'.

Focusing on formal properties of statements permits a person to ignore both their content and context. This is helpful in developing criteria for deductive validity and invalidity, and in analyzing arguments using these criteria. Complicated topics involving content and context can be safely ignored for the time being. By concentrating on the formal structure of (1) through (3), one can discuss only those general conditions that *any* statement of this structure must meet in order to be true or to be false. For example, any statement displaying the form seen in (4) is true if and only if both the statement represented by the square and in the circle are true. In all other cases the statement is false. So, (1) is true, but (2) and (3) are false. The truth or falsity of such a statement is a function of the truth or falsity of its independent statements and how they are linked by 'and' in (4).

After discussing formal properties of statements, arguments are examined from the viewpoint of deductive validity and invalidity. Several ways are developed to test for these properties of arguments. Through this study, one of the necessary requirements of a good argument is clearly seen and mastered, namely the logical relation between premises and conclusion in arguments interpreted deductively. The overall importance of establishing deductive validity and invalidity in a broad range of issues is suggested by the breadth of examples used throughout this book.

There are other benefits to be derived from a study of formal properties of statements and arguments. One of these is coming to grasp better the structure of English itself as indicated by those "little words" often taken to be relatively unimportant. Problems can arise in communication simply because the presenter or receiver does not have a command of how these words indicate the logical structure of language. There are, for example, important differences between saying 'I'll collect the final payment *if* I complete the necessary forms", 'I'll collect the final payment *only if* I complete the necessary forms' and 'I'll collect the final payment *if and only if* I complete the necessary forms'. Not recognizing these differences can lead to serious confusions and unfortunate actions based on these confusions.

Studying language from the formal viewpoint of deductive logic provides an excellent means for understanding the numerous ways that statements can be related. For example, many people read and listen primarily, if not solely, for particular, isolated facts expressed by true statements. Yet, the "data bank of information" created by this way of "reading" and "listening" has little worth if that information cannot be put together to draw conclusions and support judgments, while providing further perspectives that offer the possibilities of new avenues of profitable action. No one can be more useless in daily life and specializations such as business, management, law, science, medicine, or engineering than a person who "knows only the facts." Certainly it is necessary "to know the facts." Yet this is not sufficient either to survive or to prosper in the world.

This book begins with a quotation attributed to Confucius. Before proceeding to further chapters, read this passage once more:

> A Chinese Sage of the distant past was once asked by his disciples what he would do first if he were given power to set right the affairs of the country. He answered: "I should certainly see to it that language is used correctly." The disciples looked perplexed. "Surely," they said, "this is a trivial matter. Why should you deem it to be important?" And the master replied: "If language is not used correctly, then what is said is not what is meant; if what is said is not what is meant, then what ought to be done remains undone; if this remains undone, morals and art will be corrupted; if morals and art are corrupted, justice will go astray; if justice goes astray, then people will stand about in helpless confusion."

The proper use of language is, indeed, both of the highest moral and practical concern to one's own self, to other individuals, and to society!

## 6.  REVIEW OF NEW TERMS

**Argument:**  A series of statements some of which (the premises) are offered as providing reasons for another statement (the conclusion).

**Argument reconstruction:**   Putting an argument into standard form and making any implicit premise or conclusion explicit, following the Principle of Charity.

**Conclusion:**  The statement to be justified in an argument.

**Contradiction:** A statement that cannot possibly be true under any circumstances.

**Deductively invalid:**  An argument interpreted deductively in which the truth of the premises does not guarantee the truth of the conclusion.

**Deductively valid:**  An argument interpreted deductively in which if all the premises are true, the conclusion must also be true; that is, an argument of which it is contradictory to assert that all the premises are true but to deny the truth of the conclusion.

**Inductively strong:**  An argument interpreted inductively in which the truth of the premises provides a high probability that the conclusion is also true.

**Inductively weak:** An argument interpreted inductively in which the truth of the premises provides a low probability that the conclusion is also true.

**Logic:**  The study of the criteria for determining good and bad arguments and the practice of applying these criteria to specific arguments.

**Premise:**  A statement in an argument used to present a reason for the justification of the conclusion.

**Premise set:**  The collection of all the premises (even if only one) of an argument. The premise set represents the grounds offered in support of the truth of the conclusion of an argument.

**Principle of Charity:** That guide to understanding arguments requiring that the receiver of an argument interpret an argument in the way most favorable to it, always being as fair as possible to the presenter of the argument.

**Rational thought:** Analyzing reasons given for different statements and determining how these reasons are related in justifying other statements.

**Sound:** An argument interpreted deductively is *sound* when and only when it is both valid and all of its premises are true.

**Standard argument form:** The presentation of an argument in which each actually expressed premise is listed as a separate claim. The conclusion, introduced by a conclusion indicator word, is listed after all the premises.

**Statement:**  A linguistic entity that is either true or false, but not both. While every statement is either true or false, it might not be known by some, or any, person whether a particular statement is true or false.

# 2

# TRUTH-FUNCTIONAL LOGIC: BASIC CONCEPTS

In Chapter 1 an argument is characterized as a series of statements some of which (the premises) are offered as providing reasons for another statement (the conclusion). Chapter 2 develops in more detail some fundamental notions involved in the study of arguments viewed deductively. In particular, this chapter investigates the formal structures of truth-functional statements. Tables are introduced and used to depict the formal structures of truth-functional statements and the conditions making these statements true or false. Techniques and problems of translating from English into the notation of deductive logic are also discussed.

## 1.  TRUTH-FUNCTIONAL LOGIC

A distinction can be drawn between simple and compound statements. A *simple statement* contains no other statements as parts. A *compound statement* is constructed .out of simple statements. Consider these simple statements, not all of which are true:

(1)  Washington is the capital of China.

(2)  Rome is the capital of Italy.

(3)  Paris is the capital of France.

Compound statements can be constructed by using (1) through (3) as building blocks:

(4)  Washington isn't the capital of China.

(5)  Rome is the capital of Italy and Paris is the capital of France.

(6)  Either Paris is the capital of France or Washington is the capital of China.

(7)  Paris is the capital of France and Washington is the capital of China.

(4) through (7) share an important property. The truth or falsity of each of these, that is, their ***truth-value***, is determined solely by the truth or falsity of the simple statement(s) out of which they are constructed and specific uses of 'not', 'and', and 'Either . . . or . . . '. Given the use of 'not' in (4), and the falsity of (1), (4) is true. Since both (2) and (3) are true and are joined by 'and', (5) is also true. When (1) and (3) are connected by 'Either . . . or . . . ', the result, (6), is a true statement. Change 'Either . . . or . . . ' to 'and' and retain the same simple statements. Then (6) is transformed into the false statement, (7).

(1) through (7) exemplify truth-functional statements. A ***truth-functional statement*** is,

> **either (1) a simple statement that is true or false (never both), or (2) a compound statement whose truth or falsity is determined solely by its component simple statements and how these are built up into the compound statement.**

Some compound statements look very much like truth-functional statements but are not. The truth or falsity of these statements is not determined solely by the truth or falsity of their simple statements. Suppose a person asserted one of the following:

**(8)**  Achilles slew Hector and dragged him around the walls of Troy.

**(9)**  Caesar suppressed Rome after he conquered Gaul.

**(10)** The stock market fell because there were political pressures for higher interest rates.

**(11)** If water is poured into sulfuric acid, there will be an explosion.

**(12)** Had England recognized the Confederacy as a belligerent power, the South would have won the war.

The truth of (8) and (9) does not depend *solely* on the truth of the simple statements out of which these compound statements are constructed. (8) indicates a *temporal sequence* holding between the slaying of Hector by the son of Thetis and the sorry spectacle outside the city walls. The 'and' in (8) is understood as 'and then'. While in (9) 'after' connects two simple statements, it also suggests a temporal sequence. In (10) and (11), both a temporal sequence and a *causal relation* are suggested. (12) expresses a contrary-to-fact conditional. The truth or falsity of this claim goes beyond the truth or falsity of its simple statements. Even if 'England recognized the Confederacy as a belligerent power' had been true, 'the South would have won the war' is still open to debate. So, statements expressed in the subjunctive mood are not truth-functional.

Consider other examples that, while containing simple statements, are not truth-functional:*

---

\* Since every statement is a truth-function of itself, 'Ann believes that capital punishment or swift justice reduces crime' is true when and only when Ann does believe that capital punishment or swift justice reduces crime.

(13) Barbara hopes that oil prices will decrease and inflation remain low.

(14) Ann believes that capital punishment or swift justice reduces crime.

(15) Jane thinks that the majority of minority groups aren't fairly treated.

These examples are true or false because of the actual beliefs, hopes, and thoughts of the persons holding them. It is not the content of those hopes, beliefs, and opinions that makes (13) through (15) true or false. What is hoped, that oil prices will decrease and inflation remain low; believed, that capital punishment or swift justice reduces crime; or thought, that the majority of minority groups aren't fairly treated, are true or false *independently* of what anyone believes or thinks. It might be that 'capital punishment or swift justice reduces crime' is false. Nonetheless, the compound statement, 'Ann believes that capital punishment or swift justice reduces crime', might still be true depending on who Ann is and what she in fact believes. The truth-value of (13) through (15) is not a function solely of the truth or falsity of simple statements and the way those statements are joined into compound ones.

Many statements are not used in a purely truth-functional way. Yet such statements are important in both ordinary daily affairs and specialized areas of knowledge. Further, these statements *might also have* underlying truth-functional components necessary, even though not sufficient, for determining their overall truth-values. For instance, (8) through (15) each have essential truth-functional properties. What these properties are, and their ramifications, are studied in truth-functional logic. In this area of deductive logic, rules are established guaranteeing that if some statements are true, then other statements must also be true. Such rules do not depend on any temporal, causal, or contrary-to-fact considerations. Nor are they formulated in terms of personal beliefs, hopes, thoughts, or wishes.

The concept *function* is an important one. Imagine, for example, someone saying

(16)   The boiling point of water is a function of atmospheric pressure and temperature.

The terms 'boiling point of water', 'atmospheric pressure', and 'temperature' can be viewed as variables each of which has a specific range taking different values. For instance, the range indicated by 'temperature' has different values designated in terms of degrees Fahrenheit or Celsius. (16) asserts that there is a relation holding between particular values of temperature and atmospheric pressure that determines a value for the boiling point of water. For example, the lower the air pressure, the lower the temperature needed to bring water to a boil. Varying the value of any one of the variables in (16) changes the specific value of at least one other.*

_____

* In experimental situations, the value of one variable is often held constant while that of another is varied to observe any effect in the value of a third variable. The smaller the number of variables involved, in general the easier such experiments are to control. The following example contains four variables:

The chill factor is a function of temperature, humidity, and wind velocity.

This example and (14) in the text differ in the number of variables involved, although 'temperature' does appear in both. Any number of variables may be related in a manner such that their specific values uniquely determine the value of some other variable.

Similar examples are found in arithmetic:

$$(17)\ a + b = x$$

Let 'a' and 'b' be numerical variables. These variables can be replaced by specific numerals designating particular numbers that become the values of 'a' and 'b'. The plus sign, '+', called an 'operator', designates a rule permitting the combination of the specific values of 'a' and 'b' to determine the value of 'x'. Holding the value of any one of these variables constant while changing the value of a second determines the value of the remaining third variable. On the other hand, suppose that the specific values of 'a' and 'b' in (17) are kept, but the plus sign is changed:

$$(18)\ a \times b = x$$

Again the value of 'x' is changed.*

Expressions less complex than (17) and (18) are combinations of one operator and one variable. Yet, like (17) and (18), they determine the value of another variable. The following are examples:

$$(19)\ \sqrt{a} = x$$

$$(20)\ a^2 = x$$

The value of 'x' is determined in each case by the value of 'a' and the rules designated by the square root and exponential operators. Hence, if 'a' has the value of 3, the value of 'x' in (19) is 1.732⁺, while in (20) the value of 'x' is 9. Again, variables and operators are combined in such a way that the specific value of one variable, 'a', determines the value of another, 'x'.

Summarizing, the concept *function* is understood as

> **a combination of at least one operator and variable such that the value of the variable, in combination with the rules designated by the operator, fix the value of some other variable.**

A characterization of *truth-functional logic* is

> **the study of those statements whose truth or falsity is a function of the truth or falsity of the simple statements out of which they are constructed and connected in certain ways, and where any simple statement is a truth-function of itself.**†

## 2.   STATEMENT VARIABLES AND LOGICAL CONSTANTS

In analyzing statements, it is often helpful to isolate and display their formal properties. The concepts *variable* and *constant* make this task easier. Consider a common algebraic formula:

$$(1)\quad (a + b) = (b + a)$$

---

\* There are limiting cases to this observation. For instance, consider substituting '0' at 'a' and 'b' in both (17) and (18). In both instances, the value of 'x' remains the same.

† Truth-functional logic is also called sentential logic.

(1) is an expression of a law of commutation showing that the ordering of any two numbers does not affect the sum of those numbers. The lower-case letters 'a' and 'b' are used as numerical variables. They indicate spaces, or blank spots, that can be filled with numerical expressions used to name a number. The only restriction is that the same numerical expression must be used at each occurrence of the same variable. In general, a *variable* is

**a mark indicating a space to be filled by a name denoting some thing.**

While names are used to fill in spaces marked by variables, not just any name will do. Indeed, there are different types of names. 'Sally' and 'Paul' are names, but so are '1' and '2'. 'Rome is the capital of Italy' and 'Paris is the capital of France' are also names. They name statements. Now something can have more than one name. For instance, '7' and 'VII' both name the same number. The English, Spanish, and German sentences 'Rome is the capital of Italy', 'La capital de Italia es Roma', and 'Rom ist die Hauptstadt Italiens' each names the same statement. Sentences, often declarative sentences, are used as names of statements.* Statements are abstract linguistic objects in the sense that they are neither spatial nor temporal. It makes no sense to talk of filling in a space with an abstract object such as a statement. Strictly speaking, a sentence is used to fill in a space marked by a certain sort of variable. This sentence mentions the statement by naming it. To avoid suggesting that statements can fill in a physical space, it will sometimes be necessary to use locutions such as 'the statement name replacing the variable'.

In viewing variables as space markers to be filled in with names, two questions can be raised. *First*, what sort of name is appropriate to put in the space indicated by the variable? *Second*, of all those appropriate names, which specific one is to be selected on some particular occasion to fill that space? The first question concerns the *range* of a variable while the second concerns the *value* of a variable. The **range of a variable** is

**that group of things the name of any one of which is appropriate to fill (be substituted at) the space indicated by the variable.**

The **value of a variable**, however, is

**that specific name, having been selected from the range of the variable, that does fill (is substituted at) the space indicated by that variable.**

For instance, the range of the numerical variables 'a' and 'b' in (1) is the names of rational numbers. It is the names of these numbers that can be substituted at these

---

* When taken out of context there are examples of sentences that cannot be understood as clearly denoting a simple or compound statement. An example is 'Annye Mae and Russell went to the dance.' Is this to be understood as 'Annye Mae went to the dance and Russell went to the dance' or as 'Annye Mae and Russell, as a couple, went to the dance together'? The question cannot be answered owing to lack of context for 'Annye Mae and Russell went to the dance.' However, with sufficient context, one could say whether this sentence is used to denote a simple or compound statement. This observation underscores the importance of sensitivity to the use of sentences in specific contexts. Further notice that the type of sentence used to name a statement does not have to be a declarative sentence. Rhetorical questions, for example, can be used in particular circumstances.

numerical variables. The values of 'a' and 'b' are whatever names of specific numbers replace these variables in some particular context.

Truth-functional logic makes extensive use of *statement variables*:

> A *statement variable* **is any lower-case letter 'p', 'q', 'r', and 's' used to indicate a space to be filled by the name of some statement.**

As suggested in Chapter 1, geometrical figures could be used to indicate spaces to be filled in by statement names. Instead of the letters 'p', 'q', 'r', and 's', the following figures could be used:

A single statement variable can be replaced by any statement name, if and only if, in any particular context, the same variable is always replaced by the same statement name. A *statement name* is

> **usually, but not always, a declarative sentence in a language such as English, Greek or Spanish used to denote a statement.**

Being able to replace a statement variable with any statement name is a key factor in successfully picturing formal structures common to various statements. Having pictured these structures, comparisons can be more readily made between the formal properties of different statements. This will be of immense help in grasping how different statements are formally related.

A distinction can now be drawn between a statement and a statement form. A *statement* is

> **a nonspatial, nontemporal entity that is true or false (but not both) and often named by a declarative sentence.**

A *statement form*, on the other hand, has

> **at least one space indicated by a variable, such that when all the variables are replaced by some value from the appropriate range of that variable, the statement form is transformed into a statement.**

Statement forms contain at least one empty space indicated by a variable and, as such, are incomplete statements. It therefore makes no sense to speak of statement forms as being true or false. Statement forms, however, can be turned into statements when *all* the variables are replaced by a particular value from the range of statement variables. Consider the statement form represented by

(6)   not p

If 'p' is replaced by the name of any statement, then 'not p' represents the denial of the statement named.* Each of the following examples can be seen as an instance of 'not p'.

---

\* Instead of 'not p', it is also correct to write 'not q', 'not r', or 'not s'.

(7)  Pete Seeger isn't representative of a great many mediocre singers.

(8)  The atomic number of sulfur isn't either 18 or 21.

(9)  The United States isn't capable of both building up a strong military and also lowering the national deficit.

Using 'The following isn't the case', (7) through (9) can be re-expressed as

(10) The following isn't the case: Pete Seeger is representative of a great many mediocre singers.

(11) The following isn't the case: The atomic number of sulfur is either 18 or 21.

(12) The following isn't the case: The United States is capable of both building up a strong military and also lowering the national deficit.

When in (10) through (12) 'The following isn't the case' is abbreviated as 'not' and 'p' written in place of what follows the colon, it is *literally seen* that (10) through (12) are all **instances** of 'not p' where

> an *instance of a statement form* is some statement that is named by substituting the same statement name at the same statement variable in that statement form until all statement variables are replaced by statement names.

Now consider the notion of a **logical constant**. Logical constants, like variables, are closely connected with revealing formal structures of statements.

> **A *logical constant* is some mark referring to a fixed rule.**

The meaning and use of a logical constant is completely determined by a specific rule governing its use. This rule never changes even though applied in a wide variety of particular cases.*

There are several types of logical constants. Again consider a particular algebraic example:

$$(13)\ (2 + \sqrt{9}) = (\sqrt{9} + 2)$$

Each mark in (13) is used as a constant, even though these marks are used in different ways. The marks '+', '$\sqrt{\phantom{x}}$', '=', '(', and ')' represent algebraic constants in (13). On the other hand, **nonalgebraic constants** determine the particular content of an expression. In (13), for example, both the names '2' and '9' are nonalgebraic constants. Given the rules designated by the algebraic constants, certain operations can be performed on whatever is mentioned by the nonalgebraic constants. Thus, (14) is generated from (13):

$$(14)\ (2 + 3) = (3 + 2)$$

---

* Such rules, whether they be those of algebra or deductive logic, are similar to game rules. The rules define the game, and no matter what particular instance of the game is being played by whom, when, or where, the rules are always the same. *They* remain constant.

Continuing further, (15) is obtained from (14):

**(15)** $5 = 5$

There are two types of algebraic constants. An example of each occurs in (13). *First,* there are **operators,** designated by a mark, indicating unchanging rules to be used with a particular numerical expression. So, '$\sqrt{\phantom{x}}$' designates a rule used with 9 to produce 3. The marks '+' and '=' also designate operators. They indicate rules governing how numerical expressions are combined. Operators that designate rules governing only one expression are **monadic operators.** Operators that signify rules connecting two expressions are **dyadic operators.** The rule designated by an operator completely defines that operator. *Second,* there are **constants of punctuation** such as '(' and ')'. These logical constants designate rules determining how algebraic expressions are grouped together. Constants of punctuation also indicate in what order various operators are to be applied to these expressions.

In deductive logic, similar distinctions are made between logical and nonlogical constants. Like algebraic constants, logical constants designate fixed rules. These rules completely determine the use, and hence the meaning, of the logical constants. There are two types of logical constants: namely, *operators* and *punctuation marks.* The constants of truth-functional logic are introduced and discussed in the following sections.

## 3. TRUTH-FUNCTIONAL DENIAL

Denial holds a central place in language. It can be expressed in many ways. For instance, the word 'not' can be used to indicate the denial of

**(1)** Tim Curry is well known for his role of Dr. Frank-N-Furter in *The Rocky Horror Picture Show.*

Using 'not', the denial of (1) is

**(2)** Tim Curry is not well known for his role of Dr. Frank-N-Furter in *The Rocky Horror Picture Show.*

(1) and (2) are related in a specific way. If (1) is true, (2) is false; if (1) is false, (2) is true. (1) and (2) can be described as having *opposite truth-values* where two statements having the relation of opposite truth-values are said to be *truth-functional denials* of one another.

The mark, '~', called the **tilde,** is used to indicate truth-functional denial. Letting 'p' represent any statement, the form of truth-functional denial is depicted as

**(3)** ~p

Perhaps a square would more graphically indicate a space to be filled in by the name of some statement:

**(4)** ~ ☐

Any use of the tilde is completely governed by this rule:

> **Given any statement represented by 'p', if 'p' is true, '~p' is false, but if 'p' is false, '~p' is true.\***

The truth-functional use of '~' requires, therefore, that if the same statement is mentioned at both 'p' and '~p', a contradiction results. Thus, the statements 'Mary is a sophomore' and 'Mary isn't a sophomore', when referring to the same individual at the same time, cannot both be true or both be false.

Some uses of 'not' do not indicate truth-functional denial:

>  **(5)**  Some professors aren't kind.

is not the truth-functional denial of

>  **(6)**  Some professors are kind.

While both (5) and (6) cannot be false, they can both be true. Nor does the following use of 'not' suggest truth-functional denial:

>  **(7)**  Not only will Maria Angeles be promoted, she also will receive a substantial salary increase.

Not every appearance of the word 'not' indicates a truth-functional use of the tilde. A careful and sensitive reading is always needed to determine how 'not' is being used in a particular context.

The truth-functional rule governing the tilde can be displayed in a ***truth table***, which is

> **A diagram, or picture, systematically displaying all the truth-conditions making a statement true or false.**

Let 'p' stand for any statement, '1' for 'is true', and '0' for 'is false'. Then, since any statement is either true or false (but not both), under the 'p' write:

$$\underline{\mathbf{p}}$$
$$1$$
$$0$$

The rule governing the tilde prescribes that if 'p' is true, '~p' is false. Further, if 'p' is false, '~p' is true. This rule serves as a definition of the tilde and is pictured in the following table:

(8)

| p | ~p |
|---|---|
| 1 | 0 |
| 0 | 1 |

**RULE TABLE I**

---

\* Statement variables are neither true nor false. Yet because any statement name can be substituted at a given statement variable and because any statement that is named is either true or false, a statement variable may be spoken of *as if* it has a truth-value. This "as if" manner of speaking is often adopted in this book.

The above table is a picture showing *each particular combination* of '1' and '0' making any statement of the form '~p' true, and *each particular combination* making such a statement false. Each combination is a ***truth-condition*** of the statement.*

To achieve clarity in both understanding and visually grasping formal structure, sentences naming statements are symbolized in the notation of deductive logic. *Symbolization* is a transition from a particular language, such as English, to a specialized notation. While natural languages, such as English, are flexible, subtle, and rich in expressive force, nonetheless much of this force is abandoned in the notation of deductive logic. Someone might truthfully claim

> **(9)**   I studied hard this term and made all As.

(9) is used to suggest several things. There is the suggestion that studying hard was temporally prior to making all As. The person uttering (9) is also suggesting that studying hard was a causal factor in making all As. In truth-functional logic, temporal and causal considerations are ignored. Typically, a good deal of ordinary meaning is lost in symbolization. Be that as it may, the rewards of symbolization are considerable in analyzing statements and their relations in arguments.

Symbolization is best approached as a process of rewriting until one reaches an expression that can easily be put into the special notation. Study this example:

> **(10)**   Woody Guthrie didn't write the folk song, "Go Tell Aunt Rhody."

(10) is the denial of

> **(11)**   Woody Guthrie did write the folk song, "Go Tell Aunt Rhody."

This denial can be expressed as

> **(12)**   The following isn't the case: Woody Guthrie did write the folk song, "Go Tell Aunt Rhody."

Putting the tilde in place of 'The following isn't the case:',[†] (12) is rewritten as

> **(13)** ~: Woody Guthrie did write the folk song, "Go Tell Aunt Rhody."

Instead of writing the sentence naming a statement, a capital letter can be used as an abbreviation for that sentence. Used in this way, capital letters are *simple statement constants*. A single capital letter is viewed as a nonlogical constant used to indicate a simple statement. The letter 'G' might arbitrarily be selected as a nonlogical constant *to stand for the simple statement* expressed by that sentence, (11). Notice that while 'Guthrie' suggests the use of 'G', 'G' is not used to stand for 'Guthrie'. 'G' is used to name the entire simple statement. Nor is 'G' the only letter that could be

---

* More traditionally the capital letter 'T' is used to indicate 'is true' while 'F' indicates 'is false'. In this book '1' and '0' are used. The application of truth-functional logic to statements having two values is only one application of the binary system of logic being discussed in this book. There are other applications found in computer and information sciences, set theory, neurophysiology, and any other domain of discourse viewed primarily as forming a two-value system. The use of '1' and '0' instead of 'T' and 'F' serves as a constant reminder of the very wide range of applications of a binary logic.

† Or, 'It isn't the case that . . . ', 'The following isn't true . . . ', etc. might be used

used. 'W', suggested by 'write', is another reasonable candidate. Further, since a denied statement is considered compound,

> **single capital letters always represent nondenied statements and a tilde must be supplied to indicate the denial of a statement.**

(13) is now symbolized in truth-functional notation as

$$(14) \quad \sim G$$

---

### EXERCISES

Using the suggested capital letters, symbolize each example in truth-functional notation. Supply a tilde if appropriate.

1. Darth Vader won't finally defeat Luke. (D)
2. At first Yoda didn't wish to teach Luke the ways of the Jedi. (W)
3. Many students are now listening to the *Pet Shop Boys* from Britain. (L)
4. E. T. couldn't phone home for a long time. (P)
5. Frank-N-Furter didn't return to Transylvania with Rocky. (R)
6. Crito visited with Socrates in prison. (V)
7. Some psychologists are interested in theory construction. (I)
8. Empirical data cannot be interpreted without assuming a theory. (I)
9. The danger of projecting personal prejudices into interpretations of empirical data can't be avoided by refusing to theorize. (A)
10. Deductive logic doesn't provide a method for establishing the empirical truth of premises. (P)
11. The President insists on nominating conservative candidates for the Supreme Court. (I)
12. The principle of the steady increase of military power as a deterrent to war is in question. (Q)
13. It isn't prudent to suppose any one form of government is equally well suited for every nation. (S)
14. Revolutionary groups, such as the American Colonists, are sometimes sincere in their political promises. (S)
15. Westerners are generally unaware of the basic religious principles underlying Islam. (A)

---

## 4.  TRUTH-FUNCTIONAL CONJUNCTION

Conjunction plays an important role in language:

> **(1)**   Meat is a good source of protein and so is the soybean.
>
> **(2)**   Luke will eventually confront Darth Vader and won't be destroyed by this evil leader of the Empire.

**(3)**   Water was poured into sulfuric acid and there was an explosion.

In each example 'and' connects two simple statements. But 'and' is used ambiguously in (2) and (3). (1) represents a straightforward truth-functional use of 'and'. In (2) 'and' suggests a temporal relation. (3) indicates both a temporal and causal relation. Yet (2) and (3) have a truth-functional element. Only this truth-functional element is used in truth-functional logic.

*Truth-functional conjunction* is designated by the dot, '•', in truth-functional notation. Unlike the monadic operator, '~', the dot is a **dyadic operator**. Any dyadic operator is flanked on both its left-hand and right-hand sides by statement names, including capital letters replacing statement names, or statement variables. Selecting capital letters to stand for the simple statements in (1) through (3), the truth-functional element in each is symbolized as

**(4)**   M • S

**(5)**   C • ~D

**(6)**   P • E

Using statement variables, the general form of truth-functional conjunction is pictured as

**(7)**   p • q

Using geometrical figures, (4) through (5) can each be represented by

$$\square \;\cdot\; \bigcirc$$

Note that in (5) '~D' is being read as an instance of the single statement variable 'q'. This is literally seen in

$$\boxed{C} \;\cdot\; (\!\sim\! D)$$

The following definitional rule governs the dot and prescribes all that is meant by 'truth-functional conjunction':

> **Given any statement names substituted at 'p' and 'q', then 'p • q' is true if and only if both the statements denoted by the names at 'p' and 'q' are true. In all other cases, 'p • q' is false.**

A rule table can be constructed corresponding to the rule governing the dot. Any statement name substituted at 'p' and 'q' mentions a statement that is either true or false:

| p | q | p • q |
|---|---|---|
| 1 | 1 | |
| 1 | 0 | |
| 0 | 1 | |
| 0 | 0 | |

The definitional rule governing the dot dictates that any statement having the form 'p • q' is true if and only if each of the statements named at 'p' and 'q' is true. This truth-value assignment to 'p' and 'q' is seen in only the top row in the above partially constructed table. Therefore, only in this row can a '1' be placed in the empty column under 'p • q'. A '0' must be put in every other row. The table is completed in this way.

| p | q | p · q |
|---|---|-------|
| 1 | 1 | 1 |
| 1 | 0 | 0 |
| 0 | 1 | 0 |
| 0 | 0 | 0 |

**RULE TABLE II**

While 'and' is often used to indicate truth-functional conjunction, it has other uses:

(8)    Peaches and cream is excellent for breakfast.

(9)    Sharon and Mildred are friends.

In (8), 'and' is used to form a compound subject. It is correct to read (8) as 'Peaches are excellent for breakfast, and cream is excellent for breakfast'. What is excellent for breakfast is the combination of peaches and cream. The 'and' in (9) indicates a relation holding between Sharon and Mildred. It is incorrect to read (9) as 'Sharon is a friend and Mildred is a friend'.

'But' is another word commonly used to indicate truth-functional conjunction. 'The Lamborghini Lagonda is fast, but expensive' is an example of 'but' used as a conjunction. However, 'but' might not indicate conjunction. For instance, 'but' is used in 'It never rains but it pours'. This statement is best understood as, 'If it rains, then it pours' or 'Either it does not rain or it pours'. It is not understood as 'It never rains and it pours'. Do not suppose that every use of 'and' and 'but' suggests truth-functional conjunction.

In reading, writing, speaking, and listening, care must be taken to understand what is being said. In ordinary conversation and writing, it often makes an important difference exactly what word is used to express conjunction. Notice these examples:

(10)  She loves me and she also loves my best friend.

(11)  She loves me; nevertheless, she also loves my best friend.

(12)  She loves me despite the fact that she also loves my best friend.

Still, no matter what else is suggested by (10) through (12), this much is: If each example is to count as true, then 'She loves me' and 'she loves my best friend' must both be true. No matter what else is involved in these examples, they each minimally satisfy the condition of *truth-functional conjunction*. Because of this, each example can be symbolized truth-functionally:

(13)  M • F

*Each of the following expressions is symbolized as 'p • q' to indicate that only truth-functional conjunction is being considered:*

**(14)**

    **a)** p and q

    **b)** p and then q

    **c)** p, albeit q

    **d)** p although q

    **e)** p as well as q

    **f)** p at the same time that q

    **g)** p but q

    **h)** p, but also q

    **i)** p, but so is q

    **j)** p despite the fact that q

    **k)** p even though q

    **l)** p, further q

    **m)** p, however q

    **n)** p, in addition q

    **o)** p in spite of q

    **p)** p, moreover q

    **q)** p, nevertheless q

    **r)** not only p, but also q

    **s)** not only p, but further q

    **t)** not only p, but q as well

    **u)** p regardless of q

    **v)** p, still q

    **w)** p when q

    **x)** p, whereas q

    **y)** while p, q

    **z)** p, yet q

This list does not exhaust the various expressions that can be used to indicate truth-functional conjunction. It does, nonetheless, suggest many ways the dot can be indicated in English.

In moving from the notation of English into the notation of truth-functional logic, there are several helpful steps to take. Read the following example:

**(15)** While *AIDS* does not have a cure, nonetheless the *AZT* drug therapy is used in a significant number of cases to reduce the development of the retrovirus associated with AIDS. (C,S)

Now, reread (15) and underline every word indicating some sort of logical operator:

**(16)** <u>While</u> AIDS does <u>not</u> have a cure, <u>nonetheless</u> the AZT drug therapy is used in a significant number of cases to reduce the development of the retrovirus associated with AIDS. (C,S)

Also notice all punctuation marks in the example, such as the comma following the word 'cure' and preceding 'nonetheless'. Punctuation marks used in statement names often provide indications of how a compound statement is to be analyzed into its simple parts. Notice what capital letter suggested at the end of the example is used to represent each simple statement. In (15) 'C' is to stand for the statement '*AIDS* does have a cure' while 'S' is to represent 'the *AZT* drug therapy is used in a significant number of cases to reduce the development of the retrovirus associated with *AIDS*'. Given this information, (16) can be re-expressed as

**(17)** <u>While not</u> C, <u>nonetheless</u> S.

(17) goes easily into

**(18)** $\sim$ C $\cdot$ S

---

## *EXERCISES*

Using the suggested capital letters, symbolize each example in truth-functional notation. Indicate all cases of denial with the tilde.

1. Students in the early sixties listened to *Peter, Paul, and Mary* and to *The Kingston Trio*. (P,K)

2. Odetta is known for her interpretation of traditional folk songs while Baez has become associated with songs of social protest. (O,B)

3. Even though Piaf was the world's greatest singer of French Chanson, she didn't have a happy life. (S,L)

4. Keith Jarrett is outstanding in his contemporary piano renditions whereas John Denver captures the spirit of Appalachia with his folk guitar. (J,D)

5. Neil Diamond isn't well known in Russia despite the fact that he is very popular in Europe. (K,P)

6. Many religious fanatics preach universal love, although they certainly don't tolerate upholders of other religious beliefs. (P,T)

7. Birth control continues to be a religious issue regardless of the fact that scientific findings are often at variance with the beliefs of religious groups. (C,F)

8. Not only is the whale air-breathing but it is viviparous as well. (A,V)

9. It isn't necessary to reject Newtonian mechanics even though quantum mechanics is accepted. (R,A)

10. At one time the center of American intellectual life was located in the Northeast, nonetheless that no longer appears to be the case. (L,A)

11. The volume of a gas is inversely proportional to the pressure, the temperature remaining constant; furthermore, the pressure of a gas is proportional to the average kinetic energy of its molecules. (V,P)

12. C. L. Hull proposed his original derivation of reasoning in 1935 but repeated the proofs in 1952. (P,R)

13. Within the last decade or so, social psychology has increased the quality of its research in addition to the quantity of articles produced. (I,P)

14. Not only does theory serve as a tool in scientific investigation but also as a goal in its own right. (T,G)

15. While theory construction is a goal in its own right, still it must be related to empirical research. (C,R)

---

## 5.  TRUTH-FUNCTIONAL DISJUNCTION

Statements other than denials and conjunctions are used in truth-functional logic. Disjunctions, for example, are often constructed using 'either . . . or . . . ':

**(1)**  John Denver recorded either "Thank God I'm a Country Boy" or "Back Home Again."

**(2)**  Mikhail Baryshnikov will dance at La Scala this Friday evening or appear in the Lincoln Center then.

**(3)**  According to Werner Heisenberg, either the position or velocity of a subatomic particle can be determined with certainty.

**(4)**  Give me what I want or I'll tell the whole nasty story.

Each of these examples employs 'either . . . or . . . ', although 'either' is not actually written in (2) and (4). With capital letters, (1) through (4) can be partially symbolized as

**(5)**  Either T or B

**(6)**  Either D or A

**(7)**  Either P or V

**(8)**  Either G or T

Putting statement variables in place of capital letters displays a general pattern for (5) through (8):

**(9)**  Either p or q

Notice that 'either p or q' can be understood in two different ways. (2) states that this Friday evening Baryshnikov will dance at La Scala or appear in the Lincoln Center. But he cannot be both places at the same time. Someone familiar with quantum mechanics realizes (3) is asserting that either the position of a subatomic particle can be determined with certainty or the velocity can be determined with certainty, but not both. (1) suggests that John Denver might have recorded one or the other of the songs mentioned, and perhaps he recorded both. What of (4)? Here a blackmailer demands to receive what she wants, or the entire messy story will be made public. The victim might optimistically believe that if the blackmailer is satisfied, the story will not be told. The victim is interpreting 'either p or q' in the sense of (2) and (3). The blackmailer, however, intends to be paid off by the victim *and* to tell all. She is using 'either p or q' in the sense of (1). There are, then, two distinct truth-functional interpretations of 'either p or q':

(10) Either p or q, and perhaps both.

(11) Either p or q, but not both.

(10) is the *inclusive*, or weak, use of 'either p or q'. This use includes the possibility of both the statement names substituted at 'p' and 'q' mentioning true statements and 'either p or q' being true. (11) is the *exclusive*, or strong, use of 'either p or q'. It excludes the possibility of both the statement names substituted at 'p' and 'q' mentioning true statements and 'either p or q' being true. Using a '∨', known as the *wedge*, then the truth-functional *inclusive* sense of 'either p or q' is symbolized as

(12) p ∨ q

or even more pictorially as

(13)   □ ∨ ○

A *delta,* '∆', is used to express the truth-functional *exclusive* sense of 'either p or q':

(13) p ∆ q

or as

(14)   □ ∆ ○

In carefully worded business letters and legal documents, it is common to find 'and/or' and 'but not both'. These expressions are used to distinguish the two uses of 'either p or q' when otherwise there might be ambiguity. To avoid ambiguity in this book, the following convention is observed:

**Symbolize a disjunctive statement by using the wedge unless the exclusive use is explicitly indicated by an expression such as ' . . . but not both'.**

The marks '∨' and '∆' are both dyadic operators. The definitional rule governing 'p ∨ q' is:

**Given any statement names substituted at 'p' and 'q', 'p ∨ q' is true if and only if at least one (and perhaps both) of the statements denoted by the names at 'p' and 'q' is true.**

The definitional rule governing 'p ∆ q' is:

**Given any statement names substituted at 'p' and 'q', 'p ∆ q' is true if and only if one (but not both) of the statements denoted by the names at 'p' and 'q' is true.**

Corresponding to each of these rules is a table:

| p | q | $p \vee q$ |
|---|---|---|
| 1 | 1 | 1 |
| 1 | 0 | 1 |
| 0 | 1 | 1 |
| 0 | 0 | 0 |

**RULE TABLE III**

| p | q | $p \vartriangle q$ |
|---|---|---|
| 1 | 1 | 0 |
| 1 | 0 | 1 |
| 0 | 1 | 1 |
| 0 | 0 | 0 |

**RULE TABLE IV**

Remember that both the wedge and delta are truth-functional operators. They are used to capture only the truth-functional element of disjunctive statements. For example, someone might say

**(15)** Either I'm not going to study or I'm going to pass this course.

A native speaker of English would infer from this comment that studying is both temporally prior to, and a causal element in, passing the course. As important as these insights are, nonetheless neither temporal nor causal relations are truth-functional. Yet if (15) is true, then *minimally* it cannot be the case that 'I'm not going to study' and 'I'm going to pass the course' are both false.

---

## *EXERCISES*

Using the suggested capital letters, symbolize each example in truth-functional notation.

1. Either Pete Buck or Bill Berry, but not both, plays a blistering guitar in *R.E.M.* (P,B)

2. *R.E.M.* is America's best rock and roll band or we can't put any trust in the opinion of *Rolling Stone* magazine. (R,M)

3. Either it isn't always safe to assume tickets are available for an *R.E.M.* concert in Athens, or it's best to hear the group at the Fox in Atlanta. (S,H)

4. Either "Murmur" or "Document"—but not both—was the first album *R.E.M.* produced. (M,D)

5. *Kiss* isn't popular with the disco crowd or it is appealing to younger audiences, but not both. (P,A)

6. Bigotry isn't permitted to grow under the guise of religion, or the populace won't keep its freedoms granted under the Constitution. (P,K)

7. Society must eliminate narrow-minded fundamentalism or accept an ethical absolutism imposed by a small vocal group. (E,A)

8. Many social attitudes toward human behavior have to be modified or much of contemporary science must be recognized as hocus-pocus. (M,R)

9. In many sociopolitical situations, either the dictatorship of the Liberal or the dictatorship of the Conservative seems inevitable. (L,C)

10. Either the majority of individuals will be educated or the Republic won't survive, but not both. (E,S)

11. Education doesn't deal with the fulfillment of the individual or it isn't primarily concerned with vocational training, but not both. (D,C)

12. A student is either educated in value-oriented areas of study, or education isn't distinguishable from vocational training. (E,T)

13. The wave theory and/or the quantum theory of light is used in contemporary physics. (W,Q)

14. Heisenberg's principles are accepted or quantum mechanics isn't studied (but not both). (A,S)

15. Either Einstein eventually won the Copenhagen debates or Heisenberg didn't succeed. (W,S)

## 6.  CONSTANTS OF PUNCTUATION AND SCOPE

Consider this example:

(1)  Salaries remain constant or the government intervenes and the economy balances itself.

What is to be understood by (1)? Should it be read as

(2)  Salaries remain constant, or the government intervenes and the economy balances itself.

or as

(3)  Salaries remain constant or the government intervenes, and the economy balances itself.

Examine a parallel arithmetical example:

(4)  $2 \times 3 + 4 = y$

(4) is ambiguous because there are two distinct values of 'y', namely '14' and '10', depending on how '$2 \times 3 + 4 = y$' is interpreted. '$2 \times 3 + 4 = y$' can be viewed either as

(5)  $2 \times (3 + 4) = 14$*

or as

(6)  $(2 \times 3) + 4 = 10$

The ambiguity of (4) is dispelled by appropriate punctuation marks, just as a comma is used to dispel the ambiguity of (1).

*Constants of punctuation* are needed in the symbolism of deductive logic to avoid ambiguity. The punctuation marks used are *parentheses*, '(  )', *brackets*, '[  ]', and *braces*, '{  }'. Additional punctuation marks are supplied, as needed, by simply beginning again with parentheses. Constants of punctuation are always written in

---

* Notice that brackets are omitted, but "understood", in this example. A more pictorial way of writing '$2 \times (3 + 4) = 14$' is '$[2 \times (3 + 4)] = 14$'.

left-hand and right-hand pairs and have an order of strength. Parentheses indicate a weaker break in a statement form or symbolized statement than brackets, and brackets show a weaker break than braces. The notion of punctuation marks having an order of strength is found in English. In general, the comma is the weakest of such marks. The semicolon is stronger than the comma. The next in strength is the colon, and finally the period. In symbolizing a particular statement in logical notation, punctuation marks in English can be helpful in suggesting overall structure. Always pay careful attention to punctuation marks in both English and the notation of truth-functional logic. At the same time, remember that there are no mechanical guides for moving correctly from English into the notation of logic.

Using constants of punctuation and arbitrarily selected capital letters to name simple statements, (2) is symbolized as

$$(7) \quad C \vee (I \cdot B)$$

and (3) as

$$(8) \quad (C \vee I) \cdot B$$

The symbolism *literally shows* that (7) and (8) depict different statements.

Another ambiguous example, this one involving an unclear use of 'not', is

(9)  Russell isn't coming to the campaign conference or the governor's meeting.

Let 'C' stand for 'Russell is coming to the campaign conference' and 'G' for 'Russell is coming to the governor's meeting'. How, then, is (9) symbolized? Perhaps as

$$(10) \quad \sim C \vee G$$

(10) says 'Either Russell isn't coming to the campaign conference, or he is coming to the governor's meeting'. Perhaps (9) is to be understood as

$$(11) \quad \sim C \vee \sim G$$

(11) claims 'Either Russell isn't coming to the campaign conference, or he isn't coming to the governor's meeting'. Maybe (9) is intended as

$$(12) \quad \sim(C \vee G)$$

(12) asserts 'It isn't the case that either Russell is coming to the campaign conference or coming to the governor's meeting'; that is to say, 'Neither is Russell coming to the campaign conference nor coming to the governor's meeting'. Notice that 'neither p nor q' has two intuitively natural and equivalent interpretations; namely, '$\sim(p \vee q)$' and '$\sim p \cdot \sim q$'. For the sake of consistency in symbolizing, by *convention* '$\sim(p \vee q)$' is used in this book to symbolize any instance of 'neither p nor q'.

(1) and (9) are ambiguous because it is not clear to what the use of 'or', 'and', 'either . . . or . . . ', and 'not' applies. A more technical way of suggesting this difficulty is to say the *scope* of these words is not clear, where

**the *scope* of a particular logical operator is that part of a statement, or statement form, to which the rule designated by that operator applies.**

The possible interpretations that can be given to (1) and (9) in terms of the scope of their operators are indicated by the use of punctuation marks. In (7), the parentheses suggest the scope of the dot is 'I' and 'B', while the scope of the wedge is seen as 'C' and 'I • B'. In (8), the scope of the wedge is pictured by the parentheses as being 'C' and 'I', while the scope of the dot is 'C ∨ I' and 'B'. In (10), only 'C' is denied, while in (11) both 'C' and 'G' are denied but separately. The parentheses in (12) show that the scope of the tilde, and what is being denied, is the entirety of 'C ∨ G'.

Consider this example:

> **(13)**   Neither Princess Leia nor Han Solo is able to defeat Darth Vader single-handedly.

Given the convention of symbolizing 'neither p nor q' used in this book, (13) is translated as

$$\textbf{(14)} \sim(L \vee S)$$

Many beginners attempt to translate examples such as (13) *incorrectly* in this way:

$$\textbf{(15)} \sim L \vee \sim S$$

It is essential to note that the tilde does not function like '−1' in algebra. In logic the tilde is *never* "multiplied through" any punctuation marks.

Here is another example requiring tildes:

**(16)** Neither is Boolean logic not familiar nor trigonometry not known to Judy.

A correct way of symbolizing (16) is

$$\textbf{(17)} \sim(\sim F \vee \sim K)$$

It is not correct to symbolize (16) as '∼ ∼F ∨ ∼ ∼K'. (17) literally shows what is being denied in (16).

These conventions govern the scope of the monadic operator, the *tilde*:

> **The tilde shall apply to the smallest possible mentioned statement, or statement form, following it. This statement, or statement form, shall be indicated by parentheses, brackets, and/or braces. By convention, however, when this statement, or statement form, employs no dyadic operator, the punctuation marks shall be omitted.**

Hence, the denial of '∼F ∨ ∼K' is symbolized as '∼(∼F ∨ ∼K)'. But the denial of, say, '∼M' is symbolized simply as '∼ ∼M' because there is no dyadic operator in '∼M' but only the monadic tilde.

To depict the scope of a *dyadic operator*, the following convention is observed:

> **A dyadic operator shall operate over the smallest statement, or statement form, mentioned by the statement name flanking that operator on both its left-hand and right-hand sides. These statements, or statement forms, are indicated by constants of punctuation. By convention, however, when these**

**statements, or statement forms, employ no dyadic operators themselves, the punctuation marks shall be omitted.**

In (7), the parentheses show that the scope of the dot is 'I' and 'B', but the scope of the wedge is seen as 'C' and 'I • B'. In (8), the scope of the wedge is pictured by the parentheses as 'C' and 'I', while the scope of the dot is 'C ∨ I' and 'B'.

---

## *EXERCISES*

Using the suggested capital letters, symbolize each example in truth-functional notation.

1. Willie Nelson either plays a Martin guitar or he doesn't own a Gibson guitar. (M,G)
2. Willie Nelson either doesn't play a Martin guitar or he doesn't own a Gibson. (M,G)
3. It isn't the case that either Willie Nelson plays a Martin guitar or doesn't own a Gibson. (M,G)
4. Willie Nelson neither plays a Martin guitar nor does he own a Gibson. (M,G)
5. Last Wednesday Senator Pardessus either chaired the Arms Committee meeting or attended the Majority Caucus, or else he wasn't to be found in Washington. (C,A,F)
6. Senator Pardessus has come under close observation lately, but he neither runs from a political fight nor admits any misdeeds. (C,R,A)
7. It isn't true that Senator Pardessus is guilty of bribery and poor office management, while, on the other hand, he is highly respected in his district. (B,M,R)
8. People are either kind and altruistic, or selfish—but never both. (K,A,S)
9. The following isn't true: The majority of people are just and loving, while also being thoughtful. (J,L,T)
10. Moral betterment is not made by the egotistical while political progress is promoted by the selfish, or social fulfillment is achieved by those who care—but not both. (M,P,A)
11. Neither are most people interested in the real feelings of others nor are they incapable of such concern, but they tend to be entirely self-centered. (I,C,T)
12. Either a planet is at its closest distance to the sun, or it isn't at its perihelion and isn't moving as rapidly as when at its perihelion. (D,P,M)
13. One revolution of the earth around the sun is a sidereal year but not a tropical year, while the interval between successive spring equinoxes is a tropical year. (S,T,E)
14. The following isn't the case: Theories aren't constructed in psychology; further, it isn't true either that neither experimental nor clinical psychologists are interested in this type of work or that neither statistical nor quantitative measurement is satisfactory for representing psychological data. (T,E,C,S,Q)
15. The following isn't true: Theories aren't constructed in psychology; moreover, it isn't true that experimental or clinical psychologists are interested in this type of work and statistical or quantitative measurement is satisfactory for representing psychological data. (T,E,C,S,Q)

## 7.   CONSTRUCTING TRUTH TABLES

Consider the simple statements 'New York is the capital of Washington' and 'Sacramento is the capital of California'. The truth-values of the following compound statements can be easily calculated and displayed by truth tables.*

**(1)**   New York is the capital of Washington, while Sacramento is the capital of California. (W,C)

**(2)**   New York isn't the capital of Washington, yet Sacramento is the capital of California. (W,C)

**(3)**   It isn't the case both that New York isn't the capital of Washington and Sacramento isn't the capital of California. (W,C)

Compound truth-functional statements, such as (1) through (3), are viewed as being constructed out of building blocks held together by logical constants:

**(4)**   W · C

**(5)**   ~W · C

**(6)**   ~(~W · ~C)

Single capital letters, representing simple statements, are the basic building blocks of a truth table. These single letters are assigned the numerals '1' (for 'is true') and '0' (for 'is false'), which represent the two possible truth-values of the statements they denote. *Truth-value assignments* are placed under the initial capital letters. A truth table for (5) begins in this way:

**(7)**

| W | C | |
|---|---|---|
| 1 | 1 | |
| 1 | 0 | |
| 0 | 1 | |
| 0 | 0 | |

The truth-values of the next larger blocks are calculated according to the rules indicated by the logical constants. For instance, a tilde can be attached to a single capital letter, such as in '~W':

**(8)**

| W | C | ~W |
|---|---|---|
| 1 | 1 | 0 |
| 1 | 0 | 0 |
| 0 | 1 | 1 |
| 0 | 0 | 1 |

---

*Because the tables in this book are composed of '1's and '0's instead of 'T's and 'F's and are used in Chapter 3 as part of various methods leading to decisions about logical characteristics of truth-functional statements, arguments, and the collection of premises in those arguments, these tables are sometimes called *decision tables* instead of truth tables.

Then proceed to the next larger elements making use of dyadic operators. Continue building up larger wholes until the truth table is completed:

(9)

| W | C | ~W | ~W · C |
|---|---|----|--------|
| 1 | 1 | 0  | 0      |
| 1 | 0 | 0  | 0      |
| 0 | 1 | 1  | 1      |
| 0 | 0 | 1  | 0      |

Finishing the truth table, it is apparent what distinct combinations of truth-values of the simple statements would make the overall compound statement true or false. Each of these distinct combinations of the truth-values of the simple statements is a **truth-condition** of the statement being analyzed. For instance, '~W • C' is true only in that case where 'W' is false and 'C' true. Logicians make no claims, as logicians, concerning which of these truth-conditions in fact is the case. Logicians are not interested in the actual truth or falsity of any particular statement, but with all the possible truth-conditions making a statement true or false.*

To grasp better the construction of truth tables, it is helpful to introduce some technical terms. A horizontal string of '1's and '0's in a truth table is a *row*, while any vertical string is a **column**. A column to the left-hand side of the vertical double lines is a *lead column*, and a row to the left-hand side of the vertical double lines is a *lead row*. Each lead row represents a distinct possible *truth-condition* of the overall statement being depicted by the truth table. The '1's and '0's in the lead columns represent the initial truth-value assignments of a simple statement.

A truth table for a statement is a picture of *all possible* truth-conditions making that statement true of false[†]. Hence, a method must be established to depict every possible combination of '1's and '0's for any statement. This demand requires that the total number of both lead columns and rows be determined. There is a lead column for each *distinct* capital letter in the representation of a statement for which a truth table is constructed. In (4) through (6), 'W' and 'C' are distinct capital letters representing simple statements. A truth table for each of these examples will have exactly two lead columns. To avoid possible confusion, however, consider this example:

(10) (W ∨ C) Δ (~ W • C)

A truth table for (10) has two lead columns. While both 'W' and 'C' occur twice, the number of occurrences of a particular letter is not considered in determining the number of lead columns.

---

* Important exceptions to this general remark are necessarily true and necessarily false statements, such as tautologies and contradictions. These are discussed in later chapters.

[†] Truth table techniques can also be used with statement forms. In these cases individual statement variables always count as the basic units to which columns of '1's and '0's are first assigned.

The *number of lead rows* required by a truth table is determined by two factors. The first of these is the number of distinct letters representing simple statements. The second is the notion that each of these simple statements has only two possible truth-values. These considerations are reflected in

$$\textbf{number of rows} = \textbf{2}^{\textbf{n}}$$

where '**n**' represents the number of distinct simple statements in the compound statement to be depicted, and '2' indicates that these simple statements are either true or false, but not both. Since (4) has two distinct simple statements, represented by 'W' and 'C', the number of rows in its truth table is four, or

$$\textbf{number of rows} = \textbf{2}^{\textbf{2}} = \textbf{(2} \times \textbf{2)} = \textbf{4}$$

On the other hand, a truth table for

(11)   While Sacramento isn't the capital of Colorado, Tallahassee is either the capital of Ohio or Florida. (C,O,F)

requires eight rows:

$$\textbf{number of rows} = \textbf{2}^{\textbf{n}} = \textbf{[(2} \times \textbf{2)} \times \textbf{2]} = \textbf{8}$$

Because a truth table exhibits all possible truth-conditions of a statement, there must be a way of accounting for every possible combination of '1's and '0's in the lead rows. This book uses the following convention. To begin, divide by half the number representing the total rows needed for the truth table. Next, under the lead column furthest to the left, assign in the upper half of that column all '1's and in the lower half all '0's. Then, divide the number of '1's in the first lead column in half. In the next lead column, alternate '1's and '0's by that number until the total rows of the truth table are exhausted. If a third lead column is needed, divide the number of rows in the first group of '1's in the second lead column in half and alternate the '1's and '0's in the third lead column by that number. Proceed in this way until the last lead column in the truth table is reached. In that column, the '1's and '0's will alternate at every row.

Consider (1) and its symbolization at (4). Since there are two simple statements displayed by two capital letters, two lead columns and four lead rows are needed. Begin a truth table for 'W • C':

(12)

| W | C | W · C |
|---|---|-------|
| 1 | 1 | |
| 1 | 0 | |
| 0 | 1 | |
| 0 | 0 | |

The overall structure of (4) is a conjunction. A conjunction is true if and only if all of its conjuncts are true. Thus, look in the columns under 'W' and 'C'. When in any row there are only '1's, place a '1' under the column headed by 'W • C'. In every other row, put a '0':

(13)

| W | C | W · C |
|---|---|---|
| 1 | 1 | 1 |
| 1 | 0 | 0 |
| 0 | 1 | 0 |
| 0 | 0 | 0 |

(13) shows that only one truth-condition makes 'W • C' true; namely, when both 'W' and 'C' are true. This truth-condition is displayed in the first row. Every other truth-condition of 'W' and 'C' makes 'W • C' false.

A truth table for (6) is more complicated because of the tilde on the outside of the parentheses. Begin by constructing the lead columns. Then construct a column for any single letter coupled to a tilde. In this case, there are two. It does not matter which column, '~W' or '~C', is constructed first:

(14)

| W | C | ~W | ~C |
|---|---|----|----|
| 1 | 1 | 0 | 0 |
| 1 | 0 | 0 | 1 |
| 0 | 1 | 1 | 0 |
| 0 | 0 | 1 | 1 |

Next construct a column for '~W • ~C':

(15)

| W | C | ~W | ~C | ~W · ~C |
|---|---|----|----|---------|
| 1 | 1 | 0 | 0 | 0 |
| 1 | 0 | 0 | 1 | 0 |
| 0 | 1 | 1 | 0 | 0 |
| 0 | 0 | 1 | 1 | 1 |

A final column is generated for '~(~W • ~C)':

(16)

| W | C | ~W | ~C | ~W · ~C | ~(~W · ~C) |
|---|---|----|----|---------|------------|
| 1 | 1 | 0 | 0 | 0 | 1 |
| 1 | 0 | 0 | 1 | 0 | 1 |
| 0 | 1 | 1 | 0 | 0 | 1 |
| 0 | 0 | 1 | 1 | 1 | 0 |

And what of (11)? This compound statement is constructed out of three simple statements, as seen in this symbolization:

(17) ~C · (O ∨ F)

Hence, three lead columns and eight lead rows are required to begin its truth table. In the first lead column, write four '1's followed by four '0's; in the next column, alternate the '1's and '0's in pairs; and in the final lead column, alternate the '1's and '0's at every row:

**(18)**

| C | O | F | |
|---|---|---|---|
| 1 | 1 | 1 | |
| 1 | 1 | 0 | |
| 1 | 0 | 1 | |
| 1 | 0 | 0 | |
| 0 | 1 | 1 | |
| 0 | 1 | 0 | |
| 0 | 0 | 1 | |
| 0 | 0 | 0 | |

A column for '~C' is next developed:

**(19)**

| C | O | F | ~C |
|---|---|---|----|
| 1 | 1 | 1 | 0 |
| 1 | 1 | 0 | 0 |
| 1 | 0 | 1 | 0 |
| 1 | 0 | 0 | 0 |
| 0 | 1 | 1 | 1 |
| 0 | 1 | 0 | 1 |
| 0 | 0 | 1 | 1 |
| 0 | 0 | 0 | 1 |

A column is constructed for 'O ∨ F' before moving to the last column:

**(20)**

| C | O | F | ~C | O ∨ F |
|---|---|---|----|-------|
| 1 | 1 | 1 | 0 | 1 |
| 1 | 1 | 0 | 0 | 1 |
| 1 | 0 | 1 | 0 | 1 |
| 1 | 0 | 0 | 0 | 0 |
| 0 | 1 | 1 | 1 | 1 |
| 0 | 1 | 0 | 1 | 1 |
| 0 | 0 | 1 | 1 | 1 |
| 0 | 0 | 0 | 1 | 0 |

Finally, put '~C' and 'O ∨ F' into conjunction and generate a column for it:

**(21)**

| | C | O | F | ~C | O ∨ F | ~C · (O ∨ F) |
|---|---|---|---|----|-------|--------------|
| | 1 | 1 | 1 | 0 | 1 | 0 |
| | 1 | 1 | 0 | 0 | 1 | 0 |
| | 1 | 0 | 1 | 0 | 1 | 0 |
| | 1 | 0 | 0 | 0 | 0 | 0 |
| ⇒ | 0 | 1 | 1 | 1 | 1 | 1 |
| ⇒ | 0 | 1 | 0 | 1 | 1 | 1 |
| ⇒ | 0 | 0 | 1 | 1 | 1 | 1 |
| | 0 | 0 | 0 | 1 | 0 | 0 |

(21) shows that there are exactly three truth-conditions, marked with arrows, making '~C • (O ∨ F)' true and five making it false.

The above discussion is the basis for a decision procedure or algorithm that leads to deciding the truth-conditions of any truth-functional statement. A ***decision procedure*** or ***algorithm*** is

> **any effective and mechanical process that, when followed properly, will always lead to desired results.**

A procedure is *effective* if, and only if,

> **in a finite number of steps, when correctly followed, the procedure will always lead to the desired results.**

A procedure is *mechanical* if, and only if,

> **It is dictated by a set of rules that completely determines the mandatory and specific order of steps to be followed in applying that procedure to particular cases.**

A decision procedure or algorithm for deciding the truth-conditions of any truth-functional statement is this:

> *1. Symbolize the statement in question.*
>
> *2. Construct a truth table (decision table) for that statement.*
>
> *3. In every row in the final column of that table note the '1's and '0's. The numerals appearing in a given row of lead columns constitute the truth-condition for the '1' or '0' appearing in the final column of that same row.*

This algorithm is vital to developing decision procedures appearing in Chapter 3.

---

## EXERCISES

Construct a truth table for each of the following, clearly displaying all the truth-conditions making each example true or false. Which, if any, of the following have the same truth-value given the same truth-conditions?

1. ~(A • B)
2. ~A • ~B
3. ~(A ∨ B)
4. ~A ∨ ~B
5. ~ ~A • ~B
6. ~(~A ∨ B)
7. (~B Δ ~A) • C
8. ~(A • C) Δ B
9. B Δ (~C ∨ ~A)
10. (C ∨ ~B) • (~A ∨ D)

## 8.   HYPOTHETICAL STATEMENTS AND MATERIAL IMPLICATION

Consider the following:

**(1)**   If Sloan has the *HTLV-3* retrovirus, then Sloan has a high probability of developing *AIDS*.

**(2)**   If Turnipseed is a United States Senator, then she is at least 30 years old.

**(3)**   If 'Janet Wiess loves Brad Majors and Columbia loves Eddie' is true, then 'Columbia loves Eddie' is also true.

**(4)**   If Stalin was a good Christian, then I'm a monkey's uncle.

While different in content, (1) through (4) each makes use of 'if . . . , then . . . '. The statement name following 'if' denotes the **antecedent** of a hypothetical statement, while the statement name following 'then' denotes the **consequent**. Because a statement name follows both 'if' and 'then', statement variables can be used to display a form common to (1) through (4):

**(5)**   If p, then q

In (5) 'p' represents *any* antecedent, and 'q' *any* consequent.

But (5) is ambiguous. This can be appreciated by rereading (1) through (4). (1) suggests that having the retrovirus *HTLV-3* is both temporally prior and a causal factor in having *AIDS*. In (2), the consequent provides a constraint on the eligibility of being a United States Senator. (2) is not suggesting that the antecedent condition is either temporally prior or a causal factor to the consequent condition. Indeed, a person must be at least 30 years old *before* being a senator. Nor does (3) suggest a temporal or causal relation holding between the antecedent and consequent. Neither is some sort of constraint being imposed on the antecedent by the consequent. (3) can be seen as suggesting a relation holding between two statements as opposed to things or events in the spatiotemporal world. (4) introduces another use of 'if . . . , then . . . '. The suggestion is that an obviously false consequent emphatically dramatizes that the antecedent is also false, assuming that (4) is true.

No matter how different (1) through (4) are, they have a common truth-functional element, namely, **material implication**:

> **It is not the case in any hypothetical statement that both the antecedent is true and the consequent false if the entire statement is true.**

A truth table can be constructed to show this truth-functional feature common to hypothetical statements in the indicative mood. *First*, let 'p' stand for any antecedent and 'q' any consequent. *Second*, symbolize the antecedent as being true *and* the consequent as *not* being true in this way:

**(6)**   p · ~q

It is agreed, however, that *it is not the case that both* the antecedent is true and the consequent is not true if a hypothetical is true. This agreement can be pictured as

$$(7) \quad \sim(p \cdot \sim q)$$

(7) displays that truth-functional feature, material implication, common to all hypotheticals in the indicative mood.

The truth-value assignments of '$\sim(p \cdot \sim q)$' can be displayed. Continuing to let 'p' and 'q' represent any statements, begin a truth table with the required number of lead columns and rows:

(8)

| p | q |
|---|---|
| 1 | 1 |
| 1 | 0 |
| 0 | 1 |
| 0 | 0 |

Constructing a new column for '$\sim q$', continue the table:

(9)

| p | q | ~q |
|---|---|----|
| 1 | 1 | 0 |
| 1 | 0 | 1 |
| 0 | 1 | 0 |
| 0 | 0 | 1 |

Look at the columns under 'p' and '$\sim q$' to develop a new column under '$p \cdot \sim q$'. A truth-functional conjunction is true if and only if all the conjuncts are true. So, put a '1' under '$p \cdot \sim q$' in every case where there is a '1' in the same row under both 'p' and '$\sim q$'. Otherwise put a '0':

(10)

| p | q | ~q | p·~q |
|---|---|----|------|
| 1 | 1 | 0 | 0 |
| 1 | 0 | 1 | 1 |
| 0 | 1 | 0 | 0 |
| 0 | 0 | 1 | 0 |

Any hypothetical statement is false if it has a true antecedent, 'p', and a false consequent, 'q'. This can be represented in the table by generating a column of '1's and '0's under '$\sim(p \cdot \sim q)$'. In every row in which there is a '1' under '$p \cdot \sim q$', put a '0' under '$\sim(p \cdot \sim q)$'. And in every row where a '0' is found under '$p \cdot \sim q$', put a '1' beneath '$\sim(p \cdot \sim q)$':

(11)

| | p | q | ~q | p·~q | ~(p·~q) |
|---|---|---|----|------|---------|
| | 1 | 1 | 0 | 0 | 1 |
| ⇒ | 1 | 0 | 1 | 1 | 0 |
| | 0 | 1 | 0 | 0 | 1 |
| | 0 | 0 | 1 | 0 | 1 |

(11) literally shows that only when any antecedent, 'p', is true and any consequent, 'q', false is '$\sim(p \cdot \sim q)$' false. Every other truth-condition makes '$\sim(p \cdot \sim q)$' true.

Instead of '~ (p • ~ q)' a new dyadic operator is introduced to symbolize a hypothetical. The *horseshoe,* '⊃', is a dyadic operator flanked on both sides by statement names, capital letters used as abbreviations for statement names, or statement variable. This dyadic operator is used to picture only material implication:

$$(12)\ p \supset q$$

Again, geometric figures can be used to show spaces to be filled:

**(13)**

$$\square \supset \bigcirc$$

Since 'p ⊃ q' is a shorthand way of writing '~(p • ~q)', the truth table for 'p ⊃ q' is:

| p | q | p ⊃ q |
|---|---|-------|
| 1 | 1 | 1 |
| 1 | 0 | 0 |
| 0 | 1 | 1 |
| 0 | 0 | 1 |

**RULE TABLE V\***

The definitional rule governing the horseshoe is

> **Given any statement name at 'p' and 'q', 'p ⊃ q' is true except when the antecedent, 'p', is true and the consequent, 'q', is false.**

There are numerous ways of expressing hypotheticals in the indicative mood in English. In some cases, the antecedent is expressed after the consequent. Sometimes the word 'then' is omitted. Often some expression other than 'If . . . , then . . . ' is used. The following list represents various English expressions used to indicate hypothetical statements. Many of these suggest something more than material implication. Nonetheless, each minimally expresses at least material implication. It is this minimal expression that is captured by the horseshoe. *Each of the following is symbolized as* 'p ⊃ q' *where* 'p' *represents any antecedent and* 'q' *any consequent*:

**(14)**

      **a)** assuming p, q

      **b)** q, assuming p

      **c)** if p, q

      **d)** q, if p

---

\* 'If . . . , then . . . ' is central in computer programming. It is the heart of conditional branching. The computer is given an antecedent condition represented as either '1' or '0'. If the condition is '0', the computer is instructed to do one sort of operation, perhaps go into a "loop" until the antecedent condition is met. If the antecedent condition is '1', the computer is instructed to do something else, such as print out the results of a spreadsheet calculation.

**e)** q is necessary for p*

**f)** a necessary condition for p is q

**g)** q is a necessary condition for p

**h)** that q is a necessary condition for p

**i)** p only if q

**j)** q provided that p

**k)** p is sufficient for q

**l)** a sufficient condition for q is p

**m)** p is a sufficient condition for q

**n)** that p is a sufficient condition for q

**o)** unless q, not p

**p)** not p, unless q†

**q)** whenever p, q

**r)** q whenever p

No claim of completeness is made for this list. Nor is it suggested that these locutions are used only to express hypotheticals. 'Not p, unless q' can be rendered as '~p ∨ q', for instance. By convention, however, in this book 'p ⊃ q' is used.

To grasp *m* through *p* a person needs to understand the use of '***sufficient condition***':

> *A* **is a sufficient condition for** *B* **if and only if an occurrence of** *A* **guarantees an occurrence of** *B*.

Suppose a student has a 4.00 grade point average on a scale of 1.00 to 4.00, is majoring in history, and there is a chapter of the *Phi Beta Kappa* honorary society at her school. This is sufficient for her to be invited to join *Phi Beta Kappa*. Nothing more is required. There can be more than one sufficient condition guaranteeing something. For instance, a student might have a very high grade point average, but not a 4.00, be majoring in political science, and his school also has a chapter of *Phi Beta Kappa*. This student would be invited to join, too.

To comprehend *f* through *i*, one must understand how '***necessary condition***' is used:

> *B* **is a necessary condition for** *A* **if and only if the absence of** *B* **guarantees the absence of** *A*.

---

\* In locutions such as *e* through *h* and *k* through *n* a prepositional phrase can be used to express a statement that in other locutions can be expressed by a declarative sentence. 'That Jane Mary is excited is a necessary condition for David coming' can be expressed as 'If David is coming, then Jane Mary is excited'.

† Notice that 'unless q, p' and 'p unless q' can both be symbolized as '~p ⊃ q'. To say 'We'll go to the concert unless it has been called off' is to assert 'If we don't go to the concert, then it has been called off.'

For instance, being at least 35 years old does not guarantee being the President of the United States. But *not* being at least 35 years old does guarantee not being the President. So, being at least 35 years old is a necessary condition for being the President of the United States. But it is not a sufficient condition. The notion of a *necessary condition* is also related to *k*. To say that the team will win the game *only if* they have practiced hard is *not* to say that they will win *if* they have practiced hard. To practice hard is a necessary, but not sufficient, condition for winning the game. There are many more things required to win than simply hard practice. Yet if the team has not practiced hard, it will not win.

Capital letters found at the end of a particular example are written from left to right following the order of appearance, in that example, of the *names of the simple statements* these letters replace. This practice will be continued. To this point in the examples, the ordering of the capital letters from left to right in the symbolization of a particular statement has followed the printed order of the names of the simple statements. This will no longer always be the case. Consider this example:

**(15)** John attends the ballet whenever he has the money for a ticket. (A,H)

Letting 'A' replace 'John attends the ballet' and 'H' replace 'he has money for a ticket', 'A' is written to the left of 'H' in '(A,H)' because 'John attends the ballet' appears before 'he has money for a ticket'. But, since 'whenever' introduces the antecedent of a hypothetical statement, and the antecedent is always symbolized to the left of the horseshoe, (15) is pictured as

**(16)** H $\supset$ A

---

## EXERCISES

### Group A:

Using the suggested capital letters, symbolize each example in truth-functional notation.

1. A person might become paranoid if not able to function well in long-term situations. (B,F)

2. If human behavior is basically anticipatory rather than active, each person develops an interaction network leading into future choices. (B,N)

3. People aren't able to function maximally in a given situation unless they are basically dynamic. (F,D)

4. A society will quickly dissolve for lack of social cohesion whenever it is composed of a majority of self-centered persons. (D,C)

5. That a person can be parasitic on a society is sufficient for that society to be made up of a majority of self-centered individuals. (P,M)

6. Assuming some individuals are intellectually creative or mentally dynamic, they are intellectually creative only if they advance change in their society. (C,D,A)

7. If some persons are interested in ancient Egyptian religions or appreciative of Tolkienian mythology, then if interested in ancient Egyptian religion, they do well in "Dungeons and Dragons" episodes. (I,A,D)

8. Another team will win the World Series provided that neither the Mets nor the Yankees are the best in their league. (T,M,Y)

9. The Twins play in the World Series only if they win the American League, but winning the American League, they face the Cardinals in the World Series. (P,W,F)

10. A team plays in the World Series whenever it wins the American or National League (but not both). (S,A,N)

11. Remembering the sorry financial condition of the *PTL* is certainly sufficient for neither wishing to have the Bakkers return nor hoping their followers gain control of the organization. (R,W,H)

12. That Tammy produces a new record is sufficient to keep the *PTL* in the news, while Jimmy's not being forgotten is necessary to keep the *PTL* in the news. (P,K,F)

13. The following isn't the case: Rock Hudson suffered serious problems with his immune system, while it isn't true that he contracted *HTLV-3* only if he developed *AIDS*; but Hudson didn't develop *AIDS*. (S,C,D)

14. Assuming either that there is a possibility of a person developing *AIDS* by using dirty needles or that acquiring the retrovirus *HTLV-3* isn't augmented by casual personal contacts, then that person has neither been contaminated by dirty needles nor infected by a sex partner if that person doesn't have *AIDS*. (D,A,C,I,H)

15. A necessary condition for the Twins winning the World Series is the following: Either the Cardinals won't win and the Dodgers won't be undefeated, or neither will the Braves win nor the Yankees be undefeated. (T,C,D,B,Y)

**Group B:**

Construct truth tables for the exercises in *Group A* to determine the truth-conditions making each of these true or false.

---

## 9.    MATERIAL EQUIVALENCE

Imagine situations in which the following could be asserted:

(1)   This element is gold if and only if its atomic number is 79.

(2)   That a given number is even is a sufficient and necessary condition for it not being odd.

(3)   Annye Mae is wealthy just in case she inherited her uncle's millions.

These examples can be expressed in grammatically different ways:

(4)   This element is gold if its atomic number is 79, and the atomic number of this element is 79 if it is gold.

(5)   That a given number is even is a sufficient condition for it not being odd, and that a given number  is even is a necessary condition for it not being odd.

**(6)** If Annye Mae is wealthy, then she inherited her uncle's millions; and if she inherited her uncle's millions, then Annye Mae is wealthy.

Each of (4) through (6) can be symbolized as a conjunction of two hypotheticals:

$$\textbf{(7)} \ (N \supset G) \cdot (G \supset N)$$

$$\textbf{(8)} \ (E \supset {\sim}O) \cdot ({\sim}O \supset E)$$

$$\textbf{(9)} \ (W \supset I) \cdot (I \supset W)$$

Using statement variables, a form common to (7) through (9) is depicted as:

$$\textbf{(10)} \ (p \supset q) \cdot (q \supset p)$$

Since (7) through (9) are symbolic renderings of (1) through (3), the truth-conditions making a statement of the form '$(p \supset q) \cdot (q \supset p)$' true or false also make (1) through (3) true or false. These truth-conditions are displayed in

**(11)**

|  | p | q | $p \supset q$ | $q \supset p$ | $(p \supset q) \cdot (q \supset p)$ |
|---|---|---|---|---|---|
| $\Rightarrow$ | 1 | 1 | 1 | 1 | 1 |
|  | 1 | 0 | 0 | 1 | 0 |
|  | 0 | 1 | 1 | 0 | 0 |
| $\Rightarrow$ | 0 | 0 | 1 | 1 | 1 |

The first and fourth rows of (11) show that any statement of the form '$(p \supset q) \cdot (q \supset p)$' is true if and only if *both* the statements at 'p' and 'q' are true or *both* are false.

Instead of writing examples (1) through (3) as the conjunction of two hypotheticals, a new dyadic operator is introduced. This operator, '$\equiv$', is the **triple-bar** or **biconditional**. It is used to express **material equivalence** as

$$\textbf{(12)} \ p \equiv q$$

Geometrical figures can be used instead of statement variables:

**(13)**

Since '$p \equiv q$' is an abbreviation for '$(p \supset q) \cdot (q \supset p)$', the truth-conditions that make a statement of this form true or false also make a statement of the form '$p \equiv q$' true or false. Accordingly, the definitional rule governing the triple-bar is this:

> **Given any statement names substituted at 'p' and 'q', 'p $\equiv$ q' is true if and only if both of the statements denoted by the names at 'p' and 'q' are true or both false.**

This is the rule table corresponding to the rule of material equivalence:

| p | q | $p \equiv q$ |
|---|---|---|
| 1 | 1 | 1 |
| 1 | 0 | 0 |
| 0 | 1 | 0 |
| 0 | 0 | 1 |

**RULE TABLE VI\***

Following are some English expressions used to indicate material equivalence. *Each is rendered as 'p ≡ q'.* Note that the 'not' in (*a*) does not introduce the tilde.

**(13)**

    **a)** not p except q

    **b)** p if and only if q

    **c)** p just in case q

---

\* In literature dealing more specifically with the application of truth-functional logic to computers, the vertical columns of '1's and '0's are often reversed from bottom to top. This is done to depict better the relation of these columns to binary numerals representing various logical operators. Thus, the six basic rule tables are expressed as:

| P | $\sim$P |
|---|---|
| 0 | 1 |
| 1 | 0 |

| P | q | P·q |
|---|---|---|
| 0 | 0 | 0 |
| 0 | 1 | 0 |
| 1 | 0 | 0 |
| 1 | 1 | 1 |

| P | q | $p \vee q$ |
|---|---|---|
| 0 | 0 | 0 |
| 0 | 1 | 1 |
| 1 | 0 | 1 |
| 1 | 1 | 1 |

| P | q | $p \triangle q$ |
|---|---|---|
| 0 | 0 | 0 |
| 0 | 1 | 1 |
| 1 | 0 | 1 |
| 1 | 1 | 0 |

| P | q | $p \supset q$ |
|---|---|---|
| 0 | 0 | 1 |
| 0 | 1 | 1 |
| 1 | 0 | 0 |
| 1 | 1 | 1 |

| P | q | $p \equiv q$ |
|---|---|---|
| 0 | 0 | 1 |
| 0 | 1 | 0 |
| 1 | 0 | 0 |
| 1 | 1 | 1 |

The tilde, dot, and wedge operators are called 'Boolean gates' in computer literature. These three logical operators are especially important in computer operations. From them two other boolean gates are defined. These are the 'NAND' and 'NOR' gates. Symbolically they are represented as '$\sim$(p • q)' and '$\sim$(p ∨ q)'. The two truth tables corresponding to these are

| P | q | P·q | $\sim$(p·q) |
|---|---|---|---|
| 1 | 1 | 1 | 0 |
| 1 | 0 | 0 | 1 |
| 0 | 1 | 0 | 1 |
| 0 | 0 | 0 | 1 |

| P | q | $p \vee q$ | $\sim$(p ∨ q) |
|---|---|---|---|
| 1 | 1 | 1 | 0 |
| 1 | 0 | 1 | 0 |
| 0 | 1 | 1 | 0 |
| 0 | 0 | 0 | 1 |

Any other operator can be defined in terms of the NAND or NOR operator. This is important in computer circuitry. This circuitry is limited to (1) off-on gates, represented by the tilde, (2) parallel circuits represented by the wedge, and (3) series circuits represented by the dot.

    **d)** p is necessary and sufficient for q*

    **e)** p is a necessary and sufficient for q

    **f)** p is sufficient and necessary for q

    **g)** p is a sufficient and necessary condition for q

    **h)** p when and only when q

    **i)** p whenever and only whenever q

## *EXERCISES*

### Group A:

Using the suggested capital letters, symbolize each example in truth-functional notation.

1. Justice will be served just in those cases in which the law is followed. (S,F)

2. The civil law is obeyed when and only when doing so doesn't break the moral law. (O,B)

3. A person ought not to break the civil law except when it is in conflict with the moral law. (B,C)

4. Assuming that a person follows the moral law, then justice will be served if and only if the civil law is in accordance with the moral law. (F,S,A)

5. If in a truly just state a person follows the civil law when and only when the moral law is also obeyed, then in a truly just state an essential distinction can't be drawn between moral and civil law. (F,O,D)

6. A person doesn't have reason to break the civil law except that it is immoral to apply or unjust to follow it. (R,M,J) .

7. The advice of Apollo, "Know Thyself," will succeed just in case a person is neither insensitive to basic needs nor uneducated in values. (A,S,E)

8. Assuming John will go to the ballet just in case he has put away enough money and he has put away enough money if and only if he has saved part of his salary, then it is clear that John won't go to the ballet except that he has saved part of his salary. (G,P,S)

9. A tree is either coniferous or deciduous (but not both) when, and only when, it has either broad-veined leaves or needles (but not both). (C,D,L,N)

10. Equilibrium is reached in a solution if and only if it is the case that while the equilibrium constant is achieved nonetheless neither the temperature nor pressure is changed. (R,C,T,P)

11. That it isn't the case that a substance is an acid or a base (but not both) is sufficient and necessary for it not being water and not having a pH of 7. (A,B,W,P)

12. If water is neutral it has a pH of 7 when, and only when, basic properties do not begin before 7 and acidic properties do not exceed 7. (W,P,B,A)

13. That a mandrill is a mammal and has a spine is a sufficient condition for it being a primate if, and only if, it also both stands erect and has a true cerebrum. (M,S,P,E,C)

---

    * Notice that in *d* through *g* prepositional phrases, instead of declarative sentences, might be used to indicate statements.

14. That this substance is an acid and contains free hydrogen ions is a necessary and sufficient condition for the following—this substance is painful to the touch and sour to the taste only if it is in fact an acid and not a base. (A,I,P,S,B)

15. A cell will neither lyse nor plasmolyse whenever, and only whenever, it is the case that if it is in an isotonic solution or has an impermeable membrane to water, then water is not able to migrate and the cytoplasmic volume stays constant. (L,P,S,M,W,V)

**Group B:**

Construct truth tables for exercises 1 through 14 in *Group A* to determine the truth-conditions making each of these true or false.

---

## 10.   REVIEW OF NEW TERMS

**Abstract object:** Anything that has no spatial characteristics or properties, and no temporal characteristics or properties.

**Algorithm:** See, *Decision procedure*.

**Antecedent:** When a hypotetical statement is expressed in the form, 'If $p$, then $q$', the statement name at 'p' denotes the antecedent.

**Biconditional:** See, *Triple bar*.

**Column:** A vertical string of '1's and '0's in a truth table.

**Compound statement:** A statement constructed out of simple statements and various operators.

**Conjunction, truth-functional:** See, *Dot*.

**Consequent:** When a hypotetical statement is expressed in the form, 'If $p$, then $q$', the statement name at 'q' denotes the consequent.

**Constant:** A mark having a fixed meaning established in the context in which it occurs. Logical constants, including constants of punctuation and logical operators (monadic and dyadic), are used to picture logical form. Nonlogical constants, including statement initials, are used to express the content of a statement.

**Decision procedure:** Any effective and mechanical process that, when followed properly, will always lead to desired results; a decision procedure; *algorithm*.

**Delta:** A dyadic operator symbolized as '$\Delta$'. Any statement of the form 'p $\Delta$ q' is true if and only if 'p' and 'q' have opposite truth-values; the strong, or exclusive sense, of 'Either . . . or . . . '; *exclusive truth-functional disjunction*.

**Denial, truth-funtional:** See, *Tilde*.

**Disjunction, truth-functional:** See, *Wedge* and *Delta*.

**Dot:** A dyadic operator symbolized as '•'. Any statement of the form 'p • q' is true if and only if both 'p' and 'q' are true; *truth-functional conjunction*.

**Dyadic operator:** A logical operator that must be flanked on both its left-hand and right-hand sides by statement names, capital letters replacing statement names, or statement variables.

**Function:** A combination of at least one operator and variable such that the value of the variable, in combination with the rules designated by the operator, fix the value of some other variable.

**Horseshoe:** A dyadic operator symbolized as '⊃'. Any statement of the form 'p ⊃ q' is true except when 'p' is true and 'q' false; *material implication*.

**Instance:** The particular replacement of a variable, rule, or form pictured by the use of variables; a substitution instance.

**Material equivalence:** See, *Triple bar*.

**Material implication:** See, *Horseshoe*.

**Monadic operator:** A logical operator flanked on its right-hand side by statement names, capital letters standing for statements, or statement variables.

**Necessary condition:** Expressed by the consequent of a hypothetical statement. Some state of affairs, B, is a necessary condition for another state of affairs, A, if and only if the absence of B guarantees the absence of A.

**Operator:** A logical constant referring to an unchanging rule dictating what can be done in a specific context. There are two types of operators; namely, monadic and dyadic.

**Range of a variable:** That group of things the name of any one of which is appropriate to fill (be substituted at) the space indicated by the variable.

**Row:** A horizontal string of '1's and '0's in a truth table.

**Scope:** That part of a statement, or statement form, to which the rule designated by a logical operator applies. Scope is indicated by constants of punctuation.

**Simple statement:** A statement containing no other statements as parts.

**Statement:** A nonspatial, nontemporal entity that is true or false (but not both) and often named by a declarative sentence.

**Statement form:** Has at least one space indicated by a variable, such that when all the variables are replaced by some value from the appropriate range of that variable, the statement form is transformed into a statement.

**Statement name:** Usually, but not always, a declarative sentence in a language such as English, Greek, or Spanish used to denote a statement.

**Statement variable:** Any lower-case letter 'p', 'q', 'r', and 's' indicating spaces to be filled by statement names or capital letters representing statements.

**Sufficient condition:** Expressed by the antecedent of a hypothetical statement; some state of affairs, A, is a sufficient condition, of another state of affairs, B, if and only if an occurrence of A guarantees an occurrence of B.

**Tilde:** A monadic operator symbolized as '~'. Any statement of the form '~p' is true if and only if 'p' is false, and false if and only if 'p' is true; *truth-functional denial*.

**Triple-bar:** A dyadic operator symbolized as '≡'. Any statement of the form 'p ≡ q' is true if and only if 'p' and 'q' are both true or both false; *biconditional; material equivalence*.

**Truth-conditions:** The particular truth-value assignments of a simple statement, or those simple statements out of which a compound statement is constructed, making that statement true or false.

**Truth-functional logic:** A study of those statements whose truth or falsity is a function of the truth or falsity of the simple statements out of which they are constructed and connected in certain ways, where any simple statement is a truth-function of itself; also called *sentential logic.*

**Truth-functional statement:** (1) A simple statement that is true or false (never both), or (2) a compound statement whose truth or falsity is determined solely by its component simple statements and how these are built up into the compound statement.

**Truth table:** A diagram, or picture, systematically displaying all the truth-conditions making a statement true or false.

**Truth-value:** The truth-value of any given statement is either truth or falsity.

**Value of a variable:** That specific thing mentioned by the name substituted for a variable. The value of a variable is always selected from the range of that variable. The value of a statement variable is that statement named by a particular statement name or a capital letter used to stand for statements.

**Variable:** A mark of some sort indicating a space to be filled in by some name.

**Wedge:** A dyadic operator symbolized as '∨'. Any statement of the form 'p ∨ q' is true except when both 'p' and 'q' are false; the weak, or inclusive, sense of 'Either . . . or . . . '; *inclusive truth-functional disjunction.*

# 3

# TRUTH-FUNCTIONAL LOGIC: TRUTH TABLES

This chapter introduces truth table methods as decision procedures to determine if a particular truth-functional statement is contradictory, tautological, or contingent. Building on these distinctions, three truth table techniques are developed to decide whether truth-functional arguments interpreted deductively are valid or not. These are the shortened form truth table, the *reductio ad absurdum*, and the replacement technique. Truth tables are next used to decide if the premise set of a truth-functional argument is consistent or inconsistent. Last, truth table techniques are introduced to determine if two truth-functional statements are logically equivalent.

## 1. SHORTENED FORM TRUTH TABLES

Displaying all the truth-conditions of the following example requires a truth table having sixteen rows and nine columns!

**(1)** If water is neutral it has a pH of 7 when, and only when, base properties do not begin before 7 and acid properties do not exceed 7. (W,P,B,A)

Symbolize (1) as

$$(2) \quad (W \supset P) \equiv (\sim B \cdot \sim A)$$

Then a truth table for (2) has the following columns:

**(3)**

| W | P | B | A | $\sim$ B | $\sim$ A | $\sim$ B $\cdot \sim$ A | W $\supset$ P | (W $\supset$ P) $\equiv$ ($\sim$ B $\cdot \sim$ A) |
|---|---|---|---|---|---|---|---|---|
|   |   |   |   |   |   |   |   |   |

Unfortunately, the number of rows required for a truth table cannot be reduced. Nonetheless, the spread of the columns can be reduced somewhat.

There are four simple statements, indicated by the distinct capital letters, in (2). The capital letters representing these simple statements head the lead columns in (3). Instead of writing lead columns, make the initial truth-assignments of '1's and '0's under the single capital letters as they appear from left to right. Following the conventional method of assigning '1's and '0's, alternate the '1's and '0's by eight under 'W', by four under 'P', by two under 'B', and at every row under 'A'.*

|  | (W | ⊃ | P) | ≡ | ( ~ B | · | ~ A) |
|---|---|---|---|---|---|---|---|
| (4) |  |  |  |  |  |  |  |
|  | 1 |  | 1 |  | 1 |  | 1 |
|  | 1 |  | 1 |  | 1 |  | 0 |
|  | 1 |  | 1 |  | 0 |  | 1 |
|  | 1 |  | 1 |  | 0 |  | 0 |
|  | 1 |  | 0 |  | 1 |  | 1 |
|  | 1 |  | 0 |  | 1 |  | 0 |
|  | 1 |  | 0 |  | 0 |  | 1 |
|  | 1 |  | 0 |  | 0 |  | 0 |
|  | 0 |  | 1 |  | 1 |  | 1 |
|  | 0 |  | 1 |  | 1 |  | 0 |
|  | 0 |  | 1 |  | 0 |  | 1 |
|  | 0 |  | 1 |  | 0 |  | 0 |
|  | 0 |  | 0 |  | 1 |  | 1 |
|  | 0 |  | 0 |  | 1 |  | 0 |
|  | 0 |  | 0 |  | 0 |  | 1 |
|  | 0 |  | 0 |  | 0 |  | 0 |

Continue (4) by writing the appropriate '1's and '0's under the tildes in front of 'B' and 'A'. If 'B' has a '1' under it in some row, ' ~ B' has a '0' in that row; but if 'B' has a '0' under it, ' ~ B' has a '1'. Do the same for 'A':

(5)

| (W | ⊃ | P) | ≡ | ( ~ | B | · | ~ | A) |
|---|---|---|---|---|---|---|---|---|
| 1 |  | 1 |  | 0 | 1 |  | 0 | 1 |
| 1 |  | 1 |  | 0 | 1 |  | 1 | 0 |
| 1 |  | 1 |  | 1 | 0 |  | 0 | 1 |
| 1 |  | 1 |  | 1 | 0 |  | 1 | 0 |
| 1 |  | 0 |  | 0 | 1 |  | 0 | 1 |
| 1 |  | 0 |  | 0 | 1 |  | 1 | 0 |
| 1 |  | 0 |  | 1 | 0 |  | 0 | 1 |
| 1 |  | 0 |  | 1 | 0 |  | 1 | 0 |
| 0 |  | 1 |  | 0 | 1 |  | 0 | 1 |
| 0 |  | 1 |  | 0 | 1 |  | 1 | 0 |
| 0 |  | 1 |  | 1 | 0 |  | 0 | 1 |
| 0 |  | 1 |  | 1 | 0 |  | 1 | 0 |
| 0 |  | 0 |  | 0 | 1 |  | 0 | 1 |
| 0 |  | 0 |  | 0 | 1 |  | 1 | 0 |
| 0 |  | 0 |  | 1 | 0 |  | 0 | 1 |
| 0 |  | 0 |  | 1 | 0 |  | 1 | 0 |

*See Chapter 2, page 48.

Under the dot in ' ~ B • ~ A', write a '1' only in those rows having a '1' under both the tilde in ' ~ B' and ' ~ A':*

**(6)**

| (W | ⊃ | P) | ≡ | ( ~ | B | • | ~ | A) |
|----|----|----|----|----|----|----|----|----|
| 1 | | 1 | | 0 | 1 | 0 | 0 | 1 |
| 1 | | 1 | | 0 | 1 | 0 | 1 | 0 |
| 1 | | 1 | | 1 | 0 | 0 | 0 | 1 |
| 1 | | 1 | | 1 | 0 | 1 | 1 | 0 |
| 1 | | 0 | | 0 | 1 | 0 | 0 | 1 |
| 1 | | 0 | | 0 | 1 | 0 | 1 | 0 |
| 1 | | 0 | | 1 | 0 | 0 | 0 | 1 |
| 1 | | 0 | | 1 | 0 | 1 | 1 | 0 |
| 0 | | 1 | | 0 | 1 | 0 | 0 | 1 |
| 0 | | 1 | | 0 | 1 | 0 | 1 | 0 |
| 0 | | 1 | | 1 | 0 | 0 | 0 | 1 |
| 0 | | 1 | | 1 | 0 | 1 | 1 | 0 |
| 0 | | 0 | | 0 | 1 | 0 | 0 | 1 |
| 0 | | 0 | | 0 | 1 | 0 | 1 | 0 |
| 0 | | 0 | | 1 | 0 | 0 | 0 | 1 |
| 0 | | 0 | | 1 | 0 | 1 | 1 | 0 |

Next, assign the truth-value '1' to 'W ⊃ P' in every row except those in which 'W' has a '1' and 'P' a '0':

**(7)**

| (W | ⊃ | P) | ≡ | ( ~ | B | • | ~ | A) |
|----|----|----|----|----|----|----|----|----|
| 1 | 1 | 1 | | 0 | 1 | 0 | 0 | 1 |
| 1 | 1 | 1 | | 0 | 1 | 0 | 1 | 0 |
| 1 | 1 | 1 | | 1 | 0 | 0 | 0 | 1 |
| 1 | 1 | 1 | | 1 | 0 | 1 | 1 | 0 |
| 1 | 0 | 0 | | 0 | 1 | 0 | 0 | 1 |
| 1 | 0 | 0 | | 0 | 1 | 0 | 1 | 0 |
| 1 | 0 | 0 | | 1 | 0 | 0 | 0 | 1 |
| 1 | 0 | 0 | | 1 | 0 | 1 | 1 | 0 |
| 0 | 1 | 1 | | 0 | 1 | 0 | 0 | 1 |
| 0 | 1 | 1 | | 0 | 1 | 0 | 1 | 0 |
| 0 | 1 | 1 | | 1 | 0 | 0 | 0 | 1 |
| 0 | 1 | 1 | | 1 | 0 | 1 | 1 | 0 |
| 0 | 1 | 0 | | 0 | 1 | 0 | 0 | 1 |
| 0 | 1 | 0 | | 0 | 1 | 0 | 1 | 0 |
| 0 | 1 | 0 | | 1 | 0 | 0 | 0 | 1 |
| 0 | 1 | 0 | | 1 | 0 | 1 | 1 | 0 |

---

* The truth-assignments of 'W ⊃ P' might have been completed before assigning truth-values to ' ~ B • ~ A'.

Complete the truth table for (2). Place a '1' under the triple-bar only in those rows where both 'W ⊃ P' and ' ~ B • ~ A' have a '1' or both a '0'. In every other row, assign a '0'. The arrow beneath the truth table indicates its *final column*.

(8)

| (W | ⊃ | P) | ≡ | ( ~ | B | • | ~ | A) |
|----|----|----|----|----|----|----|----|----|
| 1 | 1 | 1 | 0 | 0 | 1 | 0 | 0 | 1 |
| 1 | 1 | 1 | 0 | 0 | 1 | 0 | 1 | 0 |
| 1 | 1 | 1 | 0 | 1 | 0 | 0 | 0 | 1 |
| 1 | 1 | 1 | 1 | 1 | 0 | 1 | 1 | 0 |
| 1 | 0 | 0 | 1 | 0 | 1 | 0 | 0 | 1 |
| 1 | 0 | 0 | 1 | 0 | 1 | 0 | 1 | 0 |
| 1 | 0 | 0 | 1 | 1 | 0 | 0 | 0 | 1 |
| 1 | 0 | 0 | 0 | 1 | 0 | 1 | 1 | 0 |
| 0 | 1 | 1 | 0 | 0 | 1 | 0 | 0 | 1 |
| 0 | 1 | 1 | 0 | 0 | 1 | 0 | 1 | 0 |
| 0 | 1 | 1 | 0 | 1 | 0 | 0 | 0 | 1 |
| 0 | 1 | 1 | 1 | 1 | 0 | 1 | 1 | 0 |
| 0 | 1 | 0 | 0 | 0 | 1 | 0 | 0 | 1 |
| 0 | 1 | 0 | 0 | 0 | 1 | 0 | 1 | 0 |
| 0 | 1 | 0 | 0 | 1 | 0 | 0 | 0 | 1 |
| 0 | 1 | 0 | 1 | 1 | 0 | 1 | 1 | 0 |
| | | | ⇑ | | | | | |

---

## *EXERCISES*

Symbolize the following using the suggested capital letters. Then construct a shortened form truth table for each.

1. ATP contains oxygen but not nitrogen. (O,N)

2. ATP doesn't contain oxygen; still, it does contain nitrogen. (O,N)

3. The following isn't true: ATP contains a peptide bond despite the fact that it doesn't contain a peptide bond. (B)

4. Rudolf Virchow believed in spontaneous generation or he believed in cellular division. (G,D)

5. It isn't the case that Rudolf Virchow believed in spontaneous generation or cellular division. (G,D)

6. If oxidation is the removal of electrons, then if reduction is the addition of electrons, oxidation is the removal of electrons. (O,R)

7. If oxidation is the removal of electrons but reduction is the addition of them, then oxidation isn't the removal of electrons only if reduction isn't the addition of electrons. (O,R)

8. Assuming this insect has a false vein, it is of the family Syrphidae; but if it doesn't have wings, it isn't of the family Syrphidae. (V,S,W)

9. That it isn't the case that this insect is a squash bug just in case it isn't of the order Hemiptera is a necessary and sufficient condition that it is a squash bug if and only if it is of the order Hemiptera. (B,H)

10. Either this is an insect and is of the order Hemiptera or it is an insect and of the order Diptera, but not both. (I,H,D)

11. If this element is zinc, then its atomic number is 30 if and only if its atomic weight is 65.37. (Z,N,W)

12. This element is krypton only if either its atomic number isn't 70 or its atomic weight is 83.80, but not both. (K,N,W)

13. West opens with one no-trump while North passes or West opens with one no-trump but East responds, or West neither opens with one no-trump nor does South pass. (W,N,E,S)

14. If South must open whenever she has a fourteen honor-point count but North cannot respond to South whenever he has a three honor-point count, and it isn't true both that North cannot respond to South and South must open, then either South doesn't have a fourteen honor-point count or North doesn't have a three honor-point count. (O,F,R,T)

15. West leads the queen only if he loses the trick to North's king, but if West leads the ace, South trumps; moreover, West makes game when and only when neither he loses the trick to North's king nor South trumps. (Q,K,A,T,G)

---

## 2.  CONTRADICTORY, TAUTOLOGICAL, AND CONTINGENT STATEMENTS

Any truth-functional statement can be categorized as *tautological*, *contradictory*, or *contingent*. Examine the following:

(1) If Mick Jagger is a successful entertainer, Springsteen isn't; but Jagger is successful, as is Springsteen. (J,S)

(2) Mick Jagger is a successful entertainer if the following is true: Both Bruce Springsteen is a successful entertainer only if Jagger is and Springsteen is successful. (J,S)

(3) Considering that Springsteen is a successful entertainer only if Jagger is, and Jagger is a successful entertainer; it then follows that Springsteen is, indeed, a successful entertainer. (S,J)

These examples can be symbolized and a truth table constructed for each. In the following, (4) represents (1), (5) pictures (2), while (6) represents (3):

(4)

| (J | ⊃ | ~ | S) | · | (J | · | S) |
|----|---|---|----|---|----|---|----|
| 1 | 0 | 0 | 1 | 0 | 1 | 1 | 1 |
| 1 | 1 | 1 | 0 | 0 | 1 | 0 | 0 |
| 0 | 1 | 0 | 1 | 0 | 0 | 0 | 1 |
| 0 | 1 | 1 | 0 | 0 | 0 | 0 | 0 |

⇑

**(5)**

| [(S | ⊃ | J) | · | S] | ⊃ | J |
|-----|----|----|----|----|----|----|
| 1 | 1 | 1 | 1 | 1 | 1 | 1 |
| 1 | 0 | 0 | 0 | 1 | 1 | 0 |
| 0 | 1 | 1 | 0 | 0 | 1 | 1 |
| 0 | 1 | 0 | 0 | 0 | 1 | 0 |
| | | | | | ⇑ | |

**(6)**

| [(S | ⊃ | J) | · | J] | ⊃ | S |
|-----|----|----|----|----|----|----|
| 1 | 1 | 1 | 1 | 1 | 1 | 1 |
| 1 | 0 | 0 | 0 | 0 | 1 | 1 |
| 0 | 1 | 1 | 1 | 1 | 0 | 0 |
| 0 | 1 | 0 | 0 | 0 | 1 | 0 |
| | | | | | ⇑ | |

Inspect (4). The final column has only '0's. It does not matter whether 'J' and 'S' are true or false, '(J ⊃ ~ S) · (J · S)' is always false. This statement is a *contradiction*.

> **A truth-functional statement is a *contradiction* if and only if there is no truth-value assignment to its simple statements making it true.**

Examine (5). Under the main horseshoe in (5) is a column of only '1's. The statement '[(S ⊃ J) · S] ⊃ J' is always true no matter if 'S' and 'J' are true or false. This statement is a *tautology*.

> **A truth-functional statement is a *tautology* if and only if there is no truth-value assignment to its simple statements making it false.**

Given the rule governing the tilde, a strict logical relation holds between contradictions and tautologies. The denial of a contradiction is a tautology and the denial of a tautology is a contradiction. '[(S ⊃ J) · S] ⊃ J' is a tautology. Therefore, ' ~ {[(S ⊃ J) · S] ⊃ J}' is a contradiction.

The final column of (6) contains both '1's and '0's. Some truth-conditions make (6) true, but others make it false. Whether '[(S ⊃ J) · J] ⊃ S' is true or false is contingent upon the actual truth-values of 'S' and 'J'. (6) is a *contingent statement*:

> **A truth-functional statement is *contingent* if and only if there is at least one truth-value assignment to its simple statements making it true and at least one truth-value assignment making it false.**

It is important to be able to distinguish between contradictions, tautologies, and contingent statements. One reason is that these distinctions become essential in developing truth table methods for deciding whether an argument is valid or not, and if the premise set of an argument is consistent or not. The distinctions between contradictory, tautological, and contingent statements are also important in developing truth table methods used to decide whether or not two statements are logically equivalent.

There are other important reasons for distinguishing between contradictory, tautological, and contingent statements. Statements are often used to present evidence for supporting some opinion or thesis. For instance, one might say, having just looked out the window, 'I am going to take my raincoat, because it's raining'. The speaker justifies 'I am going to take my raincoat' by noting 'it's raining'. Now imagine someone saying, 'I am going to take my raincoat because it may or may not rain'. The statement 'It may or may not rain' is a tautology. As such, it is true independent of any particular weather conditions. Another way of putting this is to point out that the truth of 'It may or may not rain' cannot give the least hint as to whether or not one should take a raincoat at some specific time rather than another. Tautologies are never useful in citing supporting evidence for any particular opinion or thesis about matters of fact. For similar reasons, neither are contradictions. Contingent statements are used to cite evidence for opinions, beliefs, hypotheses, and the like, about particular things and events in the world.

Often it is difficult to decide if statements are contradictory or tautological; but, to the extent they are either, no assertion of factual evidence is being offered for an opinion or thesis concerning some specific event or thing in the world. One should be skeptical about accepting factual positions "supported" by such "assertions of evidence," and even more reluctant to act in accordance with these opinions. Applications of these warnings in particular cases are often difficult. Professors, politicians, and religious leaders are not unknown to speak, and write, in tautologies and contradictions, as well as in riddles. Using a complicated style and serious tones, they easily disguise the logical forms of their comments. In these situations, they might claim to be pointing to evidence supporting opinions about topics ranging from heaven and hell to bull and bear markets.

## *EXERCISES*

Decide by shortened form truth table techniques which of the following are contradictory, tautological, or contingent. Use the suggested capital letters to symbolize the examples.

1. Either Arnold Schoenberg's *Verkaert Nacht* is his most popular work, or it isn't. (S)
2. It isn't the case that either Schoenberg was a man interested in whole-tone scales or he wasn't interested in whole-tone scales. (S)
3. If the *Pet Shop Boys* from Britain sing good pop, then the *Quiet Riot* doesn't. (P,Q)
4. Tim listens to *R.E.M.* only if he isn't uninterested in American rock and roll. (L,I)
5. Assuming it isn't true that Laura appreciates *R.E.M.* and also likes the *Police*, then she either doesn't like the *Police* or doesn't appreciate *R.E.M.* (A,L)
6. Bruce Springsteen will be in Nashville next week or Minnie Pearl will be in St. Louis, but Minnie Pearl won't be in St. Louis nor will Springsteen be in Nashville. (S,P)
7. The rock and roll crowd goes in for either *Falco* or *Genesis*, while that same crowd also goes in for *Genesis* or *Pink Floyd*. (F,G,P)
8. Assuming that either Antonio Vivaldi and J. S. Bach are musical giants or we can't trust the best of critics (but not both), then we can't trust the best of critics and either Bach or Vivaldi is a musical giant. (V,B,C)
9. J. S. Bach lived in the baroque period and composed either fugues or wrote toccatas only if either Bach lived in the baroque period and composed fugues or he lived in the baroque period and wrote toccatas. (L,C,W)

10. Provided that J. S. Bach studied with Dietrich Buxtehude, Bach mastered the organ, and he mastered the organ only if he was well received in the social circles of his day; but Bach did study with Buxtehude and yet he wasn't well received in the social circles of his day. (S,M,R)

11. Bach didn't study with Buxtehude unless he mastered the organ, while if Bach worked with the compositions of Vivaldi, he learned chamber music; yet it isn't true that Bach studied with Buxtehude only if he learned chamber music. (S,M,W,L)

12. Either it isn't the case that West takes the bid and East is dummy, or someone must play against South's strength in spades or overcome North's fourteen honor-point count. (W,E,S,N)

13. That East or North will bid at the one-suit level, or South will mention one no-trump is necessary and sufficient for West not opening with a bid of two. (E,N,S,W)

14. That the First and Third Estates were each a part of the National Assembly was sufficient for the following: Either the First Estate wasn't a part of the National Assembly only if the King supported it, and if the Third Estate wasn't a part of the National Assembly then Nobility supported it; or both the Nobility and the King supported the National Assembly. (F,T,K,N)

15. The following isn't so: It isn't true that either the King and Nobility were left helpless, or it didn't happen that both the members of the Third Estate took matters into their own hands and declared themselves the National Assembly; or if the members of the Third Estate took matters into their own hands and declared themselves the National Assembly, then the Nobility and King were left helpless. (K,N,T,A)

---

## 3.  SHORTENED FORM TRUTH TABLES: VALIDITY AND INVALIDITY

People have all sorts of opinions that they sometimes attempt to support. Often the opinions and the supporting reasons are given in declarative sentences denoting statements.* These statements can be related to one another in various ways, such as in arguments interpreted deductively. When a person presents such an argument,

---

* Statements are not always offered to give reasons, nor are statements always offered to indicate claims being supported. Imagine a teacher saying to a student, 'Chris, you ought not to cheat'. To establish this claim, the teacher cites these reasons, 'Cheating is immoral' and 'No one ought to do what is immoral'. The claim, 'Chris, you ought not to cheat' appears similar to the command, 'Chris, don't cheat'. But, commands are neither true or false. 'Cheating is immoral' might be understood as a lexical definition of the form "By 'cheating' is meant something that is immoral." Insofar as this definition is a report of how 'cheating' is actually used, it is either true or false that people do use 'cheating' in this way. But 'Cheating is immoral' should not be confused with statements such as 'Reno is a city'. And 'No one ought to do what is immoral' is a principle dictating what one ought to do. No claim is being made about what, in fact, people do. Thus, some philosophers have argued that it makes no sense to say 'No one ought to do what is immoral' is true or false. However, moral claims and principles are often presented and accepted as evidence in support of some conclusion. Indeed, most people would probably not find it difficult to say that 'One ought not to inflict needless suffering on another human being' is true. And for the sake of ease of presentation, in this book such claims are treated as if there were true or false.

some statements, perhaps only one, are if true taken as guaranteeing the truth of some other statement. Any statement given in support of a particular opinion is a *premise* of an argument. The *premise set* of an argument is the collection of all the premises even if there is only one. The *conclusion* of an argument is the statement to be supported. The relation suggested to hold between the premises and the conclusion in an argument viewed deductively is **logical entailment**:

> **One, or more, statements *logically entail* another if, whenever all the former are true, then the latter must also be true.**

If the premises do logically entail the conclusion, that argument is *deductively valid*, or simply **valid**; otherwise the argument is *deductively invalid*, or simply **invalid**.

> **An argument is *deductively valid* if the premises logically entail the conclusion; that is, when all the premises are true, the conclusion must also be true. An argument is *deductively invalid* if the conclusion is not entailed by the premises. For a deductively invalid argument there is at least one interpretation of its statements making all the premises true and the conclusion false.**

An argument interpreted deductively can be valid and have all false premises and either a true or a false conclusion. Such an argument can be deductively valid and have some true premises and some false ones while having either a true or false conclusion. Or an argument can be deductively invalid and have all true premises and a true conclusion. In no case, however, of a deductively valid argument can all the premises be true and the conclusion false.

Even though an argument can be valid and have all, or some, false premises, nonetheless such an argument is never *sound*. An argument interpreted deductively is sound if and only if it is valid and all of its premises are true. In everyday assessment of arguments, soundness is extremely important. If someone is going to give reasons for the correctness of a particular claim, it is best that those reasons be true, or at least warranted if not known to be true.*

Truth tables can be used to establish the validity, or invalidity, of any truth-functional argument. Consider this example:

(1)  Assuming the national deficit continues to rise or interest rates increase,

---

\* While every statement is either true or false, but not both, a statement might not be *known* to be either true or false by someone using it. Here the word 'known' is understood in the sense of 'known with certainty' so that there is not the least conceivable possibility, no matter how farfetched that possibility might seem, that the statement could ever, under any circumstances, be false. Indeed, there is much debate concerning whether such knowledge is possible, or if this concept of knowledge is not itself flawed. These questions are at the core of the area of philosophy known as epistemology, or the study of what is knowledge. These debates are beyond the boundaries of this book. However, this much seems clear. Any premises put forth to substantiate a conclusion are to have some evidence backing them, and evidence that is acceptable to the community receiving the argument. If not known to be true in the strict sense of 'know', even so, the premises must be warranted as if true for the community accepting them.

Wall Street will crash. We read in the papers that the national deficit continues to rise. So, we must conclude that Wall Street will crash. (R,I,C)*

Using the proposed capital letters, (1) is symbolized as

**(2)**                                                          / ∴ C

      **1)** (R ∨ I) ⊃ C  Pr

      **2)** R           Pr

The numerals '1' and '2' are written to the left of the symbolized premises. 'Pr' is found to the right. The numerals serve as *names* of the premises. 'Pr' indicates that these statements are premises and accepted *as if* true. The conclusion is symbolized and put to the upper right-hand edge of the symbolized premises. The sign of logical entailment, '/ ∴', is used to indicate the notion that if all the premises are true, then the conclusion must also be true.[†]

An argument is valid *if*, when *all* the premises are true, *then* the conclusion must also be true. Apply this notion of validity to (1) as symbolized in (2):

    **(3)**  If the premises '(R ∨ I) ⊃ C' and 'R' are both true, then the conclusion, 'C', must also be true.

(3), an 'if . . . , then . . . , statement, suggests a truth table procedure to establish the validity of (2). Put the premises of (2) into conjunction: '[(R ∨ I) ⊃ C] · R'. Let this conjunction be the antecedent of a hypothetical statement. The conclusion of (2) is the consequent:

    **(4)**  {[(R ∨ I) ⊃ C] · R} ⊃ C

(4) is the symbolization of a *statement* corresponding to the *argument*, (1). Indeed,

> **corresponding to every argument there is a hypothetical statement such that the antecedent of that statement is the conjunction of all the premises of the argument and the consequent is the conclusion of the argument[‡]**

Next, construct a truth table for (4):

**(5)**

| {[(R | ∨ | I) | ⊃ | C] | · | R} | ⊃ | C |
|------|-----|-----|-----|-----|-----|-----|-----|-----|
| 1 | 1 | 1 | 1 | 1 | 1 | 1 | 1 | 1 |
| 1 | 1 | 1 | 0 | 0 | 0 | 1 | 1 | 0 |
| 1 | 1 | 0 | 1 | 1 | 1 | 1 | 1 | 1 |
| 1 | 1 | 0 | 0 | 0 | 0 | 1 | 1 | 0 |
| 0 | 1 | 1 | 1 | 1 | 0 | 0 | 1 | 1 |
| 0 | 1 | 1 | 0 | 0 | 0 | 0 | 1 | 0 |
| 0 | 0 | 0 | 1 | 1 | 0 | 0 | 1 | 1 |
| 0 | 0 | 0 | 1 | 0 | 0 | 0 | 1 | 0 |
|   |   |   |   |   |   |   | ⇑ |   |

---

\* As, indeed, was the case on "Black Monday," 19 October 1987.

† One of the major goals of logic is to establish methods whereby logical entailment can be justified or shown to be unwarranted for particular arguments.

‡ In an argument having only one premise, that premise becomes the antecedent of the hypothetical statement corresponding to the argument.

(5) shows that (4) is a tautology. The only truth-conditions making a statement of the form 'p ⊃ q' false is when 'p' is '1' and 'q' is '0'. (4) could be false if and only if its antecedent is true and consequent false. However, in (5) there is no row in which the antecedent is '1' and the consequent '0'. If there were, (4) would not be a tautology. But the antecedent of (4) represents all the premises of (1) put into conjunction, and the consequent represents the conclusion of (1). Hence, in effect, (5) shows that there is no way of making all the premises of (1) true *and* the conclusion false. So, (1) is valid.

The following argument is similar to (1):

**(6)**  If the national deficit continues to rise and interest rates increase, Wall Street will crash. We read that the national deficit continues to rise. So, we must conclude that Wall Street will crash. (R,I,C)

Is (6) valid? *First*, symbolize (6) as

**(7)**                                    / ∴ C

    **1)** (R · I) ⊃ C   Pr

    **2)** R            Pr

*Second*, construct a hypothetical statement in which the antecedent is the conjunction of the premises and the consequent is the conclusion:

**(8)**   {[(R · I) ⊃ C] · R} ⊃ C

*Third*, develop a truth table for (8):

**(9)**

| {[(R | · | I) | ⊃ | C] | · | R} | ⊃ | C |
|------|---|----|---|----|---|----|---|---|
| 1 | 1 | 1 | 1 | 1 | 1 | 1 | 1 | 1 |
| 1 | 1 | 1 | 0 | 0 | 0 | 1 | 1 | 0 |
| 1 | 0 | 0 | 1 | 1 | 1 | 1 | 1 | 1 |
| ⇒ 1 | 0 | 0 | 1 | 0 | 1 | 1 | 0 | 0 |
| 0 | 0 | 1 | 1 | 1 | 0 | 0 | 1 | 1 |
| 0 | 0 | 1 | 1 | 0 | 0 | 0 | 1 | 0 |
| 0 | 0 | 0 | 1 | 1 | 0 | 0 | 1 | 1 |
| 0 | 0 | 0 | 1 | 0 | 0 | 0 | 1 | 0 |

                        ⇑

The truth table shows that (8) is contingent. There is a way to interpret (8) such that the antecedent is true and the consequent false. This is shown by the '0' under the horseshoe furtherest to the right in the fourth row. Thus, (6) is not valid. The truth of the premises of (6) *does not guarantee* the truth of its conclusion.

To establish the validity, or invalidity, of truth-function-al arguments with truth tables, a decision procedure can be used. Recall that a *decision procedure* or *algorithm* is a series of steps that when followed exactly will always lead to a desired result. Here is a decision procedure for establishing validity or invalidity of truth-functional arguments:

*1. Symbolize the argument.*

*2. Construct a hypothetical statement such that its antecedent is the conjunction of all the premises and its consequent is the conclusion of the argument.*

*3. Develop a truth table for this hypothetical statement.*

*4. The argument is deductively valid if and only if the hypothetical statement corresponding to it is a tautology.* \*

In using truth table techniques to demonstrate validity or invalidity, it is not uncommon to find an argument with relatively complicated premises:

**(10)**                                                                    /∴ C ⊃ B

    **1)** [A ⊃ (B ⊃ C)] • [D ⊃ (C ⊃ B)]   Pr

    **2)** D ∨ A                         Pr

    **3)** B                            Pr

    **4)** ~ C                         Pr

Putting these premises into conjunction presents problems of punctuation. The punctuation marks need to accomplish two things. *First*, they must exhibit each distinct conjunct that corresponds to a separate premise. *Second*, the punctuation marks must always manifest the form 'p•q'. Remember, conjunction is introduced in Chapter 2 as 'p•q' and not, say, '(p•q)•r'. Here are two flawed attempts to construct a hypothetical statement from the premises and conclusion in (10):

**(11)**   {[A ⊃ (B ⊃ C)] • [D ⊃ (C ⊃ B)] • [(D ∨ A)) • (B • ~ C)]} ⊃ (C ⊃ B)

**(12)**   ({[A ⊃ (B ⊃ C)] • [D ⊃ (C ⊃ B)]} • (D ∨ A) • (B • ~ C)) ⊃ (C ⊃ B)

The antecedent of (11) does not fulfill the first requirement of displaying separate premises, and the antecedent of (12) fails the second requirement of displaying the correct form, 'p • q'.

To avoid pitfalls in punctuating, a convention, *associating to the left*, is adopted:

> **Put into conjunction the first and second premises of the argument. Show by appropriate punctuation marks the conjuncts corresponding to the distinct premises, while also retaining the overall form 'p • q'. To this conjunction put into conjunction the third premise of the argument. Again, show by appropriate punctuation marks the conjuncts corresponding to the distinct premises, and also retain the overall form 'p • q'. Proceed in this way until all the premises are put into conjunction.**

Following this convention, the premises of (10) are put into conjunction:
*First*:

                          p                           q

$$\underbrace{\{[A \supset (B \supset C)] \cdot [D \supset (C \supset B)]\}} \cdot \underbrace{(D \vee A)}$$

---

\* This decision procedure, and following ones, can also be used with *argument forms* in which any statement variable is viewed *as if* it had a truth-value of '1' or '0'.

*Second*:

$$\overbrace{(\{[A \supset (B \supset C)] \cdot [D \supset (C \supset B)]\} \cdot (D \vee A))}^{p} \overbrace{\cdot B}^{q}$$

*Third*:

$$\overbrace{[(\{[A \supset (B \supset C)] \cdot [D \supset (C \supset B)]\} \cdot (D \vee A)) \cdot B]}^{p} \overbrace{\cdot \sim C}^{q}$$

The hypothetical statement corresponding to (10) is now symbolized as

$$\{[(\{[A \supset (B \supset C)] \cdot [D \supset (C \supset B)]\} \cdot (D \vee A)) \cdot B] \cdot \sim C\} \supset (C \supset B)$$

Remember that punctuation marks are used in left-hand and right-hand pairs and in the following order of strength from weakest to strongest: '( )', '[ ]', and '{ }'.

---

## *EXERCISES*

Symbolize each argument using the suggested capital letters. Then by truth table techniques decide whether the argument is valid or invalid.

1. Either the Senate comes to a bipartisan agreement to reduce the national deficit, or the dollar sinks even further against the Japanese yen. The dollar continues to sink. So, the Senate doesn't come to a bipartisan agreement to reduce the national deficit. (C,S)

2. Assuming Wall Street regains strength against the falling dollar, over the counter stocks will improve in their performance. Stock market analysts say that over the counter stocks will improve. Thus, Wall Street regains strength against the falling dollar. (R,I)

3. Wall Street doesn't regain its world leadership position only if the international market goes into general financial turmoil. However, Wall Street does regain its world leadership position. So, the international market doesn't go into general financial turmoil. (R,G)

4. A necessary condition for the Compaq family of desktop computers not selling well is that Compaq doesn't have an adequate sales force to move its product. But, on the contrary, Compaq does have an adequate sales force. Consequently, the Compaq family of desktop computers sells well. (C,F)

5. Microsoft will quickly release its own version of OS/2 or lose a great deal of long-range business to young start-up companies. Microsoft, however, won't permit itself to lose a

great deal of business. Hence, it isn't true that Microsoft will quickly release its own version of OS/2 but not lose a great deal of business to young start-up companies. (R,L)

6. The new *BIM* super desktop computers will run under either the OS/2 operating system, or under UNIX and DOS 5.0. The *BIM*, however, won't run under UNIX. So, the *BIM* super desktop computer will run under OS/2 and DOS 5.0. (O,U,D)

7. Thomas Wolfe was either a northern novelist or a southerner, but not both. He was a southerner if, and only if, he was born below the Mason-Dixon Line. Accordingly, either Wolfe was a northern novelist or he was born below the Mason-Dixon Line, but not both. (N,S,M)

8. Thomas Wolfe described real people; but also if Wolfe lived in Asheville, he wrote about southerners. So, that he described real people is a sufficient condition for Wolfe writing about southerners. (D,L,W)

9. Robert Frost was a poet but James Adams wasn't. Either Carl Sandburg was a poet or Adams was, but not both. Hence, both Frost and Sandburg were poets. (F,A,S)

10. If we're interested in northern literature, then we'll read Frost whenever we study poetry. We'll not read Frost, however. Therefore, we aren't interested in northern literature even though we do study poetry. (I,R,S)

11. If you like modern poetry, then you've read Frost only if you've studied "Birches." You don't like modern poetry. You like modern poetry or you haven't read Frost. So, you haven't studied "Birches." (L,R,S)

12. Henry James wrote short stories or poems. James wrote short stories or novels. He didn't write poems. Consequently, he wrote novels. (S,P,N)

13. Sinclair Lewis wrote *Main Street* or *Look Homeward, Angel*, but not both. He wrote *Main Street*. If he didn't write *Look Homeward, Angel*, Lewis didn't write about North Carolina. Hence, he wrote neither *Look Homeward, Angel* nor about North Carolina. (S,A,C)

14. Eugene O'Neill wrote plays, or he wrote novels and short stories. He wrote short stories or he didn't write novels. Thus, O'Neill wrote plays. (P,N,S)

15. If the choroid absorbs light but doesn't make a reflection, we see a clear image. We don't see a clear image or the choroid absorbs light. The choroid doesn't absorb light. Hence, that the choroid doesn't make a reflection is a necessary condition that it absorbs light. (A,M,S)

16. That the choroid absorbs light is a sufficient condition for the following: It reduces reflection if and only if the image is clear. If it doesn't reduce reflection, it absorbs light. But, a choroid doesn't absorb light. Therefore, the image is clear. (A,R,C)

17. The choroid doesn't absorb light. Either the choroid doesn't reduce reflection and doesn't blur the image, or the choroid does absorb light. The choroid doesn't absorb light if and only if it isn't the case that it does blur the image and doesn't reduce reflection. Hence, the choroid reduces reflection or it blurs the image, but not both. (A,R,B)

18. If actin is discovered in the myofibril, myosin is found there too; also if the muscle contracts, ATP is part of the contraction complex. It isn't true both that myosin is found in the myofibril while ATP is part of the contraction complex. The muscle does contract. So, actin is discovered in the myofibril. (D,F,C,P)

19. The following isn't true: Actin but not myosin is in the muscle filament bands. Further, it isn't true that myosin but not actin is in the muscle filament bands. If a contraction occurs,

then actin is in the muscle filament bands when and only when myosin is also in the bands. A relaxation or contraction occurs. Therefore, a relaxation occurs. (A,M,C,R)

20. If actin is in the myofibril, then so is myosin; moreover, if ATP is split, the muscle contracts. It isn't the case that actin isn't in the myofibril and ATP isn't split. The muscle doesn't contract. Therefore, myosin isn't in the myofibril. (A,M,S,C)

---

## 4.    THE *REDUCTIO AD ABSURDUM* METHOD: VALIDITY AND INVALIDITY

The concepts *valid* and *invalid arguments* are understood in this way:

> **An argument is *deductively valid* if the premises logically entail the conclusion; that is, when all the premises are true, the conclusion must also be true. An argument is *deductively invalid* if the conclusion is not entailed by the premises. For a deductively invalid argument there is at least one way to make all the premises true and the conclusion false.**

A truth table means of establishing validity and invalidity can be developed based on the notion that a valid argument cannot have *both* all true premises *and* a false conclusion. If an argument is valid, then it is contradictory both to deny the conclusion and to assert as true all the premises. So,

> **if there is at least one truth-value assignment of the conjoined premises put into conjunction with the denial of the conclusion making this entire conjunction true, the original argument is invalid. If there is not such a truth-value assignment, the original argument is not invalid but valid.**

The assumption that the argument is invalid is reduced to a contradiction, or absurdity, in the case of valid arguments. Using this *reductio ad absurdum* method, the validity of the following argument can be established:

(1)    The Yanks or the Mets will win the World Series next season if the Braves don't. However, neither the Braves nor Mets will win. So, the Yanks will. (Y,M,B)

Symbolize this argument as

$$(2) \qquad\qquad\qquad\qquad / \therefore Y$$
$$1) \quad \sim B \supset (Y \vee M) \quad \text{Pr}$$
$$2) \quad \sim (B \vee M) \qquad \text{Pr}$$

Next, put all the premises into conjunction:

$$(3) \quad [\sim B \supset (Y \vee M)] \cdot \sim (B \vee M)$$

Then, deny the conclusion and conjoin this denial with the conjunction of the premises:

$$(4) \quad \{[\sim B \supset (Y \vee M)] \cdot \sim (B \vee M)\} \cdot \sim Y$$

If there are any truth-conditions that make (4) true, then (1) is invalid. But there are no such truth-conditions, as is seen in the following truth table:

(5)

| {[ | ~ | B | ⊃ | (Y | ∨ | M)] | · | ~ | (B | ∨ | M)} | · | ~ | Y |
|---|---|---|---|---|---|---|---|---|---|---|---|---|---|---|
| | 0 | 1 | 1 | 1 | 1 | 1 | 0 | 0 | 1 | 1 | 1 | 0 | 0 | 1 |
| | 0 | 1 | 1 | 1 | 1 | 0 | 0 | 0 | 1 | 1 | 0 | 0 | 0 | 1 |
| | 0 | 1 | 1 | 0 | 1 | 1 | 0 | 0 | 1 | 1 | 1 | 0 | 1 | 0 |
| | 0 | 1 | 1 | 0 | 0 | 0 | 0 | 0 | 1 | 1 | 0 | 0 | 1 | 0 |
| | 1 | 0 | 1 | 1 | 1 | 1 | 0 | 0 | 0 | 1 | 1 | 0 | 0 | 1 |
| | 1 | 0 | 1 | 1 | 1 | 0 | 1 | 1 | 0 | 0 | 0 | 0 | 0 | 1 |
| | 1 | 0 | 1 | 0 | 1 | 1 | 0 | 0 | 0 | 1 | 1 | 0 | 1 | 0 |
| | 1 | 0 | 0 | 0 | 0 | 0 | 0 | 1 | 0 | 0 | 0 | 0 | 1 | 0 |
| | | | | | | | | | | | | ⇑ | | |

(5) shows that (4) is a contradiction. As seen in the last conjunction column of (5), there is no truth-condition making the conjunction of the premises and the denial of the conclusion true. Hence, (1) is not invalid; it is valid.

What of an invalid argument? Study this example:

**(6)** If we are going to have world peace, then we must continue talking with the Russians while also reducing the world weapons race. Certainly we do continue talking with the Russians while also reducing the world weapons race. Consequently, we are going to have world peace. (G,T,R)

(6) is symbolized as

$$(7) \qquad\qquad\qquad\qquad / \therefore G$$
$$1)\ G \supset (T \cdot R) \quad Pr$$
$$2)\ T \cdot R \qquad\qquad Pr$$

*First*, put all the premises into conjunction:

$$(8) \quad [G \supset (T \cdot R)] \cdot (T \cdot R)$$

*Second*, put the conjunction of the premises into conjunction with the *denial* of the conclusion:

$$(9) \quad \{[G \supset (T \cdot R)] \cdot (T \cdot R)\} \cdot \sim G$$

*Third*, generate a truth table for (9):

(10)

| | {[G | ⊃ | (T | · | R)] | · | (T | · | R)} | · | ~ | G |
|---|---|---|---|---|---|---|---|---|---|---|---|---|
| | 1 | 1 | 1 | 1 | 1 | 1 | 1 | 1 | 1 | 0 | 0 | 1 |
| | 1 | 0 | 1 | 0 | 0 | 0 | 1 | 0 | 0 | 0 | 0 | 1 |
| | 1 | 0 | 0 | 0 | 1 | 0 | 0 | 0 | 1 | 0 | 0 | 1 |
| | 1 | 0 | 0 | 0 | 0 | 0 | 0 | 0 | 0 | 0 | 0 | 1 |
| ⇒ | 0 | 1 | 1 | 1 | 1 | 1 | 1 | 1 | 1 | 1 | 1 | 0 |
| | 0 | 1 | 1 | 0 | 0 | 0 | 1 | 0 | 0 | 0 | 1 | 0 |
| | 0 | 1 | 0 | 0 | 1 | 0 | 0 | 0 | 1 | 0 | 1 | 0 |
| | 0 | 1 | 0 | 0 | 0 | 0 | 0 | 0 | 0 | 0 | 1 | 0 |
| | | | | | | | | | | ⇑ | | |

(10) shows that (9) is contingent. The fifth row indicates that there is at least one way to make the overall conjunction true; namely, if 'G' is false while both 'T' and 'R' are true. So, the original argument, (6), is invalid.

To use the *reductio ad absurdum* method of establishing validity follow this decision procedure:

   1. *Symbolize the argument.*
   2. *Put all the premises into conjunction, associating to the left if needed.*
   3. *Put the denial of the conclusion into conjunction with the conjoined premises.*
   4. *Develop a truth table for the entire conjunction formulated in 3.*
   5. *The original argument is valid if, and only if, this conjunction is contradictory.*

---

### *EXERCISES*

Symbolize each argument using the suggested capital letters. Then by the *reductio ad absurdum* method of truth tables decide whether every argument is valid or invalid.

   1. Iraq continues her blood bath while the United States sends more soldiers to the front. So, assuming the United States does send more soldiers to the front, Iraq continues her blood bath. (C,S)

   2. Iraq doesn't escalate hostilities in the Persian gulf unless the U.S. government continues to send military forces there. The U.S. government does continue to send military forces there. Consequently, Iraq doesn't escalate hostilities in the Gulf. (E,C)

   3. Either France or Great Britain will aid in the peace-keeping missions in the Near East. Certainly Great Britain will aid in these missions. Hence, France won't. (F,B)

   4. Russia doesn't believe that her long-range national interests are in danger in the Middle East. She won't enter into the various Middle East conflicts provided that she doesn't believe her national long-range interests are in danger. Accordingly, Russia won't enter into the various Middle East conflicts. (B,E)

   5. Wall Street regains a substantial amount of its losses or people quickly invest heavily in CDs, but not both. People quickly invest heavily in CDs. Consequently, Wall Street doesn't regain a substantial amount of its losses. (R,I)

   6. Federal securities won't fail except under the condition that the national government goes belly up. The national government isn't going belly up. Therefore, federal securities won't fail or the federal government does go belly up. (F,G)

   7. Assuming the New York Stock Exchange totters while the American Exchange is falling, the NASDAQ Exchange is in a panic. The NASDAQ Exchange is in a panic. So, the American Exchange is falling. (T,F,P)

   8. That the stock market continues in a sideways to downward path is sufficient to guarantee that investment money won't flow into Wall Street. Money won't flow into Wall Street or the banking system suffers. Accordingly, assuming the stock market continues in a sideways to downward path, the banking system will suffer. (C,F,S)

   9. Assuming the federal government imposes heavy tariffs on non-American products, either the prices of foreign goods won't escalate dramatically or many Americans lose

their jobs, but not both. The prices of foreign goods won't escalate dramatically. Thus, assuming many Americans don't lose their jobs, the federal government doesn't impose high tariffs on non-American products. (I,E,L)

10. The special bipartisan committee on the national deficit along with the President will propose budget cuts or the Gramm-Rudman Act will come into play. The President won't agree on budget cuts. Consequently, the special bipartisan committee will propose budget cuts or the Gramm-Rudman Act will come into play. (C,P,À)

11. The national deficit increases just in case that both the public sector continues to spend more than it accumulates while the private sector earns less than it charges. The private sector earns less than it charges. Consequently, the national deficit increases while the public sector continues to spend more than it accumulates. (I,C,E)

12. Expect a recession along with many investors fleeing the market if equity prices continue to rise. However, a recession isn't expected. Consequently, neither will equity prices continue to rise nor many investors flee the market. (E,F,C)

13. Going into the fourth quarter, the economy won't show modest growth except in the case that the Federal Reserve holds the line on accelerating interest rates. Furthermore, the federal government increases capital gains taxes or the Federal Reserve doesn't hold the line, but not both. Capital gains taxes surely aren't increased. So, going into the fourth quarter, the economy will show modest growth. (S,H,I)

14. Either interest rates increase as well as the national deficit worsens, or the federal government moves to immediate across the board tax increases. Neither is the national deficit worsening nor interest rates increasing. Accordingly, the federal government moves to immediate across the board tax increases or interest rates don't increase. (I,W,M)

15. It isn't true that the Mets win the National League and don't have a good shot at taking the World Series. Moreover, it isn't the case that the Mets won't probably play the Yankees as well as having a good shot at the Series. So, the Mets don't win the National League or they probably play the Yankees. (W,H,P)

16. Assuming Ole Miss wins over Alabama, then she will go to the Sugar Bowl if she also beats Georgia. Yet, neither does Ole Miss beat Georgia nor not win over Alabama. Hence, neither will Ole Miss go to the Sugar Bowl nor beat Georgia. (W,G,B)

17. If David has the retrovirus *HTLV-3* and it goes quickly into *AIDS*, then there isn't a known medical means of stopping his untimely death. That there isn't a known medical means of stopping his untimely death is both necessary and sufficient for David's dying from *AIDS*-induced complications. Unfortunately, David has the retrovirus. So, that his retrovirus *HTLV-3* will go quickly into *AIDS* is sufficient for David's dying from *AIDS*-induced complications. (H,G,M,D)

18. Assuming that *AIDS* is limited to neither homosexual males nor intravenous drug users, the general populace cannot relax in a "not me" attitude only if *AIDS* isn't widespread. So, *AIDS* isn't widespread provided that it is limited to homosexuals and intravenous drug users. (H,I,P,W)

19. That *HTLV-3* is difficult to contract as well as *AIDS* victims remain relatively few in number compared to the overall population count is sufficient for recommending that the overall population ought to condone *AIDS* victims. Either *AIDS* victims remain relatively few or they ought to be completely quarantined from the general populace, but not both. However, *AIDS* victims are not remaining relatively few in number compared to the overall population. Consequently, it is not recommended that the overall population

ought to condone *AIDS* victims, and further they ought to be completely quarantining them from the general populace. (D,R,C,Q)

20. Dramatically increasing the chances of developing *AIDS* is a sufficient and necessary condition for Pat not following exactly the advice of the Surgeon General concerning *AIDS*. Either Pat does follow exactly the advice of the Surgeon General or is put at high risk for contracting the *HTLV-3* retrovirus, but not both. Pat isn't put at high risk. Thus, it isn't true that both Pat dramatically increases the chances of developing *AIDS* and receiving *AZT* therapy to forestall the inevitable fatality of the disease. (I,F,P,R)

---

## 5.   THE REPLACEMENT METHOD: VALIDITY AND INVALIDITY

One practical limitation to truth tables is their potential length. Here is a case in point:

(1)   Nancy won't be re-elected or she complies with the policies of the county boss. She may preserve her personal integrity or not comply. Nancy won't be able to serve the people of her district if she preserves her personal integrity. If she isn't able to serve the people of her district, Nancy permits political corruption to spread. By her nature she can't permit political corruption to spread. Hence, Nancy is in the quandary of not being re-elected. (E,C,P,S,A)

Symbolize (1) as

$$(2) \qquad\qquad\qquad\qquad / \therefore\ \sim E$$

     **1)** $\sim E \vee C$    Pr

     **2)** $P \vee \sim C$    Pr

     **3)** $P \supset \sim S$    Pr

     **4)** $\sim S \supset A$    Pr

     **5)** $\sim A$        Pr

To decide by truth table methods whether (2) is valid or not, begin by constructing a hypothetical corresponding to (2):

(3)   $[(\{[(\sim E \vee C) \cdot (P \vee \sim C)] \cdot (P \supset \sim S)\} \cdot (\sim S \supset A)) \cdot \sim A] \supset \sim E$

Notice that the truth table analysis of (3) requires thirty-two rows!

An argument is valid or invalid, but not both. Is (1) valid? *Assume that (1) is invalid* and *show that this assumption cannot hold*. If it can be shown that a particular argument cannot be invalid, then that argument is valid. The definition of 'validity' is 'if all the premises are true, then the conclusion must also be true'. So, to assume an argument invalid is to assume that there is at least one truth-value assignment that makes the premises true and the conclusion false. (1) is invalid if the conclusion, ' $\sim E$', is false and all the premises true. If this truth-condition cannot be established, (1) is valid.

Does the *assumption* that (1) is invalid hold? Assuming ' ~ E' is false, 'E' is true. If 'E' is true in the conclusion, it is true whenever it occurs in the premises. But, since 'E' is assumed to be true, '~ E' in the first premise must be false. 'C' in the first premise is taken as true because the other disjunct, '~ E', is assumed false. '~ C' appears in the second premise and is understood as being false since 'C' in the first premise is interpreted as true. Because the second premise is a disjunctive statement assumed to be true, 'P' is also assumed true. The antecedent of the third premise, 'P', is therefore, true. From this it follows that '~ S', the consequent, is true. If it were not, the third premise would be false. Yet all the premises are assumed true and the conclusion false if (1) is to be shown invalid. Because '~ S' is assumed true in the third premise, it is also taken as true in the fourth. Hence, the consequent, 'A', in the fourth premise must also be understood as true. This, however, makes the fifth premise, '~ A', false. It has, accordingly, been shown that there is *no way* to interpret the conclusion of (1) as false and all the premises as true. (1) is not invalid; it is valid.

(4)               $/\therefore\ \sim E$                  $/\therefore\ 0$

     **1)**   $\sim E \lor C$                 $0 \lor 1 = 1$

     **2)** $P \lor \sim C$                 $1 \lor 0 = 1$

     **3)** $P \supset\ \sim S$                $1 \supset 1 = 1$

     **4)** $\sim S \supset A$                $1 \supset 1 = 1$

     **5)** $\sim A$                     $X \sim 1 = 0$

**TRUTH-VALUE ASSIGNMENT**

$A = 1$

$C = 1$

$E = 1$

$P = 1$

$S = 0$

'$X$' indicates the false premise given the truth-value assignments of (4).

Consider another example:

**(5)** People's moral practices are often not different from their claimed ethical system. Yet if people's moral practices are often different from their claimed ethical system, they might become psychopathic. That people might become psychopathic is sufficient for not being able to function at their best capacity. Now, people become mentally unbalanced whenever they aren't able to function at their best capacity; furthermore, if people's moral practices are often different from their claimed ethical system, social conditions are frequently the fundamental cause. Consequently, if people become mentally unbalanced, social conditions are frequently the fundamental cause. (M,P,C,U,S)

Symbolize (5) in this way:

**(6)**                                                    $/ \therefore U \supset S$

    **1)** $\sim M$                    Pr

    **2)** $M \supset P$               Pr

    **3)** $P \supset \sim C$          Pr

    **4)** $(\sim C \supset U) \cdot (M \supset S)$     Pr

*Assume* (5) is invalid. Interpret 'U ⊃ S' as false while attempting to interpret *all* the premises as true. If 'U ⊃ S' is false, 'U' is true and 'S' false. Since all the premises are assumed true, the first premise ' ~ M', is true. This means 'M' is false. Because 'M' is false, 'P' in the second premise can be either true or false, leaving the second premise true. If 'P' is true, 'C' is false and ' ~ C' true in the third premise. This would make ' ~ C' true in the fourth premise, and since 'U' is true, ' ~ C ⊃ U' would be true. Because 'M' is interpreted as false, 'M ⊃ S' is true. This guarantees the truth of the fourth premise. Consequently, there is at least one way to interpret all the premises of (5) as true and the conclusion false. Thus, the argument is invalid. This information can be pictured as

**(7)**          $/ \therefore U \supset S$              $/ \therefore 1 \supset 0$   $= 0$

    **1)** $\sim M$                          $\sim 0$           $= 1$

    **2)** $M \supset P$                     $0 \supset 1$      $= 1$

    **3)** $P \supset \sim C$                $1 \supset 1$      $= 1$

    **4)** $(\sim C \supset U) \cdot (M \supset S)$     $(1 \supset 1) \cdot (0 \supset 0)$     $= 1$

**TRUTH-VALUE ASSIGNMENT**

$$C = 0$$
$$M = 0$$
$$P = 1$$
$$S = 0$$
$$U = 1$$

There might be several other ways of assigning truth-values showing the invalidity of (6). Indeed, here is another:

**(8)**          $/ \therefore U \supset S$              $/ \therefore 1 \supset 0$   $= 0$

    **1)** $\sim M$                          $\sim 0$           $= 1$

    **2)** $M \supset P$                     $0 \supset 0$      $= 1$

    **3)** $P \supset \sim C$                $0 \supset 1$      $= 1$

    **4)** $(\sim C \supset U) \cdot (M \supset S)$     $(1 \supset 1) \cdot (0 \supset 0)$     $= 1$

**TRUTH-VALUE ASSIGNMENT**

$$C = 0$$
$$M = 0$$
$$P = 0$$
$$S = 0$$
$$U = 1$$

Remember to show that an argument is invalid, only one interpretation must be discovered in which all the premises are true but the conclusion is false.

Many arguments have conclusions that can be falsified in several ways. Some ways of falsifying a conclusion might not produce all true premises and, thereby, suggest that the argument is invalid. If the first interpretation does not show invalidity, then the other ways of making the conclusion false must be tried. This process needs to be continued until either some interpretation is found making the conclusion false and all the premises true, or all possible ways of falsifying the conclusion are shown to produce at least one false premise. To demonstrate that an argument is invalid, it is sufficient to show *at least one* way (there might be several) of falsifying the conclusion while having all true premises. If there is *no way* of showing this, that argument is valid.

---

## *EXERCISES*

Using truth table techniques developed in this section, decide which of the following are valid and which invalid.

1.                 $/ \therefore B \supset A$
   1) A    Pr

2.                 $/ \therefore A \supset B$
   1) A    Pr

3.                         $/ \therefore B$
   1) $(A \supset B) \cdot A$    Pr

4.                         $/ \therefore B$
   1) $(A \supset B) \vee A$    Pr

5.                         $/ \therefore B$
   1) $(A \supset B) \Delta A$    Pr

6.                         $/ \therefore A \supset C$
   1) $A \vee (B \cdot C)$    Pr
   2) $B \equiv C$        Pr

7.                         $/ \therefore C \cdot B$
   1) $(A \Delta B) \cdot B$    Pr
   2) $\sim (\sim A \cdot C)$    Pr

8.                         $/ \therefore A \Delta B$
   1) $(A \cdot B) \equiv C$    Pr
   2) $\sim D \supset \sim C$    Pr
   3) $B \vee A$        Pr

9.                         $/ \therefore (\sim A \cdot B) \vee (C \cdot A)$
   1) $A \supset B$        Pr
   2) $\sim (\sim C \cdot D)$    Pr
   3) $D \vee A$        Pr
   4) $(C \supset A) \cdot A$    Pr

10.                                              $/ \therefore C \lor B$
   1) $(A \equiv B) \supset [C \lor (A \cdot B)]$  Pr
   2) $(A \supset C) \cdot (C \supset B)$  Pr
   3) $(B \supset C) \cdot (C \supset A)$  Pr

11.                              $/ \therefore A \cdot B$
   1) $C \supset (A \cdot C)$  Pr
   2) $(A \cdot B) \lor B$  Pr
   3) $\sim B \triangle C$  Pr

12.                                  $/ \therefore C \triangle B$
   1) $\sim [(B \cdot \sim C) \cdot \sim A]$  Pr
   2) $\sim (A \cdot \sim B)$  Pr
   3) $\sim (\sim C \cdot \sim B)$  Pr

13.                              $/ \therefore A \supset C$
   1) $(D \lor B) \supset \sim A$  Pr
   2) $\sim (C \lor B) \supset C$  Pr

14.                              $/ \therefore A \triangle B$
   1) $(A \equiv B) \cdot (B \equiv C)$  Pr
   2) $\sim C \supset \sim D$  Pr
   3) $A \lor D$  Pr

15.                              $/ \therefore C \equiv B$
   1) $A \supset (C \supset D)$  Pr
   2) $B \triangle (D \cdot B)$  Pr
   3) $(D \cdot \sim C) \supset B$  Pr
   4) $D \cdot A$  Pr

16.                              $/ \therefore A \cdot (C \cdot B)$
   1) $(D \lor B) \supset C$  Pr
   2) $A \triangle D$  Pr
   3) $(C \lor B) \supset D$  Pr
   4) $D \supset (B \cdot \sim D)$  Pr

17.                              $/ \therefore A \supset (B \equiv C)$
   1) $\sim (D \cdot A)$  Pr
   2) $A \supset (\sim D \equiv \sim B)$  Pr
   3) $(D \cdot A) \supset C$  Pr

18.                              $/ \therefore (C \supset B) \lor \sim (B \lor C)$
   1) $(A \supset B) \supset (C \supset B)$  Pr
   2) $(D \supset C) \supset \sim (B \lor C)$  Pr

19.                              $/ \therefore (\sim B \lor D) \cdot (D \lor \sim A)$
   1) $A \equiv B$  Pr
   2) $\sim C \equiv B$  Pr
   3) $(A \lor D) \cdot \sim C$  Pr

20.                              $/ \therefore C \lor \sim E$
   1) $A \supset (B \supset C)$  Pr
   2) $\sim D \supset (E \supset \sim C)$  Pr
   3) $\sim (A \cdot D) \supset \sim (B \lor E)$  Pr
   4) $E \lor B$  Pr

## 6.   CONSISTENCY AND INCONSISTENCY

Premise sets are *consistent* or *inconsistent*, but not both.

> **The premise set of an argument is *consistent* when there is at least one truth-value assignment making the conjunction of all the premises true.**

Consequently,

> **the premise set of an argument is *inconsistent* when there is no truth-value assignment making the conjunction of all the premises true.**

Truth table techniques provide a means of deciding whether a truth-functional argument has a consistent premise set or not. The decision procedure is this:

1. *Symbolize the argument.*
2. *If there is more than one premise, put them into conjunction, associating to the left.*
3. *Construct a truth table for this conjunction.*
4. *The premise set is inconsistent if and only if the conjunction is contradictory.*

Premise sets are consistent if there is at least one truth-value assignment making all the premises true. But in step 2 the premises become the conjuncts of an overall conjunction. Hence, if the conjunction formed from the premises is contingent or tautological, there is at least one truth-value assignment making all the premises true. If this conjunction is contradictory, the premise set is inconsistent because there is at least one false conjunct in a contradictory conjunction.* That is, there is at least one false premise in the premise set.

Examine this argument:

**(1)**   Either my Zipper Gripper will hold or I'll be embarrassed, but not both. It isn't true that my Zipper Gripper will hold and I'll not be embarrassed. My Zipper Gripper will hold. Thus, I'll not be embarrassed. (G,E)

Using the recommended capital letters, symbolize (1) as

$$\textbf{(2)} \qquad\qquad\qquad\qquad / \therefore \sim E$$

| | | |
|---|---|---|
| **1)** | $G \bigtriangleup E$ | Pr |
| **2)** | $\sim (G \cdot \sim E)$ | Pr |
| **3)** | $G$ | Pr |

Is the premise set of (1) consistent? This is decided by putting the premises in

---

* *Which* premise is false might differ according to the different assignments of truth-values to the simple statements out of which the premises are built up. However, at least one premise will always be false.

conjunction, associating to the left, and constructing a truth table for that conjunction:

$$(3)\quad [(G\ \Delta\ E)\ \cdot\ \sim(G\ \cdot\ \sim E)]\ \cdot\ G$$

```
     1  0  1  0  1  1  0  0  1   0  1
     1  1  0  0  0  1  1  1  0   0  1
     0  1  1  1  1  0  0  0  1   0  0
     0  0  0  0  1  0  0  1  0   0  0
                                 ⇑
```

Inspecting (3) reveals that the final column has a '0' in every row. So, the overall conjunction is contradictory. The premise set of (1) is, therefore, inconsistent since there is no truth-value assignment making all the premises true.

Does the following argument have a consistent or inconsistent premise set?

**(4)**  It isn't the case that Jim won't live a happy life and develop financial problems. But, assuming that Jim does live a happy life, he hasn't contracted large debts. Unfortunately, either Jim does both develop financial problems while not living a happy life, or he has contracted large debts. Hence, Jim has neither developed financial problems nor will he live a happy life. (L,D,C)

Given the suggested capital letters, (4) is symbolized as

**(5)**                                         $/ \therefore\ \sim(D \vee L)$

1)  $\sim(\sim L \cdot D)$     Pr

2)  $L \supset \sim C$         Pr

3)  $(D \cdot \sim L) \vee C$  Pr

Put the symbolized premises of (5) into conjunction, associating to the left:

**(6)**    $[\sim(\sim L \cdot D) \cdot (L \supset \sim C)] \cdot [(D \cdot \sim L) \vee C]$

Construct a truth table for (6):

$$(7)\quad [\ \sim (\sim L\ \cdot\ D)\ \cdot\ (L\ \supset\ \sim C)]\ \cdot\ [(D\ \cdot\ \sim L)\ \vee\ C]$$

```
     1  0  1  0  1  0  1  0  0  1   0   1  0  0  1   1  1
     1  0  1  0  1  1  1  1  1  0   0   1  0  0  1   0  0
     1  0  1  0  0  0  1  0  0  1   0   0  0  0  1   1  1
     1  0  1  0  0  1  1  1  1  0   0   0  0  0  1   0  0
     0  1  0  1  1  0  0  1  0  1   0   1  1  1  0   1  1
     0  1  0  1  1  0  0  1  1  0   0   1  1  1  0   1  0
 ⇒   1  1  0  0  0  1  0  1  0  1   1   0  0  1  0   1  1
     1  1  0  0  0  1  0  1  1  0   0   0  0  1  0   0  0
                                    ⇑
```

(7) displays that (6) is contingent. Since the conjuncts of (6) are the premises of (5), the truth table also shows the premise set symbolized in (5) is consistent. There is at least one truth-condition, and in this case only one, making all the premises true. Of

course, in other arguments there might be more than one truth-condition making all the premises true. While (4) has a consistent set of premises, it has still not been decided if it is a valid argument or not.*

Any argument having an inconsistent premise set is valid no matter what the conclusion of that argument is. Any argument is valid if, and only if, a particular hypothetical statement constructed from the argument is tautological. The antecedent of that hypothetical statement is the conjunction of all the premises. If an argument has an inconsistent premise set, the conjunction of its premises is always false. A hypothetical statement is false, however, only when the antecedent is true and the consequent false. In the case of inconsistent premise sets, the antecedent can never be true. Consequently, the hypothetical statement can never be false. The hypothetical statement remains tautological regardless of its consequent. The argument, then, corresponding to such a hypothetical statement is valid no matter what its conclusion.

While an argument with an inconsistent premise set is valid, no argument with an inconsistent premise set is ever sound. A sound argument is not only valid, but has all true premises. From the viewpoint of soundness, any argument with an inconsistent set of premises is worthless. Such an argument permits *anything* to be deductively established. Inconsistent premise sets, like contradictions, cannot supply supporting evidence for any claim.† What if the laws of science were inconsistent? Anything could be deduced from them. What if various theories of finance were inconsistent? Anything could be shown to follow from them. Or what if someone held inconsistent political, moral, or religious opinions? Any claim could be supported. The concepts *consistency* and *inconsistency* become important, then, in guiding human activity insofar as someone is guided by her opinions and what is held to be evidence for them.

---

## EXERCISES

Symbolize each argument using the capital letters suggested. Then decide by truth table techniques which arguments have a consistent premise set and which have an inconsistent one. For extra practice, also decide which arguments are valid and which are invalid.

1. John Steinbeck wrote about itinerant farmers if and only if his works contain stories about people traveling from place to place in search of agricultural jobs. So, either Steinbeck wrote about itinerant farmers or his works contain stories about people traveling from place to place in search of agricultural jobs. (W,C)

2. William Faulkner was awarded the Nobel Prize. If Faulkner was awarded the Nobel Prize, he is considered a successful writer. Hence, Faulkner is considered a successful writer. (A,C)

---

*The argument is valid.

† Inconsistent premise sets are useful in what is known as *indirect proofs* to establish the validity of arguments. Indirect proofs are introduced in Chapter 7.

3. Edgar Allan Poe wrote either *The Pit and the Pendulum* or *Chrome Yellow*. He didn't write *Chrome Yellow*. Therefore, Poe's having written *The Pit and the Pendulum* is a sufficient reason for his having written *Chrome Yellow*. (P,Y)

4. Lord Byron wrote "Don Juan," or he wrote "The Battle of Blenheim" but not "Don Juan." So, Byron wrote "Don Juan." (J,B)

5. Percy Bysshe Shelley wrote "Don Juan" assuming that he wrote "Adonais." But, it isn't true that Shelley wrote "Adonais" and "Don Juan." Shelley didn't write "Don Juan." Thus, he wrote "Adonais" or "Don Juan." (A,J)

6. The League of Nations was valuable assuming Woodrow Wilson was correct in his anti-isolationist views. The League of Nations was valuable only if America didn't follow an isolationist policy and, moreover, Wilson was correct. Accordingly, Wilson wasn't correct unless America didn't follow an isolationist policy. (L,W,A)

7. If Woodrow Wilson and advocates of world government are correct, then the Senate accepts the League of Nations. That the advocates of world government are correct is necessary for the Senate accepting the League of Nations. Therefore, if Wilson is correct, the advocates of world government are also correct. (W,A,S)

8. Either the Senate or Woodrow Wilson was correct in their opinion of the League of Nations. It isn't the case that if Wilson wasn't correct in his opinion then the Senate was. Hence, either Wilson was correct in his opinion of the League of Nations or America wasn't prepared to have an isolationist policy. (S,W,A)

9. A strong military doesn't provide the best protection against foreign attack only if a nation isn't willing to defend itself. It isn't true that either a strong military provides the best protection against foreign attack or a militarily strong nation doesn't succumb to international pressures. Either a nation is willing to defend itself or a militarily strong nation doesn't succumb to international pressure. Hence, a strong military provides the best protection against foreign attack only if a militarily strong nation doesn't succumb to international pressures. (P,W,S)

10. A militarily strong nation succumbs to international pressure or a strong military provides the best protection against foreign attack (but not both), and certainly a strong military does provide the best protection against foreign attack. A militarily strong nation doesn't succumb to international pressure except the best use wasn't made of that nation's military power. So, the best use wasn't made of that nation's military power. (S,P,M)

11. If the most important problem of any person isn't merely to exist but to live well, we might desire to study Plato. Of course, the most important problem of any person *is* to live well. We might not desire to study Plato even though the most important problem of any person is not merely to exist. Therefore, if the most important problem of any person isn't merely to exist, then we might desire to study Plato. (E,L,D)

12. It isn't the case that either Socrates is correct or we should be unjust. Also Socrates is correct or Thrasymachus is right. Socrates is correct. Hence, we should be just despite the fact that Thrasymachus is also right. (C,J,R)

13. We're concerned with leading a morally good life provided we don't both ignore Plato and forget Aristotle. Not being concerned with leading a morally good life is necessary for forgetting Aristotle. Now we don't both forget Aristotle and ignore Plato. Hence, we're concerned with leading a good, moral life while also not forgetting Aristotle. (C,I,F)

14. If "Portrait of Leander" was written in the sixteenth century, then if "Loved by a God" was also written in the sixteenth century, the poems were written by Christopher Marlowe. Of course, "Loved by a God" was written in the sixteenth century. Furthermore, that the

poems were written by Marlowe is a sufficient reason for claiming that "Loved by a God" and "Portrait of Leander" were both written in the sixteenth century. Accordingly, that Marlowe wrote these poems is necessary and sufficient for "Portrait of Leander" having been written in the sixteenth century. (L,G,M)

15. Aldous Huxley wrote *Hadrian's Memoirs* or *Brave New World* (but not both), or Huxley was a poet and wrote "Desiderato." Huxley wrote both *Brave New World* and *Hadrian's Memoirs*, although he didn't write "Desiderato." Consequently, if he wrote "Desiderato," he also wrote *Brave New World* and was a poet. (M,W,P,D)

16. John Keats isn't a Romantic writer if and only if Robert Browning is. If Keats is a Romantic writer, he isn't a Victorian author. The poetry of Keats has Victorian characteristics or he isn't a Victorian author, but not both. Therefore, it isn't the case that Browning isn't a Romantic writer and Keats' poetry has Victorian characteristics. (K,B,A,C)

17. If adenine is a purine while uracil isn't, then quanine is a purine. It isn't true that adenine isn't a purine and quanine is. Neither uracil nor quanine is a purine. Further, it isn't the case both that quanine is a purine and thymine isn't. So, thymine is a purine. (A,U,Q,T)

18. If adenine is a purine, so is quinine. While adenine is a purine, uracil isn't. That thymine is a pyrimidine is a sufficient condition for the following not being the case; namely, if adenine is a purine, uracil isn't. That uracil is a purine is a necessary condition for quinine being a purine. Hence, thymine is a pyrimidine, and if uracil is a purine then so is quinine. (A,Q,U,T)

19. Frodo Baggins goes to the Cracks of Doom only if Gollum won't stay behind, and Frodo does go. Gollum not staying behind is a sufficient condition for Frodo both going to the Cracks of Doom and his escaping the evil creatures of Sauron the Great. Frodo escapes the evil creatures of Sauron if and only if either Frodo goes to the Cracks of Doom or Gollum doesn't stay behind. Frodo goes to the Cracks of Doom or the powers of the Ruling Ring overcome him. Frodo doesn't escape the evil creatures of Sauron. Consequently, the Ruling Ring doesn't overcome Frodo and he does go to the Cracks of Doom. (G,S,E,O)

20. That Sauron is finally defeated is necessary for the following: Bilbo Baggins recovers the lost Ruling Ring while his cousin, Frodo, becomes the Ring-bearer, and either Strider successfully helps to protect the Shire or Gandalf the Grey wards off evil from the hobbits. So, if it isn't true that Bilbo recovers the Ruling Ring and Gandalf doesn't ward off evil from the hobbits, Sauron is finally defeated. (D,R,B,H,W)

---

# 7. LOGICAL EQUIVALENCE

In proposing evidence in support of some claim, a person might say the same thing in different ways. This could be done for a number of reasons such as variation or emphasis. Semantically the statements 'Annye Mae discovered the money in the drawer' and 'Annye Mae found the money in the drawer' assert the same thing. Grammatically, the same thing can be asserted by 'Russell ate the hot dog' or 'The hot dog was eaten by Russell'. Different claims can also be used to make the same assertion because they are *logically* equivalent.

There is no difference in truth-value between saying 'If it rains, then the ground is wet' and 'Either it didn't rain or the ground is wet'. It is important to be able to establish that what is being asserted by using "other words" is the same assertion as made by the original claim. If this is not so, then a shift in meaning in either the premises or conclusion of an argument could possibly occur and not be detected. Such a shift could spoil an otherwise valid argument. When the concept *asserting the same thing* is based on logical equivalence of truth-functional statements, truth table techniques can be used to establish whether different claims are logically equivalent or not.

Two truth-functional statements are ***logically equivalent***

> **when, and only when, they each have the same truth-value if and only if they have identiical truth-conditions.**

For example, the following are logically equivalent:

(1) If a neuron is alive and fires, it contains a given minimum number of excitatory fibers. (A,F,C)

(2) If a neuron is alive, then it isn't the case that if fires and doesn't contain a given minimum number of excitatory fibers. (A,F,C)

The truth-conditions making (1) true are those that establish the truth of (2), and vice versa. Whatever conditions make (1) false also establish that (2) is false, and vice versa. A truth table method for deciding whether two truth-functional statements are logically equivalent is at hand. Follow this decision procedure:

1. *Symbolize the truth-functional statements.*

2. *From the two statements construct a statement of the form 'p ≡ q' where 'p' represents one of the statements and 'q' the other.*

3. *Generate a truth table for 'p ≡ q'.*

4. *The original two statements are logically equivalent if, and only if, 'p ≡ q' is a tautology.*

This procedure rests on the definition of 'logical equivalence' and the rule that 'p ≡ q' counts as true if and only if both statements represented by 'p' and 'q' have the same truth-value.

Return to (1) and (2). Follow steps {1} through {4}:

**{1}**

    **a)** $(A \cdot F) \supset C$

    **b)** $A \supset \sim (F \cdot \sim C)$

**{2}**   $[(A \cdot F) \supset C] \equiv [A \supset \sim (F \cdot \sim C)]$

{3}  [(A · F) ⊃ C] ≡ [A ⊃ ∼ ( F · ∼ C)]

| [ | (A | · | F) | ⊃ | C] | ≡ | [A | ⊃ | ∼ | ( F | · | ∼ | C)] |
|---|----|----|----|----|----|----|----|----|----|----|----|----|----|
|  | 1 | 1 | 1 | 1 | 1 | 1 | 1 | 1 | 1 | 1 | 0 | 0 | 1 |
|  | 1 | 1 | 1 | 0 | 0 | 1 | 1 | 0 | 0 | 1 | 1 | 1 | 0 |
|  | 1 | 0 | 0 | 1 | 1 | 1 | 1 | 1 | 1 | 0 | 0 | 0 | 1 |
|  | 1 | 0 | 0 | 1 | 0 | 1 | 1 | 1 | 1 | 0 | 0 | 1 | 0 |
|  | 0 | 0 | 1 | 1 | 1 | 1 | 0 | 1 | 1 | 1 | 0 | 0 | 1 |
|  | 0 | 0 | 1 | 1 | 0 | 1 | 0 | 1 | 0 | 1 | 1 | 1 | 0 |
|  | 0 | 0 | 0 | 1 | 1 | 1 | 0 | 1 | 1 | 0 | 0 | 0 | 1 |
|  | 0 | 0 | 0 | 1 | 0 | 1 | 0 | 1 | 1 | 0 | 0 | 1 | 0 |

⇑

**{4}** Only '1's appear under the triple bar in {3},
'[A · F) ⊃ C] ≡ [A ⊃ ∼ (F · ∼C)]' is a tautology, and '(A · F) ⊃ C' and
'A ⊃ ∼ (F · ∼C)' are logically equivalent.

---

## EXERCISES

Symbolize the following using the suggested capital letters. Then by truth table methods decide which pairs are logically equivalent and which are not.

1. a) Charles Baudelaire is a familiar French poet. (B)
   b) Charles Baudelaire isn't an unfamiliar French poet. (B)

2. a) It isn't true that Stéphane Mallarmé and Rainer Rilke are both French poets. (M,R)
   b) Either Stéphane Mallarmé isn't a French poet or Rainer Rilke isn't. (M,R)

3. a) Either a student isn't interested in Naturalism or is interested in reading Émile Zola. (N,Z)
   b) A student isn't interested in Naturalism; however, the student is interested in reading Émile Zola. (N,Z)

4. a) Neither Victor Hugo nor Théophile Gautier belong to the eighteenth century. (H,G)
   b) Théophile Gautier doesn't belong to the eighteenth century, but also Victor Hugo doesn't belong to it. (G,H)

5. a) It isn't the case that a person of letters hasn't read François René de Chateaubriand and also hasn't read Alphonse de Lamartine. (C,L)
   b) A person of letters has read either Alphonse de Lamartine or François René de Chateaubriand. (L,C)

6. a) The Feds permit interest rates to climb steeply while allowing the stock market to decline dramatically. (P,A)
   b) It isn't true that the Feds don't permit interest rates to climb steeply while not allowing the stock market to decline dramatically. (P,A)

7. a) The soothsayers of Wall Street predict there will either be a recession or the industrial index will gain, but not both. (R,I)
   b) The soothsayers of Wall Street predict that there won't be a recession if, and only if, the industrial index gains. (R,I)

8. a) Either the trade deficit balances or America's smokestack industries collapse. (B,C)
   b) Neither is it that the trade deficit doesn't balance nor America's smokestack industries don't collapse. (B,C)

9.  a) The economy regains its vitality only if individuals begin to save much more of their monthly net income. (R,S)

    b) The economy regains its vitality if individuals begin to save much more of their monthly net income. (R,S)

10. a) Stocks do well or bonds increase in value, but it isn't the case that stocks do well and bonds increase in value. (S,B)

    b) That stocks do well is a necessary condition for bonds not increasing in value; but, nonetheless, stocks don't do well and neither do bonds increase in value. (S,B)

11. a) *U2* will be on campus this weekend, while next weekend either *R.E.M.* or the *Pet Shop Boys* will be here. (U,R,P)

    b) Either *U2* will be on campus this weekend and *R.E.M.* will be here next weekend, or the *Pet Shop Boys* will be here next weekend as well as *U2* this weekend. (U,R,P)

12. a) Being interested in music of the sixties is sufficient reason to listen to both Joan Baez and *Peter, Paul, and Mary*. (S,B,P)

    b) If people are interested in music of the sixties, they'll listen to *Peter, Paul, and Mary* if they listen to Joan Baez. (S,P,B)

13. a) Most students today like both rock and acid only if they also like metal along with rock. (R,A,M)

    b) Most students today like rock, but they don't like acid unless they also like metal. (R,A,M)

14. a) Both either the murder weapon will be found or the killer won't be declared guilty, and either a motive is established or the killer won't be declared guilty. (F,D,E)

    b) Either the killer won't be declared guilty or the murder weapon will be found along with the fact that a motive is established. (D,F,E)

15. a) Provided that the defense lawyer will both plead temporary insanity on the behalf of his client and attack the death penalty, the accused murderer is a juvenile. (P,A,J)

    b) If the accused murderer is a juvenile and the defense lawyer pleads temporary insanity, then the defense lawyer will argue against the death penalty. (J,P,A)

16. a) If the accused murderer is declared guilty, this means that there will be an automatic appeal, and a new defense lawyer will be found by the court if the accused murderer is declared guilty. (D,A,F)

    b) Unless there is an automatic appeal in addition to the court finding a new defense lawyer, the accused murderer isn't declared guilty. (A,F,D)

17. a) Assuming the accused juvenile is found guilty of murder, the defendant won't be sentenced to life imprisonment except in the case that the death penalty is declared appropriate for juveniles. (F,S,D)

    b) That the accused will be sentenced to life imprisonment is necessary for both the accused juvenile being found guilty of murder as well as the death penalty being declared appropriate for juveniles. (S,F,D)

18. a) Next weekend either Vanderbilt beats Duke, or Gainesville murders North Carolina in spite of the fact that Georgia takes Alabama or Auburn stomps Clemson. (B,M,T,S)

    b) Next weekend Georgia takes Alabama or Auburn stomps Clemson at the same time that Gainesville murders North Carolina or Vanderbilt beats Duke. (T,S,M,B)

19. a) Not only does Tech take Auburn or LSU win over FSU, but further Ole Miss grinds out Virginia or South Carolina stomps Kentucky. (T,W,G,S)

    b) Either South Carolina stomps Kentucky in addition to Ole Miss grinding out Virginia, or either Tech takes Auburn or LSU wins over FSU. (S,G,T,W)

20. a) Either Georgia beats North Carolina or Texas whips Alabama, or neither Mississippi takes South Carolina nor Alabama shakes Georgia. (B,W,T,S)
    b) Mississippi never takes South Carolina but that Texas whips Alabama while Georgia beats North Carolina; and yet, unless Georgia beats North Carolina and Texas whips Alabama, Alabama doesn't shake Georgia. (T,W,B,S)

## 8. REVIEW OF NEW TERMS

**Consistent premise set:** The premise set of an argument is consistent if, and only if, there is at least one truth-value assignment making all the premises true.

**Contingent statement:** A statement having at least one truth-value assignment making it true and at least one making it false.

**Contradiction:** See, *Contradictory statement*.

**Contradictory statement:** A statement having no truth-value assignment making it true; *contradiction*.

**Inconsistent premise set:** The premise set of an argument is inconsistent if and only if there is no truth-value assignment making all the premises true.

**Invalid:** An argument interpreted deductively that is not valid.

**Logical entailment:** A premise set logically entails a conclusion if, and only if, when all the statements in the premise set are true, the conclusion must also be true.

**Logical equivalence:** Statements are logically equivalent if and only if they are each true given the same truth-value assignments and each false under the same truth-value assignments. That is, statements are logically equivalent if, and only if, they have exactly the same truth-conditions.

**Tautological statement:** A truth-functional statement having no truth-value assignment making it false; *tautology*.

**Tautology:** See, *Tautological statement*.

**Valid:** An argument interpreted deductively is valid if, and only if, when all of its premises are true, the conclusion must also be true; an argument interpreted deductively can never be valid if it can have all true premises and a false conclusion.

# 4

# TRUTH-FUNCTIONAL LOGIC: TRUTH TREES

Truth trees are introduced as a means of deciding validity and invalidity of truth-functional arguments as well as consistency and inconsistency of truth-functional premise sets. The use of truth trees is extended to test whether a truth-functional statement is contradictory, tautological, or contingent. Last, truth trees are used to decide if truth-functional statements are logically equivalent. While truth trees represent an effective decision procedure, nonetheless as presented in this chapter they are not mechanical.* This procedure is not mechanical because no set of rules is developed setting the exact order of the application of truth tree rules in particular cases. Instead strategies, or heuristics, are developed suggesting ways to proceed that will likely, but not certainly, lead to the desired results.

## 1. VALIDITY AND INVALIDITY

A *truth tree* is

**a branching diagram displaying all possible truth-conditions of a statement, or combination of statements.**

The *truth tree method* of demonstrating validity and invalidity is based on the notion that a deductively valid argument cannot have all true premises and a false conclusion. An argument is *deductively valid* or *valid* if and only if when all of its premises are true, the conclusion must also be true. An argument can never be deductively valid if it has all true premises and a false conclusion. On the other hand, an argument is

---

*As introduced in Chapter 2, Section 7, a *decision procedure* is a series of steps that, when followed exactly, always lead to a desired result.

*deductively invalid* or *invalid* if and only if it is not valid. If an argument is deductively valid and has all true premises, then its conclusion must also be true. Therefore, it is contradictory to claim that a deductively valid argument has all true premises and a false conclusion.

Assume someone arguing in this way:

> **(1)** The battle isn't lost. But either the weapons arrive on time or the battle is lost. So, the weapons arrive on time. (A,L)

Symbolize (1) as

$$
\begin{array}{lll}
\textbf{(2)} & & /\therefore \text{ A} \\
\textbf{1)} & \sim\text{L} & \text{Pr} \\
\textbf{2)} & \text{A} \lor \text{L} & \text{Pr}
\end{array}
$$

Expand the premises of (1) by asserting the denial of the conclusion as a new premise. Write 'AP' to the right-hand side of this premise to indicate that it is a new *assumed premise*:

$$
\begin{array}{lll}
\textbf{(3)} & & /\therefore \text{ A} \\
\textbf{1)} & \sim\text{L} & \text{Pr} \\
\textbf{2)} & \text{A} \lor \text{L} & \text{Pr} \\
\textbf{3)} & \sim\text{A} & \text{AP}
\end{array}
$$

(3) displays the root of the truth tree that is going to be generated. The **root** of a truth tree is

> **all of those statements, given and assumed, with which a truth tree begins.**

For an argument, the root of a truth tree is made up of all the given premises of that argument plus the new assumed premise. From the root of (3), all branches will fan out in a descending way.

Does the conjunction of the premises of (3) form a contradiction? If so, then all the premises of the original argument cannot be true, the conclusion false, and the argument valid. Or is there some assignment of truth-values to the simple statements 'A' and 'L' making all the premises of (3) true? If so, the original argument in (2) is invalid.

To answer these questions, **decompose**, or break up, the first premise of (3) into different *branches*. A **branch** of a truth tree represents a truth-value assignment that might be given to the root of that tree. (3) is decomposed into two branches:

$$
\begin{array}{lll}
\textbf{(4)} & & /\therefore \text{ A} \\
\textbf{1)} & \sim\text{L} & \text{Pr} \\
\textbf{2)} & \text{A} \lor \text{L} \quad \checkmark & \text{Pr} \\
\textbf{3)} & \sim\text{A} & \text{AP} \\
& \diagup\diagdown & \\
\textbf{4)} & \text{A} \qquad \text{L} & \text{1, ID}
\end{array}
$$

'A ∨ L' is decomposed in line 4. The '1, ID' seen in the right-hand side of line 4 indicates that the statements 'A' and 'L' come from 1 by decomposing an inclusive disjunctive statement. An inclusive disjunctive statement is always decomposed in a new line by forming separate branches out of each of its overall disjuncts. This is because an inclusive disjunctive is true if either, or both, of its disjuncts is true. The check, '✓', to the right of the statement in 2 indicates that it has been decomposed and can now be ignored. Any decomposed statement in a truth tree is marked by a check and then ignored in further development and interpretation of that tree. Decomposition continues until all branches are **terminated:**

> **A branch is terminated when, in all of its unchecked lines, only the names of simple statements and/or the names of simple statements prefixed by only one tilde are found.**

A *completed truth tree* is

> **a truth tree in which all possible branches are terminated.**

The unchecked statements in a terminated branch are to be interpreted as true. Thus, in the case of those names of simple statements prefixed by a tilde occurring in a branch, the simple statement is false because its denial is true.

Beginning with line 1, and continuing down through 3, traveling the left-hand branch, the following unchecked expressions are seen: '~ L', '~ A', and 'A'. Again, beginning with 1, moving through 3, but now going down the right-hand branch, '~ L', '~ A', and 'L' are discovered unchecked. Both branches contain a single letter representing a simple statement *and* that same letter prefixed by one tilde. Both branches lead to a contradiction. In the left-hand branch '~ A' and 'A' have opposite truth-values. They can neither both be true, nor both be false. The same situation occurs in the right-hand branch in terms of '~ L' and 'L'. A *closed branch* is

> **any branch in a truth tree containing a name of a simple statement and that statement name prefixed by one tilde.**

An *open branch* is

> **any branch that is not closed.**

To indicate a closed branch, put an 'X' at the bottom of that branch:

(5)                              /∴ A
    1)  ~ L        Pr
    2)  A ∨ L   ✓ Pr
    3)  ~ A        AP

                    ⋀
    4)  A      L    1, ID
        X      X

If every branch is closed, the premises from which those branches are generated are inconsistent. Every truth-value assignment to these premises leads to a contradiction. There is no way of making all the premises true. But the *denial* of the conclusion of the original argument symbolized at (2) is one of the premises. Thus, (5), with all closed branches, shows that there is no way of making the premises of the original argument true while also making the *denial* of its conclusion true. That is, there is no way of making all the premises true and the conclusion false. The original argument is, therefore, valid.

Consider another argument:

**(6)**  The NFL strike will end soon or the players will receive free-agent status. The hard-nosed owners are fighting free-agent status for the players and the strike won't end soon. So, the players will receive free-agent status. (E,R,F)

Put (6) into truth-functional notation:

**(7)**                                      /∴ R
  **1)** E ∨ R     Pr
  **2)** F • ~ E   Pr

Then assume the denial of the conclusion as a new premise. This forms the root of the truth tree:

**(8)**                                      /∴ R
  **1)** E ∨ R     Pr
  **2)** F • ~ E   Pr
  **3)**  ~ R      AP

Decompose the second premise by writing the conjuncts under one another in two new lines, 4 and 5. A truth-functional conjunction is true if and only if all of its conjuncts are true. That is why the conjuncts are decomposed by placing one under another in the same branch. In the right-hand side of both 4 and 5, write '2, C' to indicate that these statements come from a conjunction in line 2. Put a check after the statement, 'F • ~ E', in 2 to show that it has been decomposed and is ignored in further development of the tree:

**(9)**                                      /∴ R
  **1)** E ∨ R       Pr
  **2)** F • ~ E   ✓ Pr
  **3)**  ~ R        AP
  **4)**    F        2, C
  **5)**  ~ E        2, C

Next, decompose the first premise, using a check in line 1 and writing '1, ID' in the right-hand side of line 6:

**(10)**                                      /∴ R
  **1)** E ∨ R   ✓  Pr
  **2)** F • ~ E   ✓ Pr
  **3)**  ~ R        AP

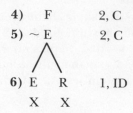

| 4) | F | 2, C |
|---|---|---|
| 5) | ~ E | 2, C |

| 6) | E    R | 1, ID |
|---|---|---|
| | X    X | |

Following the right-hand branch from 3 to 6 reveals a contradiction: ' ~ R' and 'R'. Thus, an 'X' is placed at the bottom of that branch. Similarly, the left-hand branch from 3 to 6 shows both ' ~ E' and 'E'. So, that branch is also closed, as indicated by another 'X'. Since every branch in (10) is closed, (6) is valid.

Notice that in decomposing the premises of (10) the conjunctive premise was decomposed before the disjunctive one. It is not necessary to follow this ordering, but it is usually more efficient. If the disjunctive premise is decomposed first, in order to represent all possible branches, the conjunctive premise must be decomposed in *every* new branch. While the results are the same as in (10), nonetheless (11) is more cumbersome:

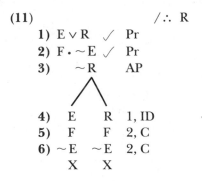

(11)                     /∴  R
1) E ∨ R  ✓  Pr
2) F • ~E  ✓  Pr
3)      ~R      AP

| 4) | E      R | 1, ID |
|---|---|---|
| 5) | F      F | 2, C |
| 6) | ~E    ~E | 2, C |
| | X      X | |

As a strategy, *decompose all conjunctive premises before disjunctive ones*.

What of invalid arguments? Here is an example:

**(12)** The fans put pressure on NFL management or the players return to the field. The fans do put pressure on management in addition to management caving in. Hence, the players return to the field. (P,R,C)

(12) can be symbolized as

(13)                     /∴  R
1) P ∨ R  Pr
2) P • C  Pr

Assume as a new premise the denial of the conclusion. This completes the root of the truth tree. Next, decompose the premises. Notice in this tree that 'P' appears twice in the same branch. It is not unusual for a letter to have multiple occurrences in a truth tree, and in different branches. These multiple occurrences are traceable to the several occurrences of that particular letter in the root.

**(14)**                                    / ∴ R

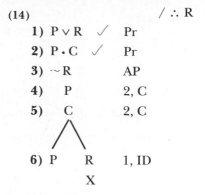

    **1)** P ∨ R   ✓    Pr

    **2)** P · C   ✓    Pr

    **3)** ~R         AP

    **4)**    P       2, C

    **5)**    C       2, C

    **6)** P     R     1, ID

            X

Starting with 3, note that while an instance of both a single letter indicating a simple statement and that letter prefixed by one tilde appear in the right-hand branch, no contradiction is seen in the left-hand branch. Hence, an 'X' is placed at the end of the terminated right-hand branch, but not at the end of the terminated left-hand one.* Since there is an open branch in (14), (13) is an invalid argument. If 'P' and 'C' are true, while 'R' is false, all the premises of (13) are true even though the conclusion is false.

Inspect this slightly more complicated argument:

**(15)** Either the stock market doesn't continue to alternate while interest rates balloon dramatically, or bond issues become highly chaotic or interest rates balloon dramatically. Interest rates don't balloon dramatically and neither do bond issues become highly chaotic. Thus, the stock market will continue to alternate. (A,B,C)

Symbolize (15) in this way:

**(16)**                                    / ∴ A

    **1)** (~A · B) ∨ (C ∨ B)    Pr

    **2)** ~B · ~C            Pr

Assuming the denial of the conclusion as a new premise, write

**(17)**                                    / ∴ A

    **1)** (~A · B) ∨ (C ∨ B)    Pr

    **2)** ~B · ~C            Pr

    **3)** ~A                AP

---

*Remember that a branch is terminated when, in all of its unchecked lines, only the names of simple statements and/or such statement names prefixed by only one tilde are found. A branch is closed when a contradiction appears in it. Hence, while the left-hand branch of (14) is terminated, it is not closed.

The strategy of first decomposing overall conjunctions dictates

(18)                                                    /∴ A
    1) ( ~A · B) ∨ (C ∨ B)    Pr
    2) ~B · ~C   ✓            Pr
    3)      ~A                 AP
    4)      ~B                 2, C
    5)      ~C                 2, C

No contradiction occurs in lines 3 through 5. So, continue by decomposing the overall disjunction in 1:

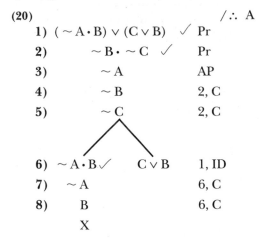

(19)                                                    /∴ A
    1) (~A · B) ∨ (C ∨ B)  ✓    Pr
    2)          ~B·~C  ✓         Pr
    3)            ~A             AP
    4)            ~B             2, C
    5)            ~C             2, C

    6)   ~A · B      C ∨ B       1, 1D

Line 6 contains two statements to be decomposed. One of these is '~A · B'. Continue by decomposing it under '~A · B':

(20)                                                    /∴ A
    1) (~A · B) ∨ (C ∨ B)   ✓   Pr
    2)          ~B · ~C  ✓       Pr
    3)            ~A             AP
    4)            ~B             2, C
    5)            ~C             2, C

    6)  ~A · B ✓     C ∨ B       1, ID
    7)   ~A                      6, C
    8)    B                      6, C
         X

An 'X' appears under 'B' in 8 because, tracing the left-hand branch of lines with no checks, ' ~B' is found in 4 and 'B' in 8. Continue by decomposing 'C ∨ B' found in 6:

(21)                                                    /∴ A
    1) (~A · B) ∨ (C ∨ B)   ✓   Pr
    2)          ~B · ~C   ✓      Pr

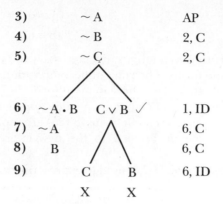

```
3)           ~ A              AP
4)           ~ B              2, C
5)           ~ C              2, C

6)   ~A•B    C∨B  ✓           1, ID
7)   ~A                       6, C
8)   B                        6, C
9)        C    B              6, ID
          X    X
```

Once again, examining lines containing no checks, each of the newly generated branches creates a situation in which only simple statement names,* or simple statement names prefixed by one tilde, are seen. Furthermore, each terminated branch displays a contradiction and is, therefore, closed. Since every possible branch of (16) is closed, (15) is a valid argument.

Until now only two implicit rules of decomposition have been used. One of these governs the decomposition of an overall conjunction, and the other an overall inclusive disjunction. These **rules of decomposition** can be pictorially represented as

**CONJUNCTION (C)**                          **INCLUSIVE DISJUNCTION (ID)**

(22)                                

Statements other than conjunctions and inclusive disjunctions also appear in truth-functional arguments. For instance, statements displaying any of these forms can appear:

(23)

      **a)** ~~p

      **b)** p Δ q

      **c)** p ⊃ q

      **d)** p ≡ q

      **e)** ~ (p•q)

      **f)** ~ (p ∨ q)

      **g)** ~ (p Δ q)

*Each simple statement name is represented by a single capital letter.

**h)** $\sim(p \supset q)$

**i)** $\sim(p \equiv q)$

In applying truth tree methods, it is necessary to be able to decompose statements exhibiting these forms. The rules of decomposition for both the dot and the wedge make it possible to replace the statement forms in (23) with expressions using only the dot and the wedge. Further, if any tilde appears, it must be coupled to a single letter only. Once the statement forms in (23) are replaced in this way, the two rules of decomposition can be applied to the new expressions generating terminating branches.

The *replacement sign*, ' :: ', is used to express the notion of replacement required in transforming the statement forms of (23) into more usable expressions:

> **If 'p' and 'q' have identical truth-values given the same truth-value assign-ments to their simple parts, then 'p' can replace 'q', and 'q' can replace 'p', at any occurrence of 'p' and 'q'. This is expressed by the notation 'p :: q'.**

For example, since 'p ⊃ q' and '∼ p ∨ q' have identical truth-values when 'p' and 'q' in each case are given identical truth-value assignments, '∼ p ∨ q' can replace 'p ⊃ q'. * This replacement is expressed as

$$p \supset q :: \sim p \vee q$$

All the replacements needed to decompose any truth-functional expression can be given:

**(24)**

**a)** $\sim\sim p :: p$

**b)** $p \triangle q :: (p \cdot \sim q) \vee (q \cdot \sim p)$

**c)** $p \supset q :: \sim p \vee q$

**d)** $p \equiv q :: (p \cdot q) \vee (\sim p \cdot \sim q)$

**e)** $\sim(p \cdot q) :: \sim p \vee \sim q$

**f)** $\sim(p \vee q) :: \sim p \cdot \sim q$

**g)** $\sim(p \triangle q) :: (p \cdot q) \vee (\sim p \cdot \sim q)$

**h)** $\sim(p \supset q) :: p \cdot \sim q$

**i)** $\sim(p \equiv q) :: (p \cdot \sim q) \vee (q \cdot \sim p)$†

---

*For the purposes of developing truth tree methods, the replacement sign '::', is read *as if* it were "one-directional" in asserting, for instance, that ' $\sim p \vee q$' may replace 'p ⊃ q'. The reason for this one-directional reading is that in constructing truth trees, one always moves to wedges and dots to decompose various statements. However, the replacement sign is actually bidirectional, as is seen in Chapter 6.

†That any named expressions flanking the ' :: ' sign are both true or both false can be established by truth tables. For instance, assuming that 'p' and 'q' represent any statements and assigning the

Any statement displaying the form on the left-hand side of the ' :: ' can be decomposed in terms of a statement displaying the form on the right-hand side of the ' :: '. Indeed, from each of these replacements a new truth tree rule of decomposition can be formulated. Take, for instance, any statement accepted as having an overall form of material equivalence:

$$(25)$$
$$\text{1) } p \equiv q$$

According to (d) in (24), 'p ≡ q' can be replaced in another line by '$(p \cdot q) \vee (\sim p \cdot \sim q)$':

$$(26)$$

**1)** $p \equiv q$  ✓                         ———*

**2)** $(p \cdot q) \vee (\sim p \cdot \sim q)$      1, replacement

Line 2 *is* an inclusive disjunction mentioning only simple statements and the denial of simple statements. Hence, 2 can be decomposed in this way:

$$(27)$$

**1)** $p \equiv q$  ✓                         ———

**2)** $(p \cdot q) \vee (\sim p \cdot \sim q)$  ✓   1, replacement

**3)** $p \cdot q$      $\sim p \cdot \sim q$        2, ID

---

same truth-value to each in the lead columns of a truth table for 'p ⊃ q' and '∼ p ∨ q' produces these results:

| p | q | p ⊃ q |   | p | q | ∼ p | ∼ p ∨ q |
|---|---|-------|---|---|---|-----|---------|
| 1 | 1 | 1 |   | 1 | 1 | 0 | 1 |
| 1 | 0 | 0 |   | 1 | 0 | 0 | 0 |
| 0 | 1 | 1 |   | 0 | 1 | 1 | 1 |
| 0 | 0 | 1 |   | 0 | 0 | 1 | 1 |

Notice that the last column in each of these truth tables has exactly the same array of '1's and '0's.

*Since (26) is not an *argument*, 'Pr' is not written to the right-hand side of 'p ≡ q'. Neither is there a '/ ∴' sign followed by a conclusion. When there is no argument involved, a dash is placed to the right-hand side of all statements in the root of the truth tree. 'Pr' is used only to indicate premises, and only arguments have premises.

The two conjunctions in 3 can be decomposed:

**(28)**

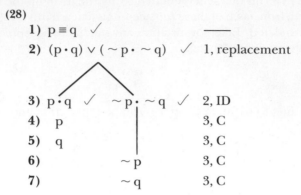

1) $p \equiv q$  ✓  ———

2) $(p \cdot q) \vee (\sim p \cdot \sim q)$  ✓  1, replacement

3) $p \cdot q$  ✓  $\sim p \cdot \sim q$  ✓  2, ID

4) $p$  3, C

5) $q$  3, C

6)  $\sim p$  3, C

7)  $\sim q$  3, C

Instead of proceeding through each step in (28) every time a material equivalence is decomposed, one can abbreviate the procedure as a rule of decomposition:

**(29)   MATERIAL EQUIVALENCE (ME)**

$$p \equiv q$$

$$p \quad \sim p$$
$$q \quad \sim q$$

Because all the replacements in (24) are expressed as statement variables, they are completely general, holding of any statement displaying these forms. This is why (29) can be accepted as picturing a *rule* of decomposition for material equivalence:

**Any statement of the form 'p ≡ q' can be decomposed into two separate branches. One of these, the left-hand branch, is composed of 'p' and 'q'. The other branch, the right-hand one, is composed of ' ~ p' and ' ~ q'.**

The pictorial expressions of the rules of decomposition, corresponding to the replacements in (24), are

**(30)   EXCLUSIVE DISJUNCTION (ED)\***    **MATERIAL IMPLICATION (MI)**

$$p \triangle q$$

$$p \quad q$$
$$\sim q \quad \sim p$$

$$p \supset q$$

$$\sim p \quad q$$

---

\*The branches for 'p ≡ q' and ' ~ (p △ q)' are the same. So are those for 'p △ q' and ' ~ (p ≡ q)'. In Chapter 2, truth-functional rules were established for the use of both 'p ≡ q' and 'p △ q'. These rules guarantee that any statements displaying the forms 'p ≡ q' and 'p △ q' are contradictory. If the statement variables, 'p' and 'q', are replaced by the name of some statement, the same name replacing each occurrence of the same variable, then the resulting statements are such that one is true and the other false. So, the denial of 'p ≡ q' or 'p △ q', but not both, is equivalent to the other.

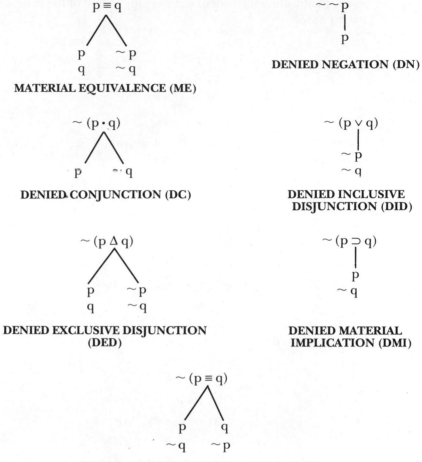

MATERIAL EQUIVALENCE (ME)

DENIED NEGATION (DN)

DENIED CONJUNCTION (DC)

DENIED INCLUSIVE
DISJUNCTION (DID)

DENIED EXCLUSIVE DISJUNCTION
(DED)

DENIED MATERIAL
IMPLICATION (DMI)

DENIED MATERIAL EQUIVALENCE (DME)

Any rule of decomposition can be used in truth trees to decide validity or invalidity. Consider another argument:

**(31)** We'll have social justice only if there is a massive reallocation, through Federal taxation, of private wealth. There is a massive reallocation, through Federal taxation, of private wealth, and, further, this newly generated tax money is used for social programs. Consequently, we'll have social justice if and only if the newly generated tax money is used for social programs. (J,R,P)

Notice how a truth tree is used to demonstrate the validity of (31). *First*, the argument is symbolized:

**(32)**  /∴ J ≡ P

1) J ⊃ R  Pr
2) R·P  Pr

*Second*, establishing the root of the tree, the denial of the conclusion is assumed as a new premise:

$$(33) \qquad\qquad /\therefore\ J \equiv P$$

1) $J \supset R$     Pr
2) $R \cdot P$     Pr
3) $\sim (J \equiv P)$   AP

Following the strategy of always first decomposing conjunctions, check the statement in 2 and decompose it in 4 and 5:

$$(34) \qquad\qquad /\therefore\ J \equiv P$$

1) $J \supset R$     Pr
2) $R \cdot P$  ✓   Pr
3) $\sim (J \equiv P)$   AP
4)     R     2, C
5)     P     2, C

The first premise is a hypothetical. Appealing to the rule of decomposition, MI, it is decomposed in 6:

$$(35) \qquad\qquad /\therefore\ J \equiv P$$

1) $J \supset R$  ✓   Pr
2) $R \cdot P$  ✓   Pr
3) $\sim (J \equiv P)$   AP
4)     R     2, C
5)     P     2, C

6)  $\sim J$     R   1, MI

Only the third premise remains to be decompsed. In order for the truth tree to be complete, '$\sim (J \equiv P)$' must be decomposed under all remaining opened branches. That is, '$\sim (J \equiv P)$' must be decomposed under both '$\sim J$' and 'R' in 6. DME is used to complete the truth tree in 7 and 8:

$$(36) \qquad\qquad /\therefore\ J \equiv P$$

1) $J \supset R$  ✓     Pr
2) $R \cdot P$  ✓     Pr
3) $\sim (J \equiv P)$  ✓     AP
4)     R     2, C

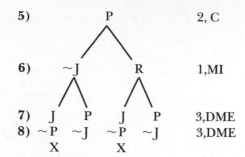

```
5)                P                2, C
                 / \
6)     ~J              R           1,MI
      / \            / \
7)   J   P          J   P          3,DME
8) ~P  ~J        ~P   ~J           3,DME
    X               X
```

After all the branches of (36) are terminated, two remain open. Examining the two open branches in (36), and ignoring repeats of expressions in each branch, reveals 'R', 'P', and ' ~ J' in every open branch. This means that if 'R' and 'P' are true and 'J' false, all the premises of (31) are true while, nonetheless, the conclusion is false. (31) is, therefore, invalid.

(34) could be continued by decomposing the third premise before the first:

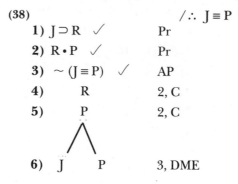

(37)                        / ∴ J ≡ P
    1) J ⊃ R          Pr
    2) R • P    ✓     Pr
    3)  ~ (J ≡ P)  ✓  AP
    4)       R        2, C
    5)       P        2, C
            / \
    6)   J     P      3, DME
    7) ~ P   ~ J      3, DME
        X

One branch is now closed *before* the decomposition of the first premise. This closure is due to 'P' in 5 and ' ~ P' in 7. The first premise is decomposed last:

(38)                        / ∴ J ≡ P
    1) J ⊃ R   ✓      Pr
    2) R • P   ✓      Pr
    3)  ~ (J ≡ P)  ✓  AP
    4)      R         2, C
    5)      P         2, C
           / \
    6)   J     P      3, DME
```
```

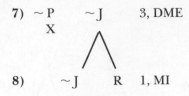

7) ~ P      ~ J      3, DME
      X

8)        ~ J      R      1, MI

Open branches remain in (38) showing that (31) is invalid. If 'R' and 'P' are true, but 'J' is false, the conclusion of (31) is false while all the premises are true.

As a *general strategy*, attempt to avoid multiple branches in developing a truth tree. *First*, decompose conjunctions and any statements that can be replaced by conjunctions. *Second*, decompose those disjunctions terminating in a closed branch. This is the guiding difference between (36) and (38). Decomposing the second premise *before* the first, even though the second is more complicated than the first, generates a closed branch more rapidly. Every time a branch is closed, there is less to generate and trace in the process of decomposition. Watch these strategies guide the development of (39) below.

The decomposition of (39) begins with line 3 because this does not create separate branches. Begin with those lines that are, or are replaceable by, conjunctions. Line 1 is treated last because it is not likely to generate closed branches if decomposed earlier. Having fewer branches will make the introduction of 1 less cumbersome. In each open branch, decomposition continues until it is terminated; that is, until only simple statement names, or simple statement names coupled to one tilde, remain. Furthermore, a terminated branch is closed with an 'X' as soon as both a letter and that letter prefixed by a single tilde occur in that branch. Finally, since a terminated open branch remains in 16, the argument is invalid. There is at least one, and in (39) only one, truth-condition making all the premises true while at the same time making the conclusion false:

(39)                                    / ∴ A Δ B

1) ~ (A ≡ B) ⊃ C   ✓   Pr
2) A ⊃ (C ⊃ ~ D)   ✓   Pr
3) ~ ( ~ A ∨ ~ D)   ✓   Pr
4) ~ (A Δ B)   ✓        AP
5)      ~ ~ A   ✓       3, DID
6)      ~ ~ D   ✓       3, DID
7)        A             5, DN
8)        D             6, DN

9)      A      ~ A      4, DED

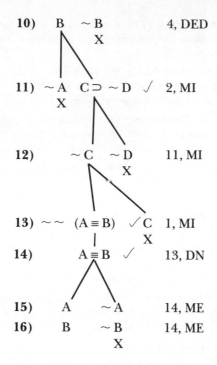

| 10) | B    ~B | 4, DED |
| 11) | ~A    C ⊃ ~D  ✓ | 2, MI |
| 12) | ~C    ~D | 11, MI |
| 13) | ~~ (A ≡ B)  ✓ C | 1, MI |
| 14) | A ≡ B  ✓ | 13, DN |
| 15) | A      ~A | 14, ME |
| 16) | B      ~B | 14, ME |

The above truth tree shows that when 'A', 'B', and 'D' are true, and 'C' is false, all the premises of (39) are true while, nevertheless, the conclusion is false. (39) is, therefore, invalid.

---

## EXERCISES

### Group A:

Using (25) through (28) as a model, coupled with the replacements in (24), establish as rules of decomposition ED, MI, DC, DID, DED, DMI, and DME. State each rule of decomposition, except ME, in English.

### Group B:

Symbolize the following arguments using the suggested notation. Then use the truth tree method techniques developed in this section to decide which of the following are valid and which invalid.

1. Assuming there is going to be world peace, it is mandatory to eliminate all nuclear weapons. All nuclear weapons are being eliminated. Hence, there is going to be world peace. (P,W)*

2. Jim Bakker didn't deny having an adulterous affair with Jessica Hahn. Now, Tammy Bakker appears to forgive easily her husband's adultery or Jim Bakker did deny having an affair. Accordingly, Tammy Bakker appears to forgive easily her husband's adultery. (D,F)

3. The *Chargers* won't lose another football game unless the *Seahawks* have a chance to win the division. Certainly, the *Seahawks* do have a chance to win the division. Therefore,the *Chargers* lose another game and the *Seahawks* have a chance to win the division. (L,W)

4. Bob Horner won't come back to the *Atlanta Braves* except that he is offered a million dollar signing bonus. The *Braves* offer Horner a million dollar signing bonus. Nonetheless, Horner won't come back to the *Atlanta Braves*. (C,O)

5. Keith Moon is neither alive nor does he still play drums for *The Who*. Thus, Moon still plays drums for *The Who* just in case he is alive. (A,P)

6. The world-wide spread of *AIDS* won't stop except that everyone is protected against the retrovirus *HTLV-3*. Yet, everyone isn't protected against this retrovirus. Accordingly, the world-wide spread of *AIDS* won't stop. (S,P)

7. People with *AIDS* don't have a good survival rate, but that a treatment of *AIDS* is at hand is a necessary condition for people with *AIDS* to have a good survival rate. Thus, there is a treatment of *AIDS* at hand and/or people with *AIDS* have a good survival rate. (S,T)

8. Neither Jessica Hahn won't pose for *Playboy* nor Jim Bakker won't be fired from the *PTL*. Moreover, Hahn told Phil Donahue, in a television interview, that she still needs money. Consequently, Jim Bakker is fired from the *PTL* despite the fact that Jessica Hahn still needs money. (P,F,N)

9. *Alabama* is a favorite country group or *Bon Jovi* is (but not both), while, of course, *Alabama* is a favorite country group. *Bon Jovi* isn't a favorite country group unless *Dead Kennedies* is. Consequently, both *Alabama* and *Dead Kennedies* are favorite country groups. (A,B,D)

10. *The Grateful Dead* will play at the Center next year if and only if they can fit a public performance into their recording schedule. *The Grateful Dead* won't play at the Center or they will release a new album, but not both. Hence, that they can fit a public performance into their recording schedule is both necessary and sufficient for *The Grateful Dead* to release a new album. (P,F,R)

11. *Mötley Crüe* is a great rock band or *Boston* is liked by everyone, but *Mötley Crüe* is a great rock band only if *Def Leppard* is tops in college concerts. However, *Def Leppard* isn't tops in college concerts. So, neither is *Mötley Crüe* a great rock band nor *Def Leppard* tops in college concerts, but nonetheless *Boston* is liked by everyone. (M,B,D)

12. Either *R.E.M.* or *U2*, but not both, is given top billing by *Rolling Stone* magazine. Neither is *U2* given top billing by *Rolling Stone* nor is *Van Halen* not recognized by *Rolling Stone*. So, *R.E.M.* is given top billing by *Rolling Stone* yet *U2* isn't, but furthermore *Van Halen* is recognized by *Rolling Stone*. (R,U,V)

13. Johann Sebastian Bach composed during the German baroque period of music and didn't write during the Italian romantic period. Bach composed during the German

---

*It is interesting to compare the following argument with the first argument in this exercise:

Assuming there is going to be world peace, it is necessary to build up a large store of strong nuclear weapons. A large store of strong nuclear weapons is being built up. Hence, there is going to be world peace. (P,W)

baroque period just in case he used German baroque musical forms. It isn't true that Bach didn't write during the Italian romantic period and didn't employ many musical embellishments. So, while employing many musical embellishments, Bach also used German baroque musical forms. (C,W,U,E)

14. It isn't true that Peter Tchaikovsky developed superb melodic lines while not also writing highly appealing music. Further, it isn't true that he didn't compose very melodic scores yet also did enjoy wide popularity. In fact, Tchaikovsky developed superb melodic lines and/or enjoyed wide popularity. Consequently, either he wrote highly appealing music or composed very melodic scores. (D,W,C,E)

15. Peter Tchaikovsky developed complicated melodic lines, and he foresaw the development of contemporary musical idioms whenever he extensively used syncopated rhythms. But Tchaikovsky neither extensively used syncopated rhythms nor didn't develop complicated melodic lines. Whenever he developed complicated melodic lines, he composed very melodic scores. Accordingly, Tchaikovsky composed very melodic scores and foresaw the development of contemporary musical idioms. (D,F,U,C)

16. It isn't true that George Harrison is attempting to regain the mystique of the *Beatles* as well as ignoring a revival of sixties music, while on the other hand, it is true that the music market is ripe for his return. Either assuming Harrison isn't ignoring a revival of sixties music, he is attempting to regain the mystique of the *Beatles*, or the music market isn't ripe for his return. Thus, Harrison isn't ignoring a revival of sixties music just in case he is attempting to regain the mystique of the *Beatles*. (A,I,R)

17. Neither do Middle Eastern political crises worsen nor do Western nations hesitate to protect their interests only if Iran suppresses Islamic fundamentalism. If Iran doesn't suppress Islamic fundamentalism, then the political crises don't worsen unless the Western nations don't hesitate to protect their interests. Iran doesn't suppress Islamic fundamentalism. Therefore, Middle Eastern political crises worsen or Western nations do hesitate to protect their interests, but not both. (W,H,S)

18. That Iraq launches a major military campaign against U.S. holdings is both necessary and sufficient for a major war beginning in the Middle East. That a major war begins in the Middle East only if Iraq launches a major military campaign against U.S. holdings is sufficient for the U.S. government attacking Iraq. A major war is beginning in the Middle East. Consequently, either the U.S. government attacks Iraq while a major war is beginning in the Middle East, or Iraq launches a major military campaign against U.S. holdings, but not both. (L,B,A)

19. Johann Sebastian Bach didn't compose in the German baroque period of music except that he used German baroque musical forms, yet he certainly did use these forms. Bach employed many musical embellishments provided that he both wrote in the Italian romantic period yet also used German baroque forms. Bach didn't employ many musical embellishments or he composed in the German baroque period. Thus, either Bach wrote in the Italian romantic period or he used German baroque musical forms, but not both. (C,U,E,W)

20. That Iraq maintains her belligerent actions in the Persian Gulf is sufficient to guarantee that neither will the U.S. government be satisfied with again going before the U.N. to seek sanctions against Iraq nor withdraw its war fleet from the Gulf. The U.S. government withdraws its war fleet provided that the government will be satisfied to see U.N. sanctions against Iraq if Iraq maintains her belligerent actions in the Gulf. Neither does the U.S. government withdraw its war fleet nor Iraq won't maintain her belligerent actions. Thus, the U.S. government will be satisfied with again going before the U.N. to seek sanctions against Iraq or withdraw its war fleet from the Gulf. (M,S,W)

## 2.   CONSISTENCY AND INCONSISTENCY

The premise set of an argument is *inconsistent* if and only if there is no truth-value assignment making all the premises true. No matter what truth-value assignment is made, at least one of the premises will be false. On the other hand, the premise set of an argument is *consistent* when and only when there is at least one truth-value assignment making all the premises true.

It is important to be able to distinguish consistent from inconsistent premise sets since inconsistent premise sets always form the basis for a valid, although unsound, argument, as in this example:

**(1)**   Cancer research is furthered, but it is furthered only if the general area of retrovirus studies is strengthened. Assuming that the general area of retrovirus studies is strengthened, more federal and state money is made available. However, for various reasons, more federal and state money is not made available. All of which substantiates the claim that cancer research is neither furthered nor more federal and state money made available. (F,S,A)

Begin by demonstrating that (1) is valid. Symbolize the argument and assume the denial of the conclusion as a new premise. This creates the root needed to generate a truth tree:

**(2)**                                         $/ \therefore \sim (F \lor A)$

  **1)** $F \cdot (F \supset S)$     Pr

  **2)** $S \supset A$         Pr

  **3)** $\sim A$          Pr

  **4)** $\sim\sim (F \lor A)$ AP

Begin with the first premise to decompose the root of (2):

**(3)**                                         $/ \therefore \sim (F \lor A)$

  **1)** $F \cdot (F \supset S)$   $\checkmark$   Pr

  **2)** $S \supset A$           Pr

  **3)** $\sim A$            Pr

  **4)** $\sim\sim (F \lor A)$   AP  AP

  **5)**      $F$               1, C

  **6)**      $F \supset S$ $\checkmark$        1, C

  **7)**  $\sim F$     $S$      6, MI
       $X$

An 'X' occurs under ' $\sim F$ ' in 7 because both 'F' and ' $\sim F$ ' appear in the same branch. Continue by decomposing the second premise:

**(4)**                                         $/ \therefore \sim (F \lor A)$

  **1)** $F \cdot (F \supset S)$   $\checkmark$   Pr

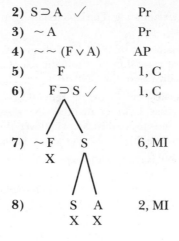

**2)**  S ⊃ A  ✓          Pr
**3)**  ∼ A              Pr
**4)**  ∼∼ (F ∨ A)       AP
**5)**      F            1, C
**6)**    F ⊃ S ✓        1, C

**7)**  ∼ F    S          6, MI
        X

**8)**        S  A        2, MI
              X  X

All branches of (4) are closed. There is no branch on the tree to append the denial of the conclusion '∼ ∼ (F ∨ A)'— *or any other conclusion.* The argument is valid no matter what conclusion it might have.

Truth trees can be used to test for consistency and inconsistency without testing for validity or invalidity. Symbolize the argument. Do *not* assume the denial of the conclusion as a new premise in the root. Use, as needed, the various rules of decomposition on the premises to generate a truth tree. If, when all decomposition is completed, every branch is closed, the premises are inconsistent. If there remains at least one open branch, the premises are consistent. It is only to such remaining open branches that the denial of a conclusion is appended and then decomposed to test for validity or invalidity. If after terminating all branches there are no open ones, then the argument is valid. Otherwise it is invalid.

An argument with a consistent premise set might be valid or invalid. However, any argument having an inconsistent premise set is always valid. While valid, arguments with inconsistent premise sets can never be sound. A sound argument is not only valid but has all true premises. But inconsistent premise sets contain premises such that at least one of them is false. This is seen in the various appearances of 'p' and '∼ p' in every branch of a truth tree whose root is made up of an inconsistent premise set. Because at least one of the premises is always false, inconsistent premise sets are, in general, worthless for supplying reasons to substantiate any conclusion.*

---

## EXERCISES

Symbolize the following arguments using the suggested notation. Then decide whether each argument has a consistent or inconsistent premise set.

1. That Wall Street is stagnating is sufficient for the GNP's falling in real dollar amounts only

---

*The Indirect Method of Proof relies on the inconsistency of a premise set of an argument to establish a conclusion. For a discussion of this type of proof see Chapter 7, Section 2.

if Wall Street is, in fact, stagnating. The GNP is falling in real dollar amounts. Accordingly, Wall Street is stagnating. (S,F)

2. Interest rates continually rise or the GNP falls in real dollar amounts. Either the GNP doesn't fall or interest rates don't continually rise. Consequently, it isn't the case that interest rates continually rise or the GNP doesn't fall in real dollar amounts. (R,F)

3. Either the GNP rises substantially or the general living standards of the country lower noticeably. It isn't the case, however, that the GNP rises substantially if the general living standards aren't lowered noticeably. So, whenever the general living standards of the country are lowered noticeably, the GNP doesn't rise substantially. (R,L)

4. It isn't true that the GNP is rising while exports are increasing dramatically. However, the GNP won't rise unless exports increase dramatically, but exports aren't increasing. Thus, since exports aren't increasing dramatically, then the GNP isn't rising. (R,I)

5. While Wall Street doesn't stagnate in any real growth change, nonetheless it does stagnate if the GNP falls in real dollar amounts. Wall Street stagnates or the GNP falls. Consequently, it is the case that neither Wall Street stagnates in any real growth change nor does the GNP fall in real dollar amounts. (S,F)

6. That Wall Street stagnates is a sufficient condition for the general living standards falling only if entry-level jobs substantially disappear. But that Wall Street stagnates only if the general standards of living fall is a necessary condition for entry-level jobs substantially disappearing. Therefore, Wall Street stagnating is sufficient to guarantee that entry-level jobs substantially disappear when and only when the general standards of living fall. (S,F,D)

7. Either the President sponsors arms legislation, or there will be a proliferation of either conventional or nuclear weapons. Assuming there is a proliferation of conventional weapons, there also is a proliferation of nuclear ones. However, there isn't a proliferation of nuclear weapons. Wherefore, the President sponsors arms legislation. (L,C,N)

8. The general living standards of the country fall just in those cases where entry-level jobs substantially disappear. Neither do entry-level jobs substantially disappear nor will living standards not fall. Hence, entry-level jobs substantially disappear and/or the general living standards of the country fall. (F,D)

9. Not only is there a widespread fear of foreign forces invading the national interests of the U.S. people, there isn't a substantial reduction in nuclear strike power. Yet, there isn't a fear of foreign forces provided that while there isn't a reduction in nuclear strike power there is a sustained development of conventional war implements. There is a sustained development of conventional war implements. So, there isn't a substantial reduction in nuclear strike power only if there is a widespread fear of foreign forces invading the national interest of the U.S. people. (F,R,D)

10. The male student typically doesn't take preventive measures against sexually transmitted diseases. Either not only does the male student contract *HTLV-3* but also eventually dies from *AIDS* complications, or the male student typically doesn't take preventive measures, and he eventually dies from *AIDS* complications. It isn't the case that both the male student has contracted *HTLV-3* and yet typically doesn't take preventive measures against sexually transmitted diseases. Hence, if the male student eventually dies, he typically didn't take preventive measures against sexually transmitted diseases and has contracted *HTLV-3*. (T,C,D)

11. Entry-level jobs never substantially disappear but that competition for remaining jobs increases radically, while the disappearance of entry-level jobs is sufficient to guarantee

that hard core individualism replaces any sustained altruism. Now, it is the case neither that hard core individualism won't replace any sustained altruism nor that competition for remaining jobs won't increase radically. Consequently, entry-level jobs substantially disappear. (D,I,R)

12. The sexual revolution starting in the sixties can't continue to grow if sexually transmitted diseases are becoming widespread in the general population, and surely sexually transmitted diseases are becoming widespread in the general population. Sexually transmitted diseases are becoming widespread in the general population provided that lack of sexual control is prevalent. The sexual revolution starting in the sixties can't continue only if there is a general return to sexual abstinence, but there is no such general return. Consequently, even though sexually transmitted diseases are becoming widespread, either lack of sexual control is prevalent and/or the sexual revolution starting in the sixties continues to grow. (C,B,L,R)

13. That Dottie leaves the States in December is a necessary and sufficient condition for her traveling to Europe for the Christmas holidays. She travels to Europe for the Christmas holidays only if she flies to the southern part of Europe, and she goes to Spain for the holidays if she flies to the southern part of Europe. Now, Dottie doesn't leave the States or she does go to Spain for the Christmas holidays. Thus, Dottie flies to the southern part of Europe if and only if she goes to Spain for the holidays. (L,T,F,G)

14. Annye Mae watches over her father's investments and/or guides his business. She watches over her father's investments only if she deals with several bankers, and moreover she handles clever vendors if she guides his business. That Annye Mae either deals with several bankers or handles clever vendors is sufficient for her taking a stubborn attitude toward competition. Accordingly, Annye Mae takes a stubborn attitude toward competition. (W,G,D,H,T)

15. Tom contracts *HTLV-3* through surgical blood transfusions only if he likely develops *AIDS*, and he will probably lead a short life if he likely develops *AIDS*. Tom does contract *HTLV-3* through surgical blood transfusion and begins to fight against social prejudices aimed at people with *AIDS*. However, if Tom contracts *HTLV-3*, then he won't fight against social prejudices if he likely develops *AIDS*. Therefore, neither will Tom likely develop *AIDS* nor probably lead a short life, or he will fight against social prejudices aimed at people with *AIDS*. (C,D,L,F)

16. Maria won't come to the States except that she leaves Barcelona, and she leaves Barcelona just in case she takes at least a month of vacation leave. Further, Maria won't purchase an airline ticket unless she leaves Barcelona. Maria, however, neither takes a month of vacation leave time nor purchases an airline ticket. So, Maria purchases an airline ticket if and only if she comes to the States. (C,L,T,P)

17. There isn't a proliferation of conventional weapons unless either the President sponsors arms legislation or there isn't a proliferation of nuclear weapons, but not both. If there is a proliferation of nuclear weapons, then the President sponsors arms legislation if there is a proliferation of conventional weapons. Neither is there a proliferation of conventional weapons nor are nuclear weapons not proliferated. So, there is a proliferation of nuclear weapons if and only if the President sponsors arms legislation. (C,L,N)

18. That either the entry-level jobs in the economy substantially disappear or the overall economic indicators point to a strengthening economy, but not both, is necessary and sufficient for the GNP substantially rising. That the overall economic indicators don't point to a strengthening economy is sufficient for either the GNP substantially rising or entry-level jobs substantially disappearing, but not both. Accordingly, that the GNP is

substantially rising is necessary for the overall economic indicators pointing to a strengthening economy. (D,P,R)

19. If the GNP falls in real dollar amounts whenever interest rates continually rise, then interest rates continually rise if the GNP falls. But the GNP doesn't fall except in those cases when interest rates don't continually rise. So, the GNP falls in real dollar amounts in addition to interest rates continually rising. (F,R)

20. If nuclear disarmament guarantees world peace even though human nature doesn't radically change from its typically bellicose attitudes, then either a powerful international police force keeps the peace or human nature does, in fact, radically change. A powerful international police force keeps the peace provided that neither the United States hinders this quasi-military force nor the United States and USSR learn to trust one another. Either human nature doesn't radically change from its typically bellicose attitudes, or neither the United States and USSR learn to trust one another nor does the United States hinder the quasi-military peace-keeping force. But neither is it the case that nuclear disarmament doesn't guarantee world peace nor that the United States and USSR don't learn to trust one another. Wherefore, it isn't true that either the United States hinders the quasi-military peacekeeping force or nuclear disarmament guarantees world peace, but not both. (G,C,K,H,L)

---

## 3.   CONTRADICTORY, TAUTOLOGICAL, AND CONTINGENT STATEMENTS

Any truth-functional statement can be classified as a contradictory, tautological, or contingent statement. A truth-functional statement is *contradictory* (or is a contradiction)

**if and only if there is no truth-value assignment making that statement true.**

For instance, (1) is a contradiction:

(1) Assuming the enemy retaliates in the Persian Gulf, the western powers will fight an all-out war; yet the western powers won't fight an all-out war even though the enemy does retaliate. (R,F)

Putting (1) into truth-functional notation produces

(2)   $(R \supset F) \cdot ( \sim F \cdot R)$

Given any truth-value assignment of 'R' and 'F', (2) will be false. A compound statement is a contradiction because of its logical form, and not simply because of the truth-values of the independent simple statements.

A truth-functional statement is *tautological*

**if and only if there is no truth-value assignment of its truth functional components making that statement false.**

An example of a tautology is

(3) Either Pat has mono and needs treatment, or Pat either doesn't have mono or doesn't need treatment—and that's that. (H,N)

(3) is symbolized as

$$(4) \quad (H \cdot N) \vee ( \sim H \vee \sim N)$$

No matter what truth-assignments are given to 'H' and 'N', (4) is true. A tautology is true because of its truth-functional form irrespective of the truth or falsity of the simple statements out of which it is constructed.

A truth-functional statement is *contingent*

> **if and only if there is at least one truth-value assignment making that statement true and at least one making it false.**

Consider this example:

> **(5)** Assuming that Michael Jackson is popular, then a great number of people will buy his records if they regularly listen to him. (P,B,L)

Using the suggested notation, (5) is symbolized as

$$(6) \quad P \supset (L \supset B)$$

The truth-value of (5)—that is, whether (5) is actually true or false—is not only a function of its logical form as indicated by the horseshoes and parentheses in (6). The truth-value of (5) also depends on the truth-values of 'P', 'L', and 'B'.

It is important to be able to distinguish between contradictions, tautologies, and contingent statements. Contingent statements are used to make assertions about particular objects, or events. These claims are true or false depending on how particular things, or events, are in the world. Suppose it is claimed that 'Pat is diabetic and needs treatment'. Further, imagine that this is a true statement about a particular person, Pat. Those hearing the claim are in a better position to know how to deal with Pat's medical condition, what treatment to seek, and what precautions to take. On the other hand, while true, (3) gives no hint of what is to be done with, for, or about Pat. Or suppose (1) is asserted. Knowing this statement is false does not help in directing any particular action or forming any testable opinion about either the situation in the Persian Gulf or anyone playing a role in that situation.

Neither contradictions nor tautologies, such as seen in (1) and (3), can guide particular actions or opinions, or provide the bases on which judgments about particular issues can be formed. Tautologies, however, often sound as if they were strong, factually true claims that must be accepted, and demand that some action be taken based on these claims. Contradictions can also appear as if they were strong, factually false claims that must be accepted and acted upon. But in neither case can these claims be accepted as making factual assertions concerning particular objects or events in the world. Hence, they cannot supply reasons for holding or not holding some particular opinion, belief, or hypothesis upon which a person acts or does not act.

Truth trees can be used to decide if statements are contradictory, tautological, or contingent. To decide if a statement is contradictory, first symbolize it. Then decompose it using the rules of decomposition introduced in Section 1. After fully decomposing the statement, if there is no terminated open branch in its truth tree, the statement is contradictory. For instance, to show that (1) is a contradiction, decompose the statement '$(R \supset F) \cdot (\sim F \cdot R)$':

| | | |
|---|---|---|
| **(7) 1)** | $(R \supset F) \cdot (\sim F \cdot R)$  ✓ | —— |
| **2)** | $R \supset F$  ✓ | 1, C |
| **3)** | $\sim F \cdot R$  ✓ | 1, C |
| **4)** | $\sim F$ | 3, C |
| **5)** | R | 3, C |

$$\bigwedge$$

| | | |
|---|---|---|
| **6)** $\sim$R       F | | 2, MI |
|      X       X | | |

Finding all the branches of (7) closed establishes that (1) is contradictory. There is not a single truth-condition of the simple statements that would make (7) true.

A tautology is true given any possible truth-value assignment to its simple statements. So, it might be tempting to suppose that if the truth tree of a statement has all open branches, that statement is tautological. This supposition is incorrect, however. Consider this straightforward example:

**(8) 1)** $A \vee B$  ✓  ——

$$\bigwedge$$

**2)** A   B        1, ID

All the branches in (8) remain open. Nonetheless, '$A \vee B$' is a contingent statement. It would be false if both 'A' and 'B' were false and true for every other truth-value assignment. However, there is a truth tree method for determining whether or not a truth-functional statement is tautological. A tautology is true under every truth-value assignment of its simple statements. Given the notion of truth-functional denial, if a tautology is a statement that is true under every truth-value assignment, the denial of a tautology is false under every truth-value assignment. That is, the denial of a tautology is a contradiction. Therefore, to decide if a truth-functional statement is tautological, first symbolize the statement. Next, assume the denial of that statement. Then, decompose that denial. If all branches are closed, the original statement is a tautology. Examine (3), symbolized as '$(H \cdot N) \vee (\sim H \vee \sim N)$' at (4). Assume the denial of this statement. Then, decompose that denial:

| | | |
|---|---|---|
| **(9) 1)** | $\sim [(H \cdot N) \vee (\sim H \vee \sim N)]$  ✓ | —— |
| **2)** | $\sim (H \cdot N)$  ✓ | 1, DID |
| **3)** | $\sim (\sim H \vee \sim N)$  ✓ | 1, DID |
| **4)** | $\sim \sim H$  ✓ | 3, DID |

---

*There are other important reasons for being able to determine whether two statements are logically equivalent or not. These reasons will become particularly clear in Chapter 6 when logically equivalent expressions are used in constructing proofs of validity.

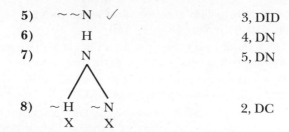

| 5) | ~~N  ✓ | 3, DID |
| 6) | H | 4, DN |
| 7) | N | 5, DN |
| 8) | ~H    ~N | 2, DC |
|  | X      X |  |

Since every branch in (9) is closed, ' ~ [(H · N) ∨ ( ~ H ∨ ~ N)]' is a contradiction. Thus, '(H · N) ∨ ( ~ H ∨ ~ N)' is a tautology.

What of contingent statements? A contingent statement is neither a contradiction nor a tautology. It is true in some cases while false in others. Thus, it might be supposed that a contingent statement would have in its truth tree some opened and some closed branches. This is not correct, however. Look at (8) once more. 'A ∨ B' is a contingent statement. Even so, there are no closed branches in (8). To use truth tree methods to decide if a statement is contingent or not, it is necessary to construct *two* truth trees. Using truth trees, first decide whether the statement is contradictory. If it is not contradictory, then assume its denial and ascertain whether it is a tautology. If the statement in question is neither contradictory nor tautological, it is contingent.

---

## *EXERCISES*

Decide by truth tree methods which of the following are contradictory, tautological, or contingent.

1. Neither is Wall Street on solid financial grounds with an overly high P/E ratio nor are bond rates escalating in proportion to weakening stock conditions; yet, on the other hand, bond rates are escalating. (S,B)

2. Either *INXS* will be at the Civic Center next week, or George Harrison won't be there unless Kenny G is too. (I,H,G)

3. While Mark caught the flu virus and is developing flu, nevertheless he hasn't caught the flu virus or isn't developing flu. (C,D)

4. Either there will be modest growth of 3% in the GNP, or there won't be modest growth in addition to the fact that Wall Street will take another beating. (G,W)

5. Assuming that the national deficit will shrink in addition to the money supply increasing, the national deficit will shrink. (S,I)

6. Michael Stipe not only writes the music but also the lyrics only if either Pete Buck sings or Stipe doesn't write the lyrics. (M,L,S)

7. Either the *HTLV-3* retrovirus will be contracted only if the advice of the Surgeon General isn't followed, or while the advice of the Surgeon General is followed, the retrovirus is contracted. (C,F)

8. If it isn't the case that *Alabama* isn't coming while *INXS* plays at the Civic Center, then *R.E.M.* not appearing is necessary for booking *Rush* at the Civic Center. (C,P,A,B)

9. That Billy Joel is coming to the Civic Center if Richard Marx is appearing at the *Stage Door*,

while Billy Joel isn't coming is sufficient for Sting being booked at the Omni if Marx appears at the Stage Door. (C,A,B)

10. The following isn't the case: John Cougar isn't appearing in concert, while the *Police* aren't opening only if some other group will come; but no other group will come. (A,O,C)

11. Madonna doesn't appear only if neither Sting plays nor Kenny G comes; yet neither does Madonna appear nor Sting not play. (A,P,C)

12. It isn't the case that there will be another "Black Monday" if massive buy-outs continue except in that case that there isn't another "Black Monday" in spite of massive buy-outs continuing. (B,C)

13. That the U.S. government continues to protect Western interests in the Persian Gulf while either the Iraqis bomb Iranian holdings along the Gulf coast or the Iranians attack non-Iranian shipping in the Gulf is necessary for the following: namely, either the Iranians attack non-Iranian shipping even though the U.S. government continues to protect Western interests, or not only does the U.S. government continue to protect Western interests in the Gulf but the Iraqis bomb Iranian holdings along the Gulf as well. (C,B,A)

14. Either neither using multiple short-term sex partners nor intravenous drugs certainly increases a person's chances for developing *AIDS*, or it's not the case that not using intravenous drugs is sufficient for multiple short-term sex partners increasing a person's chances for developing *AIDS*, but not both. (P,D)

15. If it is the case that whenever a surrogate mother lends her body to a childless couple she is performing an altruistic action, although assuming that she is compensated for services rendered she has rented her body, then it isn't true that a surrogate mother neither lends her body to a childless couple nor performs an altruistic action, or either she is compensated for services rendered or has rented her body. (L,P,C,R)

16. Neither do the Iraqis control the Persian Gulf nor oil prices skyrocket, or it isn't true that political stability doesn't degenerate further in the Middle East if the Iraqis control the Persian Gulf—but not both. (C,S,D)

17. That people will be protected from foreign intervention except in those cases where they don't follow the advice of the president is both necessary and sufficient for not following the president's advice or being protected from foreign intervention—but not both. (P,F)

18. Either someone develops lung cancer just in case that person smokes, or someone doesn't smoke when and only when that person develops lung cancer, but not both. (D,S)

19. That the GNP rises by 2–3% a year or the Feds control the money supply is sufficient for a fear of recession not keeping stock prices low while prices inflate if, and only if, both a fear of recession keeps stock prices low or prices don't inflate, and the Feds do control the money supply or the GNP rises by 2–3% a year. (R,C,K,I)

20. The U.S. Navy won't leave the Persian Gulf except that the Iraqis neither attack ships in international waters nor terrorize Kuwaitian territories, or the U.S. Navy will leave the Persian Gulf and the British will move their war fleet just in case the Iraqis don't attack ships in international waters—but not both. (L,A,T,M)

## 4.  LOGICAL EQUIVALENCE

Two statements are equivalent if and only if whatever makes one true also makes the other true, and whatever makes one false also makes the other false. Statements can be equivalent in different ways. For instance, they can be equivalent because of the rules of English grammar. Thus, if 'Sara made an A' is true, then 'An A was made by Sara' is also true. Or, two statements can be equivalent because of word usage. To say 'Russell is smart' and 'Russell is intelligent' is to make the same claim. On the other hand, two statements can be equivalent because of their logical forms. In truth-functional logic, two statements show ***logical equivalence***

> **if and only if whatever truth-conditions make one true also make the other true, and whatever truth-conditions make one false also make the other false. This is to say, truth-functional statements are logically equivalent if and only if the denial of the biconditional formed from these statements is contradictory.**

These two statements, for example, are logically equivalent:

**(1)**

    **a)** Assuming that Dottie goes to *Botin's* in Madrid, then she enjoys dinner only if she has roast suckling pig. (G,E,H)

    **b)** Assuming that Dottie goes to *Botin's* in Madrid and enjoys dinner, then she has roast suckling pig. (G,E,H)

If one of these statements is true, then so is the other; if one of them is false, so is the other.

It is often important to be able to decide if two statements are logically equivalent. It is not unusual in presenting evidence for some claim to describe the evidence in one way at one time and in a different way at another time. Perhaps the evidence is presented in statements that are believed to be logically equivalent, but that are not. Or someone might attempt to be deceptive and conceal a weakness in an argument by presenting evidence in a way that sounds as if it were logically equivalent to an acceptable statement, but is not. Because of these dangers in both presenting and receiving arguments, a way is needed to test for logical equivalence. Truth trees are helpful here.

Two statements are logically equivalent if and only if they have the same truth-value given the same truth-conditions. Furthermore, any instance of '$p \equiv q$' is tautological if and only if both '$p$' and '$q$' are replaced by names of statements having the same truth-values. These considerations lead to a truth tree method useful in testing for logical equivalence:[*]

    *1. Symbolize the two statements to be tested.*

    *2. Form a biconditional from these statements.*

    *3. Use truth tree methods to decide if this biconditional is a tautology or not.*

    *4. If the biconditional is a tautology, then the two original statements are logically equivalent, but otherwise they are not.*

---

[*]Since no mechanical procedures have been introduced to carry out step 3, the following sequence of steps is not, precisely speaking, a decision procedure. However, while not mechanical, the procedure is effective.

Apply this procedure to (1):

**(1)**

    **a)** G ⊃ (E ⊃ H)

    **b)** (G · E) ⊃ H

**(2)**   [G ⊃ (E ⊃ H)] ≡ [(G · E) ⊃ H]

**(3)**

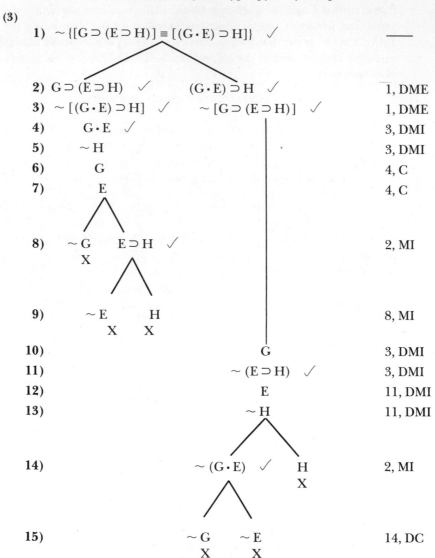

| | | | |
|---|---|---|---|
| **1)** | ~{[G ⊃ (E ⊃ H)] ≡ [(G · E) ⊃ H]} ✓ | | —— |
| **2)** | G ⊃ (E ⊃ H) ✓    (G · E) ⊃ H ✓ | | 1, DME |
| **3)** | ~[(G · E) ⊃ H] ✓  ~[G ⊃ (E ⊃ H)] ✓ | | 1, DME |
| **4)** | G · E ✓ | | 3, DMI |
| **5)** | ~ H | | 3, DMI |
| **6)** | G | | 4, C |
| **7)** | E | | 4, C |
| **8)** | ~G  E ⊃ H ✓ | | 2, MI |
| | X | | |
| **9)** | ~E  H | | 8, MI |
| | X  X | | |
| **10)** | G | | 3, DMI |
| **11)** | ~ (E ⊃ H) ✓ | | 3, DMI |
| **12)** | E | | 11, DMI |
| **13)** | ~ H | | 11, DMI |
| **14)** | ~ (G · E) ✓  H | | 2, MI |
| | X | | |
| **15)** | ~ G  ~ E | | 14, DC |
| | X  X | | |

**(4)** Since every branch in the above truth tree is closed, ' ~ {[G ⊃ (E ⊃ H)] ≡ [(G · E) ⊃ H]}' is a contradiction. However, this shows that '[G ⊃ (E ⊃ H)] ≡ [(G · E) ⊃ H]', is a tautology. In turn, this means that the statements, 'G ⊃ (E ⊃ H)' and '(G · E) ⊃ H', are logically equivalent.

## *EXERCISES*

Decide by truth tree methods which of the following pairs of statements are logically equivalent.

1.  a) Either the *Twins* win the World Series or the *Mets* tie the *Yankees*. (W,T)
    b) It isn't true that both the *Mets* tie the *Yankees* and the *Twins* win the World Series. (T,W)

2.  a) Florida goes to the Liberty Bowl or doesn't beat Clemson. (G,B)
    b) Florida doesn't beat Clemson unless she goes to the Liberty Bowl. (B,G)

3.  a) The *Braves* don't win in their league, but neither do the *Cardinals*. (B,C)
    b) It isn't the case that both the *Braves* and the *Cardinals* win in their leagues. (B,C)

4.  a) Either the *Cardinals* or the *Twins*, but not both, win the World Series. (C,T)
    b) The *Twins* win the World Series provided the *Cardinals* don't. (T,C)

5.  a) It isn't true that both Alabama doesn't play Clemson in addition to not taking on Tech. (P,T)
    b) Alabama plays Clemson or takes on Tech. (P,T)

6.  a) To appreciate Pete Buck's playing it is necessary to be familiar with good guitar. (A,F)
    b) Not being familiar with good guitar is a necessary condition for not appreciating Pete Buck's playing. (F,A)

7.  a) Georgia fumbles in the last minute of the fourth quarter or wins the game, but not both. (F,W)
    b) Georgia doesn't win the game if and only if it fumbles in the last minute of the fourth quarter. (W,F)

8.  a) Neither Alabama nor Ole Miss will play a bowl game this year. (A,M)
    b) Ole Miss won't play a bowl game this year or Alabama won't either. (M,A)

9.  a) Both *R.E.M.* and the *Police* are appearing next month. (R,P)
    b) Neither are the *Police* not appearing next month nor is *R.E.M.* not appearing. (P,R)

10. a) Assuming history is accurate, then Paul Verlaine went to prison just in case he shot Arthur Rimbaud. (H,V,R)
    b) If history is accurate and Paul Verlaine went to prison, then he shot Arthur Rimbaud. (H,V,R)

11. a) If a student is better prepared for the business world only if that student learns how to use an electronic spreadsheet, then that student is majoring in finance. (P,L,M)
    b) If a student majors in finance, then that student is better prepared for the business world if that student learns how to use an electronic spreadsheet. (M,P,L)

12. a) Whenever the American business world suffers from love of the short-term view coupled with desires for a quick profit, it falls far behind in international competition. (S,D,F)
    b) If the American business world suffers from love of the short-term view, then it never desires for a quick profit but that it falls far behind in international competition. (S,D,F)

13. a) Reading both "Les Fenêtres" and "L'Azur" is necessary to study Stéphane Mallarmé. (F,A,M)
    b) Having both studied Stéphane Mallarmé and read "Les Fenêtres" is sufficient for having read "L'Azur." (M,F,A)

14. a) Arthur Rimbaud is an exciting poet, and he wrote "Une Saison en enfer" or "Le Bateau ivre." (R,S,B)

   b) Arthur Rimbaud is an exciting poet and wrote "Une Saison en enfer," or he is an exciting poet and wrote "Le Bateau ivre." (R,S,B)

15. a) Not only will the foreign deficit increase steadily or domestic products be manufactured more efficiently, but profit margins will be cut or the foreign deficit will increase steadily. (I,M,C)

   b) Either domestic products will be manufactured more efficiently and profit margins will be cut, or the foreign deficit will increase steadily. (M,C,I)

16. a) Equity rates plummet or the Feds allow interest rates to soar, as well as the stock market moves further down or the general P/E index continues to climb unreasonably. (P,A,M,C)

   b) Either the general P/E index continues to climb unreasonably even though the stock market moves further down, or the Feds allow interest rates to soar albeit equity rates plummet. (C,M,A,P)

17. a) *Quiet Riot* or *Talking Heads* were selected by the Student Entertainment Committee, but *Quiet Riot* wasn't. (R,H)

   b) *Talking Heads* aren't selected by the Student Entertainment Committee only if *Quiet Riot* isn't either, and *Quiet Riot* isn't selected. (H,R)

18. a) Either bonds gain only a few points as well as money market investments overcome some weakness, or commodities edge up despite the fact that the market fluctuates too much. (G,O,E,F)

   b) While either money market investments overcome some weakness and bonds gain only a few points, or commodities edge up; nevertheless, the fact remains that the market fluctuates too much. (O,G,E,F)

19. a) The foreign trade ratio deepens even though the dollar continues its steep slide, or neither interest rates fly nor the deficit worsens. (D,C,F,W)

   b) Interest rates don't fly unless both the dollar continues its steep slide while the foreign trade ratio deepens; but that both the foreign trade ratio deepens and the dollar continues its deep slide is a necessary condition for the deficit worsening. (F,C,D,W)

20. a) If commodities rise when and only when bonds advance, then the market gains back some of its strength. (R,A,G)

   b) Either the market gains back some of its strength, or it isn't the case that either bonds advance or commodities don't rise (but not both). (G,A,R)

---

## 5.  REVIEW OF NEW TERMS

**Branch:**  In a truth tree, the results of a decomposition, or breaking down, of statements into their component statement parts.

**Closed branch:**  A terminated branch containing a simple statement name and that name prefixed with one tilde. A closed branch is indicated by placing an 'X' under it.

**Completed truth tree:**  A truth tree in which all possible branches are terminated.

**Conjunction (C):**  The rule of decomposition

**Consistent premise set:** The premise set of an argument is consistent if and only if there is at least one truth-value assignment making all the premises true. The premise set of an argument is consistent if and only if its truth tree decomposition yields at least one terminated open branch.

**Contingent statement:** A truth-functional statement having at least one truth-value assignment making it true and at least one making it false. A truth-functional statement is contingent if and only if there is neither a truth tree decomposition showing it to be contradictory nor one showing it to be tautological.

**Contradictory statement:** A truth-functional statement having no truth-value assignment making it true; a *contradiction*. A truth-functional statement is contradictory if and only if its truth tree decomposition yields no terminated open branch.

**Decomposition:** The breaking up, by means of the rules of decomposition, of compound statements into simple statements represented by single capital letters, or the denial of simple statements represented by single capital letters prefixed with one tilde.

**Denied Conjunction (DC):**  The rule of decomposition

**Denied Exclusive Disjunction (DED):**  The rule of decomposition

**Denied Inclusive Disjunction (DID):**  The rule of decomposition

~ (p ∨ q)

~ p
~ q

**Denied Material Equivalence (DME):**  The rule of decomposition

**Denied Material Implication (DMI):**  The rule of decomposition

**Denied Negation (DN):**  The rule of decomposition

**Exclusive Disjunction (ED):**  The rule of decomposition

**Inclusive Disjunction (ID):**  The rule of decomposition

$$p \lor q$$

$$p \qquad q$$

**Inconsistent premise set:**  The premise set of an argument is inconsistent if and only if there is no truth-value assignment making all the premises true. The premise set of an argument is inconsistent if and only if their truth tree decomposition yields no terminated open branches.

**Logical equivalence:**  Statements are logically equivalent if and only if whatever truth-conditions make one true also make the other true, and whatever truth-conditions make one false also make the other false. That is to say, truth-functional statements are logically equivalent if and only if the denial of the biconditional formed from these statements is contradictory.

**Material Equivalence (ME):**  The rule of decomposition

$$p \equiv q$$

$$
\begin{array}{cc}
p & \sim p \\
q & \sim q
\end{array}
$$

**Material Implication (MI):**  The rule of decomposition

$$p \supset q$$

$$
\begin{array}{cc}
\sim p & q
\end{array}
$$

**Open branch:**  A terminated truth tree branch that is not closed. No 'X' is placed under an open branch.

**Replacement sign:**  Expressed by the notation 'p::q'. If 'p' and 'q' have identical truth-values given the same truth-value assignments to their simple parts, then 'p' can replace 'q', and 'q' can replace 'p', at any occurrence of 'p' and 'q'.

**Root:**  The beginning expression(s) of a truth tree from which all the branches fan out.

**Tautological statement:**  A truth-functional statement having no truth-value assignment making it false; a *tautology*. A truth-functional statement is tautological if and only if a truth tree decomposition of its denial yields no terminated open branch.

**Terminated branch:**  A branch is terminated when, in all of its unchecked lines, only the names of simple statements and/or the names of simple statements prefixed with only one tilde are found.

**Truth tree:**  A branching diagram displaying all possible truth-conditions of a statement, or combination of statements.

# 5

# TRUTH-FUNCTIONAL LOGIC: ARGUMENT FORMS

Truth tables and truth trees can be used to show the validity of many arguments. However, this is not the case for all deductively valid arguments, as will be seen in later chapters. Hence, other procedures for determining validity are needed. This chapter and the next introduce rules required to construct *proofs of validity*. These *elementary rules of inference* are formulated to guarantee validity. Each of these elementary rules of inference is framed entirely in terms of the definitional rules governing the six logical operators introduced in Chapter 2. To accept these rules is to accept the elementary rules of inference introduced in this and following chapters. This chapter introduces *argument forms* and the next chapter introduces *equivalence forms* for proof construction. These rules can be viewed as tools used to construct proofs; strategies, or heuristics, are developed to guide their application in the construction of particular proofs.

## 1. ARGUMENT FORMS

An *elementary rule of inference* is

> **any logical form introduced in this and following chapters that guarantees if the premises of an argument are all true, then any new statement generated from the premises by these rules must also be true.**

There are two types of elementary rules of inference; namely *argument forms* and *equivalence forms*. Both types guarantee that *if* the premises presented as support for the conclusion are all true or accepted as true, *then* the conclusion also must be true.* This is a hypothetical way of reasoning. Even so, to accept the premises as true

---

*To simplify the discussion of deductive proofs, it is assumed that only statements are used as premises and conclusions. Thus, instead of speaking of the premises and conclusion as correct or incorrect, they are spoken of as true or false.

and reject the conclusion of a valid argument is to contradict oneself. Indeed, some or all the premises presented to support a conclusion might not be true. Further, a person is often in the situation of not knowing "for certain" if the premises are true or false. Nevertheless, it is still important to raise, and answer, *this* question: *If* all the premises are true, *then* must the conclusion also be true?

Arguments are series of statements in which at least one of the statements is presented to support the truth of another. How such statements are related to one another is the form of the argument. Thus, an *argument form* is

> **a finite sequence of statement forms of which one is the conclusion and the remainder comprise the premises, such that if all the statement variables are replaced by statements names—the same statement name replacing each occurrence of the same statement variable—an argument is obtained.**

While a particular argument is made up of a sequence of statements, an argument form is not. An argument form is composed of statement forms. This feature of argument forms is underscored by using statement variables in their symbolic representation. Since argument forms contain no statements, and only statements have a truth-value, the premises and conclusion of an argument form are not, strictly speaking, true or false. A *valid argument form*, however, results if and only if when all the statement variables are replaced with the names of true statements (the same name replacing each occurrence of the same variable) it is impossible for all the premises to be true and the conclusion false. There also are *invalid argument forms*. For these forms, there is at least one substitution of statement names for the statement variables representing the form (the same statement name being substituted at the same statement variable) that produces all true premises and a false conclusion. However, in arguing deductively and attempting to seek truth, one is interested in using only argument forms that guarantee validity while avoiding all others.*

These remarks suggest rules of substitution of statement names into both statement forms and argument forms. These rules have been implicit throughout Chapters 2, 3, and 4. The concept *substitution* is now made explicit:

> **In any statement form, a statement name can be substituted at any occurrence of a single statement variable provided that the same statement name is substituted at each occurrence of that single statement variable throughout the entire statement form.**

> **In any argument form, a statement name can be substituted at any occurrence of a single statement variable provided that the same statement name is substituted at each occurrence of that single statement variable throughout the entire argument form.**

---

*This is not so if one is arguing to deceive, manipulate, or the like. Yet, to be successful in deception and manipulation, a person has to know what forms are valid to be able to introduce invalid ones that appear valid.

Arguments often display more than one argument form. The following argument does, for instance:

**(1)**                                                    $/ \therefore \text{C} \cdot \text{D}$
   **1)**  $(\text{A} \supset \text{B}) \vee (\text{C} \cdot \text{D})$    Pr
   **2)**  $\sim (\text{A} \supset \text{B})$              Pr

(1) might be seen as displaying any of these forms:

**(2)**

$$p$$
$$\underline{q \qquad}$$
$$/ \therefore r$$

**(3)**

$$p \vee q$$
$$\underline{\sim p \qquad}$$
$$/ \therefore q$$

**(4)**

$$(p \supset q) \vee (r \cdot s)$$
$$\underline{\sim (p \supset q) \qquad}$$
$$/ \therefore r \cdot s$$

Clearly these are different argument forms. (2) is not a valid argument form whereas (3) and (4) are, as can be established by truth tables or truth trees. However, any argument is deductively valid if and only if it displays *at least one* valid argument form.

In consructing proofs of validity, however, it is convenient to distinguish between forms such as (3) and (4) above. (4) is the specific argument form of (1). The ***specific argument form*** of an argument is

> **that form that is seen if and only if every single capital letter representing a simple statement in the symbolization of an argument is replaced by a single variable letter, the same variable letter replacing the same capital letter throughout the entire symbolization.**

(3) is an elementary rule of inference introduced in *Section 3* of this chapter. A ***proof of validity*** can now be characterized as

> **a finite sequence of statements, beginning with the premises of an argument and ending with the conclusion, such that each step in the proof displays at least one elementary rule of inference.**

---

## *EXERCISES*

In each of the following argument forms, substitute 'A' for 'p', 'B' for 'q' and 'C' for 'r'. Next, substitute 'A $\vee$ B' for 'p', ' $\sim$ (C $\vee$ D)' for 'q' and ' $\sim$ [C $\supset$ (D $\supset$ B)]' for 'r'.

1.  /∴ p
    1) p • (q • r)  Pr

2.  /∴ r
    1) (p ⊃ q) Δ r  Pr
    2) ~ (p ⊃ q)  Pr

3.  /∴ q ⊃ r
    1) (p • q) ⊃ r  Pr

4.  /∴ r ⊃ p
    1) (p ≡ q) ⊃ r  Pr
    2) q ≡ p  Pr

5.  /∴ ~ p
    1) p ⊃ (q ⊃ r)  Pr
    2) ~ (q ⊃ r)  Pr

6.  /∴ (p • ~ r) ⊃ ~ q
    1) p ⊃ (q ⊃ r)  Pr

7.  /∴ r • (p ⊃ q)
    1) (p ⊃ q) • r  Pr

8.  /∴ ~ r • ~ p
    1) p ⊃ (q • q)  Pr
    2) (q • ~ q) ⊃ r  Pr

9.  /∴ ~ r ⊃ (q ⊃ p)
    1) p ⊃ q  Pr

10. /∴ ( ~ p • q) • r
    1) ~ p • (q • r)  Pr

---

## 2.  SIMPLIFICATION, COMMUTATION OF THE DOT, AND CONJUNCTION

Before discussing the first group of argument forms, it is helpful to note several features of proofs of validity. *First*, each statement is given a numerical designation that is written to the left side of the name of the statement. *Second*, a reason must be given for each statement. Two types of statements are found in a proof. There are those statements that are *accepted* as premises and *assumed to be true*. Then there are all the remaining statements obtained from the premises by using elementary rules of inference. Any statement that is assumed as a premise is indicated by writing 'Pr' to the right-hand side of the name designating it. Of a statement that is not a premise, two questions must be answered: '*From where does that statement come?*' and '*How is it obtained?*'. Every nonpremise statement must be justified by answering 'From where?' and 'How?'. The first question is answered by referring to statements already established in the proof. The second question is answered by noting what elementary rule of inference is being used to obtain the new statement. The numerical name, the statement name, and the indicated justification comprise a *line* in constructing a proof.*

---

*Remember, statements are not seen on the printed page. They are nonspatial and nontemporal. Thus, it does not make sense to speak of one statement being to the right-hand side of another or writing one statement before another. Statement names are written, seen, and heard. However, as this book proceeds, especially when no great danger of any confusion is likely, less care will be taken in distinguishing between statements and their names.

Consider this example:

**(1)**   Atlanta is the capital of Georgia and is the largest city in the state.

If (1) is true, the following must also be true:

**(2)**   Atlanta is the capital of Georgia.

If a statement of the form 'p·q' is true, then 'p' must also be true because of the rule defining the dot.* This logical truth is depicted in the following argument form:

### SIMPLIFICATION (SIMP)

$$\frac{p \cdot q}{/ \therefore p}$$

Simplification, referred to by 'Simp', dictates that if any truth-functional conjunction is true, the *left-hand* conjunct is also true. The left-hand conjunct can be asserted as a new statement in a proof. Simplification permits an overall conjunction to be "broken down" by removing the left-hand conjunct. But if (1) is true, the following must also be true:

**(3)**   Atlanta is the largest city in the state.

Yet (3) cannot be deduced from (1) by an appeal to Simplification. Using Simplification, the left-hand conjunct is removed from the overall conjunction. However, if (1) is true, so is

**(4)**   Atlanta is the largest city in the state and is the capital of Georgia.

If a statement of the form 'p · q' is true, 'q · p' must be true because of the rule governing the dot. This logical truth is expressed as

### COMMUTATION (COM)

$$\frac{p \cdot q}{/ \therefore q \cdot p}$$

Commutation, or 'Com' when referred to in proofs, asserts that truth-functional conjunction is not affected by the ordering of the separate conjuncts. Thus, if

---

*This notion of *necessity*, the 'must' in this claim, is based on two considerations. The first of these is that the claim is made within the confines of a two-value system. For instance, a statement is either true or false; a switch is either on or off; a neuron is either firing or is not. The second consideration is the acceptance of the definitional rules governing the six logical operators introduced in Chapter 2. All rules of inference in this chapter, and the next, are based on the rules of Chapter 2. Thus, the rules of inference guarantee that if all the premises of a deductive argument are true, then the conclusion of that argument *must* also be true.

statement (1) is true, Commutation guarantees the truth of (4). If (4) is true, Simplification guarantees the truth of (3).*

Study this argument:

(5)   Both *Clash* and *Squeeze* were punk, whereas *Village People* was disco. So, *Clash* was punk. (C,S,V)

Using the indicated capital letters, symbolize (5) as

        **(6)**                  / $\therefore$ C

           **1)** $(C \cdot S) \cdot V$  Pr

'C' cannot be *directly* deduced from the premise of (6) by Simplification because 'C' is *a part of* the left-hand conjunct. No argument form can be used on component statements of larger compound statements.

The premise of Simplification is an overall conjunction having exactly two conjuncts represented by 'p' and 'q'. The conclusion of this argument form is the left-hand conjunct of the premise. Applying this rule to (6) reveals 'C $\cdot$ S' to be an instance of 'p' and 'V' to be an instance of 'q'. 'C $\cdot$ S' is obtained from the premise by Simplification. The rule, Simplification, now is applied to 'C $\cdot$ S'. Here 'C' is read as an instance of 'p' and 'S' of 'q'. A correct proof for (6) is

      **(7)**                  / $\therefore$ C

        **1)** $(C \cdot S) \cdot V$  Pr

        **2)** $C \cdot S$      1, Simp

        **3)** / $\therefore$ C     2, Simp

and *not*

     **(8 )**                  / $\therefore$ C

          **1)** $(C \cdot S) \cdot V$  Pr

*WRONG X*  **2)** / $\therefore$ C     1, Simp

Notice that parentheses are not used in line 2 of (7). By convention, punctuation marks are omitted around entire statement names.

Suppose the following is true:

(9)   Georgia is the largest state east of the Mississippi River.

---

*Some logicians combine these rules into a new rule:

$$\frac{p \cdot q}{/ \therefore q}$$

This is a different rule from Simplification. This new rule could be called 'Simplification-2' and the other 'Simplification-1'. However, in this text, only Simplification-1 is introduced. While proof constructions are longer when Commutation is used, nonetheless Commutation is a useful rule to have. Thus, Simplification-2 is not needed.

Moreover, assume as true

> **(10)**  Atlanta is the capital of Georgia.

Given the truth of (9) and (10), it must further be true that

> **(11)**  Georgia is the largest state east of the Mississippi River and Atlanta is the capital of Georgia.

When two separate statements are true, their conjunction must be true:

**CONJUNCTION (CONJ)**

p

q

$/\therefore\ p \cdot q$

Imagine this situation:

**(12)** Able Leader, Inc., frequently finds itself in court litigation but Better Products, Ltd., is more conservative in its operations, while Corporate Enterprises is more productive than the others. Hence, Corporate Enterprises is more productive than the others even though Better Products, Ltd., is more conservative in its operations. (A,B,C)

Symbolize (12) as

> **(13)**                    $/\therefore\ C \cdot B$
> **1)** $(A \cdot B) \cdot C$   Pr

The conclusion of (13) is an overall conjunction. Since there is only one premise in (13), the conclusion must be constructed out of that premise if the argument is valid. The conclusion is likely constructed by a final appeal to Conjunction. The premise, like the conclusion, is a conjunction. 'C' in the conclusion is the right-hand conjunct of the premise. 'B' in the conclusion is embedded in the left-hand conjunct of the premise. To obtain 'B', begin by using Simplification:

> **(14)**                    $/\therefore\ C \cdot B$
> **1)** $(A \cdot B) \cdot C$   Pr
> **2)** $A \cdot B$        1, Simp

'B' must be isolated out of 2. Since 'A · B' is an overall conjunction and Simplification is used to obtain conjuncts out of overall conjunctions, Simplification *must* be used here. However, only left-hand conjuncts can be asserted by Simplification. So, Commutation is used before Simplification to obtain 'B':

> **(15)**                    $/\therefore\ C \cdot B$
> **1)** $(A \cdot B) \cdot C$   Pr
> **2)** $A \cdot B$        1, Simp
> **3)** $B \cdot A$        2, Com
> **4)** B              3, Simp

(15) is continued by obtaining 'C'. Again Commutation is used to prepare for a Simplification move:

$$(16) \qquad\qquad /\therefore\ C \cdot B$$

| | | |
|---|---|---|
| **1)** | $(A \cdot B) \cdot C$ | Pr |
| **2)** | $A \cdot B$ | 1, Simp |
| **3)** | $B \cdot A$ | 2, Com |
| **4)** | $B$ | 3, Simp |
| **5)** | $C \cdot (A \cdot B)$ | 1, Com |
| **6)** | $C$ | 5, Simp |

(16) shows that if the premise is true, 'B' and 'C' must also be true. However, the rule, Conjunction, guarantees that if two statements are true, the conjunction of them must also be true. This information is written in a completed proof of (13):

$$(17) \qquad\qquad /\therefore\ C \cdot B$$

| | | |
|---|---|---|
| **1)** | $(A \cdot B) \cdot C$ | Pr |
| **2)** | $A \cdot B$ | 1, Simp |
| **3)** | $B \cdot A$ | 2, Com |
| **4)** | $B$ | 3, Simp |
| **5)** | $C \cdot (A \cdot B)$ | 1, Com |
| **6)** | $C$ | 5, Simp |
| **7)** | $/\therefore\ C \cdot B$ | 6, 4, Conj |

The ordering of the numerals in a justification indicate what statement in the proof is being interpreted as an instance of what premise in that argument form being used in the justification. For instance, the justification in line 7 of (17) is '6, 4, Conj' and *not* '4, 6, Conj'. Conjunction is the rule used to justify 'C·B'. The left-hand conjunct of this conclusion is the same as the first premise of this *argument form*. The right-hand conjunct is the same as the second premise. Thus, 'C', the left-hand conjunct of the conclusion, is an instance of the first premise in Conjunction and 'B' an instance of the second. This convention is used throughout this book:

> **In justifying any nonpremise statement, the numerical names of statements answering the question, 'From where?', are written from left to right such that the leftmost name indicates the statement that is read as an instance of the first premise in the argument form being used. The next name is the name of that statement viewed as an instance of the second premise in the argument form being used, and so on.**

The validity of many arguments can be established in a number of different, but equally correct, ways. (17) is only one proof establishing the validity of (12). Another proof is

$$(18) \qquad\qquad /\therefore\ C \cdot B$$

| | | |
|---|---|---|
| **1)** | $(A \cdot B) \cdot C$ | Pr |

    **2)** C · (A · B)   1, Com
    **3)** C            2, Simp
    **4)** A · B      1, Simp
    **5)** B · A      4, Com
    **6)** B            5, Simp
    **7)** /∴ C · B   3, 6, Conj

The principal difference between (17) and (18) is the sequential order in which various rules are applied. The same statements and the same rules are found in both (17) and (18), but they are found in different arrangements. As new rules are introduced, proofs for the same argument will also differ in the rules used to construct the proofs. It is because one argument may have several different proofs establishing its validity that the "Answers" in the back of this book can be used *only as guides*.

## *EXERCISES*

### Group A:

Give the correct justification in each unjustified line of the following.

1.                     /∴ A
   1) A · (B ⊃ C)   Pr
   2) /∴ A

2.                     /∴ E
   1) (B ⊃ C) · E   Pr
   2) E · (B ⊃ C)
   3) /∴ E

3.                     /∴ D
   1) C · (D · E)   Pr
   2) (D · E) · C
   3) D · E
   4) /∴ D

4.                /∴ C · (A ⊃ D)
   1) A ⊃ D   Pr
   2) B · C    Pr
   3) C · B
   4) C
   5) /∴ C · (A ⊃ D)

5.                  /∴ B · C
   1) (A · B) · C   Pr
   2) A · B
   3) C · (A · B)
   4) C
   5) B · A
   6) B
   7) /∴ B · C

6.                                  /∴ [D · (B ⊃ C)] · (A ⊃ B)
  1)  [(A ⊃ B) · (B ⊃ C)] · D   Pr
  2)  (A ⊃ B) · (B ⊃ C)
  3)  D · [(A ⊃ B) · (B ⊃ C)]
  4)  D
  5)  A ⊃ B
  6)  (B ⊃ C) · (A ⊃ B)
  7)  B ⊃ C
  8)  D · (B ⊃ C)
  9)  /∴ [D · (B ⊃ C)] · (A ⊃ B)

7.                                  /∴ (E · F) · [(A ∨ B) ⊃ D]
  1)  (A ∨ B) ⊃ D    Pr
  2)  (C · E) · F        Pr
  3)  C · E
  4)  F · (C · E)
  5)  F
  6)  E · C
  7)  E
  8)  E · F
  9)  /∴ (E · F) · [(A ∨ B) ⊃ D]

8.                        /∴ [ ∼ (C · ∼ E) · ∼ (A · ∼ B)] · [A · ∼ (B · ∼ C)]
  1)  ∼ (A · ∼ B) · [ ∼ (B · ∼ C) · ∼ (C · ∼ E)]    Pr
  2)  (E ⊃ D) · A                                              Pr
  3)  ∼ (A · ∼ B)
  4)  [ ∼ (B · ∼ C) · ∼ (C · ∼ E)] · ∼ (A · ∼ B)
  5)  ∼ (B · ∼ C) · ∼ (C · ∼ E)
  6)  ∼ (B · ∼ C)
  7)  ∼ (C · ∼ E) · ∼ (B · ∼ C)
  8)  ∼ (C · ∼ E)
  9)  A · (E ⊃ D)
  10) A
  11) ∼ (C · ∼ E) · ∼ (A · ∼ B)
  12) A · ∼ (B · ∼ C)
  13) /∴ [ ∼ (C · ∼ E) · ∼ (A · ∼ B)] · [A · ∼ (B · ∼ C)]

9.                              /∴ [( ∼ F · D) · ( ∼ B · C)] · [(E ∨ F) · (A ∨ B)]
  1)  [(A ∨ B) · ( ∼ B · C)] · [(E ∨ F) · ( ∼ F · D)]   Pr
  2)  (A ∨ B) · ( ∼ B · C)
  3)  [(E ∨ F) · ( ∼ F · D)] · [(A ∨ B) · ( ∼ B · C)]
  4)  (E ∨ F) · ( ∼ F · D)
  5)  A ∨ B
  6)  ( ∼ B · C) · (A ∨ B)
  7)  ∼ B · C
  8)  E ∨ F
  9)  ( ∼ F · D) · (E ∨ F)
  10) ∼ F · D
  11) ( ∼ F · D) · ( ∼ B · C)
  12) (E ∨ F) · (A ∨ B)
  13) /∴ [( ∼ F · D) · ( ∼ B · C)] · [(E ∨ F) · (A ∨ B)]

10. $/ \therefore (D \cdot C) \cdot [(E \vee F) \cdot (A \vee B)]$
    1) $[(A \vee B) \cdot (\sim B \cdot C)] \cdot [(E \vee F) \cdot (\sim F \cdot D)]$  Pr
    2) $(A \vee B) \cdot (\sim B \cdot C)$
    3) $[(E \vee F) \cdot (\sim F \cdot D)] \cdot [(A \vee B) \cdot (\sim B \cdot C)]$
    4) $(E \vee F) \cdot (\sim F \cdot D)$
    5) $A \vee B$
    6) $(\sim B \cdot C) \cdot (A \vee B)$
    7) $\sim B \cdot C$
    8) $C \cdot \sim B$
    9) $C$
    10) $E \vee F$
    11) $(\sim F \cdot D) \cdot (E \vee F)$
    12) $\sim F \cdot D$
    13) $D \cdot \sim F$
    14) $D$
    15) $(E \vee F) \cdot (A \vee B)$
    16) $D \cdot C$
    17) $/ \therefore (D \cdot C) \cdot [(E \vee F) \cdot (A \vee B)]$

## Group B:

Construct a proof of validity for each of the following.

1. $/ \therefore A$
    1) $A \cdot B$  Pr

2. $/ \therefore B \cdot A$
    1) $A \cdot B$  Pr

3. $/ \therefore B$
    1) $A \cdot B$  Pr

4. $/ \therefore A \cdot B$
    1) $A$  Pr
    2) $B$  Pr

5. $/ \therefore C \cdot B$
    1) $A \cdot B$  Pr
    2) $C$     Pr

6. $/ \therefore A \vee B$
    1) $(A \vee B) \cdot (C \vee D)$    Pr

7. $/ \therefore (C \vee D) \cdot (A \vee B)$
    1) $(A \vee B) \cdot (C \vee D)$    Pr

8. $/ \therefore \sim (B \cdot \sim A)$
    1) $\sim (A \cdot \sim B) \cdot \sim (B \cdot \sim A)$    Pr

9. $/ \therefore (B \supset C) \cdot (C \supset D)$
    1) $(A \supset B) \cdot (B \supset C)$    Pr
    2) $C \supset D$          Pr

10. $/ \therefore \sim (B \cdot \sim C) \cdot [\sim (C \cdot \sim D) \cdot \sim (\sim A \cdot \sim B)]$
    1) $\sim (\sim A \cdot \sim B) \cdot \sim (B \cdot \sim C)$    Pr
    2) $\sim (C \cdot \sim D)$          Pr

**Group C:**

Symbolize the following arguments using the capital letters suggested. Then construct a proof of validity for each.

1. Game theory can be useful in learning theory, but one must understand the connection between game theory and logical networks. Hence, game theory can be useful in learning theory. (T,N)

2. General descriptions of game theory involve infinite, nonzero sum, *n*-person games; moreover, these descriptions can be developed in considerable detail. Thus, general descriptions of game theory can be developed in considerable detail. (T,D)

3. The need for learning theory is recognized by many psychologists. Further, models for learning theory are also recognized to be needed. Consequently, many psychologists recognize a need for learning theory and models for that theory. (T,M)

4. Several different models can be constructed in the area of learning theory, but the difficulty is to select an appropriate model, and this must be done in relation to the theory. Therefore, several different models can be constructed in the area of learning theory, although the difficulty is to select an appropriate model. (C,S,R)

5. Game theory and logical networks can be used as models in learning theory, although there are other devices that might be employed. So, although there are other devices that might be employed, nevertheless logical networks can be used as models in learning theory. (T,N,D)

6. Information science is a relatively new area of study; but although it needs a more theoretical foundation, nevertheless it has generated a great deal of interest and produced many useful results. Thus, while information science is a relatively new area of study, it has generated a great deal of interest. (R,N,G,P)

7. You've a regard for concrete detail and study computer programming, yet you also enjoy abstract thinking and do well in mathematics. Therefore, you study computer programming and do well in mathematics, but, moreover, you also enjoy abstract thinking as well as having a regard for concrete detail. (R,S,E,W)

8. If you're interested in information retrieval systems, you'll enjoy information science; also, if you enjoy information science, you'll need matrix algebra. However, you'll need matrix algebra only if you pursue systems design; but if you pursue systems design, you must study computers. Consequently, if you're interested in information retrieval systems, you'll enjoy information science; yet if you pursue systems design, you must study computers. (I,E,N,P,S)

9. A strong background in mathematics is desirable if you plan to study information science; moreover, you should also have a working knowledge of computers. You might also find a knowledge of neurological networks helpful along with a careful study of logic. Consequently, a strong background in mathematics is desirable if you plan to study information science, and you should also have a working knowledge of computers and a careful study of logic. (M,S,C,N,L)

10. We'll take either game theory or matrix algebra our first year and also study either systems design or numeric processing; moreover, we'll study mathematical linguistics and semantics. Wherefore, we'll study semantics as well as take either game theory or matrix algebra our first year; but even so we'll also study mathematical linguistics while studying systems design or numeric processing. (T,A,D,P,L,S)

### 3. DISJUNCTIVE SYLLOGISM, COMMUTATION OF THE WEDGE, AND ADDITION

Each argument form introduced in this section uses the wedge and applies to arguments using inclusive disjunctive statements. As discussed in Chapter 2, disjunctive statements are interpreted as inclusive unless an exclusive disjunction is explicitly indicated by an expression such as ' . . . but not both'.

Consider these statements:

   **(1)**   Unbiased medical research on cigarette smoking is wrong or the primary cause of lung cancer is smoking.

   **(2)**   Unbiased medical research on cigarette smoking isn't wrong.

Assuming the truth of (1) and (2), it follows that

   **(3)**   The primary cause of lung cancer is smoking.

(1) through (3) comprise an instance of a valid argument form:

**DISJUNCTIVE SYLLOGISM (DS)**

$$p \lor q$$
$$\underline{\sim p}$$
$$/\therefore q$$

Disjunctive Syllogism has two premises. The first is an inclusive disjunctive statement form while the second premise has exactly one more tilde than the left-hand disjunct of the first premise. The conclusion is the same as the right-hand disjunct of the first premise.

An argument displaying the form Disjunctive Syllogism must be valid because of the definitional rules governing the uses of the wedge and the tilde. Assume any statement of the form 'p ∨ q' true. Then, either 'p' is true and 'q' false, 'p' is false and 'q' true, or both 'p' and 'q' are true. Let any statement of the form ' ∼ p' be true where 'p' in ' ∼ p' is the same statement as 'p' in 'p ∨ q'. In that case, given the rule governing the tilde, 'p' is false in the first premise. Yet, if 'p' is false and 'p ∨ q' is assumed true, then 'q' must be true because of the truth-functional rule governing the wedge.

Notice that the following argument is not valid:

   **(4)**   Either Russell is taking inventory or consulting with his managers. He is taking inventory. So, Russell isn't consulting with his managers. (T,C)

Symbolizing this argument produces,

   **(5)**                              $/\therefore \sim C$
        1) $T \lor C$   Pr
        2) $T$       Pr

(5) is clearly not an instance of

$$p \lor q$$
$$\underline{\sim p}$$
$$/ \therefore q$$

Indeed, (5) is not valid because both of its premises could be true and its conclusion false. There are three interpretations making 'T ∨ C' true. One of these is if both 'T' and 'C' are true, then 'T ∨ C' is true. Russell could be both taking inventory and consulting with his managers. And while the second premise of (5) asserts that 'T' is true, it says nothing about the truth or falsity of 'C'. 'C' could be true, in which case ' ∼ C' would be false. This argument form is invalid:

$$p \lor q$$
$$\underline{p}$$
$$/ \therefore \sim q$$

Assume the following:

(5)   The atomic number of thulium is 69 or the atomic number of berkelium is 96.

Also accept (6):

(6)   The atomic number of berkelium is not 96.

Given the truth of both (5) and (6), the following cannot be asserted by Disjunctive Syllogism:

(7)   The atomic number of thulium is 69.

(7) cannot be asserted because (6) is not the denial of the *left-hand* disjunct of (5). Nor is (7) the same as the *right-hand* disjunct of (5). But if (5) is true, then (8) must also be true:

(8)   The atomic number of berkelium is 96 or the atomic number of thulium is 69.

Moving from (5) to (8), an appeal is made to this valid form:

**COMMUTATION (COM)**

$$\underline{p \lor q}$$
$$/ \therefore q \lor p$$

(8), (6), and (7), in that order, depict an instance of Disjunctive Syllogism.

   *Addition* is another argument form used in constructing proofs. Take for granted that (9) is true:

(9)   'The Refrigerator', William Perry, played for the Chicago Bears.

If (9) is true, so is (10):

(10)    'The Refrigerator', William Perry, played for the Chicago Bears or Madrid is the capital of France.

An inclusive disjunctive statement is true if *at least one* of its disjuncts is true. Since (9) is both true and one of the disjuncts of (10), (10) must be true irrespective of whether its other disjunct is true or not. Statements (9) and (10) form an instance of this valid argument form:

**ADDITION (ADD)**

$$\frac{p}{/\therefore \; p \lor q}$$

In using Addition, *any* statement (true or false) can be substituted at 'q'. The statement replacing 'q' might, or might not, be found previously in the proof. Note that Addition is the only argument form allowing capital letters not found in the symbolization of the premises to be introduced into a proof.* So, if some capital letter is found in the symbolization of a conclusion but not in the symbolization of the premises, Addition *must* be used in an attempt to construct a proof for that argument. Addition, however, *might* be used to introduce a capital letter that already appears in the symbolization of both the premises and conclusion, especially if it cannot be obtained from the premises by any other elementary rule of inference.

Here is an example in which Addition must be used:

(11) We'll either study quantum mechanics or be limited in our knowledge of the physical sciences. We shan't be limited in our knowledge of the physical sciences. Consequently, we shan't progress in our work or we'll study quantum mechanics. (S,L,P)

Symbolize (11) as

(12)                    $/\therefore \; \sim P \lor S$
  1) $S \lor L$    Pr
  2) $\sim L$      Pr

Examine the conclusion and ask these questions:

1. *What kind of overall statement is the conclusion?*

2. *Does this statement appear embedded as a whole unit in any premise?*

Looking at (14), these questions are answered:

---

*In this book, Addition is the *only* rule permitting statements not mentioned in the premises of an argument to be introduced into a proof. In different formulations of inference rules, other rules can be used to do this. For instance, some sets of rules introduce this argument form:

$$\frac{p \supset q}{/\therefore \; (p \cdot r) \supset (q \cdot r)}$$

**a)** An inclusive disjunctive statement

**b)** No

If the answer to the second question is *NO*, proceed with these questions:

3. *What rules conclude with this type of statement?*

4. *Of these rules, which is more likely to yield the desired conclusion?*

5. *To use this rule, what other statement, or statements, is needed?*

Refer to (12) and answer these questions:

**c)** Commutation and Addition

**d)** Addition followed by Commutation

**e)** 'P'

Addition must be used in constructing a proof for (12) since neither 'P' nor ' $\sim$ P' appears in the premises. Now Addition shows that a new letter is added only to the right-hand side of the wedge. Because Addition has been used, Commutation is required to obtain the ordering of the letters as seen in the conclusion. But 'S' must first be derived from the premises to use Addition. This information is displayed in (13) where the vertical line suggests the strategy of *working backwards*:

$$(13) \qquad\qquad\qquad /\therefore\ \sim P \vee S$$

| | | |
|---|---|---|
| **1)** | $S \vee L$ | Pr |
| **2)** | $\sim L$ | Pr |
| | . | |
| | . | |
| **?)** | $S$ | ?, ? |
| **?)** | $S \vee \sim P$ | ?, Add |
| **?)** | $/\therefore\ \sim P \vee S$ | ?, Com |

Before the last three statements are deduced from the premises, more information, indicated by the question marks, is needed. For instance, how is 'S' obtained? Now, ask Question 1 and 2 in relation to 'S':

1. *What kind of overall statement is needed?* [A simple statement named by a single capital letter]

2. *Does this statement appear embedded as a whole unit anywhere in any premise?* [YES]

Because the answer to the second question is *YES*, proceed this way:

3. *In what statement does the needed 'S' appear?* [The first premise]

4. *What kind of overall statement is this?* [An inclusive disjunction]

5. *Given this type of statement, what rule, or rules, begins with this type of statement and ends by isolating part of it in a line by itself?* [Disjunctive Syllogism]

6. *To use this rule, what further statements are needed?* ['L $\vee$ S' and ' $\sim$ L']

Since 'S' is *literally seen* to be embedded in a wedge expression, it is useless to attempt to call on argument forms using, say, dots or horseshoes. Of those forms using the wedge, only Disjunctive Syllogism allows a disjunct to be isolated from a disjunction. Disjunctive Syllogism shows, moreover, that the statement name to be isolated must appear on the right-hand side of the wedge. Commutation is first used with 'S ∨ L'. Then Disjunctive Syllogism can be used to assert 'S' if ' ∼ L' is found first. ' ∼ L' is the second premise, however.

$$(14) \qquad\qquad\qquad\qquad /\therefore\ \sim P \vee S$$

| | | |
|---|---|---|
| 1) | S ∨ L | Pr |
| 2) | ∼ L | Pr |
| 3) | L ∨ S | 1, Com |
| 4) | S | 3, 2, DS |
| 5) | S ∨ ∼ P | 4, Add |
| 6) | /∴ ∼ P ∨ S | 5, Com |

In (15), a common mistake is illustrated in attempting to construct a proof for this argument:

(15)   'The Refrigerator', William Perry, played for the Chicago Bears. Therefore 'The Refrigerator', William Perry, played for the Chicago Bears and they won the world title. (P,W)

Use the recommended capital letters to symbolize (10):

$$(16) \qquad\qquad /\therefore\ P \cdot W$$

1) P   Pr

The novice might now attempt to continue like this:

$$(17) \qquad\qquad\qquad\qquad /\therefore\ P \cdot W$$

| | | | |
|---|---|---|---|
| | 1) | P | Pr |
| *WRONG X* | 2) | P · W | 1, Add |

(17) is invalid because the conclusion is false even though the premise is true. Conjunctions are true only when all their conjuncts are true. However, 'The Bears won the world title' is false. So,

(18)   'The Refrigerator', William Perry, played for the Chicago Bears *and* they won the world title

is false. *Addition is used only with the wedge.*

As new elementary rules of inference are developed and more complex arguments encountered in this and following chapters, determining what rule to use at a particular move in a specific proof becomes more demanding. The above series of questions, which illustrate the strategy of *working backwards*, is often helpful in discovering those rules most likely to work in a particular move leading to a desired conclusion. No strategy, or combination of heuristics, is always successful, but the likelihood of success can be increased with the development of a sense of strategy.

A warning concerning strategy is in order. Even though strategies can increase the likelihood of success, nonetheless they can be dangerous when misused. *First*, no rules-of-thumb helpful in doing anything, whether constructing proofs, purchasing stocks, dealing in the world of business, or leading one's life, are 100 percent effective. The best that such strategies can do is increase the chances of success. *Second*, it is tempting to rely so heavily on strategies that ones's actions begin to seem quite mechanical. But there are often surprises. For instance, in some cases the obvious strategies will work but not in a very efficient way—let alone the *most* efficient way. In other cases, these strategies are not at all applicable even though it appears as if they ought to be. And, in still other cases, the obvious strategies are not only useless but harmful in that they do not lead to the desired conclusion and also prevent someone from seeing how to arrive at a desired goal. Proof construction, like many other activities, has its surprises. Good strategies will help a person become better at doing whatever it is to which the strategies are applicable. But in the end, it is insight based on a firm grasp of the activity in question, coupled with practice, that leads to becoming an excellent practitioner.

---

## *EXERCISES*

### Group A:

Give the correct justification in each unjustified line of the following.

1.                          $/ \therefore A$
   1) $\sim B$    Pr
   2) $A \lor B$    Pr
   3) $B \lor A$
   4) $/ \therefore A$

2.                          $/ \therefore D \lor E$
   1) $C \cdot D$    Pr
   2) $D \cdot C$
   3) $D$
   4) $/ \therefore D \lor E$

3.                          $/ \therefore A$
   1) $(A \lor B) \cdot \sim B$    Pr
   2) $A \lor B$
   3) $\sim B \cdot (A \lor B)$
   4) $\sim B$
   5) $B \lor A$
   6) $/ \therefore A$

4.                          $/ \therefore (C \supset D) \cdot (E \lor \sim D)$
   1) $\sim (A \lor B)$            Pr
   2) $(C \supset D) \lor (A \lor B)$    Pr
   3) $\sim D$                Pr
   4) $(A \lor B) \lor (C \supset D)$
   5) $C \supset D$
   6) $\sim D \lor E$
   7) $E \lor \sim D$
   8) $/ \therefore (C \supset D) \cdot (E \lor \sim D)$

5.                              /∴ (D ∨ A) · (E ⊃ D)
    1)  ~ (B ⊃ C) · A        Pr
    2)  (E ⊃ D) ∨ (B ⊃ C)    Pr
    3)  ~ (B ⊃ C)
    4)  A · ~ (B ⊃ C)
    5)  A
    6)  (B ⊃ C) ∨ (E ⊃ D)
    7)  E ⊃ D
    8)  A ∨ D
    9)  D ∨ A
    10) /∴ (D ∨ A) · (E ⊃ D)

6.                              /∴ D · A
    1)  (A ∨ B) · ~ C        Pr
    2)  ~ B · (C ∨ D)        Pr
    3)  A ∨ B
    4)  ~ C · (A ∨ B)
    5)  ~ C
    6)  ~ B
    7)  (C ∨ D) · ~ B
    8)  C ∨ D
    9)  B ∨ A
    10) A
    11) D
    12) /∴ D · A

7.                              /∴ G ∨ [F ∨ (C ∨ E)]
    1)  (C ∨ D) ∨ (A ⊃ B)    Pr
    2)  ~ D · ~ (A ⊃ B)      Pr
    3)  ~ D
    4)  ~ (A ⊃ B) · ~ D
    5)  ~ (A ⊃ B)
    6)  (A ⊃ B) ∨ (C ∨ D)
    7)  C ∨ D
    8)  D ∨ C
    9)  C
    10) C ∨ E
    11) (C ∨ E) ∨ F
    12) F ∨ (C ∨ E)
    13) [F ∨ (C ∨ E)] ∨ G
    14) /∴ G ∨ [F ∨ (C ∨ E)]

8.                              /∴ (A ∨ C) · F
    1)  ~ (A ∨ B) · ~ (B ∨ C)    Pr
    2)  (A ∨ B) ∨ (C ∨ E)        Pr
    3)  (F ∨ E) ∨ (B ∨ C)        Pr
    4)  ~ E                      Pr
    5)  ~ (A ∨ B)
    6)  ~ (B ∨ C) · ~ (A ∨ B)
    7)  ~ (B ∨ C)
    8)  C ∨ E
    9)  E ∨ C
    10) C

11) C ∨ A
12) A ∨ C
13) (B ∨ C) ∨ (F ∨ E)
14) F ∨ E
15) E ∨ F
16) F
17) /∴ (A ∨ C) · F

9.                              /∴ (H ∨ C) · (G ∨ I)
  1)  ~A · ~F      Pr
  2)  A ∨ (B ∨ C)  Pr
  3)  E ∨ (F ∨ G)  Pr
  4)  ~B · ~E      Pr
  5)  ~A
  6)  ~F · ~A
  7)  ~F
  8)  ~B
  9)  ~E · ~B
 10)  ~E
 11)  B ∨ C
 12)  C
 13)  C ∨ H
 14)  H ∨ C
 15)  F ∨ G
 16)  G
 17)  G ∨ I
 18)  /∴ (H ∨ C) · (G ∨ I)

10.                             /∴ (E · C) ∨ (E · D)
  1)  (~A ∨ B) · (~B · ~D)        Pr
  2)  [(A ∨ C) ∨ D] · [(E ∨ B) ∨ A]    Pr
  3)  ~A ∨ B
  4)  (~B · ~D) · (~A ∨ B)
  5)  ~B · ~D
  6)  ~B
  7)  ~D · ~B
  8)  ~D
  9)  (A ∨ C) ∨ D
 10)  [(E ∨ B) ∨ A] · [(A ∨ C) ∨ D]
 11)  (E ∨ B) ∨ A
 12)  D ∨ (A ∨ C)
 13)  A ∨ C
 14)  B ∨ ~A
 15)  ~A
 16)  C
 17)  A ∨ (E ∨ B)
 18)  E ∨ B
 19)  B ∨ E
 20)  E
 21)  E · C
 22)  /∴ (E · C) ∨ (E · D)

**Group B:**

Construct a proof of validity for each of the following.

1.                          /∴ B ∨ A
   1) A ∨ B    Pr

2.                          /∴ B
   1) ∼ A    Pr
   2) A ∨ B    Pr

3.                          /∴ A
   1) A ∨ B    Pr
   2) ∼ B    Pr

4.                          /∴ C ∨ B
   1) A ∨ B    Pr
   2) ∼ A    Pr

5.                          /∴ (C ∨ D) ∨ (B ∨ A)
   1) A ∨ B    Pr

6.                          /∴ (A · C) ∨ D
   1) A · ∼ B    Pr
   2) C ∨ B    Pr

7.                          /∴ D ∨ C
   1) A ∨ [B ∨ (C ∨ D)]    Pr
   2) ∼ B · ∼ A    Pr

8.                          /∴ (C ∨ A) · (B ∨ D)
   1) (D · C) ∨ (A · B)    Pr
   2) ∼ (A · B)    Pr

9.                          /∴ (B ∨ E) · (C ∨ F)
   1) (A ∨ B) · (C ∨ D)    Pr
   2) ∼ A · ∼ D    Pr

10.                         /∴ [(B · ∼ A) ∨ E] · [(C · ∼ D) ∨ F]
   1) (B ∨ A) · ∼ A    Pr
   2) (D ∨ C) · ∼ D    Pr

**Group C:**

Symbolize the following arguments using the capital letters suggested. Then construct a proof of validity for each.

1. We'll study either Plato or Aristotle. So, we'll study either Aristotle or Plato. (P,A)

2. Aristotle doesn't have the best literary style of the great ancient philosophers, but either Plato or Aristotle does. Thus, Plato has the best literary style of the great ancient philosophers. (A,P)

3. Plato wrote either the *Symposium* or the *Eudemian Ethics*, yet he didn't write the *Eudemian Ethics*. Hence, Plato wrote the *Lysis* or the *Symposium*. (S,E,L)

4. Either Eryximachus doesn't understand love as some cosmic principle or both Phaedrus and Alcibiades think of love in its more physical forms. Socrates isn't ignorant about love matters, and further it isn't true that Eryximachus doesn't understand love as some sort of cosmic principle. Therefore, either Phaedrus or Alcibiades thinks of love in its more physical forms, while Socrates isn't ignorant about love matters. (E,P,A,S)

5. In Plato's *Symposium* Phaedrus doesn't have a correct concept of love but neither does Eryximachus and, moreover, Agathon doesn't know what he's talking about or Phaedrus does have a correct concept of love. Either Agathon knows what he's talking about or we must listen carefully to Diotima. Consequently, Eryximachus has a correct notion of love or we must listen carefully to Diotima. (P,E,A,D)

6. The *Republic* or *Ion* is an early dialogue of Plato, but the *Lysis* or *Timaeus* is a late work. The *Republic* isn't an early dialogue and the *Lysis* isn't a late work. So, either the *Ion* or *Charmides* is an early dialogue of Plato, while the *Statesman* or *Timaeus* is a late work. (R,I,L,T,C,S)

7. We aren't interested in ancient Greek philosophy, or we'll read at least the *Timaeus* and the *Republic*. Also we'll read either the *Republic* or *Laws*, or the *Meno*. It isn't the case that we'll read at least the *Timaeus* and the *Republic*. Either we don't read the *Meno* and don't read the *Republic*, or we're interested in ancient Greek philosophy. Hence, either it isn't true that we are interested in ancient Greek philosophy and read the *Republic*, or else we'll read the *Republic* or *Laws*. (P,T,R,L,M)

8. It isn't true that Meletus testified just in case there was a public condemnation of Socrates; but also, Anytus didn't interfere or, indeed, Meletus testified if and only if there was a public condemnation of Socrates. Anytus interfered, or it isn't the case that Lycon didn't step in but yet there was a public condemnation of Socrates. Either we must believe Plato's report of the trial, or Lycon didn't step in even though there was a public condemnation of Socrates. Wherefore, we must believe Plato's report of the trial. (M,S,A,L,P)

9. Thrasymachus wasn't at Socrates' execution, but Crito was; further, while Echecrates wasn't there, Simmias was. Now, either Xanthippe didn't stay at the prison or Thrasymachus was at the execution. Furthermore, either Echecrates was at Socrates' execution, or Apollodoros was with Socrates or Xanthippe stayed at the prison. Consequently, we must not believe Plato if Echecrates was at Socrates' execution, or both Apollodoros and Simmias were with Socrates. (T,C,E,S,X,A,P)

10. Either we don't understand our contemporary world, or if we do then we study the ancient philosophers. We study the ancient philosophers and don't lose our cultural heritage, or we understand our contemporary world. It isn't the case that we understand our contemporary world only if we study the ancient philosophers; furthermore, if we don't study the ancient philosophers, we ignore a vital historic source of our civilization. Hence, we ignore a vital historic source of our civilization provided that we don't study the ancient philosophers; and also either we don't ignore a vital historic source of our civilization or we don't lose our cultural heritage. (U,S,L,I)

## 4.   MODUS PONENS AND MODUS TOLLENS

Suppose the following are true:

    **(1)**   The dollar is falling only if the national deficit is increasing.

         **(2)**   The dollar is falling.

Then (3) must also be true:

         **(3)**   The national deficit is increasing.

These statements form an instance of the valid argument form *Modus Ponens*:

**MODUS PONENS (MP)**

$$p \supset q$$
$$\underline{p}$$
$$/ \therefore q$$

Assume true a statement displaying the form 'p ⊃ q'. Because of the definitional rule governing the horseshoe, 'p' cannot be true and 'q' false. If 'p ⊃ q' and 'p' are true, 'q' must be true. The second premise of Modus Ponens does assert that 'p' is true. So, 'q' must be true.

A deductive argument form often confused with Modus Ponens is the

**FALLACY OF AFFIRMING THE CONSEQUENT**

$$p \supset q$$
$$\underline{q}$$
$$/ \therefore p$$

A *fallacy* is

**something in an argument that prohibits the premises from supporting the conclusion.**

What if a business person salvaged some capital after October 1929? Based on the following argument this person decides to put all remaining resources in the Insull Utilities Investments Corporation of Illinois:

(4)   I'll invest all I have left in the Insull Utilities Investments Corporation if I'm to regain my financial losses. I'll invest. So, I'll certainly regain my financial losses.

This argument can be pictured in this way:

(5)   $R \supset I$
$$I$$
$$\overline{/ \therefore R}$$

If (5) is taken deductively, it is invalid. That the premises are true does not guarantee the truth of the conclusion. Indeed, common shares of Insull that had been around $500 in 1930 were valued at less than four cents on the dollar by May 1932.

Assume these two statements are true:

(6)   OPEC will raise oil prices over 10% if the dollar falls more.

(7)   OPEC will not raise oil prices over 10%.

If (6) and (7) are true, the following must also be true:

(8)   The dollar doesn't fall more.

(6) through (8) comprise an instance of the valid argument form

## MODUS TOLLENS (MT)

$$p \supset q$$
$$\sim q$$
$$/\therefore \sim p$$

The first premise of Modus Tollens is a hypothetical statement form, while the second denies the consequent of the first premise. The conclusion denies the antecedent of the first premise. Any argument picturing this form is valid. If nothing but the names of true statements are substituted in the premises, then—substituting the same statement name at 'p' in both the conclusion and the premise—the conclusion must also be true. Notice that the second premise of the form asserts that ' $\sim$ q' is true, which means 'q' is false. Given the rule governing the horseshoe, if 'q' is false then 'p' must be false for 'p $\supset$ q' to be true. Since 'p' is false, it follows that ' $\sim$ p', the conclusion, must be true.*

Next, imagine that these statements are true:

**(9)**    The rate of the GNP increases rapidly only if a period of high inflation is about to begin.

**(10)**    The rate of the GNP isn't increasing rapidly.

The truth of (9) and (10) does not guarantee the truth of

**(11)**    A period of high inflation is about to begin.

(9) through (11) can be symbolized as

**(12)**                    $/\therefore$ B
    **1)** I $\supset$ B  Pr
    **2)** $\sim$ I    Pr

(12) displays an instance of the deductively invalid argument form

## FALLACY OF DENYING THE ANTECEDENT

$$p \supset q$$
$$\sim p$$
$$/\therefore \sim q$$

Since (15) does not display any valid argument form, it is deductively invalid. However, it might be considered a reasonable inductive argument supplying reasons to accept the likelihood of the truth of the conclusion.

Inspect this example of a valid argument:

**(13)** The economic middle class doesn't enjoy greater purchasing power if personal income is more heavily taxed by the federal government. Federal programs are curtailed only if the economic middle class does enjoy greater purchasing power. Personal income is more heavily taxed by the federal government while either federal programs are curtailed or the federal

---

*Once again an "as if" manner of speaking is being used—as if statement variables were either true or false.

government moves closer to economic socialism. So, the federal government moves closer to economic socialism. (E,T,C,M)

With the suggested capital letters, symbolize (10) as

$$\textbf{(14)} \qquad\qquad\qquad /\therefore\ M$$

**1)** $T \supset\ \sim E$ ⠀⠀Pr

**2)** $C \supset E$ ⠀⠀Pr

**3)** $T \cdot (C \vee M)$ ⠀⠀Pr

Begin developing a strategy for constructing a proof of (17) by asking these questions:

1. *What kind of overall statement is the conclusion?* [Simple]
2. *Does this statement appear anywhere in the premises embedded as a whole unit?* [Yes]
3. *In what premise does the needed statement, 'M', appear?* [The third]
4. *What kind of overall statement is that premise?* [A conjunction]
5. *Given this type of statement, what rule, or rules, begins with this type of statement and ends by isolating part of that statement in a line by itself?* [Simplification]
6. *To use this rule what else is needed?* ['$(C \vee M) \cdot T$]'

Only the left-hand conjunct of a conjunction can be simplified, and 'M' appears in the right-hand conjunct. Hence, use Commutation before Simplification:

$$\textbf{(15)} \qquad\qquad\qquad /\therefore\ M$$

**1)** $T \supset\ \sim E$ ⠀⠀Pr

**2)** $C \supset E$ ⠀⠀Pr

**3)** $T \cdot (C \vee M)$ ⠀⠀Pr

.

.

**?)** $(C \vee M) \cdot T$ ⠀⠀3, Com

**?)** $C \vee M$ ⠀⠀?, Simp

**?)** $/\therefore\ M$ ⠀⠀?, ?

A proof of (13) hinges on isolating 'M' out of '$C \vee M$'. Now ask:

1. *In what statement is 'M' seen?* ['$C \vee M$']
2. *What kind of overall statement is this?* [An inclusive disjunction]
3. *Given this type of statement, what rule, or rules, begins with this type of statement and ends by isolating part of that statement?* [Disjunctive Syllogism]
4. *To use this rule, what further statement is needed?* ['$\sim C$']

*Working backwards* helps to reveal that the following lines are useful to complete a proof for (13):

$$\textbf{(16)} \qquad\qquad\qquad /\therefore\ M$$

**1)** $T \supset\ \sim E$ ⠀⠀Pr

**2)** C ⊃ E          Pr
**3)** T · (C ∨ M)    Pr

.
.
.

**?)** ~ C
**?)** (C ∨ M) · T    3, Com
**?)** C ∨ M          ?, Simp
**?)** /∴ M           ?, ?, DS

To see how ' ~ C' is obtained, proceed with these questions:

1. *In what statement does ' ~ C' appear?* [None, but 'C' appears in the second premise]

2. *What kind of overall statement is this?* [A hypothetical]

3. *Given this type of statement, what rule, or rules, begins with this type of statement and ends by isolating part of that statement?* [Modus Ponens and Modus Tollens]

The third question suggests that, of all the rules, two are likely to be useful in obtaining ' ~ C'. So, new questions become:

4. *Of these possible rules, which one is more likely to yield what is wanted?* [Modus Tollens, since 'C' is the antecedent of a hypothetical statement and Modus Tollens isolates *denied* antecedents]

5. *To use this rule, what further statement is needed?* [' ~ E']

Go through the series of questions again in relation to ' ~ E':

1. *In what statement does the needed ' ~ E' appear?* [The first premise]

2. *What kind of overall statement is this?* [A hypothetical]

3. *Given this type of statement, what rule, or rules, begins with this type of statement and ends by isolating part of that statement?* [Modus Ponens and Modus Tollens]

4. *Of these possible rules, which is more likely to yield what is wanted, that is, ' ~ E'?* [Modus Ponens, since ' ~ E' is the consequent of a hypothetical statement and Modus Ponens isolates a consequent]

5. *To use this rule what further statement is needed?* ['T']

A proof for (14) begins to take shape:

**(17)**                              /∴ M
**1)** T ⊃ ~ E        Pr
**2)** C ⊃ E          Pr
**3)** T · (C ∨ M)    Pr

.
.

| ?) T | ? |
|---|---|
| ?) ~ E | 1, ?, MP |
| ?) ~ C | 2, ?, MT |
| ?) (C ∨ M) · T | 3, Com |
| ?) C ∨ M | ?, Simp |
| ?) /∴ M | ?, ?, DS |

Where is 'T' found? In the third premise. What rule is used to isolate the left-hand conjunct, 'T'? Simplification. The information needed to construct a proof for (16) is available and can be put together in this way:

| (21) | | /∴ M |
|---|---|---|
| **1)** T ⊃ ~ E | Pr | |
| **2)** C ⊃ E | Pr | |
| **3)** T · (C ∨ M) | Pr | |
| **4)** T | 3, Simp | |
| **5)** ~ E | 1, 4, MP | |
| **6)** ~ C | 2, 5, MT | |
| **7)** (C ∨ M) · T | 3, Com | |
| **8)** C ∨ M | 7, Simp | |
| **9)** /∴ M | 8, 6, DS | |

## EXERCISES

### Group A:

Given the truth-functional rules governing the horseshoe and tilde, discuss why both the Fallacy of Affirming the Consequent and the Fallacy of Denying the Antecedent are deductively invalid argument forms.

### Group B:

Give the correct justification in each unjustified line of the following.

1.                    /∴ B
   1) A ⊃ B    Pr
   2) A          Pr
   3) /∴ B

2.                    /∴ ~ ~ A
   1) ~ A ⊃ ~ B    Pr
   2) ~ ~ B          Pr
   3) /∴ ~ ~ A

3.                    /∴ B
   1) A · (A ⊃ B)    Pr
   2) A
   3) (A ⊃ B) · A

4) A ⊃ B
5) /∴ B

4.                                        /∴ ~ A
  1) (A ⊃ B) · (B ⊃ C)    Pr
  2) ~ C                  Pr
  3) A ⊃ B
  4) (B ⊃ C) · (A ⊃ B)
  5) B ⊃ C
  6) ~ B
  7) /∴ ~ A

5.                                        /∴ D
  1) (A ⊃ B) · (B ⊃ C)    Pr
  2) C ⊃ D                Pr
  3) A                    Pr
  4) A ⊃ B
  5) (B ⊃ C) · (A ⊃ B)
  6) B ⊃ C
  7) B
  8) C
  9) /∴ D

6.                                        /∴ E · B
  1) ~ A ⊃ B        Pr
  2) ~ C            Pr
  3) A ⊃ D          Pr
  4) ~ C ⊃ ~ D      Pr
  5) B ⊃ E          Pr
  6) ~ D
  7) ~ A
  8) B
  9) E
 10) /∴ E · B

7.                                        /∴ E ∨ D
  1) A ⊃ B    Pr
  2) A ∨ C    Pr
  3) B ⊃ D    Pr
  4) ~ C      Pr
  5) C ∨ A
  6) A
  7) B
  8) D
  9) D ∨ E
 10) /∴ E ∨ D

8.                                        /∴ (B · A) · (C · E)
  1) A ⊃ (B ⊃ C)    Pr
  2) (D ∨ E) ⊃ A    Pr
  3) E · B          Pr
  4) E
  5) B · E
  6) B
  7) E ∨ D

8) D ∨ E
9) A
10) B ⊃ C
11) C
12) C · E
13) B · A
14) /∴ (B · A) · (C · E)

9. /∴ G ∨ E
   1) ~ A ⊃ ~ C                              Pr
   2) ~ A · B                                Pr
   3) [A ∨ (C ∨ D)] · [(B · D) ⊃ E]          Pr
   4) ~ A
   5) B · ~ A
   6) B
   7) A ∨ (C ∨ D)
   8) [(B · D ⊃ E] · [A ∨ (C ∨ D)]
   9) (B · D) ⊃ E
   10) ~ C
   11) C ∨ D
   12) D
   13) B · D
   14) E
   15) E ∨ G
   16) /∴ G ∨ E

10. /∴ ~ B
    1) A ⊃ (B ⊃ C)         Pr
    2) A ∨ D               Pr
    3) (D ⊃ E) · (E ⊃ F)   Pr
    4) G ⊃ (~ F · ~ C)     Pr
    5) G                   Pr
    6) D ⊃ E
    7) (E ⊃ F) · (D ⊃ E)
    8) E ⊃ F
    9) ~ F · ~ C
    10) ~ F
    11) ~ C · ~ F
    12) ~ C
    13) ~ E
    14) ~ D
    15) D ∨ A
    16) A
    17) B ⊃ C
    18) /∴ ~ B

## Group C:

Construct a proof of validity for each of the following.

1. /∴ C · ~ A
   1) (A ⊃ B) · C   Pr
   2) ~ B           Pr

2.                          / ∴ C
   1)  A ∨ B            Pr
   2)  (B ⊃ C) · ~ A    Pr

3.                          / ∴ D ∨ C
   1)  (A ∨ B) ∨ C   Pr
   2)  (A ∨ B) ⊃ E   Pr
   3)  ~ E          Pr

4.                          / ∴ ~ B · ~ A
   1)  ~ (B ∨ C) ∨ A      Pr
   2)  ~ A                Pr
   3)  (D ∨ E) ⊃ (B ∨ C)  Pr
   4)  ~ B ∨ (D ∨ E)      Pr

5.                          / ∴ C
   1)  (A · B) ⊃ C         Pr
   2)  (D ⊃ A) · (E ⊃ B)   Pr
   3)  E · D               Pr

6.                          / ∴ ( ~ A · ~ B) · (C · D)
   1)  (B ⊃ A) · ( ~ B ⊃ C)  Pr
   2)  (C ⊃ D) · ~ A         Pr

7.                          / ∴ (A ∨ B) · (A · E)
   1)  (A ∨ ~ B) ⊃ ~ (C ∨ D)   Pr
   2)  (C ∨ D) ∨ (A · E)       Pr
   3)  (B ⊃ F) · ~ F           Pr

8.                          / ∴ F ∨ E
   1)  (A ⊃ B) · (C ⊃ D)       Pr
   2)  A · ~ D                 Pr
   3)  ( ~ C · B) ⊃ (E ∨ D)    Pr

9.                          / ∴ ~ G
   1)  (A · B) · (C · D)              Pr
   2)  [(B · D) ⊃ E] · [(A · C) ⊃ F]  Pr
   3)  (E · F) ⊃ ~ G                  Pr

10.                         / ∴ A · D
   1)  (A ∨ B) · (C ∨ D)            Pr
   2)  (B ⊃ E) · (C ⊃ F)            Pr
   3)  [( ~ E · ~ F) ∨ G] · ~ G     Pr

## Group D:

Symbolize the following arguments using the capital letters suggested. Then construct a proof of validity for each.

1. That we're interested in economic theory is a sufficient reason for reading the works of Thomas R. Malthus. We are interested in economic theory. So, we'll read the works of Malthus. (I,R)

2. Malthus is unfamiliar only if we aren't well-educated in economic theory. We aren't acquainted with the *First* and *Second Essay* if we aren't well educated in economic theory. We aren't unacquainted with the *First* and *Second Essay*. Consequently, Malthus isn't unfamiliar to us. (F,E,A)

3. We're not well educated in economic theory unless we've read the works of John M.

Keynes. We've studied *A Treatise on Money* provided that we've read the works of Keynes. We're well educated in economic theory, and we appreciate the economic theory of Keynes if we've studied *A Treatise on Money*. Hence, we're well educated in economic theory while also appreciating the economic theory of Keynes. (E,R,S,A)

4. Inflation continues and buying power doesn't remain stable. Price controls are established only if buying power remains stable. Certainly a sufficient condition for the middle income class to suffer is that inflation continues while price controls aren't established. So, inflation continues and the middle income class suffers. (C,R,E,S)

5. The national deficit continues to rise despite the fact that buying dwindles. That Wall Street falls is a necessary condition that either money becomes more scarce through higher interest rates or the national deficit continues to rise. Thus, buying dwindles as well as Wall Street falls. (R,D,F,S)

6. If inflation continues, taxes will increase; moreover, if taxes increase, money will become more scarce. Either money doesn't become more scarce or business will recede. That money doesn't become more scarce is a sufficient condition for the worker being happier. Business won't recede. Therefore, the worker will be happier while inflation won't continue. (C,I,S,R,H)

7. If prices rise whenever there is inflation, then the stock market won't be stable. Either the market won't be unstable or bonds will fluctuate wildly; moreover, bonds won't fluctuate wildly or federal controls are established on computer trading. Federal controls aren't established on computer trading, however. Either there is inflation only if prices rise, or we discern possible economic normality. So, we discern possible economic normality even though federal controls aren't established. (R,I,S,F,E,D)

8. Salaries stabilize or dividends remain constant, while on the other hand business isn't controlled. Business is controlled if government intervenes. If salaries stabilize and government doesn't intervene, then the economy balances itself. That dividends remain constant is a sufficient condition for business being controlled. Hence, either the economy balances itself and dividends don't remain constant, or the economy balances itself and dividends do remain constant. (S,R,C,I,B)

9. If it's neither true that time is an unimportant factor nor we aren't interested in maximizing our economic research, then we find computers interesting. That either we aren't interested in maximizing our economic research or we find computers interesting is a sufficient condition for pursuing applied mathematics. Neither is time an unimportant factor nor are we not interested in maximizing our economic research, or either we are bound to old technques of economic analysis or recent developments in logic are unfamiliar. It isn't the case that either we are bound to old techniques of economic analysis or recent developments in logic are unfamiliar. If we pursue applied mathematics or aren't bound to old techniques of economic analysis, then we should acquaint ourselves with the research of Arthur Goldberg. So, either it isn't the case that we should both acquaint ourselves with the research of Goldberg while finding computers interesting, or we find computers interesting and should acquaint ourselves with the research of Goldberg. (T,R,C,M,A,D,G)

10. If we're interested in contemporary economic theory, we must study statistical models. It isn't true that we must study statistical models or be familiar with mathematical analysis, but not both. That we need to study Boolean algebras is a necessary condition for being interested in either axiomatic systems or computer research. We're interested in axiomatic systems only if we're both acquainted with contemporary systems of logic and we're not unfamiliar with mathematical analysis. Either we're interested in contemporary economic theory or we're unfamiliar with mathematical analysis; or else we either must

study statistical models or be familiar with mathematical analysis, but not both. We're interested in axiomatic systems. Thus, we're interested in contemporary economic theory and are acquainted with contemporary systems of logic, and are also interested in axiomatic systems and need to study Boolean algebras; while, moreover, we must also study statistical models. (T,M,A,B,S,R,L)

## 5.  HYPOTHETICAL SYLLOGISM AND CONSTRUCTIVE DILEMMA

If statements (1) and (2) are true, (3) also must be true:

   **(1)**    If a person understands contemporary French literature,
            she reads the works of Jean-Paul Sartre.

 **(2)**   A person studies *No Exit* provided that she reads the works of Sartre.

   **(3)**   A person understands contemporary French literature only if
            she studies *No Exit*.

These statements form an instance of the valid argument form

### HYPOTHETICAL SYLLOGISM (HS)

$$p \supset q$$
$$q \supset r$$
$$\overline{\phantom{xxx}}$$
$$/\therefore\ p \supset r$$

Hypothetical Syllogism relates two hypothetical premises to a hypothetical conclusion. The consequent of the first premise is the same as the antecedent of the second; the antecedent of the conclusion is the same as the antecedent of the first premise; and the consequent of the conclusion is the same as the consequent of the second premise.

An argument might end with a hypothetical statement not embedded as a whole unit in the premises. Hypothetical Syllogism is a rule allowing such a conclusion to be constructed. As equivalence forms are introduced in the next chapter, there will be more ways to deduce hypothetical statements. Now, however, consider this example:

**(4)**  Estella has concern for baroque music only if she listens to the works of J. S. Bach. If she knows the compositions of Dietrich Buxtehude, then if she listens to the works of Bach, she also appreciates rich musical ornamentation. Estella knows the compositions of Buxtehude whenever she easily senses the complicated patterns of baroque music. She easily senses the complicated patterns of baroque music. Accordingly, assuming Estella has concern for baroque music, then she appreciates rich musical ornamentation. (C,L,K,A,S)

(4) is symbolized as

   **(5)**                              $/\therefore\ C \supset A$
            1) $C \supset L$        Pr

**2)** K ⊃ (L ⊃ A)    Pr
**3)** S ⊃ K    Pr
**4)** S    Pr

Begin with the heuristic of *working backwards*. Does the hypothetical conclusion appear anywhere as a whole unit in the premises? No. It seems that the conclusion must be constructed. Hypothetical Syllogism is an argument form ending in a hypothetical, and it might be used to reach 'C ⊃ A'.* Two further statements are needed to complete an instance of this form. Hypothetical Syllogism shows what these needed statements look like. They are 'C ⊃ q' and 'q ⊃ A', where the variable, 'q', has to be replaced by the name of a statement. In (5), 'C ⊃ L' is the first premise and 'L ⊃ A' the consequent of the second premise. If 'L ⊃ A' can be isolated in a separate line, Hypothetical Syllogism can then be used to establish the conclusion:

**(6)**                          / ∴  C ⊃ A
    **1)** C ⊃ L    Pr
    **2)** K ⊃ (L ⊃ A)    Pr
    **3)** S ⊃ K    Pr
    **4)** S    Pr

            .
            .

    **?)** L ⊃ A    ?
    **?)** / ∴ C ⊃ A    1, ?, HS    ↑

Since 'L ⊃ A' is the consequent of a hypothetical statement, consider using Modus Ponens. To use Modus Ponens with the second premise, 'K' is needed. 'K' is the consequent of the third premise. Once more Modus Ponens must be used if 'K' is to be asserted. To use Modus Ponens with the third premise requires 'S'. But 'S' is the fourth premise. Working backwards has shown how a proof of (4) can be constructed:

**(7)**                          / ∴  C ⊃ A
    **1)** C ⊃ L    Pr

---

*Again a word of caution is in order concerning any slavish dependency on strategies. Following is an example in which the argument has a hypothetical conclusion not appearing in the premises. But neither are there any hypothetical statements in the premises. Discovering the following proof requires insight rather than simple reliance on strategy:

                                / ∴ A ⊃ B
    **1)** ~ (A ∨ B)    Pr
    **2)** A · B    Pr
    **3)** A    2, Simp
    **4)** A ∨ B    3, Add
    **5)** (A ∨ B) ∨ (A ⊃ B)    4, Add
    **6)** / ∴ A ⊃ B    5, 1, DS

**2)** K ⊃ (L ⊃ A)    Pr
**3)** S ⊃ K    Pr
**4)** S    Pr
**5)** K    3, 4, MP
**6)** L ⊃ A    2, 5, MP
**7)** /∴ C ⊃ A    1, 6, HS

Remember, *an argument might have several different proofs* establishing its validity. Here is another proof for (4):

**(8)**                        /∴ C ⊃ A
    **1)** C ⊃ L    Pr
    **2)** K ⊃ (L ⊃ A)    Pr
    **3)** S ⊃ K    Pr
    **4)** S    Pr
    **5)** S ⊃ (L ⊃ A)    3, 2, HS
    **6)** L ⊃ A    5, 4, MP
    **7)** /∴ C ⊃ A    1, 6, HS

The final argument form to be introduced is ***Constructive Dilemma (CD)***. Assume the following are true:

**(9)**   If Roberto studies major writers in contemporary German literature, he reads Thomas Mann.

**(10)** Roberto doesn't study major writers in contemporary French literature unless Albert Camus is read.

**(11)** Roberto reads either contemporary German or French literature.

Given the truth of (9) through (11), (12) must be true:

    **(12)**   Thus, Roberto reads either Thomas Mann or Albert Camus.
These statements comprise an instance of

**CONSTRUCTIVE DILEMMA (CD)**

$$p \supset q$$
$$r \supset s$$
$$\underline{p \lor r}$$
$$/\therefore q \lor s$$

Constructive Dilemma is a valid argument form composed of three premises and a conclusion. The first two premises are hypothetical statement forms. The third premise and conclusion are inclusive disjunction statement forms. The antecedent of the first premise is exactly the same as the left-hand disjunct of the third premise. Further, the antecedent of the second premise and the right-hand disjunct of the third premise are the same. The consequent of the first premise and the left-hand disjunct of the conclusion are the same, and the consequent of the second premise is the same as the right-hand disjunct of the conclusion.

How is Constructive Dilemma used? Examine this argument:

**(13)** If Dottie appreciates the works of Igor Stravinsky, then if she also listens creatively to the compositions of Charles Ives, she grasps some of the best examples of contemporary classical music. Also, if Dottie enjoys the scores of Claudio Monteverdi, then she ponders favorably the pieces of Giovanni da Palestrina only if she recognizes some of the great heights in Italian Renaissance music. That Dottie displays keen musical sensitivity is a sufficient condition for both appreciating the works of Stravinsky and enjoying the scores of Monteverdi. Dottie does display keen musical sensitivity, while also either pondering favorably the pieces of Palestrina or listening creatively to the compositions of Ives. Thus, it follows that Dottie grasps some of the best of contemporary classical music and/or recognizes some of the great heights in Italian Renaissance music. (A,L,G,E,P,R,D)

Review how (13) is symbolized:

**(14)**                                    $/\therefore$  $G \vee R$
   **1)** $A \supset (L \supset G)$    Pr
   **2)** $E \supset (P \supset R)$    Pr
   **3)** $D \supset (A \cdot E)$    Pr
   **4)** $D \cdot (P \vee L)$    Pr

Start constructing a proof by working backwards.

The conclusion of (14) is an inclusive disjunction that does not appear in the premises. Consider obtaining 'G $\vee$ R' by using Commutation, Addition, or Constructive Dilemma since these are rules *ending* in a wedge statement. Of these possibilities, Constructive Dilemma seems most likely. What clue leads to this supposition? *Each disjunct of the conclusion appears as a consequent in a hypothetical statement* found in the premises. Isolate 'L $\supset$ G' from the first premise and 'P $\supset$ R' from the second, then a Constructive Dilemma move is almost complete:

$$L \supset G$$
$$P \supset R$$
$$\text{NEED} \quad \Rightarrow \underline{p \vee r} \quad \Rightarrow L \vee P$$
$$/\therefore \ G \vee R$$

A statement to fit the third premise of Constructive Dilemma needs to be found. The disjuncts of 'p $\vee$ r' are the same as the antecedents of the first two premises. Hence, in this application of Constructive Dilemma, 'L $\vee$ P' is needed. But 'L $\vee$ P' can be obtained from the fourth premise.

A proof of (14) hinges on isolating 'L $\supset$ G' and 'P $\supset$ R'. These appear as consequents of hypotheticals. Modus Ponens is the argument form used to isolate a consequent. If Modus Ponens is applied to 'A $\supset$ (L $\supset$ G)' to obtain 'L $\supset$ G', 'A' must first be isolated in a separate line. Similar considerations lead to using 'E' with

Modus Ponens and the second premise to assert 'P ⊃ R'. Notice 'A · E' is the consequent of the third premise. If 'A · E' can be established by using Modus Ponens, then 'A' and 'E' are established by applications of Simplification and Commutation.

Continue to work backwards, and note that 'D' needs to be asserted before Modus Ponens can be applied to the third premise to obtain 'A · E'. 'D' is the left-hand conjunct of the fourth premise. So, obtain 'D' by Simplification. All information needed for a proof of (14) is now available and can be depicted:

| | (15) | | /∴ G ∨ R |
|---|---|---|---|
| | **1)** | A ⊃ (L ⊃ G) | Pr |
| | **2)** | E ⊃ (P ⊃ R) | Pr |
| | **3)** | D ⊃ (A · E) | Pr |
| | **4)** | D · (P ∨ L) | Pr |
| | **5)** | D | 4, Simp |
| | **6)** | A · E | 3, 5, MP |
| | **7)** | A | 6, Simp |
| | **8)** | E · A | 6, Com |
| | **9)** | E | 8, Simp |
| | **10)** | L ⊃ G | 1, 7, MP |
| | **11)** | P ⊃ R | 2, 9, MP |
| | **12)** | (P ∨ L) · D | 4, Com |
| | **13)** | P ∨ L | 12, Simp |
| | **14)** | L ∨ P | 13, Com |
| | **15)** | /∴ G ∨ R | 10, 11, 14, CD |

---

## EXERCISES

### Group A:

Given the truth-functional rules governing the horseshoe and wedge, discuss why both Hypothetical Syllogism and Constructive Dilemma are deductively valid argument forms.

### Group B:

Give the correct justification in each unjustified line of the following.

1.                    /∴ C ⊃ B
   1) A ⊃ B   Pr
   2) C ⊃ A   Pr
   3) /∴ C ⊃ B

2.                    /∴ B ∨ D
   1) A ⊃ B   Pr
   2) A ∨ C   Pr

     3) C ⊃ D  Pr
     4) /∴ B ∨ D

3.                       /∴ E ⊃ B
     1) D ⊃ (A ⊃ B)  Pr
     2) D · C′        Pr
     3) C ⊃ (E ⊃ A)  Pr
     4) D
     5) C · D
     6) C
     7) E ⊃ A
     8) A ⊃ B
     9) /∴ E ⊃ B

4.                       /∴ ∼ (D ∨ E) ∨ (E ∨ D
     1) A ∨ B             Pr
     2) (B ⊃ D) · (A ⊃ E)  Pr
     3) B ⊃ D
     4) (A ⊃ E) · (B ⊃ D)
     5) A ⊃ E
     6) E ∨ D
     7) (E ∨ D) ∨ ∼ (D ∨ E)
     8) /∴ ∼ (D ∨ E) ∨ (E ∨ D)

5.                       /∴ B ∨ E
     1) (A ⊃ B) · C  Pr
     2) D ⊃ E       Pr
     3) C ⊃ D       Pr
     4) A ⊃ B
     5) C · (A ⊃ B)
     6) C
     7) C ⊃ E
     8) C ∨ A
     9) E ∨ B
     10) /∴ B ∨ E

6.                       /∴ F ∨ ∼ E
     1) A ∨ (B ∨ C)    Pr
     2) D ⊃ ∼ E       Pr
     3) ∼ A ⊃ (C ⊃ F)  Pr
     4) B ⊃ D        Pr
     5) ∼ A         Pr
     6) B ∨ C
     7) C ⊃ F
     8) B ⊃ ∼ E
     9) ∼ E ∨ F
     10) /∴ F ∨ ∼ E

7.                       /∴ D ∨ F
     1) A · B        Pr
     2) B ⊃ (C ⊃ D)  Pr
     3) A ⊃ (C ∨ E)  Pr
     4) E ⊃ F       Pr

      5) A
      6) B · A
      7) B
      8) C ⊃ D
      9) C ∨ E
   10) / ∴ D ∨ F

8.                                / ∴ C ∨ E
      1) (A ⊃ B) · (B ⊃ C)  Pr
      2) (D ⊃ E) · (D ∨ A)  Pr
      3) A ⊃ B
      4) (B ⊃ C) · (A ⊃ B)
      5) B ⊃ C
      6) D ⊃ E
      7) (D ∨ A) · (D ⊃ E)
      8) D ∨ A
      9) A ⊃ C
   10) E ∨ C
   11) / ∴ C ∨ E

9.                                / ∴ B ⊃ F
      1) A ⊃ (B ⊃ C)  Pr
      2) D ⊃ (C ⊃ F)  Pr
      3) ∼ G ⊃ D     Pr
      4) ∼ H ⊃ A     Pr
      5) H ⊃ I       Pr
      6) ∼ I ∨ J      Pr
      7) ∼ G · ∼ J   Pr
      8) ∼ G
      9) ∼ J · ∼ G
   10) ∼ J
   11) D
   12) C ⊃ F
   13) J ∨ ∼ I
   14) ∼ I
   15) ∼ H
   16) A
   17) B ⊃ C
   18) / ∴ B ⊃ F

10.                            / ∴ (C ∨ H) · I
      1) A ⊃ (B ⊃ C)          Pr
      2) D ⊃ (A · E)           Pr
      3) (B ∨ F) · (G · D)     Pr
      4) (F ⊃ H) · [(G · E) ⊃ I]  Pr
      5) B ∨ F
      6) (G · D) · (B ∨ F)
      7) G · D
      8) G
      9) D · G
   10) D
   11) F ⊃ H

12) $[(G \cdot E) \supset I] \cdot (F \supset H)$
13) $(G \cdot E) \supset I$
14) $A \cdot E$
15) $A$
16) $E \cdot A$
17) $E$
18) $B \supset C$
19) $C \vee H$
20) $G \cdot E$
21) $I$
22) $/ \therefore (C \vee H) \cdot I$

## Group C:

Construct a proof of validity for each of the following.

1.                          $/ \therefore B \vee D$
    1) $A \supset B$   Pr
    2) $C \supset D$   Pr
    3) $A \vee C$   Pr

2.                          $/ \therefore A \supset D$
    1) $A \supset B$   Pr
    2) $B \supset C$   Pr
    3) $C \supset D$   Pr

3.                          $/ \therefore D \vee B$
    1) $A \supset B$   Pr
    2) $A \vee C$   Pr
    3) $C \supset D$   Pr

4.                          $/ \therefore B \supset E$
    1) $A \vee (B \supset C)$    Pr
    2) $(C \supset E) \cdot \sim A$   Pr

5.                          $/ \therefore C \vee E$
    1) $(A \supset B) \cdot (B \supset C)$   Pr
    2) $D \supset E$    Pr
    3) $D \vee A$    Pr

6.                          $/ \therefore E \vee F$
    1) $(A \supset B) \cdot (C \supset D)$   Pr
    2) $A \vee C$    Pr
    3) $(D \supset F) \cdot (B \supset E)$    Pr

7.                          $/ \therefore (G \cdot H) \vee (G \vee H)$
    1) $[A \supset \sim (B \cdot \sim C)] \supset (D \vee E)$       Pr
    2) $[A \supset (B \supset F)] \cdot [(B \supset F) \supset \sim (B \cdot \sim C)]$   Pr
    3) $(D \vee E) \supset [(D \supset G) \cdot (E \supset H)]$       Pr

8.          $/ \therefore \{[C \vee (\sim E \vee \sim F)] \cdot [\sim (\sim G \cdot \sim H) \vee I]\} \vee [C \cdot \sim (\sim G \cdot \sim H)]$
    1) $[\sim (A \cdot B) \supset C] \cdot [D \supset (\sim E \vee \sim F)]$     Pr
    2) $[\sim (A \cdot B) \vee D] \cdot [E \vee \sim (\sim A \cdot \sim B)]$     Pr
    3) $[E \supset \sim (\sim G \cdot \sim H)] \cdot [\sim (\sim A \cdot \sim B) \supset I]$   Pr

9.                          $/ \therefore G \vee E$
    1) $[A \vee (B \cdot \sim C)] \cdot \sim A$       Pr

 2) $[B \supset (D \supset E)] \cdot [\sim C \supset (F \supset G)]$    Pr
 3) $(\sim A \vee F) \cdot (F \vee D)$    Pr

10.                                                                /∴ H ∨ F
 1) $(A \vee \sim B) \supset (C \vee D)$    Pr
 2) $[\sim E \supset (C \supset F)] \cdot [\sim G \supset (D \supset H)]$    Pr
 3) $[E \supset (H \vee I)] \cdot [G \supset (I \vee J)]$    Pr
 4) $\sim (H \vee I) \cdot \sim (I \vee J)$    Pr
 5) $(I \vee J) \vee [(H \vee I) \vee (A \vee \sim B)]$    Pr

**Group D:**

Symbolize the following arguments using the capital letters suggested. Then construct a proof of validity for each.

1. Unless we read *The Lark*, we won't read all the works of Jean Anouilh. But we'll read all the works of Anouilh or Jacinto Benavente. We'll read all of Benavente's works only if we read *The Passion Flower*. So, we'll read neither *The Lark* nor *The Passion Flower*, or we'll read *The Passion Flower* or *The Lark*. (L,A,B,F)

2. We've an interest in contemporary French theater if we read either *The Madwoman of Chaillot* or *No Exit*. We're acquainted with the works of Jean Giraudoux only if we've read *The Madwoman of Chaillot*, whereas we've read *No Exit* provided that we're acquainted with the works of Jean-Paul Sartre. We are acquainted with either the works of Sartre or Giraudoux. Thus, we've an interest in contemporary French theater or we're merely seeking to be a cultural bore. (T,C,E,G,S,B)

3. A student studies Jean-Paul Sartre provided that he studies contemporary French theater, but further a student reads *The Flies* if he studies Sartre. Assuming a student reads *The Flies*, he has a comprehension of ancient Greek mythology, whereas he has a comprehension of ancient Greek mythology only if he has a liberal education. Wherefore, whenever a student studies contemporary French theater, he has a liberal education. (S,T,F,M,E)

4. In a course in contemporary European literature Franz Kafka or Albert Camus will be studied; moreover, if Kafka is studied, *The Trial* will be read. A sense of the absurd is conveyed whenever *The Trial* is read, while if Camus is studied, the hopelessness of hope is conveyed. Consequently, either the hopelessness of hope or a sense of the absurd is conveyed. (K,C,T,A,H)

5. A student studies Kafka only if she appreciates both *The Trial* and *The Castle*. If *The Trial* is appreciated, then an absurd moral position is felt whenever *An Imperial Message* is appreciated. If *The Castle* is appreciated, then the absence of Count Westwest is understood if an absurd moral position is felt. A student studies Kafka. Therefore, if *An Imperial Message* is appreciated, the absence of Count Westwest is understood. (K,T,C,P,M,W)

6. If J. S. Bach didn't compose in the Romantic Period, his music should be played in its appropriate style if it is to be enjoyed fully. Bach composed in the Romantic Period only if he used extensively the pianoforte. If Bach didn't compose in the Romantic Period, then his music isn't interpreted properly only if it is rendered in some nonbaroque manner. Bach didn't use extensively the pianoforte; nevertheless, his music isn't interpreted properly or it is enjoyed fully. So, Bach's music should be played in its appropriate style or rendered in some nonbaroque manner. (C,P,E,U,I,R)

7. If it isn't the case that Bach both developed the German baroque style while also living in the twentieth century, then if he wrote *Le Sacre du Printemps*, Bach composed during the contemporary period. That Bach used contemporary musical idioms is a necessary

condition for his both developing the German baroque style and also living in the twentieth century. Nonetheless, Bach didn't use contemporary musical idioms, while he did either pen the *B minor Mass* or he wrote *Le Sacre du Printemps*. Bach didn't compose in the contemporary period unless he used contemporary musical idioms; yet unless he employed baroque musical ornamentation, he didn't pen the *B minor Mass*. Consequently, Bach either used contemporary musical idioms or he employed baroque musical ornamentation. (D,L,W,C,U,P,E)

8. Either Dietrich Buxtehude changed the style of Heinrich Schutz or Claudio Monteverdi influenced him, or Andre Gabrieli's music affected Schutz. Gabrieli's music didn't affect Schutz, while Schutz did use German baroque idioms only if he mastered musical ornamentation. Schutz used German baroque idioms if Buxtehude changed his style, but Schutz employed Italian themes if Monteverdi influenced him. Therefore, Schutz was either influenced by Monteverdi and affected by Gabrieli, or either he employed Italian themes or mastered musical ornamentation. (C,I,A,U,M,E)

9. The importance of the toccata is recognized if the various forms of baroque organ music are catalogued properly; moreover, the toccatas of Girolamo Frescobaldi are appreciated only if the early toccata style is understood. Either the various forms of baroque organ music are catalogued properly or the toccatas of Frescobaldi appreciated, while either the works of Buxtehude are enjoyed or German baroque music isn't studied. Whenever the organ works of Buxtehude are enjoyed, later organ compositions are grasped better, yet the music of Buxtehude becomes mysterious if German baroque music isn't studied. Hence, the importance of the toccata is recognized or the early toccata style understood, and later organ compositions are grasped better or the music of Buxtehude becomes mysterious. (R,C,A,U,E,S,G,B)

10. If the concerti of Antonio Vivaldi exemplify that form's greatest development, then *The Seasons* holds a prominent place in western music if it is a concerto written by Vivaldi. The concerti of Vivaldi do exemplify that form's greatest development or his choral works aren't some of the most moving in western music; moreover, only if the music of eighteenth century Italy should be ignored is it true that Vivaldi's choral works aren't some of the most moving in western music. The music of eighteenth century Italy shouldn't be ignored, but if it is then contemporary music loses much that is valuable. If it isn't true that Vivaldi's choral works aren't some of the most moving in western music, then either the music of eighteenth century Italy should be ignored or *The Seasons* is a concerto written by Vivaldi. Thus, either *The Seasons* holds a prominent place in western music but nonetheless, contemporary music loses much that is valuable, or either *The Seasons* holds a prominent place in western music or contemporary music loses much that is valuable. (E,H,W,M,I,L)

## 6. POINTS OF STRATEGY—A SUMMARY REVIEW

In doing some things well, it is helpful to develop a sense of strategy. Basically, a sense of strategy is grasping what is appropriate to do at a particular moment in order to be in a better position to reach some predetermined goal. There are any number of reasons why a person might succeed in sports, politics, business, living one's life, and the like. However, the chances for success are often increased if one has good strategies. Good strategies are neither mysterious nor difficult to develop, but they are often neglected. Much has already been done in this chapter to develop good strategies for constructing proofs. This has been done through the introduction of various rules-of-thumb, or heuristics, to apply to situations often found in proof construction.

The goal of proof construction is establishing validity. The goal is to show that if all the premises are true (of course, they might not be true even if accepted as true), then the conclusion must also be true. Each inference rule has its use in performing various tasks in achieving this goal. Thus, *view each rule as a tool* helpful in accomplishing a particular task. If something needs to be isolated out of a *hypothetical* statement—perhaps the consequent—rules such as Simplification or Disjunctive Syllogism are not initially considered because they do not make use of the horseshoe found in hypothetical statements. Or suppose at some point in constructing a proof the denial of the antecedent of a hypothetical statement is needed. Addition, ending with a wedge, is not going to be helpful. It is Modus Tollens that, if it can be used, produces the denial of an antecedent. On the other hand, Disjunctive Syllogism is that rule useful in isolating a disjunct out of a disjunctive statement. While Constructive Dilemma has a disjunctive premise, it does not permit the isolation of a separate disjunct in a new line of a proof. Disjunctive Syllogism does this.

Suppose that the several conjuncts of an overall conjunction are needed in separate lines. What tool is useful here? Not Hypothetical Syllogism. Hypothetical Syllogism deals with horseshoes. Of those argument forms using dots, only Simplification, in combination with Commutation, allows the separation of an overall conjunction into all of its component parts.

Perhaps a new hypothetical statement is desired in a particular move in constructing a proof. What useful tool is at hand? What rules end with a horseshoe? In this chapter, only Hypothetical Syllogism. So, if a hypothetical statement is needed, the possibility of using Hypothetical Syllogism should be considered. If a disjunctive statement is needed in a new line, two rules might be considered: Addition or Constructive Dilemma. Which of these will more likely lead to the needed wedge statement? If the name of the needed disjunctive statement contains a letter (or letters) not found in the symbolized premises, then Addition *must* be used. Of course, Addition *can* be used whenever possible. Or suppose a particular disjunctive statement is needed and the two disjuncts of that statement occur previously in the proof as the consequents of hypotheticals. Constructive Dilemma is now the rule to consider.

After symbolizing an argument to be proven valid, it is helpful to begin by examining the conclusion. Then look at the premises and ask: *Does the conclusion appear, as a whole unit, embedded in the premises?* The answer to this question will be either *YES* or *NO*. Consider this example:

**(1)**                                            /∴  C ⊃ D
    **1)** (B·A) ⊃ (C⊃D)  Pr
    **2)** A ∨ C         Pr
    **3)**  ∼ C·B       Pr

The conclusion of this argument is 'C ⊃ D'. Yes, it does appear embedded in the premises as a whole unit.

When "embedding" occurs, proceed with these questions:

> *1. In what premise is the conclusion found?*
>
> *2. What kind of overall statement is that premise?*
>
> *3. How does the conclusion occur in that premise?*

This sequence of questions often reveals what rule, or rules, is likely to be useful in obtaining the wanted conclusion. Referring to (1), the answers to these three questions are 'in the first premise', 'a hypothetical', and 'as the consequent of that hypothetical'. It is assumed that rules beginning with hypotheticals will be used because the conclusion is embedded in a hypothetical statement. This one consideration narrows the choices to Modus Ponens, Modus Tollens, Hypothetical Syllogism, and Constructive Dilemma. It is also assumed that the consequent of the hypothetical must be isolated in a new line because the desired conclusion is in the consequent position of line 1. Of the four rules mentioned, Modus Ponens is the only one used to isolate the consequent of a hypothetical.

To develop strategy, think in terms of *HAVE, WANT,* and *NEED,* coupled with that rule most likely to be *USED.* In (1), one *has* '(B·A) ⊃ (C ⊃ D)', *wants* 'C ⊃ D', and is relatively assured that Modus Ponens is going to be *used.* Hence, 'B·A' is *needed.* How is this need determined? Consider the rule Modus Ponens:

$$
\textbf{(2)} \quad
\left.
\begin{array}{l}
p \supset q \\
\underline{\phantom{xx}p\phantom{xx}} \\
/ \therefore q
\end{array}
\right\}
\text{use: MP}
$$

Write '(B·A) ⊃ (X ⊃ D)' for 'p ⊃ q', and '/∴ C ⊃ D' for '/ ∴ q'.

$$
\textbf{(3)} \quad
\left.
\begin{array}{l}
\text{have: } (B·A) \supset (C \supset D) \\
\underline{\text{need: } p \phantom{xxxxxxxxxx}} \\
\text{want: } / \therefore C \supset D
\end{array}
\right\}
\text{use: MP}
$$

One variable remains to be replaced. The same variable must be replaced by the same statement name at every occurrence of that variable in the argument form. So, write

$$
\textbf{(4)} \quad
\left.
\begin{array}{l}
\text{have: } (B·A) \supset (C \supset D) \\
\underline{\text{need: } B·A \phantom{xxxxxxxxx}} \\
\text{want: } / \therefore C \supset D
\end{array}
\right\}
\text{use: MP}
$$

'(B·A) ⊃ (C ⊃ D)' occurs as a premise. The statement *wanted* is 'C ⊃ D'. It is decided to *use* Modus Ponens to obtain this conclusion. 'B·A' is *needed* to use Modus Ponens. Certainly not every need will be met. But this is also to say that not every argument is deductively valid.

In constructing a proof for (1), 'B·A' is treated as an intermediate conclusion. The strategy questions asked of 'C ⊃ D' are now asked of 'B·A'. Does 'B·A' appear embedded anywhere in any statement *other* than the first premise? Because it is needed to combine with the first premise, 'B·A' cannot come from that premise. It must come from somewhere else and then be used in a Modus Ponens move to obtain 'C ⊃ D'. Inspection shows that, other than in the first premise, 'B • A' does not appear as a whole unit in any statement already obtained. The challenge now becomes one of *constructing* 'B • A' as opposed to isolating it out of some larger statement. To *construct* a statement, think of building it up, according to some rule, from "blocks" scattered about in statements already found in the proof.

At this juncture, ask what rules *end* in the overall type of statement exhibited by 'B • A'. Since 'B • A' is a conjunction, answer, 'Conjunction'. *IF* Conjunction is used to obtain 'B • A', that rule shows what two other statements are first needed; namely, 'B' and 'A'. These need to be found somewhere other than the first premise.

In moves requiring *constructing* a statement, ask these questions:

1. *Where do the elements of the needed statement occur in statements already established in the proof?*

2. *What kind of overall statements are these?*

3. *How does what is needed occur in these statements?*

Answer these questions in relation to 'B' and 'A'. 'B' occurs in the third premise, an overall conjunction. Here 'B' is the right-hand conjunct. 'B' needs to be isolated to use with Conjunction to obtain 'B • A'. What is the rule that permits a conjunct to be taken out of an overall conjunction? Simplification. In this case, however, Commutation is used first to prepare for Simplification.

Once more appealing to the *HAVE, WANT,* and *NEED* sequence, notice how Disjunctive Syllogism is to be *USED* to obtain 'A'. Proceed as in (2) through (4), only now suppose that Disjunctive Syllogism is the rule most likely to be used:

$$\textbf{(5)} \quad \left. \begin{array}{c} p \vee q \\ \sim p \\ \hline / \therefore q \end{array} \right\} \text{use: DS}$$

Replacing 'C ∨ A' for 'p ∨ q' and 'A' for 'q', write:

$$\textbf{(6)} \quad \left. \begin{array}{l} \text{have: } C \vee A \\ \text{need: } \sim p \\ \hline \text{want: } / \therefore A \end{array} \right\} \text{use: DS}$$

The rule shows that an instance of ' ∼ p' is needed. In the particular case of (1), a ' ∼ C' is needed to assert 'A'. ' ∼ C' is found in line 3 as the left-hand conjunct of ' ∼ C • B'. Therefore, Simplification is used to isolate ' ∼ C'. One can now *literally see* how all the elements necessary to construct a proof of (1) are obtained and put together:

**(7)** /∴  C ⊃ D

| | | |
|---|---|---|
| **1)** | (B • A) ⊃ (C ⊃ D) | Pr |
| **2)** | A ∨ C | Pr |
| **3)** | ∼ C • B | Pr |

| 4) B · ~ C | 3, Com |
|---|---|
| 5) B | 4, Simp |
| 6) ~ C | 3, Simp |
| 7) C ∨ A | 2, Com |
| 8) A | 7, 6, DS |
| 9) B · A | 5, 8, Conj |
| 10) /∴ C ⊃ D | 1, 9, MP |

The exact order of the statements in (7) is not necessary. Another proof of (1) is:

(8)                                          /∴  C ⊃ D

| 1) (B · A) ⊃ (C ⊃ D) | Pr |
|---|---|
| 2) A ∨ C | Pr |
| 3) ~ C · B | Pr |
| 4) ~ C | 3, Simp |
| 5) C ∨ A | 2, Com |
| 6) A | 5, 4, DS |
| 7) B · ~ C | 3, Com |
| 8) B | 7, Simp |
| 9) B · A | 8, 6, Conj |
| 10) /∴ C ⊃ D | 1, 9, MP |

## 7.    REVIEW OF NEW TERMS

**Affirming the Consequent, fallacy of:**  The invalid argument form,

$$p \supset q$$
$$\underline{q\qquad}$$
$$/\therefore p$$

**Addition (Add):**  A valid argument form guaranteeing that if any statement of the form 'p' is true, then 'p ∨ q' must also be true.

$$\underline{p\qquad\qquad}$$
$$/\therefore p \vee q$$

**Argument form:**  A finite sequence of statement forms of which one is the conclusion and the remainder comprise the premises, such that if all the statement variables are replaced by statement names—the same statement name replacing each occurrence of the same statement variable—an argument is obtained.

**Commutation of the Dot (Com):**  A valid argument form guaranteeing that if any statement of the form 'p · q' is true, then 'q · p' must also be true.

$$\underline{p \cdot q\qquad}$$
$$/\therefore q \cdot p$$

**Commutation of the Wedge (Com):** A valid argument form guaranteeing that if any statement of the form 'p ∨ q' is true, then 'q ∨ p' must also be true.

$$\frac{p \lor q}{/ \therefore q \lor p}$$

**Conjunction (Conj):** A valid argument form guaranteeing that if any statements of the forms 'p' and 'q' are true, then 'p · q' must also be true.

$$\frac{\begin{array}{c} p \\ q \end{array}}{/ \therefore p \cdot q}$$

**Constructive Dilemma (CD):** A valid argument form guaranteeing that if any statements of the forms 'p ⊃ q', 'r ⊃ s', and 'p ∨ r' are true, then 'q ∨ s' must also be true.

$$\frac{\begin{array}{c} p \supset q \\ r \supset s \\ p \lor r \end{array}}{/ \therefore q \lor s}$$

**Denying the Antecedent, fallacy of:** The invalid argument form,

$$\frac{\begin{array}{c} p \supset q \\ \sim p \end{array}}{/ \therefore \ \sim q}$$

**Disjunctive Syllogism (DS):** A valid argument form guaranteeing that if any statements of the forms 'p ∨ q' and ' ~ p' are true, then 'q' must also be true.

$$\frac{\begin{array}{c} p \lor q \\ \sim p \end{array}}{/ \therefore q}$$

**Elementary rule of inference:** Any logical form introduced in this and following chapters that guarantees if the premises of an argument are all true, then any new statement generated from the premises by these rules must also be true. There are two types of elementary rules of inference; namely, argument forms and logical equivalences.

**Fallacy:** Something in an argument that prohibits the premises from supporting the conclusion.

**Hypothetical Syllogism (HS):** A valid argument form guaranteeing that if any statements of the forms 'p ⊃ q' and 'q ⊃ r' are true, then 'p ⊃ r' must also be true.

$$\frac{\begin{array}{c} p \supset q \\ q \supset r \end{array}}{/ \therefore p \supset r}$$

**Instance:** Any substitution of statement names for statement variables in a statement or argument form. A statement or argument displaying the form in question.

**Invalid argument form:** An argument form that is not valid; *deductively invalid argument form.*

**Modus Ponens (MP):** A valid argument form guaranteeing that if any statements of the forms 'p ⊃ q' and 'p' are true, then 'q' must also be true.

$$p \supset q$$
$$p$$
$$/\therefore q$$

**Modus Tollens (MT):** A valid argument form guaranteeing that if any statements of the forms 'p ⊃ q' and '∼ q' are true, then '∼ p' must also be true.

$$p \supset q$$
$$\sim q$$
$$/\therefore \sim p$$

**Proof of validity:** A finite sequence of statements, beginning with the premises of an argument and ending with the conclusion, such that each step in the proof displays at least one elementary rule of inference.

**Simplification (Simp):** A valid argument form guaranteeing that if any statement of the form 'p · q' is true, then 'p' must also be true.

$$p \cdot q$$
$$/\therefore p$$

**Specific argument form:** That form which is seen if and only if every single capital letter representing a simple statement in the symbolization of an argument is replaced by a single variable letter, the same variable letter replacing the same capital letter throughout the entire symbolization.

**Valid argument form:** An argument form such that if all the premises of an argument having that form are true, then the conclusion must also be true. An argument form in which the truth of all the premises guarantees the truth of the conclusion; *deductively valid argument form.*

# 6

# TRUTH-FUNCTIONAL LOGIC: EQUIVALENCE FORMS

The introduction to Chapter 5 notes that there are two types of elementary rules of inference. The first of these, argument forms, is introduced and discussed in Chapter 5. The second type of these rules is introduced in this chapter. *Equivalence forms* differ from argument forms in two essential ways. *First*, argument forms are "one-directional." They can be applied only from top to bottom. The premise, for example, of Simplification entails its conclusion, but the conclusion does not entail the premise. The sign, '/∴', is used to indicate logical entailment between statements. However, equivalence forms are "two directional." These rules can be applied from left to right and from right to left. The ***replacement sign***, '::', is used to indicate this relation of logical equivalence. *Second*, argument forms can be used only on entire statements. Equivalence forms, on the other hand, can be used on smaller statements making up larger ones as well as on whole statements.

## 1. ASSOCIATION AND COMMUTATION

### ASSOCIATION (ASSOC)

$$p \cdot (q \cdot r) :: (p \cdot q) \cdot r$$
$$p \vee (q \vee r) :: (p \vee q) \vee r$$

### COMMUTATION (COM)

$$p \vee q :: q \vee p$$
$$p \cdot q :: q \cdot p$$
$$p \triangle q :: q \triangle p$$
$$p \equiv q :: q \equiv p$$

*Association* permits certain types of statement names to be repunctuated. If all the major connections of a statement name are wedges, ' ∨ ', or dots, '·', then punctuation marks can be moved according to the rule of Association. Accordingly, Association cannot be used on any of the following:

$$\begin{array}{ll}
\textbf{(1)} & A \cdot (B \vee C) \\
& G \supset (E \cdot F) \\
& F \vee (B \cdot H) \\
& (C \equiv H) \vee B
\end{array}$$

Association can be used on these, however:

$$\textbf{(2)} \quad [(A \supset G) \vee (B \cdot C)] \vee (E \equiv H)$$

$$\textbf{(3)} \quad [(G \supset F) \Delta H] \cdot \{[(B \vee E) \vee G] \cdot (F \Delta B)\}$$

Read (2) as an instance of '$(p \vee q) \vee r$'. Here, '$A \supset G$' is substituted at '$p$', '$B \cdot C$' at '$q$', and '$E \equiv H$' at '$r$'. Applying Association to (2), reading the rule from right to left, results in (4):

$$\textbf{(4)} \quad (A \supset G) \vee [(B \cdot C) \vee (E \equiv H)]$$

Read (3) as an instance of '$p \cdot (q \cdot r)$' where '$(G \supset F) \Delta H$' is substituted at '$p$', '$(B \vee E) \vee G$' at '$q$', and '$F \Delta B$' at '$r$'. Applying Association to (4) produces:

$$\textbf{(5)} \quad \{[(G \supset F) \Delta H] \cdot [(B \vee E) \vee G)]\} \cdot (F \Delta B)$$

Association is used on the entirety of (2) and (3). Notice that '$(B \vee E) \vee G$' occurs as part of the statement symbolized at (3). Apply Association to *only that part* of (3) and assert

$$\textbf{(6)} \quad [(G \supset F) \Delta H] \cdot \{[B \vee (E \vee G)] \cdot (F \Delta B)\}$$

To see Association used in constructing a proof, study this argument:

**(7)**   Either Greg or Mary will graduate with Honors, or Freddie will. But Greg is certainly not going to graduate with Honors. Therefore, Mary and/or Freddie will. (G,M,F)

Symbolize (7):

$$\begin{array}{lll}
\textbf{(8)} & & / \therefore M \vee F \\
& \textbf{1)} \ (G \vee M) \vee F & \text{Pr} \\
& \textbf{2)} \ \sim G & \text{Pr}
\end{array}$$

Instinctively, it seems that (7) is valid. Yet, given only the argument forms of Chapter 5, there is no way to prove its validity. Even so, there is almost a Disjunctive Syllogism holding between its premises and conclusion. Disjunctive Syllogism is not quite applicable because the second premise, '$\sim G$', is not the denial of the left-hand disjunct, '$G \vee M$', of the first premise. Nor is the conclusion, '$M \vee F$', the same as the Right-hand disjunct, '$F$', of the first premise.

Attempt using Disjunctive Syllogism to obtain the conclusion as symbolized in (8). Work backwards to discover what is needed:

$$(9) \qquad\qquad\qquad /\therefore \text{ M} \vee \text{F}$$

**1)** $(\text{G} \vee \text{M}) \vee \text{F}$    Pr
**2)** $\sim \text{G}$    Pr

.
.
.

**?)** $\text{G} \vee (\text{M} \vee \text{F})$    ?    ?
**?)** $/\therefore \text{M} \vee \text{F}$    ?, 2, DS

'$\text{G} \vee (\text{M} \vee \text{F})$' is in line 1 as transformed by Association. A complete proof of (8) is

$$(10) \qquad\qquad\qquad /\therefore \text{ M} \vee \text{F}$$

**1)** $(\text{G} \vee \text{M}) \vee \text{F}$    Pr
**2)** $\sim \text{G}$    Pr
**3)** $\text{G} \vee (\text{M} \vee \text{F})$    1, Assoc
**4)** $/\therefore \text{M} \vee \text{F}$    3, 2, DS

Because Disjunctive Syllogism cannot be used in (8), Association is required in line 3. Often equivalence forms, such as Association, are used to prepare for an application of an argument form.

Examine this argument:

**(11)**    History and Economics are interesting subjects, but so is Political Science. One will find Comparative Cultures interesting if History is interesting. So, Political Science and Comparative Cultures are interesting subjects. (H,E,P,C)

Use the capital letters suggested to symbolize (11) as

$$(12) \qquad\qquad\qquad /\therefore \text{ P} \cdot \text{C}$$

**1)** $(\text{H} \cdot \text{E}) \cdot \text{P}$    Pr
**2)** $\text{H} \supset \text{C}$    Pr

Several proofs can be constructed for (11) depending on how the first premise is used. The strategies developed in Chapter 5 suggest this approach:

$$(13) \qquad\qquad\qquad /\therefore \text{ P} \cdot \text{C}$$

**1)** $(\text{H} \cdot \text{E}) \cdot \text{P}$    Pr
**2)** $\text{H} \supset \text{C}$    Pr
**3)** $\text{H} \cdot \text{E}$    1, Simp
**4)** $\text{H}$    3, Simp
**5)** $\text{C}$    2, 4, MP

**6)** P · (H · E)    1, Com
**7)** P    6, Simp
**8)** / ∴ P · C    7, 5, Conj

The following proof is also correct:

**(14)**    / ∴  P · C

**1)** (H · E) · P    Pr
**2)** H ⊃ C    Pr
**3)** H · (E · P)    1, Assoc
**4)** H    3, Simp
**5)** C    2, 4, MP
**6)** P · (H · E)    1, Com
**7)** P    6, Simp
**8)** / ∴ P · C    7, 5, Conj

In (14), Association is used in 3 to prepare for a use of Simplification to reach 4.

Uses of ***Commutation*** are seen in Chapter 5. Since Commutation of the Wedge and Dot are previously provided, why reintroduce them now? Chapter 6 establishes Commutation not as an argument form but rather as an equivalence form so that it can be used on parts of statements symbolized in a proof. Study this:

**(15)** Making an "A" in this course is a sufficient condition for having studied and worked hard. That your grade point average is raised is a necessary condition for having worked and studied hard. Hence, assuming you make an A in this course, your grade point average is raised. (M,S,W,R)

Symbolizing (15) yields

**(16)**    / ∴  M ⊃ R
**1)** M ⊃ (S · W)    Pr
**2)** (W · S) ⊃ R    Pr

An inspection of (16) suggests using Hypothetical Syllogism to construct the conclusion, 'M ⊃ R'. This move is barred, however, because the consequent of the first premise is not the same as the antecedent of the second. Since both the consequent and antecedent are conjunctions, and are alike in all respects except for ordering of their letters, an application of Commutation to one or the other (but not both) solves the difficulty:

**(17)**    / ∴  M ⊃ R
**1)** M ⊃ (S · W)    Pr
**2)** (W · S) ⊃ R    Pr
**3)** (S · W) ⊃ R    2, Com
**4)** / ∴ M ⊃ R    1, 3, HS

Notice again how an equivalence form is used to prepare for the later use of an argument form.

## *EXERCISES*

### Group A:

Justify each of the unjustified lines in the following.

1.                    $/ \therefore A \cdot (C \cdot B)$
   1) $(A \cdot B) \cdot C$   Pr
   2) $A \cdot (B \cdot C)$
   3) $/ \therefore A \cdot (C \cdot B)$

2.                    $/ \therefore (C \lor B) \lor A$
   1) $(A \lor B) \lor C$   Pr
   2) $C \lor (A \lor B)$
   3) $C \lor (B \lor A)$
   4) $/ \therefore (C \lor B) \lor A$

3.                    $/ \therefore [(F \equiv G) \cdot (G \equiv H)] \cdot (B \cdot A)$
   1) $[(F \equiv G) \cdot A] \cdot [B \cdot (G \equiv H)]$   Pr
   2) $(F \equiv G) \cdot \{A \cdot [B \cdot (G \equiv H)]\}$
   3) $(F \equiv G) \cdot [(A \cdot B) \cdot (G \equiv H)]$
   4) $(F \equiv G) \cdot [(G \equiv H) \cdot (A \cdot B)]$
   5) $[(F \equiv G) \cdot (G \equiv H)] \cdot (A \cdot B)$
   6) $/ \therefore [(F \equiv G) \cdot (G \equiv H)] \cdot (B \cdot A)$

4.                    $/ \therefore (C \cdot B) \cdot (D \cdot A)$
   1) $(A \cdot B) \cdot (C \cdot D)$   Pr
   2) $(C \cdot D) \cdot (A \cdot B)$
   3) $(C \cdot D) \cdot (B \cdot A)$
   4) $C \cdot [D \cdot (B \cdot A)]$
   5) $C \cdot [(D \cdot B) \cdot A]$
   6) $C \cdot [(B \cdot D) \cdot A]$
   7) $C \cdot [B \cdot (D \cdot A)]$
   8) $/ \therefore (C \cdot B) \cdot (D \cdot A)$

5.                    $/ \therefore \{[A \cdot (C \cdot E)] \cdot (H \supset I)\} \cdot [(F \lor G) \cdot B]$
   1) $\{A \cdot [B \cdot (C \cdot E)]\} \cdot [(F \lor G) \cdot (H \supset I)]$   Pr
   2) $\{A \cdot [(C \cdot E) \cdot B]\} \cdot [(F \lor G) \cdot (H \supset I)]$
   3) $\{[A \cdot (C \cdot E)] \cdot B\} \cdot [(F \lor G) \cdot (H \supset I)]$
   4) $[A \cdot (C \cdot E)] \cdot \{B \cdot [(F \lor G) \cdot (H \supset I)]\}$
   5) $[A \cdot (C \cdot E)] \cdot \{B \cdot [(H \supset I) \cdot (F \lor G)]\}$
   6) $[A \cdot (C \cdot E)] \cdot \{[(H \supset I) \cdot (F \lor G)] \cdot B\}$
   7) $[A \cdot (C \cdot E)] \cdot \{(H \supset I) \cdot [(F \lor G) \cdot B]\}$
   8) $/ \therefore \{[A \cdot (C \cdot E)] \cdot (H \supset I)\} \cdot [(F \lor G) \cdot B]$

6.                    $/ \therefore (D \lor B) \lor (C \lor A)$
   1) $(A \lor B) \lor (C \lor D)$   Pr
   2) $A \lor [B \lor (C \lor D)]$
   3) $A \lor [(B \lor C) \lor D]$
   4) $A \lor [(C \lor B) \lor D]$
   5) $A \lor [C \lor (B \lor D)]$
   6) $A \lor [C \lor (D \lor B)]$
   7) $(A \lor C) \lor (D \lor B)$

    8) $(C \vee A) \vee (D \vee B)$

    9) $/ \therefore (D \vee B) \vee (C \vee A)$

7.                                       $/ \therefore [(A \vee D) \vee B] \vee [E \vee (F \vee C)]$

    1) $[A \vee (B \vee C)] \vee [(D \vee E) \vee F]$   Pr

    2) $[(A \vee B) \vee C] \vee [(D \vee E) \vee F]$

    3) $(A \vee B) \vee \{C \vee [(D \vee E) \vee F]\}$

    4) $(A \vee B) \vee \{[(D \vee E) \vee F] \vee C\}$

    5) $(A \vee B) \vee [(D \vee E) \vee (F \vee C)]$

    6) $(A \vee B) \vee \{D \vee [E \vee (F \vee C)]\}$

    7) $[(A \vee B) \vee D] \vee [E \vee (F \vee C)]$

    8) $[A \vee (B \vee D)] \vee [E \vee (F \vee C)]$

    9) $[A \vee (D \vee B)] \vee [E \vee (F \vee C)]$

    10) $/ \therefore [(A \vee D) \vee B] \vee [E \vee (F \vee C)]$

8.                                      $/ \therefore D \vee F$

    1) $[(A \cdot B) \cdot C] \supset [(D \vee E) \vee F]$  Pr

    2) $(G \supset H) \supset [(C \cdot B) \cdot A]$      Pr

    3) $G \supset (I \vee H)$                    Pr

    4) $\sim E$                           Pr

    5) $(H \vee I) \supset H$              Pr

    6) $(G \supset H) \supset [C \cdot (B \cdot A)]$

    7) $(G \supset H) \supset [C \cdot (A \cdot B)]$

    8) $(G \supset H) \supset [(A \cdot B) \cdot C]$

    9) $(G \supset H) \supset [(D \vee E) \vee F]$

    10) $(I \vee H) \supset H$

    11) $G \supset H$

    12) $(D \vee E) \vee F$

    13) $(E \vee D) \vee F$

    14) $E \vee (D \vee F)$

    15) $/ \therefore D \vee F$

9.                                      $/ \therefore (F \vee H) \vee I$

    1) $[B \cdot (A \cdot C)] \supset (A \vee D)$   Pr

    2) $(A \supset F) \cdot (E \supset D)$        Pr

    3) $(G \supset D) \supset [C \cdot (B \cdot A)]$  Pr

    4) $(D \supset I) \cdot (G \supset E)$        Pr

    5) $A \supset F$

    6) $(E \supset D) \cdot (A \supset F)$

    7) $E \supset D$

    8) $D \supset I$

    9) $(G \supset E) \cdot (D \supset I)$

    10) $G \supset E$

    11) $G \supset D$

    12) $C \cdot (B \cdot A)$

    13) $(B \cdot A) \cdot C$

    14) $B \cdot (A \cdot C)$

    15) $A \vee D$

    16) $F \vee I$

    17) $(F \vee I) \vee H$

    18) $F \vee (I \vee H)$

      19) F ∨ (H ∨ I)
      20) /∴ (F ∨ H) ∨ I

10.                                      /∴ J ∨ F
      1) ∼ [A ∨ (B ∨ C)] ∨ [D ⊃ (A ⊃ F)]  Pr
      2) ∼ ∼ [(A ∨ C) ∨ B] · (A ∨ C)  Pr
      3) (G ∨ D) ∨ H  Pr
      4) [I ∨ ∼ (G ∨ H)] ∨ A  Pr
      5) ∼ (A ∨ I) · (C ⊃ J)  Pr
      6) ∼ ∼[(A ∨ C) ∨ B]
      7) ∼ ∼[A ∨ (C ∨ B)]
      8) ∼ ∼[A ∨ (B ∨ C)]
      9) D ⊃ (A ⊃ F)
      10) G ∨ (D ∨ H)
      11) G ∨ (H ∨ D)
      12) (G ∨ H) ∨ D
      13) A ∨ [I ∨ ∼ (G ∨ H)]
      14) (A ∨ I) ∨ ∼ (G ∨ H)
      15) ∼ (A ∨ I)
      16) ∼ (G ∨ H)
      17) D
      18) A ⊃ F
      19) (C ⊃ J) · ∼ (A ∨ I)
      20) C ⊃ J
      21) (A ∨ C) · ∼ ∼ [(A ∨ C) ∨ B]
      22) A ∨ C
      23) F ∨ J
      24) /∴ J ∨ F

## Group B:

Construct a proof of validity for each of the following.

1.                      /∴ B ∨ (C ∨ A)
      1) A ∨ (B ∨ C)  Pr

2.                        /∴ (C ∨ B) ∨ (D ∨ A)
      1) (A ∨ B) ∨ (C ∨ D)  Pr

3.                      /∴ (D · A) · (B · C)
      1) (A · B) · (C · D)  Pr

4.                    /∴ {C ∨ [C · (B · A)]} ∨ D
      1) [(A · B) · C] ∨ (D ∨ C)  Pr

5.                      /∴ [(C ⊃ D) ∨ (B ≡ C)] ∨ (B Δ ∼ A)
      1) [(∼ A Δ B) ∨ (C ≡ B)] ∨ (C ⊃ D)  Pr

6.                    /∴ D ≡ E
      1) (A Δ B) ⊃ C      Pr
      2) (D ⊃ C) ⊃ (E ≡ D)  Pr
      3) D ⊃ (B Δ A)      Pr

7.                                                /∴ (F ∨ B) ∨ (D ∨ ~ C)
   1)  ~ (A ≡ B)        Pr
   2)  ~ C ∨ (B ≡ A)   Pr

8.                                                /∴ G ∨ H
   1) (A ∨ B) ⊃ (D ∨ C)       Pr
   2) E · [E ⊃ (C ⊃ G)]       Pr
   3) (B ∨ A) ⊃ (D ⊃ H)       Pr
   4) (F ∨ E) ⊃ (A ∨ B)       Pr

9.                                                /∴ E ⊃ H
   1)  ~ (A ≡ B) · ~ (B ≡ C)   Pr
   2)  ~ G ⊃ (E ⊃ F)           Pr
   3) G ⊃ (B ≡ A)             Pr
   4) I ⊃ (C ≡ B)             Pr
   5)  ~ I ⊃ (F ⊃ H)           Pr

10.                                               /∴ H ∨ (C ∨ D)
   1) [(H · G) · E] ⊃ C                        Pr
   2) A ⊃ [(G · H) · E]                        Pr
   3) (B ⊃ D) · {[F ∨ (I ∨ B)] ∨ (G ∨ A)}      Pr
   4)  ~ (I ∨ F) · ~ G                         Pr

## Group C:

Symbolize the following arguments using the suggested capital letters. Then construct a proof of validity for each.

1. Cathy needs to take a course in algebra, or she needs to take a course in statistics or logic. So, either Cathy needs to take a course in statistics or algebra, or she needs to take a course in logic. (A,S,L)

2. It isn't the case that Chris plans to do poorly in school or to avoid classes demanding good writing techniques, but not both. Chris either masters good writing techniques, or either he avoids classes demanding such techniques or plans to do poorly in school, but not both. Chris doesn't master good writing techniques unless he reads a great deal. Therefore, either Chris reads a great deal or avoids classes demanding good writing techniques. (P,A,M,R)

3. It isn't the case that Dorinda is energetic and disciplined. Assuming Dorinda isn't lazy, she is both energetic and productive. But Dorinda isn't lazy, or she is both disciplined and energetic. Consequently, Dorinda is productive. (E,D,L,P)

4. A sufficient condition for Louise's graduating is that she is a hard worker if and only if she is well disciplined. Passing all of her course requirements is a necessary condition that Louise studies long hours only if she graduates. If Louise does study long hours, then she is well disciplined if and only if she is a hard worker. Thus, Louise graduates and/or passes all of her course requirements. (G,W,D,P,S)

5. Louis neither does well in logic nor statistics. Either he doesn't do well in grammar or he does do well in statistics, or he does well in logic. Assuming that Louis likes to read and to write, he does well in grammar. However if it isn't true that he both likes to read and to

write, then he doesn't do well in logic. Consequently, Louis doesn't do well in logic, but neither does he do well in grammar. (L,S,G,R,W)

6. Either the new Byberflus computer uses crystal storage or a disk stored operating system, or it employs lasers or tapes for its operating system. Neither does the new Byberflus employ lasers nor use crystal storage unless it is an innovative piece of gear. The new Byberflus neither uses tapes nor disk storage. Hence, the new Byberflus computer is an innovative piece of gear. (C,D,L,T,G)

7. The new Byberflus computer neither uses vacuum tubes nor takes punch cards only if it represents a fifth-generation system. The new Byberflus computer neither takes punch cards nor uses vacuum tubes. That the new Byberflus computer both primarily processes alpha information and doesn't take punch cards is a necessary condition for its representing a fifth-generation system. Either the new Byberflus computer employs microchips, or it takes punch cards or it uses vacuum tubes. That the new Byberflus computer doesn't use vacuum tubes is a necessary condition for the following: The new Byberflus computer doesn't take punch cards; but either the computer uses vacuum tubes, or either it does take punch cards or employs microchips. So, the new Byberflus computer employs microchips and primarily processes alpha information. (U,T,R,P,E)

8. It isn't the case that either Don is interested in alpha applications of the computer or programs for numeric applications, but not both. Either Don programs for numeric applications or is interested in alpha applications (but not both), or he researches in Artificial Intelligence only if interested in alpha applications of the computer. While Don doesn't program for numeric applications, nonetheless he isn't interested in alpha applications unless he uses LISP programming. That Don researches in Artificial Intelligence only if he uses LISP programming is a sufficient condition for the following: Either Don programs for numeric applications, or he employs Fortran programs whenever he is concerned with mapping trajectories. Now either Don is concerned with mapping trajectories or programs for numeric applications, or he researches in Artificial Intelligence. Hence, Don uses LISP programming or employs Fortran programs. (I,P,R,U,E,C)

9. "La Machine 486" desktop computer uses for storage either floppies or tapes, or it uses either punch cards or hard disks. This computer uses neither punch cards nor tapes, and tapes are not used only if the computer uses floppies. "La Machine 486" uses floppies or hard disks only if it is the case that it is able to run expert systems programs provided that it has adequate storage. Either this computer doesn't use tapes or it does use punch cards, or either it uses tapes or has adequate storage. Thus, "La Machine 486" desktop computer is able to run expert systems programs and/or uses floppies. (F,T,C,D,P,S)

10. In planning to purchase a personal computer, the limitation of financial investment is a sufficient condition for considering the following: Either storage of data or speed of operation, or ease of use. Assuming ease of use is considered, both the limitation of financial investment and storage of data are considerations. While speed of operation may not be considered, nonetheless both types of machines available coupled with the limitation of financial investment are to be considered. If the types of machines available and/or the limitation of financial investment are considered, then storage of data is considered only if an appropriate operating system is considered. But a dedicated function of the machine is also considered if both storage of data and the limitation of financial investment are. So, either an appropriate operating system and/or storage of data is to be considered, or a dedicated function of the machine is. (I,D,O,U,T,S,F)

## 2. DOUBLE NEGATION AND TRANSPOSITION

### DOUBLE NEGATION (DN)

$$p :: \sim \sim p$$

### TRANSPOSITION (TRANS)

$$p \supset q :: \sim q \supset \sim p$$

Consider the following:

(1) Whenever Sarah doesn't study, she doesn't do well in her classes. But Sarah does well in her classes. So, Sarah studies. (S,D)

Symbolizing (1) produces

(2)                    /∴ S
  1) $\sim S \supset \sim D$   Pr
  2) D           Pr

Someone might intuit that (1) is valid. Yet, given only the elementary rules of inference introduced to this point, validity for (1) cannot be proven. Notice the conclusion, 'S', is embedded in the antecedent, '$\sim S$', in line 1 of (2). This suggests an application of Modus Tollens producing '$\sim \sim S$' followed by Double Negation to obtain the conclusion. Even so, Modus Tollens cannot yet be used in (2). Modus Tollens shows that the second premise of that argument form has *one more* tilde than the consequent of the first premise. The second premise of (2) has *one less* tilde than the consequent of the first. This situation can be remedied by using ***Double Negation***:

(3)                    /∴ S
  1) $\sim S \supset \sim D$   Pr
  2) D           Pr
  3) $\sim \sim D$       2, DN
  4) $\sim \sim S$       1, 3, MT

'S' is now asserted by a use of Double Negation:*

(4)                    /∴ S
  1) $\sim S \supset \sim D$   Pr
  2) D           Pr
  3) $\sim \sim D$       2, DN

---

* After the introduction of Transposition, a shorter proof of (2) will be available:

                   /∴ S
  1) $\sim S \supset \sim D$   Pr
  2) D           Pr
  3) $D \supset S$       1, Trans
  4) /∴ S         3,2, MP

$$4) \sim\sim S \qquad 1, 3, MT$$
$$5) /\therefore S \qquad 4, DN$$

Explore this symbolized argument:

(5) $\qquad\qquad\qquad\qquad /\therefore\ F \vee (T \cdot H)$

1) $\sim (G \cdot I) \supset O$ $\qquad$ Pr
2) $G \supset T$ $\qquad$ Pr
3) $\sim O \cdot H$ $\qquad$ Pr

Inspect the conclusion to see if it appears anywhere in the premises. It does not and must be constructed. A use of Addition is anticipated since an 'F' appears in the conclusion but not in the premises. The other disjunct of the conclusion, 'T · H', is first obtained, and then 'F' added. A final move of Commutation establishes the conclusion.

Treating 'T · H' as an intermediate conclusion, examine the premises to see if it appears there as a whole unit. It does not and must be constructed. Since 'T · H' is a conjunction, it is likely that Conjunction will be used to produce it. Before Conjunction is used to construct 'T · H', both 'T' and 'H' are needed in separate lines. Where do 'T' and 'H' appear in already established lines? 'H' appears as a conjunct in the third premise. Thus, 'H' can eventually be obtained by Simplification. 'T' is seen as the consequent of the second premise. Because Modus Ponens is the rule permitting the isolation of a consequent from a hypothetical, it is probably used to assert 'T'. The *HAVE, WANT, USE, NEED* approach suggests searching for 'G' to combine with 'G ⊃ T' in a Modus Ponens move to assert 'T'.

Other than in the second premise, 'G' appears only in the antecedent of the first premise. Modus Tollens is the only rule that permits isolation of an antecedent, and then it is the denial of the antecedent that is obtained. Modus Tollens can be used with the first premise only if the denial of its consequent can first be asserted. ' ~ O' comes from the third premise by Simplification. The results of this approach are displayed as

(6) $\qquad\qquad\qquad\qquad /\therefore\ F \vee (T \cdot H)$

1) $\sim (G \cdot I) \supset O$ $\qquad$ Pr
2) $G \supset T$ $\qquad$ Pr
3) $\sim O \cdot H$ $\qquad$ Pr
4) $\sim O$ $\qquad$ 3, Simp
5) $\sim\sim (G \cdot I)$ $\qquad$ 1, 4, MT

The 'G' needed to combine with 'G ⊃ T' by Modus Ponens comes out of line 5 after using Double Negation. (6) is now completed:

6) $G \cdot I$ $\qquad$ 5, DN
7) $G$ $\qquad$ 6, Simp
8) $T$ $\qquad$ 2, 7, MP
9) $H \cdot \sim O$ $\qquad$ 3, Com

| | | |
|---|---|---|
| **10)** | H | 9, Simp |
| **11)** | T · H | 8, 10, Conj |
| **12)** | (T · H) ∨ F | 11, Add |
| **13)** | /∴ F ∨ (T · H) | 12, Com |

Double Negation is always used to supply or remove tildes by pairs. Further, each pair of tildes must have the same scope. The following examples show common misuses of Double Negation:

**(7)**

$$\begin{array}{lll} & \mathbf{m)} \ \sim H & ?, ? \\ \textit{WRONG X} & \mathbf{n)} \ \sim \sim H & m, DN \end{array}$$

**(8)**

$$\begin{array}{lll} & \mathbf{m)} \ \sim ( \sim H \cdot O) & ?, ? \\ \textit{WRONG X} & \mathbf{n)} \ H \cdot O & m, DN \end{array}$$

While the last line in (7) displays two tildes ranging over the same statement, 'H', nonetheless Double Negation was misused with the first statement. The correct use of Double Negation yields '$\sim \sim \sim H$'. In (8) the error is different. There are two tildes in the first line of (8) but they do not have the same scope. The first tilde denies the conjunction '$\sim H \cdot O$'; the second denies only 'H'.

While no commutation rule applies to hypothetical statements, ***Transposition*** can be used to "flip over" a hypothetical provided that tildes are carefully handled. Watch how Transposition is used in constructing proofs:

**(9)** Assuming both that the Federal Reserve restricts the currency flow and the national government controls deficit spending, the prime interest rate will not escalate radically. A sufficient condition for inflation's soaring is that it is not the case that the national government controls deficit spending while the Federal Reserve restricts currency flow. If the value of the dollar does not fall, inflation will not soar. Subsequently, assuming that the prime interest rate escalates radically, the value of the dollar will fall. (R,C,E,S,F)

(9) is symbolized as

**(10)**                                                     /∴  E ⊃ F

$$\begin{array}{lll} \mathbf{1)} & (R \cdot C) \supset \sim E & Pr \\ \mathbf{2)} & \sim (C \cdot R) \supset S & Pr \\ \mathbf{3)} & \sim F \supset \sim S & Pr \end{array}$$

Again, think in terms of *HAVE, WANT, USE,* and *NEED* to help increase the chances of successfully discovering a proof. Consider the conclusion of (9) as symbolized in (10). Notice if it appears anywhere in the premises. It does not. 'E ⊃ F' must be constructed. Since the conclusion is a hypothetical statement, Hypothetical Syllogism might be used to reach it. In that case, something like this is needed:

$$\left. \begin{array}{l} \mathbf{n)} \ E \supset q \\ \mathbf{w)} \ q \supset F \end{array} \right\} \quad \text{use: HS}$$

The needed statements are not found in the premises. However, ' ~ E' is the consequent of the first premise and ' ~ F' is the antecedent of the third premise. It is possible to eliminate the tildes and to switch 'E' to an antecedent position and 'F' to a consequent position. This is done by using Transposition:

**(11)**                                         / ∴  E ⊃ F

    **1)** (R • C) ⊃ ~ E      Pr

    **2)** ~ (C • R) ⊃ S      Pr

    **3)** ~ F ⊃ ~ S      Pr

    **4)** ~ ~ E ⊃ ~ (R • C)      1, Trans

    **5)** S ⊃ F      3, Trans

Apply Transposition in line 1, reading the rule from left to right. However, in using this rule in 3, it is read from right to left. Using Double Negation in 4, 'E' is now in the antecedent position, matching its place in the conclusion:

    **6)** E ⊃ ~ (R • C)    4, DN

Moving toward a use of Hypothetical Syllogism, notice the consequent in 6 is not the same as the antecedent in 5. But this match is needed to obtain 'E ⊃ F' by Hypothetical Syllogism. The expectation of using Hypothetical Syllogism suggests that ' ~ (R • C) ⊃ S' is needed. This is almost the second premise. Use Commutation on the antecedent in 2 and complete the proof:

**(12)**                                         / ∴ E ⊃ F

    **1)** (R • C) ⊃ ~ E      Pr

    **2)** ~ (C • R) ⊃ S      Pr

    **3)** ~ F ⊃ ~ S      Pr

    **4)** ~ ~ E ⊃ ~ (R • C)      1, Trans

    **5)** S ⊃ F      3, Trans

    **6)** E ⊃ ~ (R • C)      4, DN

    **7)** ~ (R • C) ⊃ S      2, Com

    **8)** E ⊃ S      6, 7, HS

    **9)** / ∴ E ⊃ F      8, 5, HS

Line 5 is obtained by using Transposition in 3, reading the rule from right to left. However, the rule can also be read from left to right. In that application ' ~ ~ S ⊃ ~ ~ F' is generated, and Double Negation is used to eliminate tildes.

It is not unusual to find an argument having the following characteristics. *First*, there is only one premise; *second*, exactly the same letters appear in both the symbolization of the premise and the conclusion; *third*, exactly the same number of occurrences of each letter appears in the symbolization of the premise and the conclusion; and *fourth*, the premise is not a conjunction. For example:

**(13)**                         / ∴ (A ⊃ B) ⊃ {C ∨ [( ~ B ⊃ G) ∨ H]}

    **1)** ~ {H ∨ [( ~ G ⊃ B) ∨ C)]} ⊃ ~ ( ~ B ⊃ ~ A)   Pr

In such cases, it might be helpful to arrange the letters in the symbolized premise, from left to right, into the same order as they occur in the symbolized conclusion. When required, group the letters together as they appear in the symbolized conclusion. Since Commutation and Transposition govern ordering, while Association permits regrouping, expect to use these rules in applying this strategy.* Finally, if there are moves such as Double Negation, make them. Using this *ordering strategy*, observe how a proof is constructed for (13):

**(14)**                                    $/ \therefore (A \supset B) \supset \{C \vee [(\sim B \supset G) \vee H]\}$

**1)** $\sim \{H \vee [(\sim G \supset B) \vee C)]\} \supset \sim (\sim B \supset \sim A)$   Pr

**2)** $(\sim B \supset \sim A) \supset \{H \vee [(\sim G \supset B) \supset \vee C]\}$   1, Trans

**3)** $(A \supset B) \supset \{H \vee [(\sim G \supset B) \vee C]$   2, Trans

**4)** $(A \supset B) \supset \{[(\sim G \supset B) \vee C] \vee H\}$   3, Com

**5)** $(A \supset B) \supset \{[C \vee (\sim G \supset B)] \vee H\}$   4, Com

**6)** $A \supset B) \supset \{[C \vee (\sim B \supset \sim \sim G)] \vee H\}$   5, Trans

**7)** $A \supset B) \supset \{C \vee [(\sim B \supset \sim \sim G)] \vee H]\}$   6, Assoc

**8)** $/ \therefore (A \supset B) \supset \{C \vee [(\sim B \supset G) \vee H]$   7, DN

---

## *EXERCISES*

### Group A:

Give the correct justification in each unjustified line of the following.

1.                          $/ \therefore A \supset C$
   1) $A \supset \sim B$    Pr
   2) $\sim C \supset B$    Pr
   3) $\sim B \supset \sim \sim C$
   4) $\sim B \supset C$
   5) $/ \therefore A \supset C$

2.                          $/ \therefore C$
   1) $A \supset \sim B$    Pr
   2) $A \vee C$            Pr
   3) $B$                   Pr
   4) $\sim \sim B$
   5) $\sim A$
   6) $/ \therefore C$

3.                          $/ \therefore C \vee A$
   1) $\sim A \supset \sim B$    Pr
   2) $B$                        Pr

---

* Remember that strategies, no matter how good, are not infallible guides to success. So, while expectations can be raised by appealing to strategies, in logic or anywhere else, these expectations might be misguided in particular circumstances.

3) B ⊃ A
4) A
5) A ∨ C
6) /∴ C ∨ A

4.                          /∴ C ∨ A
1) ∼ A ⊃ ∼ B    Pr
2) B                Pr
3) ∼ ∼ B
4) ∼ ∼ A
5) A
6) A ∨ C
7) /∴ C ∨ A

5.                          /∴ C · D
1) A ⊃ ∼ (B ∨ C)   Pr
2) (D ∨ A) · C       Pr
3) C · (D ∨ A)
4) C
5) C ∨ B
6) B ∨ C
7) ∼ ∼ (B ∨ C)
8) ∼ A
9) D ∨ A
10) A ∨ D
11) D
12) /∴ C · D

6.                          /∴ A ⊃ E
1) ∼ (A ⊃ B) ⊃ C      Pr
2) D ⊃ (∼ E ⊃ ∼ B)   Pr
3) ∼ C · (D ∨ C)       Pr
4) ∼ C
5) ∼ ∼ (A ⊃ B)
6) A ⊃ B
7) (D ∨ C) · ∼ C
8) D ∨ C
9) C ∨ D
10) D
11) ∼ E ⊃ ∼ B
12) B ⊃ E
13) /∴ A ⊃ E

7.                          /∴ B ⊃ D
1) ∼ (∼ A ⊃ ∼ B) ⊃ ∼ E   Pr
2) E ⊃ (A ⊃ ∼ C)          Pr
3) E                      Pr
4) ∼ (∼ D ⊃ C) ⊃ ∼ E      Pr
5) E ⊃ (∼ A ⊃ ∼ B)
6) E ⊃ (∼ D ⊃ C)
7) ∼ A ⊃ ∼ B
8) B ⊃ A
9) A ⊃ ∼ C

10) B ⊃ ~ C
11) ~ D ⊃ C
12) ~ C ⊃ ~ ~ D
13) ~ C ⊃ D
14) /∴ B ⊃ D

8.                             /∴ E ∨ B

   1) A ⊃ ( ~ B ⊃ ~ C)    Pr
   2) ~ (D ⊃ E) ⊃ F      Pr
   3) C ∨ (F ∨ D)        Pr
   4) ~ F · A             Pr
   5) ~ F
   6) ~ ~ (D ⊃ E)
   7) D ⊃ E
   8) A · ~ F
   9) A
  10) ~ B ⊃ ~ C
  11) C ⊃ B
  12) (F ∨ D) ∨ C
  13) F ∨ (D ∨ C)
  14) D ∨ C
  15) /∴ E ∨ B

9.                             /∴ C ∨ F

   1) (B ⊃ ~ A) · ( ~ F ⊃ G)    Pr
   2) (E ⊃ ~ G) · ( ~ B ⊃ C)    Pr
   3) E ∨ A                   Pr
   4) B ⊃ ~ A
   5) ( ~ B ⊃ C) · (E ⊃ ~ G)
   6) ~ B ⊃ C
   7) ~ ~ A ⊃ ~ B
   8) A ⊃ ~ B
   9) A ⊃ C
  10) ( ~ F ⊃ G) · (B ⊃ ~ A)
  11) ~ F ⊃ G
  12) ~ G ⊃ ~ ~ F
  13) ~ G ⊃ F
  14) E ⊃ ~ G
  15) E ⊃ F
  16) F ∨ C
  17) /∴ C ∨ F

10.                           /∴ E ⊃ H

   1) (A ∨ B) ∨ (C ∨ D)         Pr
   2) ~ (B ∨ C)                 Pr
   3) ~ (E ⊃ F) ⊃ ~ (A ∨ D)     Pr
   4) (C ∨ B) ∨ (F ⊃ G)        Pr
   5) ~ ( ~ H ⊃ ~ G) ⊃ ~ (E ⊃ G)   Pr
   6) [(A ∨ B) ∨ C] ∨ D
   7) [A ∨ (B ∨ C)] ∨ D
   8) [(B ∨ C) ∨ A] ∨ D
   9) (B ∨ C) ∨ (A ∨ D)

10) A ∨ D
11) ~ ~ (A ∨ D)
12) ~ ~ (E ⊃ F)
13) E ⊃ F
14) ~ (C ∨ B)
15) F ⊃ G
16) E ⊃ G
17) ~ ~ (E ⊃ G)
18) ~ ~ (~ H ⊃ ~ G)
19) ~ H ⊃ ~ G
20) G ⊃ H
21) / ∴ E ⊃ H

## Group B:

Construct a proof of validity for each of the following.

1.                                    / ∴ B ⊃ ~ A
   1) A ⊃ ~ B   Pr

2.                                          / ∴ A ⊃ C
   1) (A ⊃ B) · (~ C ⊃ ~ B)   Pr

3.                                                              / ∴ [(A · B) · C] ⊃ ~ [D ⊃ (E ⊃ F)]
   1) [ ~ ( ~ F ⊃ ~ E) ⊃ ~ D] ⊃ ~ [(C · B) · A]   Pr

4.                              / ∴ B ⊃ D
   1)  ~ A ⊃ ~ B          Pr
   2) C ⊃ ( ~ D ⊃ ~ A)    Pr
   3)  ~ C ⊃ ~ E          Pr
   4) E                   Pr

5.                                          / ∴ (H ∨ F) ⊃ G
   1) B ⊃ ~ [A ∨ (C ∨ D)]        Pr
   2) A · ( ~ B ⊃ D)             Pr
   3) (A · D) ⊃ [ ~ G ⊃ ~ (F ∨ H)]   Pr

6.                              / ∴ D ∨ E
   1) (B ∨ A) ⊃ C          Pr
   2) A                    Pr
   3)  ~ (B ⊃ D) ⊃ ~ A     Pr
   4) C ⊃ (A ⊃ E)          Pr

7.                                          / ∴ B ∨ D
   1) (A ⊃ E) · (C ⊃ G)              Pr
   2) ( ~ B ⊃ ~ E) · ( ~ D ⊃ ~ G)    Pr
   3)  ~ (A ⊃ B) ∨ (A ∨ C)           Pr

8.                              / ∴ F ⊃ H
   1) B ⊃ ~ [(A ∨ C) ∨ D]    Pr
   2) A · ( ~ B ⊃ C)         Pr
   3) (A · C) ⊃ ( ~ G ⊃ ~ F)  Pr
   4) G ⊃ H                   Pr

9.                                                 /∴ ~ G ∨ D
   1) (A ⊃ G) · ~ B          Pr
   2) (G ⊃ D) · ( ~ E ⊃ A)   Pr
   3) ~ D ∨ (B ∨ ~ E)        Pr

10.                                                /∴ A ∨ C
   1) ( ~ B ⊃ ~ E) · ( ~ E ⊃ ~ A)   Pr
   2) ~ (A ∨ C) ⊃ ~ (C ⊃ B)         Pr
   3) ~ A ⊃ ~ D                     Pr
   4) ( ~ D ⊃ ~ F) · ( ~ F ⊃ ~ C)   Pr

## Group C:

Symbolize the following arguments using the suggested capital letters. Then construct a proof of validity for each.

1. That this figure isn't a square is a sufficient condition for its not having four equal angles. But this figure does have four equal angles. Consequently, it is a square. (S,A)

2. That the circumference of a figure is determined by '2πr' is necessary for its being a circle; but moreover, that a figure is an ellipse is sufficient for its circumference not being determined by '2πr'. So, a sufficient condition for a figure's not being an ellipse is that it is a circle. (D,C,E)

3. A sufficient condition for this figure's having two distinct pairs of equal opposite sides is the following: It isn't the case that if it is a parallelogram then it is a square. This figure doesn't have two distinct pairs of equal opposite sides, yet that it isn't a quadrilateral is a sufficient condition for its not being a square. So, if this figure is a parallelogram, it is also a quadrilateral. (D,P,S,Q)

4. The taxpayer demands more government services and government spending isn't brought under control. Also, the purchasing power of the dollar doesn't rise unless the rate of unemployment falls. Either the purchasing power of the dollar doesn't rise only if inflation isn't lowered, or it isn't the case that either the taxpayer demands more government services or government spending is brought under control. Hence, inflation is lowered only if the rate of unemployment falls. (D,B,R,F,L)

5. Either the taxpayer demands more government spending, or either federal programs are expanded, or inflation isn't brought under control if the rate of unemployment isn't increased. Federal programs are expanded whenever the taxpayer demands more government spending, yet federal programs aren't being expanded. Either the taxpayer demands more government spending, or federal programs are expanded or inflation is brought under control. Consequently, either the new tax program is adopted or the rate of unemployment increases. (D,E,B,I,A)

6. Assuming that inflation is brought under control, then the GNP won't strengthen only if the rate of unemployment still increases. Inflation is brought under control; yet, either the money market continues to drop, or either inflation isn't brought under control or the rate of unemployment doesn't still increase. That inflation isn't brought under control is a necessary condition for the following not being the case: The general purchasing power of the worker won't erode only if the money market doesn't continue to drop. Accordingly, the GNP will strengthen or the general purchasing power of the worker will erode. (B,S,I,D,E)

7. A sufficient condition for our being interested in Baroque architecture is the following: It isn't true that we don't appreciate fine painting only if we are aesthetically dense. Now if we overlook the Vatican, we aren't interested in Baroque architecture; but assuming we don't overlook the Vatican, we shan't miss Michelangelo's mature works. That we are unconscious of the Baroque period is a necessary condition for the following: Assuming we aren't aesthetically dense then we are appreciative of fine painting. So, if we miss Michelangelo's mature works, we are unconscious of the Baroque period. (I,A,D,O,M,C)

8. Michelangelo lived in the sixteenth century only if he didn't work for Pius II; and if Michelangelo was commissioned by Julius II, he didn't paint "Nude Descending a Staircase." On the other hand, assuming Michelangelo did sculpt "The Thinker," he wasn't commissioned by Julius II; yet, either Michelangelo worked for Pius II or he was commissioned by Julius II. So, either Michelangelo didn't live in the sixteenth century or he didn't paint "Nude Descending a Staircase"; but also either Michelangelo didn't sculpt "The Thinker" or he didn't live in the sixteenth century. (L,W,C,P,S)

9. That people are unhappy is a sufficient condition for the following: It isn't the case that assuming people love their friends, the laws of morality are followed. Either people love their friends or people balance reasoning with desiring. If people don't balance reasoning with desiring, they don't love their friends; yet, if the laws of morality aren't followed, people don't balance reasoning with desiring. The laws of morality are followed only if people respect a friend as a valuable human being. Assuming that either the laws of morality are followed or people respect a friend as a valuable human being, then people are truly useful to themselves as well as to their friends. Thus, people aren't only truly useful to themselves as well as to their friends, but furthermore they are happy. (H,L,F,B,R,U)

10. That people are unjust to their friends is a necessary condition for the following: It isn't true that assuming people are unkind to their friends, then they don't follow the laws of morality. People don't follow the laws of morality unless either they balance reasoning with desiring or are useful to their friends. Neither are such people not indifferent to their friends nor unjust to them. If people are either useful to their friends or balance reasoning with desiring, then they aren't indifferent to their friends. Either people aren't indifferent to their friends; or either they are unjust to their friends or they are just to their friends, or they do follow the laws of morality. Therefore, either people aren't indifferent to their friends, or if they do follow the laws of morality, they aren't unkind to their friends. (J,K,F,B,U,I)

## 3.  DISTRIBUTION AND DEMORGAN'S LAWS

### DISTRIBUTION (DIST)

$$p \lor (q \cdot r) :: (p \lor q) \cdot (p \lor r)$$
$$p \cdot (q \lor r) :: (p \cdot q) \lor (p \cdot r)$$

### DEMORGAN'S LAWS (DeM)

$$\sim p \lor \sim q :: \sim (p \cdot q)$$
$$\sim p \cdot \sim q :: \sim (p \lor q)$$

Consider this argument:

(1)  Assuming we're persistent in our work, we're either rewarded and honored or aren't faithful in our duties. We're persistent in our work. So, we aren't faithful in our duties or we're honored. (P,R,H,F)

Using the suggested capital letters, (1) is symbolized as

**(2)**                                                    $/\therefore \sim F \lor H$

    **1)** $P \supset [(R \cdot H) \lor \sim F]$    Pr

    **2)** $P$                       Pr

The conclusion, '$\sim F \lor H$', does not occur in the premises. Moreover, it might be difficult to see how it is constructed. In cases such as this, there are likely moves that might be useful in reaching the conclusion. For instance, are there letters that appear in the symbolization of the premises but not in the symbolization of the conclusion? If so, they need to be eliminated before reaching the conclusion. *

---

\* In some proofs, letters appearing in the symbolized premise set, but not in the symbolized conclusion, need to be retained until the last move in the proof. Here is a simple, but instructive, example:

                                       $/\therefore \sim C$

    **1)** $(B \cdot C) \lor A$   Pr

    **2)** $\sim A \cdot \sim B$    Pr

    **3)** $\sim A$           2, Simp

    **4)** $A \lor (B \cdot C)$   1, Com

    **5)** $B \cdot C$        4, 3, DS

    **6)** $B$            5, Simp

    **7)** $\sim B \cdot \sim A$   2, Com

    **8)** $\sim B$         7, Simp

    **9)** $B \lor \sim C$   6, Add

    **10)** $/\therefore \sim C$   9, 8, DS

Some logicians would shorten the above proof by combining lines. This would especially be the case in uses of commutation setting up for further moves. Using this tactic, the following proof is generated:

                                         $/\therefore \sim C$

    **1)** $(B \cdot C) \lor A$   Pr

    **2)** $\sim A \cdot \sim B$    Pr

    **3)** $\sim A$           2, Simp

    **4)** $B \cdot C$        1, 3, DS

    **5)** $B$            4, Simp

    **6)** $\sim B$         2, Simp

    **7)** $B \lor \sim C$   5, Add

    **8)** $/\therefore \sim C$   7, 6, DS

In this book, however, all moves, even if they "appear obvious," are explicitly taken.

In (2), 'P' and 'R' do not appear in the conclusion. A Modus Ponens move eliminates 'P' from further lines and also produces

$$\textbf{3)} \quad (R \cdot H) \vee \sim F \qquad 1, 2, MP$$

Several interesting features are seen in 3. *First*, while 'R' appears in 3, it is not found in the conclusion. 'R' must be removed before the conclusion is reached. *Second*, no other statement in the proof can be combined with '$(R \cdot H) \vee \sim F$' to eliminate 'R'. *Third*, the statement in 3 is not a conjunction, so Simplification cannot be used to preserve what is needed to construct the conclusion while also leaving 'R' behind. When these three features occur together, one can consider using the first rule of Distribution.* Apply this rule from left to right to eliminate any unwanted statement(s). The *distribution strategy* is used in the following sequence:

$$\textbf{4)} \quad \sim F \vee (R \cdot H) \qquad 3, Com$$
$$\textbf{5)} \quad (\sim F \vee R) \cdot (\sim F \vee H) \qquad 4, Dist$$
$$\textbf{6)} \quad (\sim F \vee H) \cdot (\sim F \vee R) \qquad 5, Com$$
$$\textbf{7)} \quad / \therefore \; \sim F \vee H \qquad 6, Simp.$$

Look at '$(R \cdot H) \vee \sim F$' in line 3. Wanting to eliminate 'R' from the remainder of the proof, someone might attempt moves like these:

|  |  |  |
|---|---|---|
|  | **3)** $(R \cdot H) \vee \sim F$ | 1,2, MP |
| *WRONG X* | **4)** $R \cdot (H \vee \sim F)$ | 3, Assoc |
|  | **5)** $(H \vee \sim F) \cdot R$ | 4, Com |
|  | **6)** $H \vee \sim F$ | 5, Simp |
|  | **7)** $/ \therefore \; \sim F \vee H$ | 6, Com |

Line 4 is incorrect. Association can only be used on statements exhibiting one side of either of these forms:

$$p \cdot (q \cdot r) :: (p \cdot q) \cdot r$$
$$p \vee (q \vee r) :: (p \vee q) \vee r$$

But there is no way of reading '$(R \cdot H) \vee \sim F$', with its mixture of a dot and wedge, as displaying either side of one of these equivalence forms.

Examine (3) to see a typical use of the second rule of Distribution:

**(3)** $\qquad\qquad\qquad\qquad\qquad\qquad / \therefore B \cdot (C \vee D)$

$\qquad$ **1)** $A \supset B \qquad\qquad$ Pr

$\qquad$ **2)** $(C \cdot A) \vee (A \cdot D) \quad$ Pr

---

* To remember the two rules of Distribution more easily, think of them as "mirror images." The same variables in each rule are found in exactly the same places. But where there is a wedge in the first rule, there is a dot in the second. And where there is a dot in the first, there is a wedge in the second. Notice also that within each rule the major connective and the connective within the parentheses reverse from dots to wedges and wedges to dots in moving from one side to the other of the replacement sign.

Since the conclusion does not appear as a whole in the premises, it has to be constructed. Further, since the conclusion is a conjunction, the odds are that Conjunction is used to reach it. To use this rule, 'B' and 'C ∨ D' are first needed. Because 'B' occurs as a consequent of a hypothetical statement, Modus Ponens might be used to obtain it. Using Modus Ponens demands that 'A' first be established in the proof. Other than in 1, 'A' occurs only in 2. Notice the second premise is an inclusive disjunction made up of two conjunctions, 'C · A' and 'A · D'. Moreover, 'A' is found in each of these conjunctions. When this situation arises, imagine using the second rule of Distribution, reading it from right to left. The following lines are generated:

| | | |
|---|---|---|
| **3)** | $(A \cdot C) \vee (A \cdot D)$ | 2, Com |
| **4)** | $A \cdot (C \vee D)$ | 3, Dist |

Line 3 prepares for the use of Distribution in 4. Distribution produces the 'A' needed for a Modus Ponens move with 2 as well as the 'C ∨ D' found in the conclusion. The proof is now completed:

| | | |
|---|---|---|
| **5)** | A | 4, Simp |
| **6)** | B | 1, 5, MP |
| **7)** | $(C \vee D) \cdot A$ | 4, Com |
| **8)** | $C \vee D$ | 7, Simp |
| **9)** | $/ \therefore B \cdot (C \vee D)$ | 6, 8, Conj |

Another important strategy in constructing proofs is the *tilde removal strategy*. If there is a tilde on the outside of punctuation marks, and there is no apparent reason to keep it, work to remove that tilde. The rationale behind this strategy is this: Of all the argument forms introduced in Chapter 4, only two display tildes. Thus, if ' $\sim (A \vee B)$ ' appears somewhere in a proof, it could only be used as an instance of the second premise of Disjunctive Syllogism or Modus Tollens, or simply as an instance of a single statement variable in some argument form. By removing tildes from in front of punctuation marks, other possibilities become available in proof construction.

The tilde removal strategy is helpful in working backwards as well as in moving from premises to conclusion. The family of rules most helpful in applying this strategy is Double Negation and ***DeMorgan's Laws***.* In particular, DeMorgan's Laws permit a move from a denied conjunction to an inclusive disjunction of separately denied disjuncts, and vice versa. These laws also allow a move from a denied inclusive disjunction to a conjunction of separately denied conjuncts, and vice versa. Thus, DeMorgan's Laws are very helpful in removing a tilde from in front of punctuation marks surrounding either an overall conjunction of an overall inclusive disjunction. Here is an example of a proof using DeMorgan's Laws:

(4)    Russell is taking Annye Mae to the symphony or opera next

---

* The two De Morgan's Laws can also be viewed as mirror images. The dots and wedges change places in the two laws while everything else remains identical.

week, or taking her to hear *The Beach Boys* and *U2*. But Russell is neither taking Annye Mae to the symphony next week nor to hear *U2*. So, he is taking her to the opera. (S,O,B,U)

Symbolize (4) as

**(5)**                                              /∴O
   **1)** $(S \lor O) \lor (B \cdot U)$   Pr
   **2)** $\sim (S \lor U)$   Pr

There is a tilde on the outside of punctuation marks in line 2 of (5). Because there is no reason to keep the tilde in that position, use *DeMorgan* to yield

   **3)** $\sim S \cdot \sim U$      2, DeM

The conclusion, 'O', appears in the first symbolized premise which is a disjunction. 'O' appears in the left-hand disjunct. If Commutation followed by Disjunctive Syllogism can be used, then 'S ∨ O' will be obtained. To use Disjunctive Syllogism after having commuted the first premise, ' ∼ (B · U)' is needed. How can this be acquired? There is a tilde on the outside of punctuation marks in ' ∼ (B · U)'. *Working backwards*, imagine what ' ∼ (B · U)' looks like when the tilde is removed by a use of DeMorgan. Using DeMorgan generates ' ∼ B ∨ ∼ U'. If ' ∼ B ∨ ∼ U' is reached, ' ∼ (B · U)' is asserted by DeMorgan and then 'S ∨ O' by Disjunctive Syllogism. Since ' ∼ B ∨ ∼ U' is an inclusive disjunction, to find it think in terms of those rules *ending* with a wedge. Addition is one of those rules. Now, ' ∼ U' is a conjunct in 3. A Simplification move prepares for Addition. Proof construction proceeds in this way:

   **4)** $\sim U \cdot \sim S$      3, Com
   **5)** $\sim U$      4, Simp
   **6)** $\sim U \lor \sim B$      5, Add
   **7)** $\sim B \lor \sim U$      6, Com
   **8)** $\sim (B \cdot U)$      7, DeM
   **9)** $(B \cdot U) \lor (S \lor O)$   1, Com
  **10)** $S \lor O$      9, 8, DS

Isolating 'O' out of 10 is straightforward:

  **11)** $\sim S$      3, Simp
  **12)** /∴ O      10, 11, DS

Another proof of (5) uses Distribution to remove 'B':

**(6)**                                              /∴ O
   **1)** $(S \lor O) \lor (B \cdot U)$   Pr
   **2)** $\sim (S \lor U)$   Pr
   **3)** $[(S \lor O) \lor B] \cdot [(S \lor O) \lor U]$   1, Dist
   **4)** $[(S \lor O) \lor U] \cdot [(S \lor O) \lor B]$   3, Com

| | | |
|---|---|---|
| **5)** | $(S \lor O) \lor U$ | 4, Simp |
| **6)** | $S \lor (O \lor U)$ | 5, Assoc |
| **7)** | $\sim S \cdot \sim U$ | 2, DeM |
| **8)** | $\sim S$ | 7, Simp |
| **9)** | $O \lor U$ | 6, 8, DS |
| **10)** | $U \lor O$ | 9, Com |
| **11)** | $\sim U \cdot \sim S$ | 7, Com |
| **12)** | $\sim U$ | 11, Simp |
| **13)** | $/\therefore O$ | 10, 12, DS |

Notice that (6) can be slightly refined by using Commutation on the right-hand disjunct, 'B · U', in line 1 before using Distribution. Then 'B', the letter to be left behind in the proof, will appear in only the right-hand conjunct after the Distribution move. This will avoid having to commute the longer expressions in line 3 above. The new proof looks like this:

**(7)**                                                          $/\therefore O$

| | | |
|---|---|---|
| **1)** | $(S \lor O) \lor (B \cdot U)$ | Pr |
| **2)** | $\sim (S \lor U)$ | Pr |
| **3)** | $(S \lor O) \lor (U \cdot B)$ | 1, Com |
| **4)** | $[(S \lor O) \lor U] \cdot [(S \lor O) \lor B]$ | 3, Dist |
| **5)** | $(S \lor O) \lor U$ | 4, Simp |
| **6)** | $S \lor (O \lor U)$ | 5, Assoc |
| **7)** | $\sim S \cdot \sim U$ | 2, DeM |
| **8)** | $\sim S$ | 7, Simp |
| **9)** | $O \lor U$ | 6, 8, DS |
| **10)** | $U \lor O$ | 9, Com |
| **11)** | $\sim U \cdot \sim S$ | 7, Com |
| **12)** | $\sim U$ | 11, Simp |
| **13)** | $/\therefore O$ | 10, 12, DS |

---

## EXERCISES

### Group A:

Give the correct justification in each unjustified line of the following.

1.                                       $/\therefore \sim A$
   1) $A \supset (B \lor C)$    Pr
   2) $\sim C \cdot \sim B$    Pr
   3) $\sim B \cdot \sim C$
   4) $\sim (B \lor C)$
   5) $/\therefore \sim A$

2.                          /∴ C
   1) (A·B) ∨ C   Pr
   2) ~ B            Pr
   3) ~ B ∨ ~ A
   4) ~ A ∨ ~ B
   5) ~ (A·B)
   6) /∴ C

3.                          /∴ C
   1) (A·B) ∨ C   Pr
   2) ~ B            Pr
   3) C ∨ (A·B)
   4) (C ∨ A) · (C ∨ B)
   5) (C ∨ B) · (C ∨ A)
   6) C ∨ B
   7) B ∨ C
   8) /∴ C

4.                          /∴ A·B
   1) (A·B) ∨ (C·A)   Pr
   2) ~ C                Pr
   3) (A·B) ∨ (A·C)
   4) A · (B ∨ C)
   5) A
   6) (B ∨ C) · A
   7) B ∨ C
   8) C ∨ B
   9) B
   10) /∴ A·B

5.                          /∴ ~ (D ∨ A) ∨ ~ (D ∨ B)
   1) ~ A ∨ ( ~ B·C)   Pr
   2) ~ D ∨ (B·A)       Pr
   3) ( ~ A ∨ ~ B) · ( ~ A ∨ C)
   4) ~ A ∨ ~ B
   5) ~ B ∨ ~ A
   6) ~ (B·A)
   7) (B·A) ∨ ~ D
   8) ~ D
   9) ~ D · ( ~ A ∨ ~ B)
   10) ( ~ D · ~ A) ∨ ( ~ D · ~ B)
   11) ( ~ D · ~ A) ∨ ~ (D ∨ B)
   12) /∴ ~ (D ∨ A) ∨ ~ (D ∨ B)

6.                          /∴ ~ B · ~ (C · ~ D)
   1) ~ (A ∨ B) ⊃ ~ C   Pr
   2) ~ B · (B ∨ ~ A)     Pr
   3) ~ B
   4) (B ∨ ~ A) · ~ B
   5) B ∨ ~ A
   6) ~ A
   7) ~ A · ~ B
   8) ~ (A ∨ B)
   9) ~ C

10)  $\sim C \vee D$

11)  $\sim \sim (\sim C \vee D)$

12)  $\sim (\sim \sim C \cdot \sim D)$

13)  $\sim (C \cdot \sim D)$

14)  $/\therefore \sim B \cdot \sim (C \cdot \sim D)$

7.                                        $/\therefore \sim (A \cdot D) \cdot \sim (E \cdot F)$

1)  $\sim A \vee (\sim D \cdot C)$     Pr

2)  $(E \supset A) \cdot (F \supset \sim C)$  Pr

3)  $(\sim A \vee \sim D) \cdot (\sim A \vee C)$

4)  $\sim A \vee \sim D$

5)  $\sim (A \cdot D)$

6)  $E \supset A$

7)  $\sim A \supset \sim E$

8)  $(F \supset \sim C) \cdot (E \supset A)$

9)  $F \supset \sim C$

10)  $\sim \sim C \supset \sim F$

11)  $C \supset \sim F$

12)  $(\sim A \vee C) \cdot (\sim A \vee \sim D)$

13)  $\sim A \vee C$

14)  $\sim E \vee \sim F$

15)  $\sim (E \cdot F)$

16)  $/\therefore \sim (A \cdot D) \cdot \sim (E \cdot F)$

8.                                        $/\therefore E \vee \sim (A \cdot C)$

1)  $(\sim A \cdot B) \vee [(A \cdot \sim C) \vee (D \cdot E)]$   Pr

2)  $(\sim A \cdot B) \vee \{[(A \cdot \sim C) \vee D] \cdot [(A \cdot \sim C) \vee E]\}$

3)  $\{(\sim A \cdot B) \vee [(A \cdot \sim C) \vee D]\} \cdot \{(\sim A \cdot B) \vee [(A \cdot \sim C) \vee E]\}$

4)  $\{(\sim A \cdot B) \vee [(A \cdot \sim C) \vee E]\} \cdot \{(\sim A \cdot B) \vee [(A \cdot \sim C) \vee D]\}$

5)  $(\sim A \cdot B) \vee [(A \cdot \sim C) \vee E]$

6)  $(\sim A \cdot B) \vee [E \vee (A \cdot \sim C)]$

7)  $(\sim A \cdot B) \vee [(E \vee A) \cdot (E \vee \sim C)]$

8)  $[(\sim A \cdot B) \vee (E \vee A)] \cdot [(\sim A \cdot B) \vee (E \vee \sim C)]$

9)  $[(\sim A \cdot B) \vee (E \vee \sim C)] \cdot [(\sim A \cdot B) \vee (E \vee A)]$

10)  $(\sim A \cdot B) \vee (E \vee \sim C)$

11)  $(E \vee \sim C) \vee (\sim A \cdot B)$

12)  $[(E \vee \sim C) \vee \sim A] \cdot [(E \vee \sim C) \vee B]$

13)  $(E \vee \sim C) \vee \sim A$

14)  $E \vee (\sim C \vee \sim A)$

15)  $E \vee \sim (C \cdot A)$

16)  $/\therefore E \vee \sim (A \cdot C)$

9.                                        $/\therefore \sim (\sim C \cdot \sim B)$

1)  $(\sim A \cdot B) \vee (C \cdot D)$                    Pr

2)  $\sim [(B \cdot E) \vee (C \cdot \sim D)] \supset (A \cdot \sim D)$  Pr

3)  $(\sim A \cdot B) \vee (D \cdot C)$

4)  $[(\sim A \cdot B) \vee D] \cdot [(\sim A \cdot B) \vee C]$

5)  $(\sim A \cdot B) \vee D$

6)  $D \vee (\sim A \cdot B)$

7)  $(D \vee \sim A) \cdot (D \vee B)$

8)  $D \vee \sim A$

9)  $\sim A \vee D$

10) $\sim \sim (\sim A \lor D)$
11) $\sim (\sim \sim A \cdot \sim D)$
12) $\sim (A \cdot \sim D)$
13) $\sim \sim [(B \cdot E) \lor (C \cdot \sim D)]$
14) $(B \cdot E) \lor (C \cdot \sim D)$
15) $[(B \cdot E) \lor C] \cdot [(B \cdot E) \lor \sim D]$
16) $(B \cdot E) \lor C$
17) $C \lor (B \cdot E)$
18) $(C \lor B) \cdot (C \lor E)$
19) $C \lor B$
20) $\sim \sim (C \lor B)$
21) $/ \therefore \sim (\sim C \cdot \sim B)$

10.                                          $/ \therefore G \lor H$

1) $\sim (C \cdot E) \cdot \sim F$          Pr
2) $\sim A \lor [B \lor (C \cdot D)]$       Pr
3) $(\sim G \supset \sim B) \cdot (\sim E \supset F)$   Pr
4) $\sim H \supset A$                       Pr
5) $\sim G \supset \sim B$
6) $B \supset G$
7) $\sim A \supset \sim \sim H$
8) $\sim A \supset H$
9) $(\sim A \lor B) \lor (C \cdot D)$
10) $(C \cdot D) \lor (\sim A \lor B)$
11) $(\sim E \supset F) \cdot (\sim G \supset \sim B)$
12) $\sim E \supset F$
13) $\sim F \cdot \sim (C \cdot E)$
14) $\sim F$
15) $\sim \sim E$
16) $\sim (C \cdot E)$
17) $\sim C \lor \sim E$
18) $\sim E \lor \sim C$
19) $\sim C$
20) $\sim C \lor \sim D$
21) $\sim (C \cdot D)$
22) $\sim A \lor B$
23) $B \lor \sim A$
24) $/ \therefore G \lor H$

## Group B:

Construct a proof of validity for each of the following.

1.                                          $/ \therefore \sim (B \lor A)$
1) $\sim A \cdot (A \lor \sim B)$   Pr

2.                                          $/ \therefore \sim (C \cdot A)$
1) $\sim A \lor (B \lor \sim C)$   Pr
2) $\sim B$                         Pr

3.                                    /∴  ~ A
   1) (A • B) ⊃ C    Pr
   2) ~ C • B         Pr

4.                                    /∴  ~ [(A • B) • (E • D)]
   1) ~ A ∨ [~ B ∨ (C • ~ D)]   Pr

5.                                    /∴  ~ (~ D ∨ ~ A)
   1) (A • B) ∨ (C • A)   Pr
   2) (C ∨ B) ⊃ D         Pr

6.                                    /∴  ~ (A • ~ C) • ~ (B • ~ C)
   1) (~ A • ~ B) ∨ (C • D)   Pr

7.                                    /∴  ~ (~ E • C) • ~ (~ C • E)
   1) A ∨ [(~ C • B) ∨ (E • D)]   Pr
   2) ~ A • ~ (E • ~ C)           Pr

8.                                    /∴  ~ (C • D)
   1) (C ⊃ ~ A) • (D ⊃ ~ B)   Pr
   2) (A • E) ∨ (E • B)           Pr

9.                                    /∴  ~ (C • E)
   1) ~ A ∨ [~ D ∨ (~ F • ~ C)]   Pr
   2) B • (E ⊃ A)                 Pr
   3) (E • D) ∨ ~ B               Pr

10.                                    /∴  ~ (~ G • ~ E)
   1) (~ A • D) ∨ (B ⊃ G)             Pr
   2) ~ (~ E ⊃ ~ C) ⊃ (~ D • ~ A)    Pr
   3) (A • B) ∨ (C • A)               Pr

## Group C:

Symbolize the following arguments using the suggested capital letters. Then construct a proof of validity for each.

1. We may appreciate Euripides' dramatic style while also understanding the political events of his time if we study carefully the *Trojan Women*. However, we don't understand the political events of Euripides' time. Consequently, we don't study carefully the *Trojan Women*. (A,U,S)

2. Aristophanes contended that democracy was destroying Athens. Now, either it isn't true that Aristophanes expressed his political views in the *Knights* while contending democracy was destroying Athens, or he sided with the old oligarchy. Therefore, Aristophanes' political views aren't expressed in the *Knights* or he sided with the old oligarchy. (C,E,S)

3. We may gather from Sophocles that the following cannot be the case: The gods aren't powerful, but either they aren't helpless in the affairs of humans or there is an objective moral order independent of the will of the gods. So, it isn't true that the gods aren't powerful and there is an objective moral order independent of the will of the gods. (P,H,O)

4. Either the gods provide a divine law and humans obey the gods, or humans follow an objective moral order independent of the will of the gods while the gods provide a divine law. Assuming that humans don't achieve happiness, then it isn't true that either humans obey the gods or they follow an objective moral order independent of the will of the gods.

Therefore, it isn't true that either the gods don't provide a divine law or humans don't achieve happiness. (P,O,F,A)

5. Humans don't desire happiness only if they don't follow an objective moral order independent of the will of the gods; but, on the other hand, humans simply seek pleasure whenever they maintain self-centered objectives in their life. Either humans follow an objective moral order independent of the will of the gods while loving their friends, or they use their friends for their own ends and maintain self-centered objectives in their life. Wherefore, humans either simply seek pleasure or they desire happiness. (D,F,S,M,L,U)

6. If either humans behave in a self-centered way or ignore completely the divine law, then neither do they appreciate the powers of Eros nor understand the moral force of Socrates' views. Either humans ignore completely the divine law, or either they grasp the importance of Plato's writings or they behave in a self-centered way. Furthermore, either humans appreciate the powers of Eros, or while following the dictates of reason they understand the moral force of Socrates' views. So, either humans grasp the importance of Plato's writings or they ignore the divine law. (B,I,A,U,G,F)

7. The following isn't true: Humans find happiness, while either the gods don't provide a divine law or humans don't obey it. Humans don't desire justice only if they don't obey the divine law; but if humans don't become miserable, they find happiness. Therefore, either humans become miserable or they desire justice. (F,P,O,D,B)

8. Either it isn't true that many of the Platonic dialogues aren't tentative and aren't conclusive, or neither are all the dialogues worthwhile nor always suggestive. Many Platonic dialogues aren't conclusive although they are always suggestive. Accordingly, many of the Platonic dialogues are tentative. (T,C,W,S)

9. If we study Aristotle's writings, then it isn't the case that we appreciate Plato's dialogues while not being infatuated with Socrates' life. The following isn't true: Neither do we appreciate Plato's dialogues nor pursue mediocrity, but we're infatuated with Socrates' life. We do study Aristotle's writings and don't pursue mediocrity. Thus, it isn't the case that we're infatuated with Socrates' life but don't appreciate Plato's dialogues, while further it isn't the case that we're not infatuated with Socrates' life but do appreciate Plato's dialogues. (S,A,I,P)

10. That we study Aristotle is a sufficient condition for the following: We accept fixed species; or we neither reject the notion of relative space nor posit a perfect universe, or we do encounter a view of evolution and develop a doctrine of relative genera. Now, either we study Aristotle and posit a perfect universe, or we reject the notion of relative space while studying Aristotle. So, either we study Aristotle and accept fixed species, or we do encounter a view of evolution while studying Aristotle. (S,A,R,P,E,D)

---

## 4.  MATERIAL IMPLICATION AND EXPORTATION

### MATERIAL IMPLICATION (IMPL)

$$p \supset q :: \sim p \vee q$$

### EXPORTATION (EXP)

$$(p \cdot q) \supset r :: p \supset (q \supset r)$$

*Material Implication* is one of the more intuitively acceptable equivalence forms. To say 'If it's cold, then I'll wear a coat', is intuitively acceptable as logically equivalent to 'Either it isn't cold or I'll wear a coat'. Indeed, there is a fundamental relation holding between horseshoes, wedges, and tildes. If beginning with a horseshoe expression, prefix the symbolization of the entire antecedent with a tilde, using appropriate punctuation marks when necessary, and then change the horse-shoe into a wedge. The reverse of this procedure also works. Starting with an inclusive disjunctive such that the left-hand disjunct is denied, change the wedge into a horseshoe and drop a tilde before what now becomes the antecedent.

In some contexts of constructing proofs, it is desirable to change a horseshoe into a wedge or a wedge into a horseshoe. It might be necessary, for instance, to remove the tilde in the expression ' $\sim (A \supset B)$ '. None of the rules studied so far can do this. If, however, the horseshoe in ' $\sim (A \supset B)$ ' is converted into a wedge, DeMorgan can be applied. Notice how Material Implication is used:

(1)

$$\textbf{m)} \quad \sim (A \supset B) \qquad ?, ?$$
$$\textbf{n)} \quad \sim (\sim A \vee B) \quad \text{m, Impl}$$
$$\textbf{o)} \quad \sim \sim A \cdot \sim B \quad \text{n, DeM}$$

An important use of Material Implication is preparing for the distribution strategy. Inspect the following:

(2)                            $/ \therefore A \supset B$
         1) $A \supset (B \cdot C)$    Pr

No matter how the conclusion, 'A ⊃ B', is finally reached, 'C' has to be left behind in the proof. The distribution strategy is helpful if the premise is first transformed into an inclusive disjunction. This move can be made by Material Implication:

(3)                            $/ \therefore A \supset B$
        1) $A \supset (B \cdot C)$         Pr
        2) $\sim A \vee (B \cdot C)$       1, Impl
        3) $(\sim A \vee B) \cdot (\sim A \vee C)$    2, Dist
        4) $\sim A \vee B$            3, Simp
        5) $/ \therefore A \supset B$        4, Impl

(4) is a more complicated example:

(4)   A necessary condition for theories in psychology not being constructed is the following: Neither experimental nor clinical psychologists are interested in this type of work, or neither statistical nor quantitative measurement is satisfactory for representing psychological data. Consequently, if experimental psychologists are interested in this type of work, then theories in psychology are constructed if statistical measurement is satisfactory in representing psychological data. (T,E,C,S,Q)

With the suggested notation, (4) is symbolized as

(5)                                $/ \therefore E \supset (S \supset T)$
      1)   $\sim T \supset [\sim (E \vee C) \vee \sim (S \vee Q)]$   Pr

The symbolized conclusion does not appear in the premise, so it must be constructed. However, it is difficult to work backwards in (5) because of the numerous ways the conclusion might be obtained. In any event, 'C' and 'Q' must be eliminated before reaching that conclusion. Since the only premise is not a conjunction, attempt to use the distribution strategy to remove 'C' and 'Q' from subsequent lines. But the premise is not an inclusive disjunction in which the right-hand disjunct is a conjunction. Notice, however, the two instances of tildes on the outside of punctuation marks in the symbolization of the premise. Remove these tildes by DeMorgan:

**2)** $\sim T \supset [(\sim E \cdot \sim C) \vee \sim (S \vee Q)]$     1, DeM

**3)** $\sim T \supset [(\sim E \cdot \sim C) \vee (\sim S \cdot \sim Q)]$     2, DeM

Convert the horseshoe in 3 into a wedge by Material Implication. Use Association to generate the following lines:

**4)** $\sim\sim T \vee [(\sim E \cdot \sim C) \vee (\sim S \cdot \sim Q)]$     3, Impl

**5)** $[\sim\sim T \vee (\sim E \sim C)] \vee (\sim S \cdot \sim Q)$     4, Assoc

Remove the double tildes and read line 5 as an instance of '$p \vee (q \cdot r)$'. Next use Distribution:

**6)** $[T \vee (\sim E \cdot \sim C)] \vee (\sim S \cdot \sim Q)$     5, DN

**7)** $\{[T \vee (\sim E \cdot \sim C)] \vee \sim S\} \cdot \{[T \vee (\sim E \cdot \sim C)] \vee \sim Q\}$     6, Dist

Simplify out the left-hand conjunct in 7. 'Q', appearing only in the right-hand conjunct, is now left behind:

**8)** $[T \vee (\sim E \cdot \sim C)] \vee \sim S$     7, Simp

Using the distribution strategy, eliminate 'C' in 8. One way to do this is first to convert the statement name in 8 into an instance of '$p \vee (q \cdot r)$'. Then use Distribution, followed by Simplification:

**9)** $\sim S \vee [T \vee (\sim E \cdot \sim C)]$     8, Com

**10)** $(\sim S \vee T) \vee (\sim E \cdot \sim C)$     9, Assoc

**11)** $[(\sim S \vee T) \vee \sim E] \cdot [(\sim S \vee T) \vee \sim C]$     10, Dist

**12)** $(\sim S \vee T) \vee \sim E$     11, Simp

Only those letters occurring in the symbolized conclusion are found in 12. Arrange these letters as they are in the conclusion:

**13)** $\sim E \vee (\sim S \vee T)$     12, Com

Compare the statement name in 13 with '$E \supset (S \supset T)$'. The needed move goes from wedges to horseshoes. Material Implication permits this:

**14)** $E \supset (\sim S \vee T)$     13, Impl

**15)** $/ \therefore\ E \supset (S \supset T)$     14, Impl

***Exportation*** can perhaps be more readily grasped by thinking of English statements. Someone could say, 'If it's thundering and raining, then I'm not going to classes'. Or a person could say, 'If it's thundering, then if it's also raining, I'm not going to classes'. These statements are logically equivalent and provide an instance of Exportation:

$$\textbf{(6)} \quad (T \cdot R) \supset \sim G :: T \supset (R \supset \sim G)$$

Notice that Exportation does not move from wedges to dots or from horseshoes to wedges. Rather, the changes come in the antecedents and consequents of the two overall hypotheticals. The antecedent of one horseshoe statement is a conjunction, whereas the consequent of the other horseshoe statement is itself a hypothetical. Further, the right-hand conjunct in the antecedent that is a conjunction becomes the antecedent of the horseshoe expression that is the consequent of the other hypothetical statement.

Suppose a proof for the following is required:

| | | |
|---|---|---|
| **(7)** | | $/ \therefore A \supset (D \supset E)$ |
| **1)** $A \supset (B \supset C)$ | | Pr |
| **2)** $(D \supset B) \cdot (\sim E \supset \sim C)$ | | Pr |

The conclusion does not appear in the premises. Since there are many possible ways of constructing a statement exhibiting the form 'p $\supset$ (q $\supset$ r)', it is not clear how the conclusion is finally obtained. Yet since neither 'B' nor 'C' appears in the conclusion, they must be left behind before the conclusion is attained.

Unlike (5), (7) has two premises, the second being a conjunction. (7) can be viewed *as if* it has three premises; namely, 'A $\supset$ (B $\supset$ C)', 'D $\supset$ B', and '$\sim$ E $\supset$ $\sim$ C':

| | | |
|---|---|---|
| **(8)** | | $/ \therefore A \supset (D \supset E)$ |
| **1)** $A \supset (B \supset C)$ | | Pr |
| **2)** $(D \supset B) \cdot (\sim E \supset \sim C)$ | | Pr |
| **3)** $D \supset B$ | | 2, Simp |
| **4)** $(\sim E \supset \sim C) \cdot (D \supset B)$ | | 2, Com |
| **5)** $\sim E \supset \sim C$ | | 4, Simp |

Observe that 'B' is the consequent in 3. The other statement (besides that in 2 from which 3 is derived) containing 'B' is the first premise. If 'B' is put in the antecedent position of the first premise, Hypothetical Syllogism could be used with 3 and 1 to eliminate 'B'. Visualize how a combination of ***Exportation*** and Commutation prepares the way for a Hypothetical Syllogism move:

| | | |
|---|---|---|
| **6)** $(A \cdot B) \supset C$ | | 1, Exp |
| **7)** $(B \cdot A) \supset C$ | | 6, Com |
| **8)** $B \supset (A \supset C)$ | | 7, Exp |
| **9)** $D \supset (A \supset C)$ | | 3, 8, HS |

'C', occurring in 5 and 9, drops out of lines in the proof before 'A $\supset$ (D $\supset$ E)' is reached. In 9, 'C' is in a consequent position, while in 5 '$\sim$ C' is a consequent. Using Transposition, 'C $\supset$ E' is available from 5, turning 'C' into an antecedent. Use

Exportation in 9 to prepare for a use of Hypothetical Syllogism, eliminating 'C' from the remainder of the proof:

|  |  |  |
|---|---|---|
| **10)** | C ⊃ E | 5, Trans |
| **11)** | (D · A) ⊃ C | 9, Exp |
| **12)** | (D · A) ⊃ E | 11, 10, HS |

The conclusion is gained by using Commutation on the antecedent in 12, followed by an Exportation move:

|  |  |  |
|---|---|---|
| **13)** | (A · D) ⊃ E | 12, Com |
| **14)** | / ∴ A ⊃ (D ⊃ E) | 13, Exp |

---

## EXERCISES

### Group A:

Give the correct justification in each unjustified line of the following.

1.                      / ∴ A ⊃ C
   1) (A · B) ⊃ C  Pr
   2) B         Pr
   3) (B · A) ⊃ C
   4) B ⊃ (A ⊃ C)
   5) / ∴ A ⊃ C

2.                      / ∴ ~ A
   1) A ⊃ (B · C)  Pr
   2) ~ B       Pr
   3) ~ A ∨ (B · C)
   4) ( ~ A ∨ B) · ( ~ A ∨ C)
   5) ~ A ∨ B
   6) B ∨ ~ A
   7) / ∴ ~ A

3.                          / ∴ D ⊃ (E ⊃ C)
   1) A ⊃ ( ~ C ⊃ ~ B)    Pr
   2) D ⊃ [(A · B) ∨ ~ E]  Pr
   3) A ⊃ (B ⊃ C)
   4) (A · B) ⊃ C
   5) D ⊃ [ ~ E ∨ (A · B)]
   6) D ⊃ [E ⊃ (A · B)]
   7) (D · E) ⊃ (A · B)
   8) (D · E) ⊃ C
   9) / ∴ D ⊃ (E ⊃ C)

4.                    / ∴ B ⊃ D
   1) ~ (A ∨ B) ∨ C  Pr
   2) C ⊃ D         Pr
   3) ( ~ A · ~ B) ∨ C
   4) C ∨ ( ~ A · ~ B)

5) $(C \lor \sim A) \cdot (C \lor \sim B)$
6) $(C \lor \sim B) \cdot (C \lor \sim A)$
7) $C \lor \sim B$
8) $\sim B \lor C$
9) $B \supset C$
10) $/\therefore B \supset D$

5.                                     $/\therefore (\sim C \lor \sim D) \cdot (C \lor D)$

1) $(C \lor D) \lor (A \cdot B)$     Pr
2) $\sim A$     Pr
3) $C \supset (\sim A \supset \sim D)$     Pr
4) $(A \cdot B) \lor (C \lor D)$
5) $\sim A \lor \sim B$
6) $\sim (A \cdot B)$
7) $C \lor D$
8) $C \supset (D \supset A)$
9) $(C \cdot D) \supset A$
10) $\sim (C \cdot D)$
11) $\sim C \lor \sim D$
12) $/\therefore (\sim C \lor \sim D) \cdot (C \lor D)$

6.                                     $/\therefore B \lor D$

1) $\sim (A \cdot \sim B)$     Pr
2) $\sim (C \cdot \sim D) \cdot (\sim A \supset C)$     Pr
3) $\sim (C \cdot \sim D)$
4) $(\sim A \supset C) \cdot \sim (C \cdot \sim D)$
5) $\sim A \supset C$
6) $\sim A \lor \sim \sim B$
7) $\sim A \lor B$
8) $A \supset B$
9) $\sim C \lor \sim \sim D$
10) $\sim C \lor D$
11) $C \supset D$
12) $\sim \sim A \lor C$
13) $A \lor C$
14) $/\therefore B \lor D$

7.                                     $/\therefore \sim C \supset D$

1) $A \supset \sim (B \cdot \sim C)$     Pr
2) $D \lor A$     Pr
3) $D \supset E$     Pr
4) $B \cdot \sim E$     Pr
5) $B$
6) $\sim E \cdot B$
7) $\sim E$
8) $\sim D$
9) $A$
10) $\sim (B \cdot \sim C)$
11) $\sim B \cdot \sim \sim C$
12) $\sim \sim B$
13) $\sim \sim C$
14) $\sim \sim C \lor D$
15) $/\therefore \sim C \supset D$

8.                                           $/\therefore\ \sim(\sim D\cdot\sim F)$

1) $(B\cdot A)\supset C$                  Pr
2) $(\sim E\vee F)\cdot(\sim A\supset E)$    Pr
3) $(C\vee\sim B)\supset D$               Pr
4) $\sim E\vee F$
5) $(\sim A\supset E)\cdot(\sim E\vee F)$
6) $\sim A\supset E$
7) $(A\cdot B)\supset C$
8) $A\supset(B\supset C)$
9) $(\sim B\vee C)\supset D$
10) $(B\supset C)\supset D$
11) $\Lambda\supset D$
12) $E\supset F$
13) $\sim\sim A\vee E$
14) $A\vee E$
15) $D\vee F$
16) $\sim\sim(D\vee F)$
17) $/\therefore\ \sim(\sim D\cdot\sim F)$

9.                                           $/\therefore\ (A\cdot G)\supset(B\supset E)$

1) $[A\supset(B\supset C)]\cdot[D\supset(\sim E\supset\sim C)]$    Pr
2) $G\supset D$                                                Pr
3) $A\supset(B\supset C)$
4) $[D\supset(\sim E\supset\sim C)]\cdot[A\supset(B\supset C)]$
5) $D\supset(\sim E\supset\sim C)$
6) $D\supset(C\supset E)$
7) $(D\cdot C)\supset E$
8) $(C\cdot D)\supset E$
9) $C\supset(D\supset E)$
10) $(A\cdot B)\supset C$
11) $(A\cdot B)\supset(D\supset E)$
12) $[(A\cdot B)\cdot D]\supset E$
13) $[D\cdot(A\cdot B)]\supset E$
14) $D\supset[(A\cdot B)\supset E]$
15) $G\supset[(A\cdot B)\supset E]$
16) $[G\cdot(A\cdot B)]\supset E$
17) $[(G\cdot A)\cdot B]\supset E$
18) $[(A\cdot G)\cdot B]\supset E$
19) $/\therefore\ (A\cdot G)\supset(B\supset E)$

10.                                          $/\therefore A\supset E$

1) $(\sim A\supset\sim B)\supset(C\cdot D)$    Pr
2) $D\supset(C\cdot E)$                      Pr
3) $\sim(\sim A\supset\sim B)\vee(C\cdot D)$
4) $\sim(\sim\sim A\vee\sim B)\vee(C\cdot D)$
5) $\sim(A\vee\sim B)\vee(C\cdot D)$
6) $(\sim A\cdot\sim\sim B)\vee(C\cdot D)$
7) $(\sim A\cdot B)\vee(C\cdot D)$
8) $[(\sim A\cdot B)\vee C]\cdot[(\sim A\cdot B)\vee D]$
9) $[(\sim A\cdot B)\vee D]\cdot[(\sim A\cdot B)\vee C]$
10) $(\sim A\cdot B)\vee D$
11) $D\vee(\sim A\cdot B)$

12) $(D \vee \sim A) \cdot (D \vee B)$
13) $D \vee \sim A$
14) $\sim A \vee D$
15) $A \supset D$
16) $\sim D \vee (C \cdot E)$
17) $(\sim D \vee C) \cdot (\sim D \vee E)$
18) $(\sim D \vee E) \cdot (\sim D \vee C)$
19) $\sim D \vee E$
20) $D \supset E$
21) $/\therefore A \supset E$

## Group B:

Construct a proof of validity for each of the following.

1.  $/\therefore C$
    1) $(A \supset B) \supset C$   Pr
    2) $\sim A$   Pr

2.  $/\therefore B \supset [C \supset (A \supset D)]$
    1) $A \supset [B \supset (C \supset D)]$   Pr

3.  $/\therefore A \supset D$
    1) $A \supset (B \cdot C)$   Pr
    2) $\sim B$   Pr

4.  $/\therefore A \supset (\sim D \supset \sim B)$
    1) $A \supset (B \supset C)$   Pr
    2) $\sim (C \cdot \sim D)$   Pr

5.  $/\therefore G \supset C$
    1) $A \supset (\sim C \supset \sim D)$   Pr
    2) $G \supset [A \cdot (B \cdot D)]$   Pr

6.  $/\therefore (B \supset \sim D) \supset \sim A$
    1) $A \supset (B \cdot C)$   Pr
    2) $A \supset (C \cdot D)$   Pr

7.  $/\therefore (F \cdot E) \supset (B \supset D)$
    1) $A \supset [B \supset (C \supset D)]$   Pr
    2) $(A \supset \sim C) \supset \sim E$   Pr

8.  $/\therefore A \supset (B \cdot D)$
    1) $A \supset (C \cdot B)$   Pr
    2) $(C \cdot D) \vee (\sim A \cdot C)$   Pr

9.  $/\therefore (A \cdot B) \supset (C \supset D)$
    1) $C \supset (E \supset D)$   Pr
    2) $E \vee F$   Pr
    3) $(F \cdot B) \supset \sim A$   Pr

10.  $/\therefore A \supset \sim C$
    1) $(A \cdot B) \supset [C \supset (D \cdot E)]$   Pr
    2) $\sim (B \supset E)$   Pr

**Group C:**

Symbolize the following arguments using the suggested capital letters. Then construct a proof of validity for each.

1. If cells make up tissue, then tissue forms an organ only if homologues are discovered in pairs. Tissue forms an organ. So, assuming cells make up tissue, homologues are discovered in pairs. (M,F,D)

2. Either it isn't the case that a particular cell doesn't divide or can't carry out photosynthesis, or we know it is a nerve cell. Thus, that a cell doesn't divide is a sufficient condition for knowing it is a nerve cell. (D,C,K)

3. Either Dottie learns Fortran and studies statistics, or she takes theory of equations while learning Fortran. She doesn't take theory of equations. Accordingly, it isn't the case that she studies statistics only if she takes theory of equations. (L,S,T)

4. If John is interested in classical ballet, then if he is appreciative of the Russian form, he is excited by *Swan Lake* if he is knowledgeable of Tchaikovsky. John is both appreciative of the Russian form and knowledgeable of Tchaikovsky. Therefore, John isn't interested in classical ballet unless he is also excited by *Swan Lake*. (I,A,E,K)

5. That Mary G. takes the case is a sufficient condition for the following; namely, if she prepares the case well this means she will win in court. Mary G. won't win in court provided that she doesn't favorably impress the court; yet, on the other hand, if Mary G. labors long hours for her client, she prepares the case well. Consequently, if Mary G. takes the case, then she labors long hours for her client only if she favorably impresses the court. (T,P,W,I,L)

6. Dottie is interested in computer software only if she studies computing machinery while mastering programming; yet, if she is proficient in "hi-tech," then she is interested in computer software if she studies computing machinery. That she studies computing machinery is a sufficient condition for Dottie's both being knowledgeable in twentieth century technology as well as mastering programming. Thus, Dottie is both proficient in "hi-tech" and studies computing machinery only if she is knowledgeable in twentieth century technology. (I,S,M,P,K)

7. Either it isn't the case that Napoleon Bonaparte escaped from Elba and didn't win at Waterloo, or he was defeated even though he escaped from Elba. Assuming that Napoleon was defeated, then if he escaped from Elba, he didn't permanently restore the Empire. Wherefore, if Napoleon permanently restored the Empire, then he didn't win at Waterloo only if he didn't escape from Elba. (E,W,D,R)

8. Assuming Wellington won at Waterloo and Napoleon was exiled to St. Helena, Europe wasn't jeopardized by French domination. Now Napoleon was both exiled to St. Helena and never returned alive to France provided that both Wellington did win at Waterloo and Europe wasn't jeopardized by French domination. So, that Wellington won at Waterloo is a sufficient condition for the following: Europe wasn't jeopardized by French domination or Napoleon wasn't exiled to St. Helena; on the other hand, Europe was jeopardized by French domination or Napoleon was exiled to St. Helena. (W,E,J,R)

9. That we both study the music of Thomas Tallis while also being familiar with "The Lamentations of Jeremiah" is a necessary condition for the following: Either we know "With Weeping and Mourning" or are familiar with "The Lamentations of Jeremiah." Hence, assuming that we know "With Weeping and Mourning" and are interested in "The Seasons," then we are familiar with "The Lamentations of Jeremiah." (S,F,K,I)

10. Assuming we study Claudio Monteverdi, then we are either interested in his laments and know "Amor" or appreciate his lyric style and are familiar with "Chiome d'oro." It isn't the case that we both know "Amor" and are interested in Monteverdi's laments. Thus, if we both know "Amor" and study Monteverdi, we aren't interested in his laments but are familiar with "Chiome d'oro." (S,I,K,A,F)

---

## 5. EQUIVALENCE AND TAUTOLOGY

### EQUIVALENCE (EQUIV)

$p \equiv q :: (p \supset q) \cdot (q \supset p)$

$p \equiv q :: (p \cdot q) \vee ({\sim}p \cdot {\sim}q)$

$p \,\triangle\, q :: (p \vee q) \cdot ({\sim}p \vee {\sim}q)$

$p \,\triangle\, q :: (p \cdot {\sim}q) \vee (q \cdot {\sim}p)$

### TAUTOLOGY (TAUT)

$p :: p \cdot p$

$p :: p \vee p$

*Equivalence* deals with statements symbolized by using either the triple bar or the delta. *Tautology* allows the number of occurrences of a statement name to be reduced or increased.

(1) If a cell is placed in a hypertonic solution, it will lyse only if it doesn't remain unchanged. Yet if a cell is placed in a hypertonic solution, it will lyse whenever it doesn't remain unchanged. Thus, if a cell is placed in a hypertonic solution, then it will lyse when and only when it doesn't remain unchanged. (P,L,R)

Symbolizing (1) yields

(2)                     $/ \therefore P \supset (L \equiv {\sim}R)$

1) $P \supset (L \supset {\sim}R)$    Pr

2) $P \supset ({\sim}R \supset L)$    Pr

Since the symbolized conclusion of (2) does not appear in the symbolized premises, and there are no conjunctions to be broken down or statements to be eliminated from the premises, work backwards. The conclusion is a hypothetical having a biconditional as its consequent. Because this biconditional does not occur in the premises, it is constructed. Going backwards, if '$P \supset [(L \supset {\sim}R) \cdot ({\sim}R \supset L)]$' is found, then '$P \supset (L \equiv {\sim}R)$' can be asserted by Equivalence:

$/ \therefore P \supset (L \equiv {\sim}R)$

1) $P \supset (L \supset {\sim}R)$    Pr

2) $P \supset ({\sim}R \supset L)$    Pr

.

.

.

?) $P \supset [(L \supset {\sim}R) \cdot ({\sim}R \supset L)]$    ??

?) $/ \therefore P \supset (L \equiv {\sim}R)$          ?, Equiv

Continue to work backwards. Notice (2) has exactly *two* premises. In moving backwards to the premises, it is possible to break up 'P ⊃ [(L ⊃ ~ R) • (~ R ⊃ L)]' into *two* statement names. Change the horseshoe into a wedge and use Distribution:

$$/\therefore P \supset (L \equiv \sim R)$$

**1)** P ⊃ (L ⊃ ~ R)   Pr
**2)** P ⊃ ( ~ R ⊃ L)   Pr

        .
        .
        .

**?)** [ ~ P ∨ (L ⊃ ~ R)] • [ ~ P ∨ ( ~ R ⊃ L)]    ?,?, Conj
**?)**  ~ P ∨ [(L ⊃ ~ R) • ( ~ R ⊃ L)]              ?, Dist
**?)** P ⊃ [(L ⊃ ~ R) • ( ~ R ⊃ L)]                ?, Impl
**?)** /∴ P ⊃ (L ≡ ~ R)                            ?, Equiv

Compare the two conjuncts obtained in the last line of working backwards with the two premises. These two conjuncts are generated from the premises by two uses of Material Implication. A complete proof is now at hand:

**(3)**                     /∴P ⊃ (L ≡ ~ R)

**1)** P ⊃ (L ⊃ ~ R)   Pr
**2)** P ⊃ ( ~ R ⊃ L)   Pr
**3)**  ~ P ∨ (L ⊃ ~ R)                              1, Impl
**4)**  ~ P ∨ ( ~ R ⊃ L)                             2, Impl
**5)** [ ~ P ∨ [(L ⊃ ~ R)] • [ ~ P ∨ ( ~ R ⊃ L)]    3,4, Conj
**6)**  ~ P ∨ [(L ⊃ ~ R) • ( ~ R ⊃ L)]              5, Dist
**7)** P ⊃ [(L ⊃ ~ R) • ( ~ R ⊃ L)]                6, Impl
**8)** /∴ P ⊃ (L ≡ ~ R)                            7, Equiv

Study this argument:

**(4)**   It isn't the case that either we accept Aristotle's cosmology or recognize his teleological viewpoint (but not both). Thus, we accept Aristotle's cosmology if and only if we recognize his teleological viewpoint. (A,R)

Use the suggested capital letters to symbolized (4):

**(5)**                     /∴ A ≡ R
**1)**  ~ (A Δ R)   Pr

While two equivalence rules can be used with the premise of (5), select

$$p \,\Delta\, q :: (p \cdot \sim q) \vee (q \cdot \sim p)$$

As a strategy, when converting statements of the form ' ~ (p ≡ q)' or ' ~ (p Δ q)', think of using the equivalence forms 'p ≡ q :: (p • q) ∨ ( ~ p • ~ q)' or 'p Δ q :: (p • ~ q) ∨ (q • ~ p)'. A conjunction can then be obtained by an appeal to DeMorgan.

Applying this strategy in (5) yields:

$$/ \therefore A \equiv R$$

| | | |
|---|---|---|
| **1)** | $\sim (A \triangle R)$ | Pr |
| **2)** | $\sim [(A \cdot \sim R) \vee (R \cdot \sim A)]$ | 1, Equiv |
| **3)** | $\sim (A \cdot \sim R) \cdot \sim (R \cdot \sim A)$ | 2, DeM |

If '$(A \supset R) \cdot (R \supset A)$' is found, '$A \equiv R$' is reached by Equivalence. Compare the statement name in 3 with '$(A \supset R) \cdot (R \supset A)$', and the following proof is suggested:

**(6)**                    $/ \therefore A \equiv R$

| | | |
|---|---|---|
| **1)** | $\sim (A \triangle R)$ | Pr |
| **2)** | $\sim [(A \cdot \sim R) \vee (R \cdot \sim A)]$ | 1, Equiv |
| **3)** | $\sim (A \cdot \sim R) \cdot \sim (R \cdot \sim A)$ | 2, DeM |
| **4)** | $(\sim A \vee \sim \sim R) \cdot \sim (R \cdot \sim A)$ | 3, DeM |
| **5)** | $(\sim A \vee R) \cdot \sim (R \cdot \sim A)$ | 4, DN |
| **6)** | $(A \supset R) \cdot \sim (R \cdot \sim A)$ | 5, Impl |
| **7)** | $(A \supset R) \cdot (\sim R \vee \sim \sim R)$ | 6, DeM |
| **8)** | $(A \supset R) \cdot (\sim R \vee A)$ | 7, DN |
| **9)** | $(A \supset R) \cdot (R \supset A)$ | 8, Impl |
| **10)** | $/ \therefore A \equiv R$ | 9, Equiv |

Cases can occur in constructing a proof in which too many occurrences of a statement appear in the proof before reaching the conclusion. These are not situations where one wishes to eliminate a statement. Rather, the number of occurrences of a statement needs to be reduced. A simple example of such a situation appears in this argument:

**(7)**   If it rains, the ground is wet. Yet if the irrigation system is operating, the ground is wet. It is either raining or the irrigation system is operating. So, the ground is wet. (R,W,O)

A use of Constructive Syllogism produces the following proof:

**(8)**                    $/ \therefore W$

| | | |
|---|---|---|
| **1)** | $R \supset W$ | Pr |
| **2)** | $O \supset W$ | Pr |
| **3)** | $R \vee O$ | Pr |
| **4)** | $W \vee W$ | 1, 2, 3, CD |

However, line 4 is not the conclusion of (7). Nor does 'W' need to be elemenated from line 4. Rather, the number of occurrences of 'W' in 4 must be reduced. In cases such as this, *Tautology* is a useful equivalence form to consider using because it allows the number of occurrences of a statement name to be reduced or increased.

Consider this more complicated argument using Tautology:

**(9)**   Tim comes only if his car is working. That Tim's car is working and he does come is a sufficient condition for Freddie's bringing the refreshments. A necessary condition for Tim's car working and his coming, while Freddie brings the refreshments, is that the party is a success. So, Tim comes only if the party is a success. (C,W,B,S)

Symbolize (9) as

**(10)**                                        $/\therefore\ C \supset S$

1) $C \supset W$                Pr

2) $(W \cdot C) \supset B$            Pr

3) $\lceil (W \cdot C) \cdot B \rceil \supset S$    Pr

Examine (10). 'W' and 'B' appear in the premises but not in the conclusion. Further, while 'C' occurs once in the conclusion, it appears three times in the premises. 'W' and 'B' must be eliminated before reaching the conclusion, while the number of occurrences of 'C' needs to be reduced. Strategically, whenever the number of occurrences of a statement found in compound statements must be reduced, consider Tautology. The *tautology strategy* is especially useful if the occurrences to be reduced appear in the same compound statement name.

How might 'W' be eliminated? Two considerations suggest a use of Hypothetical Syllogism: 'W' is found in at least two premises and each of these premises is a hypothetical. Since 'W' is the consequent in the first premise, an attempt might be made to establish 'W' as an antecedent in some other line. The second premise yields such an antecedent:

4) $W \supset (C \supset B)$  2, Exp

5) $C \supset (C \supset B)$  1, 4, HS

Then reduce the number of occurrences of 'C' in 5:

6) $(C \cdot C) \supset B$  5, Exp

7) $C \supset B$          6, Taut

'B' does not occur in the conclusion. Given 'B' in the consequent position in line 7, can 'B' be established as an antecedent of some hypothetical statement? Look at line 3 and watch how this is done:

8) $[B \cdot (W \cdot C)] \supset S$    3, Com

9) $B \supset [(W \cdot C) \supset S]$  8, Exp

10) $C \supset [(W \cdot C) \supset S]$  7, 9, HS

Once more 'C' occurs twice in a compound statement name. Move to a use of the tautology strategy and continue the proof:

11) $[C \cdot (W \cdot C)] \supset S$  10, Exp

> **12)** $[C \cdot (C \cdot W)] \supset S$    11, Com
> **13)** $[(C \cdot C) \cdot W] \supset S$    12, Assoc
> **14)** $(C \cdot W) \supset S$        13, Taut

By appealing to the third premise, 'W' has been reintroduced into the proof. However, since 'W' appears as the consequent in 1 and in the antecedent in 14, another use of Hypothetical Syllogism is at hand:

> **15)** $(W \cdot C) \supset S$    14, Com
> **16)** $W \supset (C \supset S)$    15, Exp
> **17)** $C \supset (C \supset S)$    1, 16, HS

Employing Exportation and Tautology, the proof is completed:

> **18)** $(C \cdot C) \supset S$    17, Exp
> **19)** $/ \therefore\ C \supset S$    18, Taut

Other proofs for (9) can be generated. Instead of establishing '$C \supset [(W \cdot C) \supset S]$' in 10, for example, proceed in this way:

> **10)** $(W \cdot C) \supset [\,(W \cdot C) \supset S]$    2, 9, HS
> **11)** $[(W \cdot C) \cdot (W \cdot C)] \supset S$    10, Exp
> **12)** $(W \cdot C) \supset S$    11, Taut
> **13)** $W \supset (C \supset S)$    12, Exp
> **14)** $C \supset (C \supset S)$    1, 13, HS
> **15)** $(C \cdot C) \supset S$    14, Exp
> **16)** $/ \therefore\ C \supset S$    15, Taut

Finally, the following is an even shorter proof:

**(11)**

> **1)** $C \supset W$    Pr
> **2)** $(W \cdot C) \supset B$    Pr
> **3)** $[(W \cdot C) \cdot B] \supset S$    Pr
> **4)** $[B \cdot (W \cdot C)] \supset S$    3, Com
> **5)** $B \supset [(W \cdot C) \supset S]$    4, Exp
> **6)** $(W \cdot C) \supset [(W \cdot C) \supset S]$    2, 5, HS
> **7)** $[(W \cdot C) \cdot (W \cdot C)] \supset S$    6, Exp
> **8)** $(W \cdot C) \supset S$    7, Taut
> **9)** $W \supset (C \supset S)$    8, Exp
> **10)** $C \supset (C \supset S)$    1, 9, HS

11) $(C \cdot C) \supset S$         10, Exp

12) $/ \therefore C \supset S$        11, Taut

---

## EXERCISES

### Group A:

Give the correct justification in each unjustified line of the following.

1.            $/ \therefore C$
   1) $A \supset (\sim C \supset \sim B)$    Pr
   2) $\sim C \supset (A \cdot B)$       Pr
   3) $A \supset (B \supset C)$
   4) $(A \cdot B) \supset C$
   5) $\sim C \supset C$
   6) $\sim \sim C \vee C$
   7) $C \vee C$
   8) $/ \therefore C$

2.           $/ \therefore A \, \Delta \, B$
   1) $A \equiv \sim B$    Pr
   2) $(A \supset \sim B) \cdot (\sim B \supset A)$
   3) $(\sim A \vee \sim B) \cdot (\sim B \supset A)$
   4) $(\sim A \vee \sim B) \cdot (\sim \sim B \vee A)$
   5) $(\sim A \vee \sim B) \cdot (B \vee A)$
   6) $(\sim A \vee \sim B) \cdot (A \vee B)$
   7) $(A \vee B) \cdot (\sim A \vee \sim B)$
   8) $/ \therefore A \, \Delta \, B$

3.            $/ \therefore A \supset (B \supset D)$
   1) $A \supset (B \supset C)$     Pr
   2) $(B \cdot C) \supset D$      Pr
   3) $(A \cdot B) \supset C$
   4) $(C \cdot B) \supset D$
   5) $C \supset (B \supset D)$
   6) $(A \cdot B) \supset (B \supset D)$
   7) $[(A \cdot B) \cdot B] \supset D$
   8) $[A \cdot (B \cdot B)] \supset D$
   9) $(A \cdot B) \supset D$
   10) $/ \therefore A \supset (B \supset D)$

4.            $/ \therefore A \supset \sim D$
   1) $[A \supset (B \supset C)] \cdot [A \supset (C \supset B)]$    Pr
   2) $(C \equiv B) \supset \sim D$            Pr
   3) $A \supset (B \supset C)$
   4) $[A \supset (C \supset B)] \cdot [A \supset (B \supset C)]$
   5) $A \supset (C \supset B)$
   6) $\sim A \vee (C \supset B)$
   7) $\sim A \vee (B \supset C)$
   8) $[\sim A \vee (C \supset B)] \cdot [\sim A \vee (B \supset C)]$

9) ~ A ∨ [(C ⊃ B) · (B ⊃ C)]
10) ~ A ∨ (C ≡ B)
11) A ⊃ (C ≡ B)
12) /∴ A ⊃ ~ D

5.                                         /∴ C
1) [(A · B) ⊃ C] · (E ⊃ C)   Pr
2) (A · B) ∨ (E · A)         Pr
3) (A · B) ⊃ C
4) (E ⊃ C) · [(A · B) ⊃ C]
5) E ⊃ C
6) A ⊃ (B ⊃ C)
7) (A · B) ∨ (A · E)
8) A · (B ∨ E)
9) A
10) B ⊃ C
11) (B ∨ E) · A
12) B ∨ E
13) C ∨ C
14) /∴ C

6.                                       /∴ A Δ D
1) ~ A ∨ (~ D · C)        Pr
2) (~ D ⊃ B) · (~ A ⊃ ~ B)   Pr
3) ~ D ⊃ B
4) (~ A ⊃ ~ B) · (~ D ⊃ B)
5) ~ A ⊃ ~ B
6) ~ B ⊃ ~ ~ D
7) ~ B ⊃ D
8) ~ A ⊃ D
9) ~ ~ A ∨ D
10) A ∨ D
11) (~ A ∨ ~ D) · (~ A ∨ C)
12) ~ A ∨ ~ D
13) (A ∨ D) · (~ A ∨ ~ D)
14) /∴ A Δ D

7.                                       /∴ B
1) A ⊃ (B Δ C)         Pr
2) ~ (~ D · C) · (A · ~ D)   Pr
3) (A · ~ D) · ~ (~ D · C)
4) A · ~ D
5) A
6) B Δ C
7) ~ (~ D · C)
8) ~ ~ D ∨ ~ C
9) D ∨ ~ C
10) ~ D · A
11) ~ D
12) ~ C
13) (B ∨ C) · (~ B ∨ ~ C)
14) B ∨ C

15)  C ∨ B
16)  / ∴ B

8.                                        / ∴ ~ (C ≡ D)
   1)  (A · B) ∨ (C ∨ D)    Pr
   2)  ~ A                  Pr
   3)  C ⊃ ( ~ A ⊃ ~ D)  Pr
   4)  (C ∨ D) ∨ (A · B)
   5)  [(C ∨ D) ∨ A] · [(C ∨ D) ∨ B]
   6)  (C ∨ D) ∨ A
   7)  A ∨ (C ∨ D)
   8)  C ∨ D
   9)  C ⊃ (D ⊃ A)
   10)  (C · D) ⊃ A
   11)  ~ (C · D)
   12)  ~ ~ (C ∨ D)
   13)  ~ ( ~ C · ~ D)
   14)  ~ (C · D) · ~ ( ~ C · ~ D)
   15)  ~ [(C · D) ∨ ( ~ C · ~ D)]
   16)  / ∴ ~ (C ≡ D)

9.                                        / ∴ C ≡ E
   1)  A ∨ [( ~ C · B) ∨ (E · D)]    Pr
   2)  ~ A · ~ (E · ~ C)             Pr
   3)  ~ A
   4)  ~ (E · ~ C) · ~ A
   5)  ~ (E · ~ C)
   6)  ~ E ∨ ~ ~ C
   7)  ~ E ∨ C
   8)  E ⊃ C
   9)  ( ~ C · B) ∨ (E · D)
   10)  [( ~ C · B) ∨ E] · [( ~ C · B) ∨ D]
   11)  ( ~ C · B) ∨ E
   12)  E ∨ ( ~ C · B)
   13)  (E ∨ ~ C) · (E ∨ B)
   14)  E ∨ ~ C
   15)  ~ C ∨ E
   16)  C ⊃ E
   17)  (C ⊃ E) · (E ⊃ C)
   18)  / ∴ C ≡ E

10.                              / ∴ G ⊃ D
   1)  A ⊃ (B ⊃ ~ C)    Pr
   2)  C ⊃ (B · A)       Pr
   3)  (A · C) ∨ (D · E)  Pr
   4)  (A · B) ⊃ ~ C
   5)  (B · A) ⊃ ~ C
   6)  C ⊃ ~ C
   7)  ~ C ∨ ~ C
   8)  ~ C
   9)  [(A · C) ∨ D] · [(A · C) ∨ E]
   10)  (A · C) ∨ D

11) D ∨ (A · C)
12) D ∨ (C · A)
13) (D ∨ C) · (D ∨ A)
14) D ∨ C
15) C ∨ D
16) D
17) D ∨ ~ G
18) ~ G ∨ D
19) / ∴ G ⊃ D

## Group B:

Construct a proof of validity for each of the following.

1.                      / ∴ A ⊃ C
   1) A ⊃ B         Pr
   2) (A · B) ⊃ C   Pr

2.                          / ∴ A Δ B
   1) ~ (A ≡ B)      Pr

3.                   / ∴ A ⊃ C
   1) A ≡ B        Pr
   2) C Δ ~ B     Pr

4.                          / ∴ A ∨ D
   1) ~ A ⊃ B            Pr
   2) B ⊃ ( ~ C ⊃ A)     Pr
   3) ~ D ⊃ ~ C          Pr

5.                          / ∴ ~ A ≡ D
   1) ~ (A · B) ⊃ (C · A)   Pr
   2) ~ D ∨ ~ A             Pr

6.                          / ∴ A ⊃ (B Δ C)
   1) ~ (A · B) ⊃ C   Pr
   2) ~ B             Pr

7.                          / ∴ C ⊃ D
   1) A ⊃ (B ⊃ D)   Pr
   2) C ⊃ (B ⊃ A)   Pr
   3) ~ B ⊃ ~ C     Pr

8.                          / ∴ A Δ B
   1) ~ (A ≡ ~ B) ⊃ C   Pr
   2) A ⊃ (C ⊃ ~ D)     Pr
   3) ~ ( ~ A ∨ ~ D)    Pr

9.                          / ∴ B
   1) A ≡ B              Pr
   2) C Δ ~ B            Pr
   3) ~ A ⊃ ( ~ D ⊃ C)  Pr
   4) ~ D                Pr

10.                         / ∴ C ≡ B
   1) A ⊃ ~ (B · ~ C)    Pr
   2) ~ [ ~ (B ∨ D) · C] Pr
   3) A · ~ D            Pr

**Group C:**

Symbolize the following arguments using the suggested capital letters. Then construct a proof of validity for each.

1. Cassius won't be defeated if and only if the Senate doesn't meet. The people of Rome revolt just in case Cassius isn't defeated. Accordingly, if the people of Rome revolt, the Senate won't meet. (D,M,R)

2. In accounting, either the statement of retained earnings is correct or the income statement isn't accurate, but not both. Hence, the statement of retained earnings is correct when and only when the income statement is accurate. (C,A)

3. A person can be morally good if and only if there are obtainable intrinsic values. If there are obtainable intrinsic values, then only if a person is able to put those values into practice can that person be morally good. So, if there are obtainable intrinsic values, a person is able to put these values into practice. (G,V,P)

4. Specific order cost accounting isn't used by a manufacturer except when process cost accounting is employed. Therefore, it isn't the case that either process cost accounting is employed or specific order cost accounting, but not both, is used. (U,E)

5. Increases in real wages are needed to provide workers with an adequate share of benefits or equity requires decreases in the buying power of wages, but not both. Equity requires decreases in the buying power of wages or a rise in real earnings isn't essential for the sustained growth of mass consumer markets, but not both. Consequently, increases in real wages are needed to provide workers with an adequate share of benefits or a rise in real earnings is essential for the sustained growth of mass consumer markets. (I,D,G)

6. If you pass this course, you've worked long hours and curtailed many social activities. You've either worked long hours or curtailed many social activities, but not both. If you've worked long hours, you're exhausted; but if you've curtailed many social activities, you're disappointed. Subsequently, while you haven't passed this course, nonetheless you're either exhausted or disappointed. (P,W,C,E,D)

7. Unless I wish to be happy, I don't desire to be moral; also I wish to be happy if I love my neighbor. Furthermore, either I attempt to know myself while desiring to be moral, or I love my neighbor and attempt to know myself. Hence, it isn't true that if I wish to be happy, I don't attempt to know myself. (W,D,L,A)

8. Napoleon Bonaparte was exiled to St. Helena only if he lost at Waterloo. Moreover, that Napoleon didn't lose at Waterloo is a necessary condition for the following not being the case: If Alexander, Czar of Russia, didn't form the Holy Alliance, Napoleon wasn't exiled to St. Helena. Either it isn't true that Europe was jeopardized by Napoleon although Alexander formed the Holy Alliance, or Europe wasn't jeopardized by Napoleon. So, if Napoleon was exiled to St. Helena, Europe wasn't jeopardized by him. (E,L,F,J)

9. If we are fond of baroque music and appreciate the works of J. S. Bach, then we'll enjoy the compositions of Antonio Vivaldi. Whenever we appreciate the works of Bach and enjoy the compositions of Vivaldi, we're both delighted by musical ornamentation and fond of baroque music. Therefore, if we appreciate the works of Bach, then we enjoy the compositions of Vivaldi or aren't fond of baroque music—but not both. (F,A,E,D)

10. We truly love a person when and only when we don't try to possess that person as an object; moreover, either we try to possess a person as an object or desire that person's good irrespective of our own (but not both). If truly loving a person is a necessary and sufficient condition for desiring that person's good irrespective of our own, then we don't curtail that person's moral freedom but are reasonable in our expectations of that person.

We must allow a person moral freedom or curtail it, and moreover either we aren't reasonable in our expectations of that person or we follow the dictates of reason. Consequently, we must allow a person moral freedom while also following the dictates of reason. (L,P,D,C,R,A,F)

## 6. REVIEW OF NEW TERMS

**Association (Assoc):** The equivalence forms
$$p \cdot (q \cdot r) :: (p \cdot q) \cdot r$$
$$p \vee (q \vee r) :: (p \vee q) \vee r$$

**Commutation (Com):** The equivalence forms
$$p \vee q :: q \vee p$$
$$p \cdot q :: q \cdot p$$
$$p \triangle q :: q \triangle p$$
$$p \equiv q :: q \equiv p$$

**DeMorgan's Laws (DeM):** The equivalence forms
$$\sim p \vee \sim q :: \sim (p \cdot q)$$
$$\sim p \cdot \sim q :: \sim (p \vee q)$$

**Distribution (Dist):** The equivalence forms
$$p \vee (q \cdot r) :: (p \vee q) \cdot (p \vee r)$$
$$p \cdot (q \vee r) :: (p \cdot q) \vee (p \cdot r)$$

**Double Negation (DN):** The equivalence form
$$p :: \sim \sim p$$

**Equivalence (Equiv):** The equivalence forms
$$p \equiv q :: (p \supset q) \cdot (q \supset p)$$
$$p \equiv q :: (p \cdot q) \vee (\sim p \cdot \sim q)$$
$$p \triangle q :: (p \vee q) \cdot (\sim p \vee \sim q)$$
$$p \triangle q :: (p \cdot \sim q) \vee (q \cdot \sim p)$$

**Equivalence form:** A rule of transformation that guarantees validity when all the statement variables are replaced by statement names—the same statement name replacing each occurrence of the same statement variable. An equivalence form can be read from left to right and from right to left. An equivalence form can be applied to an entire statement or a smaller statement that is a part of a larger one.

**Exportation (Exp):** The equivalence form
$$(p \cdot q) \supset r :: p \supset (q \supset r)$$

**Material Implication (Impl):** The equivalence form
$$p \supset q :: \sim p \vee q$$

**Replacement Sign ('::'):** Used in depicting equivalence forms.

**Tautology (Taut):** The equivalence forms
$$p :: p \cdot p$$
$$p :: p \vee p$$

**Transposition (Trans):** The equivalence form
$$p \supset q :: \sim q \supset \sim p$$

# 7

# TRUTH-FUNCTIONAL LOGIC: FINAL CONSIDERATIONS

By themselves, the rules introduced in Chapters 5 and 6 are not sufficient to prove the validity of every valid truth-functional argument. These rules, therefore, are not complete for truth-functional logic. Either the conditional method of proving validity or the indirect method of proving validity (but not both) is needed to complete deductive procedures in truth-functional logic.* While it will be seen that the indirect method of proving validity is a special case of the conditional method, nonetheless both these methods are introduced and developed in the first two sections of this chapter. It can be more convenient to use one rather than the other in various situations. With these new methods, a proof of validity can be constructed for any valid truth-functional argument. The next three sections introduce non-truth table and non-truth tree techniques for deciding the consistency or inconsistency of truth-functional premises, for deciding if a truth-functional statement is tautological, and for deciding if truth-functional statements are logically equivalent.

## 1. THE CONDITIONAL METHOD OF PROVING VALIDITY

Read this example:

(1) It isn't true both that our known enemies or covertly dangerous governments attack us while our allies don't come to our

---

*Some logicians introduce this argument form into the rules of the truth-functional logic:

$$\frac{p \supset q}{/ \therefore \ p \supset (p \cdot q)}$$

The rule, *Absorption*, completes truth-functional logic in the sense that any truth-functional argument that is valid can be proved valid by the rules introduced in Chapters 5 and 6 along with Absorption.

aid. Hence, assuming either our known enemies or covertly dangerous governments attack us, covertly dangerous governments or our known enemies attack us and our allies come to our aid. (E,G,A)

The validity of (1) can be established by a truth table.* Begin by symbolizing the argument:

**(2)**                                                                /∴ (E ∨ G) ⊃ [(G ∨ E) · A]
             **1)**  ~ [(E ∨ G) · ~ A]   Pr

An argument is deductively valid if and only if when all the premises are true the conclusion must also be true. Corresponding to every argument interpreted deductively is a hypothetical statement in which the conjunction of the premises is the antecedent and the conclusion is the consequent. If this hypothetical statement is

---

*The validity of this argument can also be established by the following truth tree:

/∴ (E ∨ G) ⊃ [(G ∨ E) · A]

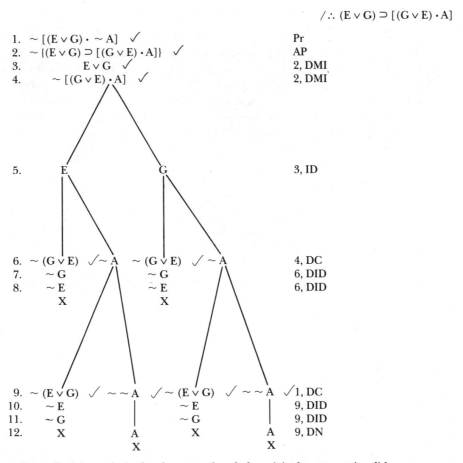

Since all of the paths in the above are closed, the original argument is valid.

tautological, the argument is valid. Otherwise, the argument is invalid. So, form a hypothetical statement corresponding to (2), and construct a truth table:

(3)

| ~ | [(E | ∨ | G) | · | ~ | A] | ⊃ | {[(E | ∨ | G) | ⊃ | [(G | ∨ | E) | · | A]} |
|---|---|---|---|---|---|---|---|---|---|---|---|---|---|---|---|
| 1 | 1 | 1 | 1 | 0 | 0 | 1 | 1 | 1 | 1 | 1 | 1 | 1 | 1 | 1 | 1 | 1 |
| 0 | 1 | 1 | 1 | 1 | 1 | 0 | 1 | 1 | 1 | 1 | 0 | 1 | 1 | 1 | 0 | 0 |
| 1 | 1 | 1 | 0 | 0 | 0 | 1 | 1 | 1 | 1 | 0 | 1 | 0 | 1 | 1 | 1 | 1 |
| 0 | 1 | 1 | 0 | 1 | 1 | 0 | 1 | 1 | 1 | 0 | 0 | 0 | 1 | 1 | 0 | 0 |
| 1 | 0 | 1 | 1 | 0 | 0 | 1 | 1 | 0 | 1 | 1 | 1 | 1 | 1 | 0 | 1 | 1 |
| 0 | 0 | 1 | 1 | 1 | 1 | 0 | 1 | 0 | 1 | 1 | 0 | 1 | 1 | 0 | 0 | 0 |
| 1 | 0 | 0 | 0 | 0 | 0 | 1 | 1 | 0 | 0 | 0 | 1 | 0 | 0 | 0 | 0 | 1 |
| 1 | 0 | 0 | 0 | 0 | 1 | 0 | 1 | 0 | 0 | 0 | 1 | 0 | 0 | 0 | 0 | 0 |

⇑

Since the hypothetical corresponding to the argument is tautological, the argument is valid. Nevertheless, given only the methods of constructing proofs introduced in Chapters 5 and 6, a proof of validity cannot be constructed for (1). *Methods of proof construction* must be augmented to include such arguments.

To discuss Conditional Proof, assume any argument having a hypothetical conclusion. Let 'P' stand for the conjunction of all the premises of that argument, 'A' the antecedent, and 'C' the consequent of the conclusion. This argument schema is produced:

(4)        / ∴ A ⊃ C
      P

Corresponding to every argument is a hypothetical statement in which the antecedent is all the premises put into conjunction, and the consequent is the conclusion of the argument. A hypothetical schema can be constructed corresponding to (4):

(5)   P ⊃ (A ⊃ C)

If whatever statement represented by (5) is tautological, the corresponding argument depicted by (4) is deductively valid. If that statement pictured by (5) is either contingent or contradictory, the argument suggested by (4) is deductively invalid. The rationale behind these relations is based on the definitional rule governing the horseshoe. The only truth-condition making a statement of the form 'p ⊃ q' false is when the antecedent is true and the consequent false. Given the relation of (5) to (4), such a situation arises if and only if at least one truth-condition makes all the premises of an argument true and the conclusion false. That is, the statement designated by (5) is not tautological just in those cases where the argument depicted by (4) is not valid.

Consider this argument schema:

(6)        / ∴ C
      P
      A

A hypothetical schema corresponds to (6):

$$\textbf{(7)} \quad (P \cdot A) \supset C$$

If '$(P \cdot A) \supset C$' represents a tautology, then

$$/ \therefore C$$
$$P$$
$$A$$

depicts an argument that is deductively valid. If '$(P \cdot A) \supset C$' stands for a contingent or contradictory statement,

$$/ \therefore C$$
$$P$$
$$A$$

pictures an argument that is deductively invalid. Now, let '$P$', '$A$', and '$C$' stand for the same statements in both '$P \supset (A \supset C)$' and '$(P \cdot A) \supset C$'. In this case '$P \supset (A \supset C)$' and '$(P \cdot A) \supset C$' are logically equivalent by Exportation. Consequently, if '$P \supset (A \supset C)$' represents a tautology, so does '$(P \cdot A) \supset C$', and vice versa. On the other hand, if '$P \supset (A \supset C)$' exemplifies a contingent or contradictory statement, so does '$(P \cdot A) \supset C$', and vice versa.

Since '$P \supset (A \supset C)$' corresponds to

$$/ \therefore A \supset C$$
$$P$$

and '$(P \cdot A) \supset C$' corresponds to

$$/ \therefore C$$
$$P$$
$$A$$

and since '$P \supset (A \supset C)$' and '$(P \cdot A) \supset C$' are logically equivalent statements, if '$P \supset (A \supset C)$' depicts a tautology, then both

$$/ \therefore A \supset C \qquad\qquad / \therefore C$$
$$P \qquad\qquad\quad and \qquad P$$
$$A$$

picture deductively valid arguments. Or, if '$(P \cdot A) \supset C$' is viewed as a tautology, then both

$$/ \therefore A \supset C \qquad\qquad / \therefore C$$
$$P \qquad\qquad\quad and \qquad P$$
$$A$$

picture deductively valid arguments. Hence, if

$$/ \therefore A \supset C$$
$$P$$

stands for an argument that is deductively valid, so does

$$/ \therefore C$$
$$P$$
$$A$$

Or, if

$$/ \therefore A \supset C$$
$$P$$

represents an argument that is deductively invalid, so does

$$/ \therefore C$$
$$P$$
$$A$$

Remember that 'P' represents the conjunction of all the premises of any specific argument, while 'A' and 'C' exemplify any statements.

**ARGUMENTS**

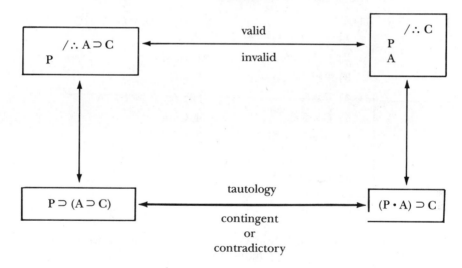

**STATEMENTS**

This diagram can be viewed as picturing the foundation for the *conditional method of proving validity*. A result of using the conditional method of proving validity is a ***Conditional Proof (CP)***.

A Conditional Proof is now available for (1). Begin by symbolizing the argument:

(8)                           $/ \therefore (E \vee G) \supset [(G \vee E) \cdot A]$
   1)  $\sim [(E \vee G) \cdot \sim A]$   Pr

Continue (8) by removing the tilde in front of the punctuation marks in line 1. Follow this by a Double Negation move to clear up further tildes.

(9)                                          $/\therefore (E \vee G) \supset [(G \vee E) \cdot A]$

1)  $\sim [(E \vee G) \cdot \sim A]$    Pr
2)  $\sim (E \vee G) \vee \sim\sim A$    1, DeM
3)  $\sim (E \vee G) \vee A$    2, DN

Expand the argument by introducing as an assumption the antecedent of the conclusion. Justify this move by writing '**CP, $/\therefore$ (G $\vee$ E) $\cdot$ A**' to the right-hand side of the symbolized assumption:

(10)                                         $/\therefore (E \vee G) \supset [(G \vee E) \cdot A]$

1)  $\sim [(E \vee G) \cdot \sim A]$    Pr
2)  $\sim (E \vee G) \vee \sim\sim A$    1, DeM
3)  $\sim (E \vee G) \vee A$    2, DN
4)  $E \vee G$    CP, $/\therefore (G \vee E) \cdot A$

The proof continues until the consequent of the conclusion, '$(G \vee E) \cdot A$', is reached. The proof is then completed in the next line:

(11)                                         $/\therefore (E \vee G) \supset [(G \vee E) \cdot A]$

1)  $\sim [(E \vee G) \cdot \sim A]$    Pr
2)  $\sim (E \vee G) \vee \sim\sim A$    1, DeM
3)  $\sim (E \vee G) \vee A$    2, DN
4)  $E \vee G$    CP, $/\therefore (G \vee E) \cdot A$
5)  $G \vee E$    4, Com
6)  $\sim\sim (E \vee G)$    4, DN
7)  A    3, 6, DS
8)  $(G \vee E) \cdot A$    5, 7, Conj

9)  $/\therefore (E \vee G) \supset [(G \vee E) \cdot A]$    4–8, CP

A vertical line in (11) indicates the *scope* of the assumption introduced in 4. The scope of an assumption includes the assumption itself and all of those statements that depend upon that assumption—totally or in part—for their justifications. In particular the statements in lines 5 through 8 depend on the assumption at 4, plus the original premise. An arrowhead is used to indicate an assumption and a horizonal line to show the end of the scope of that assumption. The first statement falling outside the scope of an assumption of a conditional proof is always a hypothetical. This hypothetical statement is said to *discharge* the assumption. A fundamental restriction of Conditional Proof is this:

**After discharging an assumption, no further statements in the proof can be justified by appealing to that assumption or any statement falling within its scope.**

Any assumption and what lies within its scope is completely isolated from supplying justifications for any other statement in the proof. As seen in (11), the assumption in 4 and its scope does not extend to the conclusion. The original premise of (8) logically entails the conclusion independently of that assumption.

In (11), line 9 shows that since '$\sim [(E \vee G) \cdot A]$' and '$E \vee G$' entail '$(G \vee E) \cdot A$', then '$\sim [(E \vee G) \cdot \sim A]$' must also entail '$(E \vee G) \supset [(G \vee E) \cdot A]$'. The justification is '4 – 8, CP' and *not* '4, 8, CP'. The *dash* used between '4' and '8' indicates that the Conditional Method is used in lines 4 *through* 8. The statement in 9 is *not* justified by an appeal to 4 *and* 8 plus some elementary rule of inference. 'CP' indicates the results of using a particular *method of proof*; not a particular elementary rule of inference.

This method of proving validity is extended to any argument whose conclusion is not hypothetical in form but is logically equivalent to a hypothetical. Note the following:

**(12)** If Batman appears whenever there is a crime, it doesn't pay to be the villain.

So, it isn't true that it pays to be the villain and Batman appears. (T,C,V)

Symbolize (12):

$$\textbf{(13)} \qquad\qquad\qquad /\therefore\ \sim (V \cdot B)$$
$$\textbf{1)}\ (C \supset B) \supset \sim V \quad Pr$$

'$\sim (V \cdot B)$' is not a hypothetical statement but it is logically equivalent to '$V \supset \sim B$'. Given '$\sim (V \cdot B)$', and working backwards, imagine a DeMorgan move with an application of Material Implication above it. Working backwards produces '$V \supset \sim B$'. So, 'V' is assumed as a new premise and '$\sim B$' becomes the new conclusion in a use of Conditional Proof. Once '$\sim B$' is established '$V \supset \sim B$' is asserted by an appeal to Conditional Proof. A conditional proof of (13) is now completed:

| | | |
|---|---|---|
| **(14)** | | $/\therefore\ \sim (V \cdot B)$ |
| **1)** | $(C \supset B) \supset \sim V$ | Pr |
| **2)** | V | CP, $/\therefore\ \sim B$ |
| **3)** | $\sim \sim V$ | 2, DN |
| **4)** | $\sim (C \supset B)$ | 1, 3, MT |
| **5)** | $\sim (\sim C \vee B)$ | 4, Impl |
| **6)** | $\sim \sim C \cdot \sim B$ | 5, DeM |
| **7)** | $\sim B \cdot \sim \sim C$ | 6, Com |
| **8)** | $\sim B$ | 7, Simp |
| **9)** | $V \supset \sim B$ | 2–8, CP |
| **10)** | $\sim V \vee \sim B$ | 9, Impl |
| **11)** | $/\therefore\ \sim (V \cdot B)$ | 10, DeM |

Notice that each line, 2 through 8, is either an assumption or depends on an assumption for its justification.

Observe how Conditional Proof can be used with arguments having a simple statement as a conclusion. Indeed, a Conditional Proof can be used with any conclusion following the techniques in the following example:

(15)  /∴ C

| | | |
|---|---|---|
| **1)** | [(A · B) ⊃ C] · (E ⊃ C) | Pr |
| **2)** | (A · B) ∨ (E · A) | Pr |
| **3)** | (A · B) ⊃ C | 1, Simp |
| **4)** | (E ⊃ C) · [(A · B) ⊃ C] | 1, Com |
| **5)** | E ⊃ C | 4, Simp |
| **6)** | (E · A) ∨ (A · B) | 2, Com |
| **→ 7)** | ~ C | CP, /∴ C |
| **8)** | ~ E | 5, 7, MT |
| **9)** | ~ E ∨ ~ A | 8, Add |
| **10)** | ~ (E · A) | 9, DeM |
| **11)** | A · B | 6, 10, DS |
| **12)** | C | 3, 11, MP |
| **13)** | ~ C ⊃ C | 7–12, CP |
| **14)** | ~ ~ C ∨ C | 13, Impl |
| **15)** | C ∨ C | 14, DN |
| **16)** | /∴ C | 15, Taut |

Combining Material Implication, Double Negation, and Tautology will always produce any conclusion of an argument.

Conditional Proof can be used several times in a proof.

(16)   Pat comes or Madge leaves and Grace goes or Larry stays only if Tim's party is a blast. Hence, whenever Pat comes, Tim's party is a blast if Grace goes. (P,M,G,L,B)

Symbolize the argument:

(17)  /∴ P ⊃ (G ⊃ T)
1) [(P ∨ M) · (G ∨ L)] ⊃ T   Pr

Assume the antecedent of the conclusion and prove for the consequent:

(18)  /∴ P ⊃ (G ⊃ T)
1) [(P ∨ M) · (G ∨ L)] ⊃ T   Pr
2) P   CP, /∴ G ⊃ T

Because 'G ⊃ T' is itself a hypothetical, 'G', the antecedent, can be assumed as another assumption helpful in deducing 'T'. In this way, two Conditional Proofs can be nested in one another:

**(19)**                                                    /∴  P ⊃ (G ⊃ T)

    **1)** [(P ∨ M) · (G ∨ L)] ⊃ T   Pr

    **2)** P                       CP, /∴ G ⊃ T

    **3)** G                       CP, /∴ T

    **4)** P ∨ M              2, Add

    **5)** G ∨ L              3, Add

    **6)** (P ∨ M) · (G ∨ L)     4, 5, Conj

    **7)** T                       1, 6, MP

    **8)** G ⊃ T               3–7, CP

    **9)** /∴ P ⊃ (G ⊃ T)       2–8, CP

When two, or more, Conditional Proofs are nested, the innermost Conditional Proof must be completed first. Then, working outward, each of the remaining assumptions is discharged with a hypothetical statement.

While assumptions and their scopes can be nested, they cannot overlap. The fundamental restriction on Conditional Proof dictates that no assumption, or statement within the scope of an assumption, can be used to justify any statement outside that scope. Hence, no legitimate proof could ever create a situation looking like this:

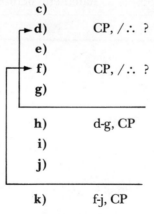

    **c)**

    **d)**       CP, /∴  ?

    **e)**

    **f)**       CP, /∴  ?

    **g)**

    **h)**       d-g, CP

    **i)**

    **j)**

    **k)**       f-j, CP

Assumptions made by using Conditional Proof do not have to be nested. Consider this argument:

    **(19)**   Bill's life is both miserable and short provided he develops lung cancer. On the other hand, Bill's life is not productive unless it is healthy and long. Consequently, if Bill develops lung cancer then his life is short, but if he is productive then his life is healthy. (M,S,A,P,L)

Symbolize (19) in this way:

(20)                                    $/\therefore\ (D \supset S) \cdot (P \supset H)$

| | | |
|---|---|---|
| 1) | $D \supset (M \cdot S)$ | Pr |
| 2) | $P \supset (H \cdot L)$ | Pr |
| 3) | D | CP, $/\therefore$ S |
| 4) | $M \cdot S$ | 1, 3, MP |
| 5) | $S \cdot M$ | 4, Com |
| 6) | S | 5, Simp |
| 7) | $D \supset S$ | 3–6, CP |
| 8) | P | CP, $/\therefore$ H |
| 9) | $H \cdot L$ | 2, 8, MP |
| 10) | H | 9, Simp |
| 11) | $P \supset H$ | 8–10, CP |
| 12) | $/\therefore (D \supset S) \cdot (P \supset H)$ | 7, 11, Conj |

Conditional Proof is commonly used when the conclusion of an argument is either a hypothetical, a conjunction of hypotheticals, or easily seen to be logically equivalent to a hypothetical or conjunction of hypotheticals. However, Conditional Proof can be used to introduce any new assumption provided that the assumption is discharged by a hypothetical statement before the conclusion of the argument is reached.

## EXERCISES

### Group A:

Without using the Conditional Method of Proving Validity, construct proofs for (12), (15), and (16) in this section.

### Group B:

Construct a Conditional Proof for each of the following.

1.                                       $/\therefore A \supset E$
   1) $A \supset B$            Pr
   2) $(B \cdot A) \supset D$            Pr
   3) $[(B \cdot A) \cdot D] \supset E$    Pr

2.                                       $/\therefore A \supset (\sim B \vee D)$
   1) $A \supset (B \supset C)$   Pr
   2) $(B \cdot C) \supset D$   Pr

3.                                          $/\therefore (A \vee B) \supset C$
   1) $[A \supset (B \cdot C)] \cdot [B \supset (D \cdot C)]$    Pr

4.                                                     /∴ B ⊃ (D ⊃ A)
  1)  ~A ⊃ [ ~ (B ∨ C) ∨ ~ (D ∨ E)]   Pr

5.                                                     /∴ D ⊃ ~A
  1)  [A ⊃ (B ⊃ C)] · [A ⊃ (C ⊃ B)]   Pr
  2)  (C ≡ B) ⊃ ~D                       Pr

6.                                                     /∴ A ⊃ (C ∨ E)
  1)  ( ~A · B) ∨ (D · C)   Pr

7.                                                     /∴ ~ B ∨ D
  1)  ~ (A ∨ B) ∨ C   Pr
  2)  C ⊃ D            Pr

8.                                                     /∴ A ⊃ · [(D · B) ∨ ~ E]
  1)  A ⊃ [ ~D ∨ ( ~B · C)]   Pr
  2)  A ⊃ (E · F)                Pr

9.                                                     /∴ ~ (A · ~ E)
  1)  ( ~A ⊃ ~B) ⊃ (C · D)   Pr
  2)  D ⊃ (C · E)              Pr

10.                                                    /∴ A ⊃ (C ⊃ E)
  1)  ( ~A · B) ∨ [(A · ~C) ∨ (D · E)]   Pr


**Group C:**

Symbolize the following arguments using the capital letters suggested. Then construct Conditional Proofs for each.

1. The following isn't the case: It isn't true that there isn't stable economic development if the money supply doesn't respond to a growing economy; yet the money supply is inelastic. There isn't stable economic development, according to some authorities. If the 1913 Federal Reserve Act is observed, then unless there is stable economic development, the money supply isn't elastic. So, the 1913 Federal Reserve Act is observed only if the money supply is inelastic. (D,R,E,O)

2. The money supply is elastic if the following is the case: The flow of currency being regular is a necessary condition for the economy being balanced toward stable growth if the money supply is elastic. Hence, the money supply is inelastic only if the following is the case: The flow of currency isn't regular; but if the economy isn't balanced toward stable growth, the money supply is inelastic. (E,R,B)

3. If the Federal Reserve performs its principal function, the flow of money is regulated and the economy is stable; moreover, if the economy is stable, both the flow of credit and money are regulated. Consequently, if either the Federal Reserve performs its principal function or the economy is stable, the flow of money is regulated. (F,M,E,C)

4. Either money isn't considered as a means of payment but is thought of as a measure of value, or currency is a form of money while money is also considered as a store of purchasing power. Also, either money is thought of as a measure of value and demand deposits are a form of money, or either currency is a form of money but money isn't considered as a store of purchasing power or currency is a form of money. Therefore,

money is never considered as a means of payment but either that currency is a form of money or demand deposits are. (P,V,C,S,D)

5. It isn't the case that a sociologist is interested in theory construction and doesn't know various systems of logic. Also, it isn't true that a sociologist is concerned only with collecting data while not being unable to make fruitful predictions; moreover, it isn't true that a sociologist isn't interested in theory construction and not concerned only with collecting data. Accordingly, a sociologist won't be able to make fruitful predictions provided that he doesn't know various systems of logic. (I,K,C,A)

6. It isn't true that we desire to organize our data although various systems of logic don't prove helpful. If we don't want to fail in our theory construction, we might find digital computers helpful in our research whenever we can't ignore logical models. We don't want to fail in our theory construction. Further, it isn't true that we might find digital computers helpful in our research while not desiring to organize our data. So, we can ignore logical models and/or various systems of logic will prove helpful. (D,P,W,F,I)

7. If we're interested in methodology, then logic doesn't prove helpful unless our scientific language is completely analyzed; moreover, if we're interested in methodology, then logic proves helpful whenever our scientific language is completely analyzed. That we aren't concerned simply with collecting data is a necessary condition for the following: Whenever scientific language is carefully analyzed, logic proves helpful. Consequently, we're interested in methodology only if we aren't concerned simply with collecting data. (I,P,A,C)

8. There isn't a finite number of positions in a game of chess provided that the following is the case: Chess isn't a finite game, albeit the rules of chess permit any move to terminate in some final move, and, further, each position in the game admits of a finite number of moves. Thus, that there is a finite number of positions in chess is a sufficient condition for the following: If each position in the game admits of a finite number of moves, then the rules of chess permit any move to terminate in some final move only if chess is a finite game. (N,G,P,A)

9. Either chess isn't a finite game and no move ever terminates in a last move, or either chess is a finite game but in principle can't be completely described as a branching tree or one can in principle scan the branching tree and find the best move to make at any juncture in the game. Hence, if chess is a finite game, then it in principle can be completely described as a branching tree only if one can find the best move to make at any juncture in the game. (G,T,D,S,F)

10. If heuristic programs are written for computers to play chess, then algorithmic methods suffice for all computer programming needs whenever and only whenever computers are massive enough to analyze all possible chess moves. It isn't true that algorithmic methods will suffice for all computer programming needs while contemporary heuristic programming authorities are examined profitably, and yet heuristic programs are written so that computers can play chess. Either Claude Shannon's approach for programming computers to construct a chess game is an important contribution to heuristic programming or heuristic programs aren't written so that computers can play chess, or our present computers are massive enough to analyze all possible chess moves. So, either Shannon's approach for programming computers to construct a chess game isn't an important contribution to heuristics or contemporary heuristic programming authorities aren't examined. (P,M,C,A,S)

## 2.   THE INDIRECT METHOD OF PROVING VALIDITY

A method useful in constructing proofs is the *indirect method of proving validity*. A result of using this method is an **Indirect Proof (IP)**. Let 'P' stand for the conjunction of all of the premises of an argument and 'C' for *any* conclusion, not necessarily a hypothetical statement nor logically equivalent to one. The supposed argument can be schematized in this way:

$$\textbf{(1)} \qquad /\therefore C$$
$$P$$

Corresponding to (1), is this hypothetical schema:

$$\textbf{(2)} \quad P \supset C$$

Assume as a new premise the denial of the *entire* conclusion of the argument represented by (1):

$$\textbf{(3)} \qquad /\therefore C$$
$$P$$
$$\sim C$$

A hypothetical schema can be constructed corresponding to (3):

$$\textbf{(4)} \quad (P \cdot \sim C) \supset C$$

If 'P $\supset$ C' pictures a tautology, then

$$/\therefore C$$
$$P$$

represents an argument that is deductively valid. If, however, 'P $\supset$ C' pictures a contingent or contradictory statement,

$$/\therefore C$$
$$P$$

represents an argument that is deductively invalid. Suppose '(P $\cdot$ $\sim$ C) $\supset$ C' pictures a tautology, then

$$/\therefore C$$
$$P$$
$$\sim C$$

exemplifies an argument that is deductively valid. But if '(P $\cdot$ $\sim$ C) $\supset$ C' represents a contingent or contradictory statement, the argument suggested by

$$/\therefore C$$
$$P$$
$$\sim C$$

is deductively invalid. Furthermore, 'P ⊃ C' and '(P · ~ C) ⊃ C' are logically equivalent:*

(5)  **(P  ⊃  C)  ≡  [(P  ·  ~  C)  ⊃  C]**

| 1 | 1 | 1 | 1 | 1 | 0 | 0 | 1 | 1 | 1 |
| 1 | 0 | 0 | 1 | 1 | 1 | 1 | 0 | 0 | 0 |
| 0 | 1 | 1 | 1 | 0 | 0 | 0 | 1 | 1 | 1 |
| 0 | 1 | 0 | 1 | 0 | 0 | 1 | 0 | 1 | 0 |

⇑

Thus, if '(P · ~ C) ⊃ C' depicts a tautology, then

/∴ C

P

~ C

pictures an argument that is deductively valid. But then

/∴ C

P

---

*A use of truth trees can also establish that 'P ⊃ C' and '(P · ~ C) ⊃ C' are logically equivalent:

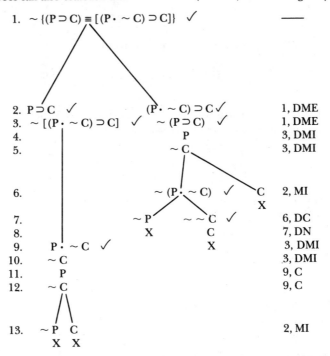

Since every branch in the above truth tree is closed, the statement in 1 is a contradiction. From this it follows that '(P ⊃ C) ≡ [(P · ~ C) ⊃ C]' is a tautology. Hence, 'P ⊃ C' and '(P · ~ C) ⊃ C' are logically equivalent.

also picture an argument that is deductively valid since 'P ⊃ C' and '(P • ~ C) ⊃ C' are logically equivalent and 'P ⊃ C' corresponds to

$$/\therefore C$$
$$P$$

This information is shown in the following diagram:

**ARGUMENTS**

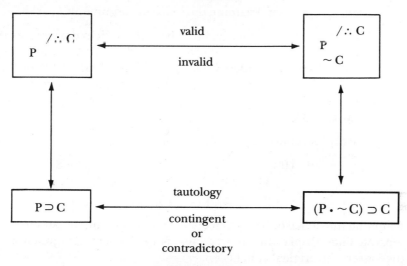

**STATEMENTS**

A close relation holds between Conditional and Indirect Proofs. Indeed, Indirect Proof is a special case of Conditional Proof. By Exportation, '(P • ~ C) ⊃ C' is logically equivalent to

(6)   P ⊃ ( ~ C ⊃ C)

Corresponding to (6) is an argument schema depicted as

(7)        /∴ ~ C ⊃ C
        P

Using the Conditional Method of Proving Validity with (7), one can assume the antecedent of the conclusion:

(8)        /∴ C
        P
        ~ C

However, (8) and (3) are identical. This relation between (7) and (8) is used in (15) of Section 1 when ' ~ C' is assumed as a new premise in order to obtain 'C'.

In constructing an Indirect Proof, it must be shown that if an argument is valid, then assuming the denial of its conclusion creates an inconsistent premise set leading to *some contradiction* depicted in lines following the assumption. To show this, move through the following five steps. First, symbolize the argument. Second, assume the denial of the *entire* conclusion no matter what that conclusion might be. Mark this assumption by writing 'IP' to its right-hand side. Third, deduce both a statement 'p' and its denial ' ~ p'. Fourth, by Conjunction, 'p • ~ p' forms a contradiction that ends the Indirect Proof. Fifth, the conclusion of the original argument is displayed in the last line of the proof. Showing a contradiction is a key step in any use of the Indirect Method of Proving Validity. For any inconsistent premise set yields a valid argument. Of course, no sound argument can have an inconsistent premise set. Examine the following argument:

(9) Tim's behavior might be viewed as basically anticipatory rather than reactive or as being environmentally controlled. Tim's behavior isn't environmentally controlled unless he is mentally deficient; but if his behavior is viewed as basically anticipatory rather than reactive, he is emotionally sensitive. It follows, then, that Tim is mentally deficient or emotionally sensitive. (A,C,D,S)

Using the capital letters suggested, symbolize (9) as

(10)                                      $/ \therefore \, D \vee S$
    1) $A \vee C$       Pr
    2) $(C \supset D) \cdot (A \supset S)$   Pr

Assuming the denial of 'D ∨ S', deduce some statement, 'p', and its denial, ' ~ p', in separate lines. Display this contradiction in the form of a conjunction, 'p • ~ p', and then assert the original conclusion.

(11)                                      $/ \therefore \, D \vee S$
    1) $A \vee C$       Pr
    2) $(C \supset D) \cdot (A \supset S)$   Pr
    3) $C \supset D$       2, Simp
    4) $(A \supset S) \cdot (C \supset D)$   2, Com
    5) $A \supset S$       6, Simp
    6) $C \vee A$       1, Com
    7) $\sim (D \vee S)$       IP
    8) $\sim D \cdot \sim S$       7, DeM
    9) $\sim D$       8, Simp
   10) $\sim S \cdot \sim D$       8, Com
 *11) $\sim S$       10, Simp*
   12) $\sim C$       3, 9, MT
   13) $A$       6, 12, DS
 *14) $S$       5, 13, MP
   15) $S \cdot \sim S$       14, 11, Conj

---

* Asterisks appearing before the name of a line are used only in this section of the text to highlight instances of 'p' and '~ p'.

    **16)** /∴ D ∨ S          3–15, IP

To mark the assumption in 7, write only 'IP', indicating the use of the Indirect Method of Proving Validity. 'IP, /∴ D ∨ S' is not written because the original conclusion of the argument is to be proved. An arrowhead is used to indicate the assumption, a vertical line to show the scope of that assumption in which the Indirect Proof takes place, and a horizonal line to indicate the end of the Indirect Proof. In (11), the assumption in line 7 is discharged at line 16. So, the original premises logically entail the conclusion independently of the assumption. As with Conditional Proof, once the assumption of an Indirect Proof is discharged, neither that assumption nor any statement within its scope is available to justify any other statement within the overall proof of which the Indirect Proof is a part.

While some contradiction must be displayed in any Indirect Proof, for a particular argument several contradictions might be obtained. For instance, examine this Indirect Proof of (9):

**(12)**                             /∴ D ∨ S

    **1)** A ∨ C                 Pr

    **2)** (C ⊃ D) · (A ⊃ S)  Pr

    **3)** C ⊃ D            2, Simp

    **4)** (A ⊃ S) · (C ⊃ D)  2, Com

    **5)** A ⊃ S            4, Simp

→  **6)** ∼ (D ∨ S)        IP

    **7)** ∼ D · ∼ S       6, DeM

 **\*8)** ∼ D              6, Simp

    **9)** ∼ S · ∼ D       6, Com

  **10)** ∼ S            9, Simp

  **11)** ∼ A            5, 10, MT

  **12)** C              1, 11, DS

**\*13)** D              3, 12, MP

  **14)** D · ∼ D       13, 8, Conj

    **15)** /∴ D ∨ S          3–14, IP

A contradiction appears in 8 and 13 in terms of 'D' and ' ∼ D'.

In an Indirect Proof what appears as the original conclusion might occur within the scope of the assumption or even as part of the generated contradiction. Consider this example:

**(13)**                             /∴ D ∨ S

    **1)** A ∨ C                 Pr

    **2)** (C ⊃ D) · (A ⊃ S)  Pr

| | | |
|---|---|---|
| **\*3)** ~ (D ∨ S) | | IP |
| **4)** C ⊃ D | | 2, Simp |
| **5)** (A ⊃ S) · (C ⊃ D) | | 2, Com |
| **6)** A ⊃ S | | 5, Simp |
| **7)** S ∨ D | | 6, 4, 1, CD |
| **\*8)** D ∨ S | | 7, Com |
| **9)** (D ∨ S) · ~ (D ∨ S) | | 8, 3, Conj |
| **10)** /∴ D ∨ S | | 3–9, IP |

Note that (13) must not stop at line 8 because that line is still within the scope of the assumption introduced in line 3. Line 10, the conclusion, falls outside the scope of 3 and is logically entailed only by the original premises.

Strategically, one of the more difficult aspects of constructing an Indirect Proof is to discover statements in terms of which a contradiction can be displayed. Former strategies of breaking down overall conjunctions and removing tildes from the outside of punctuation marks are often helpful. Further, it is often useful to look for a contradiction in terms of letters, or combinations of letters, representing statements that appear in two or more lines of the original premise set as augmented by any assumptions.

Study this argument:

**(14)** Theories in psychology aren't constructed provided the following is the case: Neither experimental nor clinical psychologists are interested in this type of work, or neither statistical nor quantitative measurement is satisfactory for representing psychological data. Consequently, if experimental psychologists are interested in this type of work, then theories in psychology are constructed if statistical measurement is satisfactory in representing psychological data. (T,E,C,S,Q)

An indirect proof for (14) can be constructed:

**(15)**                                       /∴ E ⊃ (S ⊃ T)

| | | |
|---|---|---|
| **1)** ~T ⊃ [~(E ∨ C) ∨ ~(S ∨ Q)] | | Pr |
| **2)** ~[E ⊃ (S ⊃ T)] | | IP |
| **3)** ~[~E ∨ (S ⊃ T)] | | 2, Impl |
| **4)** ~~E · ~(S ⊃ T) | | 3, DeM |
| **5)** ~~E · ~(~S ∨ T) | | 4, Impl |
| **6)** ~~E · (~~S · ~T) | | 5, DeM |
| **7)** ~~E | | 6, Simp |
| **8)** E | | 7, DN |
| **9)** E ∨ C | | 8, Add |
| **10)** (~~S · ~T) · ~~E | | 6, Com |
| **11)** ~~S · ~T | | 10, Simp |

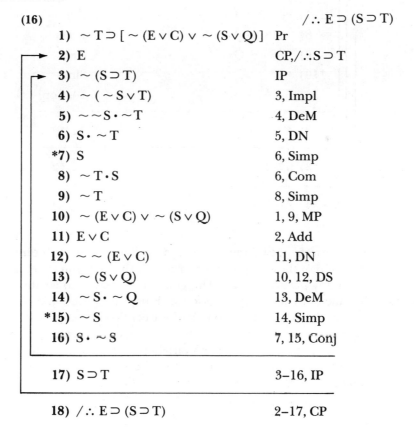

| **12)** ~ ~ S | 11, Simp |
|---|---|
| **13)** S | 12, DN |
| **14)** S ∨ Q | 13, Add |
| **14)** (E ∨ C) · (S ∨ Q) | 9, 14 Conj |
| **15)** ~ ~ [(E ∨ C) · (S ∨ Q)] | 14, DN |
| **16)** ~ [~ (E ∨ C) ∨ ~ (S ∨ Q)] | 15, DeM |
| ***17)** ~ ~ T | 1, 16, MT |
| **18)** ~ T · ~ ~ S | 11, Com |
| ***19)** ~ T | 18, Simp |
| **20)** ~ T · ~ ~ T | 19, 17, Conj |

| **21)** /∴ E ⊃ (S ⊃ T) | 2–20, IP |
|---|---|

Both Conditional and Indirect Proofs can be nested in a single proof for (14). Initiate the proof by symbolizing the argument and making two assumptions. The first of these assumptions is used with a Conditional Proof, the second with an Indirect Proof:

**(16)**                                                     /∴ E ⊃ (S ⊃ T)

| **1)** ~ T ⊃ [ ~ (E ∨ C) ∨ ~ (S ∨ Q)] | Pr |
|---|---|
| **2)** E | CP,/∴ S ⊃ T |
| **3)** ~ (S ⊃ T) | IP |
| **4)** ~ ( ~ S ∨ T) | 3, Impl |
| **5)** ~ ~ S · ~ T | 4, DeM |
| **6)** S · ~ T | 5, DN |
| ***7)** S | 6, Simp |
| **8)** ~ T · S | 6, Com |
| **9)** ~ T | 8, Simp |
| **10)** ~ (E ∨ C) ∨ ~ (S ∨ Q) | 1, 9, MP |
| **11)** E ∨ C | 2, Add |
| **12)** ~ ~ (E ∨ C) | 11, DN |
| **13)** ~ (S ∨ Q) | 10, 12, DS |
| **14)** ~ S · ~ Q | 13, DeM |
| ***15)** ~ S | 14, Simp |
| **16)** S · ~ S | 7, 15, Conj |

| **17)** S ⊃ T | 3–16, IP |
|---|---|

| **18)** /∴ E ⊃ (S ⊃ T) | 2–17, CP |
|---|---|

In (16), the antecedent of the original conclusion is first assumed in line 2. Given 'E', 'S ⊃ T' is then established by an Indirect Proof. So, the denial of 'S ⊃ T' is assumed in 3 as the assumption of an Indirect Proof. Having obtained 'S ⊃ T' by Indirect Proof, 'E ⊃ (S ⊃ T)' is established by Conditional Proof. Had an Indirect Proof been started before the Conditional Proof, this situation would occur:

**(17)**                                         / ∴  E ⊃ (S ⊃ T)
    **1)**  ~ T ⊃ [ ~ (E ∨ C) ∨ ~ (S ∨ Q)]   Pr
    **2)**  ~ [E ⊃ (S ⊃ T)]                 IP

But given (17), proof construction cannot be continued with a Conditional Proof, for there is now no antecedent to assume.

Another proof for (14) makes a nest of three assumptions;

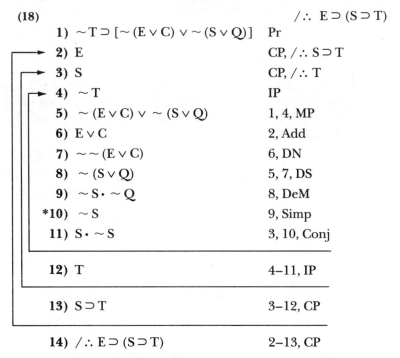

**(18)**                                         / ∴  E ⊃ (S ⊃ T)
    **1)**  ~ T ⊃ [ ~ (E ∨ C) ∨ ~ (S ∨ Q)]   Pr
    **2)**  E                             CP, / ∴ S ⊃ T
    **3)**  S                             CP, / ∴ T
    **4)**  ~ T                           IP
    **5)**  ~ (E ∨ C) ∨ ~ (S ∨ Q)         1, 4, MP
    **6)**  E ∨ C                         2, Add
    **7)**  ~ ~ (E ∨ C)                   6, DN
    **8)**  ~ (S ∨ Q)                     5, 7, DS
    **9)**  ~ S · ~ Q                     8, DeM
  **\*10)**  ~ S                           9, Simp
   **11)**  S · ~ S                       3, 10, Conj
   **12)**  T                             4–11, IP
   **13)**  S ⊃ T                         3–12, CP
   **14)**  / ∴ E ⊃ (S ⊃ T)              2–13, CP

Given various possibilities of using Conditional Proof, Indirect Proof, or some combination of these in proof construction, the question arises as to which of these to use in any particular case. The general strategy is to let the conclusion be the guiding factor in deciding. Clues for likely uses of Conditional Proof are suggested at the end of the previous section. An Indirect Proof is often used when the desired statement—the conclusion or some intermediate statement—is being interpreted as an instance of a single statement variable or as a single statement variable prefixed with one tilde. Another situation is when the wanted statement is being interpreted as an overall inclusive disjunctive statement. The assumption for an Indirect Proof will then produce a denial of an overall inclusive disjunction. Appealing to DeMorgan will produce a conjunction on which Simplification and Commutation can be used. However, when in doubt between using a Conditional or Indirect Proof, use an Indirect Proof. Because Indirect Proof is a special case of conditional Proof, the assumptions obtained in an Indirect Proof always yield those assumptions that would have been obtained had a Conditional Proof been chosen; the reverse of this, however, is not always the case.

## *EXERCISES*

### Group A:

Construct an Indirect Proof for each of the following:

1.                      /∴ ~ E ⊃ ~ B
   1) A ∨ (B ⊃ C)    Pr
   2) C ⊃ E        Pr
   3) ~ A          Pr

2.                              /∴ A ∆ B
   1) ~ A ∨ ( ~ B · C)       Pr
   2) ( ~ B ⊃ D) · ( ~ A ⊃ ~ D)   Pr

3.                   /∴ ~ ( ~ D · A)
   1) (A ∨ B) ⊃ ~ C   Pr
   2) ~ D ⊃ (C ∨ A)   Pr

4.                      /∴ D ⊃ C
   1) A ⊃ [(B · C) ∨ ~ D]   Pr
   2) A                  Pr

5.                   /∴ E ∨ D
   1) A ≡ B         Pr
   2) (C ∨ A) · ~ C   Pr
   3) B ⊃ D        Pr

6.                         /∴ E ∨ C
   1) (A ⊃ B) ⊃ C         Pr
   2) (A ⊃ D) · ( ~ B ⊃ ~ D)   Pr

7.                   /∴ D · A
   1) (A ∨ B) · ~ C   Pr
   2) ~ B · (C ∨ D)   Pr

8.                      /∴ C ∨ D
   1) (A ⊃ B) · (B ⊃ C)   Pr
   2) D ∨ A         Pr
   3) D ⊃ E        Pr

9.                     /∴ ~ ( ~ F · ~ C)
   1) A ⊃ ( ~ B ⊃ C)   Pr
   2) D ⊃ (E ⊃ F)     Pr
   3) D ⊃ ( ~ B ∆ E)   Pr
   4) D · A          Pr

10.                   /∴ F ∨ C
   1) (A ∆ B) ⊃ C   Pr
   2) ~ D · (D ∨ A)   Pr
   3) (A · B) ⊃ D     Pr

**Group B:**

Symbolize the following arguments using the capital letters suggested. Then construct an Indirect Proof for each.

1. Either information theory is a branch of probability theory with many applications to communication systems and was initiated by communication scientists, or information theory is an old discipline and yet is a branch of probability theory with many applications to communication systems. Information theory isn't an old discipline. Consequently, information theory is a branch of probability theory with many applications to communication systems, while also initiated by communication scientists. (B,I,D)

2. If a commodity needs to be tangible and communication processes are concerned with the flow of a commodity in a network, information is a tangible commodity in communication processes. Information isn't a tangible commodity in communication processes, although communication processes are concerned with the flow of a commodity in a network. Therefore, a commodity doesn't need to be tangible. (N,F,I)

3. A contrastive grammar is a teaching device if and only if it might be used as a tool in the preparation of teaching materials. Now, a contrastive grammar might be used as a tool in the preparation of teaching materials and is one in which descriptive grammars of two languages are tied together. Wherefore, while a contrastive grammar is one in which descriptive grammars of two languages are tied together, it is also a teaching device. (D,T,L)

4. Either phonemes are signs, or either various members of a writing system aren't signs of a given language's phonemes and writing systems are sign systems, or writing systems can be interpreted as meaningful but phonemes are meaningless. Phonemes aren't signs even though it isn't true that writing systems can be interpreted as meaningful and various members of a writing system aren't signs of a given language's phonemes. Consequently, either various members of a writing system are signs of a given language's phonemes or writing systems can't be interpreted as meaningful, but not both. (P,L,W,I,M)

5. Either Yiddish as a written language uses a modified Hebrew alphabet and, like Hebrew, is written from left to right, or Yiddish is basically a German dialect and as a written language uses a modified Hebrew alphabet. That Yiddish has identifying characteristics that make it a member of the Germanic language family is a necessary condition for either Yiddish being basically a German dialect or, like Hebrew, being written from left to right. Hence, neither Yiddish doesn't have identifying characteristics making it a member of the Germanic language family nor Yiddish as a written language doesn't use a modified Hebrew alphabet. (A,W,D,C)

6. If Yiddish isn't basically a German dialect except that it has identifying characteristics making it a member of the Germanic language family, then Yiddish as a written language uses the modified Hebrew alphabet; moreover, assuming that it isn't true that Yiddish has identifying characteristics making it a member of the Germanic language family just in case it is basically a German dialect, then Yiddish is completely synonymous with Hebrew. So, either Yiddish is completely synonymous with Hebrew or, as a written language, Yiddish uses the modified Hebrew alphabet. (D,C,A,S)

7. That relationships are bonds linking objects and attributes in a system process and symbiosis is a first-order relationship is a necessary condition for it not being the case that symbiosis is a first-order relationship while synergy is a second-order one. Now, either a vital relationship doesn't always hold between two similar organisms or symbiosis isn't a

first-order relationship. Therefore, symbiosis isn't a first-order relationship just in case a vital relationship always holds between two similar organisms. (B,F,S,H)

8. If risk is a measure of potential exposure to system failure in business systems analysis, then precise measures of risk are always quantifiable if high risk can be characterized by low statistical probability. Precise measures of risk aren't always quantifiable unless it isn't true that both high risk can be characterized by low statistical probability and risk is a measure of potential exposure in system failure in business systems analysis. Either risk is a measure of potential exposure to system failure in business systems analysis and high risk can be characterized by low statistical probability, or risk might be increased and emerge as a dominant characteristic of an alternative selected through miscalculation of an input-output feedback error. Thus, risk can emerge as a dominant characteristic of an alternative selected through miscalculation of an input-output feedback error and risk might also be increased. (M,Q,C,I,E)

9. If both a total system is comprised of numerous subsystems and system objectives define organizational purposes, then real-world systems are ideal only if both constraints limit system operation and system attributes are sacrificed for seemingly optimal system relationships. It isn't the case that system attributes are sacrificed for seemingly optimal system relationships whenever system objectives define organizational purposes. Accordingly, a total system isn't comprised of numerous subsystems unless real-world systems aren't ideal. (C,D,I,L,S)

10. Either it isn't the case that an essential part of a communication system is a transmitter even though the system mustn't have a receiver, or a channel conveying information from a transmitter to a receiver is vital to a communication system and an essential part of such a system is a transmitter. That a channel conveying information from a transmitter to a receiver is vital to a communication system is a sufficient condition for the following: A transmitter is an essential part of a communication system although the simplest system isn't obliged to have a feedback loop. So, a communication system must have a receiver provided that the following is true: An essential part of such a system is a transmitter and the simplest communication system is obliged to have a feedback loop. (T,R,C,L)

## Group C:

For each of the following construct a proof using both the Conditional and Indirect Methods of Proving Validity.

1.                          $/\therefore C \supset (A \supset B)$
    1) $(A \supset B) \supset [C \supset (A \supset B)]$   Pr
    2) $\sim A \vee B$                          Pr

2.                  $/\therefore \sim A \supset [\sim C \cdot (\sim B \supset \sim A)]$
    1) $[(A \supset B) \supset C] \supset A$   Pr

3.                      $/\therefore D \supset [C \supset (B \supset A)]$
    1) $[(\sim A \cdot B) \cdot C] \supset \sim D$   Pr

4.                          $/\therefore (A \cdot B) \supset C$
    1) $\sim A \vee [\sim B \vee (C \cdot D)]$   Pr

5.                 $/\therefore (B \supset \sim D) \supset \sim A$
    1) $A \supset (B \cdot C)$   Pr
    2) $A \supset (C \cdot D)$   Pr

6.                                              $/\therefore A \supset (C \vee E)$
   1) $(\sim A \cdot B) \vee (C \cdot D)$    Pr
   2) $(B \cdot E) \vee [(C \cdot \sim D) \vee C]$    Pr

7.                                              $/\therefore A \vee B$
   1) $\sim (A \vee B) \supset (C \cdot D)$    Pr
   2) $C \supset (\sim B \supset \sim D)$    Pr

8.                                              $/\therefore B \supset (C \cdot D)$
   1) $(A \cdot B) \supset (C \cdot A)$    Pr
   2) $(\sim B \cdot A) \vee (D \cdot A)$    Pr

9.                                              $/\therefore B \supset (C \cdot D)$
   1) $(A \cdot B) \supset (A \cdot C)$    Pr
   2) $(A \cdot D) \vee (\sim B \cdot A)$    Pr

10.                                             $/\therefore \sim (\sim E \cdot B)$
   1) $(A \supset B) \supset (C \supset D)$    Pr
   2) $D \supset (C \cdot E)$    Pr

## Group D:

Symbolize the following arguments using the capital letters suggested. Then construct a proof of validity using both the Conditional and Indirect Methods of Proving Validity.

1. The circumference of this figure is determined by '2 π r' if this figure is a circle; moreover, this figure is an ellipse only if its circumference isn't determined by '2 π r'. So, assuming this figure is not an ellipse, it's a circle. (D,C,E)

2. Either William Faulkner didn't write *Sanctuary* or he did write *Of Human Bondage*, or he wrote *As I Lay Dying*; nevertheless, he didn't write *Of Human Bondage*. Hence, Faulkner wrote *Sanctuary* only if he wrote *As I Lay Dying*. (S,B,D)

3. If Winslow Homer painted either "Gross Clinic" or "Life Line" (but not both), then he loved the sea. That Homer didn't paint "The Wreck" is a necessary condition for the following: It is not true that he painted "Life Line" if and only if he didn't paint "Gross Clinic." Therefore, Homer painted "The Wreck" and "Kissing the Moon" only if he loved the sea. (C,L,S,W,M)

4. Either the United Nations strongly enforces international law or European governments don't protect themselves, or Libya doesn't terrorize western nations. The United States doesn't strike against terrorist countries if the United Nations strongly enforces international law, but the United States does strike against terrorist countries. Accordingly, either Libya doesn't terrorize western nations or it isn't true that the United States doesn't strike against terrorist countries and European governments do protect themselves. (E,P,T,S)

5. Either it isn't the case that Napoleon Bonaparte escaped from Elba and didn't win at Waterloo, or he was defeated even though he escaped from Elba. If Napoleon was defeated, he escaped from Elba but didn't restore the Empire. Wherefore, Napoleon escaped from Elba and restored the empire only if he won at Waterloo. (E,W,D,R)

6. Syria attacks Israel whenever both the United States doesn't control terrorism while European countries don't enforce international law. It isn't the case that either Syria attacks Israel or Iran supports Iraq's shipping claims. Subsequently, the United States doesn't control terrorism only if either the United Nation polices the Middle East or European countries enforce international law. (A,C,E,S,P)

7. Either Libya institutes laws against international terrorism, or either Iraq blocks international terrorism or either the United States takes strong measures against terrorists or the United States controls terrorism. It isn't the case that either Iraq blocks international terrorism or Libya institutes laws against international terrorism. Hence, either the United States controls terrorism or the United States takes strong measures against terrorism. (I,B,T,C)

8. The following isn't true: We don't question the existence of Priam's Troy; moreover, we read about Heinrich Schliemann's digs, while studying George Grote's *History of Greece* and being interested in the Homeric stories. Thus, assuming we're interested in the Homeric stories only if we study Grote's *History of Greece*, then we question the existence of Priam's Troy whenever we read about Schliemann's digs. (Q,R,S,I)

9. It isn't true that terrorism continues to curse the free world while the United States does not fight back; furthermore, it isn't true that international law prevails and European countries don't bind together against extremist groups. Either terrorism continues to curse the free world or international law prevails, but not both. So, it isn't true that European countries don't bind together against extremist groups but the United States doesn't fight back. (C,F,P,B)

10. The following isn't so: We follow the dictates of reason, but also it isn't true that we attend to the needs of others if and only if we wish to be happy. Either we wish to be happy or don't try to be moral, but not both. Moreover, the following isn't the case: We don't follow the dictates of reason, yet it isn't true that we wish to be happy and don't try to be moral. So, it isn't true that we attend to the needs of others while not trying to be moral. (F,A,W,T)

---

## 3.  DEMONSTRATIONS OF INCONSISTENCY

Premises are inconsistent if there is no possible truth-assignment making them all true. Chapter 3 develops truth table methods to establish inconsistency, and Chapter 4 introduces truth tree techniques. Another way to establish the inconsistency of premises is to symbolize the argument and then move toward some statement, 'p', and its formal denial, '~ p'. The definitional rules governing the logical operators are introduced in Chapter 2. Any elementary rules of inference based on these definitional rules guarantee that if all the premises of an argument are true, any statement deduced from those premises must also be true. Yet 'p' and '~ p', while both deduced from the premises, cannot both be true. Hence, the premises can never all be true. The premises are inconsistent.

The inconsistency of (1) is established in Chapter 3 by a truth table:

(1)  Either my Zipper Gripper will hold or I'll be embarrassed, but not both. It isn't true that my Zipper Gripper will hold and I'll not be most embarrassed. Further, either I'll not be most embarrassed or my Zipper Gripper will hold. My Zipper Gripper isn't going to hold. Therefore, I'll be most embarrassed. (G,E)

Now symbolize (1) and deduce a contradiction to show that its premise set is inconsistent:

| (2) | | /∴ E |
|---|---|---|
| 1) | G △ E | Pr |
| 2) | ~ (G · ~ E) | Pr |
| 3) | ~ E ∨ G | Pr |
| 4) | ~ G | Pr |
| 5) | (G ∨ E) · ( ~ G ∨ ~ E) | 1, Equiv |
| 6) | G ∨ E | 5, Simp |
| 7) | E ∨ G | 6, Com |
| 8) | G ∨ ~ E | 3, Com |
| 9) | ~ E | 8, 4, DS |
| 10) | G | 7, 9, DS |
| 11) | G · ~ G | 10, 4, Conj |

A contradiction appears in 4 and 10 and is explicitly displayed in 11. The expression in 11 is not the conclusion of (1). It merely serves to display explicitly a contradiction entailed by the premise set of the argument. Inconsistent premise sets entail every possible statement. Once a contradiction has been established, any conclusion can be deduced by using Addition followed by Disjunctive Syllogism. Deducing some statement, 'p', and its denial, ' ~ p', from an inconsistent premise set leads to this:

| l) | p | ?,? |
|---|---|---|
| m) | ~ p | ?,? |

Let 'C' depict any conclusion. Then the above lines can be continued:

| n) | p ∨ C | l, Add |
|---|---|---|
| o) | ∴ C | n, m, DS |

However, when demonstrating that a premise set is inconsistent it is not necessary to assert a conclusion. Simply end the demonstration with a statement of the form 'p · ~ p'.

---

## EXERCISES

### Group A:

1. Given the premises of (1) prove 'Either my Zipper Gripper will hold or the party isn't a crashing bore'. (G,P)

2. Given the premises of (2) show that they are contradictory by deducing the statements 'E' and ' ~ E'.

**Group B:**

Show that each of the following arguments has inconsistent premises by deducing a contradiction.

1.                              /∴ A · ~ B
   1) A ⊃ B        Pr
   2) ~ ( ~ B · ~ A)   Pr
   3) ~ B         Pr

2.                              /∴ B ∨ C
   1) A · (B ⊃ ~ A)   Pr
   2) (C · B) ∨ (B · A)   Pr

3.                              /∴ ~ A ⊃ C
   1) ( ~ A · B) ⊃ C   Pr
   2) B         Pr
   3) ~ C · ~ A    Pr

4.                              /∴ C ⊃ A
   1) A ∨ (B ∆ C)   Pr
   2) ( ~ B · ~ C) ∨ A   Pr
   3) ~ A        Pr

5.                              /∴ B ≡ ~ A
   1) A ⊃ ( ~ B ⊃ ~ A)   Pr
   2) (B ⊃ ~ A) · A   Pr

6.                              /∴ A ⊃ C
   1) A ⊃ B     Pr
   2) ~ B · ~ C   Pr
   3) (A ≡ B) ⊃ C   Pr

7.                              /∴ B ∆ D
   1) (A · B) ∨ (C · D)   Pr
   2) ( ~ A · ~ D) ∨ ( ~ D · ~ B)   Pr

8.                              /∴ B ⊃ (C ⊃ ~ A)
   1) (A · C) ∨ ( ~ B · A)   Pr
   2) A ≡ B     Pr
   3) B ⊃ (C ⊃ ~ B)   Pr

9.                              /∴ A ≡ C
   1) (A · B) ∨ ( ~ A · ~ B)   Pr
   2) ( ~ B ⊃ ~ D) · ( ~ A ⊃ ~ C)   Pr
   3) ~ ( ~ D · ~ C) · ~ (A · B)   Pr

10.                             /∴ D ⊃ (B · C)
   1) (A ∆ B) ∨ (C · D)   Pr
   2) (B · A) · ~ D   Pr

**Group C:**

Symbolize the following arguments using the capital letters suggested. Then show that each argument has inconsistent premises by deducing a contradiction.

1. In molecular-orbital theory the energy levels of the electrons must be determined or their

orbitals described. It isn't the case that whenever the orbitals of the electrons aren't described, their energy levels must be determined. Consequently, the orbitals of electrons must be described or their density established. (L,O,D)

2. Either molecular-orbital theory assumes a molecule is comprised of nuclei fixed in space, or the electrons introduced into the nuclei's electrostatic field travel over the entire molecule while molecular-orbital theory does assume a molecule is comprised of nuclei fixed in space. Neither do the electrons introduced into the nuclei's electrostatic field travel over the entire molecule nor does molecular-orbital theory assume a molecule is comprised of nuclei fixed in space. Hence, molecular-orbital theory assumes a molecule is comprised of nuclei fixed in space. (T,E)

3. Either the principles of quantum mechanics are applied to the chemistry of molecules or molecular-orbital theory is an exciting development in chemistry (but not both), or Newtonian laws are the sole basis of contemporary chemistry. The principles of quantum mechanics are applied to the chemistry of molecules and molecular-orbital theory is an exciting development in contemporary chemistry. Now, Newtonian laws aren't the sole basis of contemporary chemistry. Accordingly, if Newtonian laws are the sole basis of contemporary chemistry, the principles of quantum mechanics aren't applied to the chemistry of molecules. (P,O,L)

4. Accepting the basic assumptions of molecular-orbital theory is sufficient for asserting that if a molecule isn't in the electrostatic field of several nuclei concurrently then an eigenfunction isn't used to represent an electron. But an eigenfunction is used to represent an electron. Further, the basic assumptions of molecular-orbital theory are accepted in spite of the fact that a molecule isn't in the electrostatic field of several nuclei concurrently. So, that the basic assumptions of molecular-orbital theory are accepted is a sufficient condition for a molecule being in the electrostatic field of several nuclei concurrently. (A,M,E)

5. If a linear velocity $v$ is associated with a particle mass $m$, a linear momentum $p$ is also associated with $m$. Linear velocity $v$ is associated with $m$ even though the acceleration $a$ of $m$ hasn't been determined. We might use Newton's second law of mechanics provided that it isn't the case $a$ of $m$ has been determined whenever $v$ is associated with $m$. A linear momentum $p$ is also associated with $m$ only if the acceleration $a$ of $m$ has been determined. Therefore, we don't use Newton's second law of mechanics, but $a$ of $m$ has been determined only if a linear momentum $p$ is associated with $m$. (V,M,A,L)

6. Either Coulomb's law is misleading, or either the force of attraction between two charged bodies is either directly proportional to the product of their charges or inversely proportional to the square of the distance between them, but not both. Now, Coulomb's law isn't misleading despite the fact that the force of attraction between two charged bodies is neither directly proportional to the product of their charges nor inversely proportional to the square of the distance between them. Thus, the force of attraction between two charged bodies is directly proportional to the product of their charges if, and only if, it is also inversely proportional to the square of the distance between them. (M,D,I)

7. If light waves are composed of photons and not atoms, we may still expect to discover an interstellar ether-type substance. Now, it isn't the case both that light waves aren't composed of photons even though we may not still expect to discover an interstellar ether-

type substance. Not only are light waves not composed of atoms, but as well we may not still expect to discover an interstellar ether-type substance. If we still may expect to discover an interstellar ether-type substance, we aren't familiar with the 1887 Michelson-Morley experiments. So, it is obvious that we aren't familiar with the 1887 Michelson-Morley experiments. (P,A,S,E)

8. Either blackbody radiation can be explained whenever quantum mechanics is accepted, or Max Planck's 1901 interpretation of his experiments isn't correct and his constant, *h*, must be revised. Planck's 1901 interpretation of his experiments is correct and quantum mechanics is accepted, but even so blackbody radiation can't be explained. Accordingly, Planck's constant, *h*, must be revised even though blackbody radiation can be explained. (R,M,I,C)

9. In a photoelectric effect if the frequency of the incident of light on a metallic electrode changes but the intensity of radiation doesn't, then either the intensity of radiation changes or the electrons' energy changes. The electrons' energy changes only if neither they are emitted from a metallic electrode nor the radiation frequency passes the value $v_o$. Either the intensity of radiation doesn't change, or neither the electrons are emitted from a metallic electrode nor does the radiation frequency pass the value $v_o$. Now, the frequency of the incident of light on a metallic electrode changes and the radiation frequency passes the value of $v_o$. Consequently, not only does the frequency of the incident of light change, but so does the intensity of radiation. (F,I,E,M,V)

10. We can't accept Louis de Broglie's 1924 "Investigations into Quantum Theory" provided that either Newtonian mechanics suffices to explain Max Planck's findings or light phenomena are explained in terms of waves. If neither the photoelectric effect can be explained nor can light phenomena be explained in terms of particles, light phenomena can be explained in terms of waves. Light phenomena can be explained in terms of either particles or waves only if we can accept de Broglie's 1924 "Investigations into Quantum Theory." Neither can the photoelectric effect nor light phenomena be explained in terms of particles, or either Newtonian mechanics suffices to explain Planck's findings or Robert Millikan in 1916 produced experimental evidence of *h*. Newtonian mechanics doesn't suffice to explain Planck's findings and Millikan didn't produce experimental evidence for *h* in 1916. Hence, if the photoelectric effect can be explained, light phenomena can be explained in terms of particles. (B,N,W,E,P,M)

## 4. DEMONSTRATIONS OF TAUTOLOGIES

In Chapter 3, truth table techniques are used to determine if a truth-functional statement is tautological. Consider this example:

(1) If the cost of living doesn't stabilize or building loans become more plentiful, while building loans become more plentiful only if there is more spending, then the cost of living will stabilize only if there is more spending. (C,B,S)

A truth table shows that (1) is tautological:*

(2)

| [( ~ | C | ∨ | B) | · | (B | ⊃ | S)] | ⊃ | (C | ⊃ | S) |
|------|---|---|----|---|----|---|-----|---|----|---|----|
| 0 | 1 | 1 | 1 | 1 | 1 | 1 | 1 | 1 | 1 | 1 | 1 |
| 0 | 1 | 1 | 1 | 0 | 1 | 0 | 0 | 1 | 1 | 0 | 0 |
| 0 | 1 | 0 | 0 | 0 | 0 | 1 | 1 | 1 | 1 | 1 | 1 |
| 0 | 1 | 0 | 0 | 0 | 0 | 1 | 0 | 1 | 1 | 0 | 0 |
| 1 | 0 | 1 | 1 | 1 | 1 | 1 | 1 | 1 | 0 | 1 | 1 |
| 1 | 0 | 1 | 1 | 0 | 1 | 0 | 0 | 1 | 0 | 1 | 0 |
| 1 | 0 | 1 | 0 | 1 | 0 | 1 | 1 | 1 | 0 | 1 | 1 |
| 1 | 0 | 1 | 0 | 1 | 0 | 1 | 0 | 1 | 0 | 1 | 0 |

$\Uparrow$

Other methods, resembling proofs, can also be used. For example, to demonstrate that a hypothetical statement is tautological, assume the antecedent and then use various elementary rules of inference to deduce the consequent. Such a procedure demonstrates that if the antecedent is true, the consequent must be true. A hypothetical statement can be false if and only if the antecedent is true and the consequent false. But if the truth of the antecedent entails the truth of the consequent, the hypothetical statement is tautological. Thus, assume the antecedent of (1) and deduce the consequent:

(3)

1) $(\sim C \vee B) \cdot (B \supset S)$   CP, / ∴ C ⊃ S
2) $\sim C \vee B$   1, Simp
3) $(B \supset S) \cdot (\sim C \vee B)$   1, Com
4) $B \supset S$   3, Simp
5) $C \supset B$   2, Impl
6) $C \supset S$   5, 4, HS

7) $[(\sim C \vee B) \cdot (B \supset S)] \supset (C \supset S)$   1–6, CP

---

*Once more, truth trees are available to demonstrate that (1) is a tautology:

| | | |
|---|---|---|
| 1. | $\sim \{[(\sim C \vee B) \cdot (B \supset S)] \supset (C \supset S)\}$ ✓ | ——— |
| 2. | $(\sim C \vee B) \cdot (B \supset S)$ ✓ | 1, DMI |
| 3. | $\sim (C \supset S)$ ✓ | 1, DMI |
| 4. | C | 3, DMI |
| 5. | $\sim S$ | 3, DMI |
| 6. | $\sim C \vee B$ ✓ | 2, C |
| 7. | $B \supset S$ ✓ | 2, C |
| 8. | $\sim C \qquad B$ | 6, ID |
| | X | |
| 9. | $\sim B \quad S$ | 7, MI |
| | X $\quad$ X | |

Since every branch in the above truth tree is closed, the statement in 1 is a contradiction. So, the statement, '$[(\sim C \vee B) \cdot (B \supset S)] \supset (C \supset S)$', is a tautology.

Because the statement asserted in 1 does entail the statement mentioned in 6, '[( ~ C ∨ B) · (B ⊃ S)] ⊃ (C ⊃ S)' can be asserted in 7. (1) is shown to be tautological since '( ~ C ∨ B) · (B ⊃ S)' does entail 'C ⊃ S'.

The scope of the statement in line 1 of (3) extends only through 6. The scope of the first statement does not extend through 7; the seventh statement is not logically dependent on the first. Indeed, the statement in 7 is not deduced from any statement in (3). The seventh statement is not the conclusion of an argument, although that it is tautological is *demonstrated* by a Conditional Proof in lines 1 through 6.

Indirect Proof can also be used to determine if some statement is tautological. Assume the denial of the statement in question and then deduce both some statement, 'p', and its denial, ' ~ p'. This establishes that the denial of the original statement is a contradiction. If the denial of the original statement can never be true, then the original statement must always be true. The original statement must be tautological. Work through this example:

**(4)** Either the computer won't function properly, or if the tapes are secured whenever the computer functions properly, the tapes are secured. (C,T)

That (4) is a tautology can be established by a truth table:*

**(5)**

| ~ | C | ∨ | [(C | ⊃ | T) | ⊃ | T] |
|---|---|---|-----|----|----|----|----|
| 0 | 1 | 1 | 1 | 1 | 1 | 1 | 1 |
| 0 | 1 | 1 | 1 | 0 | 0 | 1 | 0 |
| 1 | 0 | 1 | 0 | 1 | 1 | 1 | 1 |
| 1 | 0 | 1 | 0 | 1 | 0 | 0 | 0 |

⇑

It can also be demonstrated that (4) is tautological by using Indirect Proof. Assume the denial of ' ~ C ∨ [(C ⊃ T) ⊃ T]'. Next, work toward a contradiction:

---

*Or, by using truth trees, it can be shown that the statement, ' ~ C ∨ [(C ⊃ T) ⊃ T]', is a tautology:

| | | |
|---|---|---|
| 1. | ~ { ~ C ∨ [(C ⊃ T) ⊃ T]}  ✓ | —— |
| 2. | ~ ~ C  ✓ | 1, DID |
| 3. | ~ [(C ⊃ T) ⊃ T]  ✓ | 1, DID |
| 4. | C | 2, DN |
| 5. | C ⊃ T  ✓ | 3, DMI |
| 6. | ~ T | 3, DMI |
| 7. | ~ C      T | 5, MI |
| | X      X | |

Since every branch in the above truth tree is closed, the statement in 1 is a contradiction. Therefore, the statement, ' ~ C ∨ [(C ⊃ T) ⊃ T]', is a tautology.

**(6)**

| | | |
|---|---|---|
| **1)** | $\sim \{\sim C \vee [(C \supset T) \supset T]\}$ | IP |
| **2)** | $\sim\sim C \cdot \sim [(C \supset T) \supset T]$ | 1, DeM |
| **3)** | $\sim\sim C$ | 2, Simp |
| **4)** | $\sim [(C \supset T) \supset T] \cdot \sim\sim C$ | 2, Com |
| **7)** | $\sim\sim (C \supset T) \cdot \sim T$ | 4, Simp |
| **6)** | $\sim [\sim (C \supset T) \vee T]$ | 5, Impl |
| **7)** | $\sim\sim (C \supset T) \cdot \sim T$ | 6, DeM |
| **8)** | $(C \supset T) \cdot \sim T$ | 7, DN |
| **9)** | $C \supset T$ | 8, Simp |
| **10)** | $\sim T \cdot (C \supset T)$ | 8, Com |
| **11)** | $\sim T$ | 10, Simp |
| **12)** | $\sim C$ | 9, 11, MT |
| **13)** | $\sim C \cdot \sim\sim C$ | 12, 3, Conj |

**14)**  $\sim C \vee [(C \supset T) \supset T]$        1–13, IP

Since the denial of ' $\sim C \vee [(C \supset T) \supset T]$ ' leads to a contradiction, ' $\sim C \vee [C \supset T) \supset T]$ ' is tautological. Notice that the statement asserted in 14 does not fall within the scope of any statement in (6). Indeed, there is no premise in (6) because there is no argument. Rather, (6) is a demonstration that the statement ' $\sim C \vee [(C \supset T) \supset T]$ ' is tautological.

---

## EXERCISES

### Group A:

Employing the methods developed in this section, demonstrate that each of the following is a tautology.

1. $A \supset (B \supset A)$
2. $(A \supset B) \supset [\sim (B \cdot C) \supset \sim (C \cdot A)]$
3. $[(A \supset B) \cdot (A \supset C)] \supset [A \supset (B \cdot C)]$
4. $[(A \supset B) \supset A] \supset A$
5. $(A \vee \sim B) \vee (B \vee \sim A)$
6. $(A \supset B) \vee \sim (B \cdot A)$
7. $(A \equiv B) \vee (\sim B \equiv A)$
8. $(A \supset B) \supset [A \supset (A \cdot B)]$
9. $A \equiv [A \cdot (A \vee B)]$
10. $A \equiv [A \vee (A \cdot B)]$

### Group B:

Symbolize the following statements using the capital letters suggested. Employing the methods developed in this section, demonstrate that each of the statements is a tautology.

1. If scientists are interested not only in prediction but in explanation as well, then they are interested in either description or prediction while interested in explanation as well. (P,E,D)

2. Either it isn't the case both that government supports research but taxpayers don't, or it isn't the case both that industry doesn't support research while government also doesn't support it. (G,P,I)

3. If scientists construct theories only if they are interested in explanation, then whenever scientists construct theories and organize their findings, they are interested in explanation at the same time they organize their findings. (T,E,F)

4. The following·isn't the case: It isn't true that unless costly expenditures are important, knowledge doesn't increase with research; however, costly expenditures are important. (E,K)

5. If research is supported provided scientists collect data, then either scientists collect data or knowledge is increased whenever either research is supported or knowledge is increased. (R,S,K)

6. If scientists organize their findings whenever they collect data as well as verify their observations if they build theories, then scientists either organize their findings or verify their observations whenever they collect data or build theories. (O,C,V,B)

7. Either costly expenditures are important to support new research, or a necessary condition for sources of revenue not being found is that costly expenditures aren't important to support new research. (C,S)

8. Either it is not the case that sources of revenue are found to finance research whenever, and only whenever, the public appreciates the value of knowledge, or either sources of revenue are found to finance research or the public doesn't appreciate the value of knowledge (but not both). (S,P)

9. Either the public appreciates the value of knowledge, or costly expenditures are important to support new research only if either sources of revenue are found or the public doesn't appreciate the value of knowledge. (P,E,S)

10. That either we are not faithful in our duties or honored is a nescessary condition for the following: Assuming we persist in our work, then we either are rewarded or honored or aren't faithful in our duties; but, certainly, we do persist in our work. (F,H,P,R)

---

## 5.  DEMONSTRATIONS OF LOGICAL EQUIVALENCE

Two statements, 'p' and 'q', are logically equivalent if and only if they both have the same truth-values given the same truth-conditions. That is, 'p' and 'q' are logically equivalent if and only if the biconditional, 'p ≡ q', is tautological. For example, these statements are logically equivalent:

**(1)**

    **a)** There is a lightning discharge just in case there is an electrical discharge. (L,E)

    **b)** If there isn't a lightning discharge, there isn't an electrical discharge; moreover, there isn't a lightning discharge or there is an electrical discharge. (L,E)

That these statements are logically equivalent can be shown by a truth table.*
Symbolize (a) and (b). Then form a biconditional and construct a truth table for it:

$$(2) \quad (L \equiv E) \equiv [(\sim L \supset \sim E) \cdot (\sim L \vee E)]$$

| (L | ≡ | E) | ≡ | [(~ | L | ⊃ | ~ | E) | · | (~ | L | ∨ | E)] |
|----|---|----|---|-----|---|---|---|----|---|----|---|---|-----|
| 1 | 1 | 1 | 1 | 0 | 1 | 1 | 0 | 1 | 1 | 0 | 1 | 1 | 1 |
| 1 | 0 | 0 | 1 | 0 | 1 | 1 | 1 | 0 | 0 | 0 | 1 | 0 | 0 |
| 0 | 0 | 1 | 1 | 1 | 0 | 0 | 0 | 1 | 0 | 1 | 0 | 1 | 1 |
| 0 | 1 | 0 | 1 | 1 | 0 | 1 | 1 | 1 | 0 | 1 | 1 | 0 | 0 |

⇑

---

*Or, by a truth tree:

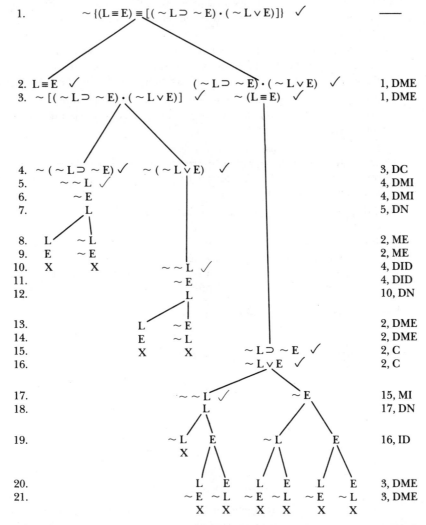

Every branch is closed in this truth tree. So, 'L ≡ E' and '( ~ L ⊃ ~ E) · ( ~ L ∨ E)' are logically
equivalent.

Section 4 develops a procedure to determine if a statement is tautological or not. Deny the statement in question. If this produces a contradiction, the original statement is tautological. A similar procedure is used to determine if two statements are logically equivalent. Symbolize the statements and form a biconditional from them. Deny this biconditional. If a contradiction can be generated from the denied biconditional, the original two statements are logically equivalent. Notice how this is done with the two statements of (1):

(3)

| | | |
|---|---|---|
| 1) | $\sim \{(L \equiv E) \equiv [(\sim L \supset \sim E) \cdot (\sim L \vee E)]\}$ | IP |
| 2) | $\sim \{(L \equiv E) \equiv [(E \supset L) \cdot (\sim L \vee E)]\}$ | 1, Trans |
| 3) | $\sim \{(L \equiv E) \equiv [(E \supset L) \cdot (L \supset E)]\}$ | 2, Impl |
| 4) | $\sim \{(L \equiv E) \equiv [(L \supset E) \cdot (E \supset L)]\}$ | 3, Com |
| 5) | $\sim [(L \equiv E) \equiv (L \equiv E)]$ | 4, Equiv |
| 6) | $\sim \{[(L \equiv E) \cdot (L \equiv E)] \vee [\sim (L \equiv E) \cdot \sim (L \equiv E)]\}$ | 5, Equiv |
| 7) | $\sim \{(L \equiv E) \vee [\sim (L \equiv E) \cdot \sim (L \equiv E)]\}$ | 5, Taut |
| 8) | $\sim [(L \equiv E) \vee \sim (L \equiv E)]$ | 7, Taut |
| 9) | $\sim (L \equiv E) \cdot \sim \sim (L \equiv E)$ | 8, DeM |

10) $(L \equiv E) \equiv [(\sim L \supset \sim E) \cdot (\sim L \vee E)]$ 　　　1–9, IP

Here is another way to show that two statements are logically equivalent. Two statements are logically equivalent if and only if they entail one another. Thus, if two statements are equivalent, this can be demonstrated by establishing that they do entail one another. For example, it can be shown that 'L ≡ E' and '($\sim$L $\supset$ $\sim$E) · '($\sim$L $\vee$ E)' are logically equivalent by demonstrating that 'L ≡ E' entails '($\sim$L $\supset$ $\sim$E) · ($\sim$L $\vee$ E)' *and* that '($\sim$L $\supset$ $\sim$E) · ($\sim$L $\vee$ E)' entails 'L ≡ E':

(4) 　　　　　　　　　　　　　　　 /∴ $(\sim L \supset \sim E) \cdot (\sim L \vee E)$

| | | |
|---|---|---|
| 1) | $L \equiv E$ | Pr |
| 2) | $(L \supset E) \cdot (E \supset L)$ | 1, Equiv |
| 3) | $(\sim \sim L \supset E) \cdot (E \supset L)$ | 2, DN |
| 4) | $(\sim L \vee E) \cdot (E \supset L)$ | 3, Impl |
| 5) | $(\sim L \vee E) \cdot (\sim L \supset \sim E)$ | 4, Trans |
| 6) | /∴ $(\sim L \supset \sim E) \cdot (\sim L \vee E)$ | 5, Com |

and 　　　　　　　　　　　　　　　　　　　　 /∴ L ≡ E

| | | |
|---|---|---|
| 1) | $(\sim L \supset \sim E) \cdot (\sim L \vee E)$ | Pr |
| 2) | $(\sim L \vee E) \cdot (\sim L \supset \sim E)$ | 1, Com |
| 3) | $(L \supset E) \cdot (\sim L \supset \sim E)$ | 2, Impl |
| 4) | $(L \supset E) \cdot (E \supset L)$ | 3, Trans |
| 5) | /∴ $L \equiv E$ | 4, Equiv |

Since (4) demonstrates that 'L ≡ E' and '($\sim$L $\supset$ $\sim$E) · ($\sim$L $\vee$ E)' mutually entail one another, these statements are logically equivalent.

## *EXERCISES*

### Group A:

Establish that each pair of expressions is logically equivalent by deducing a contradiction from the denial of the biconditional formed from them.

1.  a)  $\sim A \vee \sim B$
    b)  $\sim (A \cdot B)$

2.  a)  $A \supset B$
    b)  $\sim A \vee B$

3.  a)  $A \supset B$
    b)  $\sim B \supset \sim A$

4.  a)  $(A \cdot B) \supset C$
    b)  $A \supset (B \supset C)$

5.  a)  $A \vee (B \cdot C)$
    b)  $(A \vee B) \cdot (A \vee C)$

6.  a)  $A \cdot (B \vee C)$
    b)  $(A \cdot B) \vee (A \cdot C)$

7.  a)  $A \equiv B$
    b)  $(A \supset B) \cdot (B \supset A)$

8.  a)  $A \equiv B$
    b)  $(A \cdot B) \vee (\sim A \cdot \sim B)$

9.  a)  $A \triangle B$
    b)  $(A \vee B) \cdot (\sim A \vee \sim B)$

10. a)  $A \triangle B$
    b)  $(A \cdot \sim B) \vee (B \cdot \sim A)$

### Group B:

Symbolize the following pairs of statements using the capital letters suggested. Then demonstrate for each pair that the statements mutually entail one another.

1.  a) If there is an atom, $x$, of high electronegativity, then if $x$ approaches an atom, $y$, of low electronegativity, the very strong attraction for electrons exerted by $x$ may suffice to remove an electron from $y$. (H,L,S)
    b) If an atom, $x$, approaches an atom of low electronegativity, $y$, then if the atom $x$ of high electronegativity, the very strong attraction for electrons exerted by $x$ may suffice to remove an electron from $y$. (L,H,S)

2.  a) If two simple ions are produced by oxidation and an energy input is required, then the two original ions are at a lower state of potential energy than the two produced ones. (P,R,S)

b) Two simple ions aren't produced by oxidation unless netiher of the two original ions are at a lower state of potential energy than the two produced ones nor is an energy input not required. (P,S,R)

3. a) It isn't true that a chemical bond is ionic if and only if it is metallic. (I,M)
   b) Either a chemical bond is ionic but not metallic, or it isn't ionic while being metallic. (I,M)

4. a) If we're to understand the beginnings of Gothic architecture, we must study the life of Abbot Suger and the royal Abbey Church of Saint-Denis. (G,S,D)
   b) A necessary condition for understanding the beginnings of Gothic architecture is that we study the life of Abbot Suger; moreover, a sufficient condition for studying the royal Abbey Church of Saint-Denis is that we understand the beginnings of Gothic architecture. (G,S,D)

5. a) Either Abbot Suger was chief advisor to Louis VI or he played a small role in the creation of a powerful French monarch, but it isn't the case both that Abbot Suger played a small role in the creation of a powerful French monarch while also being chief advisor to Louis VI. (A,M)
   b) That Abbot Suger was chief advisor to Louis VI implies he didn't play a small role in the creation of a powerful French monarch; further, either Abbot Suger did play a small role in the creation of a powerful French monarch or he was chief advisor to Louis VI. (A,M)

6. a) If Abbot Suger brought the Church and monarch together against the nobility, Louis VI rewarded the Church either by supporting the Papacy against the German emperors or by rebuilding Saint-Denis in a lavish style. (S,P,D)
   b) Either Louis VI rewarded the Church by supporting the Papacy against the German emperors if Abbot Suger brought the Church and monarch together against the nobility, or Abbot Suger brought the Church and monarch together against the nobility only if Louis VI rewarded the Church by rebuilding Saint-Denis in a lavish style. (P,S,D)

7. a) The Saint-Denis of Abbot Suger is Gothic if and only if the edifice stresses both geometric planning and light. (G,P,L)
   b) The Saint-Denis of Abbot Suger isn't Gothic if and only if the edifice doesn't stress both geometric planning and light. (G,P,L)

8. a) The ambulatory of Saint-Denis is Byzantine or Romanesque (but not both) in style, or it is Gothic (but not both). (B,R,G)
   b) Either the ambulatory of Saint-Denis is Romanesque in style, or it isn't Byzantine in style if and only if it is Gothic (but not both). (R,B,G)

9. a) That Annye Mae visits Frank is a necessary condition for her also seeing Dottie whenever and only whenever she goes to Athens. (V,S,G)
   b) If Annye Mae sees Dottie only if she goes to Athens, then either she visits Frank or sees Dottie but doesn't go to Athens. (S,G,V)

10. a) If Dottie visits the West Side and the Ansonborough areas of Charleston, then she'll see either the Brandford-Horry House or the William Rhett House. (S,A,H,R)
    b) Dottie doesn't see the William Rhett House but does visit the West Side area of Charleston only if she either sees the Brandford-Horry House or doesn't visit the Ansonborough area of Charleston. (R,S,H,A)

## 6.    REVIEW OF NEW TERMS

**Conditional Proof:** A proof of validity in which the antecedent of a hypothetical conclusion, or a conclusion logically equivalent to a hypothetical, is taken as an assumption. With this assumption, coupled with the original premises, the consequent of the original conclusion becomes the conclusion to be proved. If the original premises, plus the assumption, logically entail the consequent of the original conclusion, then the original premises, without the assumption, logically entail the original conclusion.

**Indirect Proof:** A proof of validity of an argument in which the denial of the entire conclusion is assumed and from which, in combination with the original premises, a contradiction is reached. If the original premises, plus the assumption of the denial of the original conclusion, logically entail a contradiction, then the original premises, without the assumption, logically entail the conclusion of the argument.

**Scope:** The scope of an assumption consists of those statements in a proof that depend on that assumption for their deduction.

# 8

# CATEGORICAL LOGIC: STATEMENTS AND IMMEDIATE INFERENCES

The validity or invalidity of many arguments cannot be established by using only truth-functional logic. Here are two examples:

**(1)** Some toxic chemicals aren't industrial waste products. Consequently, some nonindustrial waste products aren't toxic chemicals.

**(2)** No failing student earns a degree. But anyone who gets a good-paying job earns a degree. So, no failing student will get a good paying job.

All of the statements in (1) and (2) are simple. None of them is built up out of two or more smaller statements. Consequently, given only the techniques of truth-functional logic, (1) can be symbolized in this way:

**(3)**          / ∴ P
     1) C   Pr

And the two premises and conclusion of (2) can be truth-functionally symbolized in this way:

**(4)**          / ∴ F
     1) S   Pr
     2) J   Pr

While both (1) and (2) are valid arguments, no hint of this is found in (3) or (4). Fortunately, however, several ways can be developed to establish the validity or invalidity of these arguments and others like them. Methods dealing with arguments such as (1) are developed in this chapter. In the next chapter these methods are extended to include arguments such as (2).

## 1. CATEGORICAL STATEMENTS AND VENN DIAGRAMS

Each of the statements in (1) and (2) above is a *categorical statement*:

**A categorical statement asserts that a relation holds between two classes, or categories.**

A *class* is understood as

**a collection of individuals having some common characteristic(s).**

Categorical statements can be reduced to four different, basic forms. These basic forms are named '*A*', '*E*', '*I*', and '*O*'.* Each of the following simple statements is an example of a different basic form of categorical statement:

> **(1)**  All mammals are animals.
> No whales are fish.
> Some nurses are men.
> Some viruses are not harmful organisms.

Using capital letters to name the classes mentioned in these statements, the statements can be classified and symbolized as

> **(2)**  A: All M are A.
> E: No W are F.
> I: Some N are M.
> O: Some V are not O.

'All mammals are animals' is an *A* statement, and 'No whales are fish' is an *E*. 'Some nurses are men' is an *I* statement, while 'Some viruses are not harmful organisms' is an *O*.

Suppose that each of the four basic forms of categorical statements was used to make an assertion about the same two classes. For instance, someone could say

> **(3)**  All students are intelligent.
> No students are intelligent.
> Some students are intelligent.
> Some students are not intelligent.

Not all of these statements can be true, nor can they all be false. For example, if 'Some students are not intelligent' is true, then 'All students are intelligent' must necessarily be false. Or suppose it is false that, 'No students are intelligent'. Then, 'Some students are intelligent' must be true. Very often the truth-value of one categorical statement determines the truth-value of others. The truth-value relations holding between categorical statements becomes critical in constructing proofs of arguments involving categorical statements.

The logical forms of categorical statements occurring in an argument are determining factors in the deductive validity of that argument. So, in analyzing an argument for deductive validity or invalidity, it is useful to clarify the logical form of

---

* These letters are from the Latin '*AffIrmo*', 'I affirm', and 'n*EgO*', 'I deny'.

those statements involved in the argument. This can be done with categorical statements by first putting them into **standard form**. A categorical statement is in standard form if and only if it is expressed in one of the following ways:

> *A*: **All S are P***
> *E*: **No S are P**
> *I*: **Some S are P**
> *O*: **Some S are not P†**

Both the capital letters 'S' and 'P' represent a *term* where

> **a term is indicated by a linguistic expression that can be used as the subject of a declarative sentence.**

In (1) above the following statements are found:

> All mammals are animals.
> No whales are fish.
> Some nurses are men.
> Some viruses are not harmful organisms.

The words 'mammals', 'whales', 'nurses', and 'viruses' indicate *subject terms* of the statements while the words 'animals', 'fish', 'men', and 'harmful organisms' denote *predicate terms*. Categorical statements often have more complicated subject and predicate terms than theses examples. The phrase 'conscientious students who work hard and schedule their time properly' is the subject term and 'people who are usually successful in their school work and social activities' is the predicate term in

> **(4)** All conscientious students who work hard and schedule their time properly are people who are usually successful in their school work and social activities.

The logical form of a categorical statement is a function of its *quality* and *quantity*. Every categorical statement has an *affirmative* or *negative quality*. The quality is affirmative just in case the classes denoted by the terms of the statement are completely, or partially, *included* in one another. Hence, *A* and *I* statements are affirmative. The quality of a categorical statement in negative when and only when

---

* Note that 'All S are not P' is not a standard form categorical statement. What 'All S are not P' asserts is not clear. 'All S are not P' could mean either 'No S are P' or 'Some S are not P'. How 'All S are not P' is understood depends on the context in which it is used.

† Another way to render *A*, *E*, *I*, and *O* statements is by

> SAP
> SEP
> SIP
> SOP

Categorical statement names are flanked on the left by subject terms and on the right by predicate terms.

the classes denoted by the terms of the statement are completely, or partially, *excluded* from one another. So, *E* and *O* statements are negative.

The *quantity* of a categorical statement is either *universal* or *particular*. A categorical statement is *universal* if and only if the entire class denoted by the subject term is either completely included in, or excluded from, the class denoted by the predicate term. Thus, *A* and *E* statements are universal. *I* and *O* statements are *particular*. These statements are used to assert that the class denoted by the subject term is either partially included in, or excluded from, the class denoted by the predicate term. The quantity of categorical statements in standard form is suggested by the words 'all', 'no', or 'some'. These words are used to indicate *how many* individuals in the class that the subject term denotes are, or are not, members of the class named by the predicate term. Since these words answer, in a general way, 'How many?' they are known as **quantifiers**.

The quantity and quality, and thus the logical form, of each basic type of categorical statement can be summarized:

| QUANTITY | QUALITY |
|---|---|
| *A*: **Universal** | **Affirmative** |
| *E*: **Universal** | **Negative** |
| *I*: **Particular** | **Affirmative** |
| *O*: **Particular** | **Negative** |

Some form of the verb 'to be' is used to express the relation said to hold between the subject and predicate terms. This use of 'to be' expresses the **copula** of a categorical statement. Two points should be noted about the logical concept *copula*. *First*, the copula is tenseless, although it is traditionally expressed by the present tense of 'to be'. *Second*, the copula is neither singular nor plural, being expressed by either 'is' and 'is not' or 'are' and 'are not'. Simply as a convention to assure consistency of expression, in this book 'are' and 'are not' are used.

Remember that categorical statements assert something about relations holding between two classes. *A* statements assert that one class is *completely included in* another. 'All mammals are animals', says that the entire class *mammals* is included in the class *animals*. *E* statements claim that a class in *completely excluded from* another class. 'No whales are fish' says that the class *whales* is completely excluded from the class *fish*. *I* statements affirm that a class is *partially included in* another class. To declare, 'Some nurses are men' is to maintain that part of the class *nurses* is included in the class *men*. *O* statements contend that one class is *partially excluded from* another. 'Some viruses are not harmful organisms' claims that part of the class *viruses* is not included in the class *harmful organisms*.

John Venn introduced a pictorial method of representing relations holding between classes called *Venn diagrams*.* Let two circles represent the classes men-

---

* John Venn, 1834–1923, was an English mathematician and logician.

tioned in a categorical statement. Four areas are created by overlapping these circles:

(5)

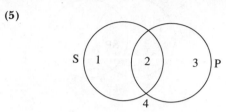

Let '*S*' represent any class and '*P*' some other class. Then area 1 represents the class of all things that are an *S* but not a *P*. Area 2 portrays the class of all things that are both an *S* and a *P*. Area 3 depicts the class of all things that are a *P* but not an *S*. And, finally, area 4 represents all things that are neither an *S* nor a *P*. All of this information is pictured in the two overlapping circles.*

Before Venn diagrams can be used to analyze categorical statements, the notion of the ***complement of a class*** needs to be introduced:

> **The complement of any class, *S*, is that class, *non-S*, having as its members all those things that are not members of *S*.**

The complement of the class *women* contains such individuals as men, pigs, desks, books, and any other thing that is not a woman. Expressions that denote *contrary classes* must not be confused with expressions that denote class complements. For instance, the classes *white* and *black* are contrary classes. The class *white things* contains only things that are white and the class *black things* only things that are black. No one thing can be both white and black at the same time and in the same way. Nonetheless, many things are neither white nor black. If 'W' denotes the class *white things*, then 'non-W' denotes *non-white things*; namely, the complement of the class *white things*.† More subtle and dangerous examples of confusion between class contraries and complements are often found in discussions concerning the classes *morally good actions* and *morally bad actions*. While these classes are contraries, they are not complements. Because some action is not morally good it does not follow that it is morally bad. The action might be neither morally good nor morally bad. The bar, '—', is used to represent the complement of a class. Thus, '$\overline{\text{W}}$' represents the complement of the class *women*. The information represented by the overlapping circles in (5) can now be displayed in this way:

---

\* In the remainder of this chapter, for ease of reference, each area of a Venn diagram will continue to be numbered.

† By convention the complement of the class *non-white things* is understood as *white things*, represented by 'W', and not *non-non-white things*. A rule of "double complement" is implicitly assumed to yield the class *white things*.

**(6)**

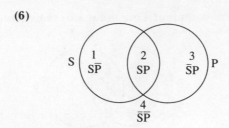

The four standard forms of categorical statements can now be pictured by using overlapping circles. Consider the four categorical assertions that can be made about the classes *surgeons* and *physicians*.

'All surgeons are physicians', for instance, says that anything that is an *S* (a surgeon) is also a *P* (a physician). This is equivalent to asserting 'No surgeons are not physicians', or 'Anything that fails to be a surgeon also fails to be a physician'. What is asserted by 'All S are P' can be diagrammed as

**(7)**

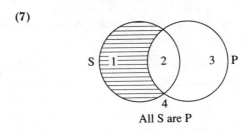

All S are P

Shading an area indicates an ***empty class***; that is, a class having no members.* With area 1 shaded, the only remaining part of *S* is area 2, which is also in the *P* circle. Area 2, known as the *intersect*, or *lens*, of *S* and *P*, is where any individual would be found, if such an individual exists, who is both a surgeon and a physician. Notice that *not shading* an area indicates only that nothing is known concerning whether the class pictured by that area is empty or not. That class might or might not have members.

'No surgeons are physicians', or 'No S are P', asserts that there is nothing common to *S* and *P*:

**(8)**

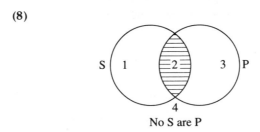

No S are P

———————————

* The empty class is also sometimes called the *null class*. The class *unicorns* has no members, but it is no less a class for that.

What of examples such as 'Some surgeons are physicians'? One problem in understanding clearly what is being claimed is the vagueness of 'some'. When Annye Mae says to Russell, 'Some of us are going to the dance', just how many are going? To avoid this vagueness, 'some' is used in logic in the minimal sense of 'there is at least one'. That is, 'Some S are P' declares that there is at least one thing that is both an S and a P. There might be surgeons who are not physicians, or physicians who are not surgeons. This is why neither areas 1 nor 3 are shaded in (9) below. Nonetheless, at least one surgeon, perhaps more, is a physician. An 'X' is drawn in area 2 to represent this individual or these individuals:

**(9)**

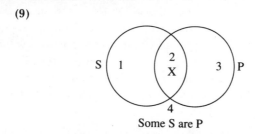

Some S are P

'Some surgeons are not physicians' maintains there is at least one surgeon who is not a physician.* There might be someone who is a surgeon and a physician, or who is a physician but not a surgeon. 'Some S are not P' leaves these possibilities undetermined. Hence, areas 2 and 3 are not shaded. Even so, there is an 'X' in area 1 picturing the information asserted in 'Some S are not P':

**(10)**

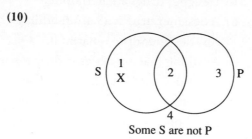

Some S are not P

---

## EXERCISES

Assert at least one A, E, I, and O statement in each of the following areas: International politics, domestic politics, studies or school, social life, and sports. This will be a total of twenty statements. Put each statement in standard form. Using (2) as a paradigm, symbolize each statement. Then picture what each statement asserts by drawing a Venn diagram representing the relation said to hold between the classes denoted by the subject and predicate terms.

---

* A podiatrist, for example, might perform surgery without having an M.D.

## 2. NON-STANDARD FORM CATEGORICAL STATEMENTS

Categorical statements encountered in ordinary contexts are often not in standard form. Such statements, however, can be translated into standard form. While *there are no mechanical rules for translating categorical statements into standard form*, it is often reasonably clear what is being asserted. Such reasonability is based on insights of the topic under discussion, the context in which the discussion is taking place, and sensitivity to vocabulary and grammar. The better the insights anyone has into these sorts of matters, the less likely there will be confusion in understanding and, hence, in translating. Coupled with these insights, there are rules-of-thumb that can be helpful in many cases of translation. This section discusses techniques of translation. Remember that clarity in what one says and how one hears what is said are key elements in raising the probability that harmful actions will be avoided.

In everyday contexts, categorical statements often do not start with one of the quantifiers 'all', 'no' or 'some'. An *A* statement, for instance, can be expressed in many ways. In talking about *designer drugs* and *harmful things*, the following *A* statement is in standard form:

> **(1)** All designer drugs are harmful things.
> (All D are H)

While none of the following is in standard form, each, among many others, expresses the same thing as (1):

**(2)**

    **a)** Designer drugs are harmful.

    **b)** A designer drug is a harmful thing.

    **c)** Any designer drug is harmful.

    **d)** Anything that is a designer drug is harmful.

    **e)** Every designer drug is harmful.

    **f)** Everything that is a designer drug is harmful.

    **g)** None but harmful things are designer drugs.*

    **h)** Only harmful things are designer drugs.

    **i)** The designer drug is a harmful thing.

    **j)** Whatever is a designer drug is harmful.

*E* statements are expressed in a number of ways. Imagine talking about the classes *designer drugs* and saying this:

> **(3)** No designer drugs are safe.
> (No D are S)

---

* Consider the example, 'All presidents of the United States have been men'. This can be expressed as 'None but men have been president of the United States' or 'Only men have been president of the United States'.

Here are some nonstandard ways to express (3):

**(4)**

    **a)** A designer drug is never safe.

    **b)** None of the designer drugs are safe.

    **c)** Not even one designer drug is safe.

    **d)** Not a single designer drug is safe.

    **e)** Nothing that is a designer drug is safe.

    **f)** The designer drugs are not safe.

In discussing the classes *machines* and *robots* this standard form *I* statement might be asserted:

**(5)**   Some machines are robots.

       (Some M are R)

Each of the following expresses (5) differently:

**(6)**

    **a)** Certain machines are robots.

    **b)** A few machines are robots.

    **c)** A suitable number of machines are robots.

    **d)** Some things that are machines are also robots.

    **e)** There exist machines that are robots.

    **f)** There is a machine that is a robot.

    **g)** There are machines that are robots.

When referring to the classes *automobile* and *sports car*, this *O* claim can be made:

**(7)**   Some automobiles are not sports cars.

       (Some A are not C)

In different circumstances, each of the following can function to assert the same thing as (7):

**(8)**

    **a)** A certain number of automobiles are not sports cars.

    **b)** A few automobiles are not sports cars.

    **c)** Not all automobiles are sports cars.

    **d)** Not everything that is an automobile is a sports car.

    **e)** There exist automobiles that are not sports cars.

    **f)** There is an automobile that is not a sports car.

    **g)** There are automobiles that are not sports cars.

Remember that there are no mechanical rules for translating categorical statements into standard form. For example, the articles 'a', 'an' and 'the' do not automatically indicate an *I* or *O* statement. They are also correctly used in *A* or *E* statements. 'A whale is a mammal' is an *A* statement and 'The whale is not a fish' is an *E* statement. Another troublesome word is 'only' used to indicate a predicate term:

> **(9)**   Only women are heroines.

> **(10)**   The only graduating students are passing seniors.

(9) goes into standard form as

> **(11)**   All heroines are women.

In standard form (10) is rendered as

> **(12)**   All passing seniors are graduating students.

Confusion can also occur with 'a few' and 'few':

> **(13)**   A few persons are saints.

> **(14)**   Few persons are saints.

(13) is normally understood as

> **(15)**   Some persons are saints.

The meaning of (14), however, is expressed in a conjunction of two categorical statements:

> **(16)**   Some persons are saints *and* some persons are not saints.

Care must be taken not to confuse statements such as

> **(17)**   All athletes are energetic people.

with statements like

> **(18)**   All but the lazy succeed.

(18) is not translated into a standard form categorical statement. It moves into a conjunction of two categorical statements:

> **(19)**   All things that are lazy are things that do not succeed *and* all things that do not succeed are things that are lazy.

A categorical statement might not be in standard form because the subject or predicate term is not expressed by a noun phrase. Or perhaps the copula is not signified by 'are' or 'are not'. Consider these examples:

> **(20)**
> **a)** Fish swim.
> **b)** Whoever works profits.
> **c)** There has never been a cheap war.
> **d)** Hard drugs frequently lead to a wasted life.
> **e)** Occasionally one finds cheating students.

**f)** Not everywhere is safe from terrorists.

**g)** People with *AIDS* don't live very long.

**h)** Certain mammals lay eggs.

**i)** Not every yuppie drives a BMW.

It is often possible to translate a categorical statement into standard form in several ways. Following is one way in which this can be done for the examples in (20):

**(21)**

**a)** All fish are things that are swimmers.*

**b)** All persons who work are persons who profit.

**c)** No wars are cheap things.

**d)** Some hard drugs are things that lead to a wasted life.

**e)** Some persons who are students are persons who are cheaters.

**f)** Some places are not places safe from terrorists.

**g)** No persons with *AIDS* are persons who live very long.

**h)** Some mammals are things that lay eggs.

**i)** Some yuppies are not persons who drive a BMW.

The words 'always', 'never', 'occasionally', 'frequently', 'seldom', and 'sometimes' can be used to indicate the quantity of a categorical statement. Such words also suggest temporal considerations.

**(22)**   A tiger never changes its stripes.

(22) is not in standard form. Nonetheless, it can be recast as

**(23)**   No animals that are tigers are animals that change their stripes.

(22) can also be put into standard form as

**(24)**   No times are times during which a tiger changes its stripes.

Which rendition is preferable depends upon the context of the statement and what is being emphasized in that context.

Categorical statements are used to make claims about relations said to hold between two classes. Hence, strictly speaking, they cannot be used to make assertions about a particular individual.† Rather, a **singular statement** is utilized to make

---

* The phrases 'things that are—', 'times that are—', and 'places that are—' can be helpful in constructing noun phrases used to denote classes

† What is to count as an individual in one context may be understood, in another context, as having other individuals as its components. The individual, George Bush, has various individual parts such as arms, legs, lungs, cells that make up his body. One must always look to the context in which a statement is used to ascertain what is to count, in that context, as an individual.

assertions about a particular individual, thing, event, action, or the like. A *singular statement*

**asserts that a particular individual is, or is not, a member of a specific class.**

Here are several examples of singular statements:

(25)

   a) Annye Mae is an executive.

   b) The killer of Ann Orr was caught.

   c) July 4, 1776 is an important date in American history.

   d) Russell will be in his garden.

'Annye Mae' is a proper name used to mention a particular person. 'The killer of Ann Orr' is a description denoting a particular individual. 'July 4, 1776' refers to a particular segment of time. Both 'Russell' and 'his garden' refer to a particular individual—the former, a person; the latter, a location.* None of the examples in (25) suggest a relation holding between two classes of individuals. An assertion about, say, a particular individual can, nonetheless, be interpreted as an assertion about classes. The claim 'Annye Mae is an executive' can be understood as 'All persons who are identical to Annye Mae are persons who are executives'. 'Annye Mae' can be viewed as denoting that class of individuals having exactly one member, namely Annye Mae. 'July 4, 1776' is understood as denoting that class of particular things having that time segment named by 'July 4, 1776'. Thus, 'All times that are identical to July 4, 1776, are times that are important in American history' is a categorical statement.

---

## EXERCISES

Translate each of the following into standard categorical form. Then, using the capital letters suggested in the parentheses, symbolize each of the statements. For each example, draw the appropriate Venn diagram corresponding to that statement.

1. Certain politicians are mendacious. (P,M)

2. John Venn was an English logician. (V,L)

3. Every cat is gray in the dark. (C,G)

4. Most students who are poor in their studies are not happy in their social life. (S,H)

5. There are goals of life not obtainable by everyone. (G,O)

6. Anyone who is a friend in time of need is a real friend. (F,R)

7. Several self-centered people ruined the class. (S,R)

---

* Names, descriptions, and the like are used to denote individual things and events. However, the meaning of a name is not that individual purported to be denoted by the name, as seen in such examples as 'Zeus is a mighty god'. While the name 'Zeus' is meaningful, it does not denote an existing ancient Greek god.

8. Henry Kissinger was Secretary of State under two presidents. (K,S)

9. No ignorant person is ever truly free. (I,F)

10. A few sincere professors are concerned about their students. (P,C)

11. A person who hates anyone will never be content. (H,C)

12. *R.E.M.* began in Athens, Georgia. (R,A)

13. None but the diligent are rewarded. (D,R)

14. Various experiences of life are bitterly absurd. (E,A)

15. The silent person hears the most. (S,H)

16. Many nosey people are lonely. (N,L)

17. A few people aren't belligerent toward their enemies. (P,B)

18. There are people rewarded by society for no good reason. (P,R)

19. Try as they may, certain people never succeed. (P,S)

20. No moral person can suffer real disgrace. (M,D)

21. Any understanding friend is valuable to have. (U,V)

22. George Boole introduced the hypothetical interpretation of categorical statements. (B,I)

23. The only persons in the audience will be students. (P,S)

24. The majority of business majors want to make a great deal of money. (B,W)

25. Knowledge is power. (K,P)

26. Only those students who work hard pass. (W,P)

27. Most students desire good job training. (S,T)

28. November 1988 was an important month for the Democrats. (N,M)

29. Inside trading became a Wall Street scandal in 1987. (T,S)

30. The reduction of nuclear armament increases the cost of conventional national defense. (R,I)

---

## 3. EXISTENTIAL IMPORT AND THE SQUARE OF OPPOSITION

*A* and *E* statements are ambiguous. Compare 'Heroes are brave persons' and 'Abominable snowmen are large bipeds'. When asserting or hearing 'Heroes are brave persons' someone would assume, given her experience of the world, that both heroes and brave persons exist. That is, it would be assumed that the classes *heroes* and *brave persons* are not empty. This might not be the case in saying 'Abominable snowmen are large bipeds'. Perhaps the speaker is not suggesting that abominable snowmen actually do exist. The class *abominable snowmen* might be empty. Whether there are abominable snowmen or not is a question yet to be answered. Which classes are empty or not is not a matter determined by logic only, but also by experiences of the world.

In traditional categorical logic, *A* and *E* statements are understood as having **existential import**. It is assumed that the classes denoted by the terms of these statements are not empty. The claim 'All jazz artists have a strong sense of rhythm', not only asserts that all the members of the class *jazz artists* are included in the class *things with a strong sense of rhythm*. It also assumes that jazz artists and things with a strong sense of rhythm in fact exist. Assuming existential import, represented by 'EI', various truth-value relations that necessarily hold between *A*, *E*, *I*, and *O* statements are depicted by the ***traditional square of opposition***:

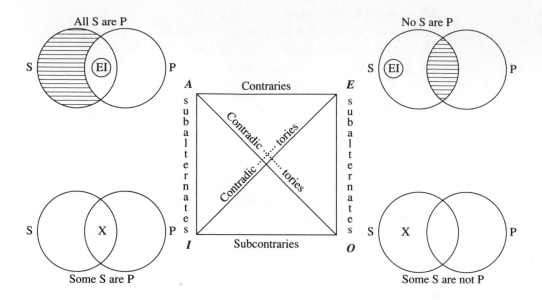

Based on these necessary truth-value relations, proofs known as immediate inferences can be constructed. An ***immediate inference*** is

> **a proof made up of only two simple categorical statements, one of which is the premise and the other the conclusion.**

Notice how the above diagram pictures necessary truth-value relations holding between *A*, *E*, *I*, and *O* statements and allows for immediate inferences. Let 'S' and 'P' represent the same subject and predicate terms throughout the above diagram. For instance, 'S' might stand for 'hard drugs' and 'P' for 'dangerous substances'. Then 'All hard drugs are dangerous substances' and 'Some hard drugs are not dangerous substances' are ***contradictory***. 'No hard drugs are dangerous substances' and 'Some hard drugs are dangerous substances' are also contradictory:

> **Two statements are contradictory if and only if they can neither both be true nor both be false; that is, if they must have opposite truth-values.**

With this relation at hand, someone could argue

> **(1)**   Since some hard drugs are dangerous substances, it follows that it's false that no hard drugs are dangerous substances.

Because *O* and *A* statements are contradictory, the truth of 'Some hard drugs are dangerous substances' immediately guarantees that 'No hard drugs are dangerous substances' is false. So, 'It's false that no hard drugs are dangerous substances' must be true.

'All hard drugs are dangerous substances' and 'No hard drugs are dangerous substances' are *contraries*:

> **Two statements are contrary if and only if both of them cannot be true but both can be false. That is, two statements are contrary if and only if at least one of them must be false.**

If 'All mammals are air-breathing' is true, then 'No mammals are air-breathing' must be false. The following argument is, therefore, valid:

> **(2)** All mammals are air-breathing. So, it isn't the case that no mammals are air-breathing.

But this argument is invalid:

> **(3)** It's false that all contemporary communists are atheists. Consequently, no contemporary communists are atheists.

If it is false that all contemporary communists are atheists, then the truth-value of 'No contemporary communists are atheists' is undetermined. This statement could be either true or false and the requirement that *at least one* of the *A* or *E* statements is false be satisfied. (3) is an example of *the fallacy of illicit contraries.*

'Some hard drugs are dangerous substances' and 'Some hard drugs are not dangerous substances' are neither contradictory nor contrary. These *I* and *O* statements are *subcontraries*:

> **Two statements are subcontraries if and only if both of them cannot be false but both can be true. That is, two statements are subcontraries if and only if at least one of them must be true.**

'Some murders are legal' is a false *I* statement. Since *I* and *O* statements are subcontraries, it necessarily follows that 'Some murders are not legal' is true. But what of the following example? Suppose the *I* statement, 'Some killings are morally acceptable' is true. Then nothing concerning the truth-value of the *O* statement, 'Some killings are not morally acceptable', *necessarily* follows. In particular, this argument is deductively invalid:

> **(4)** Some killings are morally acceptable. So, some killings are also not morally acceptable.

It *might* be true, 'Some killings are not morally acceptable'. But the truth of this claim is not necessarily guaranteed by the truth of 'Some killings are morally acceptable'. Nor is (5) deductively valid:

> **(5)** Some killings are morally acceptable. So, it's false that some killings are also not morally acceptable.

(4) and (5) are examples of *the fallacy of illicit subcontraries.* Certainly someone might wish to argue for the truth of the conclusion of (4) or (5). But whether either

conclusion is true is not guaranteed by the truth of 'Some killings are morally acceptable'.

Another relation holding between categorical statements is *subalternation*:

> **Two statements are subalternates if and only if the following conditions are met: (1) one of these statements is an *A* and the other an *I*, or one of the statements is an *E* and the other is an *O*; (2) the truth of the universal statement, the *superaltern*, guarantees the truth of the particular statement, the *subaltern*; and (3) the falsity of the particular statement guarantees the falsity of the universal statement.**

If 'All hard drugs are dangerous substances' is true, assuming hard drugs exist, it also must be true that 'Some hard drugs are dangerous substances'. Suppose that it is false, 'All hard drugs are dangerous substances', assuming that there are hard drugs. From this the truth-value of 'Some hard drugs are dangerous substances' is undetermined. Even though not all hard drugs are dangerous substances, some of them might be. Nor does the truth of 'Some hard drugs are dangerous substances' guarantee the truth of 'All hard drugs are dangerous substances'. Yet if 'Some hard drugs are dangerous substances' is false, then 'All hard drugs are dangerous substances' must be false. In the necessary truth-value relation of subalternation, truth moves from the universal to the particular while falsity moves from the particular to the universal. To break these relations in an argument is to create an instance of *the fallacy of illicit subalternation*. Here is an example of this fallacy:

> (6)    Most people certainly cheat. Thus, it must be the case that all people do.

Even assuming the existence of many people who cheat, it does not necessarily follow that all people cheat.

The necessary truth-value relations holding between categorical statements, assuming existential import, can be summarized like this:

> Assume *A* is true; then *E* is false, *I* is true, and *O* is false.

> Assume *E* is true; then *A* is false, *I* is false, and *O* is true.

> Assume *I* is true; then *A* is undetermined, *E* is false, and *O* is undetermined.

> Assume *O* is true; then *A* is false, *E* is undetermined, and *I* is undetermined.

A chart can be given to display this information:*

_____

* This and the following chart were suggested by a reviewer of this book.

assume true

|   | A | E | I | O |
|---|---|---|---|---|
| A | — | F | T | F |
| E | F | — | F | T |
| I | U | F | — | U |
| O | F | U | U | — |

Assume $A$ is false; then $E$ is undetermined, $I$ is undetermined, and $O$ is true.

Assume $E$ is false; then $A$ is undetermined, $I$ is true, and $O$ is undetermined.

Assume $I$ is false; then $A$ is false, $E$ is true, and $O$ is true.

Assume $O$ is false; then $A$ is true, $E$ is false, and $I$ is true.

assume false

|   | A | E | I | O |
|---|---|---|---|---|
| A | — | U | U | T |
| E | U | — | T | U |
| I | F | T | — | T |
| O | T | F | T | — |

Contemporary logic, introduced by George Boole, differs from traditional categorical logic concerning $A$ and $E$ statements.* The classes designated by the terms in $A$ and $E$ statements are not assumed, from the viewpoint of contemporary logic, to have members. Indeed, one might make some assertions hoping that certain things do not exist. Suppose a physician says to a patient, 'Any cancerous cells you have will be treated'. According to the Boolean view, the physician is saying, 'If you have any cancerous cells, then those cells will be treated'. The patient might or might not have cancerous cells. Or a physicist might say 'All point masses are absolutely elastic'. In asserting this, she is not committing herself to any assertion concerning the existence of point masses or absolutely elastic things.† Similar comments are to be made concerning $E$ statements. 'No poorly qualified student is interviewed' is understood as saying, 'Given anyone at all, if he is a poorly qualified student, then he is not interviewed'. Of course there are poorly qualified students and things interviewed. That such things do exist, however, is established by empirical considerations and not simply by logic.

---

* George Boole, 1815–1864, was an English mathematician and logician. The logic developed out of his work is known as *Boolean Logic*, or *Boolean Algebra*. *Boolean Algebra* is foundational in computer development for both the areas of hardware and software.

†From the point of view of physics, she is doing the very opposite. So-called *point masses* are "theoretical constructs" that are assumed not to exist as spatial-temporal things. Such constructs are seen as helpful in talking about those particular things that do exist in the spatial-temporal world. Nothing is taken actually to be absolutely elastic.

Under the ***Boolean interpretation***, *I* and *O* statements still carry the assumption that at least one thing of the type mentioned exists. To say 'There are jazz artists with a strong sense of rhythm' is to assert that, in fact, there is at least one thing that is both a jazz artist and a thing with a strong sense of rhythm. *O* statements such as 'Some dragons are fire-breathing animals' also carry the assumption of existence under a Boolean interpretation.*

Not assuming existential import, only the truth-value relation of contradiction remains in the Boolean square of opposition and the immediate inferences based on this relation:

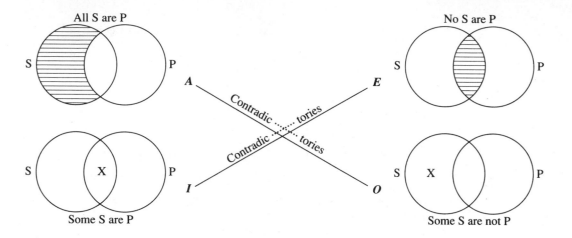

*A* and *E* statements are no longer contraries under the Boolean interpretation. If nothing is assumed about the existence of dragons, it is equally true to say 'All dragons are fire-breathing animals' and 'No dragons are fire-breathing animals'. Further, given the Boolean interpretation, *I* and *O* statements cannot be subcontraries. Not assuming anything about the existence of dragons, the 'Some dragons are fire-breathing animals' and 'Some dragons are not fire-breathing animals' are both false. And finally, the relation of subalternation cannot hold between *A* and *I* statements or between *E* and *O* statements. Precisely because no existential assumption is made about dragons, 'All dragons are fire-breathing animals' is true, while 'Some dragons are fire-breathing animals' is false. Supposing that dragons do not exist, 'No dragons are fire-breathing animals' is true but 'Some dragons are not

---

* Assumptions can be ill-founded and the statements based on them false. To assume the existence of dragons and fire-breathing animals is one thing. For them to exist is another. Considerations concerning the relations of logic to the spatial-temporal world and observations of it go beyond the range of what is included in logic only. More exacting views concerning these relations are found in areas of philosophy known as *metaphysics* and *epistemology*.

fire-breathing animals' is false.* Assuming a Boolean interpretation of *A* and *E* statements, any attempted inferences other than those based on the contradictory relation holding between *A* and *O,* and *E* and *I,* statements will be an instance of *the fallacy of existential import.* This fallacy consists in assuming something to exist as asserted by *A* and *E* statements when such assumptions are not warranted.

As a rule-of-thumb in real life-situations when analyzing categorical statements, assume a traditional interpretation if the classes mentioned in the statements are known to have members. If members are known not to exist, assume a Boolean interpretation. When in doubt about the existence of individuals of a class, follow a principle of simplicity dictating that the less assumed the better. Even so, not knowing whether a class is empty or not, it might be *interesting* to suppose that such individuals do in fact exist. Then determine by appealing to the traditional square of opposition what further statements can be asserted given this assumption of existence.

---

## EXERCISES

### Group A:

*First,* translate the following examples into standard form. Then symbolize each using the suggested capital letters and draw a Venn diagram for each. *Second,* assume each statement is

---

\* Assuming the Boolean interpretation of *A* and *E* statements, another method of symbolization is at hand. Let 'S' represent any subject and 'P' any predicate term. Let '0' indicate an empty class. A bar, '–', drawn over a capital letter represents the complement of the class designated by that letter. 'All S are P' says that a class that is both an S and a non-P is empty, or 'S$\overline{\text{P}}$ = 0'. 'No S are P' asserts that any class that is both *S* and *P* is empty, or 'SP = 0'. 'SP ≠ 0' asserts that any class that is both *S* and *P* is not empty, or 'Some S are P'. Finally, 'Some S are not P' is rendered as 'S$\overline{\text{P}}$ ≠ 0' and says that a class that is *S* and *non-P* is not empty. In terms of Venn diagrams, this method of symbolizing categorical statements, assuming the Boolean interpretation, is shown in the following:

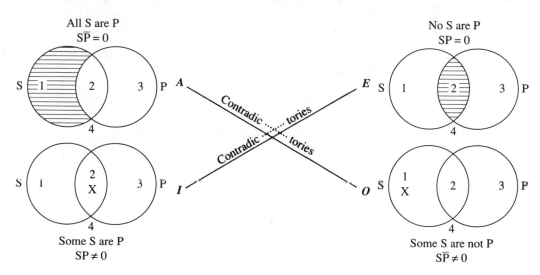

true. Appealing to the traditional square of opposition, determine what other statement(s) must be true or must be false. What further statements are there, if any, whose truth or falsity cannot be determined by an appeal to the traditional square of opposition? *Third*, assume each statement is false. Once more, appealing to the traditional square of opposition, determine what other statement(s) must be true or must be false. What further statements are there, if any, whose truth or falsity cannot be determined by an appeal to the traditional square of opposition?

1. Every Iraqi is mendacious. (I,M)
2. Most Iraqis want war with Israel. (I,W)
3. Relatively few Americans exercise their privilege to vote. (A,E)
4. Many bureaucrats in local government are not competent decision makers. (B,D)

**Group B:**

*First*, translate the following examples into standard form. Then symbolize each using the suggested capital letters and draw a Venn diagram for each. *Second*, assume each statement is true. Appealing to the Boolean square of opposition, determine what other statement(s) must be true or must be false. What further statements are there, if any, whose truth or falsity cannot be determined by an appeal to the Boolean square of opposition? *Third*, assume each statement is false. Once more, appealing to the Boolean square of opposition, determine what other statement(s) must be true or must be false. What further statements are there, if any, whose truth or falsity cannot be determined by an appeal to the Boolean square of opposition?

1. A good many intravenous drug users will develop *AIDS*. (U,D)
2. Lazy people never achieve very much. (L,A)
3. Not all *STD*s are successfully treatable. (S,T)
4. A sizable number of cigarette smokers will not survive lung cancer. (C,S)

## 4.    CONVERSION, OBVERSION, AND CONTRAPOSITION

There are other types of immediate inferences besides those based on the squares of opposition. Three of these types are *conversion*, *obversion*, and *contraposition*. The rule of *simple conversion* is this:

> **The simple converse of an *E* or *I* categorical statement is obtained by exchanging subject and predicate terms.**

Here is an instance of simple conversion, or *conversion*, involving two *E* statements. Consider (1) as the premise and (2) the conclusion.

**(1)**   No pop musicians are opera singers.
(No M are S)

**(2)**   No opera singers are pop musicians.
(No S are M)

The beginning statement, (1), is the *convertant* and the resulting statement, (2), is the *converse*. (2) is generated from (1), by conversion. A Venn diagram representing (1) is

**(3)**

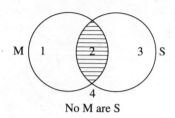

No M are S

While a Venn diagram for (2) is

**(4)**

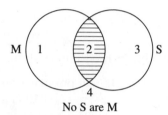

No S are M

Notice in both (3) and (4) the lens is shaded while areas 1 and 3 are not. These diagrams show that 'No M are S' and 'No S are M' assert exactly the same thing.
  Conversion can also be used with *I* statements:

**(5)**  Some students are punctual people.
(Some S are P)

Replacing subject and predicate terms with one another yields

**(6)**  Some punctual people are students.
(Some P are S)

Again appealing to a Venn diagram, (5) can be pictured as

**(7)**

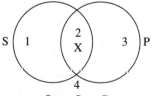

Some S are P

(6) is diagrammed like this:

**(8)**

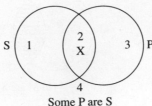

Some P are S

Once more the diagrams are identical, showing that 'Some S are P' and 'Some P are S' make the same assertion.

Simple conversion cannot be used with *A* statements such as

> **(9)**   All athletes are popular heroes.
>               (All A are H)

From (9) it cannot be correctly inferred that

> **(10)**   All popular heroes are athletes.
>                (All H are A)

Even if (9) were true, this would not guarantee that (10) is true. This pair of Venn diagrams illustrates that (9) and (10) are not logically equivalent:

**(11)**

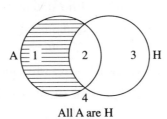

All A are H

**(12)**

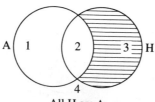

All H are A

However, if existential import is assumed for (9), an *I* statement is logically entailed by (9):

**(13)**   Some popular heroes are athletes.
(Some H are A)

The move from (9) to (13) is an instance of *conversion by limitation*. Notice that conversion by limitation holds only by assuming existential import for *A* statements. Examine these Venn diagrams:

**(14)**

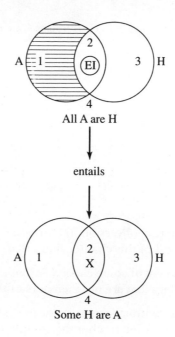

All A are H

entails

Some H are A

To use conversion by limitation, apply this rule:

> **(1) switch the subject and predicate terms of an *A* statement, and (2) change the quantifier of the statement from 'All' (universal) to 'Some' (particular).**

Assuming existential import the convertant, an *A* statement, logically entails the converse, an *I* statement.

No rule of conversion can be used with *O* statements, as can be seen in the following *O* statements:

**(15)**   Some cats are not lions.
(Some C are not L)

**(16)**   Some lions are not cats.
(Some L are not C)

(15) is true, but (16) is not. Here are the corresponding Venn diagrams:

**(17)**

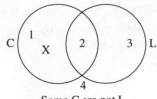

Some C are not L

**(18)**

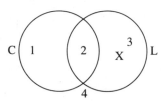

Some L are not C

Before considering obversion, the notion of the *complement of a class* needs to be reviewed. Section 1 of this chapter states that

> **the complement of some class, *S*, is that class, *non-S*, having as its members all those things that are not members of the class *S*.**

Terms denoting contrary classes must not be confused with terms denoting class complements. Moreover, neither the complement nor the contrary of a class is to be confused with the denial of a statement. For instance, *E* and *O* statements deny that some relation holds between two classes. The claim 'No active alcoholics are non-drinkers' denies that any member of the class *active alcoholic* is also a member of the class *non-drinkers*. This same information is asserted in 'All active alcoholics are drinkers'. To say 'Some politicians are not non-ethical',* where 'not' is part of the copula, claims that there is at least one member of the class *politicians* that fails to be a member of *non-ethical things*. To fail to be a member of the class *non-ethical things* is to be a member of the class *ethical things*. That is, to suggest 'Some politicians are not non-ethical' is the same as saying 'Some politicians are ethical'.

Observe how complements of classes can be represented using Venn diagrams. The complement of a class is everything not belonging to that class. So, the complement of *P* in the following diagram is everything not in the area 1:

---

* Or 'unethical' might be used instead of 'non-ethical'.

**(19)**

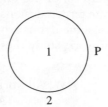

That is, everything outside the circle represents non-*P*. Now suppose a second class, *S*, overlaps *P*:

**(20)**

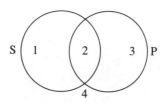

Non-*P* is represented by areas 1 and 4. Thus, 'All S are non-P' is diagrammed in this way:

**(21)**

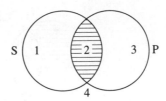

'Some non-S are P' is pictured like this:

**(22)**

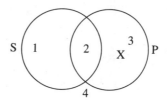

Having the concept *class complement*, the rule *obversion* can be stated in this way:

**(1) change the quality of the original categorical statement and (2) replace the predicate term with its complement.**

Suppose the predicate term of the obvertant is designated by 'P'. Replace it with 'non-P'. If this predicate term is designated by 'non-P', replace it with 'P'. A "double complement" rule is assumed, thus avoiding writing 'non-non-P'.

To see obversion at work, study these examples where (23) is the *obvertant* and (24) the *obverse*:

> **(23)**   All workers are taxpayers.
> (All W are T)

> **(24)**   No workers are non-taxpayers.
> (No W are non-T)

The operation can be reversed, treating (24) as the obvertant and (23) as the obverse. So, (23) and (24) are logically equivalent, as is seen in these Venn diagrams:

**(25)**

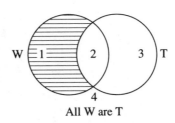

All W are T

**(26)**

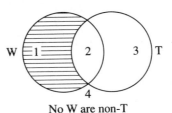

No W are non-T

Obversion can be used with all four standard forms of categorical statements. Here are all of the Venn diagrams representing obversion:

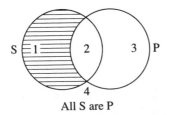

All S are P

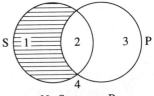

No S are non-P

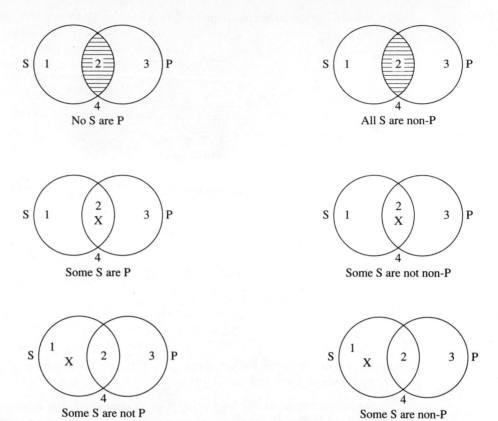

*Simple contraposition* is used with only *A* and *O* statements and is a way of combining conversion and obversion. Imagine this assertion:

> **(27)**  All wars are costly activities.
> (All W are C)

The obverse of (27) is

> **(28)**  No wars are non-costly activities.
> (No W are non-C)

Simple conversion can be applied to (28):

> **(29)**  No non-costly activities are wars.
> (No non-C are W)

A final use of obversion on (29) yields

> **(30)**  All non-costly activities are non-wars.
> (All non-C are non-W)

The Venn diagram corresponding to (27) is

**(31)**

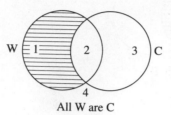

All W are C

(30) is pictured by this Venn diagram:

**(32)**

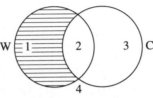

All non-C are non-W

Instead of going through each of these steps, (30) can be immediately obtained from (27) by *simple contraposition* in which

> **the subject term of the beginning *A* or *O* statement, the *contrapositant*, is replaced by the complement of the predicate term and the predicate term is replaced by the complement of the subject term to obtain the *contrapositive*.**

*Contraposition by limitation* is used with *E* statements if existential import is assumed. To use contraposition by limitation, first apply obversion to 'No S are P'. This produces 'All S are non-P'. Conversion is next applied. Only conversion by limitation, assuming existential import, can be used on *A* statements. This move produces 'Some non-P are S'. The final use of obversion yields 'Some non-P are not non-S', and this can be viewed as the results of contraposition by limitation applied to *E* statements. Examine this Venn diagram:

(33)

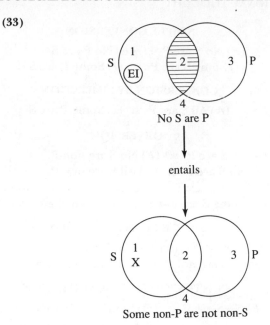

No S are P

entails

Some non-P are not non-S

No form of contraposition can be used with *I* statements. Attempting to apply contraposition to an *I* statement first produces, by obversion, an *O* statement. *O* statements, however, have no converse. So, the sequence of moves (obversion-conversion-obversion) necessary to obtain the contraposition of an *I* statement cannot be completed.

Simple conversion for *E* and *I* statements, obversion for all categorical statements, and simple contraposition for *A* and *O* statements are *equivalence forms* guaranteeing that the statements related by these rules are logically equivalent; that is, they have the same truth-values. Statements related in this way can be interchanged in a proof without altering its validity. Thus, to say 'No vipers are animals' is to say the same thing, as far as truth or falsity is concerned, as 'No animals are vipers'. On the other hand, conversion by limitation for *A* statements and contraposition by limitation for *E* statements are *argument forms*. These rules guarantee that if one statement is true then a second must also be true, but the truth of the second statement does not guarantee the truth of the first. Statements related in this way do not have the same truth-values. They are not mutually interchangeable. Assuming existential import, the truth of 'All cats are animals' guarantees the truth of 'Some animals are cats'. Nonetheless, the truth of 'Some students are brilliant persons' does not logically entail the truth of 'All brilliant persons are students'.

Conversion, obversion and contraposition are now summarized. The sign '::' indicates the statements flanking the sign are logically equivalent and can mutually replace one another in a proof. So, any rule expressed by using a '::' can be read from left to right and from right to left. On the other hand, the sign '∴' indicates the statement on the left-hand side of the sign logically entails the statement on the right-hand side, but that the reverse does not hold.

**SIMPLE CONVERSION**

(*E*) No S are P  ::  (*E*) No P are S
(*I*) Some S are P  ::  (*I*) Some P are S

**CONVERSION BY LIMITATION**

(*A*) All S are P  ∴  (*I*) Some P are S

**OBVERSION**

(*A*) All S are P  ::  (*E*) No S are non-P
(*E*) No S are P  ::  (*A*) All S are non-P
(*I*) Some S are P  ::  (*O*) Some S are not non-P
(*O*) Some S are not P  ::  (*I*) Some S are non-P

**SIMPLE CONTRAPOSITION**

(*A*) All S are P  ::  (*A*) All non-P are non-S
(*O*) Some S are not P  ::  (*O*) Some non-P are not non-S

**CONTRAPOSITION BY LIMITATION**

(*E*) No S are P  ∴  (*O*) Some non-P are not non-S

Assuming a Boolean interpretation of *A* and *E* statements, the relations between the four standard categorical statements, immediate inferences discussed in this section, and validity and invalidity can be pictured in this way:*

|   | conversion | obversion | contraposition |
|---|------------|-----------|----------------|
| A | invalid    | valid     | valid          |
| E | valid      | valid     | invalid        |
| I | valid      | valid     | invalid        |
| O | invalid    | valid     | valid          |

Assuming existential import also adds the two implication rules of conversion by limitation and contraposition by limitation.

Conversion, obversion, and contraposition can now be used in constructing proofs of validity, and thus in substantiating claims. Such proofs establish that if some statement, the premise, is true, then another statement, the conclusion, must also be true.

(**34**) No non-smokers are people at high risk to have lung cancer. Hence, all people at high risk to have lung cancer are smokers. (S,P)

Using the suggested capital letters, (34) can be symbolized as

(**35**)                            / ∴ All P are S
  1) No non-S are P   Pr

Begin by examining the conclusion. This statement is a universal affirmative in which 'P' is on the left-hand side of the copula and 'S' of the right-hand side. Compare this information to what is asserted by the premise. In the premise, 'P' is

---

* This chart was suggested by the same reviewer who suggested those charts found on page 279 of this chapter.

found on the right of the copula and 'non-S' on the left side. Further, while the premise is universal, nonetheless it is negative. First, to put 'P' on the left of the copula and 'S' on the right, as found in the conclusion, simple conversion can be used on the premise:

| (36) | | / ∴ All P are S |
|---|---|---|
| 1) No non-S are P | Pr | |
| 2) No P are non-S | 1, simple conversion | |

The differences between line 2 and the conclusion are in their quality and the complement of the predicate term. Both of these differences, however, can be eliminated by a use of obversion:

| (37) | | / ∴ All P are S |
|---|---|---|
| 1) No non-S are P | Pr | |
| 2) No P are non-S | 1, simple conversion | |
| 3) All P are S* | 2, obversion | |

Often there is more than one way of constructing a proof for an argument. Here is another proof for (36):

| (38) | | / ∴ All P are S |
|---|---|---|
| 1) No non-S are P | Pr | |
| 2) All non-S are non-P | 1, obversion | |
| 3) All P are S | 2, simple contraposition | |

---

## EXERCISES

### Group A:

Translate the following into standard form. Next, symbolize each using the suggested capital letters. Then, when appropriate, state the converse of each. Indicate if conversion by limitation is used.

1. Certain chemical changes are endothermic. (C,E)
2. There are chemical substances not in liquid form. (S,L)
3. Each heat-releasing chemical change is exothermic. (C,E)
4. Chemical elements never represent an ambiguous species of matter. (E,R)
5. Energy is the capability of a body to bring about changes in other bodies. (E,C)

### Group B:

Translate the following into standard form, symbolizing them using the suggested capital letters. Then give the obverse of each.

1. A person who has *AIDS* is not expected to live more than several years. (A,L)

---

* Here 'non-non-P' is replaced by 'P'.

2. The retrovirus, *HTLV-3*, is the causal agent of *AIDS*. (H,A)

3. A sizable number of persons infected with *HTLV-3* aren't inflicted with *AIDS*. (H,A)

4. The greatest proportion of *AIDS* cases now reported is a result of using contaminated needles in various drug practices. (A,N)

5. Terminally ill persons deserve our compassion. (I,C)

## Group C:

Translate the following into standard form, symbolizing them using the suggested capital letters. Then, when appropriate, form the contrapositive of each. Indicate if contraposition by limitation is used.

1. There are non-taxable financial investments. (T,I)

2. Many start-up businesses don't remain privately controlled. (B,C)

3. Federal securities are never non-redeemable. (S,R)

4. Treasury notes can be used to create safe investments in a bear market. (N,I)

5. Certain junk stocks aren't sound investments. (S,I)

## Group D:

With (34) through (38) as a paradigm, using conversion, obversion and contraposition establish the validity of each of the following arguments. Indicate any use of conversion by limitation or contraposition by limitation.

1. Some chemical substances are homogeneous substances. Hence, some homogeneous substances are not non-chemical substances. (C,H)

2. All chemical substances are discretely structured. Thus, no non-discretely structured things are chemical substances. (C,D)

3. No chemical substances are phlogistic substances. Accordingly, some non-phlogistic substances are chemical substances. (C,P)

4. Some chemical substances are not heterogeneous substances. Wherefore, some non-heterogeneous substances are chemical substances. (C,H)

5. All atomic elements are chemical substances. So, some chemical substances are not non-atomic elements. (E,S)

---

## 5.   REVIEW OF NEW TERMS

**Argument form:** Guarantees that if one statement is true then a second must also be true, but the truth of the second statement does not guarantee the truth of the first.

**Boolean interpretation:** Not assuming in *A* and *E* categorical statements that there are any members in the classes denoted by the terms in those statements; represented in the Boolean Square of Opposition.

**Categorical statement:** A statement asserting that a certain relation does, or does not, hold between two classes.

**Class:** A collection of individuals having some common characteristic(s).

**Complement of a class:** The class, *non-S*, that has as its members all those things not members of the class *S*.

**Contradictory statements:** Two statements that both cannot be true or both cannot be false.

**Contraposition, simple:** An operation in which the subject term of either an *A* or *O* statement is replaced by the complement of the predicate term and the predicate term by the complement of the subject term; an *equivalence rule*.

**Contraposition by limitation:** An operation in which (1) the quantity of an *A* statement is reversed and (2) the subject term is replaced by the complement of the predicate term and the predicate term by the complement of the subject term; an *implication rule*.

**Contrary statements:** Two statements that cannot both be true although they might both be false.

**Conversion, simple:** An operation in which the subject term of an *E* or *I* statement is replaced by the predicate term and the predicate term by the subject term; an *equivalence rule*.

**Conversion by limitation:** An operation in which (1) the quantity of an *E* statement is reversed and (2) the subject term is replaced by the predicate term and the predicate term by the subject term; an *implication rule*.

**Copula:** In a standard form categorical statement the words 'are' and 'are not' connecting the subject and predicate terms of that statement.

**Empty class:** A class having no members; the *null class*.

**Equivalence form:** Guarantees that any statements related by such a rule are logically equivalent; that is, these statements have the same truth-values.

**Existential import:** An assumption that there exists at least one member of the classes denoted by the terms of a categorical statement; existential import interpretation of *A* and *E* statements in the traditional square of opposition.

**Immediate inference:** A proof made up of only two simple categorical statements, one of which is the premise and the other the conclusion.

**Obversion:** An operation in which (1) the quality of a categorical statement is changed and (2) the predicate term is replaced with its complement; an *equivalence rule*.

**Predicate term:** In a standard form categorical statement the term following the copula.

**Quality:** That property of a categorical statement when it is viewed as either affirming or denying certain relations holding between two classes; the quality of a categorical statement affirming a relation is *affirmative* and of a categorical statement denying a relation is *negative*.

**Quantifier:** Any word indicating how many individuals are being designated by the subject term of a categorical statement; in standard form categorical statements the words 'all', 'no' and 'some'.

**Quantity:** A property of a categorical statement when it is viewed as either *universal* or *particular*; the quantity of a categorical statement is universal if it makes an assertion about all the individuals of the class denoted by its subject term and particular if it makes an assertion about less than all of those individuals.

**Singular statement:** Asserts that a particular individual is, or is not, a member of a specific class.

**Square of opposition:** A diagram depicting various logical relations holding between categorical statements having the same subject and predicate terms but having different qualities and quantities; the Boolean and the traditional squares of opposition.

**Standard form categorical statement:** Any categorical statement expressed as 'All *S* are *P*', 'No *S* are *P*', 'Some *S* are *P*', or 'Some *S* are not *P*' where 'S' designates any subject term and 'P' any predicate term.

**Subalternates:** Two statements are subalternates if and only if the following conditions are met: (1) one of these statements is an *A* and the other an *I*, or one of the statements is an *E* and the other is an *O*; (2), assuming existential import, the truth of the universal statement, the *superaltern*, guarantees the truth of the particular statement, the *subaltern*; and (3) the falsity of the particular statement guarantees the falsity of the universal statement.

**Subcontrary statements:** Two statements that cannot possibly both be false but might both be true.

**Subject term:** In a standard form categorical statement the term following the quantifier and proceeding the copula.

**Terms:** Any linguistic expression that can be used as a grammatical subject in a declarative sentence. In categorical logic those linguistic expressions denoting classes.

**Venn diagram:** A diagram of circles, each area displayed by these circles representing a distinct class, used to picture all possible relations holding between those classes.

# 9

# CATEGORICAL LOGIC: SYLLOGISMS, ENTHYMEMES, AND SORITES

The last chapter introduces categorical statements along with methods to picture what these statements assert. Arguments having only one premise—a simple categorical statement—are discussed and techniques developed to determine the validity or invalidity of these types of arguments. This chapter builds on that foundation and introduces more complicated categorical arguments. Methods of determining the validity or invalidity of these arguments are explored, as well as techniques helpful in the actual construction of such arguments in real-life situations. For it is in real-life situations that a person must guard against misguided, misleading, and harmful claims that might influence actions leading to painful results.

## 1. CATEGORICAL SYLLOGISMS

Categorical statements can be related in a *categorical syllogism*:

> **A categorical syllogism is an argument viewed deductively having a sequence of three categorical statements, such that (1) two of these are the premises and one the conclusion, (2) exactly three terms appear in these statements, and (3) each term appears in only two statements.**

Consider this argument:

(1)  All sources of high energy are dangerous.
All nuclear power plants are sources of high energy.
Thus, all nuclear power plants are dangerous.

Using capital letters to replace the terms and separating the premises from the conclusion by a horizontal line, (1) can be visualized more easily as

> **(2)**    All S are D
> All P are S
> ———————
> All P and D*

(1) exemplifies the defining characteristics of a syllogism. The truth of the premises is presented as guaranteeing the truth of the conclusion. The argument has three statements, two of which are premises and one the conclusion. The sequence of statements has three terms. Finally, each of the three terms appears in only two statements.

Here is an argument that appears to be a syllogism but is not:

> **(3)**    All good parents are people who love children.
> All child molesters are people who love children.
> So, all good parents are child molesters.

The phrase, 'people who love children', occurs in each of the premises as if it designated a single term. These words, however, are used differently in each of the premises. Hence, (3) contains more than three terms. Symbolizing (3) results in something like this:

> **(4)**    All P are C
> All M are L
> ———————
> All P are M

(3) is an instance of the ***fallacy of four terms,*** also known as the ***fallacy of equivocation.***[†]

Naming the various parts of syllogisms makes it easier to discuss them. The predicate term of the conclusion is the ***major term*** of a syllogism. The subject term of the conclusion is the ***minor term***. The major term found in the conclusion is also found in one of the premises. This premise is the ***major premise***. Similarly, the minor term of the conclusion is found in the remaining premise. This is the ***minor premise***. The ***middle term*** appears twice in the premises, "mediating" between the subject and predicate terms in the premises to establish the conclusion.[‡] Thus, beginning with

---

* (1) can also be symbolized by these notations:

$$\frac{\begin{array}{l} \text{SAD} \\ \text{PAS} \end{array}}{\text{PAD}} \quad \text{and} \quad \frac{\begin{array}{l} \text{S}\overline{\text{D}} = 0 \\ \overline{\text{P}}\text{S} = 0 \end{array}}{\overline{\overline{\text{PD}}} = 0}$$

†This argument also displays the fallacy of undistributed middle discussed in Section 2 of this chapter.

‡Syllogistic arguments are *mediating arguments,* as opposed to *immediate arguments* having no middle term and discussed in the previous chapter.

the conclusion, the major and minor terms are identified. This, in turn, determines which premise is the major and which the minor. Finally, one is then able to determine which premise to write down first—the major—and which second—the minor—before expressing the conclusion.

A syllogism is in *standard form* if and only if it displays these two conditions:

> *First*, **all the premises and the conclusion are in standard form;** *second*, **the major premise is mentioned first, next the minor premise, and last the conclusion.**

In analyzing a syllogism it is helpful to put it into standard form. Then every logical detail will be laid out and displayed in a regular way. Techniques for establishing validity and invalidity can thus be more easily applied in a consistent manner.

(1), above, is in standard form. *First*, the premises and the conclusion are in standard form. *Second*, the predicate term, 'dangerous things', of the conclusion, 'All nuclear power plants are dangerous', is found in the first premise. This premise, 'All sources of high energy are dangerous', is, therefore, the major premise. *Third* the subject term, 'nuclear power plants', of the conclusion is found in the second premise, 'All nuclear power plants are sources of high energy'. Thus, this is the minor premise and is correctly expressed after the major premise. The middle term of (1), 'sources of high energy', appears in both premises but not in the conclusion.

The validity of a syllogism depends solely on its form. The *form of a categorical syllogism* is determined by

> **(1) the logical forms of its categorical statements (their quantity and quality) and (2) the way the subject, predicate, and middle terms are arranged in the syllogism.**

In more technical language, the logical form of a syllogism is determined by its *mood* and *figure*. The *mood* of a syllogism is specified by

> **writing the name of each type of categorical statement used in that syllogism, beginning with the major premise, followed by the minor premise, and then the conclusion.**

The mood of (1) is indicated by writing 'AAA'.

The *figure* of a syllogism is a function of the arrangement of the terms of that syllogism expressed in standard form. There are four possible syllogistic figures. Let 'S' represent any subject term, 'P' any predicate term and 'M' any middle term appearing in both premises. The four figures can be displayed as

| M–P | P–M | M–P | P–M |
|-----|-----|-----|-----|
| S–M | S–M | M–S | M–S |
| S–P | S–P | S–P | S–P |
| **FIGURE 1** | **FIGURE 2** | **FIGURE 3** | **FIGURE 4** |

The following "shirt collar" diagram is helpful in remembering the placement of terms:

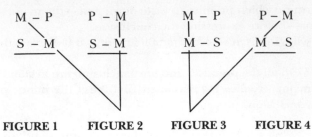

**FIGURE 1      FIGURE 2      FIGURE 3      FIGURE 4**

Since the logical form of a syllogism is completely determined by a combination of its mood and figure, both must be mentioned when indicating its form. The form of (1) is *AAA-1*.

There are exactly 256 syllogistic forms. The major and minor premises of a syllogism can only be *A*, *E*, *O*, or *I* statements. Thus, there are $4 \times 4 = 16$ combinations of major and minor premises. The conclusion can also be an *A*, *E*, *I*, or *O* statement. Hence, there are $16 \times 4 = 64$ possible moods for any syllogism. Because each mood can be in one of four figures, there are $64 \times 4 = 256$ syllogistic forms. However, assuming existential import, only 24 of these forms produce valid syllogisms. Under a Boolean interpretation, there are only 15 valid syllogistic forms. To protect oneself from being duped by invalid arguments, it is important to determine which forms produce valid syllogisms and which do not. The following sections introduce ways to determine if a syllogism is valid or invalid.

A syllogism has only three terms. Some arguments, however, having more than three terms can be rewritten as syllogisms:

> **(5)**   Anyone who breaks the law is a criminal. Human beings who
> intentionally and without legal consent take the life of anoth-
> er human being break the law. So, murderers are criminals.

(5) can be symbolized as

> **(6)**   All B are C
>          All I are B
>          ---------
>          All M are C

(6) has four terms. Yet these four terms can be reduced to three by appealing to a definition permitting the replacement of an expression with a single but synonymous word:

> **'murderer' = def. 'a human being who intentionally takes the life of another human being without legal consent'**

The subject term in the second premise is now changed to read

> All murderers are human beings who break the law.

(6) can be rewritten as

$$
\begin{array}{ll}
\textbf{(7)} & \text{All B are C} \\
& \text{All M are B} \\
\hline
& \text{All M are C}
\end{array}
$$

Watch for *synonym replacements* to reduce terms.

An argument might have more than three terms because of terms used to denote the complement of a class. This argument has six terms:

**(8)** Every reptile is a non-mammal. Mammals are non-viperous. Thus, vipers are never non-reptilian.

(8) moves into symbols as

$$
\begin{array}{ll}
\textbf{(9)} & \text{All R are non-M} \\
& \text{All M are non-V} \\
\hline
& \text{No V are non-R}
\end{array}
$$

Since (8), as seen in (9), does not have three terms, it is not a syllogism. However, if contraposition is applied to the second premise and obversion to the conclusion, (8) can be transformed into this standard form syllogism:

**(10)** All reptiles are non-mammalian animals.
All vipers are non-mammalian animals.
_____
All vipers are reptiles.

(10), having exactly three terms, is symbolized in this way:

$$
\begin{array}{ll}
\textbf{(11)} & \text{All R are non-M} \\
& \text{All V are non-M} \\
\hline
& \text{All V are R*}
\end{array}
$$

---

\* While (10) is a syllogism having all true premises and a true conclusion, it is, nonetheless, an invalid syllogism. This can be seen by using the same logical form of (10) with different terms such that both premises are true but the conclusion false:

All humans are non-reptilian.
All dogs are non-reptilian.
_____
All dogs are humans.

This counter-example shows that the truth of the premises of an argument displaying the form of (10) does not guarantee the truth of the conclusion. That is, any argument having this form is invalid. Using counter-examples, as done here, is a powerful method to show the invalidity of invalid syllogisms.

## EXERCISES

### Group A:

Put the following arguments into standard syllogistic form, reducing the number of terms where necessary. Then, using the suggested capital letters, symbolize each example. Name the form of each by stating both its mood and figure.

1. Rock stars are never jazz players. A few jazz players are classically trained musicians. So, there're classically trained musicians who aren't rock stars. (R,J,C)

2. That none of the country singers in Nashville are punk musicians is evident for two reasons. First, punk musicians never do jazz. Second, not even one country singer in Nashville does jazz. (C,P,J)

3. Members of *U2* are Irish. Further, several of the *U2* members are non-dreamers. It follows that at least several Irish aren't dreamers. (M,I,D)

4. Sixties rock stars were never musicians into acid. This is evident for two reasons. First, musicians into acid are non-punk players. Second, sixties rock stars were not punk players. (R,A,P)

5. Paul Evans is a lead guitarist in a famous rock band. And any lead guitarist in a famous rock band has a lot of money. So, Paul Evans is wealthy. (E,L,M,W)

6. Controlled economic growth is never potentially harmful to the stock market. However, anything bringing about inflationary pressures is capable of being injurious to the stock market. Thus, certain controlled economic growth doesn't create inflationary pressures. (G,H,P,I)

7. Not a single treasury bond is speculative. This is evident because every treasury bond is a note backed by the federal government. But further, no notes backed by the federal government are speculative. (B,S,N)

8. Junk stock is likely to have quick price fluctuation in an unsteady market. Some blue chip stocks are likely to have quick price fluctuations in an unsteady market. So, a few blue chip stocks are junk stocks. (J,F,B)

9. Every financial newsletter is an expensive business tool. Further, many of these newsletters aren't good market predictors. Hence, there're expensive business tools that aren't good market predictors. (L,T,P)

10. Each eighteenth century harpsichord is a baroque musical instrument. Not a single eighteenth century harpsichord was pitched on A-440. Accordingly, no baroque musical instrument is pitched on A-440. (H,I,P)

11. A few symphonic pieces are not non-atonal works. Baroque musical compositions are non-symphonic pieces. Hence, there're atonal works that are not baroque musical compositions. (P,W,C)

12. A psychedelic drug is a life-threatening substance. Any life-threatening substance is harmful. So, certain harmful things are psychedelic drugs. (D,S,H)

13. Heroin is dangerous to use. Moreover, it is controlled by the *FDA*. Wherefore, anything controlled by the *FDA* is dangerous to use. (H,D,C)

14. Any illegal drug is an expensive substance. Also illegal drugs are never safe to use. Thus, certain expensive substances aren't safe to use. (D,E,U)

15. Alcoholics suffer from a potentially deadly disorder. Many persons who drink beer are

alcoholics. Accordingly, quite a few persons suffering from a deadly disorder drink beer. (A,D,B)

**Group B:**

Construct a syllogism, in non-standard form, for each of the following forms. Use different topics and grammatical variations in constructing your arguments.

1. EAE-1
2. AEO-4
3. EAE-2
4. OAO-3
5. IOI-4
6. EIO-2
7. AAI-3
8. AII-4
9. AEO-1
10. AOO-2

## 2.  VALIDITY AND VENN DIAGRAMS

A syllogism suggests relations holding between three classes. In the previous chapter Venn diagrams are introduced as a means to picture all possible relations holding between two classes. This technique can be expanded to depict all possible relations holding between three classes:

**(1)**

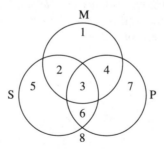

The three overlapping circles form eight distinct areas, each area representing a distinct class.* In this book, the circle representing that class denoted by the subject

---

\* In the remainder of this section, for ease of reference, each area of a Venn diagram will continue to be numbered.

term, 'S', is always the lower left-hand one; the circle representing that class denoted by the predicate term, 'P', is always the lower right-hand circle; and the circle representing that class denoted by the middle term, 'M', is always the upper circle shown between the 'S' circle and the 'P' circle.

Venn diagrams are used to determine if a syllogism is valid or not. Consider this example:

> **(2)**  All mathematicians are pliable people.
> All statisticians are mathematicians.
> So, all statisticians are pliable people.

Using 'M', 'P', and 'S', (2) can be symbolized as

> **(3)**  All M are P
> All S are M
> ―――――――――
> All S are P*

(3) portrays the form *AAA-1*. Does the truth of the premises, if they are true, guarantee the truth of the conclusion?

To answer this question, draw a Venn diagram representing (3). The circle 'M' represents the class *mathematicians*, the circle 'P' stands for the class *pliable people*, and the circle 'S' pictures the class *statisticians*. Thus, each area in the diagram represents a specific class of individuals. Area 1 represents the class *mathematicians* that is neither *statisticians* nor *pliable people*. Area 2 depicts the class *mathematicians* that is also *statisticians* and *non-pliable people*. Area 3 pictures the class *mathematicians* that is both *statisticians* and *pliable people*. Area 4 illustrates the class *mathematicians* that is *pliable people* and *non-statisticians*. Indicated by area 5 is the class *statisticians* that is neither *mathematicians* nor *pliable people*. The class *statisticians* that is also *pliable people* and *non-manthematicians* is pictured in area 6. Area 7 represents the class *pliable people* that is *non-statisticians* and *non-mathematicians*. The class that is *non-mathematicians, non-statisticians,* and *non-pliable people* is designated by area 8. This information can be pictured in this way, where a bar, '—', is drawn over a letter designating the complement of a class:

**(4)**

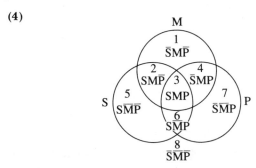

――――――――――――

* Alternative ways of symbolizing (2) are

| MAP | | $M\overline{P} = 0$ |
|---|---|---|
| SAM | and | $S\overline{M} = 0$ |
| ――― | | ――――― |
| SAP | | $S\overline{P} = 0$ |

In using a Venn diagram to determine whether a categorical syllogism is valid, first assume a Boolean interpretation of any universal premises. If the syllogism is invalid assuming a Boolean interpretation, then make whatever *existential assumptions* necessary to establish the validity of that argument. If the argument is invalid under a Boolean interpretation and, furthermore, no existential assumption makes the syllogism valid, the argument is invalid under any possible interpretation. Remember that an argument might be valid given certain existential assumptions yet, nonetheless, not be sound. That is, all the premises might not be true.

Begin analyzing (2) by assuming a Boolean interpretation of the universal premises. The major premise asserts that any mathematician is a pliable person. Shading an area indicates that the class represented by that area is empty. Consequently, that area of *M*—1 and 2 in (4)—not overlapping *P* in (5) is shaded to show that no mathematicians fail to be pliable persons. Any major premise that is an *A* or *E* statement will be shaded in a Venn diagram with *horizontal slash marks*. Here is that part of (4) picturing the major premise of (2):

**(5)**

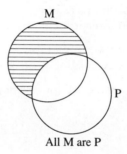

All M are P

The minor premise claims that any statistician is a mathematician. Areas 5 and 6 of (4) are shaded to picture the claim that no statisticians fail to be mathematicians. A minor premise that is an *A* or *E* statement will be shaded with *diagonal slash marks*. The minor premise of (2) is pictured like this:

**(6)**

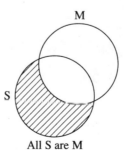

All S are M

The diagrams in (5) and (6) can now be overlaid to complete a Venn diagram representing the entire argument, (2):

**(7)**

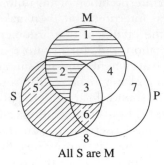

All S are M

(7) represents exactly what is claimed by the premises of (2). (7) also represents what is asserted in the conclusion. The only part of the circle S that is not shaded is area 3. This shows that all statisticians, if there are any, are pliable people, if there are any. The truth of the premises does guarantee the truth of the conclusion. (2) is a valid syllogism given a Boolean interpretation of its premises. No existential assumptions are necessary to establish this validity.

Assuming a Boolean interpretation, consider this argument:

**(8)** Philosophers are metaphysicians. Scientists are never meta-physicians. Accordingly, no scientists are philosophers.

Let 'P' stand for *philosophers*, 'M' for *metaphysicians*, and 'S' for *scientists*. (8) can then be depicted as

**(9)** All P are M
No S are M
——————————
No S are P*

Is (8) valid?

To determine whether (8) is valid, draw a Venn diagram:

**(10)**

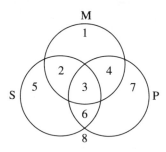

_____

* (7) can also be symbolized as

PAM                    $\overline{PM} = 0$
SEM          and       $SM = 0$
SEP                    $SP = 0$

The major premise asserts that every philosopher is a metaphysician. To depict this claim, shade in areas 6 and 7 with horizontal slash marks. (11) shows that no philosopher fails to be a metaphysician:

**(11)**

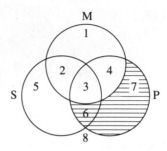

The minor premise says that any scientist fails to be a metaphysician. So, shade areas 2 and 3 with diagonal slash marks:

**(12)**

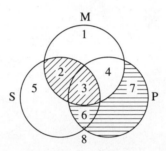

In (12) every part of the circle representing the class *scientists* that overlaps the circle picturing the class *philosophers* is shaded. So, no scientists are philosophers and (8) is valid under a Boolean interpretation.

Syllogisms having *I* or *O* statements introduce further considerations in using Venn diagrams to determine validity.

> **(13)**  Some marine animals are porpoises.
> All marine animals are sea creatures.
> Wherefore, some sea creatures are porpoises.

(14) displays the logical form of (13) as *IAI-3*:

> **(14)**  Some M are P
> All M are S
> ―――――――――
> Some S are P*

---

* These are alternative symbolizations for (12):

$$\begin{array}{ccc} \text{MIP} & & \text{MP} \neq 0 \\ \underline{\text{MAS}} & \text{and} & \underline{\overline{\text{MS}} = 0} \\ \text{SIP} & & \text{SP} \neq 0 \end{array}$$

The minor premise asserts that nothing that is a marine animal fails to be a sea creature:

**(15)**

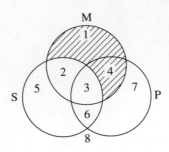

The major premise says that there is at least one marine animal which is a porpoise. To show there is something that is both a marine animal and a porpoise, put an 'X' in area 3:

**(16)**

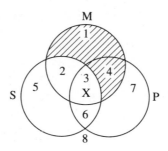

(16) shows that there is at least one sea creature that is a porpoise. Since this is the conclusion of (13), it is valid.

When diagramming a syllogism containing both universal and particular premises, always first picture the universal premise. This procedure is followed in diagramming (13). If this procedure were not followed, the question of where to put an 'X' would arise. Would an 'X' be placed in area 3 or 4? No 'X' can be put in a shaded area. When the universal premise is depicted by the shading in area 4, the 'X' must be placed in area 3.

The following syllogism has a term denoting the complement of a class:

> **(17)** All non-mammals are cold-blooded animals. No cold-blooded animals are creatures that suckle their young. Accordingly, no creatures that suckle their young are non-mammals.

(17) can be put into symbols in this way:

> **(18)** All non-M are C
> No C are S
> ———————
> No S are non-M

The class *non-mammal* is represented in a Venn diagram:

**(19)**

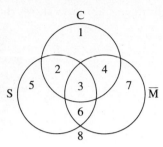

Shading in the appropriate areas shows that (17) is valid given a Boolean interpretation of its universal premises:

**(20)**

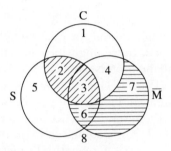

Work through this example:

**(21)** Engineers are alert people. Smart people are also alert people. So, all smart people are engineers.

(21) can be symbolized as

**(22)** All E are A
All S are A
——————
All S are E

The major premise, given a Boolean interpretation, says that if any person is an engineer, that person is alert. To show that no engineer fails to be an alert person, use horizontal slash marks to shade areas 6 and 7:

**(23)**

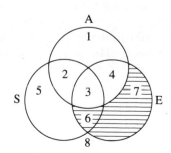

The minor premise claims that all smart people are alert people. Shading in areas 5 and 6 of (22) with diagonal marks shows that no smart person fails to be mentally alert:

**(24)**

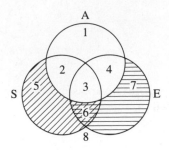

What does (24) exhibit about the relation between *smart people* and *engineers*? Since area 2 is *not* shaded, there might be smart people who are not engineers. Consequently, even if all the premises of (21) were true, that would not guarantee the truth of its conclusion. Thus, (21) is an invalid argument.

Since (21) is an invalid argument given a Boolean interpretation, assume existential import for its premises. In particular, given (24), assume that smart people exist. Even if smart people are assumed to exist, the placement of an 'X' is ambiguous. Does it go in area 2, area 3, or both? To picture this ambiguity, put an 'X' on that segment of the circle separating areas 2 and 3:*

**(25)**

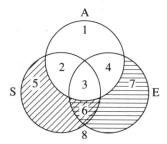

Since an 'X' could go only in area 2 if (21) were valid, the conclusion, 'All smart people are engineers', does not necessarily follow from the assumed truth of the premises. (21) is invalid under both a Boolean and an existential interpretation.

An *O* statement is asserted in the following argument:

---

* Any syllogism is invalid if its corresponding Venn diagram contains an 'X' drawn on an arc of any circle, one of its areas is double shaded, or both.

**(26)**   There are philosophers who are metaphysicians. Not one metaphysician is a scientist. Hence, some scientists are not philosophers.

(26) displays the form *IEO-4*:

> **(27)**   Some P are M
> No M are S
> ———————
> Some S are not P

Accept a Boolean interpretation of the second premise and use Venn diagrams to
determine if (26) is valid:

**(28)**

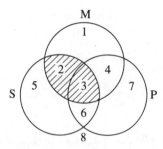

(28) shows that any metaphysician fails to be a scientist. The major premise states
that there is at least one philosopher who is a metaphysician. Area 4 represents all
those things that are both philosophers and metaphysicians. Put an 'X' in that area:

**(29)**

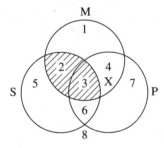

'Some scientists are not philosophers', does not necessarily follow from the truth of
the premises. Area 5 in (29) represents all those things that are scientists but non-
philosophers. If (26) were a valid argument, an 'X' would be found in area 5.

Nor will an existential interpretation of the second premise of (26) establish
validity. Assuming scientists do exist, where is an 'X' to be placed in (30)? Does it go
in area 5 or area 6?

**(30)**

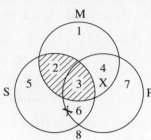

(26) would be valid under an existential interpretation only if there were no place to draw an 'X' but area 6.

Next, examine this syllogism:

**(31)** Every puritanical person is malicious. Many malicious people are shrewd. So, many shrewd people are puritanical.

(31) can be displayed as having the form *AII-4*:

**(32)** All P are M
Some M are S
───────────
Some S are P

Is (31) valid? In a Venn diagram, first display the assertion of the major premise giving it a Boolean interpretation:

**(33)**

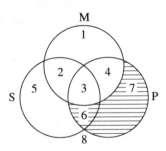

In the minor premise, *both* areas 2 and 3 in (33) represent 'Some malicious people are shrewd'. To diagram exactly what is asserted by the minor premise, set an 'X' on the arc of the circle separating areas 2 and 3:

**(34 )**

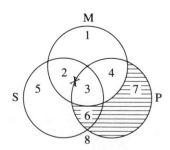

An 'X' indicates that there is a malicious person who is shrewd. It is not known, assuming the premises are all true, whether this person is found in area 2, area 3, or both. There could be a person who is shrewd and malicious but non-puritanical.

(31) is invalid under a Boolean interpretation. Nor is the argument valid if an existential viewpoint is taken. In asserting that all puritanical people are malicious, and assuming the existence of puritanical people, where does an 'X' go? In area 3 or area 4?

**(35)**

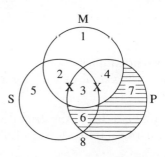

Since the 'X' could be in area 4, the truth of the premises of (31), assuming the premises are true, does not guarantee that some shrewd people are puritanical.

There are syllogisms invalid under a Boolean interpretation of their universal premises that are valid if existential import is assumed. Here is an example:

**(36)**   Any psychopathic person is miserable. Not a single saint is miserable. So, the majority of saints are not psychopathic.

This syllogism can be symbolized in standard form:

**(37)**   All P are M
No S are M
─────────────
Some S are not P

Given a Boolean interpretation of (36), the following is drawn:

**(38)**

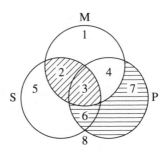

Area 5 represents those things that are saints but not psychopathic persons and not miserable. (38) shows that (36) is invalid because area 5 is empty.

Now assume existential import for (36). In particular, assume that saints exist. Using an 'X' to indicate this assumption, the Venn diagram for (36) is this:

**(39)**

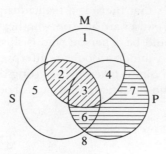

Since it is assumed that saints exist, it follows that there is at least one thing that is a saint and not a psychopathic person.

Here is another syllogism invalid under a Boolean interpretation, but valid given an existential one:

    **(40)**   Alcohol is a drug. Any drug can be harmful. Consequently, certain harmful things are alcoholic.

(40) is pictured in standard form:

           **(41)**   All A are D
                   All D are H
                   —————————
                   Some H are A

If the premises of (40) are true, must the conclusion be true?

    **(42)**

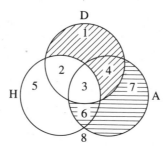

(42) does not establish the validity of (40). Since area 3 is empty, there might or might not be harmful things that are alcoholic drinks. However, assuming the existence of alcoholic drinks, (40) is valid as seen in the following:

**(43)**

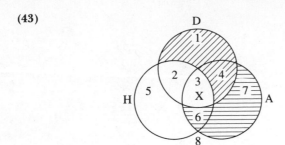

The 'X' in area 5 indicates that there is at least one harmful drug that is an alcoholic drink.

Study one more syllogism that is invalid under a Boolean stance, yet valid assuming existential import:

**(44)**  Extraterrestrial creatures are never humorous. Extraterrestrial creatures come from outer space. Hence, some creatures from outer space aren't humorous.

The form of (44), *EAO-3*, is displayed in

**(45)**  No E are H
All E are S
―――――――――
Some S are not H

Given a Boolean understanding of (45), (46) is constructed:

**(46)**

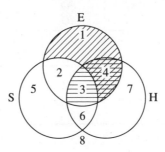

Areas 2 and 5 represent *creatures from space who are non-humorous*. Since both of these areas are empty, the conclusion of (44) is not guaranteed by the premises. Following is a Venn diagram of (44) assuming existential import:

(47)

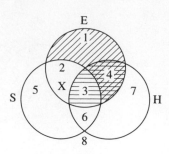

Supposing that extraterrestrial creatures do in fact exist, an 'X' appears in area 2. This shows that there is at least one individual who is a creature from outer space but not humorous. (44) is valid given an existential interpretation.

In summary, Venn diagrams establish that any syllogism having one of the following forms is valid under a Boolean interpretation:

| Figure 1 | Figure 2 | Figure 3 | Figure 4 |
|----------|----------|----------|----------|
| AAA | AEE | AII | AEE |
| EAE | EAE | EIO | EIO |
| AII | AOO | IAI | IAI |
| EIO | EIO | OAO | |

Assuming existential import, any syllogism having one of the following forms is also valid:

| Figure 1 | Figure 2 | Figure 3 | Figure 4 | Assumption |
|----------|----------|----------|----------|------------|
| AAI | AEO | | AEO | Ss exist |
| EAO | EAO | | | |
| | | AAI | EAO | Ms exist |
| | | EAO | | |
| | | | AAI | Ps exist |

## EXERCISES

### Group A:

Assuming a Boolean interpretation, determine by Venn diagrams if the arguments in *Group A* of Section 1 are valid. Next, determine which of the invalid arguments, if any, are valid assuming existential import.

### Group B:

Translate each of the following arguments into standard form, reducing terms if necessary. Identify the logical form of each. Next, assuming a Boolean interpretation, determine by using Venn diagrams which of the arguments are valid and which invalid. Finally, for those arguments invalid under a Boolean interpretation, determine, again by using Venn diagrams, which are valid if existential import is assumed. State what existential assumptions are needed to establish validity if any such assumptions are necessary.

1. A few people betting on the Mets are non-winners. Anyone pulling for the Buffalos is a winner. Accordingly, some people betting on the Mets aren't pulling for the Buffalos. (B,W,P)

2. There're scholars who are also college athletes. Yet pro football players are never college athletes. So, many scholars are not pro football players. (S,A,P)

3. It is the case that some Raider fans aren't also Giant supporters. This is obvious because no Giant supporters root for Dallas. Furthermore, quite a few Raider fans do root for Dallas. (R,G,D)

4. It is obvious that Senator Kennedy is a big tax spender. After all, no big tax spender is a non-liberal. Moreover, Senator Kennedy is a liberal. (K,S,L)

5. Many diplomats are expected to be strictly honest in their work. Yet not even one seller of political influence is expected to be strictly honest in his work. Hence, many diplomats aren't sellers of political influence. (D,H,S)

6. It is true that certain of the current candidates want to throw mud during an election year. This is evident from two considerations. Each one of today's candidates is a politician. Moreover, any politician wants to throw mud during an election year. (C,W,T,P)

7. None of the particles explainable by the laws of quantum mechanics are considered to be Newtonian atoms. Any Newtonian atom is viewed as being completely located simultaneously in space and time. Thus, there exist things viewed as being completely located simultaneously in space and time that aren't particles explainable by the laws of quantum mechanics. (P,A,L)

8. Not one of the discoveries in quantum mechanics is understandable solely in terms of atoms in motion. Things understandable solely in terms of atoms in motion are explainable in classical mechanics. Accordingly, there're findings in quantum mechanics that aren't explainable in classical mechanics. (D,U,E,F)

9. Some index arbitrage is blamed for injecting sudden price swings into stock purchase plans. Of course, index arbitrage is a very controversial form of program trading in the stock market. So, there're things blamed for injecting sudden price swings into stock purchase plans that are very controversial forms of program trading in the stock market. (A,S,T)

10. Sales of stocks in one market and purchase of stock index futures in another market are a form of index arbitrage. Certain forms of index arbitrage are permissible in a consistently steady market. Therefore, certain permissible things in a consistently steady market are sales of stock in one market and purchase of stock index futures in another market. (S,A,P)

11. Every baroque building is very ornate. None but buildings filled with a great deal of light are baroque. Thus, a building filled with a great deal of light is very ornate. (B,O,L)

12. Durham Cathedral is an example of Norman architecture. Each example of Norman architecture is noted for its massive strength. Accordingly, Durham Cathedral is noted for its massive strength. (D,N,S)

13. There're many examples of pre-Palladian architecture that are Gothic structures. Any building designed by Christopher Wren is an example of non-pre-Palladian architecture.

Hence, many examples of Gothic structures aren't designed by Christopher Wren. (P,G,W)

14. Not even one example of a Saxon structure has Norman origins. Many ancient, currently used, English cathedrals aren't Norman in origin. Consequently, there're examples of Saxon structures that aren't ancient, currently used, cathedrals in England. (S,N,C)

15. Non-pre-Gothic buildings are non-Norman structures. Ancient English cathedrals are non-pre-Gothic buildings. So, some ancient English cathedrals are Norman structures. (G,N,C)

---

## 3.   VALIDITY AND CATEGORICAL RULES

Venn diagrams are useful in determining whether a syllogism is valid or not. They are less helpful in actually constructing valid syllogisms or pinpointing specifically what is logically wrong with invalid syllogisms. But a person needs to be able to construct new arguments that are valid as well as determine whether an argument presented to him is valid or not. *Syllogistic rules of validity* are helpful not only in determining the validity, or invalidity, of syllogisms. They are also important guides in the construction of both syllogisms and longer arguments made up of categorical statements. Analyzing and constructing such longer arguments are tasks discussed in the next section.

Different sets of rules are employed to determine the validity of any syllogism. The following set is commonly used:

> *Rule 1*: **The middle term must be distributed at least once in the premises of a valid syllogism.**

> *Rule 2*: **Any term distributed in the conclusion of a valid syllogism must also be distributed in the premises.**

> *Rule 3*: **Any valid syllogism having a negative premise must have a negative conclusion, and any valid syllogism having a negative conclusion must have a negative premise.**

> *Rule 4*: **No valid syllogism can have two negative premises.**

Rule 5 is used only with a Boolean interpretation:

> *Rule 5*: **Any valid syllogism having only universal premises must have a universal conclusion, and a valid syllogism with a universal conclusion must have two universal premises.**

The first two rules introduce the concept *distributed term*. A term is distributed when, and only when, because of the form of the statement in which it appears, that term refers to every member of the class it names. In the *A* statement, 'All illegal substances are dangerous products', the subject term is distributed. Every illegal substance is being referred to in this statement. However, the predicate term does not refer to every dangerous product. The predicate term is not distributed. The *E* statement, 'No cigarettes are safe for the lungs', distributes both the subject and predicate terms. Every cigarette fails to be safe for the lungs, and all things safe for the lungs fail to be cigarettes. In the *I* statements, 'Some people are cruel', neither the subject nor the predicate term is distributed. What of the *O* statement, 'Some stocks are not financially productive'? The subject term is not distributed. The predicate term is considered distributed, however. The predicate term says something about all financially productive things; namely, there is at least one stock excluded from the class *financially productive things*. In summary,

**the subject term of a universal statement is distributed and the predicate term of a negative statement is distributed**

| | SUBJECT TERM | PREDICATE TERM |
|---|---|---|
| *A*: | distributed | undistributed |
| *E*: | distributed | distributed |
| *I*: | undistributed | undistributed |
| *O*: | undistributed | distributed |

Accepting this view of distribution, an intuitive rationale can be given for the first two syllogistic rules of validity.

The first rule demands that in a valid syllogism the middle term is distributed at least once in the premises. The function of the middle term is to mediate between, or bring together in the conclusion, those classes named by the subject and predicate terms. Suppose some classes *S*, *P*, and *M* are being considered. The ways in which *S* and *P* can be related in the conclusion depend upon how they are related to *M* in the premises. If *M* is distributed in one of the premises, then either the predicate term or the subject term is related to the whole of the distributed *M*. For instance, it might be said that 'All M are P'. This is to assert that everything in the class *M* is included in the class *P*. Suppose, further, the claim that 'All S are M'. Then everything that is in *S* is in *M*. Since everything in *M* is in *P*, everything in *S* must necessarily be in *P*. Or it might be said that 'Some S are M'. Then, that part of *S* which is in *M* must be in *P*, since all of *M* is in *P*. Similar remarks are appropriate if one begins with 'All M are S'.

Any syllogism that breaks the first rule of syllogistic validity is an instance of the *fallacy of undistributed middle*:

(1) Gossips are malicious people. Certain malicious people are dangerous. It follows that there are dangerous people who are gossips.

The middle term, 'malicious people', is not distributed in either premise. Hence, the premises of (1) cannot guarantee any relation holding between the classes *dangerous people* and *gossips*. Even though the conclusion is true, this is not established by the evidence of the premises.

The second rule also relies on the concept *distribution*. Suppose the predicate term is distributed in the conclusion but not in the major premise. In this case, the major premise could only make a claim about part of the members of *P* while the conclusion would make a claim about all those members. However, that something is the case about some members of a class does not guarantee that it holds for all members of that class. The same is true for the subject term if it is distributed in the conclusion but not in the minor premise. In general, if a conclusion is understood as making an assertion about all the members of a class, then the corresponding premise must also make an assertion about all the members of that same class.

In the following example, while the predicate is distributed in the conclusion, it is not distributed in the major premise. This is an instance of the *fallacy of the illicit major*:

(2)    There are professional golfers who are very wealthy. However, a middle-class person is never wealthy. Consequently, some middle-class persons aren't professional golfers.

In the following example, (3), the subject term is distributed in the conclusion, but not in the minor premise. This is an instance of the *fallacy of the illicit minor*:

(3)    The heroes of today's youth are entertainment stars. Further, entertainment stars are rich people. Hence, it is rich people who are the heroes of today's youth.

The third syllogistic rule of validity deals with negative premises and conclusions. Assume that all the premises of a syllogism are affirmative. An affirmative statement asserts that one class is either entirely or partially included in another. If all the premises assert class inclusion, in whole or in part, no conclusion can be drawn that necessarily establishes the exclusion, in whole or in part, of two classes. If, on the other hand, the conclusion is an *E* or *O* statement, it asserts that one class is wholly or partially excluded from another. Such claims, however, cannot be based on assertions maintaining solely that the classes designated in the conclusion are wholly or partially included in one another. So, a negative conclusion demands, in a valid syllogism, a negative premise. The following example violates the third rule of syllogistic validity:

(4)    Certain technically skilled people aren't good strategists. Yet many sports persons are good strategists. Therefore, there are sports persons who are technically skilled.

(4) is an instance of the *fallacy of inferring a positive conclusion from a negative premise*. Attempting to infer a negative conclusion from all positive premises is the *fallacy of inferring a negative conclusion from positive premises*.

The fourth rule requires that no valid syllogism have two negative premises. A negative categorical statement denies that one class is completely or partially included in another. Imagine a major premise in which *P* is completely or partially excluded from *M*. Also assume that *S*, in the minor premise, is completely excluded from *M*. In the case of complete exclusion from *M*, there could be no relation between *P* and *S*. In the situation of partial exclusion from *M* there might, or might not, be a partial overlap between *P* and *S*. Thus, no conclusion concerning any relation between *P* and *S* can necessarily be drawn from two negative premises. Any syllogism with two negative premises is said to be an instance of the *fallacy of exclusive premises*. This is an example:

(5)    Drugs that are effective and safe to use are never placebos. Not even one illegal designer drug is a placebo. Thus, no illegal designer drug is effective and safe to use.

The final syllogistic rule of validity applies to syllogisms understood from a Boolean interpretation of *A* and *E* statements. If a syllogism fails in *only* this rule, then it is valid from an existential stance but not from a Boolean one. If all the premises of a syllogism are universal and supposing a Boolean viewpoint, then no existence claim is being made. Now, no claim concerning the existence of anything can necessarily follow from premises making no existence claim. Hence, neither *I* nor *O* conclusions are entailed by only *A* or *E* premises interpreted in a Boolean way. Similar considerations establish why a syllogism with a universal conclusion must have all universal premises. A violation of this rule is an instance of the *fallacy of existential import*:

(6)    Cigarette smokers consume cancer-causing agents. Every consumer of cancer-causing agents is at high risk of developing cancer. Accordingly, many at high risk of developing cancer are cigarette smokers.

Certainly it is not problematic "to assume" that there are cigarette smokers. But the acceptance of this assumption is based on observation and not on logic. If the supposition is not made, however, (6) is invalid.

---

## EXERCISES

### Group A:

In each case of an invalid argument in *Group A* of Section 1 give the syllogistic rule(s) for validity that is broken and name the fallacy that is committed. Do the same for *Group B* of Section 2.

### Group B:

Put the following syllogisms into standard form, stating the form of each. Then, under the Boolean interpretation, determine by an appeal to the syllogistic rules of validity which of the following are valid and which are invalid. For those arguments, if any, that are invalid under the Boolean interpretation, determine which are valid under the existential interpretation. In all cases cite the specific rule(s) that is broken and name any fallacy that is committed.

1. Jazz musicians never use a great deal of metal. On the other hand many hard acid players do use a great deal of metal. Consequently, some jazz musicians aren't hard acid musicians. (J,M,A)

2. None of the rock music heard today was known during the fifties. Further, much jazz also wasn't known during the fifties. Hence, it can be inferred that some jazz isn't the rock music heard today. (R,K,J)

3. There're punk players who are funky entertainers. No classical performer is a funky entertainer. It follows that there're non-funky entertainers who aren't non-classical performers. (P,F,C)

4. A good many rock 'n' roll musicans are guitarists. but no folk singers are rock 'n' roll musicans. In which case, it follows that there're guitarists who are also folk singers. (R,G,F)

5. Some metabolic processes aren't anabolic. None but metabolic processes are organic

growth processes. So, certain organic growth processes aren't anabolic. (M,A,O)

6. There're metabolic processes that are anabolic. The anabolic process, however, is an organic growth process. Consequently, there're metabolic processes that are also organic growth processes. (M,A,O)

7. There exist hawks supporting international trade quotas to protect U.S. industries. This can be substantiated by pointing to many conservatives supporting international trade quotas in order to protect U.S. industries. Moreover, some conservatives are hawks. (H,S,C)

8. Every non-conservative is a non-fundamentalist. Moreover, each fundamentalist tends toward the Republican Party. Thus, many who tend toward the Republican Party are fundamentalists. (C,F,R)

9. One concludes that a few Dixie Democrats are political liberals. Obviously, several strong supporters of expanding federal welfare programs are Dixie Democrats. Further, strong supporters of expanding federal welfare programs are never non-liberals. (D,L,S)

10. Any chlorine is a non-metallic Group VIIB element. Now, chlorine is a halogen. Hence, each non-metallic Group VIIB element is a halogen. (C,E,H)

11. Sodium chloride is a salt. Salt is found widely in nature. Consequently, some sodium chloride is found widely in nature. (C,S,N)

12. Compounds exist such as sodium chloride that are salt. Further, salt is a chief natural source of chlorine. So, compounds such as sodium chloride are a chief natural source of chlorine. (C,S,N)

13. High school students are non-college graduates hoping to have a profitable life. Not a single person with a baccalaureate degree is a high school student. Wherefore, there're persons with a baccalaureate degree who aren't college graduates hoping to have a profitable life. (S,G,D)

14. Every college student looks forward to great personal success after graduation. Not even one college student expects to fail in life. Hence, many anticipate great success after graduation who aren't expecting to fail in life. (C,S,F,A)

15. Everyone hoping to find a good-paying job is eagerly awaiting graduation. Each senior hopes to find a good-paying job. So, everyone eagerly awaiting graduation is a senior. (J,G,S)

---

## 4.  ENTHYMEMES AND SORITES

One or both premises might not be stated in presenting a syllogism. Or perhaps the conclusion is omitted. In some instances, both a premise and conclusion are left unasserted. Any syllogism having such omissions is an ***enthymeme***.*

Imagine someone claiming this:

> **(1)**  Simon Kirke is wealthy. After all anyone who is a member of a
> very popular rock 'n' roll band is wealthy.

---

\* The concept *enthymeme* can be broadened to include not only syllogisms but any argument with missing premises, a missing conclusion, or both.

Interpreting (1) as a deductive argument, the premise, 'anyone who is a member of a very popular rock 'n' roll band is wealthy', is not sufficient to guarantee the truth of the conclusion, 'Simon Kirke is wealthy'. There is another claim needed as a premise. This new premise is 'Simon Kirke is a member of the very popular rock 'n' roll band'. (1) can now be rewritten in standard form as

> **(2)** All persons who are members of a very popular rock 'n' roll band are wealthy.
>
> All persons identical to Simon Kirke are members of a very popular rock 'n' roll band.
>
> ————————————————————
>
> All persons who are identical to Simon Kirke are wealthy.

(2) can be put into symbols in this way:

> **(3)** All M are W
> All K are M
> ————————
> All K are W

(3) displays the valid syllogistic form, AAA-1.*

Perhaps in arguing, someone omits a conclusion taken to be obvious:

> **(4)** Certainly it's true that no unorganized student is going to pass the course. It's the case that Jennifer is an unorganized student. I don't believe that it's necessary to say anything more!

The conclusion of (4) is not difficult to supply. The claims in (4) give evidence to support the assertion, 'Jennifer isn't going to pass the course'. (4) can be depicted in symbols as

> **(5)** No non-O are P
> All J are non-O
> ——————————
> No J are P

(5) displays the valid syllogistic form, *EAE-1*.

Or consider a mother insisting to her daughter,

> **(6)** No long-haired tramp is marrying my daughter.

(6) could serve either as a premise or as a conclusion, depending upon the context in which it is asserted. Suppose that the mother is talking about Sean, a guitarist in the local heavy metal band. Imagine, further, that Sean and the daughter are in a serious relationship. The implicit argument might be this:

> **(7)** No long-haired tramp is marrying my daughter. Sean is a long-haired tramp. So, Sean isn't marrying my daughter.

---

*The validity of (2) can be confirmed by constructing a Venn diagram.

(7) can be put into syllogistic notation:

**(8)**   No T are M
All S are T
———————
No S are M

The valid syllogistic form, *EAE-1*, is seen in (8).

Appealing to the rules of syllogistic validity, notice how (8) is constructed. The task is to construct a valid syllogism in which the terms 'persons marrying my daughter' and 'persons identical to Sean' appear in the conclusion as denoting classes excluded from one another. 'No long-haired tramp is marrying my daughter' is presented in support of the conclusion about the daughter and her relation with Sean. Since the explicit premise, (6), is negative, by rule 3 the conclusion must be negative. And this is in keeping with the position of the mother. A good hypothesis for the conclusion is 'Sean isn't marrying my daughter', or 'No persons identical to Sean are persons marrying my daughter'.

Given the conclusion, 'No persons identical to Sean are persons marrying my daughter', 'persons identical to Sean' is the minor term and must appear in the minor premise. Similarly, 'persons marrying my daughter' is the major term and must appear in the major premise. Thus, the claim actually stated, 'No long-haired tramp is going to marry my daughter', is the major premise. Rule 4 demands that no valid syllogism can have more than one negative premise. To comply, the remaining premise must be either an *A* or *I* statement. The conclusion, however, is a universal statement. Observing rule 5, the minor premise cannot be a particular statement. Excluding the possibility of an *I* statement, the minor premise must be an *A* statement. Can anything more be said about the minor premise? Yes.

The term 'long-haired tramp' appears in that one statement presented as evidence for the conclusion, 'Sean isn't marrying my daughter'. Since it does not appear in the conclusion, 'long-haired tramp' must serve as the middle term in the premises. Notice that this term is already distributed in the major premise, thus satisfying rule 1. The remaining term in the minor premise must be 'persons identical to Sean'. Is the minor premise 'All long-haired tramps are persons identical to Sean' or 'All persons identical to Sean are long-haired tramps'? The second of these possibilities is more likely. There is a compelling logical reason, however, not to select 'All long-haired tramps are persons identical to Sean'. The term 'persons identical to Sean' is not distributed in this claim, but it is distributed in the conclusion. Rule 2 demands that any term distributed in the conclusion must also be distributed in the premises. This rule is not broken if 'All persons identical to Sean are long-haired tramps' is the minor premise.

Sometimes a person asserts a specific claim and is asked to give evidence for it. One should attempt to realize two important goals in presenting evidence. The first is to offer premises that are logically related to that claim in question. The other is to offer premises that are true or at least acceptable to those engaged in the arguing process. That is, any supplied claims ought to make the syllogism not only valid, but, if possible, sound or acceptable. To be guided by these goals is to follow the *Principle of Charity* in constructing, and interpreting, arguments. Syllogistic rules are powerful guides in discovering valid syllogisms while avoiding invalid ones. Venn diagrams are useful as independent means of confirming the results suggested by the rules. On the other hand, careful attention to facts, acceptable principles, and correct definitions is demanded in establishing the soundness or acceptability of an argument.*

There are cases, nonetheless, where a syllogism cannot be supplied that is valid, sound, and interesting. Assume someone asserts

**(9)**   Every gay is a child molester.
(All G are C)

What acceptable evidence can support this assertion, establish a valid syllogism, and retain interest in (9)? Because the conclusion is a universal statement, no particular statement can be a premise. Since the conclusion is affirmative, by rule 4 no premise can be negative. Further, because 'gay' is distributed as the minor term in the conclusion, it must be, by rule 2, distributed in the minor premise. These two observations limit the minor premise to an *A* statement:

**(10)**   All .. C ..
All G are M
———————
All G are C

The major premise needs to be completed. Rule 1 requires that the middle term must be distributed at least once in the premises. Since the middle term is not distributed in the minor premise, it must be distributed in the major. 'No M are C' is precluded by rule 1, leaving only

**(11)**   All M are C
All G are M
———————
All G are C

(11) pictures a valid syllogistic form, *AAA-1*, although it does not yet represent a syllogism. In (11), 'M' is merely a reminder of where a middle term is to be placed *when* there is a middle term. Suppose the middle term is 'people who sexually abuse children'. (11) is then interpreted in standard form as

**(12)**   All people who sexually abuse children are child molesters.
All gays are people who sexually abuse children.
———————————————————————————
All gays are child molesters.

(12) is a valid argument exhibiting the form *AAA-1*. Even so, the argument is not sound because the second premise is false. The minor premise can be replaced with this true statement, 'Some gays are people who sexually abuse children'. However, the resultant argument is invalid because, while 'gays' is distributed in the conclusion, it is not distributed in the new minor premise. The conclusion might next be changed to form a valid argument:

---

* Topics concerning the acceptability of premises are discussed further in Chapters 13–15.

> **(13)** All people who sexually abuse children are child molesters.
> Some gays are people who sexually abuse children.
> _____
> Some gays are child molesters.

(13) is both valid and sound, but so is this argument:

> **(14)** All people who sexually abuse children are child molesters.
> Some non-gays are people who sexually abuse children.
> _____
> Some non-gays are child molesters.

The combined consideration of (13) and (14) does not suggest anything uniquely interesting or horrific about gays.

Sometimes two, or more, enthymemes will be chained together to form a more complicated argument. Such chains of enthymemes are called sorites. A *sorites* is

**a series of categorical statements in which there are more than two premises and more than three terms.**

However, as in a syllogism, each term will occur only twice and only once in any statement in which it does appear. Here is an example of a sorites:

> **(15)** Conservative financial investments are wise acquisitions in an inflationary period. A few municipal notes aren't wise acquisitions in an inflationary period. Only conservative financial investments are bonds. Thus, some municipal notes aren't bonds.

In analyzing a chain of categorical statements making up sorites, begin by putting each of the statements into standard form:

> **(16)** All conservative financial investments are wise acquisitions in an inflationary period.
> Some municipal notes aren't wise acquisitions in an inflationary period.
> All bonds are conservative financial instruments.
> _____
> Some municipal notes aren't bonds.

Then, to visualize the argument better, symbolize it:

> **(17)** All I are A
> Some N are not A
> All B are I
> _____
> Some N are not B

(17) is not a syllogism. It has more than two premises and more than three terms. Nonetheless, (17) is a chain of enthymemes.

This chain is more obvious if (17) is put into something like standard syllogistic form. To do this, rearrange the premises so that the first premise will contain the predicate term of the conclusion and the second premise will contain the other term of the first premise:

> **(18)**   All B are I
> All I are A
> . . . ??? . . .
> _____
> Some N are not B

The remaining premise of (17) contains the subject term of the conclusion. It also contains that term, in this case 'A', of the previous premise not having been mentioned twice:

> **(19)**   All B are I
> All I are A
> Some N are not A
> _____
> Some N are not B

The first two premises of (19) can be viewed as the two premises in an enthymeme:

> **(20)**   All B are I
> All I are A
> _____
> . . . ??? . . .

'I', the middle term, is distributed in the second premise. Since both of the premises are universal affirmative, the conclusion must also be universal affirmative according to the rules of syllogistic validity. This conclusion, however, cannot be 'All A are B' because the subject term would be distributed in the conclusion but not in the premises. Hence, the conclusion of (20) must be 'All B are A'. (21) is a valid syllogism:*

> **(21)**   All B are I
> All I are A
> _____
> All B are A

The conclusion of (21) is next used as a premise, coupled with the third premise of (19), to produce a second enthymeme:

> **(22)**   All B are A
> Some N are not A
> _____
> . . . ??? . . .

The middle term, 'A', is distributed in the second premise, and at least one premise is affirmative. Hence, rules 1 and 3 of syllogistic validity are met. The conclusion must be negative since one of the premises is negative. Yet the conclusion can be neither 'No B are N' nor 'No N are B' because while 'N' is distributed in both these statements, it is not distributed in the premises. Combining these demands, the conclusion must be 'Some B are not N' or 'Some N are not B'. However, the conclusion cannot be 'Some B are not N' since, while 'B' is distributed in the first

---

* The validity of (21) can be confirmed by constructing a Venn diagram.

premise, it is not distributed in 'Some B are not N'. Therefore, the conclusion to (22) must be 'Some N are not B':

> **(23)**   All B are A
> Some N are not A
> ———————————
> Some N are not B

Since this is the conclusion of the original sorites, (15) is valid.*

(15) is a sorites composed of two valid syllogisms presented as enthymemes. A sorites might contain more than two enthymemes. To test for the validity of the entire sorites demands analyzing the chain into its component enthymemes, supplying the missing conclusion of each enthymeme, checking to see if each enthymeme is valid, and using the conclusion of a previous enthymeme as a premise in the next. If, at any stage of analysis, an enthymeme is invalid, then the entire sorites is invalid.

---

## *EXERCISES*

### Group A:

Put each of the statements in the following enthymemes into standard form. Next, supply any missing premise, conclusion, or premise and conclusion. Following the Principle of Charity, attempt to supply claims making the resulting syllogism both valid and sound. Using the suggested capital letters, symbolize the completed syllogism and specify its form. For any invalid syllogisms state both the syllogistic rule of validity broken and name the fallacy that is committed.

1. Anything that instills great fear of breaking the law greatly reduces the crime rate. Certainly, then, the death penalty greatly reduces the crime rate. (I,R,D)

2. Every victimless crime involves a non-violent act. So, crimes exist that don't involve violent acts. (V,A,C)

3. Many civil crimes aren't immoral acts. Evidence for this is simply that many immoral acts are non-punishable under the civil law. (C,M,P)

4. Bands using a great deal of metal are never non-loud. Consequently, many rock 'n' roll bands use a great deal of metal. (M,L,R)

5. Punk bands use violent lyrics. Obviously, then, there're bands using violent lyrics that are acid. (P,V,A)

6. More than a few politicians are corrupt. This isn't surprising considering that every one of them is a scoundrel. (P,C,S)

7. It's well known that not a single straightforward person thrives in politics. This comment is based on the fact that honest persons are straightforward. (S,T,H)

8. There're a few politicians who are honest. After all, a small number of politicians aren't liars. (P,H,L)

---

\* The validity of (23) can be confirmed by constructing a Venn diagram.

9. Many conservative people aren't unreasonable. So, many unreasonable people aren't Democrats. (C,R,D)

10. It's certainly true that many Republicans are wealthy. On top of that, quite a few fundamentalists are Republicans. This supports my contention about wealthy fundamentalists. (R,W,F)

## Group B:

Analyze each of the following sorites for validity. First, put the categorical statements into standard form. Second, using the suggested capital letters, symbolize the sorites and then put it into standard form. Reduce the number of terms, where necessary, to two occurrences of each term. Third, determine whether the sorites is valid or not by using the syllogistic rules of validity and Venn diagrams to test the validity, or invalidity, of each enthymeme making up the sorites. Fourth, name the rule broken and the fallacy exemplified in any invalid enthymeme.

1. Anyone who can grasp the relations of evidence to assertive conclusions is an asset in business. Everyone who reads comprehensively can grasp the relations of evidence to assertive conclusions. Anyone who is an asset in business is a valuable employee. Wherefore, everyone who reads comprehensively is a valuable employee. (G,A,R,V)

2. No one with a strong minor in marketing is going to fail in sales. Quite a few students majoring in the humanities take a strong minor in marketing. Further, anyone majoring in the humanities has a good grasp of communication skills. So, many students with a good grasp of communication skills aren't going to fail in sales. (M,S,H,C)

3. Only those persons concerned with long term systems approaches to market conditions are top managers. Not a single business graduate will fail in the world of finance. Unfortunately, however, there're business graduates not concerned with long term systems approaches to market conditions. It follows that some who fail in the world of finance won't be successful top managers. (A,M,B,F)

4. Any products dangerous to a person's well-being are non-conducive to a person's good health. This conclusion is supported by the following considerations. Products conducive to a person's good health are never forbidden by the *FDA*. Not even one product to be avoided is non-forbidden by the *FDA*. Every product dangerous to a person's well-being is to be avoided. (D,C,F,A)

5. Not one tobacco product is healthy for humans. There are even tobacco products causally related to lung cancer. On the other hand, products conducive to a clean air environment are healthy for humans. Accordingly, products exist causally related to lung cancer that aren't conducive to a clean air environment. (T,H,C,A)

6. There're drugs sold on the streets that are cocaine products. Now, every non-potentially fatal substance is a non-cocaine product. Further, every designer drug is sold on the street. So, safely enough, many deisgner drugs aren't potentially fatal substances. (S,C,P,D)

7. Every ornamented musical composition is non-simple in musical design. Simple fugues exist, however. On the other hand, baroque compositions are never non-ornamented. It therefore follows that there are fugues that aren't baroque compositions. (O,S,F,B)

8. Simplistic compositions are never complex in structure. Not a single elegant baroque composition of J. S. Bach is non-complex in structure. Every non-ingenious work of Bach is a non-elegant baroque composition. Each ingenious work of Bach is an example of baroque music. Thus, each example of baroque music is a non-simplistic composition. (S,C,E,I,M)

9. Mikhail Gorbachev is a liberal politician. Every non-liberal politician is non-accepted by Gorbachev. Further, Gorbachev takes a non-traditional approach to internal affairs in the USSR. There're traditional approaches to internal affairs in the USSR that aren't likely to survive under Gorbachev. So, there're non-accepted politicians who aren't likely to survive under Gorbachev. (G,L,A,T,S)

10. Social liberals are never non-political activists. Only persons engaged in political reforms are political activists. Now, it's the case that a few social liberals are financial moderates. Financial moderates are careful with the tax dollar. Anyone who is non-interested in lowering the national deficit is non-careful with the tax dollar. Consequently, anyone interested in lowering the national deficit is engaged in political reforms. (L,A,E,M,C,I)

**Group C:**

List several claims, asserted in categorical statements, that you hold true. Following the syllogistic rules of validity and Principle of Charity, cite evidence for each of these claims. In each case your results must be either a *sound* argument (not merely a valid argument) or the abandonment of your original claim. You might have to supply reasons for someone to accept the evidence you introduce as premises justifying your original claims.

## 5.   REVIEW OF NEW TERMS

**Categorical syllogism:** An argument viewed deductively having a sequence of three categorical statements such that only three terms appear in these statements with each term appearing in only two statements.

**Distributed term:** A term that, because of the form of the categorical statement in which it appears, refers to every member of the class it denotes.

**Enthymeme:** A syllogism with an unstated premise or conclusion.

**Equivocation, fallacy of:** Fallacy of four terms.

**Exclusive premises, fallacy of:** A categorical syllogism with two negative premises.

**Existential import, fallacy of:** Under a Boolean interpretation of categorical statements, a categorical syllogism with all universal premises and a particular conclusion.

**Figure of a categorical syllogism:** That property of a syllogism determined by the arrangement of its three terms.

**Form of a categorical syllogism:** Determined by the combination of the mood and figure of a categorical syllogism.

**Four terms, fallacy of:** An argument posing as a syllogism but which has four, instead of three, terms; fallacy of equivocation.

**Illicit major, fallacy of the:** A categorical syllogism in which the predicate term is distributed in the conclusion but not in the major premise.

**Illicit minor, fallacy of the:** A categorical syllogism in which the subject term is distributed in the conclusion but not in the minor premise.

**Inferring a positive conclusion from a negative premise, fallacy of:** A categorical syllogism in which a positive conclusion is drawn from premises of which at least one is negative.

**Inferring a negative conclusion from positive premises, fallacy of:** A categorical syllogism in which a negative conclusion is drawn from all positive premises.

**Major premise:** That premise of a categorical syllogism in which the major term is mentioned.

**Major term:** The predicate term of the conclusion of a categorical syllogism; any use of that term in the syllogism.

**Middle term:** The term found in both premises but not in the conclusion of a categorical syllogism.

**Minor premise:** That premise of a categorical syllogism in which the minor term is mentioned.

**Minor term:** The subject term of the conclusion of a categorical syllogism; any use of that term in the syllogism.

**Mood:** That property of a categorical syllogism determined by the qualities of its categorical statements.

**Sorites:** A series of enthymemic syllogisms.

**Standard form categorical syllogism:** A categorical syllogism in which (1) all the statements are in standard form, (2) the major premise is mentioned first, (3) the minor premise is mentioned second, and (4) the conclusion is mentioned last.

**Undistributed middle, fallacy of:** A categorical syllogism in which the middle term is not distributed at least once.

**Venn diagram:** A diagram of circles, each area representing a distinct class, used to picture all possible relations holding between those classes; used to determine the validity or invalidity of categorical syllogisms.

# 10

# PREDICATE LOGIC: BEGINNINGS

Truth-functional and categorical logic are powerful tools for analyzing arguments viewed deductively. Both are limited, however. Many arguments fall outside their scope of application because of the types of statements used in these arguments. For instance, each of the following arguments is deductively valid, yet there is no truth-functional means of establishing this validity:

(1)   All entrepreneurs are risk-takers. Marlene is an entrepreneur. So, Marlene is a risk-taker.

Either some people are vicious or there isn't a person who isn't kind. That all persons are kind isn't true. Hence, some people are vicious.

Certain people are appreciated by everyone. Thus, some people appreciate themselves.

Lies are falsehoods. Consequently, whoever tells a lie tells a falsehood.

While the first of these examples can be shown valid by methods developed in categorical logic, the others cannot. This chapter introduces a new area of logic to analyze statements and arguments such as the first example in (1), as well as the others. This realm of logic is *predicate logic*:*

**Predicate logic is that part of deductive logic dealing with the interior structure of simple statements as well as the structure of compound statements.**

---

*Predicate logic, also known as *quantification logic*, is becoming increasingly important in programming languages being developed in work with Artificial Intelligence and Expert Systems.

Chapters 8 and 9 also deal with the interior structures of simple statements. Indeed, many of the topics developed in those chapters are taken up into Chapters 10 and 11.* But predicate logic goes far beyond the boundaries of truth-functional and categorical logic in ways that will be pointed out as this and further chapters develop.

Predicate logic, then, is a more powerful tool than either truth-functional or categorical logic. This is not to suggest, however, that it is a more useful tool in some situations. A person does not need a scalpel to cut butter. A butter knife will do nicely. Yet, in some cases, scalpels *are* needed. A wise person will have many and various tools at her disposal and will also know the appropriate use of each one. For example, the validity of the argument

> **(2)**  All entrepreneurs are risk-takers. Marlene is an entrepreneur.
> So, Marlene is a risk-taker.

might be established using techniques developed in categorical logic rather than using methods introduced in coming chapters. Yet,

> **(3)**  Lies are falsehoods. Consequently, whoever tells a lie tells a falsehood.

cannot be proven valid using categorical logic. However, the logical machinery necessary to establish the validity of (3) will also prove the validity of (2).

## 1.  INDIVIDUALS, PROPERTIES, AND SINGULAR STATEMENTS

In truth-functional logic, no matter how far a statement is broken down into its component parts, those parts are always statements. 'Marlene is an entrepreneur' is an example of a basic unit of analysis in truth-functional logic. No uses of 'not p', 'p and q', 'if p, then q', 'either p, or q', etc., indicate that it is a compound statement analyzable into further statements. 'Marlene is an entrepreneur' is a simple statement symbolized by using a single capital letter, such as 'M'. Yet 'Marlene is an entrepreneur' can be further analyzed from another viewpoint. The statement asserts that a specific individual, Marlene, has the property of being an entrepreneur. It is common to claim that some particular thing does or does not have some property or another. Statements used to make such assertions are ***singular statements***:

> **A statement used to assert that at least one specific individual (thing) has, or has not, a certain property or properties.**[†]

---

* A good introduction to Chapter 10 is Sections 1 and 2 of Chapter 8.

[†] What is to count as an individual in a given context of language may itself have other particular individuals as its components. The city of Barcelona is itself composed of particular people, buildings, automobiles, plants, and so on. And each of these is further made up of individual parts. But note also that the individual George Bush has various parts such as arms, legs, lungs, and cells that make up his body. One must always look to the context in which a statement is asserted to ascertain what is to count, in that context, as an individual. Moreover, a distinction may be drawn between *concrete individuals* and *abstract individuals*. Roughly speaking, concrete individuals are those of which it is meaningful to say that spatial and/or temporal properties do, or do not, hold. Abstract individuals are those of which it is not meaningful to say that spatial and/or temporal properties do, or do not, hold. Nor is it the case that spatial and/or temporal properties have to be of a certain type, such as Newtonian.

Notice that in this book 'individual' is used to include not only persons, but other things as well.

A simple statement has an interior structure that can be analyzed and symbolized. Categorical logic provides one way of doing this. For example, in Section 2 of Chapter 8 assertions about particular individuals, dates, and places are translated into categorical statements. Given the techniques discussed there, 'Marlene is an entrepreneur' can be restated as 'All things identical to Marlene are things that are entrepreneurs'. Predicate logic develops another method of analyzing and symbolizing the interior structure of simple statements. If one were only going to face arguments made up solely of truth-functional or categorical statements, one would not need to venture into predicate logic. But the everyday world poses arguments of a much more complex nature, and a person needs the additional weaponry of predicate logic to protect himself against invalid arguments and the harm they can bring when acted upon.

The notation of predicate logic is based on a distinction between an *individual,* such as Marlene, and a *property,* such as being an entrepreneur.* Lower-case letters 'a' through 'v' are used as names of individuals. These letters used as names are ***individual constants***. A convention is adopted in selecting individual constants. When possible, the individual constant corresponds to the first letter of the name of the individual denoted. Properties affirmed or denied to hold of an individual are symbolized by capital letters 'A' through 'Z'. Capital letters used in this way are known as ***predicate letters***. As a convention, predicate letters are selected, when possible, to correspond to the first letter of the word, or key word in a phrase, used to mention a property.

With an individual constant and predicate letter, 'Marlene is an entrepreneur' can be rewritten as

**(1)**   m is an E.

The expression 'is an E' is a *predicate*. A convention is adopted to rewrite expressions such as 'is an E' in (1). In expressions using both individual constants and predicate letters, write the predicate letter followed by the individual constant. (1) is now displayed as

**(2)**   Em

(2) is read, 'E is a property of m', 'E holds of m', or 'm is an E'.

Several properties can be affirmed of the same individual. Someone might say

**(3)**   Feathernut is a knowledgeable teacher but not interesting.

This statement cannot be symbolized in categorical logic. It is an example of why another approach is needed to analyze many statements and arguments. (3) is an

---

*In this book, the distinction between individuals and properties is considered a logical one. No position is taken concerning, for instance, the "real existance" of individuals independent of their properties, or properties independent of some individual.

assertion about the specific individual, Feathernut. Several properties are said to hold of Feathernut. He is knowledgeable and a teacher. However, one property, being interesting, does not hold of Feathernut. (3) can be symbolized as

**(4)**   (Kf · Tf) · ~ If

In truth-functional logic, the single lower-case letters 'p', 'q', 'r', and 's' are used as statement variables in picturing statement forms. These letters continue to be used in this way although now when written to the immediate right of a predicate letter they can be understood as individual constants. In any event, a predicate letter followed by one or more individual constants represents a singular statement that can replace a statement variable in any of the statement forms introduced in Chapter 2. So, any truth-functional statement form displayed with the help of statement variables can be used in symbolizing singular statements, as seen in (4). Suppose it is claimed

**(5)**   Either Barcelona is a large, industrial metropolis, or it isn't wealthy.

The dot, wedge, and tilde are used in symbolizing (5):

**(6)**   [(Lb · Ib) · Mb] ∨ ~ Wb

Someone might suggest

**(7)**   Jane isn't being a responsible politician unless she listens.

Using the horseshoe to capture 'unless p not q', (9) can be put into predicate logic notation as

**(8)**   (Rj · Pj) ⊃ Lj

Or one of Mario's friends might comment

**(9)**   If Mario is pleasant, then he has a good time just in case he doesn't drink too much.

(9) can be symbolized in this way:

**(10)**   Pm ⊃ (Gm ≡ ~ Dm)

A singular statement can mention more than one individual. After interviewing several candidates for one job opening, a personnel manager might advise this:

**(11)**   Either Alice, a worker and capable student, is to be hired, or Bill, who is average but charming, is.

(11) can be symbolized in predicate logic notation as

**(12)**   {[Wa · (Ca · Sa)] · (Ab · Cb)} · (Ha Δ Hb)

Notice that (11) does not explicitly state that Bill, like Alice, is a student. Hence, 'Sb' is not found in (12). If, however, Bill is a student, this information is easily included:

**(13)**   {[Wa · (Ca · Sa)] · [(Ab · Cb) · Sb]} · (Ha △ Hb)

In symbolizing singular statements in predicate logic, use all of the techniques and strategies developed for symbolizing truth-functional statements. Of course, instead of using single capital letters in symbolizing statements, use predicate notation.

Any argument made up exclusively of singular statements can be analyzed solely by truth-functional methods. For example, someone might present this argument:

**(14)**   If Juan is being funny, then Teresa is happy just in case Juan doesn't drink too much. Neither is Juan drinking too much nor is he not being funny. So, Teresa is happy.

(14) can be symbolized in predicate logic and a proof of its validity constructed:

**(15)**                                            / ∴ Ht

1) Fj ⊃ (Ht ≡ ~ Dj)      Pr
2) ~ (Dj ∨ ~ Fj)         Pr
3) ~ Dj · ~ ~ Fj         2, DeM
4) ~ ~ Fj · ~ Dj         3, Com
5) ~ ~ Fj                4, Simp
6) Fj                    5, DN
7) Ht ≡ ~ Dj             1, 6, MP
8) (Ht ⊃ ~ Dj) · (~ Dj ⊃ Ht)   7, Equiv
9) (~ Dj ⊃ Ht) · (Ht ⊃ ~ Dj)   8, Com
10) ~ Dj ⊃ Ht            9, Simp
11) ~ Dj                 3, Simp
12) / ∴ Ht               10, 11, MP

If nothing more were involved than singular statements in predicate logic, it would not be needed. But much more is involved.

---

## EXERCISES

Using the suggested predicate logic notation, symbolize each of the following.

1. Even though W. H. Auden is a poet, he isn't dull. (D,P;a)
2. Steve Pelluer either passes or runs for the Dallas Cowboys. (P,R;p)
3. Tammy was the winner despite the fact that Lewis was favored. (W,F;t,l)
4. Amadeus Mozart wasn't successful but for his musical brilliance. (S,B;m)
5. In Britain either Margaret Thatcher is loved or she is despised, but not both. (L,D;t)
6. If George Bush is a strong politician, Mikhail Gorbachev is a clever one. (S,P,C;b,g)
7. The world-famous athlete, Stefan Edberg, is a tennis player. (W,A,T;e)
8. Bishop David E. Jenkins of Durham is considered a contemporary theologian or a heretic. (C,T,H;j)

9. The famous singer, Prince, appears frequently on television. (F,S,A;p)

10. While Yasser Arafat becoming peaceful is a necessary condition for the *PLO* to recognize the rights of Israel, Arafat must also be a diplomat in dealing with the Western powers. (P,R,D;a,p)

11. Paul Taylor is the director of a major ballet troupe if and only if he is also a brilliant choreographer. (D,B,C;t)

12. Aristotle, who studied philosophy with Plato, changed the course of history but wasn't highly respected in ancient Athens. (S,C,R;a)

13. T. S. Eliot is neither a dramatist nor poet unless he is known in literary circles. (D,P,K;e)

14. Dorothy Gordy, a specialist in information management and a known international consultant, matriculated at the Georgia Institute of Technology. (S,K,M;g)

15. Either Nick Faldo is a golfer who wasn't beatable, or he wasn't the winner of the 1990 Masters Tournament, but not both. (G,B,W;l)

16. The metal band, *Hot Heads*, doesn't play unless given a great deal of money. (M,B,P,G;h)

17. Sam Nunn is either a diplomat who is astute, or a crass politician, but certainly not both. (D,A,C,P;n)

18. Turnipseed stays and works if, and only if, either Mustardgreen puts forth an effort or at least defrays expenses. (S,W,P,D;t,m)

19. Claes Oldenburg, born in Stockholm but educated at Yale, is a humorous artist. (B,E,H,A;o)

20. If Boris Becker is a world-famous tennis player, then he competes at Wimbeldon only if he is in fit form. (W,T,C,F;c)

21. Either the philosopher John Locke isn't famous or he is both widely read and studied. (F,P,R,S;l)

22. The boxer, Evander Holyfield, doesn't win except for the fact that he is a savage fighter. (B,W,S,F;t)

23. George Bush will run and garnish the conservative vote of both parties provided Michael Dukakis is the Democratic choice. (R,G,D,C;b,d)

24. Albert Einstein, a physicist, either won the Copenhagen debates, or else Werner Heisenberg beat Einstein only if Heisenberg was convincing in his arguments—but, of course, not both. (P,W,B,C;e,h)

25. Assuming that Merlyn Evans is neither well-known nor understood, he is a painter not appreciated by the general public. (W,U,P,A;e)

26. Edward Hopper was either an American Realist painter or a French Impressionist, but hardly both. (A,R,P,F,I;h)

27. Pierre Auguste Renoir, a French Impressionist painter, wasn't an admirer of Delacroix unless he was also a user of oriental motifs. (F,I,P,A,U;r)

28. Juan Carlos is either a Bourbon monarch much admired by his people, or a Hanoverian impostor who will be overturned, but not both. (B,M,A,H,I,O;c)

29. Wilmerding is neither a prosecutor nor a defendant in the case provided that Hinkeldink is either a foreign spy or a government agent. (P,D,F,S,G,A;w,h)

30. The famous American outlaw, Jesse James, was killed only if the American gunman, Robert Ford, was a sharpshooter. (F,A,O,K,G,S;j,f)

## 2.   GENERAL STATEMENTS—I

The study of general statements is an essential part of predicate logic. Here are examples of general statements:

> **(1)**   All students are energetic.
>     No professor is cranky.
>     Some books are exciting.
>     Some lectures were not worthless.
>     Something is noisy.
>     Everything is in motion or at rest, but not both.
>     No one likes a cheater.

A *general statement* is

> **a statement used to assert that at least one unspecified individual has, or has not, a certain property or properties.**

This section emphasizes statements like the first four in (1).* Following sections will discuss statements like the last three examples.

General statements can be classified as either universal or particular. That a general statement is either universal or particular comprises the *quantity* of that statement. For instance, the first two examples in (1), as well as the last two, are *universal statements*:

> **A statement used to assert that all unspecified individuals have, or have not, a certain property or properties.**

The other examples in (1) are *particular statements*:

> **A statement used to assert that at least one unspecified individual has, or has not, a certain property or properties.**

'Sam Nunn is a Senator' makes a claim about the specified individual, Sam Nunn. To say 'Some professor is understanding' also makes a claim about at least one individual. However, *which* professor has the property of being understanding is unspecified. Universal and particular statements can also be affirmative or negative. That a general statement is affirmative or negative comprises the *quality* of that statement. If a general statement affirms that some property, or properties, holds of an unspecified individual, it is affirmative. If it denies that some property, or properties, holds of an unspecified individual, it is negative.

How are universal and particular statements, affirmative or negative, symbolized

---

*These statements are examples of the four types of categorical statements studied in categorical logic; namely,

> A:  All S are P.
> E:  No S are P.
> I:  Some S are P.
> O:  Some S are not P.

in predicate logic? Consider the first example in (1). From the viewpoint of contemporary logic, 'All students are energetic' is interpreted as asserting

(2)   Given any thing in the universe, *IF* it is a student, *THEN* it is energetic.

This is the *Boolean*, or *hypothetical, interpretation* of universal statements.* The position of contemporary logic is that, in asserting a universal statement, no commitment is made concerning the existence of individuals mentioned in that statement. If someone says 'All unicorns are magnificent animals', the speaker is not committing herself to the existence of unicorns. The assertion is that *IF* there are any unicorns, *THEN* they are magnificent animals.

Moving toward a symbolization of (2), the concept *individual variable* is introduced:

> **An individual variable is a lower-case letter, 'w' through 'z', marking a space that can be filled in by the name of a specific individual.**

Individual variables are analogous to pronouns. Used properly, they both must have a referent, or be replaced by the name of an individual. Neither 'It is blue' nor 'Sydney likes him' asserts anything true or false. Neither a referent nor a context of any sort suggests the name of a particular individual to replace 'it' or 'him'. Hence, these pronouns act only as indicators of a space to be filled. Such expressions can be turned into statements—some true, some false—when the pronouns have a referent or are replaced by the name of an individual. For instance, 'The Indian Ocean is blue' and 'Sydney likes Leslie' are both statements.

Use the individual variable, 'x', to rewrite (2) as

(3)   Given anything in the universe, if x is a student, then x is energetic.

The expression 'Given anything in the universe . . . ' indicates that (3) is a universal statement. This phrase also includes the subject of the statement, 'anything'. In predicate logic, a *universal quantifier* replaces 'Given anything in the universe . . . '. A monadic operator, it is known as a *quantifier* because it addresses the question 'How many?'[†] It is the *universal* quantifier because it is used to symbolize statements referring to all individuals having a certain property or properties. The universal quantifier is formed by placing an individual variable in parentheses. '(w)', '(x)', '(y)', and '(z)' are universal quantifiers. By convention, when only one individual variable is used in symbolizing a statement, 'x' is selected. So, in (3), the individual

---

*See Chapter 8, Section 3 for a discussion of the traditional and Boolean interpretations of universal statements.

[†]Recall this distinction made in Chapter 2, Section 2:

> **Operators that designate rules governing only one expression are *monadic operators*.**
> **Operators that signify rules connecting two expressions are *dyadic operators*.**

To this point in the study of logic, only the tilde is a monadic operator. Quantifiers are now included.

variable, 'x', is used to form the universal quantifier and to replace every occurrence of 'it' referring back to the subject embedded in that quantifier:

$$\text{(4)} \quad \text{(x) if x is a student, then x is energetic.}$$

Continue the symbolization of (3) by introducing predicate letters:

$$\text{(5)} \quad \text{(x) if x is an S, then x is an E.}$$

Rewriting 'x is an S' and 'x is an E' produces

$$\text{(6)} \quad \text{(x) if Sx, then Ex.}$$

The horseshoe is now introduced to move (6) further into logical notation:

$$\text{(7)} \quad \text{(x) Sx} \supset \text{Ex}$$

(7) is not yet the final symbolization of 'All students are energetic'. That final symbolization is

$$\text{(8)} \quad \text{(x)(Sx} \supset \text{Ex)}$$

Like the pronouns it replaces, each 'x' following a predicate letter must refer back to the subject embedded in a quantifier. In (7), the 'x' of 'Ex' does not refer back to the quantifier, but is analogous to a dangling pronoun. Such variables do not fall under the scope of any quantifier. Any individual variable that does not refer to some quantifier is a *free individual variable*. Any individual variable that does refer back to some quantifier is **bound**, or *captured*, by the quantifier under whose scope it falls. Expressions containing free variables, such as 'Sx', 'Ex' and 'Sx $\supset$ Ex', are examples of *statement functions*:*

> **A statement function is an expression containing a predicate letter followed by one or more free individual variables, or such expressions coupled to truth-functional operators.**

In a symbolized statement, as contrasted with a statement function, there can be no free individual variable. Indeed, no type of variable can occur in a statement. Statements are either true or false. But, containing at least one free variable, no statement function can be either true or false. Suppose someone said, 'It swims', symbolized as 'Sx'. It would make no sense to ask whether this is a true or false statement as long as 'it' had no referent or was not replaced by the name of a specific individual.

Visually, the only difference between '(x) Sx $\supset$ Ex' and '(x)(Sx $\supset$ Ex)' is the parentheses. Punctuation marks are introduced in Chapter 2, Section 6, to display the scope of logical operators. The *scope* of an operator is understood as that part of

---

*In discussions of the programming languages *LISP* ("*LIS*t Processing") and *PROLOG* ("*PRO*gramming in *LOG*ic") predicates letters, sometimes called *functors*, are used in expressing functions. The lower-case letters following functors are *arguments*. Functors followed by arguments are said to represent facts, and information is built up out of facts by the use of predicate logic. *LISP* and *PROLOG* are two powerful programming languages of Artificial Intelligence and Expert Systems work.

a statement, or statement function, governed by the rule indicated by the logical operator in question—which, in the case of '(x)(Sx ⊃ Ex)', is the universal quantifier. Punctuation conventions governing the scope of quantifiers are parallel to those governing the tilde:

> **A quantifier operates over the smallest statement function following it. This statement function is indicated by parentheses, brackets, and/or braces. By convention, however, when the statement function following a quantifier employs no dyadic operators, punctuation marks are omitted.**

In moving from (6) to (7), a horseshoe is introduced in which the statement functions 'Sx' and 'Ex' are substituted at the statement variables in 'p ⊃ q'. Accordingly, the range of the statement variables 'p', 'q', 'r', and 's' introduced in truth-functional logic is broadened to include not only statements but also statement functions. Broadening the range of statement variables introduces *all* the rules and strategies of truth-functional logic into predicate logic.

In symbolizing statements, attention must always be paid to the plausible meaning of what is being asserted. There are no mechanical rules guaranteeing a correct symbolization in moving from everyday language into logical symbols. There is, nevertheless, a step-by-step procedure that often proves helpful. This procedure is seen at work in (1) through (8) above. Such help is possible, however, only in the context of an overall sensitivity to the uses of vocabulary and grammar. An understanding and mastery of everyday language is of utmost importance in symbolizing. On the other hand, symbolization also helps one to grasp better the structures and uses of everyday language.

'All students are energetic' can be expressed in various ways. Here are some examples:

**(9)**

    **a)** A student is energetic.

    **b)** Any student is energetic.

    **c)** Every student is energetic.

    **d)** Students are energetic.

    **e)** None but the energetic are students.*

    **f)** Only those who are energetic are students.

Each of these examples is symbolized as '(x)(Sx ⊃ Ex)'.

The words 'any' and 'every' are often used to suggest the notion of *all* and, thereby, a universal quantifier. However, do not automatically use a universal quantifier to capture the meaning of these words. For instance, compare 'Jeff won't win every contest' and 'Jeff won't win any contest'. The first example suggests that of the contests Jeff enters, there is at least one he will not win. The second example suggests that of the contests Jeff enters, he will not win a single one.

---

*Compare the statement 'All fathers are males'. This can be expressed as 'None but males are fathers' or 'Only males are fathers'.

Take care in using 'a', 'an', and 'the'. They can indicate either universal or particular statements. 'The gazelle is a mammal' or 'A gazelle is a mammal' can be used to assert the same statement as 'All gazelles are mammals'. To say 'A thief was caught' or 'The thief was caught' is not understood as 'All thieves were caught'.* Other examples are even more open to various interpretations. What is to be understood by 'The student is pressed for more knowledge'? Only a context surrounding the claim can supply the conditions needed to answer this question. Contexts in which claims are used are always essential to consider in coming to understand what a claim asserts.

Any statement must be understood within a ***universe of discourse***, or *domain*, in which it is used, where

> **the universe of discourse is a finite or infinite collection of individuals to which, either implicitly or explicitly, the statement(s) used in a particular context refers.**

For instance, in its broadest sense, 'given anything in the universe . . . ' denotes everything that is logically possible. Roughly, something can be thought of as logically possible if it does not correspond to a contradiction of some sort. Or the universe of discourse might be more limited. For example, in the assertion 'Everyone who studies hard in this course will pass', the universe of discourse is *people*. In many situations, the universe of discourse is often not made explicit. Much of the time speakers and hearers find no need to do this. In the statement 'Anyone found using cocaine will be arrested' it is implicit that the statement is about *persons* because of the pronoun 'anyone'. However, a demand for clarity often requires, when symbolizing in predicate logic, that the universe of discourse is be made explicate in the symbolization.

The second example in (1) is 'No professor is cranky'. This asserts that any individual having the property of being a professor fails to have the property of being cranky. This can be said in various ways. Here are several examples:

**(10)**

    **a)** A professor is never cranky.

    **b)** None of the professors are cranky.

    **c)** Not even one professor is cranky.

    **d)** Not a single professor is cranky.

    **e)** Professors are not cranky.

These examples can each be symbolized as

**(11)**   $(x)(Px \supset \sim Cx)$

The next two assertions in (1)—namely, 'Some books are exciting' and 'Some lectures were not worthless'—are examples of *particular statements*. Each uses the

---

* 'A thief was caught' is normally understood as a particular statement asserting 'Some thief or another was caught'. 'The thief was caught' is normally understood as a singular statement in which 'the thief' acts as a name of a specific individual.

word 'some'. 'Some' is vague in everyday usage. How many things does it take to constitute *some* things? To avoid vagueness, in predicate logic, 'some' is understood as 'there is *at least one thing* in the universe such that . . . '. This use of 'some' provides a minimal answer to the question 'How many?'. 'Some' can be expressed in different ways. Any of the following can be used, given appropriate surroundings, to make the same assertion as 'Some books are exciting':

**(12)**

    **a)** A few books are exciting.

    **b)** A suitable number of books are exciting.

    **c)** Certain books are exciting.

    **d)** Some things that are books are also exciting.

    **e)** There exist books that are exciting.

    **f)** There is an exciting book.

    **g)** There are books that are exciting.

Each of these examples can be understood as asserting

**(13)** There is at least one thing in the universe such that it is a book and it is exciting.

The expression 'There is at least one thing in the universe such that . . . ' signifies the use of the ***existential quantifier***. Unlike the universal quantifier, the existential quantifier indicates the claim that something does exist. This monadic operator is formed by writing '∃' followed by an individual variable, both of which are surrounded by parentheses. Each of these is an existential quantifier: '(∃w)', '(∃x)', '(∃y)' and '(∃z)'. Using an existential quantifier and the individual variable, 'x', (13) can be rendered as

**(14)** (∃x) x is a book and x is exciting.

Introducing predicate letters and writing them before the individual variable yields

**(15)** (∃x) Bx and Ex

The 'and' is replaced by the dot and the scope of the quantifier indicated by appropriate punctuation marks to produce

**(16)** (∃x) (Bx · Ex)

Each example in (12) can be symbolized by (16).

Beginners frequently find it tempting to symbolize statements such as 'Some books are exciting' in the same way they would symbolize 'All students are energetic'; that is, as '(∃x) (Bx ⊃ Ex)'. This is incorrect. By material implication, '(∃x) (Bx ⊃ Ex)' is equivalent to '(∃x) (~ Bx ∨ Ex)' which says 'There is at least one thing in the universe such that either it is not a book or it is exciting'. This assertion is uninteresting in that almost anything named makes the statement true. For example, a particular desk is not a book. Thus, the statement is true of that desk.

The fourth assertion in (1), 'Some lectures were not worthless', can be expressed in various ways. 'A few lectures were not worthless' is one. No matter how the statement is expressed, the claim made is that at least one thing having the property of being a lecture fails to have the property of being worthless. All such assertions say

**(17)**   There is at least one thing in the universe such that it is a lecture and it is not worthless.

(17) goes into predicate logical notation as

**(18)**   $(\exists x)(Lx \cdot \sim Wx)$

Universal and existential quantifiers are used in expressing general statements. If, however, the universe of discourse of a general statement is finite and every thing in that universe can be given a unique name, then quantifiers are not necessary. For example, the universal quantifier can be *expanded* into a series of conjuncts. Suppose someone said, 'Every swan is white'. Also imagine that there are exactly four individuals in the entire universe named Alice, Bruce, Connie and Dwight. Then, 'Every swan is white' can be expressed as 'If Alice is a swan, then Alice is white; AND if Bruce is a swan, then Bruce is white; AND if Connie is a swan, then Connie is white; AND if Dwight is a swan, then Dwight is white'. Now, instead of symbolizing 'Every swan is white' as '$(x)(Sx \supset Wx)$', it can be symbolized in this way:

**(19)**   $(Sa \supset Wa) \cdot (Sb \supset Wb) \cdot (Sc \supset Wc) \cdot (Sd \supset Wd)*$

Suppose someone claimed, 'Some members of the seminar are juniors'? Again, assume a finite universe of exactly four individuals such that each individual can be given a unique name. Existentially quantified statements, under these conditions, can be expanded into a series of disjuncts. 'Some members of the seminar are juniors' can be asserted as 'Alice is a member of the seminar and Alice is a junior, *OR* Bruce is a member of the seminar and Bruce is a junior, *OR* Connie is a member of the seminar and Connie is a junior, *OR* Dwight is a member of the seminar and Dwight is a junior':

**(20)**   $(Ma \cdot Ta) \vee (Mb \cdot Tb) \vee (Mc \cdot Tc) \vee (Md \cdot Td)†$

Both quantifiers are retained and predicate logic developed because there are assertions that are not limited to a finite universe of discourse, or if they are, the

---

*This is not quite correct. In expanding a universal quantified statement into a series of conjuncts, a final statement seems to be needed to close the expansion by declaring 'And this is every member of the universe'. There are difficulties in formulating such a statement, however. Is it, in some sense, itself a member of that series it declares to be completed? If so, it seems that yet another statement is needed to say that *that* series is completed, and so on *ad infinitum*. On the other hand, if this "closing statement" is not a part of that series, then it is not a descriptive statement about particular things in that universe under consideration and, consequently, cannot say all members of that universe have been listed. Issues such as these stand at the intersection of logic and philosophy of language.

†Once more, a final statement appears to be needed to declare that this is the end of the series. Once again, serious problems are encountered in attempting to satisfy this need.

members of that universe cannot be uniquely named. 'Any prime number is divisible only by *1* or itself without remainder' is an assertion about an infinite universe of individual numbers. 'Every star that still burns is a sun' is, presumably, about a finite number of objects. Even so, *stars* denotes an immense universe of discourse making it a practical impossibility to give each member a unique name.

Four types of general statements have been examined in the above discussion concerning symbolization into predicate logic notation. These types can be pictured by the following schemata in which '$\alpha$' represents any individual variable, and '$\Phi$' and '$\Psi$' any predicate letters:

$$(21) \quad (\alpha)(\Phi\alpha \supset \Psi\alpha)$$
$$(\alpha)(\Phi\alpha \supset \sim \Psi\alpha)$$
$$(\exists\alpha)(\Phi\alpha \cdot \Psi\alpha)$$
$$(\exists\alpha)(\Phi\alpha \cdot \sim \Psi\alpha)$$

If any general statement can be reworded to display one of these forms, its symbolization will be made easier by referring to its corresponding schema in (21).

Consider this example:

**(22)** Unhappy people are lonely and not self-accepting.

(22) is a universal claim. It asserts something about all unhappy people; namely, that they are lonely and not self-accepting:

**(23)** All unhappy people are lonely and not self-accepting.

This statement matches the first pattern in (21). Therefore, the final symbolization of (22) can be expected to look something like

$$(24) \quad (\alpha)(\Phi\alpha \supset \Psi\alpha)$$

The symbolization is approached by first writing

**(25)** Given anything in the universe, if it is a person and it is not happy, then it is lonely and not self-accepting.

Continue by introducing the universal quantifier and replacing each occurrence of 'it' with an individual variable:

**(26)** (x) if x is a person and x is not happy, then x is lonely and x is not self-accepting.

Standard predicate notation can now be introduced to create

**(27)** (x) if Px and not Hx, then Lx and not Sx.

Use the dot to replace 'and' and the tilde to replace 'not':

**(28)** (x) if Px $\cdot \sim$ Hx, then Lx $\cdot \sim$ Sx.

Parentheses indicate the scope of both dots:

**(29)** (x) if (Px $\cdot \sim$ Hx), then (Lx $\cdot \sim$ Sx).

Introduce the horseshoe to replace 'if p, then q' and brackets to show the scope of the quantifier:

(30)   $(x)[(Px \cdot \sim Hx) \supset (Lx \cdot \sim Sx)]$

It is incorrect to symbolize (22) as

(31)   $(x)(Px \cdot \sim Hx) \supset (Lx \cdot \sim Sx)$

Because of the free variables occurring in 'Lx · ~ Sx', (31) is not a statement, but a statement function. This statement function is transformed into a statement when the free individual variables in 'Fx · ~ Sx' are bound to the quantifier by appropriate punctuation marks as seen in (30).

Follow how the next example is symbolized:

(32)   Anything beautiful or expensive is never unnoticed if wanted.

(32), a universal negative statement, can be reexpressed in this way:

(33)   Nothing that is beautiful or expensive is unnoticed if wanted.

Viewing (33) as displaying '$(\alpha)(\Phi\alpha \supset \sim \Psi\alpha)$', it is rewritten as

(34)   Given anything in the universe, if it is beautiful or it is expensive,
       then it is not not noticed if it is wanted.

Introducing the universal quantifier, predicate letters, and the individual variable 'x' yields

(35)   $(x)$ if Bx or Ex, then not not Nx if Wx.

'Nx' is read as 'x is noticed'. The first 'not' in 'not not Nx' is the denial suggested by 'Nothing' in (33). While 'Nothing' appears at the beginning of (33), this does not indicate that a *statement* is being denied. What is denied is that some property, or properties, hold of an individual. The second 'not' captures the denial suggested by 'un-' in 'unnoticed'. The symbolization of (32) is completed as

(36)   $(x)[(Bx \vee Ex) \supset (Wx \supset \sim \sim Nx)]$

Following is an affirmative particular statement:

(37)   There are clever and expensive machines that if programmed
       properly save time.

(37) can be reexpressed in this way:

(38)   Some things that are clever and expensive machines are
       things that if they are programmed properly save time.

(38) displays the form, '$(\exists\alpha)(\Phi\alpha \cdot \Psi\alpha)$', and is remolded as

(39)   There is at least one thing in the universe such that it is clever and it is
       expensive and it is a machine; and if it is programmed properly then it
       saves time.

Using predicate logic notation, (39) is rewritten as

**(40)**   (∃x)Cx and Ex, and Mx; and if Px then Sx.

Final operators and punctuation marks produce

**(41)**   (∃x){[(Cx · Ex) · Mx] · (Px ⊃ Sx)}

What of particular statements denying that some property, or properties, hold of an unspecified individual? Here is an example:

**(42)**   A sizeable number of painters are not artists who, nevertheless, are craftsmen and decorators only if they have an eye for color balance.

(42) can be expressed to resemble more closely '(∃α)(Φα · ~ Ψα)':

**(43)**   Some painters who are craftsmen and decorators only if they have an eye for color balance are not artists.

(43) is restated as

**(44)**   There is at least one thing in the universe such that it is a painter, and if it is a craftsman and it is a decorator then it has an eye for color balance; and it is not an artist.

Introducing predicate logic notation produces

**(45)**   (∃x)Px, and if Cx and Dx then Bx; and not Ax.

From (45) move to

**(46)**   (∃x)({Px · [(Cx · Dx) ⊃ Bx]} · ~ Ax)

---

## EXERCISES

Using the suggested predicate logic notation, symbolize each of the following.

1. A few mammals lay eggs. (M,L;x)

2. Glucose is not a double sugar. (G,D;x)

3. Many students are not punctual. (S,P;x)

4. None but dreamers are artists. (D,A;x)

5. Some flagellates don't have outer cellulose cell walls. (F,C;x)

6. Only things composed of protoplasm are unicellular. (C,U;x)

7. Some students caught cheating will not be expelled. (S,C,E;x)

8. A sizable number of illegal aliens return each year to their native country. (L,A,R;x)

9. Certain chemical transformations are seen to be endothermic. (C,T,E;x)

10. Brown algae never survive in fresh water. (B,A,S;x)

11. A few professors who are committed to their research show sincere concern for their students. (P,C,S;x)

12. There are always those few fortunate people who will not be discouraged no matter what happens to them. (F,P,D;x)

13. Anything which is vulgar or unseemly can never be found acceptable in a civilized society. (V,S,A;x)

14. A large number of sports car enthusiasts who are very knowledgeable concerning automobile construction still rank the Morgan as superior in classic design. (E,K,R;x)

15. A sizable number of OTC stocks have terrible growth potential, and this is coupled with a low earning ratio. (S,P,R;x)

16. Stocks never fluctuate whenever they remain constant. (S,F,C;x)

17. Certain molecular structures are not predictable by the "octet rule." (M,S,P;x)

18. Nobody is compassionate who both gossips and is intolerant. (P,C,G,T;x)

19. No person who is wise and good will suffer real disgrace. (P,W,G,S;x)

20. Any mammal that is linguistic and rational is human. (M,L,R,H;x)

21. There are many modern painters who are neither craftsmen nor artists. (M,P,C,A;x)

22. An instrument suitable for measuring temperatures close to absolute zero degrees will never be a mercury column thermometer. (I,S,M,T;x)

23. Most mammals that are risible if human are linguistic bipeds. (M,R,H,L,B;x)

24. Nothing that is a reptile or fish while also being cold-blooded and scaly is viviparous. (R,F,C,S,V;x)

25. A tolerant and understanding person is generally happy if not selfish. (T,U,P,H,S;x)

26. Certain chemicals that are acids or bases taste bitter only if they aren't sweet. (C,A,B,T,S;x)

27. Habit-forming drugs are not prescribed and monitored by a physician if not safe to use. (H,D,S,P,M;x)

28. Some things that are chlorine sources if they are ordinary salt produced by evaporation of sea water are neither fluorine nor bromine sources. (C,O,S,P,F,B;x)

29. None of the various chemicals that are either phosphoric or nitric if acid are both slick to the touch while being high on the pH scale. (C,P,N,A,S,H;x)

30. Any acid that corrodes electro-positive metals and releases hydrogen is a proton donor only if it gives up protons easily while also being strong. (A,C,R,D,G,S;x)

---

## 3.   GENERAL STATEMENTS—II

Every statement studied in the previous section displays one of these patterns:

**(1)**   $(\alpha)(\Phi\alpha \supset \Psi\alpha)$
$(\alpha)(\Phi\alpha \supset \sim \Psi\alpha)$
$(\exists\alpha)(\Phi\alpha \cdot \Psi\alpha)$
$(\exists\alpha)(\Phi\alpha \cdot \sim \Psi\alpha)$

However, not every general statement is an instance of a form in (1). The following, for example, are not:

**(2)**   A thing is either red or it isn't.

**(3)**   Some things are either squares or circles, but never both.

Both of these are universal statements yet neither makes a hypothetical claim.

Rather, they move into predicate logic notation in this way:

**(4)**   (x)(Rx ∨ ~ Rx)

**(5)**   (∃x)(Sx △ Cx)

There are more complicated statements not exhibiting any form in (1). Some examples are explored in the following discussion.

In discussing the triple-bar in Chapter 2, different ways of expressing material equivalence are suggested. One of these is the use of *exceptive statements*. 'Clara will do well except when she follows Steve's advice' is symbolized truth-functionally as 'C ≡ ~ S'. Exceptive statements can also be general statements:

**(6)**   Everything is interesting except when it is boring.

Use of the universal quantifier, predicate logic notation, and the triple-bar permits (6) to be symbolized as

**(7)**   (x)(Ix ≡ ~ Bx)

(4), (5), and (7) are simple statements. However, many statements involving quantifiers are compound. Imagine being told

**(8)**   Every poet is sensitive only if any artist is creative.

(8) is reexpressed as

**(9)**   If everything that is a poet is sensitive, then anything that is an artist is creative.

(9) is a compound statement composed of these simple statements:

**(10)**   everything that is a poet is sensitive

**(11)**   anything that is an artist is creative.

(10) is symbolized in predicate logic notation as

**(12)**   (x)(Px ⊃ Sx)

while (11) is symbolized as

**(13)**   (x)(Ax ⊃ Cx)

In (8), the simple statements are joined together by 'only if'. So, the complete symbolization of (8) is

**(14)**   (x)(Px ⊃ Sx) ⊃ (x)(Ax ⊃ Cx)

(14) is an instance of 'p ⊃ q' and is, thus, compound.

In symbolizing (8), it might be tempting to write

**(15)**   (x)[(Px ⊃ Sx) ⊃ (Ax ⊃ Cx)]

(15) cannot be a correct reading of (8). While (8) has two subjects, there is only one in (15). In general statements, subjects are always embedded in a quantifier, each

quantifier representing exactly one subject. There is only one quantifier in (15), and, hence, only one subject in *that* statement. So, (15) cannot be a correct symbolization of (8), which has two subjects.

Another way to see the difference between (14) and (15), and their relation to (8), is to grasp what (15) does assert. Exportation and Commutation used on the statement in (15) yield

$$(16)\quad (x)\{[Ax \cdot (Px \supset Sx)] \supset Cx\}$$

Because (16) is logically equivalent to (15), if (15) is a correct symbolization of (8), then (16) must assert the same thing as (8). Putting (16) into English produces

**(17)**   Any artist who if a poet is sensitive is creative.

(8) and (17) do not assert the same thing. (8) and (14) do.

A different example of a compound general statement is

**(18)**   Some figures are squares and some figures are circles.

Moving toward a symbolization of (18), first write

**(19)**   There is at least one thing in the universe such that it is a figure and it is a square, and there is at least one thing in the universe such that it is a figure and it is a circle.

(19) is an overall conjunction of two particular statements:

$$(20)\quad (\exists x)(Fx \cdot Sx) \cdot (\exists x)(Fx \cdot Cx)$$

(18) cannot be correctly symbolized as

$$(21)\quad (\exists x)[(Fx \cdot Sx) \cdot (Fx \cdot Cx)]$$

(21) asserts, falsely, that there is at least one figure in the universe such that it is *both* a square *and* a circle. As in (8), the number of quantifier words in (18) indicates the number of distinct subjects that must remain distinct when put into logical notation. In more technical terms, caution must always be taken in ascertaining, and properly displaying, the scope of any quantifier.

Another example of a general statement is

**(22)**   Fish and beef are served.

It is reasonable to suppose that it is not being suggested that *all* the fish and beef in the universe are to be served. Rather, (22) appears to be an existential statement asserting

**(23)**   Some fish and beef are served.

Someone might be tempted to symbolize (23) as

$$(24)\quad (\exists x)[(Fx \cdot Bx) \cdot Sx]$$

(24) is incorrect, however. (24) suggests that there is some particular thing that is *both* fish *and* beef, and furthermore it is served. The intended meaning of (22) is

expressed symbolically like this:

$$(25) \quad (\exists x)(Fx \cdot Sx) \cdot (\exists x)(Bx \cdot Sx)$$

Look at an example similar to (22):

**(26)**   Triangles and circles are figures.

Unlike (22), this example is used to make a universal claim:

**(27)**   All triangles and circles are figures.

A rash move to what might appear as a proper symbolization of (26) yields

$$(28) \quad (x)[(Tx \cdot Cx) \supset Fx]$$

(28) cannot be a correct rendering of (27). (28) says that if anything at all is *both* a triangle *and* a circle, then it is a figure. However, nothing is both a triangle and a circle. The intended meaning of (26) is captured by

$$(29) \quad (x)[(Tx \vee Cx) \supset Fx]$$

(26) can also be interpreted correctly as

$$(30) \quad (x)(Tx \supset Fx) \cdot (x)(Cx \supset Fx)$$

In no case is (26) symbolized as (28).

Confusion can occur in using 'a few' and 'few':

**(31)**   A few persons are rich and kind.

**(32)**   Few persons are rich and kind.

(31) is normally understood as

**(33)**   Some persons are rich and kind.

This is expressed as

$$(34) \quad (\exists x)[Px \cdot (Rx \cdot Kx)]$$

The meaning of (32), on the other hand, is captured in a conjunction of two statements:

**(35)**   Some persons are rich and kind *and* some persons are
neither rich nor kind.

This assertion goes into symbols as

$$(36) \quad (\exists x)[Px \cdot (Rx \cdot Kx)] \cdot (\exists x)[Px \cdot \sim (Rx \vee Kx)]$$

Care must be taken not to confuse statements such as

**(37)**   All athletes are energetic people.

with statements like

**(38)**   All but the lazy student will pass.

(38) is not symbolized as a single general statement. It moves into a conjunction of two universal negative statements:

**(39)** No students who are lazy will pass *and* no students who will pass are lazy.

(39) can be symbolized as

**(40)** $(x)[(Sx \cdot Lx) \supset \sim Px] \cdot (x)[(Sx \cdot Px) \supset \sim Lx]$

General statements can be denied. For example, the denial of

**(41)** All drug trafficking will be eliminated.

is the statement

**(42)** It is not the case that all drug trafficking will be eliminated.

(41) can be symbolized as

**(43)** $(x)(Dx \supset Ex)$

(42), the denial of (41), is put into notation in this way:

**(44)** $\sim [(x)(Dx \supset Ex)]$

Two important points must be understood about these examples. First, the denial of 'All drug trafficking is eliminated' is not 'No drug trafficking is eliminated'. The denial of any statement displaying the form, '$(\alpha)(\Phi\alpha \supset \Psi\alpha)$', is not a statement having the form, '$(\alpha)(\Phi\alpha \supset \sim \Psi\alpha)$'. An English equivalent of the denial of (41) is 'Some drug trafficking is not eliminated'. That is, the denial of a statement displaying the form, '$(\alpha)(\Phi\alpha \supset \Psi\alpha)$', is equivalent to a statement of the form, '$(\exists\alpha)(\Phi\alpha \cdot \sim \Psi\alpha)$'. The second point to be emphasized concerns the scope of the tilde. In (44), the scope of the tilde, shown by an overt use of brackets, is '$(x)(Dx \supset Ex)$'. However, no ambiguity concerning the scope of the tilde results if these brackets are omitted:

**(45)** $\sim (x)(Dx \supset Ex)$

Techniques in predicate logic for symbolizing statements not displaying any form in (1) have been augmented to include these truth-functional forms:

$$\sim p$$
$$p \cdot q$$
$$p \vee q$$
$$p \, \Delta \, q$$
$$p \supset q$$
$$p \equiv q$$

Possibilities for symbolization are broadened further by combining singular statements with general ones in an overall *hybrid statement*:

**A statement used to assert that at least one specific individual has, or has not, a certain property or properties, and also at least one unspecified individual has, or has not, a certain property or properties.**

Consider for instance

    **(46)** If every person is straightforward and honest, Dottie is such a person.

(46) is a hypothetical statement. The antecedent is 'every person is straightforward and honest'. This can be symbolized as

$$\textbf{(47)} \quad (x)[Px \supset (Sx \cdot Hx)]$$

The consequent is 'Dottie is such a person'. That is, it is claimed, 'Dottie is a person who is straightforward and honest'. This is symbolized

$$\textbf{(48)} \quad Pd \cdot (Sd \cdot Hd)$$

Joining (47) and (48) by the horseshoe produces

$$\textbf{(49)} \quad (x)[Px \supset (Sx \cdot Hx)] \supset [Pd \cdot (Sd \cdot Hd)]$$

Instead of asserting (46), someone might say this:

    **(50)** If any person is straightforward and honest, Dottie is such a person.

While perhaps ambiguous, the antecedent of (50) can be read

    **(51)** There is at least one person in the universe who is straightforward and honest.

Thus, (50) goes into symbols as

$$\textbf{(52)} \quad (\exists x)[Px \cdot (Sx \cdot Hx)] \supset [Pd \cdot (Sd \cdot Hd)]$$

Here is another example of a general statement combined with a singular one:

    **(53)** Either Helmut Kohl speaks, or no concerned person listens (but not both).

(53) is a compound statement displaying the form 'p $\Delta$ q'. The antecedent, 'Helmut Kohl speaks', is symbolized

$$\textbf{(54)} \quad Sk$$

To move toward a symbolization of the consequent, first reexpress 'no concerned person listens':

$$\textbf{(55)} \quad (x)[(Cx \cdot Px) \supset \sim Lx]$$

Using the delta, combine (51) and (52):

$$\textbf{(56)} \quad Sk \, \Delta \, (x)[(Cx \cdot Px) \supset \sim Lx]$$

---

## *EXERCISES*

Using the suggested predicate logic notation, symbolize each of the following.

1. Not every war is just. (W,J;x)

2. There aren't any just wars. (J,W;x)

3. Either Murray Gell-Mann is correct or there aren't any quarks. (C,Q;x,g)

4. Anything is composite except a quark. (C,Q;x)

5. Everything is ultimately composed of quarks or structured pions, but not both. (C,S;x)

6. Solomon was wise or anyone who has ever been powerful has never been wise. (W,P;x,s)

7. That T.S. Eliot is an exciting poet is a sufficient condition for there being poets who are exciting. (E,P;x,e)

8. It is simply not true that every poet is ethically radical, although some poets are. (P,R;x)

9. Each student progresses rapidly whenever Allan Bloom teaches. (S,P,T;x,b)

10. Every employee is happy if Trump or Iacocca proposes a raise. (E,H,P;x,t,i)

11. There aren't any vertebrate creatures that don't have hearts. (V,C,H;x)

12. Unless a person repents, he cannot enter the Kingdom of Heaven. (P,R,E;x)

13. If everyone is rich, then not only is someone rich but influential as well. (P,R,I;x)

14. Only if the saints are joyful has some person repented. (S,J,P,R;x)

15. Not every person is wise who is rich or famous. (P,W,R,F;x)

16. Assuming President Johnson was correct, then there has been at least one just war and Vietnam was it. (C,J,W;x,j,v)

17. That numerous gaseous substances aren't odoriferous is both sufficient and necessary for not all substances being odoriferous if gaseous. (G,S,O;x)

18. Any act is good except one which is either selfish or harmful. (A,G,S,H;x)

19. Each mammal has lungs only if it has a bloodstream, or certain mammals with lungs don't have a bloodstream, but not both. (M,L,B;x)

20. Not one of the philosophers uninfluenced by Ludwig Wittgenstein is a metaphysician except those who have been tempered by traditional thinkers. (P,I,M,T;x)

21. If all metals expand whenever heated, then copper, a metal, expands if heated. (M,E,H,C;x)

22. That numerous metals are conductors is a sufficient condition for some things being electrical conductors or insulators. (M,C,E,I;x)

23. Each man and woman is equal under the law except those not having citizenship. (M,W,E,C;x)

24. If anything is gold, it melts if heated to 1063°C, or else some gold heated to 1063°C doesn't both vaporize and melt, but not both. (G,M,H,V;x)

25. Not every philosopher who has come under the influence of Positivism finds the study of the history of philosophy worthless, although there aren't any philosophers coming under its influence who don't recognize the importance of language. (P,I,F,R;x)

26. No philosopher is an Idealist who is a follower of the Vienna Circle and adheres to American Pragmatism if, and only if, it isn't true that some philosophers are followers of the Vienna Circle while also adhering to American Pragmatism and being Idealists. (P,I,F,A;x)

27. A substance that is a gas never has a definite boundary of its own or no liquid substance has a definite boundary of its own. (S,G,B,L;x)

28. Some gases are dense or certain gases are colorless when, and only when, there are either some dense or colorless things that are gases or liquids. (G,D,C,L;x)

29. That humanists or scientists disagree whenever conversing is a necessary condition for C.P. Snow being right in his analysis of Western education. (H,S,D,C,R;x,s)

30. There isn't some gas that is either pure or mixed such that it isn't true that it closely approaches the specifications of Boyle's Law if, and only if, it isn't both under high pressure but can still be represented by that Law. (G,P,M,A,H,R;x)

---

## 4.    STATEMENTS INVOLVING RELATIONS

Thus far only *one-place predicate letters* have been used in predicate logic symbolization. A one-place predicate letter is a capital letter followed by only one lower-case letter. However, a predicate letter can be followed by two or more lower-case letters. In such cases, the predicate letter represents a *relational predicate* representing a relation said to hold, or not, between individuals. Quantifiers, predicate letters, individual variables and constants, and the notation of truth-functional logic are used to symbolize statements asserting relational claims. To suggest strategy useful in symbolizing, the remainder of this section introduces and discusses a series of examples. Each new example reflects themes developed in previous ones while also advancing symbolization skills further.

Imagine cases in which something like this is asserted:

(1)    Jack works for Naomi.

*Working for* is a relation holding between two individuals. Using 'W' to represent 'works for', 'j' to stand for 'Jack', and 'n' in place of 'Naomi', (1) is symbolized as a singular statement:

(2)    Wjn

The ordering of the individual constants in (2) is important. By convention, the name of the subject of the statement is written immediately after the predicate letter. Hence, it is incorrect to symbolize (1) as

(3)    Wnj

By convention, (3) asserts 'Naomi works for Jack'.

A further example indicating a two-place relation is

(4)    London is east of Cardiff.

(4) is correctly symbolized as

(5)    Elc

It is incorrect to symbolize (4) as

(6)    Ecl

(6) asserts 'Cardiff is east of London'.

An example of a three-place relation is

**(7)**   Dottie bought a Pininfarina for Frank.

Let the relation of someone's buying something for someone else be represented by 'B'. Introducing individual constants, (7) can then be symbolized as

**(8)**   Bdpf

The ordering of the lower-case letters again is important. By convention, after the predicate letter first write the name of the subject of the statement, then the name of the direct object, and next the name of the indirect object.

**(9)**   Bdfp

is interpreted as 'Dottie bought a Frank for Pininfarina'.*

Instead of a predicate letter being followed by names of individuals, individual variables can be used. For instance, 'x fights with y' is written as

**(10)**   Fxy

Distinct individual variables are used in (10). This is to display the relation '*fights with*' holding between two individuals. It is essential that the logical notation is able to distinguish distinct individuals between which some relation might, or might not, hold. For example, let the relation '*mother of*' be represented by 'M'. If distinct individual variables are not used with 'M', then

**(11)**   Mxx

says 'x is the mother of x', or 'x is its own mother'. What is required is

**(12)**   Mxy

Using different individual variables in (10) does not preclude such interpretations as 'Tim fights with Tim', or 'Tim fights with himself'. The same individual constant must always be substituted at each occurrence of the same individual variable in order to transform a statement function into a statement. Nevertheless, the same individual constant can be substituted at different individual variables provided that such substitutions are consistent throughout the entire statement function and in keeping with various rules introduced in later chapters.

The use of individual variables, individual constants, and quantifiers permits the symbolization of the hybrid statement

**(13)**   Something loves Freddie.

A stepwise handling of (13) yields

**(14)**   There is at least one thing such that it loves Freddie.

The next step is to introduce the existential quantifier and to replace 'it' with 'x':

---

*While a predicate letter may be followed by any finite number of lower-case letters, only one-place and two-place predicate letters are used in this book. This is a matter of pedagogical expediency. This decision imposes no limitations on predicate logic.

**(15)**   (∃x) x loves Freddie.

A final symbolization of (13) is obtained by introducing a two-place predicate letter, 'L', and an individual constant, 'f':

**(16)**   (∃x)Lxf

On the other hand, it might be suggested

**(17)**   Freddie loves something.

(17) is reexpressed as

**(18)**   There is at least one thing such that Freddie loves it.

With the existential quantifier and an individual variable, (19) is written:

**(19)**   (∃x) Freddie loves x.

The final move in symbolization is

**(20)**   (∃x) Lfx

Perhaps Julia is extremely popular and

**(21)**   Everyone loves Julia.

The word 'everyone' suggests that persons love Julia. To indicate this universe of discourse, first write

**(22)**   Given anything in the universe, if it is a person, then it loves Julia.

The symbolization of (22) continues by introducing a universal quantifier and individual variables:

**(23)**   (x) if x is a person, then x loves Julia.

(23) is symbolized as

**(24)**   (x)(Px ⊃ Lxj)

Perhaps Steve is exceptionally good-natured, and

**(25)**   Steve loves everyone.

Again showing the universe of discourse, the strategy of moving step-by-step produces

**(26)**   Given anything in the universe, if it is a person, then Steve loves it.

With a universal quantifier and an individual variable, (26) shifts into

**(27)**   (x) if x is a person, then Steve loves x.

And (27) is symbolized as

**(28)**   (x)(Px ⊃ Lsx)

Predicate logic notation can be extended even further by using several quantifiers in combination, permitting them to fall within the scope of one another. Consider this example of a general statement:

> **(29)**    Everything is related to something.

(29) can be rewritten as

> **(30)**    Given anything in the universe, it is related to something.

Introducing a universal quantifier and replacing 'it' with 'x' produces

> **(31)**    (x) x is related to something.

Next, the notion of 'something' in (31) needs to be expressed. Note that (32) retains the meaning of (31):

> **(32)**    (x) there is at least one thing in the universe such that
> x is related to it.

In (32), an existential quantifier can replace 'there is at least one thing in the universe such that', while 'y' replaces the occurrence of 'it':

> **(33)**    (x)($\exists$y) x is related to y.

In a final move, (33) is goes into:

> **(34)**    (x)($\exists$y)Rxy

It is important to grasp why the universal quantifier is written before the existential one in (34). In considering this, the ambiguity of (29) becomes apparent. (29) might be symbolized as

> **(35)**    ($\exists$y)(x)Rxy

depending upon what is being asserted. (34) suggests everything is related to something but not necessarily to the same thing. Once any $x$ is selected, some $y$ is found such that 'x is related to y' including the individual, $x$, being related to itself. (35) maintains

> **(36)**    There is something to which everything is related, and they all
> are related to the same individual.

Once some $y$ is selected, every $x$ is related to $y$. (34) and (35) do not express logically equivalent statements.

The ordering of quantifiers is logically unimportant when they are all the same type. Suppose someone says

> **(37)**    Everything is related to everything.

(37) is indifferently symbolized either as

> **(38)**    (x)(y)Rxy

or

> **(39)**    (y)(x)Rxy

Similarly,

        **(40)**    Something is related to something.

is put in predicate logic notation either as

        **(41)**    $(\exists x)(\exists y)Rxy$

or

        **(42)**    $(\exists y)(\exists x)Rxy$

Pronouns such as 'everyone', 'anyone', 'someone', 'nobody', and the like tacitly indicate the property of being a person. As seen in (22) and (26) above, such tacit assumptions can be made explicit:

        **(43)**    Everyone talks with someone.

It is not difficult to rewrite (43) as

        **(44)**    Given anything in the universe, if it is a person, then it talks with some person.

Use the universal quantifier and 'x' to write

        **(45)**    (x) if x is a person, then x talks with some person.

(45) can be expressed as

        **(46)**    $(x)(Px \supset$ x talks with some person$)$.

Next 'x talks with some person' is symbolically rendered:

        **(47)**    There is at least one thing in the universe such that it is a person and x talks with it.

Continue this step-by-step strategy and move to

        **(48)**    $(\exists y)(y$ is a person and x talks with y$)$.

Go from (48) to

        **(49)**    $(\exists y)(Py \cdot Txy)$

Combine (46) and (48) to complete the symbolization of (43):

        **(50)**    $(x)[Px \supset (\exists y)(Py \cdot Txy)]$

It is instructive to compare the next example with (43):

        **(51)**    Someone talks with everyone.

The meaning of (51) is captured in

        **(52)**    There is at least one thing in the universe such that it is a person and it talks with every person.

Reformulate (52) as

        **(53)**    $(\exists x)$ x is a person and x talks with every person.

(53) moves to

**(54)** $(\exists x)(Px \cdot x \text{ talks with every person})$.

The expression 'x talks with every person' can be rewritten as

**(55)** Given anything in the universe, if it is a person, then
x talks with it.

Use a universal quantifier and an appropriate individual variable to produce

**(56)** (y) if y is a person, then x talks with y

A complete symbolization of (56) is

**(57)** $(y)(Py \supset Txy)$

Combining (54) and (57) yields a symbolization of (51):

**(58)** $(\exists x)[Px \cdot (y)(Py \supset Txy)]$

Here is a more complicated example to symbolize:

**(59)** Whoever plays sport also enjoys games.

'Whoever' indicates that the universe of discourse is *persons*. First express (59) as

**(60)** Given anything in the universe, if it is a person, then if it
plays sports then it enjoys games.

Using appropriate predicate logic notation, next write

**(61)** (x) if x is a person, then if x plays sports then x enjoys games.

In (61), 'sports' is understood as 'some sport', and 'games' as 'some game'. Thus, (61) becomes

**(62)** (x) if x is a person, then if x plays some sport then x enjoys
some game.

Reexpress 'x plays some sport' as

**(63)** there is at least one thing in the universe such that it is a
sport and x plays it.

Transform (63) into symbolic notation:

**(64)** $(\exists y)(Sy \cdot Pxy)$

In a similar manner

**(65)** x enjoys some game

is symbolically expressed as

**(66)** $(\exists y)(Gy \cdot Exy)$

Having the sundry pieces at hand, (59) is now symbolized:

**(67)** $(x)\{Px \supset [(\exists y)(Sy \cdot Pxy) \supset (\exists y)(Gy \cdot Exy)]\}$

The existential quantifier, '(∃y)', appears twice in (67). The first of these occurrences ranges over the statement function 'Sy · Pxy' and the second over 'Gy · Exy'. Since the individual variable, 'y', in these two statement functions falls under the scope of different quantifiers, they do not necessarily refer to the same thing.

Consider a final example:

> **(68)**   Anyone who lives in a glass house shouldn't throw stones.

(68) is reexpressed as

> **(69)**   Given anything in the universe, if it is a person and it lives in a glass house, then it should not throw stones.

Using a universal quantifier and individual variables, move to

> **(70)**   (x) if x is a person and x lives in a glass house, then x should not throw stones.

Next, examine this expression:

> **(71)**   x is a person and x lives in a glass house.

The first part of this conjunction becomes

> **(72)**   Px

The second part can be reworded as

> **(73)**   there is at least one thing in the universe such that it is glass and it is a house, and x lives in it

(73) is expressed:

> **(74)**   (∃y) y is glass and y is a house, and x lives in y.

Supplying predicate letters and punctuation completes (74):

> **(75)**   $(\exists y)[(Gy \cdot Hy) \cdot Lxy]$

Conjoining (72) and (75) produces

> **(76)**   $Px \cdot (\exists y)[(Gy \cdot Hy) \cdot Lxy]$

Returning to (70), the following needs to be symbolized

> **(77)**   x shouldn't throw stones.

(77) is transformed into

> **(78)**   given anything in the universe, if it is a stone, then x should not throw it.

(78) is restated in symbols as

> **(79)**   (z) if z is a stone, then x should not throw z.

(79) is now completed:

> **(80)**   $(z)(Sz \supset \sim Txz)$

(76) and (80) are connected with a horseshoe:

**(81)**   $\{Px \cdot (\exists y)[(Gy \cdot Hy) \cdot Lxy]\} \supset (z)(Sz \supset \sim Txz)$

(81) is still a statement function needing a final universal quantifier. This is supplied in

**(82)**   $(x)(\{Px \cdot (\exists y)[(Gy \cdot Hy) \cdot Lxy]\} \supset (z)(Sz \supset \sim Txz))$

---

## *EXERCISES*

Using the suggested predicate logic notation symbolize each of the following.

1. Everything contains itself. (C;x)

2. Something contains something. (C;x,y)

3. Something circumscribes everything. (C;x,y)

4. Everything is circumscribed by something. (C;x,y)

5. There is something attracted by everything. (A;x,y)

6. Nothing attracts everything. (A;x,y)

7. There isn't something that everything attracts. (A;x,y)

8. There is something that everything doesn't repel. (R;x,y)

9. Nothing repels nothing. (R;x,y)

10. Something doesn't repel something. (R;x,y)

11. Every natural number other than zero is a successor of zero.
    'Nx' = 'x is a natural number other than zero'
    'Sxa'= 'x is a successor of zero,

12. Zero is not the successor of any natural number.
    'Nx' = 'x is a natural number'
    'Sax'= 'zero is the successor of x'

13. A loving person is God's friend.
    'Lx' = 'x is loving'
    'Px' = 'x is a person'
    'Fxg' = 'x is a friend of God'

14. The successor of any number is a number.
    'Nx' = 'x is a number'
    'Ny' = 'y is a number'
    'Sxy' = 'x is the successor of y'

15. No successor of an even number is an even number.
    'Nx' = 'x is an even number'
    'Ny' = 'y is an even number'
    'Sxy' = 'x is the successor of y'

16. All numbers are succeeded by some number or another.
    'Nx' = 'x is a number'
    'Ny' = 'y is a number'
    'Sxy' = 'x is succeeded by y'

17. Everyone needs some friend or another.
    'Fy' = 'y is a friend'
    'Px = 'x is a person'
    'Nxy' = 'x needs y'

18. To err is human.
    'Ey' = 'y is an error'
    'Hx' = 'x is human'
    'Mxy' = 'x makes y'

19. To forgive an error is divine.
    'Ey' = 'y is an error'
    'Dx' = 'x is divine'
    'Fxy' = 'x forgives y'

20. The silent person still endures injustice.
    'Iy' = 'y is injustice'
    'Px' = 'x is a person'
    'Sx' = 'x is silent'
    'Exy' = 'x still endures y'

21. A few students appreciate all their teachers.
    'Sx' = 'x is a student'
    'Ty' = 'y is a teacher'
    'Axy' = 'x appreciates y'
    'Tyx' = 'y is a teacher of x'

22. Anyone lonely knows no friend.
    'Fy' = 'y is a friend'
    'Lx' = 'x is lonely'
    'Px' = 'x is a person'
    'Kxy' = 'x knows y'

23. Students do not like every course they take.
    'Sx' = 'x is a student'
    'Cy' = 'y is a course'
    'Lxy' = 'x likes y'
    'Txy' = 'x takes y'

24. Those persons who wrong others wrong themselves.
    'Px' = 'x is a person'
    'Py' = 'y is a person'
    'Wxx' = 'x wrongs x'
    'Wxy' = 'x wrongs y'

25. Whoever loves his neighbor loves God.
    'Px' = 'x is a person'
    'Py' = 'y is a person'
    'Lxg' = 'x loves God'
    'Lxy' = 'x loves y'
    'Nxy' = 'y is a neighbor of x'

26. A friend in need is a friend indeed.
    'Fy' = 'y is a friend'
    'Gy' = 'y is genuine'
    'Px' = 'x is a person'

'Py' = 'y is a person'
'Nxy' = 'x is in need of y'

27. Not all students entering a university receive a degree.
'Dz' = 'z is a degree'
'Sx' = 'x is a student'
'Uy' = 'y is a university'
'Exy' = 'x enters y'
'Rxz' = 'x receives z'

28. Idiots go where angels fear to tread.
'Az' = 'z is an angel'
'Py' = 'y is a place'
'Ix' = 'x is an idiot'
'Fzy' = 'z fears to tread to y'
'Gwy' = 'w goes to y'

29. Certain materials used by scientists conduct electrical impulses.
'Ly' = 'y is an electrical impulse'
'Mx' = 'x is a material'
'Sz = 'z is a scientist'
'Cxy' = 'x conducts y'
'Uxy' = 'x is used by z'

30. If any unbalanced force does not act on some body, that body continues in a state of rest or uniform motion (but not both).
'By' = 'y is a body'
'Fx' = 'x is a force'
'Mw' = 'w is a state of uniform motion'
'Rz' = 'z is a state of rest'
'Ux' = 'x is unbalanced'
'Axy' = 'x acts on y'

---

## 5. REVIEW OF NEW TERMS

**Bound individual variable:** An individual variable that refers back to some quantifier. An individual variable that falls under the scope of a quantifier. In a correctly symbolized statement, every individual variable must be bound to some quantifier or another.

**Existential quantifier:** A monadic operator in predicate logic formed by placing an '∃' before an individual variable and flanking the results of this with left- and right-hand parentheses. '(∃x)' is an example of an existential quantifier. This operator is read, 'There is at least one thing in the universe such that . . . '.

**Free individual variable:** An individual variable that does not refer back to some quantifier. An individual variable that does not fall under the scope of a quantifier. There can be no free variables in a correctly symbolized statement.

**General statement:** A statement used to assert that individuals have, or have not, a certain property or properties; statements mentioning only unspecified individuals.

**Hybrid statement:** A statement used to assert that at least one specific individual has, or has not, a certain property or properties, and also at least one unspecified individual has, or has not, a certain property or properties; statements mentioning both specific and unspecified individuals.

**Individual constant:** A lower-case letter 'a' through 'v' used in predicate logic as a name of an individual. Individual constants comprise the range of individual variables.

**Individual variable:** A lower-case letter 'w' through 'z' used in predicate logic to mark a space that can be filled by the name or description of a specific individual. Individual variables in predicate logic are analogous to pronouns in everyday language.

**Particular statement:** A statement used to assert that at least one unspecified individual has, or has not, a certain property or properties; statements mentioning only at least one unspecified individual.

**Predicate letter:** Any capital letter 'A' through 'Z' used in predicate logic to mention some property that is said to hold, or not hold, of an individual or hold, or not hold, between individuals.

**Predicate logic:** The part of deductive logic that deals with the interior structure of simple statements as well as the structure of compound statements.

**Quantifier:** In predicate logic, a monadic operator answering the question 'How many?'; an operator used to express an indefinite subject of a statement.

**Singular statement:** A statement used to assert that at least one specific individual has, or has not, a certain property or properties; statements mentioning only specific individuals.

**Statement function:** An expression containing a predicate letter followed by one or more individual variables, or such expressions coupled with truth-functional operators.

**Universal quantifier:** A monadic operator in predicate logic formed by flanking an individual variable with left- and right-hand parentheses. '(x)' is an example of a universal quantifier. This operator is read, 'Given any thing in the universe . . . '.

**Universal statement:** A statement used to assert that all unspecified individuals have, or have not, a certain property or properties; statements mentioning only all unspecified individuals.

**Universe of discourse:** A finite or infinite collection of individuals to which, either implicitly or explicitly, the statement(s) being used in a particular context refer.

# 11

# TRUTH TREES AND PREDICATE LOGIC

Chapter 4 develops truth tree rules and strategies to determine the validity or invalidity of truth-functional arguments and consistency or inconsistency of premise sets; to decide whether truth-functional statements are contradictory, tautological, or contingent; and to show if truth-functional statements are logically equivalent or not. These rules and strategies are now expanded to use in predicate logic. This expansion requires new rules and strategies governing the universal and existential quantifier.

## 1. VALIDITY AND INVALIDITY

This argument shows a simple use of truth trees in predicate logic to establish validity:

(1) If Ed lies to Bill and Mary hears Ed, then she speaks to Bill. Mary hears Ed but doesn't speak to Bill. Consequently, Ed doesn't lie to Bill.

First, symbolize (1):

(2)                         /∴ ~ Leb

    **1)** $(Leb \cdot Hme) \supset Smb$    Pr

    **2)** $Hme \cdot \sim Smb$    Pr

Assume the denial of the conclusion:

(3)                         /∴ ~ Leb

    **1)** $(Leb \cdot Hme) \supset Smb$    Pr

    **2)** $Hme \cdot \sim Smb$    Pr

    **3)** $\sim \sim Leb$    AP

Proceed by developing a truth tree for (3):

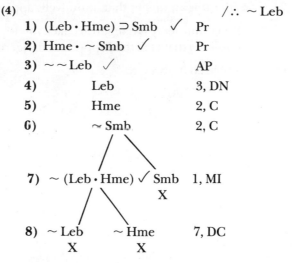

**(4)**                                          /∴ ~ Leb

     **1)** (Leb · Hme) ⊃ Smb ✓    Pr

     **2)** Hme · ~ Smb ✓    Pr

     **3)** ~ ~ Leb ✓    AP

     **4)**       Leb      3, DN

     **5)**       Hme      2, C

     **6)**      ~ Smb      2, C

     **7)** ~ (Leb · Hme) ✓   Smb    1, MI

                              X

     **8)** ~ Leb    ~ Hme      7, DC

        X        X

Every branch of (4) is closed, and (1) is valid.*

Examine another use of truth trees to establish validity:

     **(5)**    Every student is passing or some students aren't doing well. Not all students are passing. So, some students aren't doing well.

This argument can be symbolized as

     **(6)**                                    /∴ (∃x)(Sx · ~ Dx)

     **1)** (x)(Sx ⊃ Px) ∨ (∃x)(Sx · ~ Dx)    Pr

     **2)** ~ (x)(Sx ⊃ Px)    Pr

In (6), every quantified statement can be read as an instance of a single statement variable or a single statement variable prefixed by one tilde. So, all the rules introduced in Chapter 4 are directly applicable in (6). In line 3, assume the denial of the conclusion. Then decompose line 1:

     **(7)**                                    /∴ (∃x)(Sx · ~ Dx)

     **1)** (x)(Sx ⊃ Px) ∨ (∃x)(Sx · ~ Dx) ✓   Pr

     **2)**     ~ (x)(Sx ⊃ Px)      Pr

     **3)**     ~ (∃x)(Sx · ~ Dx)      AP

     **4)** (x)(Sx ⊃ Px)    (∃x)(Sx · ~ Dx)      1, ID

          X               X

(5) is valid because all the branches in (7) are closed.

---

*As discussed in Chapter 4, a closed branch is a terminated branch containing a simple statement and that simple statement prefixed by one tilde. That is, a closed branch is one containing a contradiction. In (4) both 'Leb' and 'Hme' are simple statements, and ' ~ Leb' and ' ~ Hme' are these simple statements prefixed by one tilde.

Many truth tree applications in predicate logic are not as straightforward as (1) and (5). Consider this argument that, intuitively, appears valid:

**(8)**    Every murderer is dangerous. Jack the Ripper was a murderer. It follows that Jack the Ripper was dangerous.

(8) can be symbolized in this way:

**(9)**                                                  $/ \therefore Dj$
    **1)** $(x)(Mx \supset Dx)$    Pr
    **2)** Mj                        Pr

The premises and conclusion in (8) are simple statements. Rewriting (8) in terms of truth-functional notation yields

**(10)**                $/ \therefore J$
    **1)** D    Pr
    **2)** M    Pr

Unfortunately, none of the rules introduced in Chapter 4 are applicable in (10) to establish the validity of (8). What is needed is some rule that can transform '$(x)(Mx \supset Dx)$' in (9) into a compound statement mentioning Jack the Ripper. This rule is *Universal Instantiation*.

Universal Instantiation permits a universal quantifier to be dropped from a universally quantified statement when that quantifier ranges over the entire statement. The rule further permits all the individual variables bound to the quantifier to be changed into a name of a specific individual. Assume that 'Every murderer is dangerous' is true. Suppose, further, that there are only four individuals in the universe of discourse under discussion, namely *persons*. These individuals are named 'Allison', 'Bruce', 'Cathy', and 'Dave'. Then, if 'Every murderer is dangerous' is true, each of these statements must also be true:

**(11)**    If Allison is a murderer, then Allison is dangerous.
        If Bruce is a murderer, then Bruce is dangerous.
        If Cathy is a murder, then Cathy is dangerous.
        If Dave is a murderer, then Dave is dangerous.

A universally quantified statement is true if and only if every member of the universe of discourse has the properties mentioned by that statement. Thus, an instance of a universal statement can be taken by dropping the universal quantifier appearing at the beginning of the statement and replacing every individual variable bound to that quantifier by the name of an individual, being sure to replace each freed variable by the same name of the same individual.

The rule, *Universal Instantiation*, can now be expressed. Let '$(\alpha)$' represent any universal quantifier, '$\alpha$' any individual variable, and '$\Phi$' any predicate, or combination of predicates:

**UNIVERSAL INSTANTIATION (UI)**

$$(\alpha)\Phi\alpha$$
$$|$$
$$\Phi\beta$$

'$\Phi\beta$', an *instance* of '$(\alpha)\Phi\alpha$', is appended to every open branch in which '$(\alpha)\Phi\alpha$' occurs. Further, (1) '$\beta$' represents the name of an individual, and (2) '$\beta$' occurs in just those places where '$\alpha$' occurs as a free individual variable in '$\Phi\alpha$'. Let '$(\alpha)\Phi\alpha$' represent

> **(12)**   Every murderer is dangerous.

or, in symbols

> **(13)**   $(x)(Mx \supset Dx)$

View (13) as displaying '$(\alpha)\Phi\alpha$'. Then, an instance of '$\Phi\beta$' is 'If Jack the Ripper is a murderer, then Jack the Ripper is dangerous'. Instances of (13) could be generated as long as individuals in the universe of discourse, persons, remain to be mentioned. However, (8) mentions a specific murderer, Jack the Ripper. So, if (8) is assumed to be true, by Universal Instantiation (14) must also be true:

> **(14)**   If Jack the Ripper is a murderer, then Jack the Ripper is dangerous.

(9) can be continued by assuming the denial of the conclusion and then taking an instance of the first premise:

> **(15)**                                    $/\therefore Dj$
> **1)** $(x)(Mx \supset Dx)$        Pr
> **2)** $Mj$                               Pr
> **3)** $\sim Dj$                          AP
> **4)** $Mj \supset Dj$                 1, UI

After Universal Instantiation is used to obtain line 4, a check is not put to the right of '$(x)(Mx \supset Dx)$'. This is because line 4 does not exhaust the information asserted in 1. There are many more instances of '$(x)(Mx \supset Dx)$' than '$Mj \supset Dj$', and some of this information might be needed later in constructing a truth tree. Further, any of these many instances could have been correctly written at line 4. However, since the argument mentions the individual, Jack the Ripper, no other instance would be useful in establishing the validity of (8). As a strategy, introduce by UI the name of an individual previously mentioned in the branch to which that instance of the universally quantified statement is being appended. If there is no previously mentioned individual, introduce the name 'a'. Now, one could continue to apply UI to '$(x)(Mx \supset Dx)$' as long as there were distinct individuals in its universe of discourse. In an infinitely large universe, this process would never come to an end. Nor is it feasible in other universes of discourse. Thus, stop applying UI to a universally quantified statement as soon as it has been instantiated for every name on the path in which it is found.* A truth tree for (15) can now be completed:

> **(16)**                                    $/\therefore Dj$
> **1)** $(x)(Mx \supset Dx)$        Pr
> **2)** $Mj$                               Pr

---

*As will be seen later (e.g., (45) below), in some cases this leads to a nonterminating branch.

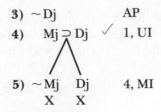

Because every path in (16) is closed, (8) is valid.

Here is a slightly more complicated argument:

(17)   Students are expelled if caught cheating. Unfortunately, both Jeff and Martha are students caught cheating. The result is that they're both expelled.

(17) can be symbolized as

(18)                                              / ∴ Ej · Em
　　　1) (x)[Sx ⊃ (Cx ⊃ Ex)]   Pr
　　　2) (Sj · Cj) · (Sm · Cm)    Pr

Begin a truth tree by assuming the denial of the conclusion:

(19)                                              / ∴ Ej · Em
　　　1) (x)[Sx ⊃ (Cx ⊃ Ex)]   Pr
　　　2) (Sj · Cj) · (Sm · Cm)    Pr
　　　3) ~ (Ej · Em)               Ap

Following the strategies in Chapter 4, first fully decompose 2:

(20)                                              / ∴ Ej · Em
　　　1) (x)[Sx ⊃ (Cx ⊃ Ex)]       Pr
　　　2) (Sj · Cj) · (Sm · Cm)  ✓   Pr
　　　3) ~ (Ej · Em)                   Ap
　　　4)     Sj · Cj  ✓                 2, C
　　　5)     Sm · Cm  ✓               2, C
　　　6)       Sj                         4, C
　　　7)       Cj                         4, C
　　　8)       Sm                        5, C
　　　9)       Cm                        5, C

Continue the truth tree by decomposing the assumed premise:

(21)                                              / ∴ Ej · Em
　　　1) (x)[Sx ⊃ (Cx ⊃ Ex)]       Pr
　　　2) (Sj · Cj) · (Sm · Cm)  ✓   Pr
　　　3) ~ (Ej · Em)  ✓               Ap
　　　4)     Sj · Cj  ✓                 2, C

|     |           |       |
|-----|-----------|-------|
| **5)** | Sm · Cm  ✓ | 2, C |
| **6)** | Sj        | 4, C |
| **7)** | Cj        | 4, C |
| **8)** | Sm        | 5, C |
| **9)** | Cm        | 5, C |

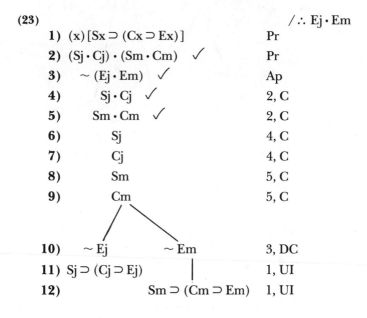

|     |           |       |
|-----|-----------|-------|
| **10)** | ~Ej      ~Em | 3, DC |

Since the first premise is accepted as true about everything, it is true about Jeff and Martha:

**(22)**

    **a)** Sj ⊃ (Cj ⊃ Ej)

    **b)** Sm ⊃ (Cm ⊃ Em)

Universal Instantiation must be used twice on line 1 to introduce these statements into the developing tree. Let the left-hand branch of the tree mention Jeff and the right-hand one, Martha. Put information about Jeff in the "Jeff branch" and about Martha in the "Martha branch":

**(23)**                                                             / ∴ Ej · Em

| | | |
|---|---|---|
| **1)** | (x) [Sx ⊃ (Cx ⊃ Ex)] | Pr |
| **2)** | (Sj · Cj) · (Sm · Cm)  ✓ | Pr |
| **3)** | ~ (Ej · Em)  ✓ | Ap |
| **4)** | Sj · Cj  ✓ | 2, C |
| **5)** | Sm · Cm  ✓ | 2, C |
| **6)** | Sj | 4, C |
| **7)** | Cj | 4, C |
| **8)** | Sm | 5, C |
| **9)** | Cm | 5, C |
| **10)** | ~Ej        ~Em | 3, DC |
| **11)** | Sj ⊃ (Cj ⊃ Ej) | 1, UI |
| **12)** | Sm ⊃ (Cm ⊃ Em) | 1, UI |

After line 11 is generated, a '✓' is not placed to the right of '(x) [Sx ⊃ (Cx ⊃ Ex)]'. Had this been done, no further information could have been obtained from the first premise. But information concerning Martha is needed in 12.

Continue (26) by decomposing lines 11 and 12:

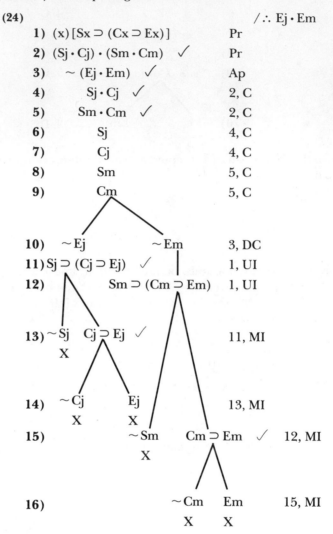

(24)                       /∴ Ej·Em

1) (x)[Sx ⊃ (Cx ⊃ Ex)]       Pr

2) (Sj·Cj) · (Sm·Cm) ✓      Pr

3)    ∼ (Ej·Em) ✓           Ap

4)        Sj·Cj ✓            2, C

5)       Sm·Cm ✓          2, C

6)          Sj                4, C

7)          Cj                4, C

8)         Sm               5, C

9)        Cm              5, C

10)    ∼Ej        ∼Em      3, DC

11) Sj ⊃ (Cj ⊃ Ej) ✓          1, UI

12)       Sm ⊃ (Cm ⊃ Em)    1, UI

13) ∼Sj   Cj ⊃ Ej ✓         11, MI
     X

14)    ∼Cj    Ej            13, MI
       X     X

15)         ∼Sm    Cm ⊃ Em ✓   12, MI
          X

16)            ∼Cm   Em      15, MI
            X    X

Every path in (24) is closed, and (17) is valid.

Examine this argument using existentially quantified statements:

(25)   Some compassionate people are successful in business. Compassionate people are thoughtful. Thus, some people successful in business are thoughtful.

(25) can be symbolized this way:

**(26)**                                  /∴ $(\exists x)[(Px \cdot Sx) \cdot Tx]$

    **1)** $(\exists x)[(Cx \cdot Px) \cdot Sx]$    Pr

    **2)** $(x)[(Cx \cdot Px) \supset Tx]$    Pr

Begin a truth tree by assuming the denial of the conclusion:

**(27)**                                  /∴ $(\exists x)[(Px \cdot Sx) \cdot Tx]$

    **1)** $(\exists x)[(Cx \cdot Px) \cdot Sx]$    Pr

    **2)** $(x)[(Cx \cdot Px) \supset Tx]$    Pr

    **3)** $\sim (\exists x)[(Px \cdot Sx) \cdot Tx]$    AP

Before continuing (27), it is necessary to discuss two topics. First, how can the existential quantifier in line 1 be removed to obtain '(Ca • Pa) • Sa'? Second, because of the tilde prefixed to the quantifier, how is line 3 to be decomposed? Answering these questions will introduce new rules needed to construct truth trees in predicate logic. The first of these rules is *Existential Instantiation* and the second is *Quantificational Denial*.

Assume that the first premise of (25) is true:

**(28)**   Some compassionate people are successful in business.

The truth of (28) does not entail the truth of

**(29)**   Joan, a compassionate person, is successful in business.

The specific individual, Joan, might or might not be a compassionate person successful in business. Nonetheless, assuming (28) is true, it is true that there is at least one individual who is a compassionate person successful in business. While it is not known which specific individual this is, even so, that individual can be assigned a name. For example, that individual might be called 'Jane Doe'. 'Jane Doe' is understood as an ***ambiguous name*** referring to that individual who is both a compassionate person and a success in business.

**EXISTENTIAL INSTANTIATION (EI)**

$(\exists\alpha)\Phi\alpha$

$\Phi\beta$

'$\Phi\beta$', an instance of '$(\exists x)\ \Phi\alpha$', is appended to every open path in which '$(\exists\alpha)\ \Phi\alpha$' is found, and '$\beta$' is replaced by an ambiguous name in '$\Phi\beta$'. At each of its occurrences corresponding to the free '$\alpha$' in '$\Phi\alpha$'. The truth of any statement displaying the schema '$(\exists x)\ \Phi\alpha$' guarantees that there is at least one individual having the property denoted by '$\Phi$' even though it is not known which specific individual that is. This is why '$\beta$' is replaced by an ambiguous name. In predicate logic, new symbols, such as 'σ', 'δ', 'ζ', and 'η', could be used as ambiguous names. Yet no confusion occurs in developing truth trees if lower-case letters are viewed as ambiguous names when introduced by Existential Instantiation.

Another restriction is placed on 'β' when introduced into a truth tree by Existential Instantiation. 'β' can never be a name already appearing in a branch to which 'Φβ' is appended. Given the truth of (28) there might be two, or more, individuals who are compassionate persons successful in business. Not knowing what other properties these individuals might or might not have, they are assigned different ambiguous names. Consider this argument in which 'Alfonso' is understood as an ambiguous name:

**(30)**   Some cats meow. Some dogs bark. Hence, Alfonso is both
a cat and a dog.

If the second restriction on 'β' is not observed, the following truth tree can be developed:

**(31)**                                          / ∴ Ca · Da

$$
\begin{array}{lll}
\textbf{1)} & (\exists x)(Cx \cdot Mx) \;\; \checkmark & Pr \\
\textbf{2)} & (\exists x)(Dx \cdot Bx) \;\; \checkmark & Pr \\
\textbf{3)} & \sim (Ca \cdot Da) & AP \\
\textbf{4)} & Ca \cdot Ma \;\; \checkmark & 1, EI \\
\textbf{5)} & Da \cdot Ba \;\; \checkmark & 2, EI \\
\textbf{6)} & Ca & 4, C \\
\textbf{7)} & Ma & 4, C \\
\textbf{8)} & Da & 5, C \\
\textbf{9)} & Ba & 5, C \\
\end{array}
$$

*WRONG X* appears beside line **5)**.

**10)**    ∼ Ca        ∼ Da        3, DC
            X            X

Given (31), (30) is a valid argument. Since all the premises of (30) are true, the conclusion must also be true. But 'Alfonso is both a cat and a dog' cannot be true. Beginning with true premises, the use of the rules in (31) has led to a false conclusion. Something is wrong with the rules as they stand. Using EI, 'a' is introduced as an ambiguous name into 4. The mistake occurs when 'a' is again introduced by EI as an ambiguous name into 5. Logic supplies no guarantees that the individual having the properties of being a cat and meowing is the same individual as that having the properties of being a dog and barking. Hence, two distinct ambiguous names must be used when naming these individuals.

(27) can be continued using Existential Instantiation:

**(32)**                                          / ∴ (∃x)[(Px · Sx) · Tx]

$$
\begin{array}{lll}
\textbf{1)} & (\exists x)[(Cx \cdot Px) \cdot Sx] \;\; \checkmark & Pr \\
\textbf{2)} & (x)[(Cx \cdot Px) \supset Tx] & Pr \\
\end{array}
$$

**3)** $\sim (\exists x)[(Px \cdot Sx) \cdot Tx]$     AP

**4)** $(Ca \cdot Pa) \cdot Sa$     1, EI

A check is placed to the right of '$(\exists x)[(Cx \cdot Px) \cdot Sx]$' after EI is used to obtain line 4. Continue (32):

**(33)**                                   $/ \therefore (\exists x)[(Px \cdot Sx) \cdot Tx]$

**1)** $(\exists x)[(Cx \cdot Px) \cdot Sx]$   ✓   Pr

**2)** $(x)[(Cx \cdot Px) \supset Tx]$     Pr

**3)** $\sim (\exists x)[(Px \cdot Sx) \cdot Tx]$     AP

**4)** $(Ca \cdot Pa) \cdot Sa$   ✓   1, EI

**5)**     $Ca \cdot Pa$   ✓   4, C

**6)**     $Sa$   4, C

**7)**     $Ca$   5, C

**8)**     $Pa$   5, C

**9)**   $(Ca \cdot Pa) \supset Ta$   2, UI

**10)**  $\sim (Ca \cdot Pa)$  ✓  $Ta$   9, MI

**11)**  $\sim Ca$     $\sim Pa$   10, DC
       X          X

The name 'a' is introduced in 9 by UI. Any other name might have been introduced since it is assumed that the statement in 2 is true of everything. However, given line 4, the argument is about 'a'. Remember, whenever a new statement is appended to a branch by UI, replace '$\beta$' in '$\Phi\beta$' by the name of an individual already used in that developing branch. Stop using UI only when every name previously mentioned in the branch to which '$(\alpha)\Phi\alpha$' is appended is introduced as an instance of '$\Phi\alpha$'.*

While no restrictions on the rules of instantiation are broken in (33), examine this truth tree:

**(34)**                                   $/ \therefore (\exists x)[(Px \cdot Sx) \cdot Tx]$

**1)** $(\exists x)[(Cx \cdot Px) \cdot Sx]$   ✓   Pr

**2)** $(x)[(Cx \cdot Px) \supset Tx]$     Pr

**3)** $\sim (\exists x)[(Px \cdot Sx) \cdot Tx]$     AP

**4)** $(Ca \cdot Pa) \supset Ta$     2, UI

*WRONG X*  **5)** $(Ca \cdot Pa) \cdot Sa$     1, EI

EI is misused in going to 5 because 'a' has already occurred in 4. As a strategy, when using both EI and UI to develop a branch, use EI first to preserve the restrictions on EI.

---

*Remember that following this requirement will sometimes generate a nonterminating branch.

What is to be done with ' $\sim (\exists x)[(Px \cdot Sx) \cdot Tx]$' in 3 of (34)? The tilde ranges over all of '$(\exists x)[(Px \cdot Sx) \cdot Tx]$' and not merely '$(\exists x)$'. As long as a tilde is prefixed to any quantifier there can be no application of EI or UI. Such tildes, however, can be removed by this rule:

### QUANTIFICATIONAL DENIAL (QD)

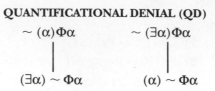

where '$(\exists \alpha) \sim \Phi \alpha$' or '$(\alpha) \sim \Phi \alpha$' is appended to every open branch in which '$\sim (\alpha) \Phi \alpha$' or '$\sim (\exists \alpha) \Phi \alpha$' occurs. To use Quantificational Denial, change the quantifier and move the tilde. If the quantifier is a universal one, change it to an existential quantifier. But if the quantifier is existential, change it to a universal one. Take the tilde that is prefixed to the quantifier and suffix it to that quantifier. These moves can be grasped intuitively by interpreting '$\Phi \alpha$' as, say, 'x is expensive' and reading each pair in English. For instance, if '$\sim (\alpha) \Phi \alpha$' is read as 'Not all things are expensive', then '$(\exists \alpha) \sim \Phi \alpha$' is understood as 'Some things are not expensive'. And 'It is not the case that some things are expensive' can be understood as 'All things are not expensive' or 'Everything is not expensive'.*

Viewing line 3 in (33) as displaying the schema '$\sim (\exists \alpha) \Phi \alpha$', the truth tree is continued:

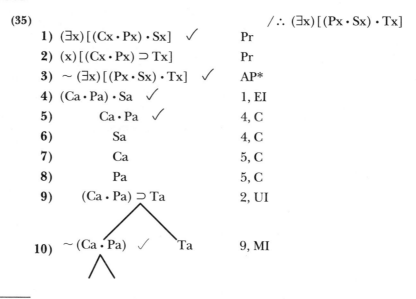

(35)

/∴ $(\exists x)[(Px \cdot Sx) \cdot Tx]$

1) $(\exists x)[(Cx \cdot Px) \cdot Sx]$ ✓    Pr

2) $(x)[(Cx \cdot Px) \supset Tx]$    Pr

3) $\sim (\exists x)[(Px \cdot Sx) \cdot Tx]$ ✓    AP*

4) $(Ca \cdot Pa) \cdot Sa$ ✓    1, EI

5) $Ca \cdot Pa$ ✓    4, C

6) $Sa$    4, C

7) $Ca$    5, C

8) $Pa$    5, C

9) $(Ca \cdot Pa) \supset Ta$    2, UI

10) $\sim (Ca \cdot Pa)$ ✓    $Ta$    9, MI

*Without sufficient context, 'All things are not expensive' is ambiguous. Suppose someone were going with a friend to the store to make some purchases. The friend asks about the price range of the items in a store and the reply is 'Everything is not expensive'. This sentence could mean either 'Nothing is expensive' or 'Some things are not expensive'. In the context of Quantificational Denial, however, the ambiguity is avoided by laying down the rule that any statement of the form '$\sim (\exists \alpha) \Phi \alpha$' entails a statement of the form '$(\alpha) \sim \Phi \alpha$'.

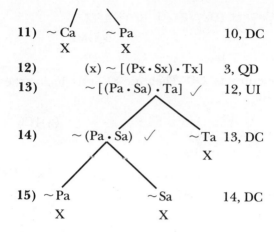

**11)**  ~Ca        ~Pa                    10, DC
         X          X

**12)**         (x) ~ [(Px · Sx) · Tx]    3, QD

**13)**           ~ [(Pa · Sa) · Ta] ✓    12, UI

**14)**      ~ (Pa · Sa) ✓        ~Ta      13, DC
                                   X

**15)**  ~Pa              ~Sa              14, DC
         X                 X

Since no path remains open in (35), (25) is valid.

Is the following argument valid?

**(36)**                                    / ∴  (w) [Cw ⊃ (z) (Dz ⊃ Bwz)]
  **1)** (x) (y) (Axy ⊃ Byx)        Pr
  **2)** (x) [Cx ⊃ (y) (Dy ⊃ Axy)]   Pr

Begin a truth tree by assuming the denial of the conclusion:

**(37)**                                    / ∴  (w) [Cw ⊃ (z) (Dz ⊃ Bwz)]
  **1)** (x) (y) (Axy ⊃ Byx)        Pr
  **2)** (x) [Cx ⊃ (y) (Dy ⊃ Axy)]   Pr
  **3)** ~ (w) [Cw ⊃ (z) (Dz ⊃ Bwz)]    AP

Remove the tilde prefixed to the quantifier in the third premise:

**(38)**                                    / ∴  (w) [Cw ⊃ (z) (Dz ⊃ Bwz)]
  **1)** (x) (y) (Axy ⊃ Byx)        Pr
  **2)** (x) [Cx ⊃ (y) (Dy ⊃ Axy)]   Pr
  **3)** ~ (w) [Cw ⊃ (z) (Dz ⊃ Bwz)]    AP
  **4)** (∃w) ~ [Cw ⊃ (z) (Dz ⊃ Bwz)]   3, QD

Continue the tree by using EI on 4 followed by DMI:

**(39)**                                    / ∴  (w) [Cw ⊃ (z) (Dz ⊃ Bwz)]
  **1)** (x) (y) (Axy ⊃ Byx)        Pr
  **2)** (x) [Cx ⊃ (y) (Dy ⊃ Axy)]   Pr
  **3)** ~ (w) [Cw ⊃ (z) (Dz ⊃ Bwz)]    AP
  **4)** (∃w) ~ [Cw ⊃ (z) (Dz ⊃ Bwz)]   3, QD

---

*Notice when QD is used on a statement a check, '✓', is placed after that statement.

5)  ~ [Ca ⊃ (z)(Dz ⊃ Baz)]    ✓    4, EI
6)              Ca                    5, DMI
7)  ~ (z)(Dz ⊃ Baz)                   5, DMI

Remove the tilde in 7 by QD. Then use EI, introducing the ambiguous name 'b', followed by DMI:

(40)                                    / ∴ (w)[Cw ⊃ (z)(Dz ⊃ Bwz)]

1)  (x)(y)(Axy ⊃ Byx)                 Pr
2)  (x)[Cx ⊃ (y)(Dy ⊃ Axy)]           Pr
3)  ~ (w)[Cw ⊃ (z)(Dz ⊃ Bwz)]         AP
4)  (∃w) ~ [Cw ⊃ (z)(Dz ⊃ Bwz)]       3, QD
5)  ~ [Ca ⊃ (z)(Dz ⊃ Baz)]    ✓       4, EI
6)              Ca                     5, DMI
7)      ~ (z)(Dz ⊃ Baz)                5, DMI
8)  (∃z) ~ (Dz ⊃ Baz)    ✓             7, QD
9)      ~ (Db ⊃ Bab)    ✓              8, EI
10)             Db                     9, DMI
11)           ~Bab                     10, DMI

To show (36) is valid, a truth tree must be generated in which every branch is closed. This can be done in (40) if ' ~ Ca', ' ~ Db', or 'Bab' can be produced from lines 1 and 2 for every branch of the tree. Hence, in using UI think of changing individual variables in ways that, coupled with truth tree rules, will yield either ' ~ Ca', ' ~ Db', or 'Bab'. For instance, using UI with 1 the individual variables can be changed so that the line produced will contain 'Bab':

(41)                                    / ∴ (w)[Cw ⊃ (z)(Dz ⊃ Bwz)]

1)  (x)(y)(Axy ⊃ Byx)                 Pr
2)  (x)[Cx ⊃ (y)(Dy ⊃ Axy)]           Pr
3)  ~ (w)[Cw ⊃ (z)(Dz ⊃ Bwz)]         AP
4)  (∃w) ~ [Cw ⊃ (z)(Dz ⊃ Bwz)]       3, QD
5)  ~ [Ca ⊃ (z)(Dz ⊃ Baz)]    ✓       4, EI
6)              Ca                     5, DMI
7)      ~ (z)(Dz ⊃ Baz)    ✓           5, DMI
8)  (∃z) ~ (Dz ⊃ Baz)    ✓             7, QD
9)      ~ (Db ⊃ Bab)                   8, EI
10)             Db                     9, DMI
11)           ~Bab                     10, DMI
12)     (y)(Aay ⊃ Bya)
13)         Aab ⊃ Bba                  12, UI

Applying MI to 13 closes one branch of the tree:

(**42**)                                                     /∴ (w)[Cw ⊃ (z)(Dz ⊃ Bwz)]

  **1)**   (x)(y)(Axy ⊃ Byx)           Pr

  **2)**   (x)[Cx ⊃ (y)(Dy ⊃ Axy)]     Pr

  **3)**   ~ (w)[Cw ⊃ (z)(Dz ⊃ Bwz)]   AP

  **4)**   (∃w) ~ [Cw ⊃ (z)(Dz ⊃ Bwz)]   3, QD

  **5)**   ~ [Ca ⊃ (z)(Dz ⊃ Baz)]   ✓    4, EI

  **6)**              Ca                5, DMI

  **7)**     ~ (z)(Dz ⊃ Baz)  ✓    5, DMI

  **8)**     (∃z) ~ (Dz ⊃ Baz)  ✓    7, GD

  **9)**       ~ (Db ⊃ Bab)        8, EI

**10)**            Db               9, MI

**11)**          ~ Bab           10, DMI

**12)**    (y)(Aay ⊃ Bya)       1, UI

**13)**      Aab ⊃ Bba       12, UI

                   /\

**14)**   ~ Aba    Bab       13, MI

                 X

Can the left-hand branch be closed? Using UI on 2, changing 'x' to 'a', produces another closed branch:

(**43**)                                                     /∴ (w)[Cw ⊃ (z)(Dz ⊃ Bwz)]

  **1)**   (x)(y)(Axy ⊃ Byx)           Pr

  **2)**   (x)[Cx ⊃ (y)(Dy ⊃ Axy)]     Pr

  **3)**   ~ (w)[Cw ⊃ (z)(Dz ⊃ Bwz)]   AP

  **4)**   (∃w) ~ [Cw ⊃ (z)(Dz ⊃ Bwz)]   3, QD

  **5)**   ~ [Ca ⊃ (z)(Dz ⊃ Baz)]   ✓    4, EI

  **6)**              Ca  ✓           5, DMI

  **7)**     ~ (z)(Dz ⊃ Baz)  ✓    5, DMI

  **8)**     (∃z) ~ (Dz ⊃ Baz)  ✓    7, QD

  **9)**       ~ (Db ⊃ Bab)        8, EI

**10)**            Db               9, DMI

**11)**          ~ Bab           10, DMI

**12)**    (y)(Aay ⊃ Bya)       1, UI

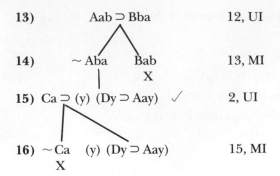

| 13) | Aab ⊃ Bba | 12, UI |
|---|---|---|
| 14) | ~ Aba    Bab | 13, MI |
| |          X | |
| 15) | Ca ⊃ (y) (Dy ⊃ Aay)  ✓ | 2, UI |
| 16) | ~Ca    (y) (Dy ⊃ Aay) | 15, MI |
| | X | |

In line 16, '(y)(Dy ⊃ Aay)' remains to be decomposed. UI followed by MI will produce two branches. If one of these contains '~ Db', that branch will be closed because of 'Db' appearing in it at 10. But the other branch will contain 'Aab', and there is nothing in the now terminated branch to close it. Hence, (36) is invalid. An argument is invalid if and only if when all the branches of its corresponding truth tree are terminated there is at least one open branch.

**(44)**                                            /∴ (w) [Cw ⊃ (z) (Dz ⊃ Bwz)]

| 1) | (x)(y)(Axy ⊃ Byx) | Pr |
|---|---|---|
| 2) | (x)[Cx ⊃ (y)(Dy ⊃ Axy)] | Pr |
| 3) | ~ (w)[Cw ⊃ (z)(Dz ⊃ Bwz)] | AP |
| 4) | (∃w) ~ [Cw ⊃ (z)(Dz ⊃ Bwz)] | 3, QD |
| 5) | ~ [Ca ⊃ (z) (Dz ⊃ Baz)]  ✓ | 4, EI |
| 6) | Ca | 5, DMI |
| 7) | ~ (z) (Dz ⊃ Baz) | 5, DMI |
| 8) | (∃z) ~ (Dz ⊃ Baz)  ✓ | 7, QD |
| 9) | ~ (Db ⊃ Bab)  ✓ | 8, EI |
| 10) | Db | 9, DMI |
| 11) | ~ Bab | 10, DMI |
| 12) | (y) (Aay ⊃ Bya) | 1, UI |
| 13) | Aab ⊃ Bba | 12, UI |
| 14) | ~ Aba    Bab | 13, MI |
| |          X | |
| 15) | Ca ⊃ (y) (Dy ⊃ Aay)  ✓ | 2, UI |

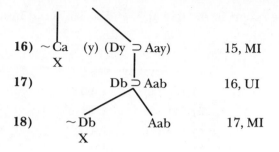

| 16) | ~Ca    (y) (Dy ⊃ Aay) | 15, MI |
| | X | |
| 17) | Db ⊃ Aab | 16, UI |
| 18) | ~Db        Aab | 17, MI |
| | X | |

Some statements in truth trees produce branches that are nonterminating. Consider this example:

$$(45) \quad (x)(\exists y)Lxy$$

Applying UI to (45) generates

**(46)**
1) $(x)(\exists y)Lxy$ ——
2) $(\exists y)Lay$    1, UI

EI can now be used with 2, but in doing so a name other than 'a' must be introduced:

**(47)**
1) $(x)(\exists y)Lxy$ ——
2) $(\exists y)Lay$ ✓ 1, UI
3) Lab    2, EI

Since a new name is introduced into the developing branch and '$(x)(\exists x)Lxy$' is assumed true of everything, UI needs to be used again with line 1 to mention 'b':

**(48)**
1) $(x)(\exists y)Lxy$ ——
2) $(\exists y)Lay$ ✓ 1, UI
3) Lab    2, EI
4) $(\exists y)Lby$    1, UI

A new existentially instantiated statement is now introduced at 4. Existential Instantiation must be applied to this line, taking care not to introduce a name that has already been mentioned:

**(49)**
1) $(x)(\exists y)Lxy$ ——
2) $(\exists y)Lay$ ✓ 1, UI
3) Lab    2, EI
4) $(\exists y)Lby$ ✓ 1, UI
5) Lbc    4, EI

Another new name occurs in the tree at 5, and so Universal Instantiation is once more applied to line 1:

(50)

1) $(x)(\exists y)Lxy$ ——
2) $(\exists y)Lay$ ✓ 1, UI
3) $Lab$ 2, EI
4) $(\exists y)Lby$ ✓ 1, UI
5) $Lbc$ 4, EI
6) $(\exists y)Lcy$ 1, UI

This move necessitates an EI move on 6, again making sure not to introduce a name already appearing in the developing branch. The procedure continues *ad infinitum*. There is no last line, and so it can never be determined whether the last line of the branch does, or does not, contradict some other line in that branch.

Any truth tree producing a **nonterminating** branch is invalid:

(51)   All men hate some person. Hence, there're men who hate themselves.

Symbolize (51) as

(52)                                    / ∴ $(\exists x)(Mx \cdot Hxx)$
1) $(x)[Mx \supset (\exists y)(Py \cdot Hxy)]$   Pr

Begin a truth tree for (52) by assuming the denial of the conclusion as a new premise and using QD on that assumption:

(53)                                    / ∴ $(\exists x)(Mx \cdot Hxx)$
1) $(x)[Mx \supset (\exists y)(Py \cdot Hxy)]$   Pr
2) $\sim (\exists x)(Mx \cdot Hxx)$   AP
3) $(x) \sim (Mx \cdot Hxx)$   2, QD

Continue the tree by taking an instance of line 1, introducing the name 'a' at every occurrence of 'x' in 'Mx ⊃ (∃y)(Py · Hxy)':

(54)                                    / ∴ $(\exists x)(Mx \cdot Hxx)$
1) $(x)[Mx \supset (\exists y)(Py \cdot Hxy)]$   Pr
2) $\sim (\exists x)(Mx \cdot Hxx)$   AP
3) $(x) \sim (Mx \cdot Hxx)$   2, QD
4) $Ma \supset (\exists y)(Py \cdot Hay)$   1, UI

Apply MI to 4:

(55)                                    / ∴ $(\exists x)(Mx \cdot Hxx)$
1) $(x)[Mx \supset (\exists y)(Py \cdot Hxy)]$   Pr
2) $\sim (\exists x)(Mx \cdot Hxx)$ ✓   AP

**3)** (x) ~ (Mx · Hxx)                           2, QD
**4)** Ma ⊃ (∃y) (Py · Hay)  ✓  1, UI

**5)** ~Ma          (∃y) (Py · Hay)  4, MI

The existential quantifier in '(∃y)(Py · Hay)' is removed by a use of EI. An 'a' already occurs in the branch of '(∃y)(Py · Hay)' Hence, the ambiguous name, 'b', is introduced in line 6:

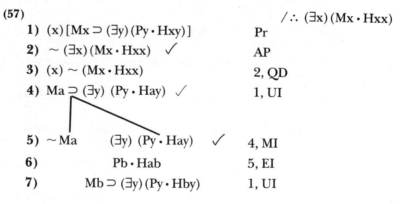

**(56)**                                        / ∴ (∃x) (Mx · Hxx)
    **1)** (x) [Mx ⊃ (∃y) (Py · Hxy)]      Pr
    **2)** ~ (∃x) (Mx · Hxx)  ✓      AP
    **3)** (x) ~ (Mx · Hxx)       2, QD
    **4)** Ma ⊃ (∃y) (Py · Hay)  ✓   1, UI

    **5)** ~Ma      (∃y) (Py · Hay)  ✓   4, MI

    **6)**          Pb · Hab       5, EI

Line 6 introduces the name of an individual not previously mentioned in that branch. But since line 1 is true of every individual, it is also true of that individual named 'b', and, hence, another instance on line 1 is required:

**(57)**                                        / ∴ (∃x) (Mx · Hxx)
    **1)** (x) [Mx ⊃ (∃y) (Py · Hxy)]      Pr
    **2)** ~ (∃x) (Mx · Hxx)  ✓      AP
    **3)** (x) ~ (Mx · Hxx)       2, QD
    **4)** Ma ⊃ (∃y) (Py · Hay)  ✓   1, UI

    **5)** ~Ma      (∃y) (Py · Hay)  ✓   4, MI
    **6)**          Pb · Hab       5, EI
    **7)**      Mb ⊃ (∃y) (Py · Hby)   1, UI

Line 7 is now decomposed, introducing '(∃y)(Py · Hby)'. Using EI on '(∃y)(Py · Hby)' introduces a new name, 'c', into the branch, requiring another use of UI on line 1—*ad infinitum*:

**(58)**                                        / ∴ (∃x) (Mx · Hxx)
    **1)** (x) [Mx ⊃ (∃y) (Py · Hxy)]      Pr
    **2)** ~ (∃x) (Mx · Hxx)  ✓      AP
    **3)** (x) ~ (Mx · Hxx)       2, QD

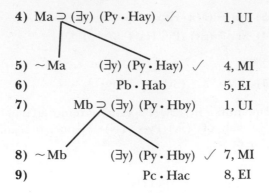

**4)**  Ma ⊃ (∃y) (Py · Hay)  ✓        1, UI

**5)**  ~Ma        (∃y) (Py · Hay)  ✓    4, MI
**6)**              Pb · Hab            5, EI
**7)**         Mb ⊃ (∃y) (Py · Hby)      1, UI

**8)**  ~Mb        (∃y) (Py · Hby)  ✓    7, MI
**9)**              Pc · Hac            8, EI

(58) contains a nonterminating branch, and so (51) is invalid.

---

## *EXERCISES*

Symbolize the following arguments using the suggested predicate logic notation. Then by truth tree methods determine if each argument is valid or invalid.

1. Some cocaine users are hooked. Hugh is a cocaine user. Hence, Hugh is hooked. (U,H;x,h)

2. No drug addict is fully productive. There're drug addicts. Consequently, some things aren't fully productive. (D,P;x)

3. Jennifer isn't an illegal drug user. Illegal drug users are stupid. Therefore, Jennifer isn't stupid. (U,S;x,j)

4. Every drug addict is miserable. Anything that's miserable is pitiable. It follows that drug addicts are pitiable. (D,M,P;x)

5. Only men are profootball players. There're athletes who are profootball players. So, some athletes are men. (M,P,A;x)

6. Any athlete is competitive. Everything motivated is competitive. Dave isn't an athlete. Thus, Dave isn't motivated. (A,C,M;x,d)

7. Every athlete is motivated only if anything motivated is skillful. Athletes are skillful. Wherefore, any skillful athlete is motivated. (A,M,S;x)

8. If every body is in motion, only those things changing are in motion. Whatever is a body is changing, while whatever is changing is in motion. Consequently, everything in motion is changing. (B,M,C;x)

9. Any nation has a large population of poor people or a substantial middle class. Every large population of poor people is accompanied by a high rate of suicide. Certain nations don't have a high rate of suicide. Consequently, some nations have a substantial middle class. (N,P,C,R;x)

10. Any loving person is ignorant to some degree only if selfish. Some persons aren't selfish. Every person is ignorant to some degree. Accordingly, a few people are loving. (L,P,I,S;x)

11. An action is good just in case it is neither selfish nor harmful. There're good actions. Hence, not every action is harmful. (A,G,S,H;x)

12. It isn't the case that some harmful actions are selfish. Actions are harmful and mean if selfish. Wherefore, there isn't some action of which it isn't true to claim that it's selfish if it's harmful. (H,A,S,M;x)

13. There isn't something vicious that is an action but not mean. It isn't true that some mean action isn't cruel. Consequently, all vicious actions are cruel. (V,A,M,H,C;x)

14. Any understanding or tolerant person is compassionate. There isn't some person who is understanding but also not both virtuous and compassionate. So, not all tolerant persons are compassionate. (U,T,P,C,V;x)

15. Some students are admired by every student. Consequently, some students admire themselves. (Sx,Ayx,Avy)

16. No person is his own father. So, anyone who was the father of every person isn't a person. (Px,Fxy,Fxx)

17. Every person appreciates someone. Therefore, some person is appreciated by everyone. (Px,Axy)

18. Every student enjoys some course. Steve is a student who will work at anything if he enjoys it. So, Steve will work at some course. (Sx,Cy,Exy,Esx,Wsx;s)

19. Nothing is a lie unless it is a falsehood. Thus, whoever tells a lie tells a falsehood. (Lx,Fx,Txy,Txz)

20. All people are critical of a few new ideas. Therefore, if anything is a new idea, some people are critical of it. (Px,Nx,Ix,Cxy,Cyx)

---

## 2.  CONSISTENCY AND INCONSISTENCY

An argument has an inconsistent premise set if there is no interpretation making all its premises true. If there is at least one interpretation making all the premises true, that premise set is consistent. Chapter 4 introduces truth tree techniques for establishing consistency and inconsistency. These methods, coupled with Universal Instantiation, Existential Instantiation, and Quantificational Denial, are used in predicate logic to determine consistency.

In using truth trees to determine consistency or inconsistency, symbolize the argument if it is not already in symbolized form. Do *not* assume the denial of the conclusion as a new premise. Using truth tree rules, decompose all the premises. If every branch terminates and is also closed, the premise set is inconsistent. If there is at least one open terminated branch, or at least one nonterminating branch, the premise set is consistent.

Consistent premises are found in both valid and invalid arguments. But if a premise set is inconsistent, that argument is valid although it is unsound. A sound argument is one that is not only valid but also has all true premises. An inconsistent premise set can never have, under any interpretation, all true premises. Arguments with inconsistent premises, while valid, are generally not useful in establishing the truth of a conclusion.*

---

*The Indirect Method of Proof relies on the inconsistency of a premise set of an argument to establish a conclusion. For a discussion of this type of proof, see Chapter 7, Section 2.

Follow how truth tree techniques are used to determine whether or not (1) has consistent premises:

**(1)** Every person is motivated or not. Anyone is motivated only if he succeeds. Some motivated persons won't succeed, however. Therefore, there're people who aren't motivated.

Symbolize (1) in this way:

**(2)**                       $/ \therefore (\exists x)(Px \cdot \sim Mx)$

   **1)** $(x)[Px \supset (Mx \vee \sim Mx)]$    Pr

   **2)** $(x)[Px \supset (Mx \supset Sx)]$    Pr

   **3)** $(\exists x)[(Mx \cdot Px) \cdot \sim Sx]$    Pr

In using truth tree techniques to establish consistency or inconsistency, do not assume the denial of the conclusion as a new premise. Instead, decompose the premises, beginning with existentially quantified statements if there are any:

**(3)**                       $/ \therefore (\exists x)(Px \cdot \sim Mx)$

   **1)** $(x)[Px \supset (Mx \vee \sim Mx)]$    Pr

   **2)** $(x)[Px \supset (Mx \supset Sx)]$    Pr

   **3)** $(\exists x)[(Mx \cdot Px) \cdot \sim Sx]$   ✓   Pr

   **4)**    $(Ma \cdot Pa) \cdot \sim Sa$   ✓    3, EI

   **5)**      $Ma \cdot Pa$   ✓    4, C

   **6)**      $\sim Sa$    4, C

   **7)**       $Ma$   ✓    5, C

   **8)**       $Pa$    5, C

Next, decompose any universally quantified premises, introducing names, when possible, to match those introduced by any use of EI:

**(4)**                       $/ \therefore (\exists x)(Px \cdot \sim Mx)$

   **1)** $(x)[Px \supset (Mx \vee \sim Mx)]$    Pr

   **2)** $(x)[Px \supset (Mx \supset Sx)]$    Pr

   **3)** $(\exists x)[(Mx \cdot Px) \cdot \sim Sx]$   ✓   Pr

   **4)**    $(Ma \cdot Pa) \cdot \sim Sa$   ✓    3, EI

   **5)**      $Ma \cdot Pa$   ✓    4, C

   **6)**      $\sim Sa$    4, C

   **7)**       $Ma$   ✓    5, C

   **8)**       $Pa$    5, C

   **9)**    $Pa \supset (Ma \vee \sim Ma)$   ✓    1, UI

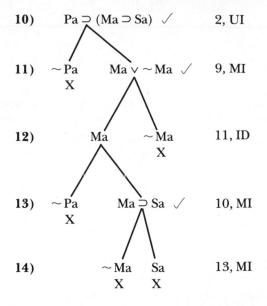

10)      Pa ⊃ (Ma ⊃ Sa)  ✓        2, UI

11)   ~Pa      Ma ∨ ~Ma  ✓        9, MI
        X

12)        Ma        ~Ma          11, ID
                        X

13)   ~Pa      Ma ⊃ Sa  ✓         10, MI
        X

14)          ~Ma   Sa             13, MI
              X     X

Each branch in (4) is closed, and (1) has consistent premises.

Does the following argument have consistent or inconsistent premises?

> **(5)**   Every dog chases some animal or another. Dogs are animals.
> Hence, some dogs chase themselves.

(5) can be symbolized like this:

**(6)**                                    / ∴ (∃x) (Dx · Cxx)

    **1)** (x) [Dx ⊃ (∃y) (Ay · Cxy)]   Pr
    **2)** (x) (Dx ⊃ Ax)             Pr

If a truth tree is begun by decomposing the first premises, this is the result:

**(7)**                                    / ∴ (∃x) (Dx · Cxx)

    **1)** (x) [Dx ⊃ (∃y) (Ay · Cxy)]   Pr
    **2)** (x) (Dx ⊃ Ax)             Pr
    **3)** Da ⊃ (∃y) (Ay · Cay)  ✓    1, UI

    **4)** ~Da     (∃y) (Ay · Cay)  ✓   3, MI
    **5)**           Ab · Cab         4, EI

The name, even though an ambiguous one, of a new individual has been introduced in line 5. So, UI again needs to be used on the first premise, changing the variable 'x' to the name 'b'. This move, however, will produce '(∃y) (Ay · Cby)' calling for a further use of EI that, in turn, will introduce yet another new name into the expanding tree. Indeed, a nonterminating branch is developing. Thus, the premises of (5) are consistent.

## *EXERCISES*

### Group A:

Symbolize the following arguments, using the suggested notation. Then, by truth tree techniques, determine whether each argument has consistent or inconsistent premises.

1. Musicians practice. Few who don't practice are musicians. Consequently, there're those who practice or aren't musicians. (M,P;x)

2. Barbara is a practicing guitarist. A guitarist is a musician. Thus, Barbara is a practicing musician. (P,G,M;b,x)

3. Guitarists practice. Musicians also practice. So, guitarists are musicians. (G,P,M;x)

4. It isn't the case that some cocaine isn't harmful. Harmful things aren't safe. Wherefore, cocaine is harmful. (C,H,S;x)

5. Crack is a drug. Anything is harmful or not a drug. Nonetheless, some drugs aren't harmful. Thus, some drugs aren't crack. (C,D,H;x)

6. It isn't true that everything is harmful or safe. Anything isn't safe only if it is harmful. Consequently, it isn't true that everything isn't both safe and not harmful. (H,S;x)

7. Cocaine is an illegal drug. Any drug is illegal if harmful. So, cocaine is a harmful drug. (C,I,D,H;x)

8. Drugs are harmful if not used properly. There're drugs that aren't used properly. So, some drugs aren't harmful. (D,H,U;x)

9. Some stocks that aren't profitable are, nonetheless, useful tax deductions. Anything that's a useful tax deduction is profitable. Consequently, some profitable stocks aren't useful tax deductions. (S,P,D;x)

10. Penny stocks are cheap investments. Not every penny stock, however, is cheap. Thus, not every penny stock is an investment. (S,C,I;x)

11. An investment is safe or risky, but not both. Many safe investments are profitable. It follows that some risky investments aren't profitable. (I,S,R,P;x)

12. Investments are profitable only if they're safe. Many investments are neither safe nor not profitable. Hence, there're profitable investments that aren't safe. (I,P,S;x)

13. Earnings are safe when and only when they're guaranteed. Not all earnings are risky or profitable. So, few guaranteed earnings are profitable. (E,S,G,P;x)

14. Anything grave is dangerous if ignored. Cases of herpes are ignored or grave. Cases of herpes are grave. Numerous cases of herpes aren't ignored. Therefore, a few cases of herpes aren't dangerous. (G,D,I;x)

15. A great number of heterosexual students ignore *AIDS* to their own peril. A student who ignores *AIDS* to her own peril is at risk of developing it. Any student at risk of developing *AIDS* ought to be careful in her activities. So, heterosexual students ought to be careful in their activities. (H,S,I,R,C;x)

16. Unfortunately, scleroderma exists. Scleroderma will be eliminated only if there is a drug that cures it. Scleroderma will be eliminated. Consequently, there will be a drug that cures scleroderma. (Sx,Ex,Dy,Cyx)

17. Everyone believes something only if they aren't cynical. Yet some cynical people believe everything. So, there're people who believe something yet aren't cynics. (Px,Cx,Bxy)

18. No one who ruins some person is trustworthy. Many cynics are people who ruin some person or another. Hence, no cynic is trustworthy. (Px,Cx,Py,Tx,Rxy)

19. A few draconian cuts will be taken against all projects. Draconian cuts are severe moves. So, something severe will be taken against every project. (Dx,Cx,Px,Sx,Mx,Txy)

20. There aren't government projects not overly expensive. Anything spent on something overly expensive is wasted. There're taxes spent on some government projects. Consequently, some taxes are wasted. (Gx,Px,Ex,Wx,Tx,Sxy)

**Group B:**

For those arguments in *Group A* having a consistent premise set determine which are valid and which invalid.

---

## 3. CONTRADICTIONS, LOGICALLY TRUE STATEMENTS AND CONTINGENT STATEMENTS

Chapter 4 introduces truth tree techniques to determine if truth functional statements are contradictory, tautological, or contingent. These same techniques, coupled with truth tree rules governing quantifiers, can be used in predicate logic to determine if a statement is contradictory, logically true, or contingent. In predicate logic, a statement is *contradictory* just in case there is no possible interpretation making it true. A statement in predicate logic is *logically true* when and only when there is no possible interpretation making that statement false. And a statement in predicate logic is *contingent* if and only if it is neither contradictory nor logically true.

Suppose someone said

> **(1)** Instructors are disagreeable or helpful, yet even so a few instructors, while not helpful, aren't disagreeable.

Is (1) contradictory, logically true, or contingent? To answer this question, first put (1) into predicate logic notation:

> **(2)**  $(x)[Ix \supset (Dx \lor Hx)] \cdot (\exists x)[(Ix \cdot \sim Hx) \cdot \sim Dx]$

Next, develop a truth tree for (2):

**(3)**

| | | |
|---|---|---|
| 1) | $(x)[Ix \supset (Dx \lor Hx)] \cdot (\exists x)[(Ix \cdot \sim Hx) \cdot \sim Dx]$ ✓ | —— |
| 2) | $(x)[Ix \supset (Dx \lor Hx)]$ | 1, C |
| 3) | $(\exists x)[(Ix \cdot \sim Hx) \cdot \sim Dx]$ ✓ | 1, C |
| 4) | $(Ia \cdot \sim Ha) \cdot \sim Da$ ✓ | 3, EI |
| 5) | $Ia \cdot \sim Ha$ ✓ | 4, C |
| 6) | $\sim Da$ | 4, C |
| 7) | $Ia$ | 5, C |
| 8) | $\sim Ha$ | 5, C |

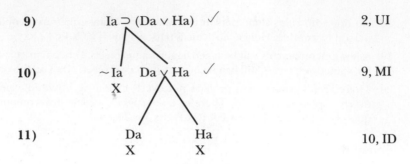

| | | |
|---|---|---|
| **9)** | Ia ⊃ (Da ∨ Ha)  ✓ | 2, UI |
| **10)** | ~Ia    Da ∨ Ha  ✓ | 9, MI |
|  | X | |
| **11)** | Da      Ha | 10, ID |
|  | X       X | |

Since there are no open branches in (3), (1) is contradictory.

Imagine hearing this rather cheerless remark:

>   **(4)**   If there're people who hate everything, there're people who hate themselves.

Is (4) contradictory, logically true, or contingent? First, symbolize (4):

>   **(5)**   (∃x)[Px · (y)Hxy] ⊃ (∃x)(Px · Hxx)

Second, determine by truth tree methods whether (5) is contradictory or not:

**(6)**

| | | |
|---|---|---|
| **1)** | (∃x)[Px · (y)Hxy] ⊃ (∃x)(Px · Hxx)  ✓ | ‒‒‒ |
| **2)** | ~ (∃x)[Px · (y) Hxy]          (∃x)(Px · Hxx)  ✓ | 1, MI |
| **3)** | (x) ~ [Px · (y) Hxy] | 2, QD |
| **4)** | ~ [Pa · (y) Hay]  ✓ | 3, UI |
| **5)** | ~ Pa   ~ (y) Hay  ✓ | 4, DC |
| **6)** | (∃y) ~ Hay  ✓ | 5, QD |
| **7)** | ~ Hab | 6, EI |
| **8)** | Pa · Haa  ✓ | 2, EI |
| **9)** | Pa | 8, C |
| **10)** | Haa | 8, C |

(6) shows that (5) is not contradictory. Next, assume the denial of (5) and develop a truth tree for that statement. If the denial of (5) is contradictory, then (5) must be logically true.

**(7)**

| | | |
|---|---|---|
| **1)** | ~ {(∃x)[Px · (y)Hxy] ⊃ (∃x)(Px · Hxx)}  ✓  ‒‒‒ | |
| **2)** | (∃x)[Px · (y)Hxy]  ✓ | 1, DMI |
| **3)** | ~ (∃x)(Px · Hxx)  ✓ | 1, DMI |

| | | |
|---|---|---|
| **4)** | (x) ~ (Px · Hxx) | 3, QD |
| **5)** | Pa · (y)Hay  ✓ | 2, EI |
| **6)** | Pa | 5, C |
| **7)** | (y)Hay | 5, C |
| **8)** | Haa | 7, UI |
| **9)** | ~ (Pa · Haa)  ✓ | 4, UI |
| **10)** | ~ Pa        ~Haa | 9, DC |
| | X            X | |

Every path in (7) is closed. The denial of (5) is a contradiction. Therefore, (5) must be logically true.

Contingent statements are neither contradictory nor logically true. Two truth trees are needed to establish that a statement is contingent. Consider this example:

> **(8)**   Every person wants something or another only if there are
> some goals wanted by everyone.

(8) can go into symbols as

$$\textbf{(9)}\quad (x)[(\exists y)(Px \cdot Wxy) \supset (\exists y)(Gy \cdot Wxy)]$$

Begin by attempting to show that (3) is contradictory:

**(10)**

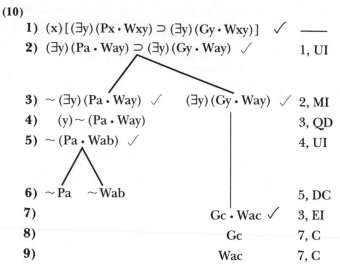

| | | |
|---|---|---|
| **1)** | (x)[(∃y)(Px · Wxy) ⊃ (∃y)(Gy · Wxy)]  ✓ —— | |
| **2)** | (∃y)(Pa · Way) ⊃ (∃y)(Gy · Way)  ✓ | 1, UI |
| **3)** | ~ (∃y)(Pa · Way)  ✓      (∃y)(Gy · Way)  ✓ | 2, MI |
| **4)** | (y) ~ (Pa · Way) | 3, QD |
| **5)** | ~ (Pa · Wab)  ✓ | 4, UI |
| **6)** | ~ Pa    ~Wab | 5, DC |
| **7)** | Gc · Wac  ✓ | 3, EI |
| **8)** | Gc | 7, C |
| **9)** | Wac | 7, C |

The open paths show that '(x)[(∃y)(Px · Wxy) ⊃ (∃y)(Gy · Wxy)]' is not contradictory. However, is it logically true? Assume the denial of this statement and proceed to generate a truth tree:

**(11)**

**1)**  ~ (x)[(∃y)(Px · Wxy) ⊃ (∃y)(Gy · Wxy)]  ✓ ——

| | | | |
|---|---|---|---|
| **2)** | $(\exists x) \sim [(\exists y)(Px \cdot Wxy) \supset (\exists y)(Gy \cdot Wxy)]$ ✓ | 1, QD |
| **3)** | $\sim [(\exists y)(Pa \cdot Way) \supset (\exists y)(Gy \cdot Way)]$ ✓ | 2, EI |
| **4)** | $(\exists y)(Pa \cdot Way)$ ✓ | 3, DMI |
| **5)** | $\sim (\exists y)(Gy \cdot Way)$ ✓ | 3, DMI |
| **6)** | $(y) \sim (Gy \cdot Way)$ | 5, QD |
| **7)** | $Pa \cdot Wab$ ✓ | 4, EI |
| **8)** | $\sim (Gb \cdot Wab)$ ✓ | 6, UI |
| **9)** | $Pa$ | 7, C |
| **10)** | $Wab$ | 7, C |

$$
\begin{array}{ccc}
& \diagup \quad \diagdown & \\
\textbf{11)} \qquad Gb & \qquad \sim Wab & \qquad 8, DC
\end{array}
$$

'$(x)[(\exists y)(Px \cdot Wxy) \supset (\exists y)(Gy \cdot Wxy)]$' is not logically true since its denial is not a contradiction. Because (8) is neither contradictory nor logically true, it must be contingent. Note that any statement generating a truth tree with a nonterminating path is contingent.

---

## EXERCISES

Symbolize the following statements, using the suggested notation. Then, by truth tree techniques, determine whether each statement is contradictory, logically true, or contingent.

1. Everything is expensive only if some things are. (E;x)

2. Nothing expensive is cheap. (E,C;x)

3. A few expensive things are neither not cheap nor expensive. (E,C;x)

4. When every person loves anything at all, then each person loves something. (Px,Lxy)

5. If every person wants something or another, some persons want everything. (Px,Wxy)

6. Drugs are useful, yet some things are not drugs but are useful. (D,U;x)

7. Every drug is harmful or a few aren't—but not both. (D,H;x)

8. While many things are harmful, not every drug is. (H,D;x)

9. Not all drugs aren't harmful if, and only if, some are. (D,H;x)

10. Some potent drugs aren't beneficial if not every drug is potent or beneficial. (P,D,B;x)

11. Some potent things are beneficial drugs. (P,B,D;x)

12. There're potent drugs that aren't beneficial even though drugs are beneficial. (P,D,B;x)

13. Every student makes a few good grades. (Sx,Gy,Mxy)

14. Some students don't attend any classes. (Sx,Cy,Axy)

15. Students are industrious or lazy (but not both), and while some students aren't lazy, neither are they industrious. (S,I,L;x)

16. Not every student makes a few good grades, but most do. (Sx,Gy,Mxy)

17. Any student makes a few good grades or some students don't make all good grades. (Sx,Gy,Mxy)

18. Many lazy students don't achieve when and only when every lazy student does achieve. (L,S,A;x)

19. Every teacher enjoys some students, but no teacher enjoys every student. (Tx,Sy,Exy)

20. Assuming some people are critical of new ideas, then if anything is a new idea, there're people critical of it. (Px,Ny,Iy,Cxy)

---

## 4.   LOGICAL EQUIVALENCE

Two statements are logically equivalent if and only if a biconditional statement formed from those statements is logically true. To use truth trees to show that two statements are logically equivalent, first form a biconditional composed of those statements. For example, are the following two statements logically equivalent?

**(1)**

    **a)** $(\exists x)(Ax \lor Bx)$

    **b)** $(\exists x)Ax \lor (\exists x)Bx$

Form a biconditional from these statements:

**(2)**   $(\exists x)(Ax \lor Bx) \equiv [(\exists x)Ax \lor (\exists x)Bx]$

If (2) is logically true, the statements in (1) are logically equivalent. To determine whether (2) is logically true, generate a truth tree for the *denial* of (2). If the denial of (2) is contradictory, (2) is logically true:

**(3)**

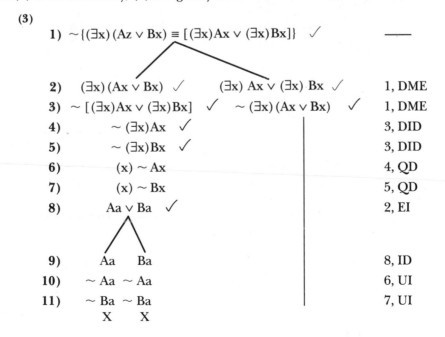

| | | | |
|---|---|---|---|
| 1) | $\sim\{(\exists x)(Az \lor Bx) \equiv [(\exists x)Ax \lor (\exists x)Bx]\}$ ✓ | | —— |
| 2) | $(\exists x)(Ax \lor Bx)$ ✓     $(\exists x)Ax \lor (\exists x)Bx$ ✓ | | 1, DME |
| 3) | $\sim[(\exists x)Ax \lor (\exists x)Bx]$ ✓   $\sim(\exists x)(Ax \lor Bx)$ ✓ | | 1, DME |
| 4) | $\sim(\exists x)Ax$ ✓ | | 3, DID |
| 5) | $\sim(\exists x)Bx$ ✓ | | 3, DID |
| 6) | $(x)\sim Ax$ | | 4, QD |
| 7) | $(x)\sim Bx$ | | 5, QD |
| 8) | $Aa \lor Ba$ ✓ | | 2, EI |
| 9) | $Aa$    $Ba$ | | 8, ID |
| 10) | $\sim Aa$   $\sim Aa$ | | 6, UI |
| 11) | $\sim Ba$   $\sim Ba$ | | 7, UI |
| | X     X | | |

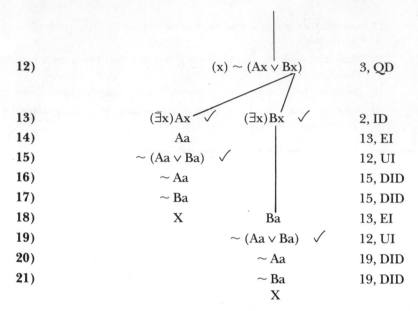

| | | | |
|---|---|---|---|
| **12)** | (x) ~ (Ax ∨ Bx) | | 3, QD |
| **13)** | (∃x)Ax ✓    (∃x)Bx ✓ | | 2, ID |
| **14)** | Aa | | 13, EI |
| **15)** | ~ (Aa ∨ Ba) ✓ | | 12, UI |
| **16)** | ~ Aa | | 15, DID |
| **17)** | ~ Ba | | 15, DID |
| **18)** | X | Ba | 13, EI |
| **19)** | | ~ (Aa ∨ Ba) ✓ | 12, UI |
| **20)** | | ~ Aa | 19, DID |
| **21)** | | ~ Ba | 19, DID |
| | | X | |

Every branch in (3) is closed and ' ~ {(∃x)(Ax ∨ Bx) ≡ [(∃x)Ax ∨ (∃x) Bx]}' is a contradiction. So, **'(∃x)(Ax ∨ Bx) ≡ [(∃x)Ax ∨ (∃x)Bx]'** is logically true. Thus, the statements in (1) are logically equivalent.

---

## *EXERCISES*

Symbolize the following pairs of statements, using the suggested notation. Then, by truth tree techniques, determine whether each pair is logically equivalent or not.

1.  a) Computers are fast. (C,F;x)
    b) It isn't true that there're computers that aren't fast. (C,F;x)

2.  a) Anything is either fast or not a computer. (F,C;x)
    b) Many things that aren't computers are fast. (C,F;x)

3.  a) Some things are fast computers. (F,C;x)
    b) Some things are fast and some things are computers. (F,C;x)

4.  a) There isn't something infected with herpes that is, nonetheless, healthy. (I,H;x)
    b) Nothing infected with herpes is healthy. (I,H;x)

5.  a) Many things not infected with Crohn's disease aren't healthy. (I,H;x)
    b) Not everything is healthy or infected with Crohn's disease. (H,I;x)

6.  a) Not everything infectious is deadly. (I,D;x)
    b) Many infectious things aren't deadly. (I,D;x)

7.  a) Not all illnesses are deadly. (I,D;x)
    b) No illnesses are deadly. (I,D;x)

8. a) Anything is both temporal and spatial. (T,S;x)
   b) Everything is temporal and all things are spatial. (T,S;x)

9. a) Every spatial thing is temporal. (S,T;x)
   b) Every temporal thing is spatial. (T,S;x)

10. a) Anything is spatial or temporal. (S,T;x)
    b) Anything is spatial or everything is temporal. (S,T;x)

11. a) Anyone is kind if loving. (P,K,L;x)
    b) No unkind person is loving. (K,P,L;x)

12. a) Everyone loves someone or another. (Px,Lxy)
    b) Someone loves everyone. (Px,Lxy)

13. a) Everyone is kind or hateful, but not both. (P,K,H;x)
    b) There isn't a person who is hateful if and only if kind. (P,H,K;x)

14. a) Everyone who dislikes himself is disliked by someone else. (Px,Dyx)
    b) Everyone who is disliked by someone else dislikes himself. (Px,Dxy)

15. a) There're people who, trusting no one, don't trust themselves. (Px,Txy)
    b) Not all people who trust themselves don't trust anyone. (Px,Txy)

---

## 5.  REVIEW OF NEW TERMS

**Ambiguous name:**  The name of an individual introduced into a truth tree by EI where nothing is known concerning the individual mentioned by this name except those properties mentioned in the existentially quantified statement upon which EI was used to introduce the ambiguous name.

**Consistent premises:**  The premises of an argument are consistent if and only if there is at least one interpretation making all the premises true.

**Existential Instantiation (EI):**  The rule of decomposition—

### EXISTENTIAL INSTANTIATION

$$(\exists\alpha)\Phi\alpha$$
$$|$$
$$\Phi\beta$$

where (1) '$\beta$' occurs in '$\Phi\beta$' at all those places where '$\alpha$' occurs free in '$\Phi\alpha$', (2) '$\beta$' is an ambiguous name, (3) this name has not previously occurred in the branch to which '$\Phi\beta$' is appended, and (4) '$\Phi\beta$' is appended to every branch in which '$(\exists\alpha) \Phi\alpha$' previously appears.

**Instance:**  Any statement introduced into a truth tree by either EI or UI.

**Nonterminating branch:**  A branch in a truth tree that never resolves into only simple statements and simple statements prefixed with one tilde.

**Quantificational Denial (QD):**  The rule of decomposition—

### QUANTIFICATIONAL DENIAL

$$\sim (\alpha)\Phi\alpha \qquad\qquad \sim (\exists\alpha)\Phi\alpha$$
$$|\qquad\qquad\qquad\qquad |$$
$$(\exists\alpha) \sim \Phi\alpha \qquad\qquad (\alpha) \sim \Phi\alpha$$

**Universal Instantiation (UI):**  The rule of decomposition—

### UNIVERSAL INSTANTIATION

$$(\alpha)\Phi\alpha$$
$$|$$
$$\Phi_\beta$$

where (1) '$\beta$' is the name of an individual that (2) occurs in '$\Phi_\beta$' at all those places where '$\alpha$' occurs free in '$\Phi\alpha$'.

# 12

# PREDICATE LOGIC: PROOF CONSTRUCTION

Chapter 9 introduces predicate logic and discusses techniques useful in symbolizing. To symbolize an argument is not to construct a proof, however. This chapter develops new elementary rules of inference. These rules, coupled with those of truth-functional logic, provide the tools required to construct proofs in predicate logic. Strategies developed in terms of *HAVE*, *WANT*, *USE*, and *NEED* are retained and refined. New strategies for further, more advanced, proof construction are also introduced.

## 1.  GETTING STARTED

To develop new rules of transformation in predicate logic, it is convenient to continue using several Greek letters. Let 'α and 'β' stand for any individual variable or individual constant. If 'α' and 'β' represent individual variables, then 'Φα' and 'Φβ' stand for any statement function containing at least one free occurrence of 'α' or 'β'. Each of the following statement functions is an instance of 'Φα' or 'Φβ':

$$Ax$$
$$Ax \supset Bx$$
$$(y)Ay \equiv Dx$$
$$Ax \supset (\exists y)Bxy$$

Notice that each example in (1) has at least one predicate letter followed by a free individual variable. Hence, each example is a statement function.*

---

* To review the concept *statement function*, see Chapter 10, Section 2.

If '$\alpha$' and '$\beta$' stand for individual constants, '$\Phi\alpha$' or '$\Phi\beta$' depict statements such as

$$\sim Aa$$
$$Ab \triangle Bb$$
$$(Aa \cdot Bc) \supset Dac$$

Let '$(\alpha)$' represent any universal quantifier. Then '$(\alpha)\Phi\alpha$' pictures any universally quantified statement. Examples are:

$$(x)(Ax \equiv Bx)$$
$$(y)[(Ay \cdot By) \supset Cy]$$
$$(z)[Az \supset (\exists w)(Bzw \triangle Czw)]$$

If '$(\exists\alpha)$' pictures any existential quantifier, '$(\exists\alpha)\Phi\alpha$' portrays any existentially quantified statement. Here are some examples:

$$(\exists x)(Ax \cdot Bx)$$
$$(\exists x)(y)Axy$$
$$(\exists z) \sim [(Az \cdot Bz) \vee Cz]$$

In both '$(\alpha)\Phi\alpha$' and '$(\exists\alpha)\Phi\alpha$' the quantifier extends over the entire statement. '$(\alpha)\Phi\alpha$' does not depict '$(x)(Px \supset Lx) \supset Pj$' nor does '$(\exists\alpha)\Phi\alpha$' portray '$Ag \equiv (\exists x)Ax$'.

The concept *substitution instance* is essential in discussing rules and strategies in predicate logic:

> A *substitution instance* of a statement function '$\Phi\alpha$' is the result of replacing every free occurrence of '$\alpha$' in '$\Phi\alpha$' by the same individual constant or the same individual variable.

Assume that '$Ax \supset Bx$' is a statement function represented by '$\Phi\alpha$'. Then both '$Ac \supset Bc$' and '$Ag \supset Bg$' are substitution instances of '$\Phi\alpha$', as is '$Aw \supset Bw$'. But '$Aa \supset Bx$' and '$Af \supset Bi$' are not substitution instances of '$\Phi\alpha$'. Nor is '$Ax \supset By$'. Notice in '$Aa \supset Bx$' not *every* free occurrence of '$\alpha$', namely '$x$', is replaced by an individual constant. '$Af \supset Bi$' fails as a substitution instance of '$\Phi\alpha$' because not every free occurrence of '$\alpha$' is replaced by the *same* individual constant. In '$Ax \supset By$' every free occurrence of '$\alpha$' is not replaced by the *same* individual variable '$y$'. It is necessary to follow every substitution restriction in applying each of the elementary rules of inference introduced in this chapter.

## 2. UNIVERSAL INSTANTIATION AND UNIVERSAL GENERALIZATION

Assuming a statement, '$(\alpha)\Phi\alpha$', is true of every member of some universe of discourse, then a particular substitution instance of '$\Phi\alpha$' must also be true for any specific member of that universe.* Accept the following as true:

(1)   All humans are risible.

---

* To review the concept *universe of discourse*, see Chapter 10, Section 2.

(1) can be symbolized as

$$(2) \quad (x)(Hx \supset Rx)$$

Since (1) is accepted as true, any substitution instance of the statement function, 'Hx ⊃ Rx', must be true. For example, each of the following must be true:

**(3)**  If Annye Mae is human, then Annye Mae is risible.
     If Bob is human, then Bob is risible.
     If Carlos is human, then Carlos is risible.
     If Debbra is human, then Debbra is risible.

Each statement mentioned in (3) is symbolized as a substitution instance of 'Hx ⊃ Rx':

**(4)**  Ha ⊃ Ra
     Hb ⊃ Rb
     Hc ⊃ Rc
     Hd ⊃ Rd

In general

'$(\alpha)\Phi\alpha$' is true if and only if every possible substitution instance of an individual constant in '$\Phi\alpha$' at every occurrence of '$\alpha$' turns '$\Phi\alpha$' into a true statement.

This observation leads to the first of two rules governing the universal quantifier.
*Universal Instantiation* is an argument form that, under certain circumstances, permits the removal of a universal quantifier:

### UNIVERSAL INSTANTIATION (UI)

$$\frac{(\alpha)\ \Phi\alpha}{/\therefore\ \Phi_\beta}$$

Let '$\beta$' represent any individual constant. That is, '$\beta$' stands for the name of an individual in the universe of discourse to which '$(\alpha)\Phi\alpha$' refers. Beginning with a universally quanitfied statement, an *instance* of that statement is obtained by first removing the universal quantifier. Next, the same individual constant is substituted in the resulting statement function, '$\Phi\alpha$', at each occurrence, and only those occurrences, of the individual variable, '$\alpha$', originally bound to the removed quantifier. Following these steps, a universally quantified statement is *instantiated* as '$\Phi_\beta$'. Note that because Universal Instantiation is an argument form, indicated by '$\therefore$', it can be read only from top to bottom and must be applied to entire statements when used in constructing a proof of validity.

Once a universal quantifier is removed, any elementary rule of inference in truth-functional logic, as well as any truth-functional strategies, might possibly be used with '$\Phi_\beta$'. Examine this argument:

**(5)**  All Rotarians are helpful. Mike is a Rotarian.
     Accordingly, Mike is helpful.

Symbolizing (5) produces

**(6)**                                           / ∴ Hm

**1)** (x)(Rx ⊃ Hx)     Pr

**2)** Rm                      Pr

The first premise declares something to be true of anything in the universe. No matter what that thing is, if it is a Rotarian, then it is also helpful. If the first premise is true of every possible thing, then it is true of Mike, mentioned in the second premise. Thus, (6) can be continued and the new statement justified by an appeal to Universal Instantiation:

**(7)**                                           / ∴ Hm

**1)** (x)(Rx ⊃ Hx)     Pr

**2)** Rm                      Pr

**3)** Rm ⊃ Hm            1, UI

The conclusion, 'Hm', of the argument is the consequent in 3. Line 2 asserts the antecedent found in 3 is true. So, an appeal to Modus Ponens establishes the conclusion:

**(8)**                                           / ∴ Hm

**1)** (x)(Rx ⊃ Hx)     Pr

**2)** Rm                      Pr

**3)** Rm ⊃ Hm            1, UI

**4)** / ∴ Hm                3, 2, MP

If the first premise of (5) is true, it can be instantiated in terms of any individual. Alice might be mentioned at line 3:

**(9)**                                           / ∴ Hm

**1)** (x)(Rx ⊃ Hx)     Pr

**2)** Rm                      Pr

**3)** Ra ⊃ Ha             1, UI

Line 3 is correct in the sense that Universal Instantiation is properly used. However, 'Ra ⊃ Ha' is not helpful in obtaining 'Hm'. Only by instantiating the first premise in terms of 'm' is the conclusion reached. An important strategy in using Universal Instantiation is this. If a specific individual is mentioned in a premise or the conclusion of an argument, consider instantiating universally quantified statements in terms of the name of that individual.

As an argument form, Universal Instantiation can be used only on whole statements in a proof. For instance, each of the following moves from 1 to 2 is incorrect:

**(10)**

**1)** (∃z)Az ⊃ (x)Cx     Pr

*WRONG X* **2)** (∃z)Az ⊃ Ca          1, UI

In (10) an attempt is made to use Universal Instantiation on only the consequent of the statement mentioned in 1. But Universal Instantiation can never be used on part of a statement.

**(11)**

1) $(x)Bx \supset (\exists y)By$    Pr

*WRONG X*   2) $Bd \supset (\exists y)By$       1, UI

Notice that in (11) an attempt is made to use Universal Instantiation on only the antecedent of a statement. Again, this is an incorrect move because Universal Instantiation can only be used on entire statements.

The following use of Universal Instantiation is also incorrect:

**(12)**                          $/ \therefore Ag \supset Cg$

1) $(x)(Ax \supset Bx) \cdot (x)(Bx \supset Cx)$    Pr

*WRONG X*   2) $(Ag \supset Bg) \cdot (x)(Bx \supset Cx)$       1, UI

While Universal Instantiation must never be used on parts of a statement, a proof for (12) can be constructed:

**(13)**                         $/ \therefore Ag \supset Cg$

1) $(x)(Ax \supset Bx) \cdot (x)(Bx \supset Cx)$    Pr

2) $(x)(Ax \supset Bx)$              1, Simp

3) $Ag \supset Bg$                   2, UI

4) $(x)(Bx \supset Cx) \cdot (x)(Ax \supset Bx)$    1, Com

5) $(x)(Bx \supset Cx)$              4, Simp

6) $Bg \supset Cg$                   5, UI

7) $/ \therefore Ag \supset Cg$            3, 6, HS

The concept substitution instance also permits the substitution of an individual variable, instead of an individual constant, at every free occurence of '$\beta$' in '$\Phi\beta$' in Universal Instantiation. Each of the following is a legitimate use of UI:

**(14)**

1) $(x)(Px \supset Dx)$    Pr

2) $Px \supset Dx$         1, UI

1) $(x)(Px \supset Dx)$    Pr

2) $Py \supset Dy$         1, UI

1) $(x)(Px \supset Dx)$    Pr

2) $Pz \supset Dz$         1, UI

In using UI to introduce free individual variables into a proof, '$\beta$' must occur free in '$\Phi\beta$' at all those places, and only those places, where '$\alpha$' is free in '$\Phi\alpha$'. *Remember,

---

* The need for this restriction becomes clear in Section 6.

Universal Instantiation permits moves from general statements to singular ones as well as from statements to statement functions. But why introduce free individual variables into a proof?

Suppose a proof is being constructed in which no particular individual is mentioned in the premises or conclusion. In such a case, one is not concerned with a specific individual. Rather, one is interested in properties shared by all individuals of a certain sort. To show this general concern, no specific individual constant is introduced into the proof. Instead, individual variables are used as substitution instances of 'α' in 'Φα'. This results in introducing a statement function into a proof. Remember that a statement function is neither true nor false. Yet any statement function introduced into a proof by Universal Instantiation can be converted into a true statement. This is done by consistently substituting the same name of an individual at every occurrence of any individual variable originally bound to that quantifier removed by an application of UI. No matter what individual constant is substituted 'α' in 'Φα', that substitution instance converts 'Φα' into a true statement. So, a statement function derived by Universal Instantiation can be treated as if it were a statement for purposes of a proof of an argument.*

---

* This procedure of introducing statement functions containing individual variables into a proof is similar to a practice common in constructing proofs in Euclidian geometry. Suppose a proof is to be constructed for "Proposition 6" of *Book I* of Euclid's *Elements*:

> If two angles of a triangle be equal to one another, the sides also which subtend, or are opposite to, the equal angles, shall be equal to one another.

The first step in the proof is

> Let ABC be a triangle having the angle ABC equal to the angle ACB: the side AC shall be equal to the side AB.

Of course *ABC* is *any* triangle having certain properties. But then a *specific* triangle appears in the scholium of the text:

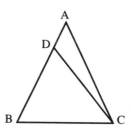

The actual proof is carried through in relation to this specific triangle. The final assertion is the general theorem to be proved. The proof assumes that the particular triangle drawn in the scholium is completely representative of all other triangles of a certain sort; namely, those in which "∠ ABC = ∠ ACB" holds. Thus, what is proven to be the case about this specific, but completely representative, triangle is also held to be proven about all other triangles of that type. A legitimate use of Universal Instantiation can be viewed as introducing the name of an individual completely representative of all individuals of a certain sort.

In Chapter 10, Section 2, the range of the statement variables 'p', 'q', 'r', and 's', is extended to include not only statements, but statement functions as well. This extension of the range of statement variables is vital for predicate logic. However, coupled with the need to extend the range of these varables, there is also a demand to broaden the concept *proof of validity* introduced and developed in Chapter 5. There, in Section 1, the notion of a proof of validity is introduced as

> a finite sequence of statements, beginning with the premises of an argu-
> ment and ending with the conclusion, such that each step in the proof
> displays at least one elementary rule of inference.

With the introduction of Universal Instantiation and the extension of the range of statement variables, this notion of *proof* is expanded in this way:

> **A** *proof of validity* **is a finite sequence of statements and/or statement
> functions each of which is either a premise or obtained from a premise, or
> premises, by some rule of transformation. While all premises and the
> conclusion must be statements, in other lines statement functions can
> appear.**

The second argument form governing the universal quantifier is *Universal Generalization*. Consider this argument:

> **(15)**   Every poet is an artist. None but dreamers are artists.
> So, each poet is a dreamer.

(15) is symbolized as

> **(16)**                                   $/\therefore (x)(Px \supset Dx)$
> **1)** $(x)(Px \supset Ax)$   Pr
> **2)** $(x)(Ax \supset Dx)$   Pr

Since no specific individual is mentioned in (15), use Universal Instantiation to obtain

> **3)** $Px \supset Ax$   1, UI
> **4)** $Ax \supset Dx$   2, UI

An appeal to Hypothetical Syllogism establishes

> **5)** $Px \supset Dx$   3, 4, HS

The conclusion of (16), '$(x)(Px \supset Dx)$', is the statement function '$Px \supset Dx$', universally quantified.

Notice how '$(x)(Px \supset Dx)$' is obtained. No free individual variable is found in 3, 4 or 5 that is not introduced into the proof by Universal Instantiation. The statement function in 5 is produced by using Hypothetical Syllogism. Thus, assuming the truth of the premises, '$Px \supset Dx$' can be transformed into a true statement. This is done by substituting *any* individual constant at 'x', the same individual constant being substituted at each occurrence of 'x'. Since '$Px \supset Dx$' can be converted into a true statement by mentioning *any* individual, it can be viewed as true of *all* individuals. A complete proof of (16) is now constructed:

| (17) | | /∴ (x)(Px ⊃ Dx) |
|---|---|---|
| **1)** (x)(Px ⊃ Ax) | Pr | |
| **2)** (x)(Ax ⊃ Dx) | Pr | |
| **3)** Px ⊃ Ax | 1, UI | |
| **4)** Ax ⊃ Dx | 2, UI | |
| **5)** Px ⊃ Dx | 3, 4, HS | |
| **6)** /∴ (x)(Px ⊃ Dx) | 5, UG | |

Universal Generalization in proof construction permits, under certain restrictions, a universal quantifier to be appended to a statement function containing free individual variables:

### UNIVERSAL GENERALIZATION (*UG*)

$$\frac{\Phi\beta}{/\therefore \ (\alpha)\Phi\alpha}$$

Important restrictions are placed on using Universal Generalization. These restrictions are : (1), '$\beta$' is an individial variable that occurs free in '$\Phi\beta$' at all, and only, those places where '$\alpha$' is an individual variable that occurs free in '$\Phi\alpha$' *; (2), '$\Phi\beta$' is obtained only from statements in which '$\beta$' does not occur as a free individual variable, and (3), no free individual variable, coming from an existentially quantified statement, can occur in '$\Phi\alpha$'. This third restriction is to prevent moves from true assertions about *some* individuals having a given property to a false claim about *all* individuals having that same property.

Examine this proof:

| (18) | | /∴ (x){[Ax · (Bx · Ex)] ⊃ Dx} |
|---|---|---|
| **1)** (x){[Ax · (Bx · Cx)] ⊃ Dx} | Pr | |
| **2)** (x)[(Bx · Ex) ⊃ Cx] | Pr | |

Both premises and the conclusion of (18) are universally quantified statements. This conclusion can be obtained by Universal Generalization if

**(19)**

**n)** [Ax · (Bx · Ex)] ⊃ Dx

is first secured. To reach (19), a free individual variable, such as 'x', must be

---

* Notice that while '$\alpha$' is bound in '$(\alpha)\Phi\alpha$', it is free in '$\Phi\alpha$'. In '$(\alpha)\Phi\alpha$' the first occurrence of '$\alpha$' is in the quantifier, while its second occurrence falls under the scope of the quantifier. In '$\Phi\alpha$', '$\alpha$' is found in neither the quantifier nor bound to any quantifier. Hence '$\alpha$' occurs free in '$\Phi\alpha$'.

introduced into the proof by Universal Instantiation. The next two lines in a proof of (18) are, therefore, these:

**(20)**

3) $[Ax \cdot (Bx \cdot Cx)] \supset Dx$    1, UI
4) $(Bx \cdot Ex) \supset Cx$           2, UI

Once the premises are instantiated, any truth-functional rule of inference can be used to construct (19).

Continuing a proof for (18), compare the statement functions in 3 and 4 of (20) with (19). 'Cx' must be eliminated before reaching (19). The statement functions in 3 and 4 are hypotheticals with 'Cx' in the antecedent of one and in the consequent of the other. So, anticipate a use of Hypothetical Syllogism:

**(21)**

5) $[Ax \cdot (Cx \cdot Bx)] \supset Dx$    3, Com
6) $[(Cx \cdot Bx) \cdot Ax] \supset Dx$    5, Com
7) $[Cx \cdot (Bx \cdot Ax)] \supset Dx$    6, Assoc
8) $Cx \supset [(Bx \cdot Ax) \supset Dx]$  7, Exp
9) $(Bx \cdot Ex) \supset [(Bx \cdot Ax) \supset Dx]$    4, 8, HS

Next, reduce the number of occurrences of 'Bx' in 9 by a use of Tautology:

**(22)**

10) $[(Bx \cdot Ex) \cdot (Bx \cdot Ax)] \supset Dx$    9, Exp
11) $\{[(Bx \cdot Ex) \cdot Bx] \cdot Ax\} \supset Dx$    10, Assoc
12) $\{[Bx \cdot (Bx \cdot Ex)] \cdot Ax\} \supset Dx$    11, Com
13) $\{[(Bx \cdot Bx) \cdot Ex] \cdot Ax\} \supset Dx$    12, Assoc
14) $[(Bx \cdot Ex) \cdot Ax] \supset Dx$            13, Taut

The conclusion is now established in two steps:

**(23)**

15) $[Ax \cdot (Bx \cdot Ex)] \supset Dx$              14, Com
16) $/ \therefore (x)\{[Ax \cdot (Bx \cdot Ex)] \supset Dx\}$    15, UG

'$[Ax \cdot (Bx \cdot Ex)] \supset Dx$' is a statement function. However, it is obtained from only universally quantified statements using Universal Instantiation properly coupled with other elementary rules of inference. Hence, this statement function can be universally generalized, and this is done in line 16.

A common mistake is seen in

**(24)**

15) $[Ax \cdot (Bx \cdot Ex)] \supset Dx$              14, Com
*WRONG X*  16) $/ \therefore (x)[Ax \cdot (Bx \cdot Ex)] \supset Dx$   15, UG

Line 16 is incorrect. There is a free 'x' in the consequent, 'Dx'. In applying Universal

Generalization, remember that every free occurrence of '$\alpha$' in '$\Phi\alpha$', and only those occurrences, must fall under the scope of the quantifier in '$(\alpha)\Phi\alpha$'.

## *EXERCISES*

### Group A:

Give the correct justification in each unjustified line of the following.

1.                          /∴ Ba
    1) (x)(Ax ⊃ Bx)   Pr
    2) Aa             Pr
    3) Aa ⊃ Ba
    4) /∴ Ba

2.                          /∴ Aa
    1) ~ Ba          Pr
    2) (x)(Ax ∨ Bx)   Pr
    3) Aa ∨ Ba
    4) Ba ∨ Aa
    5) /∴ Aa

3.                          /∴ Aa ⊃ Ca
    1) (x)(Ax ⊃ Bx)   Pr
    2) (x)(Bx ⊃ Cx)   Pr
    3) Aa ⊃ Ba
    4) Ba ⊃ Ca
    5) /∴ Aa ⊃ Ca

4.                          /∴ (x)(Ax ⊃ Cx)
    1) (x)(Bx ⊃ Cx)   Pr
    2) (x)(Ax ⊃ Bx)   Pr
    3) Ax ⊃ Bx
    4) Bx ⊃ Cx
    5) Ax ⊃ Cx
    6) /∴ (x)(Ax ⊃ Cx)

5.                          /∴ ~ Aa ∨ ~ Ba
    1) (x)[(Ax · Bx) ⊃ ~ Cx]   Pr
    2) Ca                Pr
    3) (Aa · Ba) ⊃ ~ Ca
    4) ~ ~ Ca
    5) ~ (Aa · Ba)
    6) /∴ ~ Aa ∨ ~ Ba

6.                          /∴ Ca
    1) Aa ⊃ (x)(Bx ⊃ Cx)   Pr
    2) Ba · Aa           Pr
    3) Aa · Ba
    4) Aa
    5) (x)(Bx ⊃ Cx)
    6) Ba ⊃ Ca

    7) Ba
    8) /∴ Ca

7.                                              /∴ (x)(Bx ∨ Dx)
    1)  (x)(Ax ⊃ Bx) · (x)(Cx ⊃ Dx)    Pr
    2)  (x)(Cx ∨ Ax)                    Pr
    3)  (x)(Ax ⊃ Bx)
    4)  (x)(Cx ⊃ Dx) · (x)(Ax ⊃ Bx)
    5)  (x)(Cx ⊃ Dx)
    6)  Cx ⊃ Dx
    7)  Ax ⊃ Bx
    8)  Cx ∨ Ax
    9)  Dx ∨ Bx
    10) Bx ∨ Dx
    11) /∴ (x)(Bx ∨ Dx)

8.                                              /∴ (x)[(Ax · Dx) ⊃ Bx]
    1)  (x)[Ax ⊃ (Bx ∨ Cx)]    Pr
    2)  (x)(Cx ⊃ ∼ Dx)         Pr
    3)  Ax ⊃ (Bx ∨ Cx)
    4)  Cx ⊃ ∼ Dx
    5)  Ax ⊃ (∼ ∼ Bx ∨ Cx)
    6)  Ax ⊃ (∼ Bx ⊃ Cx)
    7)  (Ax · ∼ Bx) ⊃ Cx
    8)  (Ax · ∼ Bx) ⊃ ∼ Dx
    9)  Ax ⊃ (∼ Bx ⊃ ∼ Dx)
    10) Ax ⊃ (Dx ⊃ Bx)
    11) (Ax · Dx) ⊃ Bx
    12) /∴ (x)[(Ax · Dx) ⊃ Bx]

9.                                              /∴ (x)(Ax ⊃ Dx) · (x)(Cx ⊃ Dx)
    1)  (x)(Ax ⊃ Bx) ⊃ (x)(Bx ⊃ Dx)    Pr
    2)  (x)(Ax ⊃ Cx) · (x)(Cx ⊃ Bx)    Pr
    3)  (x)(Ax ⊃ Cx)
    4)  (x)(Cx ⊃ Bx) · (x)(Ax ⊃ Cx)
    5)  (x)(Cx ⊃ Bx)
    6)  Ax ⊃ Cx
    7)  Cx ⊃ Bx
    8)  Ax ⊃ Bx
    9)  (x)(Ax ⊃ Bx)
    10) Bx ⊃ Dx
    11) Bx ⊃ Dx
    12) Cx ⊃ Dx
    13) (x)(Cx ⊃ Dx)
    14) Ax ⊃ Dx
    15) (x)(Ax ⊃ Dx)
    16) /∴ (x)(Ax ⊃ Dx) · (x)(Cx ⊃ Dx)

10.                                             /∴ (x)[Ax ⊃ (Dx ⊃ Cx)]
    1)  (x)(Ax ⊃ Bx) · (x)(Bx ⊃ Cx)    Pr
    2)  (x)(Ax ⊃ Bx)
    3)  (x)(Bx ⊃ Cx) · (x)(Ax ⊃ Bx)
    4)  (x)(Bx ⊃ Cx)

5) Ax ⊃ Bx
6) Bx ⊃ Cx
7) Ax ⊃ Cx
8) ∼ Ax ∨ Cx
9) ( ∼ Ax ∨ Cx) ∨ ∼ Dx
10) ∼ Dx ∨ ( ∼ Ax ∨ Cx)
11) ( ∼ Dx ∨ ∼ Ax) ∨ Cx
12) ∼ (Dx · Ax) ∨ Cx
13) (Dx · Ax) ⊃ Cx
14) (Ax · Dx) ⊃ Cx
15) Ax ⊃ (Dx ⊃ Cx)
16) /∴ (x)[Ax ⊃ (Dx ⊃ Cx)]

## Group B:

Construct a proof for each of the following.

1.                                   /∴ Aa
   1) ∼ Ba            Pr
   2) (x)( ∼ Ax ⊃ Bx)   Pr

2.                                   /∴ ∼ Aa ∨ ∼ Ba
   1) (x)[(Ax · Bx) ⊃ ∼ Cx]   Pr
   2) Ca                       Pr

3.                                   /∴ Ca
   1) (x)(Ax ⊃ ∼ Bx)   Pr
   2) Aa               Pr
   3) (x)(Bx ∨ Cx)     Pr

4.                                   /∴ (x)[(Ax · Bx) ∨ Cx]
   1) (x)(Ax ∨ Cx) · (x)(Bx ∨ Cx)   Pr

5.                                   /∴ (x)(Ax ⊃ Bx)
   1) (x)[(Ax · ∼ Bx) ⊃ Cx]   Pr
   2) (x)(Cx ⊃ Bx)            Pr

6.                                   /∴ ∼ (Aa · Ba)
   1) (x)[(Ax ⊃ Bx) ⊃ ∼ Cx]   Pr
   2) Ca                       Pr

7.                                   /∴ ∼ Ba
   1) (x)[(Ax · Bx) ≡ ∼ Cx]   Pr
   2) Aa · Ca                 Pr

8.                                   /∴ ∼ Aa · Ca
   1) (x){[Ax · (Bx ∨ Cx)] ⊃ ∼ Dx}   Pr
   2) (x)( ∼ Dx ⊃ ∼ Ax)               Pr
   3) Ca                              Pr

9.                                   /∴ (x)[(Ax · Cx) ⊃ ∼ Dx]
   1) (x){[Ax · (Bx ∨ Cx)] ≡ ∼ Dx}   Pr

10.                                  /∴ (x)[(Cx ∨ Ax) ⊃ Dx]
   1) (x)[Ax ⊃ (Bx · Cx)]   Pr
   2) (x)(Cx ⊃ Dx)          Pr

### Group C:

Symbolize the following arguments using the suggested predicate logic notation. Then construct a proof for each.

1. Every logician is highly trained. Anyone who is highly trained is skillful. Alonzo Church is a logician. So, Church is skillful. (L,T,S;x,c)

2. Everything is extended or it isn't. Only those things having mass are extended. Nothing which isn't extended is physically locatable. Hence, anything has mass or isn't physically locatable. (E,M,L;x)

3. If every body is in motion, only those things changing are in motion. Whatever is a body is changing, while whatever is changing is in motion. Consequently, everything in motion is changing. (B,M,C;x)

4. Squares and circles are extended. Accordingly, circles are extended. (S,C,E;x)

5. The student who is both industrious and clever will pass. While Elizabeth is a student, nonetheless she won't pass. Elizabeth is clever. Therefore, Elizabeth isn't industrious. (S,P,I,C;x,e)

6. No student will benefit from work who is lazy whenever made to perform. Karl will benefit from work although he is lazy. Wherefore, Karl isn't a student. (S,B,L,M;x,k)

7. Anyone can use a computer who is facile with mathematical manipulations or interested in symbolic operations except those not trained in programming. Marsha is a person who is neither trained in programming nor can't use a computer. Therefore, Marsha is neither facile with mathematical manipulations nor trained in programming. (P,U,F,I,T;x,m)

8. Whoever is intemperate is neither slow to anger nor quick to forgive when aroused or contradicted. So, whoever is contradicted is temperate when quick to forgive. (P,T,S,Q,A,C;x)

9. Everyone who isn't understanding when not compassionate is truly happy and benevolent. Anyone benevolent is both truly happy and forgiving. Consequently, whoever is compassionate is forgiving. (P,U,C,H,B,F;x)

10. All persons who are 18 years old must register for the draft if they are males and not aliens. Any person who registers for the draft isn't exempt from military service if an 18-year-old male. Thus, all non-alien males are not exempt from the draft if they are persons 18 years old. (P,O,R,M,A,E;x)

---

## 3. EXISTENTIAL GENERALIZATION AND EXISTENTIAL INSTANTIATION

Two argument forms govern the existential quantifier. *Existential Instantiation* is one of these argument forms. This rule can be shown as

**EXISTENTIAL INSTANTIATION (EI)**

$$(\exists\alpha)\Phi\alpha$$
$$/\therefore \Phi\beta$$

Two restrictions are placed on '$\beta$' in using Existential Instantiation to construct proofs. To understand these restrictions and appreciate their need, consider two arguments. Here is the first of these:

> **(1)**  Some students are wealthy. Therefore, Melissa, who is a student, is wealthy.

The premise of (1) is true. Yet the truth of this premise guarantees nothing about the truth of the conclusion of (1). Suppose that there is a student named 'Melissa'. It does not follow that she is wealthy. The premise asserts that *part* of those individuals having the property of being a student also have the property of being wealthy. That is, some students are wealthy and some are not. To which part, the wealthy or the non-wealthy, does Melissa belong? The truth of 'Some students are wealthy' cannot guarantee the truth of 'Melissa is wealthy' even though Melissa is a student. Because some members of a class have a certain property, it does not follow deductively that a specific member of that class has that property. Thus, '$\beta$' in Existential Instantiation must always be viewed as an individual variable and never as the name of a specific individual. Hence, no individual constant can ever be introduced into a proof by Existential Instantiation. The first restriction of Existential Instantiation is this:

> '$\beta$' **represents an individiaul variable that is free at all those places, and only those places, where '$\alpha$' is free in $\Phi\alpha$'.**

The need for the second restriction on '$\beta$' in Existential Instantiation is clearly shown in the following argument:

> **(2)**  Some mammals are dangerous. Some reptiles are dangerous. So, there are mammals that are reptiles.

All the premises of (2) are true, but the conclusion is false. Thus, (2) cannot be valid. However, someone might attempt to construct a "proof" for (2) in this way:

|  | **(3)** |  | $/ \therefore (\exists x)(Mx \cdot Rx)$ |
|---|---|---|---|
|  | **1)** | $(\exists x)(Mx \cdot Dx)$ | Pr |
|  | **2)** | $(\exists x)(Rx \cdot Dx)$ | Pr |
|  | **3)** | $Mx \cdot Dx$ | 1, EI |
| *WRONG X* | **4)** | $RX \cdot Dx$ | 2, EI |
|  | **5)** | $Mx$ | 3, Simp |
|  | **6)** | $Rx$ | 4, Simp |
|  | **7)** | $Mx \cdot Rx$ | 5, 6, Conj |
|  | **8)** | $/ \therefore (\exists x)(Mx \cdot Rx)$ | 7, EG |

What has gone wrong in (3)? Of course there is some individual that has the property of being both a mammal and being dangerous. There is also some individual that has the property of being both a reptile and being dangerous. Admittedly, both these individuals have the property of being dangerous. Yet from this fact nothing follows deductively about their having other properties in common. More especially, it does not follow that there is some individual that has the property of being both a mammal and a reptile. This sort of situation is avoided by the second restriction on Existential Instantiation:

> **Whatever individual variable '$\beta$' represents in the context of a particular proof, that individual variable cannot previously appear in the proof as a free variable.**

Line 4 in (3) is incorrect because 'x' already appears previously in 3 as a free variable. Breaking this second restriction on '$\beta$' in Existential Instantiation permits a move from true premises to a false conclusion.

While (2) is not a deductively valid argument, the following is:

> **(4)** Some mammals are dangerous. Some reptiles are dangerous.
> So, there are mammals and there are reptiles.

One proof of (4) is this:

**(5)**                           $/\therefore (\exists x)Mx \cdot (\exists y)Ry$

| | | |
|---|---|---|
| **1)** | $(\exists x)(Mx \cdot Dx)$ | Pr |
| **2)** | $(\exists x)(Rx \cdot Dx)$ | Pr |
| **3)** | $Mx \cdot Dx$ | 1, EI |
| **4)** | $Ry \cdot Dy$ | 2, EI |
| **5)** | $Mx$ | 3, Simp |
| **6)** | $Ry$ | 4, Simp |
| **7)** | $(\exists x)Mx$ | 5, EG |
| **8)** | $(\exists y)Ry$ | 6, EG |
| **9)** | $/\therefore (\exists x)Mx \cdot (\exists y)Ry$ | 7, 8, Conj |

Existential Instantiation is used to obtain 3 and 4. However, neither of the free variables introduced by these moves previously appears in the proof as a free variable.

Consider this argument:

> **(6)** Computer circuitry is based on Boolean Algebras. Computing circuitry is important. There are computer circuits. So, there are important Boolean Algebras.

(6) is symbolized as

**(7)**                             $/\therefore (\exists x)(Ix \cdot Bx)$

| | | |
|---|---|---|
| **1)** | $(x)(Cx \supset Bx)$ | Pr |
| **2)** | $(x)(Cx \supset Ix)$ | Pr |
| **3)** | $(\exists x)Cx$ | Pr |

Innocently enough, having properly symbolized the argument, an incorrect move might be attempted:

**(8)**

|  |  |  |
|---|---|---|
|  | 4) Cx ⊃ Bx | 1, UI |
|  | 5) Cx ⊃ Ix | 2, UI |
| *WRONG X* | 6) Cx | 3, EI |
|  | 7) Bx | 4, 6, MP |
|  | 8) Ix | 5, 6, MP |
|  | 9) Ix · Bx | 8, 7, Conj |
|  | 10) /∴ (∃x)(Ix · Bx) | 9, EG |

Line 6 is incorrect because it breaks the second restriction on 'β' in Existential Instantiation. The free individual variable, 'x', in line 6 previously occurs as a free individual variable. Yet the following proof of (6) is acceptable:

**(9)**  /∴ (∃x)(Ix · Bx)

| | | |
|---|---|---|
| 1) | (x)(Cx ⊃ Bx) | Pr |
| 2) | (x)(Cx ⊃ Ix) | Pr |
| 3) | (∃x)Cx | Pr |
| 4) | Cx | 3, EI |
| 5) | Cx ⊃ Bx | 1, UI |
| 6) | Cx ⊃ Ix | 2, UI |
| 7) | Bx | 5, 4, MP |
| 8) | Ix | 6, 4, MP |
| 9) | Ix · Bx | 8, 7, Conj |
| 10) | /∴ (∃x)(Ix · Bx) | 9, EG |

None of the restrictions on 'β' is broken in 4. In particular 'x' does not occur anywhere before 4 as a free variable. Lines 5 and 6 are also acceptable. The 'β' of Universal Instantiation is not restricted in the same way as the 'β' of Existential Instantiation. As a general strategy, whenever a premise set contains both universally and existentially quantified statements, use EI before using UI.

The other argument form governing the existential quantifier is ***Existential Generalization***. Existential Generalization prefixes an existential quantifier to a statement function. This argument form is displayed as

### EXISTENTIAL GENERALIZATION (EG)

$$\frac{\Phi\beta}{/\therefore (\exists\alpha)\Phi\alpha}$$

In using this rule in constructing proofs, first, 'β' represents either an individual constant or an individual variable in 'Φβ' and, second, 'α' is a free individual variable in 'Φα' at all, and only, those places where 'β' occurs in 'Φβ'.

PREDICATE LOGIC: PROOF CONSTRUCTION

Consider why Existential Generalization is a valid argument form. Suppose an instance of '$\Phi\beta$' is found in some line of a proof. First, assume that '$\beta$' is an individual constant, in which case '$\Phi\beta$' is an assertion about a specific individual. In the proof, '$\Phi\beta$' must be either a premise of deduced from premises. In either case, '$\Phi\beta$' is accepted as true, assuming the truth of the premises. In this case, then, it is true that there is at least one individual in the universe such that it has the property designated by '$\Phi$'. This is to say, '$(\exists\alpha)\,\Phi\alpha$' is true. Second, assume that '$\beta$' is an individual variable. Then '$\Phi\beta$' is a statement function deduced from the premises by either Universal Instantiation of Existential Instantiation. What if '$\Phi\beta$' is introduced into a proof by Universal Instantiation? Then the name of any individual consistently substituted at '$\beta$' in '$\Phi\beta$' transforms '$\Phi\beta$' into a true statement. Hence, there is at least one individual having the property '$\Phi$'. That is, $(\exists\alpha)\Phi\alpha$' is true. Or, if '$\Phi\beta$' is introduced into a proof by Existential Instantiation as discussed below, there is at least one unspecified individual having the property '$\Phi$'. Once again, '$(\exists\alpha)\Phi\alpha$' is true.

Consider this argument:

> **(10)**   All saints are virtuous and Augustine of Hippo is a saint.
> So, there are virtuous saints.

A proof can be constructed using Existential Generalization:

**(11)**                           $/\therefore (\exists x)Vx$

| | | |
|---|---|---|
| **1)** | $(x)(Sx \supset Vx) \cdot Sa$ | Pr |
| **2)** | $(x)(Sx \supset Vx)$ | 1, Simp |
| **3)** | $Sa \cdot (x)(Sx \supset Vx)$ | 1, Com |
| **4)** | $Sa$ | 3, Simp |
| **5)** | $Sa \supset Va$ | 2, UI |
| **6)** | $Va$ | 5, 4, MP |
| **7)** | $Va \cdot Sa$ | 6, 4, MP |
| **8)** | $/\therefore (\exists x)(Vx \cdot Sx)$ | 6, EG |

For a final insight into Existential Generalization, consider this argument:

> **(12)** All vipers are snakes. So, there is something such that if it is a viper, then it is also a snake.

A proof of this argument is straightforward:

**(13)**                           $/\therefore (\exists x)(Vx \supset Sx)$

| | | |
|---|---|---|
| **1)** | $(x)(Vx \supset Sx)$ | Pr |
| **2)** | $Vx \supset Sx$ | 1, UI |
| **3)** | $/\therefore (\exists x)(Vx \supset Sx)$ | 2, EG |

This argument, and its proof, is trivial in the sense that almost anything satisfies the conclusion. Since '$(\exists x)(Vx \supset Sx)$' is logically equivalent to '$(\exists x)(\sim Vx \vee Sx)$',

'(∃x)(Vx ⊃ Sx)' is true of anything that is either not a viper or is a snake—or both. Indeed, assuming a Boolean interpretation, any statement of the form, '(∃α)(Φα ⊃ Ψ$_β$)', is commonly prohibited from proofs of validity. '(∃α)(Φα ⊃ Ψ$_β$)' asserts that 'There exists at least one thing, α, in the universe such that if α is Φ then α is Ψ'. But under a Boolean interpretation, existence assertions are not coupled with hypotheticals in this way. One is not to confuse 'If anything is Φ, then it is Ψ' with 'Since something is Φ, it is also Ψ'.

## *EXERCISES*

### Group A:

Give the correct justification in each unjustified line of the following.

1.                                    / ∴ (∃x)[(Ax ∨ Cx) · Bx]
   1)  (∃x)(Ax · Bx)    Pr
   2)  Ax · Bx
   3)  Ax
   4)  Ax ∨ Cx
   5)  Bx · Ax
   6)  Bx
   7)  (Ax ∨ Cx) · Bx
   8)  / ∴ (∃x)[(Ax ∨ Cx) · Bx]

2.                                    / ∴ (∃x)Cx
   1)  (x)(Ax ⊃ Bx)          Pr
   2)  (∃x)Ax                Pr
   3)  (x)(∼ Cx ⊃ ∼ Bx)     Pr
   4)  Ax
   5)  Ax ⊃ Bx
   6)  ∼ Cx ⊃ ∼ Bx
   7)  Bx ⊃ Cx
   8)  Ax ⊃ Cx
   9)  Cx
   10) / ∴ (∃x)Cx

3.                                    / ∴ (∃x)(Bx · Cx)
   1)  (x)(Ax ⊃ Bx) · (∃x)(Ax · Cx)    Pr
   2)  (x)(Ax ⊃ Bx)
   3)  (∃x)(Ax · Cx) · (x)(Ax ⊃ Bx)
   4)  (∃x)(Ax · Cx)
   5)  Ax · Cx
   6)  Ax ⊃ Bx
   7)  Ax
   8)  Bx
   9)  Cx · Ax
   10) Cx
   11) Bx · Cx
   12) / ∴ (∃x)(Bx · Cx)

4.                                                        $/\therefore (\exists x) \sim Ax$

   1) $(x)\{[Ax \cdot (Bx \lor Cx)] \supset Dx\}$  Pr
   2) $(\exists x)(Cx \cdot \sim Dx)$         Pr
   3) $Cx \cdot \sim Dx$
   4) $[Ax \cdot (Bx \lor Cx)] \supset Dx$
   5) $Cx$
   6) $\sim Dx \cdot Cx$
   7) $\sim Dx$
   8) $\sim [Ax \cdot (Bx \lor Cx)]$
   9) $\sim Ax \lor \sim (Bx \lor Cx)$
  10) $\sim (Bx \lor Cx) \lor \sim Ax$
  11) $Cx \lor Bx$
  12) $Bx \lor Cx$
  13) $\sim\sim (Bx \lor Cx)$
  14) $\sim Ax$
  15) $/\therefore (\exists x) \sim Ax$

5.                                                        $/\therefore (\exists x) \sim (Dx \lor Ax)$

   1) $(x)(Ax \supset Bx)$     Pr
   2) $(\exists x)(\sim Bx \cdot Cx)$  Pr
   3) $(x)(Dx \supset \sim Cx)$  Pr
   4) $\sim Bx \cdot Cx$
   5) $Ax \supset Bx$
   6) $Dx \supset \sim Cx$
   7) $\sim Bx$
   8) $Cx \cdot \sim Bx$
   9) $Cx$
  10) $\sim Ax$
  11) $\sim\sim Cx$
  12) $\sim Dx$
  13) $\sim Dx \cdot \sim Ax$
  14) $\sim (Dx \lor Ax)$
  15) $/\therefore (\exists x) \sim (Dx \lor Ax)$

6.                                                        $/\therefore (\exists x)[Cx \lor (Dx \cdot Ax)]$

   1) $(\exists x)(Ax \cdot \sim Bx)$        Pr
   2) $(x)\{[Ax \cdot \sim (Cx \lor Dx)] \supset Bx\}$  Pr
   3) $Ax \cdot \sim Bx$
   4) $[Ax \cdot \sim (Cx \lor Dx)] \supset Bx$
   5) $Ax$
   6) $\sim Bx \cdot Ax$
   7) $\sim Bx$
   8) $\sim [Ax \cdot \sim (Cx \lor Dx)]$
   9) $\sim Ax \lor \sim\sim (Cx \lor Dx)$
  10) $\sim Ax \lor (Cx \lor Dx)$
  11) $Ax \supset (Cx \lor Dx)$
  12) $Cx \lor Dx$
  13) $Ax \lor Cx$
  14) $Cx \lor Ax$
  15) $(Cx \lor Dx) \cdot (Cx \lor Ax)$
  16) $Cx \lor (Dx \cdot Ax)$
  17) $/\therefore (\exists x)[Cx \lor (Dx \cdot Ax)]$

7.                                                  / ∴ (∃x)(Ax · Dx)
   1)  (x)[(Ax · Bx) ⊃ ~ Cx]   Pr
   2)  (∃x)(Ax · Cx)           Pr
   3)  (x)[(Ax · ~ Bx) ⊃ Dx]   Pr
   4)  Ax · Cx
   5)  (Ax · Bx) ⊃ ~ Cx
   6)  (Ax · ~ Bx) ⊃ Dx
   7)  Ax
   8)  Cx · Ax
   9)  Cx
   10) ~ ~ Cx
   11) ~ (Ax · Bx)
   12) ~ Ax ∨ ~ Bx
   13) ~ ~ Ax
   14) ~ Bx
   15) Ax · ~ Bx
   16) Dx
   17) Ax · Dx
   18) / ∴ (∃x)(Ax · Dx)

8.                                                  / ∴ (∃x)[Ax · ~ (Dx · Ex)]
   1)  (∃x)[Ax · ~ ( ~ Bx ∨ Cx)]   Pr
   2)  (x)[(Ax · Dx) ≡ ~ Bx]       Pr
   3)  Ax · ~ ( ~ Bx ∨ Cx)
   4)  (Ax · Dx) ≡ ~ Bx
   5)  Ax
   6)  ~ ( ~ Bx ∨ Cx) · Ax
   7)  ~ ( ~ Bx ∨ Cx)
   8)  ~ ~ Bx · ~ Cx
   9)  [(Ax · Dx) ⊃ ~ Bx] · [ ~ Bx ⊃ (Ax · Dx)]
   10) (Ax · Dx) ⊃ ~ Bx
   11) Ax ⊃ (Dx ⊃ ~ Bx)
   12) Dx ⊃ ~ Bx
   13) ~ ~ Bx
   14) ~ Dx
   15) ~ Dx ∨ ~ Ex
   16) ~ (Dx · Ex)
   17) Ax · ~ (Dx · Ex)
   18) / ∴ (∃x)[Ax · ~ (Dx · Ex)]

9.                                                  / ∴ (∃x)(Ex ∨ Gx)
   1)  (∃x)[Ax · ( ~ Bx · Cx)]     Pr
   2)  (x)[Ax ⊃ (Dx ⊃ Ex)]         Pr
   3)  (x)[(Cx · Fx) ⊃ Gx]         Pr
   4)  (x)[( ~ Dx · ~ Fx) ⊃ Bx]    Pr
   5)  Ax · ( ~ Bx · Cx)
   6)  Ax ⊃ (Dx ⊃ Ex)
   7)  (Cx · Fx) ⊃ Gx
   8)  ( ~ Dx · ~ Fx) ⊃ Bx
   9)  Ax
   10) ( ~ Bx · Cx) · Ax

11) ~ Bx · Cx
12) ~ Bx
13) Cx · ~ Bx
14) Cx
15) Dx ⊃ Ex
16) Cx ⊃ (Fx ⊃ Gx)
17) Fx ⊃ Gx
18) ~ ( ~ Dx · ~ Fx)
19) ~ ~ (Dx ∨ Fx)
20) Dx ∨ Fx
21) Ex ∨ Gx
22) / ∴ (∃x)(Ex ∨ Gx)

10.                                          / ∴ (∃x)[Bx · (Hx · ~ Fx)]
1) (x)[(Ax ∨ Bx) ⊃ Cx]       Pr
2) (x)[(Cx ∨ Dx) ⊃ Ex]       Pr
3) (∃x)[Ax · ~ (Gx ∨ Hx)]    Pr
4) (x)[Ex ⊃ (Fx · Gx)]       Pr
5) Ax · ~ (Gx ∨ Hx)
6) (Ax ∨ Bx) ⊃ Cx
7) (Cx ∨ Dx) ⊃ Ex
8) Ex ⊃ (Fx · Gx)
9) Ax
10) ~ (Gx ∨ Hx) · Ax
11) ~ (Gx ∨ Hx)
12) ~ Gx · ~ Hx
13) Ax ∨ Bx
14) Cx
15) Cx ∨ Dx
16) Ex
17) Fx · Gx
18) Gx · Fx
19) Gx
20) ~ Gx
21) Gx ∨ (∃x)[Bx · (Hx · ~ Fx)]
22) / ∴ (∃x)[Bx · (Hx · ~ Fx)]

## Group B:

Construct a proof for each of the following.

1.                                          / ∴ (∃x) ~ Ax
1) (x)[Ax ⊃ (Bx ∨ Cx)]   Pr
2) (∃x)( ~ Cx · ~ Bx)    Pr

2.                                          / ∴ (∃x)(Ax · Cx)
1) (∃x)(Ax · Bx)   Pr
2) (x)(Bx ⊃ Cx)    Pr

3.                                          / ∴ (∃x) ~ Bx
1) (x)[(Ax · Bx) ⊃ Cx]   Pr
2) (x)(Cx ⊃ ~ Bx)        Pr
3) (∃x)Ax                Pr

4.                                                        / ∴ (∃x)[Bx ∨ (Cx · Dx)]
  1)  (x)[Ax ⊃ (Bx ∨ Cx)] · (x)[Ax ⊃ (Bx ∨ Dx)]  Pr
  2)  (∃x)Ax                                                      Pr

5.                                                        / ∴ (∃x)(Cx ∨ Ax)
  1)  [(∃x)Ax · (∃x)Bx] ⊃ (∃x)(Cx ∨ Ax)  Pr
  2)  (x)[Cx ⊃ (Ax · Bx)]                            Pr
  3)  (x)(Dx ⊃ Cx)                                  Pr
  4)  (∃x)Dx                                        Pr

6.                                                        / ∴ (∃x)[Ax · (Bx △ Cx)]
  1)  (x){Ax ⊃ [Bx ∨ (Cx · Dx)]}  Pr
  2)  (∃x)(Ax · ∼ Cx)                Pr

7.                                                        / ∴ (∃x) ∼ (Dx · Ax)
  1)  (x)[(Ax · Bx) ≡ ∼ Cx]  Pr
  2)  (∃x)(Cx · Bx)           Pr

8.                                                        / ∴ (∃x)( ∼ Cx ∨ ∼ Ax)
  1)  (x)(Ax ⊃ Bx)              Pr
  2)  (x)[(Bx · Cx) ⊃ Dx]     Pr
  3)  (x)[(Ax · Dx) ⊃ Ex]     Pr
  4)  (∃x) ∼ Ex              Pr

9.                                                        / ∴ (∃x)[ ∼ Ax · (Bx ∨ Ex)]
  1)  (x)[Ax ⊃ ∼ (Bx ⊃ Cx)]  Pr
  2)  (x)[Bx ⊃ (Cx ∨ Dx)]       Pr
  3)  (∃x)[ ∼ Dx · (Bx △ Ex)]   Pr

10.                                                       / ∴ (∃x)(Ex △ Dx)
  1)  (∃x)[(Ax ⊃ Cx) · ∼ Bx]              Pr
  2)  (x)(Cx ⊃ Dx) · (x)( ∼ Ex ⊃ Ax)     Pr
  3)  (x)[Dx ⊃ (Ex ⊃ Bx)]                Pr

## Group C:

Symbolize the following arguments using the suggested predicate logic notation. Then construct a proof for each.

1. Artificial satellites are useful in meteorology and communications. There are artificial satellites. Thus, there are artificial satellites useful in meteorology. (S,M,C;x)

2. Every man-made satellite is an important technological achievement even though some man-made satellites aren't American inventions. So, certain important technological achievements aren't American inventions. (S,A,I;x)

3. If some things are important or useful, then surely every advancement in human understanding is beneficial. Certain things are both important and also advancements in human understanding. Hence, some things are beneficial. (I,U,A,B;x)

4. Any nation has either a large population of poor people or a substantial middle class. Every large population of poor people is accompanied by a high rate of suicide. Certain nations don't have a high rate of suicide. Consequently, some nations have a substantial middle class. (N,P,C,R;x)

5. Nations are economically backward whenever poor. However, some poor nations are developing their resources. Wherefore, certain nations that are economically backward are developing their resources. (N,B,P,D;x)

6. Anyone who isn't loving is ignorant to some degree only if selfish. Some persons aren't selfish. Everyone is ignorant to some degree. Accordingly, loving people exist. (P,L,I,S;x)

7. Succubi and/or incubi are demons. Now, demons and/or ghosts are occult things. But some things are not occult. Therefore, some things are neither ghosts nor incubi. (S,I,D,G,O;x)

8. There exist Chordates that are mammals or reptiles only if every tortoise is a reptile. If some Chordates are mammals or vertebrates, all reptiles are vertebrates. Certain Chordates are mammals. Hence, every tortoise is a vertebrate. (C,M,R,T,V;x)

9. Certain poetry is neither understandable nor readable. Further, no poetry or novel is factual. If anything is neither factual nor readable, it's bunk. Therefore, some poetry is bunk and neither readable nor understandable. (P,U,R,N,F,B;x)

10. Anything that wrote the Scriptures must have been either a good person or a bad one, or a Deity. Anything that wrote the Scriptures preached virtue while saying "Thus saith the Lord." Whatever said "Thus saith the Lord" and wasn't a Deity was fabricating. No good person fabricates but no bad person preaches virtue. Obviously, someone wrote the Scriptures. Consequently, there is a Deity who wrote the Scriptures. (S,G,P,B,D,V,L,F;x)

## 4.   QUANTIFICATIONAL DENIAL

It is not necessary to introduce both the universal and existential quantifier into predicate logic. Nor does it matter logically which quantifier is used. With the aid of the tilde, one quantifier can be converted into the other. It is convenient, however, in symbolization and proof construction to have both. To grasp intuitively the relationships holding between quantifiers, consider these examples:

(1)
    **a)** Something is expensive.

    **b)** Not everything is inexpensive.

The examples in (1) are symbolized as

(2)
    **a)** $(\exists x)Ex$

    **b)** $\sim (x) \sim Ex$

Let '$(\exists \alpha)$' represent any existential quantifier and '$\Phi \alpha$' any statement function containing some free variable '$\alpha$'. Then, **a** of (2) is an instance of

(3)   $(\exists \alpha)\Phi \alpha$

If '$(\alpha)$' pictures any universal quantifier and '$\Phi \alpha$' any statement function, then $b$ of (2) is an instance of

(4)   $\sim (\alpha) \sim \Phi \alpha$

The two statements in (1) are equivalent. Whatever conditions make one true, or false, makes the other true, or false. This observation holds for any quantified statements having the same general forms '$(\exists \alpha)\Phi \alpha$' and '$\sim (\alpha) \sim \Phi \alpha$' where '$\Phi \alpha$' is interpreted the same way in both cases. Hence, a new *equivalence form* is introduced, where '∷' indicates that this is a replacement rule that can be read from left to right and from right to left:

**QUANTIFICATIONAL DENIAL**

$$(\exists\alpha)\Phi\alpha \;::\; \sim(\alpha)\sim\Phi\alpha$$
$$(\exists\alpha)\sim\Phi\alpha \;::\; \sim(\alpha)\Phi\alpha$$
$$\sim(\exists\alpha)\Phi\alpha \;::\; (\alpha)\sim\Phi\alpha$$
$$\sim(\exists\alpha)\sim\Phi\alpha \;::\; (\alpha)\Phi\alpha$$

To use Quantificational Denial, first, change the quantifier. If the quantifier is existential, replace it by a universal quantifier. If the quantifier is universal, change it to an existential one. Second, deal with the tildes. Imagine an empty space both prefixed and suffixed to the quantifier:

$$\square\,(\exists\alpha)\,\square \;::\; \square\,(\alpha)\,\square$$

If there is a tilde in that space, remove it. If there is no tilde in that imaginary space, put one there.

Continuing to let 'Φα' represent 'x is expensive', the above four forms can be interpreted like this:

**(5)**  Something is expensive.  ∷  Not everything is inexpensive.

Something is inexpensive.  ∷  Not everything is expensive.

It isn't the case that
 something is expensive.  ∷  Everything is inexpensive.

It isn't the case that
 something is inexpensive.  ∷  Everything is expensive.

Examine this argument to see a use of Quantificational Denial:

**(6)**  Not all rodents are mice. So, certain rodents aren't mice.

Read carefully the premise of (6). A common mistake in moving into logical notation is to confuse such expressions as 'not all', 'not any', and 'not every' with words such as 'no' and 'nothing'. 'Not all rodents are mice' and 'No rodents are mice' are quite different assertions. While the former is true, the latter is not. Such distinctions must be portrayed in the symbolic representation of statements. Symbolize (6) as

**(7)**                                                    $/ \therefore (\exists x)(Rx \cdot \sim Mx)$
  **1)**  $\sim(x)(Rx \supset Mx)$   Pr

The scope of the tilde in 1 is '$(x)(Rx \supset Mx)$'. Hence, because of the tilde prefixed to the universal quantifier, '$\sim(x)(Rx \supset Mx)$' cannot be instantiated by Universal

Instantiation.* This tilde, however, can be removed and '(x)' converted to '(∃x)' by a use of Quantificational Denial. Then a proof of (6) is constructed:

(8)                                              /∴ (∃x)(Rx • ~ Mx)

   **1)** ~ (x)(Rx ⊃ Mx)     Pr

   **2)** (∃x) ~ (Rx ⊃ Mx)   1, QD

   **3)** ~ (Rx ⊃ Mx)       2, EI

   **4)** ~ ( ~ Rx ∨ Mx)    3, Impl

   **5)** ~~Rx • ~ Mx      4, DeM

   **6)** Rx • ~ Mx        5, DN

   **7)** /∴ (∃x)(Rx • ~ Mx)   6, EG

Not only does Quantificational Denial permit the removal of tildes in front of quantifiers, it also allows the prefixing of tildes to quantifiers. For instance, it can be argued that

   **(9)** Only reptiles are snakes. Some snakes are poisonous. So, not every reptile is nonpoisonous.

Symbolize (9) as

   **(10)**                                      /∴ ~ (x)(Rx ⊃ ~ Px)

    **1)** (x)(Sx ⊃ Rx)   Pr

    **2)** (∃x)(Sx • Px)   Pr

Because of the tilde prefixed to the quantifier, ' ~ (x)(Rx ⊃ ~ Px)' cannot be reached by Universal Generalization. If '(∃x) ~ (Rx ⊃ ~ Px)' is acquired, however, the conclusion can be established by Quantificational Denial. '(∃x) ~ (Rx ⊃ ~ Px)' is established by Existential Generalization if ' ~ (Rx ⊃ ~ Px)' is first obtained. Further, working backwards, it is discovered that 'Px' and 'Rx' are needed:  ·

   **(11)**                                      /∴ ~ (x)(Rx ⊃ ~ Px)

    **1)** (x)(Sx ⊃ Rx)        Pr

    **2)** (∃x)(Sx • Px)      Pr

            ·

            ·

    ?**)** Rx                ?

    ?**)** Px                ?

    ?**)** Rx • Px        ?, ?, Conj

    ?**)** ~~ (Rx • Px)    ?, DN

    ?**)** ~ ( ~ Rx ∨ ~ Px)  ?, DeM

    ?**)** ~ (Rx ⊃ ~ Px)    ?, Impl

    ?**)** (∃x) ~ (Rx ⊃ ~ Px)  ?, EI

    ?**)** /∴ ~ (x)(Rx ⊃ ~ Px)  ?, QD

---

* Compare attempting to use Simplification on ' ~ (A • B)'.

To connect the premises with the results of working backwards, take instances of both premises. Observe all the restrictions on the instantiation rules. Next, use truth-functional moves to produce 'Rx' and 'Px'. A complete proof of (9) is

| (12) | | $/ \therefore \sim (x)(Rx \supset \sim Px)$ |
|---|---|---|
| **1)** | $(x)(Sx \supset Rx)$ | Pr |
| **2)** | $(\exists x)(Sx \cdot Px)$ | Pr |
| **3)** | $Sx \cdot Px$ | 2, EI |
| **4)** | $Sx \supset Rx$ | 1, UI |
| **5)** | $Sx$ | 3, Simp |
| **6)** | $Px \cdot Sx$ | 3, Com |
| **7)** | $Rx$ | 4, 5, MP |
| **8)** | $Px$ | 6, Simp |
| **9)** | $Rx \cdot Px$ | 7, 8, Conj |
| **10)** | $\sim \sim (Rx \cdot Px)$ | 9, DN |
| **11)** | $\sim (\sim Rx \lor \sim Px)$ | 10, DeM |
| **12)** | $\sim (Rx \supset \sim Px)$ | 11, Impl |
| **13)** | $(\exists x) \sim (Rx \supset \sim Px)$ | 12, EG |
| **14)** | $/ \therefore \sim (x)(Rx \supset \sim Px)$ | 13, QD |

Consider one more example:

**(13)**  Either some people are vicious or it isn't true that there are people who are unkind. That all persons are kind isn't true. So, some people are vicious.

(13) is symbolized as

| (14) | | $/ \therefore (\exists x)(Px \cdot Vx)$ |
|---|---|---|
| **1)** | $(\exists x)(Px \cdot Vx) \lor \sim (\exists x)(Px \cdot \sim Kx)$ | Pr |
| **2)** | $\sim (x)(Px \supset Kx)$ | Pr |

The conclusion is the left-hand disjunct of the first premise. This suggests using Commutation on line 1, followed by Disjunctive Syllogism. '$\sim \sim (\exists x)(Px \cdot \sim Kx)$' is then required to apply Disjunctive Syllogism. This is obtained by a use of Double Negation if '$(\exists x)(Px \cdot \sim Kx)$' is first established. So, attempt to convert the second premise into '$(\exists x)(Px \cdot \sim Kx)$'.

| (15) | | $/ \therefore (\exists x)(Px \cdot Vx)$ |
|---|---|---|
| **1)** | $(\exists x)(Px \cdot Vx) \lor \sim (\exists x)(Px \cdot \sim Kx)$ | Pr |
| **2)** | $\sim (x)(Px \supset Kx)$ | Pr |
| **3)** | $\sim (\exists x)(Px \cdot \sim Kx) \lor (\exists x)(Px \cdot Vx)$ | 1, Com |
| **4)** | $(\exists x) \sim (Px \supset Kx)$ | 2, QD |
| **5)** | $(\exists x) \sim (\sim Px \lor Kx)$ | 4, Impl |

| | |
|---|---|
| **6)** (∃x) (~ ~Px • ~Kx) | 5, DeM |
| **7)** (∃x) (Px • ~Kx) | 6, DN |
| **8)** ~ ~ (∃x) (Px • ~Kx) | 7, DN |
| **9)** /∴ (∃x) (Px • Vx) | 3, 8, DS |

As a strategy, whenever there is a tilde prefixed to a quantifier and there is no evident reason to keep it there, remove it. Quantificational Denial is often helpful in carrying out this plan of action.

---

## EXERCISES

### Group A:

Give the correct justification for each unjustified line of the following.

1.                                           /∴ (x) (Ax ⊃ ~ Bx)
   1) (x) ~ (Ax • Bx) ∨ (x) (Cx ⊃ Bx)    Pr
   2) (∃x) (Cx • ~ Bx)               Pr
   3) ~ (x) ~ (Cx • ~ Bx)
   4) ~ (x) ( ~ Cx ∨ ~ ~ Bx)
   5) ~ (x) ( ~ Cx ∨ Bx)
   6) ~ (x) (Cx ⊃ Bx)
   7) (x) (Cx ⊃ Bx) ∨ (x) ~ (Ax • Bx)
   8) (x) ~ (Ax • Bx)
   9) (x) ( ~ Ax ∨ ~ Bx)
   10) /∴ (x) (Ax ⊃ ~ Bx)

2.                                           /∴ (x) (Ax ⊃ ~ Cx)
   1) ~ (∃x) (Ax • ~ Bx)    Pr
   2) (x) (Bx ⊃ ~ Cx)      Pr
   3) (x) ~ (Ax • ~ Bx)
   4) Bx ⊃ ~ Cx
   5) ~ (Ax • ~ Bx)
   6) ~ Ax ∨ ~ ~ Bx
   7) ~ Ax ∨ Bx
   8) Ax ⊃ Bx
   9) Ax ⊃ ~ Cx
   10) /∴ (x) (Ax ⊃ ~ Cx)

3.                                           /∴ (∃x)Cx
   1) ~ (x) ~ (Ax • Bx)    Pr
   2) (x) (Bx ⊃ Cx)       Pr
   3) (∃x) (Ax • Bx)
   4) Ax • Bx
   5) Bx ⊃ Cx
   6) Bx • Ax

7) Bx
8) Cx
9) /∴ (∃x)Cx

4.                                                          /∴ (x)(Ax ⊃ Cx)

1) ∼ (∃x)(Ax · ∼ Bx) · ∼ (∃x)(Bx · ∼ Cx)    Pr
2) ∼ (∃x)(Ax · ∼ Bx)
3) ∼ (∃x)(Bx · ∼ Cx) · ∼ (∃x)(Ax · ∼ Bx)
4) ∼ (∃x)(Bx · ∼ Cx)
5) (x) ∼ (Ax · ∼ Bx)
6) (x) ∼ (Bx · ∼ Cx)
7) ∼ (Ax · ∼ Bx)
8) ∼ (Bx · ∼ Cx)
9) ∼ Ax ∨ ∼ ∼ Bx
10) ∼ Ax ∨ Bx
11) Ax ⊃ Bx
12) ∼ Bx ∨ ∼ ∼ Cx
13) ∼ Bx ∨ Cx
14) Bx ⊃ Cx
15) Ax ⊃ Cx
16) /∴ (x)(Ax ⊃ Cx)

5.                                       /∴ ∼ (x)(Cx ∨ Bx)

1) ∼ (x)(Ax ∨ Bx)      Pr
2) (x)(Cx ⊃ Bx)      Pr
3) (∃x) ∼ (Ax ∨ Bx)
4) ∼ (Ax ∨ Bx)
5) Cx ⊃ Bx
6) ∼ Ax · ∼ Bx
7) ∼ Bx · ∼ Ax
8) ∼ Bx
9) ∼ Cx
10) ∼ Cx · ∼ Bx
11) ∼ (Cx ∨ Bx)
12) (∃x) ∼ (Cx ∨ Bx)
13) /∴ ∼ (x)(Cx ∨ Bx)

6.                                       /∴ (x)(Bx ⊃ Dx)

1) ∼ (∃x) ∼ (Ax ∨ Bx)      Pr
2) (x)[(Ax ∨ Cx) ⊃ Dx]      Pr
3) (x)(Ax ∨ ∼ Bx)
4) (Ax ∨ Cx) ⊃ Dx
5) Ax ∨ ∼ Bx
6) ∼ Bx ∨ Ax
7) Bx ⊃ Ax
8) ∼ (Ax ∨ Cx) ∨ Dx
9) ( ∼ Ax · ∼ Cx) ∨ Dx
10) Dx ∨ ( ∼ Ax · ∼ Cx)
11) (Dx ∨ ∼ Ax) · (Dx ∨ ∼ Cx)
12) Dx ∨ ∼ Ax
13) ∼ Ax ∨ Dx
14) Ax ⊃ Dx

    15)  Bx ⊃ Dx

    16)  /∴ (x)(Bx ⊃ Dx)

7.                                           /∴ (∃x)(Ax · ~ Bx)

    1)  (x)(Ax ⊃ Bx) ⊃ (x)(Cx ⊃ Bx)    Pr

    2)  (x)(Dx ⊃ Cx)    Pr

    3)  ~ (x)(Dx ⊃ Bx)    Pr

    4)  (∃x) ~ (Dx ⊃ Bx)

    5)  ~ (Dx ⊃ Bx)

    6)  ~ ( ~ Dx ∨ Bx)

    7)  ~ ~ Dx · ~ Bx

    8)  Dx · ~ Bx

    9)  Dx ⊃ Cx

    10)  Dx

    11)  ~ Bx · Dx

    12)  ~ Bx

    13)  Cx

    14)  Cx · ~ Bx

    15)  (∃x)(Cx · ~ Bx)

    16)  ~ (x) ~ (Cx · ~ Bx)

    17)  ~ (x)(~ Cx ∨ ~ ~ Bx)

    18)  ~ (x)( ~ Cx ∨ Bx)

    19)  ~ (x)(Cx ⊃ Bx)

    20)  ~ (x)(Ax ⊃ Bx)

    21)  (∃x) ~ (Ax ⊃ Bx)

    22)  (∃x) ~ ( ~ Ax ∨ Bx)

    23)  (∃x) (~ ~ Ax · ~ Bx)

    24)  /∴ (∃x)(Ax · ~ Bx)

8.                                           /∴ (x)[(Cx ∨ Ax) ⊃ Dx]

    1)  (x)[Ax ⊃ (Bx · Cx)]    Pr

    2)  ~ (∃x)[Cx · ( ~ Dx ∨ ~ Ex)]    Pr

    3)  (x) ~ [Cx · ( ~ Dx ∨ ~ Ex)]

    4)  Ax ⊃ (Bx · Cx)

    5)  ~ [Cx · ( ~ Dx ∨ ~ Ex)]

    6)  ~ Cx ∨ ~ ( ~ Dx ∨ ~ Ex)

    7)  ~ Cx ∨ ~ ~ (Dx · Ex)

    8)  ~ Cx ∨ (Dx · Ex)

    9)  ( ~ Cx ∨ Dx) · ( ~ Cx ∨ Ex)

    10)  ~ Cx ∨ Dx

    11)  Cx ⊃ Dx

    12)  ~ Ax ∨ (Bx · Cx)

    13)  ~ Ax ∨ (Cx · Bx)

    14)  ( ~ Ax ∨ Cx) · ( ~ Ax ∨ Bx)

    15)  ~ Ax ∨ Cx

    16)  Ax ⊃ Cx

    17)  Ax ⊃ Dx

    18)  ~ Ax ∨ Dx

    19)  Dx ∨ ~ Cx

    20)  Dx ∨ ~ Ax

    21)  (Dx ∨ ~ Cx) · (Dx ∨ ~ Ax)

22) Dx ∨ ( ∼ Cx · ∼ Ax)
23) ( ∼ Cx · ∼ Ax) ∨ Dx
24) ∼ (Cx ∨ Ax) ∨ Dx
25) (Cx ∨ Ax) ⊃ Dx
26) / ∴ (x) [(Cx ∨ Ax) ⊃ Dx]

9.                                           / ∴ ∼ (∃x)(Dx · ∼ Bx)

1) ∼ (∃x)[(Cx ∨ Dx) · ∼ Ax]   Pr
2) ∼ (∃x)(Ax · ∼ Bx)           Pr
3) (x) ∼ [(Cx ∨ Dx) · ∼ Ax]
4) (x) ∼ (Ax · ∼ Bx)
5) ∼ [(Cx ∨ Dx) · ∼ Ax]
6) ∼ (Cx ∨ Dx) ∨ ∼ ∼ Ax
7) ∼ (Cx ∨ Dx) ∨ Ax
8) (Cx ∨ Dx) ⊃ Ax
9) ∼ (Ax · ∼ Bx)
10) ∼ Ax ∨ ∼ ∼ Bx
11) ∼ Ax ∨ Bx
12) Ax ⊃ Bx
13) (Cx ∨ Dx) ⊃ Bx
14) ∼ (Cx ∨ Dx) ∨ Bx
15) ( ∼ Cx · ∼ Dx) ∨ Bx
16) Bx ∨ ( ∼ Cx · ∼ Dx)
17) Bx ∨ ( ∼ Dx · ∼ Cx)
18) (Bx ∨ ∼ Dx) · (Bx ∨ ∼ Cx)
19) Bx ∨ ∼ Dx
20) ∼ Dx ∨ Bx
21) Dx ⊃ Bx
22) (x)(Dx ⊃ Bx)
23) ∼ (∃x) ∼ (Dx ⊃ Bx)
24) ∼ (∃x) ∼ ( ∼ Dx ∨ Bx)
25) ∼ (∃x) ∼ (∼ Dx ∨ ∼ ∼ Bx)
26) ∼ (∃x) ∼ ∼ (Dx · ∼ Bx)
27) / ∴ ∼ (∃x)(Dx · ∼ Bx)

10.                                          / ∴ ∼ (∃x)[(Ex · Bx) · ∼ Dx]

1) ∼ (∃x)[Ax · ∼ (Bx ⊃ ∼ Cx)]        Pr
2) ∼ (∃x)( ∼ Dx · ∼ Cx) · ∼ (∃x)(Ex · ∼ Ax)   Pr
3) ∼ (∃x)( ∼ Dx · ∼ Cx)
4) ∼ (∃x)(Ex · ∼ Ax) · ∼ (∃x)( ∼ Dx · ∼ Cx)
5) ∼ (∃x)(Ex · ∼ Ax)
6) (x) ∼ [Ax · ∼ (Bx ⊃ ∼ Cx)]
7) (x) ∼ ( ∼ Dx · ∼ Cx)
8) (x) ∼ (Ex · ∼ Ax)
9) ∼ [Ax · ∼ (Bx ⊃ ∼ Cx)]
10) ∼ ( ∼ Dx · ∼ Cx)
11) ∼ (Ex · ∼ Ax)
12) ∼ Ax ∨ ∼ ∼ (Bx ⊃ ∼ Cx)
13) ∼ Ax ∨ (Bx ⊃ ∼ Cx)
14) Ax ⊃ (Bx ⊃ ∼ Cx)

15)  ~~Dx ∨ ~~Cx
16)  ~~Dx ∨ Cx
17)  ~Dx ⊃ Cx
18)  ~Ex ∨ ~~Ax
19)  ~Ex ∨ Ax
20)  Ex ⊃ Ax
21)  Ex ⊃ (Bx ⊃ ~Cx)
22)  (Ex · Bx) ⊃ ~Cx
23)  ~Cx ⊃ ~~Dx
24)  ~Cx ⊃ Dx
25)  (Ex · Bx) ⊃ Dx
26)  (x)[(Ex · Bx) ⊃ Dx]
27)  ~(∃x)~[(Ex · Bx) ⊃ Dx]
28)  ~(∃x)~[~(Ex · Bx) ∨ Dx]
29)  ~(∃x)[~~(Ex · Bx) · ~Dx]
30)  /∴  ~(∃x)[(Ex · Bx) · ~Dx]

## Group B:

Construct a proof for each of the following.

1.                                              /∴ (∃x) ~Ax
   1)  ~(∃x)(Ax · ~Bx) · ~(x)Bx    Pr

2.                                              /∴ (x)(Bx ⊃ Cx)
   1)  ~(∃x)[(Ax ⊃ Bx) · ~Cx]   Pr

3.                              /∴ ~(x)(Cx ⊃ Ax)
   1)  ~(∃x)~(Ax ⊃ Bx)   Pr
   2)  ~(x)(Cx ⊃ Bx)     Pr

4.                                              /∴ (x)[Ax ⊃ (Dx ⊃ Bx)]
   1)  ~(∃x)[(Ax · Bx) · (Cx ∨ Dx)]   Pr

5.                                      /∴ ~(∃x)[Bx · (Ax · ~Dx)]
   1)  ~(∃x)[(Ax · Bx) · ~Cx]   Pr
   2)  (x)[Cx ⊃ (Ax ⊃ Dx)]            Pr

6.                          /∴ ~(x)[(Cx ∨ Dx) ⊃ Bx]
   1)  ~(x)~Ax           Pr
   2)  ~(∃x)(Ax · Bx)    Pr
   3)  (x)(Bx △ Cx)      Pr

7.                                              /∴ (∃x)(Cx · Ax) ∨ (∃x)(Cx · Dx)
   1)  ~(∃x)[~Ax · (~Bx · Cx)]   Pr
   2)  ~(x)(Cx ⊃ Bx)                   Pr

8.                                      /∴ (∃x)[Ax · (Cx · Ex)]
   1)  ~(x)(Ax ⊃ Bx)                   Pr
   2)  (x)(Ax ⊃ Cx)                    Pr
   3)  ~(∃x)[(~Bx · ~Ex) · (Dx ∨ Cx)]   Pr

9.                                                            /∴ ~ (∃x) ( ~ Cx · ~ Fx)
    1)   ~ (∃x) (Ax · ~ Bx) · ~ (∃x) (Bx · ~ Cx)  Pr
    2)   (x) ( ~ Ax ≡ Dx)  Pr
    3)   (x) (Dx ⊃ Ex) · (x) (Ex ⊃ Fx)  Pr

10.                                                          /∴ (x) ( ~ Cx ⊃ Fx)
    1)   ~ (∃x) [(Ax · Bx) · ~ Cx]  Pr
    2)   (x) [Dx ⊃ ( ~ Bx ≡ Ex)]  Pr
    3)   ~ (∃x) [(Dx · Ex) · ~ Fx]  Pr
    4)   ~ (x) (Dx ⊃ ~ Ax)  Pr

**Group C:**

Symbolize the following arguments using the suggested predicate logic notation. Then construct a proof for each.

1. Everything is harmful or safe but not everything is safe. Consequently, some things are safe and not harmful. (H,S;x)

2. There aren't Aristotelians who aren't empiricists; but further there isn't someone who isn't an Aristotelian but is a naturalist. Thus, there aren't naturalists who aren't empiricists. (A,E,N;x)

3. None but teleologists are Aristotelians. It isn't true that there are teleologists who aren't both interested in ethics while maintaining a doctrine of the supreme good for human beings. So, there aren't Aristotelians who fail to be interested in ethics. (T,A,I,M;x)

4. It isn't the case that some harmful actions aren't selfish. Actions are harmful and mean when selfish. Wherefore, there isn't some action of which it isn't true to claim that it's selfish when and only when it's harmful. (H,A,S,M;x)

5. Any action is good if and only if it is neither selfish nor harmful. There are good actions. Hence, not every action is harmful. (A,G,S,H;x)

6. Anyone who is a Realist holds that sets exist if he is a mathematician. Not everyone who is a mathematician holds that sets exist. Every Logicist is a Realist or holds that sets exist. Therefore, someone isn't a Realist and not a Logicist. (P,R,S,M,L;x)

7. There isn't something vicious which is an action but not mean. It isn't true that some action which is mean isn't both harmful as well as cruel. Consequently, all actions are harmful if vicious. (V,A,M,H,C;x)

8. Not everyone is compassionate who is understanding or tolerant. There isn't someone who is understanding but also either not virtuous or not compassionate. Thus, not everyone is compassionate who is tolerant. (P,C,U,T,V;x)

9. There aren't some pleasurable things in the world of which it isn't true to say that they ought to be avoided just in case they aren't harmful. It isn't the case that all pleasurable things in the world ought to be done. There isn't something beneficial that ought not to be done and there isn't something that ought to be avoided that isn't harmful. So, some pleasurable things in the world are harmful. (P,A,B,D,H;x)

10. There isn't some person who truly loves his neighbor but doesn't either understand or gossip (but not both). Not every person who truly loves his neighbor isn't compassionate. It isn't the case that there is some person who is compassionate but of whom it isn't true

that he understands when and only when he is virtuous. No person is compassionate who both gossips and is intolerant. Hence, not every person is both not virtuous and intolerant. (P,L,U,G,C,V,T;x)

---

## 5.  CONDITIONAL AND INDIRECT PROOFS

Both the Conditional Method and Indirect Method of proving validity can be expanded for use in predicate logic. Imagine an argument whose conclusion is some statement '$(\alpha)(\Phi\alpha \supset \Psi\alpha)$'. This is not a hypothetical statement. However, any statement function represented by '$\Phi\alpha \supset \Psi\alpha$' is hypothetical. So, as a new premise, assume '$\Phi\alpha$' and deduce '$\Psi\alpha$'. Then obtain '$\Phi\alpha \supset \Psi\alpha$' by Conditional Proof. The conclusion is reached by using Universal Generalization. In using an Indirect Proof, the denial of the conclusion is assumed as a new premise and then a contradiction is deduced from the augmented premise set. If the conclusion is an undenied universally or existentially quantified statement, QD very likely might be applied to the assumption introduced by Indirect Proof to obtain a contradiction.

Problems not found in truth-functional logic can be encountered when using CP or IP in predicate logic. If care is not taken a "proof" can be constructed for an invalid argument. To guard against the possibility of deducing a false conclusion from all true premises, the restrictions on Universal Generalization must be extended:

### UNIVERSAL GENERALIZATION (UG)

$$\Phi\beta$$
$$\overline{/\therefore (\alpha)\Phi\alpha}$$

(1), '$\beta$' is an individual variable that occurs free in '$\Phi\beta$' at all, and only those, places where '$\alpha$' is a variable that occurs free in '$\Phi\alpha$'; (2), '$\beta$' does not occur free in any statement function, $\Phi\alpha$, obtained by Existential Instantiation; and (3), '$\beta$' *is a variable that does not occur free in an assumption within whose scope '$\Phi\beta$' lies.*

Why is the third restriction needed? Consider this example:

**(2)**  Everything is dangerous only if everything is wicked. Consequently, everything is wicked if dangerous.

The premise of this argument, symbolized as '$(x)Dx \supset (x)Wx$', is true because the antecedent is false for everything in the universe.* Nonetheless, the conclusion is false. There are many dangerous things that are not wicked. However, if the third

---

* Assuming a Boolean interpretation, any hypothetical statement is true if it has a false antecedent. 'If Hilda is a unicorn, then Hilda is fleet of foot' is true because, there being no unicorns, 'Hilda is a unicorn' is false. While true, such hypotheticals are *vacuously* true. In a similar way, since 'Given anything in the universe it is dangerous' is false, 'Everything is dangerous only if everything is wicked' is true.

restriction on UG is not observed, then the following "proof" can be generated for (2):

**(3)**                                          / ∴ (x)(Dx ⊃ Wx)

             **1)** (x)Dx ⊃ (x)Wx   Pr

             **2)** Dx                   CP, / ∴ Wx

*WRONG X*    **3)** (x)Dx             2, UG

             **4)** (x)Wx            1, 3, MP

             **5)** Wx                   5, UI

             **6)** Dx ⊃ Wx        2–5, CP

             **7)** (x)(Dx ⊃ Wx)   6, UG

The conclusion of (3) is a simple statement involving a universal quantifier. Quantifiers can also be used in the symbolization of compound statements. Consider this argument:

**(4)**   All cats are furry. Accordingly, if everything is a cat, then everything is furry.

(4) can be symbolized and a legitimate proof constructed for it using Conditional Proof:

**(5)**                                          / ∴ (x)Cx ⊃ (x)Fx

          **1)** (x)(Cx ⊃ Fx)   Pr

          **2)** Cx ⊃ Fx       1, UI

          **3)** (x)Cx          CP, / ∴ (x)Fx

          **4)** Cx             3, UI

          **5)** Fx             2, 4, MP

          **6)** (x)Fx        5, UG

          **7)** / ∴ (x)Cx ⊃ (x)Fx   2–6, CP

UG is used in line 6 to generalize over 'x'. And 6 is within the scope of the assumption introduced in 2. Nevertheless, 'x' does not occur as a free variable in line 2. Hence, the restriction on Universal Generalization is not violated.

If the statement function leading to a conclusion is logically equivalent to a hypothetical statement function, Conditional Proof can be used provided that all of the restrictions on UG are observed:

**(6)**                                          / ∴ ~ (∃x) ~ [(Ax ⊃ Dx) ∨ Bx]

      **1)** (x)[Ax ⊃ (Bx ∨ Cx)]   Pr

      **2)** (x)(Cx ⊃ Dx)         Pr

      **3)** Ax ⊃ (Bx ∨ Cx)        1, UI

      **4)** Cx ⊃ Dx           2, UI

| | | |
|---|---|---|
| **5)** | Ax · ~ Dx | CP, / ∴ Bx |
| **6)** | Ax | 5, Simp |
| **7)** | ~ Dx · Ax | 5, Com |
| **8)** | ~ Dx | 7, Simp |
| **9)** | Bx ∨ Cx | 3, 6, MP |
| **10)** | Cx ∨ Bx | 9, Com |
| **11)** | ~ Cx | 4, 8, MT |
| **12)** | Bx | 10, 11, DS |
| **13)** | (Ax · ~ Dx) ⊃ Bx | 5–12, CP |
| **14)** | ~ (Ax · ~ Dx) ∨ Bx | 13, Impl |
| **15)** | (~Ax ∨ ~~ Dx) ∨ Bx | 14, DeM |
| **16)** | ( ~ Ax ∨ Dx) ∨ Bx | 15, DN |
| **17)** | (Ax ⊃ Dx) ∨ Bx | 16, Impl |
| **18)** | (x) [(Ax ⊃ Dx) ∨ Bx] | 17, UG |
| **19)** | / ∴ ~ (∃x) ~ [(Ax ⊃ Dx) ∨ Bx] | 18, QD |

Caution must also be taken in using Indirect Proof. Here is an argument in which all the premises are true but the conclusion false:

> **(7)** Every cat is an animal. Either there are animals or there are cats. So everything is an animal.

Suppose someone attempted to use an indirect proof to generate this "proof" of (7):

**(8)** / ∴ (x)Ax

| | | | |
|---|---|---|---|
| | **1)** | (x)(Cx ⊃ Ax) | Pr |
| | **2)** | (∃x)Ax ∨ (∃x)Cx | Pr |
| *WRONG X* | **3)** | ~ Ax | IP |
| *WRONG X* | **4)** | (x) ~ Ax | 3, UG |
| | **5)** | ~ (∃x)Ax | 4, QD |
| | **6)** | (∃x)Cx | 2, 5, DS |
| | **7)** | Cx | 6, EI |
| | **8)** | Cx ⊃ Ax | 1, UI |
| | **9)** | Ax | 8, 7, MP |
| | **10)** | ~ Ax | 4, UI |
| | **11)** | Ax · ~ Ax | 9, 10, Conj |
| | **12)** | Ax | 1–11, IP |
| | **13)** | / ∴ (x)Ax | 12, UG |

Two lines are incorrect in (7). First, line 3 is not the denial of the conclusion. The denial of the conclusion of (7) is ' ~ (x)Ax'. Second, even if ' ~ Ax' were the denial of the conclusion of (7), line 4 introduces an illegitimate use of Universal Generalization. Here the third restriction on Universal Generalization is broken because the individual variable 'x' generalized in 6 is introduced as free in the assumption at line 3.

Examine the following Conditional Proof in which each of the restrictions on UG is observed:

(9)                                          / ∴ (x)[Ax ⊃ (Dx ⊃ Cx)]

   **1)** (x)(Ax ⊃ Bx) · (x)(Bx ⊃ Cx)      Pr
   **2)** (x)(Ax ⊃ Bx)      1, Simp
   **3)** (x)(Bx ⊃ Cx) · (x)(Ax ⊃ Bx)      2, Com
   **4)** (x)(Bx ⊃ Cx)      3, Simp
   **5)** Ax ⊃ Bx      2, UI
   **6)** Bx ⊃ Cx      4, UI
   **7)** Ax ⊃ Cx      5, 6, HS
→ **8)** Ax      CP, / ∴ Dx ⊃ Cx
   **9)** Cx      7, 8, MP
  **10)** Cx ∨ ~ Dx      9, Add
  **11)** ~ Dx ∨ Cx      10, Com
  **12)** Dx ⊃ Cx      11, Impl

  **13)** Ax ⊃ (Dx ⊃ Cx)      8–12, CP
  **14)** / ∴ (x)[Ax ⊃ (Dx ⊃ Cx)]      13, UG

And here is a proof correctly using Indirect Proof:

(1)                                           / ∴ (∃x)( ~ Ax · ~ Dx)

   **1)** (x)[Ax ⊃ (Bx ⊃ Cx)]      Pr
   **2)** (∃x)(Bx · ~ Cx)      Pr
   **3)** (x)[Dx ⊃ (Ax ∨ Cx)]      Pr
   **4)** Bx · ~ Cx      2, EI
   **5)** Ax ⊃ (Bx ⊃ Cx)      1, UI
   **6)** Dx ⊃ (Ax ∨ Cx)      3, UI
   **7)** Bx      4, Simp
   **8)** ~ Cx · Bx      4, Com
   **9)** ~ Cx      8, Simp
  **10)** (Ax · Bx) ⊃ Cx      5, Exp
  **11)** ~ (Ax · Bx)      10, 9, MT
  **12)** ~ Ax ∨ ~ Bx      11, DeM

| | | |
|---|---|---|
| **13)** | $\sim Bx \lor \sim Ax$ | 12, Com |
| **14)** | $\sim\sim Bx$ | 7, DN |
| **15)** | $\sim Ax$ | 13, 14, DS |
| → **16)** | $\sim (\exists x)(\sim Ax \cdot \sim Dx)$ | IP |
| **17)** | $(x) \sim (\sim Ax \cdot \sim Dx)$ | 16, QD |
| **18)** | $\sim (\sim Ax \cdot \sim Dx)$ | 17, UI |
| **19)** | $\sim\sim (Ax \lor Dx)$ | 18, DeM |
| **20)** | $Ax \lor Dx$ | 19, DN |
| **21)** | $Dx$ | 20, 15, DS |
| **22)** | $Ax \lor Cx$ | 6, 21, MP |
| **23)** | $Cx$ | 22, 15, DS |
| **24)** | $Cx \cdot \sim Cx$ | 23, 9, Conj |

**25)** $/\therefore (\exists x)(\sim Ax \cdot \sim Dx)$    16–24, IP

## EXERCISES

### Group A:

Construct an Indirect Proof for each of the following.

1.  $/\therefore \sim (x)(Bx \supset \sim Cx)$
    1) $(x)(Ax \supset Bx)$    Pr
    2) $(\exists x)(Ax \cdot Cx)$    Pr

2.  $/\therefore (x)(Bx \supset Cx)$
    1) $(x)[(Ax \lor Bx) \supset Cx]$    Pr

3.  $/\therefore (\exists x)(Ax \cdot Bx)$
    1) $(x)[Ax \supset (Bx \cdot Cx)]$    Pr
    2) $(\exists x)Ax$    Pr

4.  $/\therefore (x)(Bx \supset Cx)$
    1) $(x)(Ax \supset Bx) \supset (x)(Bx \supset Cx)$    Pr
    2) $(x)(Ax \supset Cx) \cdot (x)(Cx \supset Bx)$    Pr

5.  $/\therefore (\exists x)(Bx \cdot \sim Cx)$
    1) $(x)(Ax \supset Bx) \cdot (\exists x)(Ax \cdot \sim Cx)$    Pr

6.  $/\therefore \sim (Ba \lor Da)$
    1) $(x)\{[Ax \cdot (Bx \lor Cx)] \equiv Dx\}$    Pr
    2) $\sim (Da \lor \sim Aa)$    Pr

7.  $/\therefore (\exists x)[(Ax \cdot Bx) \cdot (Ex \cdot Cx)]$
    1) $(\exists x)[(Ax \cdot Bx) \cdot (Cx \cdot Dx)]$    Pr
    2) $(x)(Ax \supset Ex)$    Pr

8.  $/\therefore (\exists x)(Ax \cdot Cx)$
    1) $(x)(Ax \supset (Bx \lor Cx)]$    Pr
    2) $(x)(Bx \supset Dx)$    Pr
    3) $(\exists x)(Ax \cdot \sim Dx)$    Pr

9.                                                    $/ \therefore (x)(Bx \lor \sim Cx)$
   1) $(x)(Ax \lor \sim Ax)$      Pr
   2) $(x)(Ax \equiv Bx)$        Pr
   3) $\sim (\exists x)(Cx \cdot \sim Ax)$   Pr

10.                                                   $/ \therefore (x)[Cx \supset (Ex \supset Ax)]$
   1) $(x)\{ \sim Ax \supset [(Bx \lor Cx) \supset \sim (Dx \lor Ex)]\}$     Pr

**Group B:**

Symbolize the following arguments using the suggested predicate logic notation. Then construct a Conditional Proof for each.

1. No drug that is habit-forming is either safe or beneficial if not prescribed by a physician. Hence, any habit-forming drug is either prescribed by a physician or isn't beneficial. (D,F,S,B,P;x)

2. Anything not safe to use without a prescription might not be harmful even though it isn't beneficial. Everything that is safe to use without a prescription is trustworthy. So, everything is trustworthy or not beneficial. (S,H,B,T;x)

3. Every body is spatially extended. Any body is spatially extended only if it obeys the laws of physics. Each spatially extended body can be described and explained if it obeys the laws of physics. Thus, any body can be described and explained. (B,S,O,D,E;x)

4. If anything is either knowable or understandable, it is a proper object of scientific study. Everything is either understandable or both not explainable and not describable. Consequently, anything explainable is a proper object of scientific study. (K,U,O,E,D;x)

5. Anyone who is a scientist or technician is respected only if well-educated and knowledgeable. Therefore, anyone who is a scientist is well-educated if respected. (P,S,T,R,E,K;x)

6. Acids that corrode the more electropositive metals while releasing hydrogen are proton donors only if they give up protons easily and are strong. Accordingly, acids that corrode the more electropositive metals release hydrogen only if they are strong whenever they are proton donors. (A,C,R,D,G,S;x)

7. Nothing that is either a reptile or fish while also being cold-blooded and scaly is viviparous. Hence, anything viviparous is both cold-blooded and scaly only if it isn't a fish. (R,F,C,S,V;x)

8. Nothing that is both cold-blooded and has a shell is viviparous. Anything that isn't oviparous is viviparous. Turtles are cold-blooded. So, turtles are oviparous if they have shells. (C,S,V,O,T;x)

9. No chemical that is an acid only if either phosphoric or nitric is both slick to the touch while also being high on the pH scale. Therefore, no chemical that is slick to the touch and high on the pH scale is either phosphoric or nitric. (C,A,P,N,S,H;x)

10. No contestant will be either noticed or judged who is either not over twenty-one years old or married. Consequently, any noticed contestant isn't married. (C,N,J,O,M;x)

---

## 6.   ARGUMENTS INVOLVING RELATIONS

Predicate letters can be followed by one, or more, individual variables, individual constants, or both. Further, quantifiers can fall within the scope of other quantifiers in a single statement. These features can produce difficulties in attempting to use the quantificational rules introduced in this chapter. Indeed, particular attention to the restrictions on these rules is demanded with relational predicates and quantifiers falling within the scope of other quantifiers.

Consider this argument:

**(1)** Every person has a mother. Persons exist. Accordingly, something is its own mother.

(1) can be symbolized and an abortive proof attempted:

**(2)**                                    / ∴ (∃y)(My · Hyy)

             **1)** (x)[Px ⊃ (∃y)(My · Hxy)]    Pr

             **2)** (∃x)Px                   Pr

             **3)** Py                        2, EI

*WRONG X*    **4)** Py ⊃ (∃y)(My · Hyy)      1, UI

             **5)** / ∴ (∃y)(My · Hyy)      4, 3, MP

What is wrong with line 4? Notice that every 'x' in the first premise of (2) is under the scope of the universal quantifier, '(x)'. In 4, however, each 'x' is changed to 'y'. So, the 'x' in 'Hxy' becomes a 'y' and falls under the scope of the existential quantifier, '(∃y)'. Now, examine this argument:

**(3)** Some people are wise in every act. Thus, every act is itself a wise one.

Note the following "proof" of (3):

**(4)**                                 / ∴ (y)(Ay ⊃ Wyy)

             **1)** (∃x)[Px · (y)(Ay ⊃ Wxy)]    Pr

*WRONG X*    **2)** Py · (y)(Ay ⊃ Wyy)       1, EI

             **3)** (y)(Ay ⊃ Wyy) · Py       2, Com

             **4)** / ∴ (y)(Ay ⊃ Wyy)       3, Simp

Once more an individual variable originally bound by one quantifier has become bound by another. In (4) the illegitimate move occurs in going from the premise to the statement function in 2. Such moves break restrictions placed on Universal and Existential Instantiation. The restriction violated in both (2) and (4) is this:

> **Let 'Φα' be some statement function under the scope of either a universal quantifier, '(α)', or an existential quantifier, '(∃α)'. Then if 'Φβ' is obtained either by Universal or Existential Instantiation and 'β' is some individual variable, then 'β' must remain free in 'Φβ' at all those places where 'α' is free in 'Φα'.**

Analogous to the mistakes in (2) and (4) are those sometimes made when appealing to Universal or Existential Generalization. Study the following example:

**(5)** Given anything at all, there is something from which it is distinguishable. So, given anything at all, it is distinguishable from itself.

A "proof" for (5) might be attempted in this way:

**(6)** /∴ (y)Dyy
**1)** (x)(∃y)Dxy    Pr
**2)** (∃y)Dxy    1, UI
**3)** Dxy    2, EI
*WRONG X* **4)** /∴ (y)Dyy    3, UG

The errors in (6) are not the result of the Existential Instantiation move in 3. Even though Universal Instantiation is used before 3, 'y' does not appear free before 3. Two restrictions placed on Universal Generalization are violated, however. First, the statement function to be generalized, 'Dxy', is obtained by Existential Instantiation. Second, the free 'x' in 'Dxy' becomes bound in 4 as does the free 'y'. The move from 3 to the conclusion allows the quantifier to capture too much in its scope. A similar mistake is found in

**(7)** /∴ (∃y)Dyy
**1)** (x)(∃y)Dxy    Pr
**2)** (∃y)Dxy    1, UI
**3)** Dxy    2, EI
*WRONG X* **4)** /∴ (∃y)Dyy    3, EG

Too much becomes bound by the quantifier in 4. However, restrictions implicit in Sections 1 and 2 prohibit this illicit move. The particular restriction violated is this:

Let '$\Phi\beta$' be some statement function and '$\beta$' an individual variable. If '$(\alpha)\Phi\alpha$' is obtained from '$\Phi\beta$', then '$\alpha$' must be bound in '$\Phi\alpha$' at only those occurrences of free '$\beta$' in '$\Phi\beta$'. Or if '$(\exists\alpha)\Phi\alpha$' is obtained from '$\Phi\beta$' by Existential Generalization, then '$\alpha$' must be bound in '$\Phi\alpha$' at only those occurrences of '$\beta$' free in '$\Phi\beta$'.

Here is an argument in which all the rules are correctly used:

**(8)** Airplanes are means of transportation. So, anyone using an airplane uses a means of transportation.

Intuitively, (8) is valid. To prove its validity the argument must first be symbolized. The premise goes into

**(9)**
**1)** (x)(Ax ⊃ Tx)    Pr

The conclusion is more complicated. The word, 'anyone', suggests the universe of discourse is *persons*. For the sake of simplicity, in working through this example, assume this universe of discourse as part of the tacit background in which the conclusion is asserted. So, 'x is a person' is not explicitly included in this symbolization of the conclusion. Further, since no person uses every airplane, in the conclusion 'airplane' is understood as 'some airplane'. In a similar manner 'a means of transportation' is understood as 'some means of transportation'. Symbolize 'some airplane' as

(**10**)   (∃y)Ay

Symbolize 'some means of transportation' as

(**11**)   (∃y)Ty

The entire conclusion is now symbolized as

(**12**)   (x)[(∃y)(Ay · Uxy) ⊃ (∃y)(Ty · Uxy)]

(9) and (12) are now put together in the format of an argument and a proof constructed:

(**13**)                              /∴ (x)[(∃y)(Ay · Uxy) ⊃ (∃y)(Ty · Uxy)]

   **1)**  (x)(Ax ⊃ Tx)      Pr
→**2)**  (∃y)(Ay · Uxy)      CP, /∴ (∃y)(Ty · Uxy)
   **3)**  Ay · Uxy      3, EI
   **4)**  Ay      3, Simp
   **5)**  Ay ⊃ Ty      1, UI
   **6)**  Ty      5, 4, MP
   **7)**  Uxy · Ay      3, Com
   **8)**  Uxy      7, Simp
   **9)**  Ty · Uxy      6, 8, Conj
**10)**  (∃y)(Ty · Uxy)      9, EG

**11)**  (∃y)(Ay · Uxy) ⊃ (∃y)(Ty · Uxy)           2–10, CP
**12)**  /∴ (x)[(∃y)(Ay · Uxy) ⊃ (∃y)(Ty · Uxy]    11, UG

In moving from the premise to line 5 by Universal Instantiation the bound variable, 'x', is changed to the free variable, 'y'. In proof construction in previous sections, when using Universal, or Existential, Instantiation the bound variables are not changed as the quantifier is dropped. This is only a matter of convenience. The rules of instantiation permit changing a bound variable to any free variable provided that every restriction on these rules is observed. A change of variables is required within (13) in going to 5 to prepare for a Modus Ponens move. Also notice that the scope of '(x)' in the conclusion is the entire hypothetical, (∃y)(Ay · Uxy) ⊃ (∃y) (Ty · Uxy)'. First use Conditional Proof to obtain this hypothetical. Then, end the proof with a use of Universal Generalization.

The strategy of changing individual variables is slightly more complicated if the conclusion of (1) is symbolized as

(**14**) (x)[(∃y)(Ay · Uxy) ⊃ (∃z)(Tz · Uxz]

Review the following proof:

**(15)**                                   / ∴ (x) [(∃y) (Ay · Uxy) ⊃ (∃z) (Tz · Uxz)]

**1)** (x) (Ax ⊃ Tx)        Pr

**2)** (∃y) (Ay · Uxy)      CP, / ∴ (∃z) (Tz · Uxz)

**3)** Az · Uxz            2, EI

**4)** Az ⊃ Tz            1, UI

**5)** Az                  3, Simp

**6)** Tz                  4, 5, MP

**7)** Uxz · Az            3, Com

**8)** Uxz                7, Simp

**9)** Tz · Uxz            6, 8, Conj

**10)** (∃z) (Tz · Uxz)     9, EG

**11)** (∃y) (Ay · Uxy) ⊃ (∃z) (Tz · Uxz)            2–10, CP

**12)** / ∴ (x) [(∃y) (Ay · Uxy) ⊃ (∃z) (Tz · Uxz]    11, UG

When moving from the statement in 2 to the statement function in 3, the bound variable, 'y', is changed to 'z'. This is done to obtain 'Uxz' appearing in the conclusion. Further, a 'z' is introduced in 4 to deduce 'Az' in 5. 'Az' is needed for a Modus Ponens move with 'Az ⊃ Tz' to establish 'Tz' in the conclusion.

## *EXERCISES*

### Group A:

Construct a proof for each of the following using Conditional Proof when appropriate.

1.                                   / ∴ ~ Bba

1) Aab                Pr
2) (x) (Bxa ⊃ ~ Aax)  Pr

2.                                   / ∴ (∃z) Bzz

1) (x) [(∃y) Ayx ⊃ Bxx]  Pr
2) (∃x) [(∃y) Ayx · Bxy]  Pr

3.                                   / ∴ (y) [Ay ⊃ (∃w) Cyw]

1) (x) [Ax ⊃ (∃z) (Bz · Cxz)]  Pr

4.                                   / ∴ (z) (Dz ⊃ ~ Bz)

1) (x) [Ax ⊃ (y) (By ⊃ Cxy)]     Pr
2) Aa                             Pr
3) (x) [Ax ⊃ (w) (Dw ⊃ ~ Cxw)]   Pr

5.                                   / ∴ (∃x) (y) ( ~ Cx ⊃ ~ By)

1) (∃x) (y) [(Axy ⊃ By) ⊃ Cx]  Pr

6.                                   / ∴ (w) [Cw ⊃ (z) (Bz ⊃ Awz)]

1) (x) (y) (Axy ⊃ Ayx)          Pr
2) (x) [Bx ⊃ (y) (Cy ⊃ Axy)]    Pr

7.                                        / ∴ ~ (y)(Ay ⊃ Bxy)
   1) (x){[Ax · (y)(Ay ⊃ Bxy)] ⊃ Bxx}   Pr
   2) ~ (x)(Ax ⊃ (∃y)Bxy)           Pr

8.                                      / ∴ (∃y)(By · ~ Dy)
   1) (x)[Ax ⊃ (∃y)(By · Cxy)]   Pr
   2) Aa                         Pr
   3) (x)[Ax ⊃ (y)(Dy ⊃ ~ Cxy)]   Pr

9.                               / ∴ (∃x)[Bx · (y)(Ay ⊃ Cyx)]
   1) (x)[Ax ⊃ (∃w)(Bw · Cxw)]        Pr
   2) (∃x)(Bx · (y){[Ay · (∃z)(Bz · Cyz)] ⊃ Cyx})   Pr

10.                       / ∴ (y){(By · Dy) ⊃ (x)[(Ax · Dx) ⊃ Cyx]}
   1) (x)(y)[(Ax ∨ By) ⊃ (Cxy ≡ Cyx)]   Pr
   2) (x){(Ax · Dx) ⊃ (y)[(By · Dy) ⊃ Cxy]}   Pr
   3) (∃x)Ax · (∃y)By                  Pr

## Group B:

Symbolize the following arguments using the suggested predicate logic notation. Then construct a proof for each. Use Condition Proof when appropriate.

1. Any friend of Maria is a friend of Dottie. Paco is a friend of Maria. So, Paco is also a friend of Dottie.

   'Fpm' = 'Paco is a friend of Maria'
   'Fxd' = 'x is a friend of Dottie'
   'Fxm' = 'x is a friend of Maria'

2. Someone appreciates everything. Therefore, everything is appreciated by someone.

   'Px' = 'x is a person'
   'Axy' = 'x appreciates y'

3. For any two numbers 'x' and 'y', if 'x' is greater than 'y', 'y' is not greater than 'x'. Now, 7 is greater than 3. Hence, 3 is not greater than 7.

   'Gxy' = 'x is greater than y'
   'Gyx' = 'y is greater than x'
   'G₇₃' = '7 is greater than 3'

4. Certain poets are appreciated by every poet. Consequently, some poets appreciate themselves.

   'Px' = 'x is a poet'
   'Py' = 'y is a poet'
   'Ayx' = 'y appreciates x'

5. Everything that hates Smaug appreciates Bilbo. Anything that trusts William the Troll isn't trusted by Bilbo. Thorin appreciates everything that trusts Gandalf. Thus, Gandalf trusts William the Troll only if Thorin doesn't hate Smaug.

   'Atx' = 'Thorin appreciates x'
   'Axb' = 'x appreciates Bilbo'

'Hxs' = 'x hates Smaug'
'Tbx' = 'Bilbo trusts x '
'Txg' = 'x trusts Gandalf'
'Txa' = 'x trusts William the Troll'

6. Every student enjoys some course or another. Tom is a student and, moreover, he will work at anything if he enjoys it. So, Tom will work at something.

'Cy' = 'y is a course'
'St' = 'Tom is a student '
'Sx' = 'x is a student '
'Exy' = 'x enjoys y'

7. No person is his own father. Hence, any person who was the father of every person would not be a person.

'Px' = 'x is a person'
'Py' = 'y is a person'
'Fxx' = 'x is the father of x'
'Fxy' = 'x is the father of y'

8. All lies are falsehoods. Thus, whoever tells a lie tells a falsehood.

'Fx' = 'x is a falsehood'
'Fy' = 'y is a falsehood'
'Lx' = 'x is a lie'
'Ly' = 'y is a lie'
'Txy' = 'x tells y'

9. Some people are critical of any new idea. Therefore, if anything is a new idea, not all people aren't critical of it.

'Iy' = 'y is an idea'
'Ny' = 'y is new'
'Px' = ' is a person'
'Cxy' = 'x is critical of y'

10. Unless Michael's sister helps him trim his sails, he won't row a boat ashore. Only if he finds the land of milk and honey will Michael row a boat ashore. Rachael, a person who is Michael's sister, helps him trim his sails. Any person who trims Michael's sails helps him. So, Michael will find the land of milk and honey.

'By' = 'y is a boat'
'Lx' = 'x is the land of milk and honey'
'Px' = 'x is a person'
'Fmx' = 'Michael finds x '
'Hxm' = 'x helps Michael'
'Rmy' = 'Michael rows y'
'Srm' = 'Rachael is a sister of Michael'
'Txm' = 'x trims the sails of Michael'

## 7.   REVIEW OF NEW TERMS

**Existential Instantiation (EI):** An argument form permitting, under certain restrictions, the existential quantifier to be removed from an existentially quantified statement:

$$\frac{(\exists\alpha)\Phi\alpha}{/\therefore\ \Phi\beta}$$

**Existential Generalization (EG):** An argument form permitting, under certain restrictions, the existential quantifier to be appended to a statement or statement function:

$$\frac{\Phi\beta}{/\therefore\ (\exists\alpha)\Phi\alpha}$$

**Proof of validity:** A finite sequence of statements and/or statement functions each of which is either a premise or obtained from a premise, or premises, by some rule of transformation. The last statement in such a sequence is the conclusion. While all premises and the conclusion of a proof must be statements, statement functions can occur in other lines.

**Quantificational Denial (QD):** A logical equivalence permitting the replacement of universal quantifiers by existential quantifiers and vice versa under certain conditions of denial:

$$(\exists\alpha)\Phi\alpha\ ::\ \sim(\alpha)\sim\Phi\alpha$$
$$(\exists\alpha)\sim\Phi\alpha\ ::\ \sim(\alpha)\Phi\alpha$$
$$\sim(\exists\alpha)\Phi\alpha\ ::\ (\alpha)\sim\Phi\alpha$$
$$\sim(\exists\alpha)\sim\Phi\alpha\ ::\ (\alpha)\Phi\alpha$$

**Statement variable:** Lower-case 'p', 'q', 'r', and 's' used to indicate various spaces that can be filled by statement names, statement initials, or statement functions.

**Substitution instance:** The result of replacing every free occurrence of '$\alpha$' in '$\Phi\alpha$' by the same individual constant or the same individual variable, using the same constant or variable at every occurrence of '$\alpha$'.

**Universal Generalization (UG):** An argument form permitting, under certain restrictions, the universal quantifier to be appended to a statement function:

$$\frac{\Phi\beta}{/\therefore\ (\alpha)\Phi\alpha}$$

**Universal Instantiation (UI):** An argument form permitting, under certain restrictions, the universal quantifier to be removed from a universally quantified statement:

$$\frac{(\alpha)\Phi\alpha}{/\therefore\ \Phi\beta}$$

# 13

# LANGUAGE, MEANING, AND DEFINITIONS

Even if the premises support, in a purely formal way, the conclusion of an argument, nevertheless that argument could still be a bad one. For instance, arguments have premises and conclusions that are asserted in some particular language such as English, Spanish, or German. Language can be misused in ways preventing anyone from being able to say what, if anything, is being asserted. Sentence structure might be faulty, or individual words or phrases poorly used. For an argument to be a good one, the premises must be acceptable. But from the viewpoint of rational thought, premises can neither be accepted nor rejected unless they are first understandable. Chapter 13 discusses fundamental issues—*language, meaning,* and *definition*—related to understanding and, hence, to accepted or to rejecting premises and conclusions.

## 1. LANGUAGE

Up to now, emphasis in this book has been placed on formal properties of statements and arguments. Statements are neither written nor spoken. They are not spatial and temporal, but are abstract objects. Nonetheless, they can be named and asserted through the use of particular languages. It is the names of statements that are written or spoken at a particular time and place in some specific context. Viewed as declarative sentences, 'Rome is the capital of Italy', 'The capital of Italy is Rome', 'La capital de Italia es Roma', and 'Rom ist die Hauptstadt Italiens' all name the same statement. And any attempt to write down that statement would simply result in producing another name for it.

Error can be introduced into attempts to understand statements through a misuse of the sentences naming them. Suppose someone asks what sort of guarantee the computer, *Generic Super 486*, carries. A salesperson replies that 'The machine is absolutely guaranteed to work throughout its useful lifetime'. What is one to understand by this remark? What is it for the computer to be absolutely guaranteed? If someone becomes particularly irate while writing a paper and smashes the computer, will it be replaced? And how is 'useful lifetime' to be understood? What if the computer breaks down? Does that mark the end of its useful lifetime? If so, it has no guarantee at all. Or is 'useful lifetime' to be understood as a specific number of years? Why, then, did the salesperson not say so? Since language can be misused as a tool for naming and asserting statements, it becomes an important topic for anyone wishing to think rationally.

Language, either spoken or written, can be thought of as beginning with basic signs such as sounds, gestures, and marks. These basic signs are related to one another according to various accepted rules, conventions, and customs. In this way, larger signs or words are constructed. Words are arranged into sentences, and sentences into even larger units. Sentences are used by different people within the context of a common language to describe, inform, predict, argue, persuade, command, question, emote, evaluate, direct, perform ceremonies, and engage in a host of other activities. Broadly, then, *language* can be viewed as

> **a set of accepted rules, conventions, and customs that relate a set of signs (1) to one another, (2) to any referent these signs might have, and (3) to the users of those signs.**

The relations holding between the various signs in a language are the *syntactical properties* of that language. **Syntax** is

> **the study of the relations of the signs to one another in a language.**

In studying the rules, conventions, and customs governing how the signs of a language are correctly joined, a person is concentrating on the formal structures of that language. It is correct, because of English syntax, to write 'The environment is important' but not 'Environment important the is'.

An appropriate use of language requires not only that it be a well-ordered collection of signs. These signs need an interpretation permitting them to refer to various things. Such interpretations cannot be provided by appealing solely to the syntactical properties of a language. Suppose Robert said, 'A stackie steals the wickem'. This sentence is syntactically correct. Yet before any English-speaker can understand this comment, she has to know to what 'stackie' and 'wickem' mean. She needs to have a grasp of the semantic properties of the sentence. Here **semantics** is understood as

> **the study of the rules, customs, and conventions determining the interpretations of various linguistic expressions, such as words, phrases, and sentences in a language.**

Since semantics is a study of the interpretations of language, it includes inquiries into the general conditions under which a statement is true or false. *Being true* and *being false* are semantic properties of statements. When the '1's and '0's in the tables in Chapters 2 and 3 are read as 'true' and 'false', they indicate semantic properties of statements.

Language is more than a syntactically correct arrangement of interpreted expressions. There are also important relations of language to its users. ***Pragmatics*** is

**a study of the rules, customs, and conventions relating language to its users.**

Sarah might say, 'I believe that people ought to be kind to one another'. Assuming that she knows how to use English properly and is not being deceptive, *belief* is the relation Sarah has to what she says. People accept, reject, know, believe, and ponder specific claims. Pragmatics includes the study of those rules, customs, and conventions by which a person is related to those claims she makes.

Language never functions in a vacuum. It is always used by some person in a specific context. Within a context, a sentence can be used to do several things at once. Someone might say, 'Professors are crass and self-centered'. This sentence could be understood as expressing a statement. But it could be understood as suggesting defining properties of 'professor'. Or, the sentence might be the emotional outburst of a failing student. Before one can understand what is being done with 'Professors are crass and self-centered', one must grasp the context in which this sentence is placed. Insofar as any sentence is expressed in a specific context, it is being used by a particular person on a certain occasion to do something. The more of the specific context one grasps, the better position one is in to say how that sentence is being used and what is to be understood by it.

This section has touched upon important notions useful in grasping a clearer comprehension of language and the areas in which something might go wrong when a person expresses himself linguistically. Indeed, it is important to understand language and to use it well if one wishes to think rationally and to protect oneself from being led into foolish and dangerous situations. To be able to use language well is closely related to the ability one has to assert statements and to construct arguments. The following sections in this chapter take the study of language and its connections with arguments further by discussing *meaning* and *definition*. Then the last two chapters examine some specific ways in which language is misused and how these misuses hinder an argument from supplying reasons to support conclusions.

---

## *EXERCISES*

### Group A:

Suppose that the chairman of the Chinese Communist party said, "I support democratic interaction and individual freedoms." What if the prime minister of Great Britain uttered those sounds? Would both persons be asserting the same statement? Explain your answer.

### Group B:

Invent and describe several specific contexts in which each of the following sentences might be used. Describe how each sentence might perform different jobs in these different contexts. Be creative, *even outlandish*, in the contexts you invent and describe.

1. I went to see him while she was gone.

2. It isn't fair that you made it and I didn't.

3. The Tigers are the best ever.

4. Take a flying leap!

5. He was turned on and attracted a good deal of their attention.

6. She's up today.

7. She went over to his place for an affair.

8. This group only went to the beach.

9. Rosa argues regularly with Roldan.

10. All I want is your heart.

11. If you pass it, then everything will go smoothly.

12. Mary G. is responsible.

13. She told him that she would if he could.

14. He said to him that he didn't mind doing it with him so long as no one found out about it.

15. He sent it to him on the fly.

16. Unless you do it for me, I shan't give you this.

17. The blind person came to the house to do some repairs.

18. The note was high, but he took it anyway.

19. A tank mysteriously appeared in the yard.

20. Rolling his drum, he kept in step.

---

## 2. MEANING

The important question, 'What does that mean?', is asked of linguistic expressions. If the meaning of individual words is not known, the expression in which those words appear will be unclear. The meaning of the word 'viviparous' has to be known before one can understand 'The whale is a viviparous creature'. A person who does not understand the sentence cannot say whether a statement named by that sentence is true or false. In general, meaning is rationally prior to giving consent or withholding it. 'What does that mean?' has layers of answers. One way to approach these layers is suggested in the last section. The syntactic, semantic, and pragmatic properties of language each contribute to meaning.

How does *syntax* contribute to the meaning of a sentence? Suppose someone said

(1)   It millied the willie and it dillied the tillie.

Assuming English syntax, there are nine clusters of letters or words in (1). Of these only 'it', 'the', and 'and' are recognizable English words. Two words, 'millied' and 'dillied', end with '-ed', which is an identifiable way in English syntax to represent the past tense of a verb. From these observations of the syntactic properties of (1), this information is gleaned:

(2)   It [verb in the past tense] the willie and it [verb in the past tense] the tillie.

English syntax dictates that a verb must have a subject. In (2), the two occurrences of 'it' suggest the grammatical subject for each verb. Further, English syntax requires that 'the' be followed by a noun or noun phrase. Thus, 'willie' and 'tillie' must be used like nouns. Given this insight, (2) can be rewritten:

> **(3)** [subject] [verb in the past tense] the [noun] and [subject] [verb in the past tense] the [noun].

A verb must be transitive when noun-like words follow it. The noun following the verb is the object of the action suggested by the verb. (3) now becomes

> **(4)** [subject] [transitive verb in the past tense] the [noun-object] and [subject] [transitive verb in the past tense] the [noun-object].

The word 'and' is used in several ways in English. For instance, it can be used to form a compound subject or a compound sentence. In (4), 'and' is being used to connect two sentences in which 'it' appears as the subject in both sentences. So, by following the dictates of English syntax, a good deal can be grasped about (1). A flaw in the grammar of (1) could hinder grasping the syntactical meaning of any word in it.

Not all grammatical flaws, however, hinder communication. Imagine a specific context. What if Bubba, a good old country boy, says

> **(5)** 'I ain't going 'cause I ain't got no money'.

Following the rules of English syntax, this sentence would be rewritten as 'I am not going because I have money'. And this might be, in a particular set of circumstances, what Bubba wants to say. Knowing his weakness for gambling, Bubba is not going to the take his weekly salary to the race track. On the other hand, a more likely interpretation of (5) is 'I am not going because I do not have any money'. The unacceptable syntactic structure of (5) does not prevent a speaker of English from understanding it. For the most part, these speakers realize that, informally, double negation is sometimes incorrectly used to indicate denial. So, while the syntax of a language provides at least minimal meaning, as in the case of (1), breaking that syntax in specific contexts does not necessarily prevent a sentence from being meaningful.

What is more commonly understood by 'meaning' can be discussed under the heading of *semantics*. It is convenient to begin this discussion by introducing the notion of **term**:

> A *term* is any linguistic expression that could be used as a grammatical subject in a sentence.

'Chemistry professor' can be used as a grammatical subject in a sentence, as in, 'The chemistry professor was late to class'. While a term is a linguistic expression that could be used as a grammatical subject, that expression might not be used as a subject in a particular sentence. For instance, 'chemistry professor' is not used as a subject in 'Jane saw her chemistry professor in the office'.

Terms are characterized in two ways; namely, as **singular terms** and **general terms**:

> A *general term* refers to a class of individuals whereas a *singular term* refers to a particular individual.

Terms can be either *concrete* or *abstract* depending on the type of referent of the term:

> A *concrete term* **refers to things that are locatable in space and time whereas** *abstract terms* **refer to things that are nonspacial and nontemporal.**

Examples of concrete general terms are 'student' and 'teacher' since the members of the class of students and of teachers can be located in a particular place at a particular time. On the other hand, 'number' and 'honesty' are abstract general terms. Neither numbers nor honesty is the sort of thing that is locatable in space and time. Singular terms are used to pick out a particular individual from a group. Both *proper names*, such as 'William Henry Harrison', and *definite descriptions*, such as 'the dog that saved Susie's life', are concrete singular terms. For the devout Muslim, 'Allah' is an abstract singular term.

Every *general term* having an appropriate and accepted use in a particular language—that is, every *concept**—has both an *extension* and an *intension*:

> The *extension* **of a general term is the class of individuals having the property or properties comprising the intension of that term.**

The extension or reference of 'red' is every red thing—past, present, and future. The extension of 'dog' is every dog—past, present, and future. On the other hand,

> The *intension* **of a general term is whatever it is that something must have to be included in the extension of that term.**

Properties, characteristics, or attributes constitute the intension of that term. The property of being red is the intension of 'red'. The intension of 'dog' includes, but is not exhausted by, the properties of being mammalian, four-legged, and carnivorous. The *intensional meaning* of a general term is the intension determining the extension of that term. The *extensional meaning* of a general term is the class of all those things named by that term. For example, the intensional meaning of 'dog' is those properties anything is held to have to be called a dog. The particular dogs Rex, Rover, Lassie, and Spot are part of the extensional meaning of 'dog'.

General terms having the same extension, can have different intensions. Consider 'equilateral triangle' and 'equiangular triangle'. These terms have identical extensions. However, they have different intensions and, hence, different intensional meanings. The general terms 'elf' and 'griffin' also have the same extension. The extension of both is that class of individuals having no members; namely, the null or empty class. Nonetheless, these terms have different intensional meanings. While some general terms have an empty extension, no term can have an empty intension. This is because the intension of a term determines its extension. Suppose some term could have an empty intension. Imagine some "term," 'ZEQ', that refers to no properties at all. Then that "term" would have no intentional meaning. Referring to no properties, there could be no way of identifying any class of things, empty or not, to which that term might refer. In this sense, the intensional meaning of a term is

---

*A *concept* is the appropriate and accepted use of a general term in a particular language.

logically prior to any extensional meaning the term might have and is the primary meaning of the term.

The extension of a *singular term* is the particular individual referred to, or named, by that term. The extension or referent of the proper name, 'George Bush', is that individual, George Bush. The definite description, 'the president of the United States in 1990', has the same extension as 'George Bush'. Both of these singular terms, therefore, have the same referent. Now, a singular term can have an extension even if it does not refer to any presently existing thing. 'The first president of the United States was married to Martha' refers to two individuals who no longer exist. Nonetheless, the statement is meaningful. Or a singular term might refer to an individual who has never existed, does not now exist, and never will exist. 'Zeus' has such an extension. The extension of 'Zeus' is that class having no members.

The intension of a singular term is those properties that permits two or more singular terms to have the same extension.* As with general terms, the intensional meaning of a singular term is logically prior to any extensional meaning the term might have and is the primary meaning of that term. If this were not so, then neither 'George Washington was married to Martha' nor 'Zeus is the father of Apollo' could be meaningful. Remember, the primary meaning of a term is its intensional meaning, and the intension of a term, generally speaking, determines the extension of that term.

There are further important relations holding between the extension and intension of a term. Two terms have

> *identical meanings* **if and only if those properties comprising their intensions are the same.**

For instance, the general terms 'cat' and 'feline' mean the same thing in English, not because they have the same extension, but because they have the same intension. The rules, conventions, and customs governing the use of 'cat' and 'feline' in English are the same. Two general terms not having identical meanings, nonetheless, might have **compatible meanings** in a particular language.

> **Two general terms, 'γ' and 'δ' have** *compatible meanings* **if and only if those properties comprising the intension of 'γ' are included in those formulating the intension 'δ'. Two general terms have** *incompatible meanings* **when and only when part of those properties comprising the intension of one cannot be included in those properties comprising the intension of the other.**

'Animal' and 'cat' are examples of terms having compatible meanings. 'Circle' and 'square' are examples of general terms having incompatible meanings. While both 'circle' and 'square' are compatible with 'figure', part of the intension of 'circle' cannot be included in the intension of 'square' and vice versa.

---

*The intension of a singular term is sometimes called the *sense* of that term. While 'George Washington', 'the first president of the United States', and 'the husband of Martha Washington' each refer to the same individual, nevertheless they each mean something different. What is involved in this difference of meanings is the sense of these singular terms.

If two or more general terms are compatible, often they can be ranked as having greater or less intension or greater or less extension. For instance, the intension of 'cat' is greater than the intension of 'animal'. All of the properties held necessary for anything to be an animal are also properties of anything to be a cat. Yet there are more properties held necessary for anything to be a cat than to be an animal. Thus, for any two general terms γ and δ, γ *has greater intension than* δ just in case γ and δ are compatible and all of the properties comprising the intension of δ are part of the intension of γ, but not all of the properties of γ are part of the intension of δ. So *cat* has a greater intension than *animal*. On the other hand, *animal* has a greater extension than *cat*. There are more animals than cats. Of two compatible terms, the one with the smaller intension usually has the greater extension.

Generally speaking, the more defining properties a general term has, the more semantic meaning is conveyed by that term. This observation leads to the ***inverse rule of meaning***:

> **Given a series of compatible general terms, then the order of increasing intension and decreasing extension are identical as are those of increasing extension and decreasing intension.**

There are exceptions to this rule. These exceptions occur when, while the intensions of compatible general terms are different, their extensions are the same. Consider this list:

**elf, elf with pointed ears, elf with pointed ears wearing green shoes**

This list displays an order of increasing intension. However, since each general term has the same extension, namely the null class, its extension cannot be decreasing. Here is another list of general terms, each having the same extension but each also having a different intension:

**mammals, mammals with hearts, mammals with hearts and lungs**

There is an increasing intension among the expressions. But each of the general terms has the same extension; namely, the class *mammals*.

The intension and extension of terms can be related to the notion of ***semantic information***. Here the concept ***semantic information*** is understood as the intension of a term. There are more properties determining what is to count as a coin than as a metal object. Thus, 'Dan has some metal objects in his pocket' conveys less semantic information than 'Dan has some coins in his pocket'. Declarative sentences and the information they convey can also be related to truth values. One declarative sentence, 'p', conveys more information that another, 'q', if and only if there are more ways to falsify the statement named by 'p' than by 'q'. Thus, 'It's raining and the ground is wet' conveys more information than 'Either it's raining, or the ground is wet'.

The third element of meaning in a linguistic expression is *pragmatics*. It is here that the importance of the context within which a person finds herself becomes more apparent. Within such contexts are found customs and conventions, usually unstated, governing how individual language users are related to what is said and heard. Suggesting, inferring, knowing, believing, accepting, rejecting, counting as justification or evidence are all pragmatic relations holding between the speaker and what she says.

To grasp the importance of pragmatics, visualize this situation. It is evening. Al and Bill are in their apartment watching a ball game on television. The following conversation takes place:

(8)  **Al:** We're out of beer.
  **Bill:** My keys are on the table in the kitchen.
  **Al:** I don't get my check 'til tomorrow.
  **Bill:** There's money in my wallet by the keys.
  **Al:** OK! We're on! I'll be back soon.
  **Bill:** Hurry! This is a great game! And I'm thirsty.

Al makes a claim to which Bill replies. From this response, Al infers that he may drive Bill's car to fetch some beer and bring it back to the apartment. Al presents another claim and, given Bill's reply, infers that Bill is paying for the beer. Al signals agreement with this arrangement and then says that he will be back soon. From Bill's further response, Al infers that he ought to come straight back with the beer.

What are the bases for the inferences that Al makes? Consider the first two remarks and the unstated inference Al draws:

(9)  **Al:** We're out of beer.
  **Bill:** My keys are on the table in the kitchen.

---

  **Al:** Therefore, I may drive Bill's car to fetch the beer
  and bring it back to the apartment.

In (9), there are no syntactic relations holding between the first two remarks and the conclusion that warrant this inference. Nor are there any semantic relations, say, between terms such as *beer* and *keys*. The conversation continues. Al says that he does not receive his check until tomorrow. Bill then infers that if any beer is bought, he will pay for it. Once more, this inference is based on considerations of neither syntax nor semantics. When Bill says, 'There's money in my wallet', Al infers that Bill is suggesting that he will pay for the beer but that Al will have to get the money from the wallet. Again, this is not an inference based on syntax or semantics.

From the viewpoint of syntax and semantics, the conversation in (8) is strange if not unintelligible. The following is even stranger:

(10)  **Al:** We're out of beer.
  **Bill:** My toothbrush is on the sink.
  **Al:** Liz called yesterday.
  **Bill:** There's oil in the garage.
  **Al:** I need the cash as soon as possible.
  **Bill:** Hurry! This is a great game! And I'm thirsty.

Individually, each of the comments in (10) is syntactically and semantically meaningful. Yet none seem related either syntactically or semantically. There might be some context in which these comments would permit inferences to be made. But such a context is not quickly evident to speakers of English. To explain how (8) is meaningful while (10) is not requires moving further into the area of pragmatics. It is necessary to comprehend the relation between language and its users in different contexts.

In (8), Al makes several assumptions, no doubt without being aware of them, in order to establish his conclusions. First, he assumes that Bill knows how to speak English in a syntactically and semantically adequate way for their conversation. Second, Al assumes that Bill is responding to 'We're out of beer' and later to 'I don't get my check 'til tomorrow'. Third, Al assumes that Bill, when replying, is telling the truth to the best of his ability. Fourth, Al assumes that Bill is relating sufficient information, instructions, and so on, needed to make the inferences in question. This, fifth, requires that Al assume Bill recognizes sundry relations holding between keys, cars, fetching and bringing, wallets, money, buying, and the like. These *assumptions of meaningful discourse* can be generalized in this way:

1. Both the speaker and hearer in a conversation assume that each knows how to speak English in a syntactically and semantically adequate way for the conversation to proceed.

2. Each assumes that the other is responding to comments offered at some point in the conversation.

3. Each assumes that the other is telling the truth or saying something correct when replying.

4. Each assumes that the other is relating sufficient information required to make the inferences in question.

5. Each assumes the other shares a common background relevant to the conversation.

To the extent that at least one of these assumptions fails in (10) between each comment, no inferences can be made.

Semantic meaning can be confused with pragmatic meaning. A more flagrant case of this is found when *emotive meaning*, properly a topic of pragmatics, is confused with *cognitive meaning*, properly a topic of semantics. Someone might say, 'Shane is a tightwad bureaucrat'. Another person could say, 'Shane is a public servant who conserves public money'. Or, think of this pair of assertions: 'The Communists spread propaganda' and 'The free world disseminates information'. Or what of 'Abortion is killing a baby' and 'Abortion is terminating a pregnancy'. Each assertion in these pairs of examples semantically says the same thing. Nonetheless, from a pragmatic viewpoint, they have very different meanings.

When emotive meaning is confused with cognitive meaning, it can appear that someone is offering evidence to support a conclusion when no evidence at all is being offered. What is a person arguing in this example:

(15) It is a shame, to say nothing of being highly dangerous, to phase out the farsighted national defense effort, Star Wars, that President Reagan so strongly supported. This ought not to be done, even considering the lessening of political tensions with Russia. After all, if anything is going to protect the freedoms of this great God-fearing nation from the attacks of our atheistic enemies, it is a strong defense against their terrible weapons.

Contemporary technology, which has given us so much in the way of higher living standards, is the only sure answer to our national defense needs. Anything that has provided so many benefits to all of us ought to be supported and continued.

The major thesis of (15) seems to be, 'The defense effort, Star Wars, ought not to be phased out'. But what evidence is given in support of this opinion? Very little. Even if it is granted that a strong defense is the best protection against enemy attack, it does not follow that Star Wars is the best sort of defense to have. Admittedly, there is a great deal of rhetoric and emotion in (15) that might be taken as evidence. Yet little evidence is presented in support of the author's position.

---

## EXERCISES

### Group A:

Assuming correct English syntax, determine in each of the following how every "word" (that is, group of letters separated by spaces) likely functions.

1. Who wearies the wounded weasel waxes wibbly.
2. The wimble wasps the waddled wips from wite to wate.
3. Tiddled toward the trik, Tilley tolled the tarry tuk.
4. While a sak sot the smearth, a jammer jots the jees.
5. An iglee iraa for the boosic is a coosta ceepa.

### Group B:

Using the syntactic structure established for each example in *Group A*, turn every example into an English sentence that is semantically meaningful.

### Group C:

Each of the following contains a group of compatible general terms. Rank these terms in increasing intension beginning with the term having the smallest intension.

1. Cat, living organism, animal, mammal
2. Molecule, substance, hydrogen, atom
3. Human, bachelor, adult, male
4. Building, house, cottage, edifice
5. Fiction, written work, poem, epic

### Group D:

Which of the following terms have the same extension?

1. The present king of France
2. The Morning Star

3. Dog

4. Water

5. London

6. The Evening Star

7. Juno, consort of Jupiter

8. Canine

9. The capital of England

10. $H_2O$

## Group E:

Suggest a partial intension and extension for each of the following general terms.

1. Illegal drug

2. Ballet

3. Novel

4. Nation

5. United States senator

6. Wine

7. Communist government

8. Opera

9. Democratic government

10. University

## Group F:

In each of the following groups of exercises, rank the sentences in order of the amount of information conveyed; beginning with the sentence conveying the least information.

1. Barcelona is a Spanish city.
   Barcelona is a Spanish port city.
   Barcelona is a city.

2. Steve owns a vehicle.
   Steve owns a Ferrari.
   Steve owns a sports car.

3. Mike saw a human.
   Mike saw a Susie.
   Mike saw a woman.

4. Any wimble-wop is a mammal.
   Any wimble-wop is a marsupial.
   Any wimble-wop is an animal.

5. XYZ is a social organization.
   XYZ is a college fraternity.
   XYZ is a private club.

### Group G:

From a pragmatic viewpoint, discuss what, if anything, you believe fails to hold between each comment in the following dialogues. Next attempt to construct some pragmatic background, even a bazar one, in which these conversations appear reasonable.

1.  **Al:** We're out of beer.
    **Bill:** My toothbrush is on the sink.
    **Al:** Liz called yesterday.
    **Bill:** Good! There's oil in the garage.
    **Al:** OK! I need the cash.
    **Bill:** Hurry! This is a great game! And I'm thirsty.

2.  **Tammy:** Do you have any money with you?
    **Cathy:** Look! There goes Dave!
    **Tammy:** He certainly is handsome.
    **Cathy:** Yes, he has buck teeth and crossed eyes.
    **Tammy:** I don't like buck teeth.
    **Cathy:** Well, it is beginning to rain.

3.  **Pat:** It's hot in here.
    **Sloan:** Turn down the thermostat.
    **Pat:** Why do you always have to be argumentative about anything I say?
    **Sloan:** Modus ponens is a valid argument form.
    **Pat:** But I can't study because of all the noise.
    **Sloan:** Like I said, turn down the thermostat.

### Group H:

Rewrite each of the following avoiding as much emotional language as you can while retaining what you think is the cognitive meaning of the claim.

1. The stupid bureaucrats in Washington shovel mountains of paper.
2. Having murdered her unborn baby, Mary was thrown out of the apartment by her live-in.
3. The harvesting of deer is needed each year to foster the healthy growth of the deer population.
4. Jean's gaudy red and yellow dress was an eyesore to everyone at the snooty cotillion.
5. The fascist government of General Franco in Spain has only recently been replaced by forward-looking but conservative democratic institutions.
6. The cunning extortion of honestly earned money by unscrupulous junk bond brokers must be stopped if confidence in the stock market is to be restored.
7. Every communist government guarantees socioeconomic oppression for the hordes of people who are crushed by dictatorial central management.
8. Many emerging nations need American loans both to provide aid for the needy and combat the onslaught of socialistic governments.
9. The United States maintains a network of intelligence agents to obtain from other countries information that is sensitive to its national security.
10. Benjamin Franklin was a great American patriot and freedom fighter who served his country by gathering information from foreign sources.

## 3.  DEFINITIONS

Words and phrases can have unclear meanings that become stumbling blocks in rational thought. Clarifying the meanings of words and phrases is often accomplished by defining them:

> A *definition* is a way to indicate the meaning of a word or phrase not used as a proper name.

A definition of a word or phrase is not its meaning, but an indication of that meaning. View a definition as a guide to the appropriate use of a word or phrase. In discussing a definition, the word or phrase being defined is the *definiendum*. The word or phrase used to indicate the meaning of the definiendum is the *definiens*. Consider this definition:

> 'Synergy' means the action of at least two substances, organs, or organisms to achieve an effect of which each is individually incapable.

'Synergy' is the definiendum while 'the action of at least two substances, organs, or organisms to achieve an effect of which each is individually incapable' is the definiens. In many definitions, the definiens is made up of words, but there are instances where this is not so. 'Quadrilateral' can be defined as follows: 'Quadrilateral' means anything that is similar to

A *definiendum* is always a word or phrase.* Things, events, institutions, and the like are not defined. Yet a definition can be presented in a misleading way suggesting that things, events, etc., are being defined. For example, a definition for 'horse' can be presented as either

> **(1)**  'Horse' means a four-legged, solid-hoofed, herbivorous animal.

or

> **(2)**  A horse is a four-legged, solid-hoofed, herbivorous animal.

Both (1) and (2) define the word 'horse'. In (1), 'horse' is the definiendum and 'a four-legged, solid-hoofed, herbivorous animal' the definiens. (1) uses single quotes to show clearly that a word is being defined. Not using some device such as single quotes can lead to confusing definitions with sentences indicating contingent statements:

---

*Instead of writing 'word and phrase' or 'words and phrases', for the sake of brevity, 'word' or 'words' will be used as an abbreviation. Thus, both 'acid' and 'Norman English monarch' are examples of the sorts of things that can be defined.

> A *contingent statement* is one whose truth or falsity is determined by taking into consideration particular things in the world.

Lacking single quotes or the like, (2) might be viewed as a contingent statement and not a definition. If viewed as a statement, (2) is appropriately considered an *analytic statement*:

> An *analytic statement* is one whose truth or falsity is determined solely by the definitions of the words in the sentence naming that statement.

That is, (2) is a statement that is true by definition. Since the criteria for the acceptability of definitions and statements differ, it is preferable to set off clearly the definiendum being defined. In this book, single quote marks are used.

Definitions can be used to clarify words used in a *vague* or *ambiguous* way in a particular context.

> A linguistic expression is *vague* if and only if its meaning is too imprecise within a specific context for a person to understand whether it is applicable in that context or not.

> A linguistic expression is *ambiguous* if and only if it has two or more distinct meanings and the context in which it is being used does not determine which meaning is to be understood.

Roughly, vagueness might be viewed as a difference of degree whereas ambiguity is a difference of kind. Suppose a piece of legislation reads like this:

**(3)** Any student who is claimed as a tax deduction by a parent and comes from a family in the middle-class income bracket shall receive only 50% of full financial aid from "The Department of Student Loans and Aid."

(3) is vague. What is to be understood by 'the middle-class income bracket'? How much income does the family of a student need to be declared 'middle-class' for the purposes of this legislation? $20,000, $22,000, $30,000? A definition of 'middle-class' could be introduced to clarify this vagueness. On the other hand, the following sentence is ambiguous:

**(4)** Bobby saw Frank leaving Ann's shop with a file in his hand.

For example, what is to be understood by the word 'file' in (4)? Is it a folder containing papers or a tool used to remove rough edges? (4) supplies no context that can be cited to answer this question.

Definitions are not only used to clarify the meaning of a word. They are also used to introduce new meanings for old words used in new situations, and to establish new meanings for new words used in new contexts. In that a *concept* is the appropriate and accepted use of a general term within a particular language, definitions can relate various concepts to one another. And in relating concepts, new or old, definitions organize and expand a language. The word 'lightning' was used acceptably before Benjamin Franklin flew his kite. He took the old word, 'lightning', and defined it in a new way that related it to 'electricity'. However, 'quark' is a new word introduced into contemporary physics. This word is used, among other ways, to relate the concepts *electric charge* and *elementary particles*. These are examples of how definitions can organize and expand a language.

Definitions are also used to clarify in the sense of settling disputes. Controversies that can be settled by introducing definitions might seem "merely verbal". However, it is not the case that all verbal disputes are capricious, unimportant, or uninteresting. Imagine a situation in which the owner of a water craft is attempting to collect damages from her insurance company. In describing coverage, her insurance policy uses 'water craft'. Further, the craft was damaged in a way that appears clearly covered by this policy. The owner of the craft, however, is having difficulty in collecting and seeks the help of a lawyer. The case eventually appears in court. The court learns that the damaged water craft is an amphibious airplane. Admittedly, when in use, the majority of the time the craft is in the air. Nonetheless, it cannot fly if it does not take off from and land on a body of water. The question before the court is whether this amphibious airplane is to be considered a water craft or not. If the court decides that the amphibious airplane is a water craft, the insurance company has to pay damages. Otherwise, the owner will collect nothing.

Here is an example of a verbal dispute having important consequences. The issue before the court is not a factual one in the sense that there is any need to examine amphibious airplanes more closely. In that someone already knows what an amphibious airplane is and how it functions, he does not need to collect further evidence supporting a factual claim. The dispute is verbal in that its outcome rests on how 'amphibious airplane' and 'water craft' are defined and related. Yet once some decision has been made concerning these definitions, there will be factual consequences for the owner and the insurance company.

Another use of definitions is to increase the vocabulary of someone already speaking a language. *Vocabulary* generally suggests the correct use of individual words. It also indicates words suitably used in interrelated conceptual schemes. Learning the meaning of 'dog' permits one to point correctly to Lassie and not to Garfield. But it also allows a person to grasp relations holding between, say, the concepts *dog, animal, pet, worker, hunter,* and *protector.* The words a person uses correctly are, in large part, those concepts and their relations forming the ways in which that person grasps the world. Therefore, increasing one's vocabulary is more than merely increasing the number of words that one can use. It involves introducing and relating concepts in an expanding view of the world.

The meaning of a word can be indicated in different ways depending on the purposes to be fulfilled by using that word in a specific context. A definition can be used in different ways to accomplish different ends. Since a word might have intensional and extensional meaning, some types of definitions stress the one and some the other. Many of the more common types and uses of definitions are discussed in the remainder of this section.

A typical way of defining words is to suggest other words which mean the same, or approximately, the same thing.

**A *synonymous definition* indicates the intensional meaning of a word by presenting another word having the same or approximate intensional meaning as the first.**

The word 'feline' could be defined by saying that 'feline' means 'cat'. One could say that 'instructor' means 'teacher' or that 'obfuscate' means 'obscure'. While synonymous definitions are common, they are often not helpful in clarifying the meaning of a definiendum. *First*, the meaning of the synonym might not itself be clear. To say that 'recalcitrant' means 'obstinately defiant' is not helpful in grasping its meaning unless the meaning of 'obstinately defiant' is already understood. *Second*, even if the definiens is clear, it might not have exactly the same meaning as the definiendum. For instance, the words 'physician' and 'doctor' do not have identical meanings. Notice that while every physician is a doctor, not every doctor is a physician. All dentists and many clergy and university professors are doctors, but relatively few of them are physicians. So, types of definitions other than synonymous ones are needed to clarify words.

*Lexical definitions*, typically found in dictionaries, are commonly used when the meaning of a word needs to be learned.

> **A *lexical definition* is a report of the actual or normative meanings of a word at a given time in the ongoing development of a language.**

Since lexical definitions are reports of actual usage, they, like any report, can be true or false. Suppose, for instance, that someone is unclear concerning the meaning of 'carapace'. In *Webster's New Collegiate Dictionary*, the following definition is found:[1]

> **car•a•pace** *n* [F, fr. Sp *carapacho*] **1** : a bony or chitinous case or shield covering the back or part of the back of an animal (as a turtle or crab) **2** : a hard protective outer covering; *esp* : an attitude or state of mind (as indifference) serving to protect or isolate from external influence.

This is a true report of how 'carapace' is used. It indicates that 'carapace' has two distinct intensional meanings. While a lexical definition is a report about the meaning(s) of a word, it does not follow that the word being defined has any referent. For instance, the word 'mermaid' is defined in this way:[2]

> **mer•maid** *n* : a fabled marine creature usu. represented with a woman's body to the hips and a fish's tail instead of legs.

This is a true report of the meaning of 'mermaid' but not a true report about any existing creature. For, while 'mermaid' has an intension, it has no extension.

Lexical definitions not only report the actual meanings of words, but also report what meanings are considered normative. The normative meaning of a word is reflected in the use of that word by persons who are considered, because of education, profession, social position, or the like, to use the word correctly. Some actual uses conflict with normative ones. It is likely that more people use 'lay' in such sentences as, 'Mary lays down for a nap every afternoon' than use 'lie' as in, 'Mary lies down for a nap every afternoon'. Even so, 'Mary lays down for a nap every afternoon' displays an incorrect use of 'lay'. Of course, it is correct to say, 'Mary lays down her burdens every afternoon to lie down for a nap'. There can, therefore, be a strain between the normative and more widespread actual meanings of a word.

A *stipulative definition* can be viewed either as a distinct type of definition, or as some type of definition being used in a certain way:

> A *stipulative definition* **is a definition, or a use of a definition, that specifies the intensional meaning of a word within a particular context irrespective of how that word might be commonly used, if used at all.**

A stipulative definition, or a definition used stipulatively, typically eliminates or reduces both ambiguity and vagueness. This is done by specifying those properties anything must have to be denoted by the definiendum. Because it specifies meaning, a stipulative definition is not a report and, hence, is neither true nor false. A stipulative definition represents a decision to request or command that a word be used in a particular way, within a given context. While representing a decision to specify meaning for a word, stipulative definitions are not capricious. The next section of this chapter introduces criteria that can be used to judge whether such definitions are acceptable.

There are two types of stipulative definitions, or two ways in which definitions might be used stipulatively. The first of these is a *reforming definition*:

> A *reforming definition* **is a stipulative definition, or a definition used stipulatively, that (1) specifies a new intensional meaning for an old word used in new circumstances or (2) extends the intensional meaning of an old word.**

For example, in *Webster's New Collegiate Dictionary*, seven entries are found for 'person'.[3] None of these are readily related to the definition of 'zygote'; namely,

> **a cell formed by the union of two gametes;** *broadly***: the developing individual produced from such a cell'.**[4]

Yet currently there is great debate over what amounts to reforming the definition of 'person' to include the property of being a human zygote.*

Notice how reforming definitions can be used to reduce the vagueness of a word. A lexical definition of 'murder' is 'to kill (a human being) unlawfully and with premeditated malice'.[5] Imagine a case in which a human has irreversible brain

---

*Many of the arguments taking place between "Pro-Lifers" and "Pro-Choicers" can be seen as attempts to reform definitions of 'person', 'zygote', 'fetus', and 'human being' by stipulative definition. Notice that such questions as 'Is the zygote, or fetus, of a human really a person or not?' is not a question that can be answered by any further collection of facts and information. Rather, it is a question calling for a decision. And making that decision will involve introducing stipulative definitions of a reforming sort.

damage and is being kept alive solely by mechanical means. Is it murder to remove the life support machinery and allow that human to die? Or suppose a human has been in a coma for fifteen years and there are no medical reasons to expect any reversal in this situation. The only life support system involved is that the patient is being fed through a tube. Is it murder to withdraw this tube and permit the patient to starve to death? Reforming definitions of 'murder' are needed in resolving these issues. No doubt borderline cases will continue to occur where no one will know, literally, quite what to say. Even so, many of these cases can be resolved, as they arise, by means of good reforming definitions.

The second sort of stipulative definition, or stipulative use of a definition, is a *theoretical definition*:

> A *theoretical definition* is a stipulative definition, or definition used stipulatively, that specifies the intensional meaning of a word in some specialized discipline, such as physics.

A definition is called 'theoretical' when a particular theory is exemplified in it in such a way that to understand the definition is to understand the theory of which it is a part. 'Quark' was not a meaningful word until introduced into the language of physics by Murray Gell-Mann. In establishing 'quark' as a new word in physics, Gell-Mann was free to define it as he wished. Based on his work in physics, he had specific uses to which he wished to put 'quark'. These are reflected in his definition. On the other hand, 'force' had an established meaning before Isaac Newton wrote *Principia*. Newton redefined 'force' in terms of his concepts *mass* and *acceleration*. In their new roles, both 'quark' and 'force' reflect entire systems of physics.

Like stipulative definitions, *precising definitions* can be seen as either a distinct type of definition or as a type of definition used in a particular way:

> A *precising definition* is a definition, or a use of a definition, that makes more exact the already established intensional meaning of a word.

It is not unusual for a word vaguely used in more ordinary conversation or writing to need a more precise definition in specific circumstances. While in college, because her family could not afford it, Jennifer was not able to join a sorority, did not have a new car, and could not buy her clothes from stores such as Sak's and Lord & Taylor. While some students consider her family to be poor, the Internal Revenue Service did not classify her family as poor. The *IRS* provides a precising definition to establish exactly what it means by 'poor'. Given this meaning, Jennifer could not apply for many student loans.

Precising definitions should not be confused with stipulative ones. Stipulative definitions represent decisions to use old words in new ways or to introduce new words and their meanings into specific areas of language. While not capricious, stipulative definitions are arbitrary in a way in which precising definitions are not. Great care must be taken in formulating precising definitions because they are used to clarify the already existing meaning of a word. A boat is clearly a water craft. A hydrofoil is less clearly an example of a boat, but an example nonetheless. It must be decided whether or not an amphibious airplane is an instance of a water craft by comparing it to other things that are considered water crafts, the ways in which these things function, whether they can function without a body of water, and the like. Decisions based on such considerations make the meaning of both 'amphibious airplane' and 'water craft' more precise in a specific context. They do not stipulate a new meaning for the words.

Definitions can be given by citing **genus and species**. Such definitions are also known as *analytical definitions*.

> A *definition by genus and species* gives the intensional meaning of a word by (1) specifying the type of thing being defined and (2) by listing those properties that distinguish that thing from other things of the same type.

A concrete example will make this type of definition clearer. Suppose that 'wife' is defined by genus and species. Anything that is a wife is also a female. The word 'female' indicates the genus or type to which all wives belong. But many types of things other than wives are females. Daughters, for example, are also females. So, for a definition of 'wife' to be successful, some property or properties must be stated to differentiate wives from daughters. These properties are the *differentia*. Being married is one property differentiating being a wife from being a daughter. Hence, 'wife' can be partially defined by genus and species as a married female, where 'female' indicates the genus and 'married' the differentia.

In logic, the concepts *genus* and *species* are relative ones. A type of individual is said to be a genus in relation to some second type, a species, when and only when all of the properties of the second type are included in the first but all of the properties of the first are not included in the second. Thus, all whales are included in the type of all those things that are mammals, but all mammals are not included in the type of all whales. On the other hand, the type of all those things that are mammals is itself included in the type of all those things that are animals, but not all animals are included in the type of those things that are mammals. What is to count as a genus or a species, then, is always determined in relation to something else. Not only are *genus* and *species* relative, a genus is usually made up of various species. For instance, species indicated by the words 'wife', 'husband', 'daughter', 'son', and 'dentist' can each be understood as species of the genus *human*. So, insofar as species have extensions, a particular individual, Annye Mae, could be a mammal, human, daughter, wife, mother, and business executive.

In general, what is accepted as a clear definition is determined by the particular context in which a definition is used. This is the case with definitions by genus and species. In discussing whales and fish, it might be sufficient to say that 'whale' means an air-breathing animal. In this definition, 'animal' denotes the genus and 'air-breathing' the differentia. However, humans, horses, cats, and dogs are also air-breathing animals. Thus, in certain contexts, 'whale' might be defined as an aquatic air-breathing animal. But what of porpoises and dolphins? While they are not whales, they are aquatic air-breathing animals. A definition by genus and species can continue as long as there is need for more clarity within a specific context.

One important type of intensional definition does not provide properties in its definiendum:

> An *operational definition* **clarifies or establishes the intensional meaning of a word by citing various techniques or methods governing whether or not that word applies to some thing or event.**

Note that operational definitions do not list properties that something must have to be denoted by the definiendum. Rather, they supply tests that something must meet to be part of the referent of the definiendum. These definitions have limitations. Generally, they capture only a part of the usual meaning of a word, or they cannot be applied successfully in cases where it would seem appropriate to use them.

Here is an example in which an operational definition captures only a part of the usual meaning:

> A human is said to be 'dead' if and only if when connected to an electroencephalograph (EEG) machine that human registers no brain activity on the machine.

Lesley, recently in a serious accident, has been placed on life support systems. No vital signs such as pulse or heartbeat can be detected. On the back of her driver's license, Lesley has signed her permission for authorities to remove any useful organs at her death. Is Lesley now dead or alive? To answer this question, the attending physicians examine the EEG machine connected to Lesley. No brain activity is registered. Lesley is, by operational definition, dead. The otherwise vague word, 'dead', is given a precise meaning in this operational definition by relating it to specific empirical techniques. But surely, to be 'dead' means more than not registering brain activity on an EEG machine.

The application of some operational definitions is problematic:

> Two objects are said 'to have the same mass' if and only if when one is put in one pan of a pan balance and the other in the second pan, neither of the two pans drops below the other.

Now, the earth has more mass than its moon. However, given the above operational definition of 'to have the same mass', it is meaningless to say, 'The earth has more mass than its moon'. Imagine the size of the pan balance that would be required to make sense out of this claim! And even if there were such a pan balance, on what could it be placed and who would do the measuring? Now, there are other operational definitions of 'mass' that are more appropriate when speaking of the mass of the earth and moon. But if another operational definition is used and this operation establishes a distinct definition for 'mass', then how are the two uses of 'mass' related? For surely it seems to be the case that the property of mass an object has that can be put in the pan of a balance is the same property of mass that the earth has.

There are three useful types of definitions that do not establish the intension of a word, but rather its extension. *Ostensive definitions, enumerative definitions*, and *definitions by subclass* are all extensional definitions. First consider *ostensive definitions*:

> An *ostensive definition* **of a word is provided by pointing to particular examples of those things denoted by that word.**

A father is teaching his child the meaning of 'chair'. The father points to various examples of chairs, saying 'This is a chair, and that is a chair'. Those chairs the father uses as standard examples of chairs are the *paradigms* to which all other examples are compared. In the process of learning how to use 'chair', the child might come to believe that a chair is anything on which to sit. This would be wrong. To avoid this misunderstanding, the father points to things that are not chairs, such as stools, cushions, and hassocks, and says, 'And this is not a chair'. If this process of pointing to various objects is successful, eventually the child will begin to use 'chair' correctly.

The success of an ostensive definition requires both that the learner master the activity of pointing and that the word being learned has an extension to which one can point. Suppose that someone does point to a chair, saying, 'That's a chair'. While pointing to the chair, the person is also pointing to the materials out of which the chair is made, the color of the chair, where the chair is located, and many other things. Which of these is being pointed out is not fully determined simply by more pointing. Further, an ostensive definition is of little use in attempting to define 'snow' for a child who has always lived in Egypt. Moreover, ostensive definitions are useless in defining abstract words such as 'freedom' and 'number' that have no extension to which one can point.

In some extensional definitions the definiens is a list of the members of the class referred to by the definiendum.* Such a list can be provided in two ways. The first is to give an *enumerative definition*:

> An *enumerative definition* of a word is provided by listing those things denoted by the definiendum.

'Major American automobile companies' can be given an enumerative definition by listing 'Chrysler', 'Ford', and 'General Motors'. This is a *complete* enumerative definition of those things denoted by 'major American automobile companies'. Often only *partial* enumerative definitions are given:

> 'American poet' means Walt Whitman, Emily Dickinson, Sidney Lanier, Robert Frost, and the like.

*Definition by subclass* is a third kind of extensional definition:

> A *definition by subclass* is one in which (1) the definiens denotes classes having fewer members than the class denoted by the definiendum, and (2) the definition provides a list of those subclasses that are the members of the class denoted by the definiendum.

Definitions by subclass can be either *complete* or *partial*. An example of a complete definition by subclass is this:

> 'North American marsupial' means an opossum.

---

*Because of this referring use, extensional definitions are also called *referential definitions*. Those things referred to are said to be the *denotation* of the definiendum. Since an extension definition denotes the particular things making up the definiens, these definitions are also known as *denotive definitions*.

Here is an example of a partial definition by subclass:

'Mammal' means an elephant, cat, dog, human, and so on.

Enumerative definitions and definitions by subclass are limited in their ability to avoid ambiguity and vagueness. *First*, vagueness and ambiguity are eliminated only to the extent that a definiens is complete. However, cases of complete extensional definitions are often limited in practice. Imagine attempting to provide an extensional definition for 'American citizen' or 'natural number'. *Second*, providing an extensional definition depends on a prior definition determining those properties required of anything if it is to be included in or excluded from that list comprising the definiens. Suppose an enumerative definition of 'passing student' is given for some particular class by listing the names of those students taking that class who are passing. Before this list can be supplied, it is necessary to know those properties that something must have to be a passing student. This is another reminder that the extension of a term depends on its intension. And *third*, extensional definitions have no use in defining words having no extension. Another type of definition is required for them.

'The', 'for', 'and', 'not', and '— only if . . . ' are examples of words that do not have extensions. Such words are not used to refer to things, events, or properties, either real or imaginary. Not one of them designates properties that anything must have to be denoted by that word. They can be explicitly defined by using synonymous definitions. For instance, '— only if . . . ' means 'if —, then . . . '. They can also be defined implicitly by the use of *contextual definitions*:

> A *contextual definition* defines a word by either (1) providing the function of that word, (2) providing the truth-value of statements named by the sentence using that word, or (3) providing an expression equivalent in meaning to the one in which that word is used.

*First*, examples might be given of how a word is used in context. Here is a contextual definition for 'and':

> 'And' is a word used to connect sentence elements of the same grammatical type or function, as in 'Dan went to class and the store' and 'Bring paper, pencils, and a ruler to class'.

*Second*, 'and' might be defined as a word that connects declarative sentences naming statements so that the result is a compound sentence naming a compound statement that is true if and only if both of its simple statements are true. In this way, the truth-value for the compound statement is determined. This type of contextual definition is, for example, displayed in truth tables introduced in Chapter 2. *Third*, a further type of contextual definition introduces an expression equivalent in meaning to the expression in which the definiendum is used:

> 'The ground is wet whenever it rains' and 'It rains only if the ground is wet' both mean the same as 'If it rains, then the ground is wet'.

This type of contextual definition is also introduced in Chapter 2.

In general, a definition can be used either to clarify or to persuade:

**A *persuasive definition* is any type of definition used to convince the receiver to accept or reject a claim in which the definiendum occurs.**

Persuasive definitions are not primarily employed to clarify ambiguity or vagueness, to introduce new meanings for words, to extend the meanings of old ones, or to report the actual use of words. Persuasive definitions might appear to be used to do any of these things. But their primary function is to convince. So, persuasive definitions are often couched in emotional language, either positive or negative. Consider two examples of persuasive definitions by genus and species:

> (5) 'Democracy' means a form of government guaranteeing those personal freedoms cherished by all individuals as they each seek to achieve the fulfillments of their own great potentials.

And 'communism' might be defined in this way:

> (6) 'Communism' means a form of government suppressing those personal freedoms necessary to achieve the fulfillment of one's potential and replacing these freedoms with the authoritative dictates of a totalitarian government.

Accepting these definitions, a person could now say, 'Democracy is a freer form of government than communism'. This claim is true "by definition." There would have been no evidence or argument presented to substantiate this claim. Rather, persuasive definitions presented in emotional language are given in place of evidence or argument to convince someone that a claim is true.

---

## EXERCISES

### Group A:

Determine what kind of definition each of the following is. Give reasons for your answers.

1. 'Cetacean' means a whale, porpoise, or dolphin.
2. 'I shall go to the theater and/or the ballet next week' means the same as 'Either I shall go to the theater or the ballet next week, and perhaps I shall go to both'.
3. 'Pacific states of the United States' means Washington, Oregon, and California.
4. 'Illegal' means 'unlawful'.
5. 'Building' means house, skyscraper, apartment house, cottage, and the like.
6. 'Odeum' (*pl* odea) [L & Gk:] 1: a small roofed theater of ancient Greece and Rome 2: a theater or concert hall.
7. 'Poor' means anyone with an annual income of less than $5,000.00.
8. 'Viable human life' means that time when brain activity of a fetus can be determined.
9. 'Felicitous' means 'pleasant' or 'delightful'.
10. 'Rich' means any person with an annual income of over $250,000.00.

11. 'United States President' means George Washington, Thomas Jefferson, Benjamin Harrison, Richard Nixon, Jimmy Carter, etc.

12. 'Triangle' means a , , , and so on.

13. 'Domestic cat' means a feline with retractable claws.

14. 'Scald' 1: an injury to the body caused by scalding 2: an act or process of scalding.

15. 'Charm' means a subatomic particle considered to be one of the basic building blocks of matter.

16. 'Atlanta is the capital of Georgia but Albany is the capital of New York' means the same as 'Atlanta is the capital of Georgia, yet Albany is the capital of New York'.

17. 'Weight' means the reading on a scale of a weighing device when an object is put on that scale.

18. 'Recrudescent' means 'renewal'.

19. 'Vinyl' means a synthetic textile fiber that is a long-chain polymer consisting largely of vinyl alcohol units.

20. 'Tiger' means a large carnivorous mammal of the cat family having a tawny coat and darker strips.

21. 'Feline' means a domestic cat, tiger, lion, bobcat, etc.

22. 'Edifice' means 'large building'.

23. 'Noise' means the lack of information transmitted over electronic lines or airwaves as a result of static.

24. 'National capital' means Paris, London, Prague, Madrid, etc.

25. 'Nanotechnology' means the ability to build complex objects on a molecular scale, with atom-by-atom precision; control over and building up complex objects from smaller objects measured on the scale of a nanometer (billionth of a meter).

## Group B:

Which of the following do you believe is an example of a definition used persuasively? Give your reasons for each example.

1. 'Vendue' means a public sale.

2. 'Clever' means witty but lacking depth.

3. 'Communist' means an ungodly person who lies at every opportunity to further the cause of the state.

4. 'Neuron' means a granular cell that has specialized processes and that is the fundamental functioning unit of nervous tissue.

5. 'Religion' means that wonderful experience one feels when abandoning himself completely to the strong arms of God.

6. 'Conifer' means an evergreen tree with true cones.

7. 'Socialist' means a lazy person who lets the government take care of him.

8. 'Entrepreneur' means a hard-working and clever person who makes a great deal of money in her own business.

9. 'Bureaucrat' means a slow-paced and rather dim-witted government worker.

10. 'Diplomat' means a highly intelligent person who is also very persuasive in getting others to do what he wants.

---

## 4.  CONSTRUCTING DEFINITIONS

There is a wide range of different types of definitions used for diverse purposes. Acknowledging this variation, there are important general considerations guiding the construction of definitions acceptable in rational thought. These guidelines grow out of the various purposes to which definitions can be put. Some of these purposes are (1) reporting the uses of words in a language, (2) clarifying the uses of words in a language by eliminating vagueness and ambiguity, (3) making the uses of words more precise, (4) introducing new words or new uses of old words into a language, and (5) relating various concepts in a language. Following are guidelines useful in constructing definitions that are in keeping with these purposes.

*First*, a definition should be neither too broad nor too narrow. A definition is too broad if it permits including things in its referent that ought not to be included. A definition is too narrow if it omits things from its referent that ought to be included. Suppose 'university' is defined as an institution from which one can receive instruction and training in particular fields of expertise. This definition of 'university' is too broad because it includes in the referent of 'university' not only universities, but secondary schools, trade schools, and vocational schools. Next, imagine someone defining 'chair' as anything having legs and a back on which a person is intended to sit. This definition is too narrow because it excludes chairs having arms. A definition can be both too broad and too narrow. This would be the case if someone defined 'love' to mean an emotion evoked in one human by another human. This definition is too narrow because love can be evoked in a human by all sorts of things besides another human. A pet dog, for instance, can invoke love in a human. The definition is too broad because there are many emotions that are evoked in one human by another human that are not love. Hate and envy are two examples.

An important way to determine whether a term is defined too narrowly, too broadly, or perhaps both, is to seek a *counterexample* for the proposed definition. A counterexample for a definition that is too narrow is an instance of something that should be included in the referent of a term but is excluded because of the proposed definition. A definition is too broad when there is an instance of something that should not be included in the referent of a term, but is included because of the proposed definition. Counterexamples are used in the above paragraph to show that a definition of 'university' is too broad, a definition of 'chair' is too narrow, and a definition of 'love' is both too broad and too narrow.

*Second*, a definition should not be viciously circular. In discussing circularity, it is not unusual to find this sort of restriction: The word being defined, some other grammatical form of it, or a synonym, cannot occur in the definiens. But this restriction is not acceptable. For example, a person might say 'sooty' means of, relating to, or producing soot. This definition is circular in the sense that the noun, 'soot', appears in the definiens. Yet the definition is permissible when 'soot' is not in turn defined in terms of 'sooty'. In constructing definitions, *viciously circular definitions* are to be avoided.

> A *viciously circular definition* is one in which a word defined, or a synonym, is found in some form in the definiens *AND* that word in the definiens is itself defined in terms of the definiendum.

Thus, if 'owner' is defined as a person who possesses something and in turn 'a person who possesses something' is defined as an owner, the definitions would be viciously circular. A viciously circular definition explains nothing about how a word is used or how it is related to other words. Nor does a viciously circular definition clarify any meaning a word might have. If someone does not know how to use 'owner', the above attempted definition is not helpful in grasping the correct use.

*Third*, an acceptable definiens should not use negative words when positive ones can be used. In general, to know what is *not* the referent of a word is not to know what *is* its referent. To use an extreme example, suppose someone said that 'car' means something that is not a tree, house, or book. This would tell the person ignorant of the meaning of 'car' very little. A more useful attempt at defining 'car' would be to say that 'car' means a motorized vehicle, the primary purpose of which is to transport one or more persons by land from one place to another. Note that this definition is itself too broad because it includes such things as motorcycles in its extension. Nonetheless, it is more useful than a negative definition.

Some definitions, however, are best presented in a negative form. Indeed, some words seem to require a negative definiens. A definiens for 'bachelor' is 'any unmarried male human over the age of consent'. While 'unmarried' is a negative word, it is appropriate in this definition. There are no unbending rules determining when it is proper to introduce a negative definiens. There is this guideline, however. Always define the definiendum in the way that gives the most information about its appropriate use. In most cases, a positive definition will more likely satisfy this guideline.

*Fourth*, a definition should avoid vague, ambiguous, obscure, or figurative language. This requirement extends to the use of correct grammar in a definition. To determine what is to count as obscure, vague, ambiguous, or figurative one must consider the context in which a word is to be used. For instance, a botanist would not find obscure the definition of 'protonema' as the filamentous thalloid stage of the gametophyte in mosses and in some liverworts comparable to the prothalium in ferns. Nor could a less technical definition be constructed and remain as accurate and useful as this one. Suppose someone defines 'pencil' as an elongated cylinder originally constructed of organic materials having a core of graphite and found useful in written communications. This definition ignores the guideline of avoiding obscurity. Nor should a definition be figurative. What if a person defines 'happiness' by saying that happiness is a warm, fuzzy teddy bear? This would be of little help in coming to a clear understanding of the meaning of 'happiness'.

*Fifth*, the language of a definition should be as emotionally neutral as possible. Someone could say 'communism' means a government run by perverts and godless people in pursuit of the destruction of individual rights while glorifying the state.

However, this definition is too emotional to be useful in clarifying the concept *communism*. Such attempts at definitions might be effective in persuading people to believe certain things and even to act on their beliefs. Even so, the primary purpose of a definition for rational thought is not to persuade but to clarify linguistic expressions.

*Sixth*, a definition should indicate the appropriate context in which the definiendum is used if there is likelihood of confusion concerning that context. This requirement is necessary to avoid possible ambiguity. Suppose, for example, that a definition for 'love' is required. The word 'love' has various meanings in different contexts. For example, there are those meanings of 'love' in the context of human emotions. But there is also the meaning of 'love' in the context of tennis. A good definition of 'love' will clearly distinguish these contexts, and any others, in which 'love' is defined.

These six guidelines for constructing acceptable definitions in rational thought are helpful in achieving good communication. Constructing definitions demands a sensitivity for the type of definition needed to do a particular job in a specific context. In constructing specific types of definitions, further guides ought to be considered. For instance, a lexical definition ought to be true. In giving a stipulative definition, or a definition used stipulatively, consider introducing an entirely new word as the definiendum. This will remove the likelihood of confusing the old meaning of a word with its new one. And in constructing a definition by genus and species, take care to give differentia that clearly distinguish one species from another in the same genus.

---

## *EXERCISES*

### Group A:

In each of the following definitions at least one of the six general guidelines for constructing acceptable definitions has not been observed. For each example state which guideline(s) has been ignored. Give reasons substantiating which guidelines have been ignored.

1. 'Strike' means to swing at, but not hit, a ball.
2. 'Pen' means a cylindrical, monofunctional information delivery system.
3. 'Ship' means a form of transportation through water.
4. 'To snatch' means to grab something.
5. 'Fear' means a bad feeling in the pit of your stomach.
6. 'Love' means a cozy fire on a cold night.
7. 'Homophlant' means a featherless quadruped.
8. 'Hard rock music' means a cacophonous disturbance that is pure trash.
9. 'Parent' means a person who is not without a child.
10. 'Wife' means a person who has a husband.
11. 'Religion' means the formalized worship of God.
12. 'Time' means what is measured by a timing device such as a clock or watch.

13. 'Peace' means the absence of war.

14. 'Taxation' means a formalized method of revenue enhancement employed by a legally constituted body of elected governmental officials.

15. 'Communism' means a form of government in which the government owns the principal means of manufacturing of goods.

### Group B:

Provide a precising definition for each of the following as they might apply to persons. Be certain to observe all of the guidelines for constructing acceptable definitions:

1. 'Strong'

2. 'Intelligent'

3. 'Short'

4. 'Efficient'

5. 'Old'

### Group C:

Provide a definition by genus and species for each of the following, being certain to observe all of the guidelines for constructing acceptable definitions:

1. 'Lying'

2. 'Rug'

3. 'Cheating'

4. 'Computer'

5. 'Poem'

### Group D:

Provide an operational definition for each of the following, being certain to observe all of the guidelines for constructing acceptable definitions:

1. 'Density'

2. 'Weight'

3. 'Length'

4. 'Temperature'

5. 'Hunger'

### Group E:

Provide a complete enumerative definition for each of the following, being certain to observe all of the guidelines for constructing acceptable definitions.

1. 'Central American country'

2. 'United States state bordering Canada'

3. 'Warsaw Pact nation'

4. 'Major United States political party'

5. 'Post World War II United States President'

**Group F:**

Provide a partial definition by subclass for each of the following, being certain to observe all of the guidelines for constructing acceptable definitions:

1. 'Contemporary popular music'

2. 'Printed material'

3. 'Motorized vehicle'

4. 'Tree'

5. 'Sexually transmitted disease'

---

## 5.    REVIEW OF NEW TERMS

**Ambiguous:** A linguistic expression that has two or more non-overlapping meanings and the context in which the expression is being used does not determine which meaning is to be understood.

**Analytic statement:** A statement whose truth-value (truth or falsity) is determined solely by the definitions of the words used in expressing that statement.

**Compatible meaning:** Two general terms, 'γ' and 'δ', such that those properties comprising the intension of 'γ' are included in those properties comprising the intension of 'δ'.

**Concept:** The appropriate and accepted use of a general term in a particular language.

**Contextual definition:** Defines a word or phrase—the definiendum—by either (1) providing the function of the definiendum, (2) providing the truth-value of statements named by the sentence using the definiendum, or (3) providing an expression equivalent in meaning to the one in which the definiendum is used.

**Contingent statement:** A statement whose truth or falsity is determined by taking into consideration particular things in the world.

**Definiendum:** The word or phrase to be defined in a definition.

**Definiens:** In a definition, that which indicates the meaning of the definiendum.

**Definition:** Some means used to indicate the meaning of a word or phrase not used as a proper name.

**Enumerative definition:** An extensional definition that provides a list of those things denoted by the definiendum. There are both *complete* and *partial* enumerative definitions depending on whether all those things denoted by the word are listed or only a part of them.

**Extension:** What an expression is about; that is, its referent.

**Genus and species, definition by:** An intensional definition that defines a word or phrase by (1) specifying the type of thing being defined and (2) by listing those properties that distinguish that thing from other things of the same type; *analytical definition.*

**Identical meaning:** Two general terms γ and δ such that those properties comprising the intentions of both are the same.

**Incompatible meaning:** Two general terms γ and δ such that part of the rules, conventions, and customs formulating the intension of one cannot be included in those rules, conventions, and customs formulating the intension of the other.

**Intension:** Whatever determines the extension of an expression.

**Inverse rule of meaning:** Given a series of compatible general terms, then the order of increasing intension and decreasing extension are identical as are those of increasing extension and decreasing intension.

**Language:** A set of accepted rules, conventions, and customs that relate a set of signs (1) to one another, (2) to any referent these signs might have, and (3) to the users of those signs.

**Lexical definition:** A report of the actual or normative meanings of a word or phrase at a given time in the ongoing development of a language.

**Operational definition:** Clarifies or establishes the intensional meaning of a word or phrase by citing various techniques, methods, or the like governing whether or not that word or phrase applies to some thing, event, or the like.

**Ostensive definition:** An extensional definition that is provided by pointing to particular examples of those things denoted by a word.

**Persuasive definition:** Any type of definition used to convince the receiver to accept or reject a claim in which the definiendum occurs.

**Pragmatics:** A study of the rules, customs, and conventions relating language to its users.

**Precising definition:** A definition or a use of a definition that makes more exact the already established intensional meaning of a term.

**Reforming definition:** A stipulative definition, or a definition used stipulatively, that (1) specifies a new intensional meaning for an old word used in new circumstances or (2) extends the intensional meaning of an old word.

**Semantic information:** The intension of a linguistic expression.

**Semantics:** The study of the rules, customs, and conventions determining the interpretations of various linguistic expressions, such as words and sentences.

**Stipulative definition:** A definition or a use of a definition that specifies the intensional meaning of a word or phrase within a particular context irrespective of how that word or phrase might be commonly used, if used at all.

**Subclass, definition by:** An extensional definition in which (1) the definiens denotes classes having fewer members than the class denoted by the definiendum, and (2) the definition provides a list of those subclasses that are the members of the class denoted by the definiendum.

**Synonymous definition:** Indicates the intensional meaning of a word or phrase by presenting another word or phrase having the same or approximate intensional meaning as the first.

**Syntax:** The study of the relations of the signs of a language independent of any interpretations these signs might have.

**Term:** Any linguistic expression that can be used as a grammatical subject in a sentence. Terms may be *general* or *singular, concrete* or *abstract*. A general term refers to a class of individuals whereas a singular term refers to a particular individual. A concrete term refers to individuals that are locatable in space and time whereas abstract terms refer to things that are non-spatial and nontemporal.

**Theoretical definition:** A stipulative definition or definition used stipulatively that specifies the intensional meaning of a word or phrase in some specialized discipline, such as physics.

**Vague:** A linguistic expression whose meaning is too imprecise within a specific context for one to understand whether it is applicable in that context or not.

**Viciously circular definition:** One in which the word or phrase defined, or a synonym, is found in some form in the definiens *AND* that word or phrase in the definiens is itself defined in terms of the definiendum.

---

## ENDNOTES

1. Webster's New Collegiate Dictionary (G. & C. Merriam Company; Springfield, Massachusetts, 1981), p. 164.
2. *Ibid.,* p. 713.
3. *Ibid.,* p. 848.
4. *Ibid.,* p. 1355.
5. *Ibid.,* p. 751.
6. *Ibid.,* p. 1100.

# 14

# THINGS THAT CAN GO WRONG: FALLACIES OF RELEVANCE

## 1. COGENT AND FALLACIOUS ARGUMENTS

In that a person thinks rationally and presents arguments, those arguments must be cogent. A *cogent argument* must satisfy these requirements:

**(1) the premises support the conclusion; (2) only considerations relevant both to the justification and rejection of the conclusion are taken into account by those arguing; and (3) the premises are rationally acceptable.**

A *fallacious argument* is one that is not cogent. There are, therefore, three broad ways in which an argument can be fallacious. These types of flaws in arguments can be categorized as fallacies of *logical relation*, *relevance*, and *rationality*. Whenever analyzing an argument, it is helpful to think in terms of these *Three Rs*. Chapters 1 through 12 discuss important topics concerning logical relation. Attention is now turned to the other demands of cogency. These requirements focus on the content of arguments, the context in which they are placed, and those people presenting and receiving the arguments. Both the presenter and receiver of an argument can commit a *fallacy*; that is,

**an error that (1) occurs in an argument and (2) adversely affects the ability of the premises to supply evidence for the conclusion.**

The presenter can commit a fallacy by initiating one, and the receiver by accepting a fallacy as if it were a legitimate part of an argument.

The demand of *relevance* stresses the *content* of statements presented in arguments and how that content is perceived by those arguing to be related to the conclusion.

Those, and only those, claims having a bearing in content on establishing or rejecting the conclusion are to be considered in an argument. For example, the following argument does not meet the requirement of logical relation, and the requirement of relevance is, at best questionably met:

(1)   American industry has created one of the highest standards of living found in the world today. Not only workers and managers but also investors have profited in numerous ways from the growth of industry. So, the protection of minnows, owls, forests, and shrinking clean environments are of little importance to the well-being of the American people.

Even if the premises of (1) are true, this is not a cogent argument. Today's perceived material affluence brought about by industry bears minimal, if any, relevance as evidence to support the claim that protection of the environment is of *little* importance to the *continued* well-being of the American people.

Relevant claims are not only those that give reasons for the justification of a conclusion. Equally important are claims that suggest reasons for its rejection. Imagine this argument:

(2)   More hospitals use brand 'X' pain reliever than any other. In cases of your own personal pain, you ought to do what hospitals do. Therefore, you ought to use brand 'X' to relieve your pain.

Suppose, as part of the content of (2), the receiver assumes the primary function of a hospital is to serve in healing and restoring health. This person further assumes that hospital administrators select medications primarily on the basis of their medical effectiveness in fulfilling this function. What if it is discovered that the motive of hospital administrators to use brand 'X' is basically financial. The manufacturer of 'X' supplies it without charge. Then, this discovery is relevant in weighing the acceptability of (2).

Logical relation and relevance are necessary, but not sufficient, for an argument to be cogent. Consider this example:

(3)   If country Z is stockpiling a great many dangerous weapons to initiate a surprise attack against the United States, American citizens ought to demand rapid and decisive action be taken against Z. Z is stockpiling a great many dangerous weapons to initiate a surprise attack against the United States. So, American citizens ought to demand rapid and decisive action be taken against Z.

For an argument to be cogent, it seems appropriate to demand that *all* its premises be true. Even so, there is a difference between demanding that a statement be true and actually knowing whether a particular statement is true or false. Often in presenting or receiving an argument a person is not in a position to know whether a premise is actually true or not. This is the case with the second premise of (3). Further, in some types of argument at least one of the premises is assumed to be false. This is seen in *reductio ad absurdum* arguments, and in those arguments in which a claim known to be false is assumed to explore what conclusions it would sustain if it were true. In general, anyone arguing ought to demand that all the premises of an argument are true. But in actual practice, this requirement is often too stringent.

Yet it can be required that premises by *rationally acceptable*. Following are guidelines to judge whether a premise is rationally acceptable or not. While each guideline is to be considered in assessing the rational acceptability of any premise, there will be particular instances of their application when one will be given more weight than another. Good judgment, based on past experiences coupled with the way a person interprets these experiences, is always needed in applying guidelines.

*First*, if a premise is known to be true, it is rationally acceptable.\* And, insofar as a premise is known to be false, then, in general, it cannot be rationally acceptable. When an argument is being used merely to persuade and not in an attempt to establish the truth of some claim, this requirement of rational acceptability is often ignored. An ideologue, for instance, wants to persuade someone to accept his views. People of this sort might, knowingly or not, "stretch the truth" of their premises for purposes of persuasion. In rational thought, however, the primary purpose of an argument is to provide evidence for a conclusion. Persuading and giving evidence are distinct activities.

*Second*, for a premise to be rationally acceptable it must be *coherent*. A premise must be integrated into the order and sense established by the content of the argument and the context in which the argument is placed. An ancient Aztec might coherently present as rationally acceptable in some argument, 'The Sun, in order to rise each morning, needs the blood of many humans'. A twentieth century person educated and trained in the technological West could not coherently make this claim. It simply does not fit his contemporary world view.† Nor are the claims of soothsayers, astrologers, and the like generally acceptable as rational in the twentieth century West because they are not coherent in that world view.

*Third*, for a premise to be rationally acceptable it must be *adequate* itself or in conjunction with other claims to supply reasons for substantiating a conclusion. Some premises are relevant but not adequate. Suppose Peter Wimsey is attempting to establish that Rumpple murdered Sir Alex. Wimsey might say this:

(4)   It is evident that Rumpple is our murderer. After all, he was
       found in the same location as Sir Alex's body.

Wimsey is concluding, 'Rumpple is the murderer of Sir Alex'. As evidence, he says that Rumpple was found in the same location as the body of Sir Alex. To establish the whereabouts of the murderer is relevant in solving the crime. Yet it is not adequate evidence for Wimsey to support his conclusion.

*Fourth*, for a premise to be rationally acceptable, it must be *relatively simple*. This concept of *simplicity* is not to be confused with grammatical simplicity, the use of

---

\* If an argument interpreted deductively is sound, all of its premises are rationally acceptable because they are all true.

†The world view of a person or group of people is that interacting network of beliefs held to have universal and indisputable application. These beliefs form the background against which claims are interpreted, and accepted or rejected.

simple vocabulary, or the lack of psychological complexity. The concept *relative simplicity* is understood in terms of the number of suppositions needed to support a conclusion. Consider these two arguments each concluding with 'So, Erica has no doubt been lost':

   **(5)** If Erica ran into foul weather, her small boat was likely destroyed. Assuming her boat was destroyed, she no doubt has been lost. There was alleged foul weather where Erica was sailing. So, Erica has no doubt been lost.

   **(6)** If Erica ran into foul weather or UFOs, her small boat was likely destroyed. Assuming her boat was destroyed, she no doubt has been lost. There were known foul weather and alleged UFOs where Erica was sailing. So, Erica has no doubt been lost.

The premises in (6) suppose both UFOs and foul weather conditions for Erica to be lost. In (5), only the existence of foul weather is assumed. Thus, (5) is simpler than (6).

---

## EXERCISES

### Group A:

Which of the following arguments do you intuitively suppose are cogent and which fallacious? Appealing to the Three Rs, give reasons for your answers.

1. I cheated on the test. The course was not a required course in my major but only part of the stupid core curriculum. And I usually cheat on courses not in my major.

2. Premarital sex ought to be outlawed in the United States because it is a sin from the perspective of the religious traditions on which this nation is built.

3. Social programs backed by federal tax dollars need to be strengthened. That is the only way that minorities and women are able to compete in a white male-dominated society.

4. If I do well in my course in logic, I look forward to a successful law practice. An essential skill needed by all lawyers is the ability to reason well.

5. Don't trust any arms reduction plan the Russians agree to accept. From Stalin to right now, they have not kept a single one of them.

6. Yes, I am studying tonight. I know I'm not going to pass the exam tomorrow unless I study. But since I'm studying, I'm going to pass that exam.

7. If the United States government stops supporting the Contras, Mexico will be the next to go. A familiar pattern will follow the last hopes of democracy in Central America as communism topples one freedom-loving country after another.

8. Blonds are airheads. It isn't hard to figure that one out. Just go to a couple of their parties or see them with their parents at a country club.

9. Since there is no known cure for *AIDS* and it is a fatal disease, all persons with *AIDS* ought to be completely isolated from the rest of the population.

10. What's the matter with drinking a few beers every night to loosen up? The pressure around here is pretty tough. Anyway, everybody has a couple now and again.

11. Holly is weird. Don't get mixed up with her. She studies a lot, for one thing. And when you take her out and pay for everything, you don't get a thing in return except maybe a goodnight kiss.

12. Bryan must really be into the needle scene since I hear he is being tested for drug abuse.

13. Two weeks ago David told Jane Mary that she ought to invest in North-Western Mining and Drill Company. He said to her that if she were not only going to save her principal, but also make a fortune in the market, she ought to invest in North-Western. He is glad to see that she followed his advice. She is bound to make a fortune.

14. The United States government has exactly two choices in its support of any Central American government. It can support communism or it can support local dictatorship. And everyone knows which of these is the better. Thus, we know exactly what to do with Panama.

15. Owing to the conservative nature of the Midwest and South, coupled with the high regard for religious fundamentalism in both areas, it is very probably the case that a conservative Republican will win the nomination for any national office. So, we can look forward to the Rev. Feelgood taking the political field in these regions.

**Group B:**

List some claims you believe are rationally acceptable. *Why* do you hold that these specific claims are rationally acceptable? What are *your* general criteria for defining *rational acceptability*? For instance, do you believe that some claim is rationally acceptable because acting on it makes you feel good or it is to your personal advantage to do so?

**Group C:**

Have you ever been tricked into accepting a fallacious argument as if it were cogent and then acting on what you believed to be a justified claim? If so, what was the fallacious argument that tricked you? Appealing to the Three Rs, explain why you now suppose it was fallacious.

---

## 2. CLASSIFYING FALLACIES

A common practice is to classify fallacies as formal or informal. *Formal fallacies* are determined solely by the form, or structure, of an argument. Any invalid argument form, such as the following, is a formal fallacy. That the premises of an argument having this form are correct does not guarantee that the conclusion is:

> **(1)** If [sentence $A$], then [sentence $B$]
> But [sentence $B$]
> Therefore, [sentence $A$]

Here are two arguments displaying this form:

> **(2)** If there is to be world peace, nuclear armaments are to be reduced. Nuclear armaments are being reduced. Therefore, there is to be world peace.

> **(3)** If there is to be world peace, nuclear armaments are to be increased. Nuclear armaments are being increased. Therefore, there is to be world peace.

The form in (1) does not guarantee the validity of any argument. Even if all the premises in (2) and (3) were true, this would not guarantee that the conclusion is true. Any argument displaying the form in (1) is an instance of the fallacy of Affirming the Consequent.*

An *informal fallacy*, on the other hand, is based on considerations of the context and content of an argument. Here is an example of that worn question, 'How could you do this after all we've done for you?'

**(4)** Lee, you ought to feel ashamed if you go that party tonight and not study so you can ace your exam tomorrow. All of the brothers, including me, are counting on you to pull up your GPA. We've all done a lot for you. Missing a party and studying for us is the least you can do.

Whether it is correct or not that Lee should miss the party and study is not substantiated by the emotions of his fraternity brothers or how much they have done for him. Lee might feel guilty or threatened if he does not study. Such feelings, however, are considerations of motivation and not evidence in support of some claim.

The formal-informal distinction, however, is not an exclusive one because both types of flaws might be found combined in an argument. Suppose someone argues like this:

**(5)** If Sam is a good brother, he loves his sister. But if Sam loves his sister, then he ought to be accused of incest. So, if Sam is a good brother, he ought to be accused of incest.

(5) is not a cogent argument. There is an equivocal use of 'loves' in the premises. This equivocation prohibits (5) being interpreted as having this form:

**(6)** If [sentence $A$], then [sentence $B$]
If [sentence $B$], then [sentence $C$]
So, if [sentence $A$], then [sentence $C$]

Since 'loves' is used in one way in the first premise and in a very different way in the second, it cannot consistently stand in place of 'sentence $B$' in both premises. This is the actual form of (6):

**(7)** If [sentence $A$], then [sentence $B$]
If [sentence $C$], then [sentence $D$]
So, if [sentence $A$], then [sentence $D$]

Is (5) fallacious because of faulty form or faulty content? Because of examples like (5), fallacies cannot universally be classified as *exclusively* formal or informal. Even so, the formal-informal distinction is an important practical distinction useful in

---

* Another frequently used formal fallacy is Denying the Antecedent:

If [sentence $A$], then [sentence $B$]
But not [sentence $A$]
Therefore, not [sentence $B$]

learning to analyze arguments from the viewpoint of rational thought.

The fallacies discussed in Chapters 14 and 15 are common in the everyday world. The scheme used to classify them grows out of the notion of an argument being cogent. For instance, if what is being asserted in a premise is not clear because of faulty grammar, or improper or vague uses of words, then that premise cannot be accepted as relevant to any conclusion. Not knowing what is being asserted, a person cannot say if it is relevant in an argument. Indeed, the less clear a claim is, the less likely it can be used to supply evidence in support of some conclusion. *Ambiguity, equivocation, vagueness,* and *relative words* presented in sections 5 through 8 of this chapter are examples of ***FALLACIES OF FAULTY GRAMMAR.*** Often premises are presented as relevant to a conclusion when they are not. Four common types of ***IRRELEVANT APPEALS*** are appeals to *irrelevant authority,* to *pity,* to *popular opinion,* and to *special interests.* Sections 9 through 12 of this chapter deal with these fallacies. It is also inappropriate not to introduce a claim as a premise in an argument when that claim is relevant to the acceptability of a conclusion. ***FALLACIES OF MISSING EVIDENCE*** typically occur in appeals to *ignorance, fake precision, hasty conclusions,* and *neglect of relevant evidence.* These are discussed in Sections 13 through 16 of this chapter.

***FALLACIES OF RATIONAL ACCEPTABILITY*** can be collected into groupings of *coherence, adequacy, simplicity,* and *contradiction.* The *ad hominem, tu quoque, red herring,* and *straw man* fallacies can be thought of as ***FALLACIES OF INCOHERENCE.*** Each interjects into an argument a *diversionary tactic* that does not "fit with" the conclusion or the overall topic under debate. These fallacies are discussed in Chapter 15, Sections 1 through 4. Nor can a premise be useful in establishing a conclusion if it is in some way unwarranted. The *is-ought, deceptive alternative, wishful thinking,* and *novelty* fallacies are types of ***UNWARRANTED PREMISES.*** These fallacies are introduced in Sections 5 through 9 of Chapter 15. Fallacies grouped under the concept *simplicity* are seen operating in various ***CAUSAL FALLACIES.*** *Confusing necessary and sufficient conditions,* citing *questionable causes,* introducing a *slippery slope,* and using the *gambler's fallacy* are examples. Causal fallacies are examined in Sections 9 through 12 of Chapter 15. Finally, fallacies that tend to introduce either a ***CONTRADICTORY OR VACUOUS CLAIM*** into an argument are *circularity, inconsistency, factual certainty,* and *question begging.* These are discussed in the last four sections of Chapter 15.

## 3.  HINDRANCES TO GRASPING FALLACIES

In many ways, perpetrators of fallacies are to language what magicians are to vision. Both create illusions of what is correct. For the most part, however, a person is not taken in by the tricks of the magician. The magician is on stage and clearly set apart from those watching. The audience waits for the tricks, is entertained by them, and perhaps even attempts to figure out how they are done. Fallacies are verbal illusions, but they are not set apart from what is taken as correct. Nor are they woven into arguments to entertain. Rather, they are often used to persuade when there is insufficient evidence on which to establish a claim. While the tricks of the magician are taken for what they are, this is seldom the case with instances of fallacies. Imagine this argument:

(1) Anyone who proposes legalized gun control is anti-American. After all, the possession of guns by the general populace is a fundamental right, guaranteed by the Constitution, of all peace-loving people. Furthermore,

the procession of arms is an essential part of the American way of life.

Little is offered in (1) to support the conclusion. Just how little support is given should become clearer as this and the next chapter are studied.

Fallacies are also found in circumstances in which there is slight interest in pursuing a topic or there is seemingly insufficient time to do so. Imagine a student who has recently been suffering from lower back pains. He takes time from his study schedule and goes to the school health clinic. After examining him, the physician says the following:

> **(2)**   Mister Smith, you're to take two of these pills three times a day
> for your pain. My diagnosis is that you have a mild kidney infec-
> tion and this medication will cure it.

Few people have sufficient interest, time, or ability to pursue medical training. Generally, the advice of the physician is taken at face value without the patient's seeking a second opinion. And in some cases, it is appropriate to accept opinion on authority. Yet in some cases it is not.

Fallacies take much of their strength from the fact that they are similar to legitimate cases of reasoning. Consider this example. If someone wants to give evidence in support of a claim in relativity physics, that person can correctly appeal to what Einstein has to say. If, on the other hand, the person wants to supply evidence for upholding a particular claim dealing with social justice, an appeal to Einstein is unwarranted unless it can be established that Einstein is also an authority in *that* field. Because a person is an authority in one area, it does not follow that he is one in another. He might be; he might not. A judgment on the part of the person analyzing the argument is demanded. Indeed, good, sensitive judgment is always demanded to analyze an argument and determine whether it is fallacious or not.

There are typical limitations making it difficult to see fallacies. A lack of strong linguistic abilities is one. The firmer a grasp someone has of vocabulary and grammar, the less likely he will miss fallacies. For instance, *to censor* and *to censure* are concepts often confused. 'Censor' means the repression, by a recognized authority, of something objectionable. 'Censure' means moral disapproval of something. A person might censure any disrespect of the American flag but not demand legislative action making it illegal to burn that flag or wear it as decoration on the back side of swim shorts.

Another common stumbling block to grasping fallacies is lack of a broad range of experiences needed to come into intimate contact with other cultures and world views. A person well trained in a particular specialty can display a mental narrowness prohibiting her from realizing various ways of interpreting an argument. The broader and deeper an individual's *general* knowledge, the more likely she will be aware of faulty reasoning. Imagine someone well trained in chemical engineering who has traveled little and has few interests outside of her own field of expertise. She is a target for the verbal charlatan:

> **(3)**   Certainly you shouldn't hire Orientals and Indians. They can't be
> trusted. After all, they are raised in godless religions, and this
> can't help but shape their attitudes and behavior.

Much of the persuasive force this argument might have is related to ignorance of world religions such as Hinduism, Buddhism and Taoism. What does this chemical engineer know of the moral demands of these world religions? Enough to counter the argument being presented?

It is common to accept or reject some claim simply because of an emotional predisposition toward that claim. Someone, intentionally or not, can play on the feelings of the listener. One can say either 'Abortion during the first week of pregnancy is murdering a baby' or 'Abortion during the first week of pregnancy is removing a zygote'. A primary goal of using emotional language is to persuade, independently of solid evidence, someone to accept a claim. A claim can be made more acceptable when the desires and beliefs of the hearer are heightened by emotionally charged language. It does not seem necessary to demand evidence for what is considered obvious. Yet particular claims and arguments should never be accepted simply because they concur with already held opinions. Nor should they be rejected simply because they are not in keeping with particular beliefs. In everyday practice, however, both situations occur too frequently.

In coming to distinguish fallacious arguments from cogent ones,

> *there might be more than one reason why an argument is fallacious. Being able to state those reasons clearly is important in rational thought.*

It is important to be able *to explain why* an argument is fallacious. To do this, it is helpful to recognize quickly some of the more common fallacies. A person who can recognize bad arguments is in a better position to argue successfully. Anyone who finds it difficult to comprehend instances of fallacies can fall prey to the illusions of verbal tricksters.

## 4.  GUIDES TO CATCHING FALLACIES

In attempting to isolate fallacies, it is good strategy to follow these steps.* *First*, put the argument into **standard argument form**. Rewrite the argument so that all premises, both explicit and implicit, are stated, followed by a clear statement of the conclusion. This is not always easy to do. People are sometimes not clear in what they are attempting to support. Sometimes they are trying to support several assertions at the same time. In attempting to establish the conclusion of an argument, it is not unusual to find subsidiary conclusions in passages used to support the main contention of the arguer. Watch for these subsidiary conclusions. Attempt to ascertain what is the overall topic being discussed by the arguer, the main conclusion, and any subsidiary conclusions. Also, remember that not every claim in a passage containing an argument is essential to that argument. In analyzing an argument, look for **essentially used** claims and words:

> **A claim or word is *essentially used* in an argument if and only if without it the conclusion could not be justified or have the appearance of being justified.**

Claims or words must be essentially used in an argument to introduce fallacies.

---

* In conjunction with this section, review Chapter 1, Section 2 concerning argument reconstruction and the Principle of Charity.

*Second*, having put the argument into standard form, *reconstruct* it. Notice if there appear to be any claims that are implicitly understood, but not actually stated. Such claims might be either premises or the conclusion of an argument. Make explicit all implicit claims essential to the argument. Do not attempt, however, to avoid fallacies by supplying claims not in keeping with the likely views of the arguer and the context in which the argument is placed. The purpose of supplying missing premises is *to clarify* and *to complete* the argument as the arguer most likely would. To accomplish this purpose, follow the ***Principle of Charity***. The Principle of Charity requires that the receiver of an argument assumes that the arguer is attempting to provide a cogent argument. So, always analyze an argument as fairly as possible, within the surroundings of the argument and the known views of the presenter. Even so, the purpose of reconstruction is not to turn a bad argument into a good one, but to clarify and complete it.

Applying the Three Rs of *logical relation*, *relevance*, and *rationality* is useful in reconstructing arguments. Imagine hearing this:

> **(1)** You won't find Pat doing drugs. This is because Pat hates drugs. Further, he hates doing anything that he thinks is detrimental to his health.

It appears that an argument is being presented in which 'Pat hates drugs' and 'Pat hates doing anything that he thinks is detrimental to his health' are offered as premises in support of the conclusion, 'You won't find Pat doing drugs'. In standard form, (1) looks like this:

**(2)**
1) Pat hates drugs.
2) Pat hates doing anything that he thinks is detrimental to his health.
3) So, you won't find Pat doing drugs.

There appears to be a gap between the premises and the conclusion. One way of bridging this gap is to suggest a suppressed premise claiming 'Pat thinks drugs are detrimental to his health'. (2) is now reconstructed as

**(3)**
1) Pat hates drugs.
2) Pat hates doing anything that he thinks is detrimental to his health.
3) Pat thinks that drugs are detrimental to his health.
4) So, you won't find Pat doing drugs.

The third premise of (3) closes the gap between the explicit premises in (1) and its conclusion. Thus, this premise is relevant to the argument.

But how does the inclusion of this new information survive under the criterion of *rationality*? Is, for example, too much being included in (3)? Does Pat ever take a legal drug? He might not. But then again, he might. And if it is likely that he does take an aspirin now and then, (1) can be better stated as

(4)

    1) Pat hates drugs.

    2) Pat hates doing anything that he thinks is detrimental to his health.

    3) Pat thinks that illegal drugs are detrimental to his health.

    4) So, you won't find Pat doing illegal drugs.

The Principle of Charity is a guiding force in interpreting (1). It is assumed that in the context of the argument the arguer is talking about illegal drugs and that he wishes to present a cogent argument. Further, in the actual reconstruction of (1) the Three Rs are used as guides. The premises logically relate to the conclusion, they are relevant to the conclusion, and they are rationally acceptable.

The steps followed above provide a powerful strategy to help discover fallacies. However, like all guides, these steps do not guarantee uncovering any fallacy that might be in an argument. The process still depends on the judgments of the person putting the argument into standard form and reconstructing it. These judgments themselves are based on fundamental linguistic abilities, broadness of background experience, and general knowledge. A weakness in any of these areas can result in a faulty reconstruction and a fallacy escaping detection.

## EXERCISES

### Group A:

Report some arguments you have recently heard that you believe are fallacious. Explain why you believe that these arguments are flawed. Save your work. After you have further studied fallacies, evaluate the reasons you give in support of your beliefs concerning the arguments that you say are fallacious.

### Group B:

Find examples of arguments in newspapers, magazines, trade journals, textbooks, and the like that you believe are fallacious. Explain why you believe that these arguments are flawed. Again save your work. After you have studied fallacies, evaluate the reasons you give in support of your beliefs concerning the arguments that you say are fallacious.

### Group C:

Imagine that you want to deceive someone to accept some claim. To do this you present a fallacious argument that appears to justify your claim. Think of several such claims. One possibility is 'Legalized gun control is a step toward totalitarian government'. Then, appealing to the Three Rs, create a fallacious, but persuasive, argument for each claim. Explain why you believe each argument is fallacious. When you have finished studying various types of fallacies, return to your work in this exercise and examine rationally what you have said.

## 5. AMBIGUITY

> *Fallacies of Ambiguity* occur when either (1) a claim introduced as a premise is ambiguous and no reasonable interpretation of that premise within the context of the argument supports the conclusion, or (2) a claim introduced as the conclusion is ambiguous and no reasonable interpretation of that conclusion within the context of the argument is supported by the premises.

A claim is ambiguous if it can be interpreted in two or more distinct ways and the context in which it appears does not indicate which interpretation is to be taken as the proper one. There are two types of ambiguity; namely, *syntactical ambiguity* and *semantic ambiguity*.

*Syntactical ambiguity* occurs when different interpretations of a sentence result from unclear grammatical structure. An example of syntactical ambiguity, or *amphibole*, is 'Dottie never talks to her mother when she is irritated with her'. Is Dottie, or her mother, irritated, and who is it that never talks with whom under such circumstances? This example, of course, is not an instance of a fallacy because it is not used in an argument to support a conclusion. Consider this, however:

**(1)** Since deceitful public manipulation only guarantees the election of our candidate, it ought to be avoided on moral grounds and our candidate not be elected.

(1) can be rewritten in standard form like this:

**(2)**
1) Deceitful public manipulation only guarantees the election of our candidate.
2) Therefore, it ought to be avoided on moral grounds and our candidate not be elected.

Is the premise to be interpreted as 'Deceitful public manipulation guarantees only the election of our candidate' or as 'Only deceitful public manipulation guarantees the election of our candidate'?

In either case, (2) needs to be restructured and missing premises supplied:

**(3)**
1) Deceitful public manipulation only guarantees the election of our candidate.
2) Deceitful public manipulation is morally wrong.
3) If something is morally wrong, then it ought to be avoided.
4) Therefore, deceitful public manipulation ought to be avoided and our candidate not be elected.

Even if the premises are relevant and rationally acceptable, (3) is deductively invalid. That the premises are rationally acceptable does not guarantee that the conclusion is. Nor is (3) likely to be interpreted as an inductive argument. Evidence is not being presented in support of the probability of the conclusion being correct. What of the second interpretation of the ambiguous first premise of (1)?

**(4)**

    **1)** Only deceitful public manipulation guarantees the election of our candidate.

    **2)** Deceitful public manipulation is morally wrong.

    **3)** If something is morally wrong, then it ought to be avoided.

    **4)** Therefore, deceitful public manipulation ought to be avoided and our candidate not be elected.

(4) is deductively valid, but not cogent. The first premise is questionable. This premise is equivalent to claiming, 'Anything that elects our candidate is public manipulation'.\* This claim, however, could reasonably be rejected by those supporting the candidate. They might argue that hard work, coupled with ability and some luck, can elect their candidate.

*Semantic ambiguity* occurs when an expression has two or more distinct meanings *and* the context in which that expression is used does not clarify its use. Imagine hearing, 'Ellen has a file'. What does Ellen have? The context in which 'Ellen has a file' is used, coupled with the experiences of the person making the claim and those hearing it, might clarify any ambiguity. Realizing Ellen is the office manager who keeps various records, and seeing her with a folder in hand, at once sets the stage for understanding 'Ellen has a file'. The context of the comment eliminates any ambiguity. Possible ambiguity could also be eliminated by introducing different words for different concepts now indicated by 'file'. One could say, 'Ellen has a folder'.

Ambiguity occurs in ways that are neither clarified by considerations of context nor in which different words could be readily introduced to distinguish easily different concepts. An instance of ambiguity can occur in arguments making them fallacious. Here is an instance:

    **(5)** The communist people of Russia vote for their national political leaders. So, the national political leaders of Russia are elected by the people of Russia.

What is to be understood by 'the communist people of Russia'? There are at least two interpretations. *First*, the phrase might mean 'those people living under the Russian communistic form of government'. The phrase, 'the people of Russia', appearing in the conclusion encourages this interpretation. Then, while (5) is deductively valid, nevertheless it is not cogent. The premise is incoherent with Russian law. *Second*, 'the communist people of Russia' might mean 'those people who are members of the Russian Communist Party'. Suppose the phrase, 'the people of Russia', found in the conclusion means *all* the people of Russia. Then, while the premise is coherent with Russian law, (5) is deductively invalid. If, on the other hand, 'the people of Russia'

---

\* Consider this claim: 'Only the hard worker will succeed'. This does not assert, 'If anyone is a hard worker, then that person will succeed'. Many people work hard at something but do not succeed at it. Rather, 'Only the hard worker will succeed' says 'If anyone succeeds, then that person is a hard worker'.

refers only to the members of the Communist Party, (5) is circular.

Notice how (5) is analyzed. *First*, the ambiguous phrase is interpreted in a distinct way. The entire argument is then understood in accordance with this interpretation. But this interpretation introduces a fallacy. The whole argument is next understood in light of another interpretation of the ambiguous phrase. This new interpretation introduces a different fallacy. Every interpretation of an ambiguous claim *appropriate to the argument* should be considered. In some arguments containing ambiguity, various interpretations might introduce fallacies and others not. Any clarification of ambiguity should be relevant and rationally acceptable. Often the interpreter of the argument has to rely heavily on the content of the argument and what is known about the arguer to interprete fairly an argument. Consider an American saying

> **(6)**  We need one more woman for dinner tonight, Let's have
>     Melissa. She is a sweet, tender person everyone will like.

Typically, an American would interpret (6) as asserting something such as that Melissa is a kind-hearted person who is a comfortable guest. Count Dracula might have altogether different ideas!

## 6.  EQUIVOCATION

> The *Fallacy of Equivocation* occurs when justifying the conclusion of an argument depends on the meaning of a single ambiguous expression shifting between two or more claims within the argument.

A shift of meaning is at the heart of the fallacy of equivocation. For such a shift to flaw an argument, the following three features have to be present. (1) Some word or phrase has to be essentially used in an argument; (2) that expression must occur in at least two distinct premises or in at least one premise and the conclusion; and (3) the expression in question must have different meanings in at least two of its occurrences.

While the fallacy of equivocation depends on ambiguity, it is not to be confused with fallacies of ambiguity. Examine this example of equivocation:

> **(1)**  Anything obtuse is dull-witted. Some triangles are obtuse.
>     Hence, there are dull-witted triangles.

In (1) 'obtuse' is essentially used in two different premises and is used differently in each case. Few native English speakers would be caught in the verbal trickery of (1). Yet what of (2)?

> **(2)**  Whatever is recognized as a law must be obeyed. However, sci-
>     ence is a body of recognized laws. So, the laws of science must
>     be obeyed.

The word 'law' is used in two different ways in (2). A law that must be obeyed is like a civil law prescribing how one should act, to avoid sanctions, in certain situations. Laws of science, however, do not prescribe how one should act to avoid sanctions. Laws of science are more like broad generalizations used in describing, explaining, or predicting how things usually act.

Here is another instance of equivocation:

**(3)**  Considering all pregnant women, only a relatively few have unnatural abortions. That is, a medically induced abortion is not the natural, or normal, way of terminating a pregnancy. What is unnatural, of course, falls outside the general mainstream of social action. But something is harmful and repugnant if it falls outside the mainstream of social action. Certainly, society ought legally to guard itself against what is repugnant and harmful to it. So, abortion ought to be outlawed by society.

The argument begins by using 'natural' and 'normal' in a statistical sense. Throughout (3), however, there is a shift to a moral sense of 'natural' and 'normal'. Only if this shift is ignored can anyone suppose that the premises support the conclusion.

## 7.  VAGUENESS

**The *Fallacy of Vagueness* occurs when either a vague premise is understood in an arbitrarily precise way while attempting to maintain an illusion of a broad meaning to substantiate a specific conclusion, or a vague conclusion is understood in an arbitrarily precise way while attempting to maintain an illusion of a broad meaning to be supported by some specific evidence.**

A claim is vague when its meaning is not clear because of some word or phrase used in a vague way in the claim. A word or phrase is *vague* when the boundaries of its application are not clear. Just because a word or phrase used in expressing an argument is vague, it does not follow that the argument is flawed. However, vague claims can be deceptive when used in presenting evidence to support a more specific conclusion. The difficulty is to determine whether a vague claim is relevant to the more specific conclusion.

Suppose someone says

**(1)**  Since Joan is a Christian, she ought not dance, wear anything but plain and simple clothes, smoke, and certainly never drink alcoholic beverages.

Rewrite (1) in standard form:

**(2)**
>   **1)** Joan is a Christian.
>
>   **2)** Hence, she ought not dance, wear anything but plain and simple clothes, smoke, and certainly never drink alcoholic beverages.

How is 'Joan is a Christian' relevant in supporting the conclusion? Conservative Baptists are Christians, but so are liberal Episcopalians. Some Baptists might accept (2), but most Episcopalians would not. The word 'Christian' is used in too vague a way to support the specific conclusion of (2). Certainly someone can define a word in any way she wishes. Someone could define 'Christian' as 'a person who believes in the divinity of Jesus as the Christ'. This definition is, however, itself vague.* In any event, it is not clear how this definition could be related to precluding smoking, dancing, wearing fashionable clothes, drinking alcoholic beverages, or the like, and still be acceptable to *ALL* those calling themselves 'Christians'.†

Vague conclusions also typically lead to arguments that are not cogent. Suppose someone says, 'The Judeo-Christian tradition has led to more hatred than love'. What claims are specific enough to count as presenting evidence for or against this assertion? This question presupposes at least that a reasonable account can be given of 'Judeo-Christian tradition' that does justice to all the diverse, even incompatible, beliefs, movements, rituals, and so on, suggested by this phrase. And then there are the words 'hatred' and 'love'! Before evidence can be offered for a claim, that claim has to be specific enough for a person to judge what evidence can or cannot count as relevant.

## 8.    RELATIVE WORDS

> The *Fallacy of Relative Words* occurs when a distinct situation in which a word can be used appropriately is confused with another distinct but related situation in which that same word can be appropriately used in a different but related way.

Typical examples of words found in instances of this fallacy are 'big', 'expensive', 'good', 'heavy', 'intelligent', 'large', 'normal', and 'poor'. Relative words can be understood in different but related ways when used in different but related contexts. Relative words are not to confused, however, with ambiguous or vague words. While 'expensive' can be viewed as a vague word, it is not the vagueness of that word that supplies the basis for the flaw in (1):

(1)   Since a cracker costing $22.98 is expensive, it follows that a sports car costing $22.98 is also expensive.

Or, someone might argue

(2)   A flea is an insect. Thus, a large flea is a large insect.

---

* In Christian theology, there is the important area of *Christology*. Christology raises questions such as how, from the Christian viewpoint, can Jesus be both fully human *and* fully God; what is meant by claims that Jesus is divine; specifically, how is Jesus related to the Divinity? There is no universal agreement on answers to such questions among those calling themselves Christians.

† This argument avoids the vagueness of (2):

No fundamentalist Christian ought to dance, wear anything but plain and simple clothes, smoke, and certainly never drink alcoholic beverages. Joan is a fundamentalist Christian. Hence, she ought not to dance, wear anything but plain and simple clothes, smoke, and certainly never drink alcoholic beverages.

It is doubtful that anyone would accept (1) or (2) as cogent. The next example is more tricky:

> **(3)** In Mozambique and Ethiopia there is real poverty. There are no economic conditions in the United States even remotely comparable to those in Mozambique and Ethiopia. Hence, in the United States there is no real poverty.

'Poverty' is used as a relative word in (3). Admittedly, what counts as poverty in the United States is seen as abundance in other parts of the world. From this observation, however, it does not follow that there is no real poverty in the United States.*

## EXERCISES

### Group A:

Consider each of the following examples. Determine which are arguments and which are not. Then, for those that are arguments, isolate, name, and explain any fallacy, or fallacies, that the arguments have. Remember, some arguments might be cogent.

1. ... and Mr. Quayle appears to be one of the least qualified candidates to appear on a national ticket in modern times. That's not just because of his youth, lack of experience, questionable academic record and Vietnam War record; it's more importantly because of the immaturity, verbal infelicity and ignorance he has demonstrated so far in his campaign. [*The New York Times*; 4 October 1988]

2. I do not advocate federal action on all irritations faced by the average American. But pornography is a matter of public health, and just as federal action is necessary in other areas of public health, so too is it required here. [*National Review*; 6 June 1986]

3. A research team led by psychologist Lawrence A. Fehr has concluded that the level of generalized guilt jurors feel is important in judging the fate of the defendant. Jurors who experience more guilt may find it difficult to mete out harsh sentences .... [The] cases were designed to show that the defendants were clearly guilty of the charges .... The researchers found that the more guilt the jurors felt themselves, the less likely they were to deal harshly with the defendants. [*Psychology Today*; October 1987]

4. No matter what our political view, a kinder, gentler nation means caring for and about others—not killing them .... Once the doctor becomes the killer, we won't know if the syringe he bears in his hand as he comes through the door contains needed medication or the lethal dose. Physician-assisted suicide should never be legal. [*USA Today*; 6 April 1989]

5. People should feel responsible for themselves as they grow older. Of course, we must do what we can for the less fortunate. But there's only so much that we should expect others to be responsible for. Health care is about to bankrupt us, mainly because people aren't taking better care of themselves. [*USA Today*; 12 January 1989]

---

* A less forceful conclusion could avoid the fallacy in (3). Here is an example:

> In Mozambique and Ethiopia there is real poverty. There are no economic conditions in the United States even remotely comparable to those in Mozambique and Ethiopia. Hence, poverty in the United States is far less extreme than that found in Mozambique.

6. Moles found that generally there has been no increase in crimes against students in the past decade. The incidence of assault has remained steady, robberies have dropped off in recent years, and thefts have continued a long decline . . . . The most disturbing trend to emerge was a sharp increase in the possession of weapons on school property . . . . Schools have not become more dangerous over the past decade, then, but the widespread possession of weapons means the potential for violence in our schools, as in the rest of society, remains very real. [*Psychology Today*; March 1988]

7. The quote "Spare the rod and spoil the child" does not refer to physical punishment. A rod is a device by which standards are measured. It is 'rod' from which we derive the term canon, or law. The canon of Scripture was measured against known facts. In this proverb, the term refers to the biblical Law of Moses: The Law is to be taught to the child, and the child is to be reared by these standards. [*Psychology Today*; June 1988]

8. Like millions of other people around the world, I, too, became entranced by the plight of the whales . . . . Only by the joint humanitarian effort of two of the most powerful nations on earth were we able to bring freedom to those whales. If we can do that for two whales, why can't we do it for mankind? Most human beings, no matter where they live, want nothing more than what was given to those whales—the chance to live in freedom. Freedom from the threat of war, starvation and tyranny. [*U.S. News and World Report*; 14 November 1988]

9. Although a point can be raised that it is always desirable to attempt to bring opposing sides of a dispute together, this line of reasoning does not apply with regard to apartheid. Apartheid is simply not a difference of opinion between gentlemen, but a satanic ideology, akin to Nazism. Those who practice and maintain apartheid must first reject it, clearly and adamantly. [*The Atlanta Journal and Constitution*; 17 January 1988]

10. What right have we got to preach human rights to others when we deny the right to life to 1,500,000 Americans each year through abortion? Yes, they are persons who have the physical pain of a cruel and inhuman death. There are no rights for unborn Americans here at home and you say nothing about that. [*Spotlight*; 18 July 1988]

## Group B:

Present arguments for four claims you support. In each argument, use one of the fallacies discussed in Sections 5 through 8, using a different fallacy in each argument. Make these arguments as persuasive as possible. Next, construct a cogent argument for each of your original four claims. Test your arguments by having them criticized by members of your class.

## Group C:

Find an example of each of the four fallacies discussed in Sections 5 through 8 in newspapers, magazines, textbooks, or the like.

## 9.  APPEAL TO IRRELEVANT AUTHORITY

The *Fallacy of Appealing to Irrelevant Authority* occurs when either (1) a recognized authority in one field is cited as supplying evidence for a conclusion in another field, or (2) when someone is assumed to be

**an authority when not and is appealed to as supplying evidence for a conclusion.**

Consider this example:

(1)    Einstein said we use only 5% of our brain. This means there is still 95% to develop. BRAIN BOGGLERS, Inc. offers a unique course in expansion and development of brain power for those interested in using that other 95%. Call toll free 1-(800)-BOGGLER.

As in all advertisements, there is the implicit conclusion, 'You ought to purchase our product'. An argument is presented to persuade the reader to use the services of BRAIN BOGGLERS, Inc. to improve the unused 95% of the brain. And how is this figure of 95% obtained and substantiated?* By appealing to Einstein who said that 'we use only 5% of our brain'. Of course, Einstein is one of the "great brains" of all ages! Thus, an appeal to authority is made in (1). The appeal, however, is unacceptable as supplying evidence to support the conclusion. Einstein is not a relevant authority in neurophysiology or psychology. It is appropriate to appeal to Einstein concerning physics. The fallacy of appealing to irrelevant authority does not consist in simply appealing to an authority. Yet because a person is an authority in one field it does not follow that he is an authority in another.

Who is a relevant authority? Guidelines can be suggested. A relevant authority must be in a position by experience, training, or education to be knowledgeable, and expertise to use that knowledge, relative to the topic in question. Suppose someone is seeking financial advice beneficial to herself. Many people are willing to be helpful—parents, friends, casual acquaintances, and people advertising themselves as financial advisers. However, these sources might have only the minimal abilities required to make sound investment recommendations. Imagine, on the other hand, a certified broker with a university degree who has worked successfully for many years in a large financial firm. The advice of this person would, under most circumstances, be relevant to a person seeking sound financial counsel. Yet it is reasonable to accept the advice of this broker only if there is no reason to suspect that she is biased, dishonest, prejudiced, or fraudulent in ways that would bring her financial advice into question. In situations where dishonesty, prejudice, fraud, or the like are suspected on the part of the authority, the claims of that authority should not be accepted as relevant evidence.

An instance of appeal to irrelevant authority can occur in citing an authority in a field concerning an issue on which there is not general agreement among the authorities. For example, reading the business section of newspapers and magazines, one discovers many cases of different financial pundits disagreeing with one another. A fallacy occurs when one authority is cited as supplying relevant evidence in support of some claim while an equally authoritative figure who disagrees is ignored. If legitimate authorities in the same area are in conflict, the nature of this conflict must be brought out in any argument appealing to one of the conflicting authorities. Otherwise relevant evidence is suppressed.

---

* An instance of the fallacy of fake precision also seems to be at work here. See below, Section 14.

To guard against accepting irrelevant authority, further considerations ought to be taken into account. There should be a legitimate need for some sort of information, advice, or service before seeking an authority. Not only should a person have legitimate needs, but also the lack of time, ability, or desire for that person to gain the authoritative expertise for himself. Someone might need the professional aid of a dentist. Rarely would there be the time needed to become an expert in this field, or the ability if there were the time, or the desire if there were both the time and the ability. These considerations, nonetheless, do not excuse a person in need of authoritative advice from becoming as knowledgeable as time and ability permit in order not to be duped by a pseudo or unscrupulous authority.

## 10. APPEAL TO PITY

> The *Fallacy of Appealing to Pity* occurs to the extent that, instead of giving evidence to support a conclusion, an arguer appeals merely to the pity of the receiver to accept the conclusion.

Appealing to pity can be an effective way to persuade someone to accept a claim. Yet no matter how pitiful the circumstances of a person might be, merely appealing to such circumstances cannot serve as evidence used to establish claims. Now an argument might contain premises raising a sense of pity without creating an instance of an appeal to pity. This would be the case, for example, if the pity raised was not used in place of evidence to support some claim. Remember, the purpose of an argument is not to persuade someone of something but to supply evidence in support of a claim.

Instances of appeals to pity are traditionally found in the courts. The defending lawyer, all but weeping, might declare

(1) My client did in fact murder Carlos Cervera in an attempted robbery. And you have justly found him guilty of that crime. No matter what you do now, Mr. Cervera cannot be returned from the dead. Yet my client has young children. Think of your own children when you vote on whether to sentence my client to be executed or not. Therefore, I beg you not to sentence my client to death.

Touching as this scene might be, merely appealing to the pity of the jury is irrelevant to support the conclusion of the defense lawyer. Whether the defendant ought to be executed or not is a matter of applying the law in a consistent way to a particular situation. Of course, in a particular case there might be legitimate considerations mitigating against imposing the death penalty. But merely feeling pity for that individual is not one.

There are situations, however, in which appeals to pity do not necessarily flaw an argument. Usually these arguments have a moral ought-claim somewhere in their premises and conclude with a moral recommendation. Picture a student missing an important test for an instructor who has a strong policy of "no make-up" on tests. Going to the instructor, the student says this:

(2) I missed your test last week because I recently discovered my parents

are divorcing. This was when I had to go home to see my brother who was just in a car crash. Otherwise I would have been prepared for your test and would have taken it. I know you have a "no make-up" policy. But I really couldn't help what has happened to my parents and brother. It is only fair to permit me to make up a missed quiz. One ought to do what is fair. So, you ought to allow me to take the test.

Several considerations are presented in (2) that do not appear merely to appeal to the pity of the instructor. There is the recent discovery of parents divorcing. But how recently did the student discover this? And there is the mentioning of the brother in a car crash. How serious was this crash and to what extent was the brother injured? Answers to these sorts of questions are needed before the legitimacy of the considerations introduced in (2) can be properly evaluated. And there is the essentially used premise, 'One ought to do what is fair'. This is not merely an appeal to pity. A moral appeal is being made.

## 11.  APPEAL TO THE MASSES

> The *Fallacy of Appealing to the Masses* occurs when merely the beliefs or actions of a group, large or small, are substituted for evidence for or against some claim.

A general principle of rational thought is that simply because people believe that some claim is correct, or act in a way suggesting that some claim is correct, does not make that claim correct. Certainly a group of people might be correct in what they believe or what they do. But, then again, they might not. The issue here is what can count as evidence in support of some claim. Appealing to the beliefs or actions of others for evidence to support a claim ignores the possibility that even large groups can be wrong and, thus, can introduce irrelevant claims or faulty evidence.

People commit this fallacy for various reasons. The belief that a group is right, peer pressure, the desire to be accepted and popular are a few motivations underlying the use and acceptance of this fallacy. Picture a student having been caught cheating on a test. There is no doubt that she did cheat. The student is brought before the student council and pleads her case like this:

(1)    Yes, I cheated on my chemistry quiz. But I shouldn't be punished for that. What's wrong with cheating? That's the way most students get their grades in this school.

The student is arguing that she should not be punished. However, to substantiate this claim she must first argue that her offense, cheating on a test, is not a punishable one. The only evidence that she gives is that most students do, in fact, cheat.

Here is an appeal to the masses found in the political-military arena. In the aftermath of the Persian Gulf war it was not unusual to hear something like this:

(2) George Bush must be a superior military leader since that is what everybody is saying.

George Bush may, or may not, be a superior military leader. But evidence to support the claim that he is cannot be merely what everybody is saying. "Everybody" could be wrong. The success of Bush in the Persian Gulf could have been a fluke, or what appears to be his decisions might have been those of others which he only mouthed. While Bush may be a superior military leader, just because the great majority say so is not evidence to support the claim that he is.

## 12. APPEAL TO SPECIAL INTERESTS

Many tricks can be used in arguments to avoid offering relevant evidence. An appeal to special interests is one.

> The *Fallacy of Appealing to Special Interests* occurs when evidence for some conclusion is presented or accepted merely because of some special interests the presenter or receiver of the argument has.

In general, those interests that are peculiar to either an individual or group do not supply relevant evidence for substantiating a conclusion. They are, rather, motivations explaining why someone might wish a claim to be correct. It can normally be expected that a person arguing would have a special interest in the argument he is presenting. Otherwise, why present it? More specifically someone might have a special interest in seeing a conclusion being accepted. Further, to address a person or a group that is interested in what is being said is not to create an instance of the fallacy of appeal to special interests. An instance of this fallacy occurs when special interests are offered as evidence, or in place of evidence, in the premises to support some conclusion.

Special interest groups use this fallacy heavily. Since the presidency of Franklin D. Roosevelt, federal social services and benefits have grown immensely. Many have been extended far beyond the purposes for which they were first envisioned. None of these services and benefits are free. They are paid for, in very large part, by deductions taken out of the pay of those presently working. Large groups of people are now benefitting from these federal programs and a large number of people foresee themselves as being aided by them. It is to these people that special interest organizations appeal in lobbying for, say, catastrophic national medical insurance to be underwritten by the federal government:

> **(3)** While it is the case that social security deductions have risen considerably in the last ten years, nonetheless, you ought to support the *XYZ* in its move to put political pressure on the federal government for a catastrophic health insurance program. It is you who are going to benefit most from it.

Merely whether someone is going to benefit from such a federally sponsored program—even if a very large number of people are to benefit from it—is not in itself relevant evidence for substantiating the merits of a federally sponsored program. The same benefits might be supplied more efficiently and at less cost through, for instance, private insurance policies.

## *EXERCISES*

### Group A:

Consider each of the following examples. Determine which are arguments and which are not. Then, for those that are arguments, isolate, name, and explain any fallacy, or fallacies, that the arguments have. Remember, some arguments might be cogent.

1. After reading your article, "Should Teenagers Be Executed?" (March, 1988), my heart felt heavy for Paula Cooper. I think it's a shame that someone close to my age is sentenced to death row. I know that she committed murder, but everyone makes mistakes. She even admitted that she was wrong. The life she had before prison was a terrible one. [*Ebony*; July 1988]

2. If we [gun owners] are to turn the tide and win the war, we have only one choice and that is to unite on a common front. As I see it, and it is with prejudice of course, we must have a National Rifle Association that is 10 million strong in short order, and even more, I believe that every lawabiding, gun-owning citizen who cares must be a member of the NRA. [*Guns and Ammo*; December 1989]

3. "I promised earlier this year that we would respond in a constructive way to Mr. Gorbachev's proposals on the International Court of Justice, and we have done so," the State Department's chief legal counsel, Abraham D. Sofaer, who prepared the proposal, said in a telephone interview. [*The New York Times*; 6 October 1988]

4. Parents do have the right to more information . . . . and the power to get more involved. There is good reason to encourage more studies on the impact of music; [Tipper] Gore [wife of Senator Albert Gore] is correct that "Music is the most unexpected medium, and rock music has shown perhaps the least willingness to show self-restraint." Gore is also reasonable in encouraging moderate parents to get involved in the debate over pornography and violence in the media. [*Psychology Today*; September 1987]

5. It is pleasing to note that a basketball purist like Wolff can recognize the entertainment value of the three-point shot. He joins the company of another observer of the game who once advocated that, under certain circumstances, a goal scored from afar be worth more points than a shot made from in close. That suggestion, made 52 years ago, came from Dr. James Naismith. [*Sports Illustrated*; 27 March 1989]

6. "Lowdown on highways: Repair them," and the study upon which it was based hit the nail on the head: The USA's infrastructure is deteriorating. As any American motorist will tell you, our overburdened roads and highways need a major facelift, not only to better handle increasing traffic, but to promote safety. The nation's truckers strongly agree. [*USA Today*; 26 July 1988]

7. Is it right to believe in the sanctity of life and protect the lives of innocent children? My opponent says no—but I say yes. We must change from abortion to adoption. I have an adopted granddaughter. The day of her christening we wept with joy. I thank God her parents chose life. [*Vital Speeches of the Day*; 15 October 1988]

8. In the six weeks that followed, Swaggart's fate became a matter of church politics. The state council of his denomination, the Assemblies of God, was controlled by Swaggart's close associates and relatives . . . . They met and announced that their repentant brother would be removed from the pulpit for three months, not the usual full year. [*Rolling Stone*; 14 July 1988]

9. Earlier this year, a petition drive, conducted jointly by The Moral Majority and *The Old*

*Time Gospel Hour*, gathered approximately 2 million names of voting-age Americans in support of an unconditional presidential pardon of Oliver North . . . . More recently, we have heard impassioned pleas for a pardon from Sen. Orrin Hatch, R-Utah, Rep. Henry Hyde, R-Ill., Paul Harvey and countless others. In my opinion, there is very broad national support for such a pardon, and now is the time. [*USA Today*; 1 December 1988]

10. Dr. Stephen Bryen, who was Deputy Under Secretary of Defense for Technology Security, is a strong critic of the State Department and its policies—he says that State admits anyone unless they are *certified* as spies—or at least admit to being one. [Bryen says] the State Department routinely grants Soviet visitors access to universities, research centers, and high-tech laboratories . . . . Bryen says that the State Department is the worst federal agency to make determinations about whether or not a visitor is a spy. [*The American Sentinel*; 15 March 1989]

11. There are many single-parent women in this country who are making the minimum wage. Employers have a responsibility to pay them more. But students working a summer job shouldn't expect a raise. We can't afford to put small businesses out of business simply because a youth needs more money. [*USA Today*; 12 July 1988]

12. Dr. Vernon Mark, a neurosurgeon at Harvard Medical School, advocates a program for Massachusetts that includes an intensive 90-day public-education campaign—after which AIDS victims who continue to engage in dangerous sexual practices would be quarantined. [*U.S. News and World Report;* 25 November 1985]

13. Let's get one point straight: The vast majority of U.S. scientists wouldn't fund the super-collider. In a democratic society, that is a key reason for Congress to put this scientifically impudent and fiscally absurd claim out of its misery. [*USA Today*; 20 December 1988]

14. What did she think of the suggestion that the sex [telephone call-in] lines should be banned? "What do you expect me to say? No, I don't agree with it. It's my bread and butter and a lot of other people's besides. Okay, some people make a lot of money out of the whole business of sex, and I don't like a lot of pornography for the way it treats women—I'm a feminist really, you know, I think a lot of us are in this game. But I don't think the sex lines should be banned." [*New Statesman & Society*; 7 April 1989]

15. I simply believe that childbirth can be a greater crime than abortion and, sometimes, giving life ought to be a criminal offense. "Nice" little words such as head traumas, dehydration and oral venereal disease dress up what is actually happening to the 1 million *reported* victims of child abuse and neglect, according to federal studies. These children are being thrown up against walls, tortured with cigarette butts, burned in scalding water and sexually abused in their cribs. Recently, a 9-week old child, born to a cocaine addict here, was brought into a hospital dead from head wounds and infections from diaper sores so bad that hospital workers cried. If birth control fails, how are torture and starvation superior to an abortion? [*USA Today*; 23 September 1988]

## Group B:

Present arguments for four claims you support. In each argument, use one of the fallacies discussed in Sections 9 through 12, using a different fallacy in each argument. Make these arguments as persuasive as possible. Next, construct a cogent argument for each of your original four claims. Test your arguments by having them criticized by members of your class.

## Group C:

Find an example of each of the four fallacies discussed in Sections 9 through 12 in newspapers, magazines, textbooks, or the like.

## 13. APPEAL TO IGNORANCE

> The *Fallacy of Appeal to Ignorance* occurs when either a conclusion is said to be correct merely because there is no known evidence to establish that it is not, or when a conclusion is said to be incorrect merely because there is no known evidence to establish that it is correct. In both cases, only this lack of evidence is used to support a conclusion.

Suppose someone says

> **(1)**   Even though I have high blood pressure, my physician didn't say not to drink coffee. So, I'll continue to drink as much as I want.

Or imagine hearing this:

> **(2)**   Ron has never said anything concerning minority rights. Therefore, he obviously doesn't support them.

(1) is an instance of the first version of appealing to ignorance. Merely that the doctor did not say anything about not drinking coffee is appealed to as the only evidence in support of the claim that it is all right to drink coffee. (2) is an instance of the second version. This argument suggests that it is correct to claim Richard does not support minority rights merely because there is no evidence to establish that he does. This lack of evidence is itself appealed to as evidence in support of another claim. Neither of these arguments is cogent.

If a claim is correct solely because there is no evidence to reject it, as an appeal to ignorance assumes, then equally a claim can be incorrect solely because there is no evidence to support it. This observation leads to curious results:

> **(3)**   It's evident that capital punishment does nothing to lower the crime rate. After all, no one has been able to produce conclusive evidence that it does.

> **(4)**   It's evident that capital punishment lowers the crime rate. After all, no one has been able to produce conclusive evident that it doesn't.

At best the combination of (3) and (4) suggests an open attitude should be maintained toward capital punishment and its relation to lowering the crime rate. In appeals to ignorance, an attempt is made to cite all lack of evidence for one claim as positive evidence for another. As the combination of (3) and (4) suggests, this attempt can be a dangerous two-edged sword.

The fallacy of appealing to ignorance gains much of its strength from confusion with legitimate cases of arguing that appear similar to it. Image a team of expert cosmologists asserting that there are black holes in a certain sector of the sky. The scientists proceed to look for evidence of these black holes. Over time, using methods accepted by the scientific community, coupled with the best relevant technology of the day, no evidence is found. It is reasonable, then, to suggest 'No black holes occur in that part of the sky'. Here is an example of not finding evidence for one claim tending to substantiate another claim. The difference between this case and a fallacy of appealing to ignorance is that in science the evidence, or lack of it, is weighed in light of its place in a larger scheme of theory, methodology, technology, and what is acceptable, or not, within a wider scientific community. This is not merely a matter of lack of evidence for something.

There are more ordinary examples of arguments that appear to be appealing to ignorance, but are not. Suppose someone observed

(5)  Pat is a very honest person. We know this because in her whole life she has never been caught lying, stealing, or cheating.

Assume more or less mutually acceptable uses of 'lying', 'cheating', and 'stealing' on the part of those who have observed Pat over the years. Then, their consistent reports of not finding any instances of these stand as very strong evidence that Pat is an honest person. Certainly, they could be wrong in their assessment. Those observing Pat might not have looked in the right places at the right time. But the same can be said of the cosmologists in their search for black holes.

Another exception to the fallacy of appealing to ignorance is found in cases where the burden of proof rests on whoever initiates a claim. Consider, for example, the U.S. legal system. Not to find evidence of someone committing a crime sometimes provides good reasons to claim the person innocent. The burden of proof is on the prosecutor, not the defendant, in a court of law. If the prosecutor cannot supply evidence that a person did commit a crime, the accused does not then have to provide evidence of innocence. Or suppose Jim claims that Sean is a liar. The burden of proof rests with Jim. Sean is under no logical obligation to have to supply evidence that Jim is wrong. Certainly, from a practical viewpoint, a person might seek to discredit his accuser and protect himself from false charges and gossip. That is another matter, however.

## 14.  FAKE PRECISION

The *Fallacy of Fake Precision* occurs when a claim seeming to have a mathematical, or statistical, precision that is impossible, or very likely impossible, to have is used as evidence in support of a conclusion.

If an American newspaper reporter claims 21.43% of the inhabitants of Africa have the slimming disease, then suspicion is in order. Imagine reading this in a newspaper:

(1)  It is imperative that medical supplies and personnel be sent to Africa to help control the spread of the slimming disease. Alarmingly it is true that 21.43% of the total African population has the slimming disease. This is an intolerably high percentage for the safety of the world population.

The figure 21.43% is not likely very meaningful, although it does carry with it a persuasive air of precision. Consider the extensive pockets of isolated African population and the political difficulties encountered in obtaining this information. Nonetheless, there is still an apparent legitimatizing of factual claims because of the introduction of a spurious numerical value suggesting precision when it is highly unlikely that such information can be obtained.

Notice how the following argument appeals to what seems to be large, and precise, statistical support for its conclusion:

(2)    You ought to use brand 'B' pain reliever because more than     |
       73% of all doctors use it.

Following the Principle of Charity, (2) can be reconstructed in this way:

(3)

1) In matters concerning the relief of pain you ought to use what doctors use most.

2) More than 73% of all doctors use brand 'B'.

3) So, you ought to use brand 'B'.

How is '73% of all doctors' to be interpreted, even assuming that 'doctor' means a physician? What is to be understood by 'all'? Are these physicians 73% of all the physicians in the world, in the western world, in the United States, in California, at the Mayo Clinic, or at the County Regional Clinic? And by what methods was '73%' obtained? Why was it not '71%'? Unfortunately, not one of these questions is answered. Even so, 73% can be persuasive because of its apparent precision.

## 15.  HASTY CONCLUSION

> The *Fallacy of Hasty Conclusion* occurs when a conclusion is drawn from premises that, while relevant to establishing the conclusion, do not supply enough evidence to establish the conclusion.

This fallacy, like others, provides only an illusion of cogency. *In general*, someone cannot say what is enough evidence to establish a conclusion. What counts as enough evidence is closely tied to the particular context of an argument. In a particular argument, these background considerations can be brought into focus well enough to determine what is to count as evidence sufficient to establish a conclusion. However, there are typical cases in which the evidence presented, while relevant to the conclusion, is not enough to support it.

A hasty conclusion can be based on *first impressions*:

(1)    I watched the senatorial candidates last night on TV. This was the first time I've seen Joe Jones. From the way he handled himself, it is evident he is an honest, hard-working man. He'd be a good senator.

It might be that Jones is both honest and hard-working. While relevant, this impression obtained from watching him once on television is not enough to establish the conclusion that he would be a good senator.

Hasty conclusions can occur in arguments interpreted inductively that conclude with universal claims such as 'Every mutual fund is a safe economic investment' and 'No jocks are intelligent'. In hasty conclusions, the evidence offered to justify a universal claim is relevant to the conclusion but not sufficient to justify it. For instance, pet prejudices and stereotypes can become the universal conclusion of an argument:

(2)  No mideastern leader can be trusted. All of them I've heard
      anything about are hard-core liars.

Imagine (2) being presented by someone whose only opinions of mideastern leaders
are based on reports and editorials found in U.S. news media. It is not unreasonable
to suppose that some bias is at work in these editorials and reports. Hasty conclusions
can also result from small samples of, or limited experience with, something. Here is
a similar example:

(3)  Of course all gays are effeminate. What evidence do I have?
      Why, every one of them I've ever known has been.

For the sake of argument, suppose approximately 10% of the national population is
homosexual. This supposition places the number of homosexuals in the United
States, based on the 1980 national census, at 2,265,458 when the population count
was 226,545,805. Just 1% of this figure is 22,654. It is doubtful that a person
presenting (3) would know even 1% of the estimated number of homosexuals in the
United States. Thus, (3) represents a hasty conclusion.

On the other hand, simply having a very large sample of some population is not
sufficient to support many conclusions. Consider this argument:

(4)  No mammal lays eggs. This claim is amply supported by an immense
      number of observations of mammals in Europe and the Far and Near East.
      Similar observations have been made in North, Central and South America.

This sampling of mammals is very large. However, it is not *representative* of all
mammals. Mammals in Australia and Tasmania where the duck-billed platypus, an
egg-laying mammal, is found have not been included. A sample of any population
must be representative of the entire population to supply sufficient evidence to
justify a conclusion. And the more representative a sample is of a particular
population, the smaller that sample needs to be. Pollsters often do a credible job
with relatively small samples. When they do not, it is frequently because of problems
involving the selection of samples of a sufficient size and representation of a
population.

## 16.  NEGLECT OF RELEVANT EVIDENCE

The *Fallacy of the Neglect of Relevant Evidence* occurs when considerations
unfavorable to a conclusion are ignored or considered in a way less
important to that conclusion than they are.

It is often the case that evidence relevant to the *overthrow*, or *weakening*, of a claim is
ignored or minimized by an arguer. The reasons for ignoring unfavorable relevant
evidence are not difficult to appreciate. Many people consider persuasion to be their
primary goal in arguing. If the goal of arguments is persuasion, then it is appropriate
to ignore or deemphasize counterevidence to any claim set forth. Yet if the goal of
arguments is not to persuade, but to provide relevant and rationally acceptable
evidence to substantiate a conclusion, then no relevant evidence can safely be
ignored or considered unimportant. And, from the viewpoint of rational thought, the

primary purpose of an argument is to provide relevant and rational evidence for the substantiation of some claim. As a general guide of rational thought, the arguer ought to set forth the strongest available version of an argument. To do this, however, requires a sensitivity to relevant factors that could count against the claim being suggested. The arguer then needs to address, and resolve, any counterevidence. If this cannot be done, it is better, at least tentatively, to suspend accepting or rejecting the conclusion of the original argument.

The following appears in a letter to the editors. The writer, Liu Chen-bao, argues that Tibet is not a country occupied by China, but is an integral part of China:

> Your report on Tibet . . . gives the impression that it is an occupied country. On the contrary, Tibet has been an integral part of China for generations. Even the Tibetan language belongs to the Chinese-language family. The idea of an independent Tibet is a fantasy. Any attempt to sever Tibet from China will be doomed to failure and considered an unfriendly act toward China. [*Time Magazine*; 16 November 1987]

The author fails to mention that Tibet was annexed by China in 1965 and that the Dalai Lama had to escape from the country while a puppet government was set up by China. Nor does the author mention the various uprisings of the Tibetan people against China and the military actions taken by the Chinese government against the Tibetans. While the above letter might serve to persuade someone that Tibet is an integral part of China, it does not serve to substantiate that the claim is correct.*

---

## EXERCISES

### Group A:

Consider each of the following examples. Determine which are arguments and which are not. Then, for those that are arguments, isolate, name, and explain any fallacy, or fallacies, that the arguments have. Remember, some arguments might be cogent.

1. But often this pile of medical money has not bought better care or increased access. Instead, it has fueled a profoundly wasteful and inefficient system. "Thirty percent of what we do in health care is of no apparent benefit . . . " says Marion [*Time Magazine*; 31 October 1988]

2. In remarks to reporters en route to a speaking engagement in Florida, Quayle said he had known Tower for eight years while both were in the Senate and had never seen him drunk . . . . Quayle, who served with Tower on the Armed Services Committee, said, "I have never seen him inebriated. I have never seen drinking being a factor in John Tower's life other than a social glass of wine. There is absolutely no reason he should not be confirmed." [*The Washington Post*; 11 February 1989]

3. If the autoworkers want jobs, what they have to recognize is that one out of every four people on the assembly line, according to statistics I have, is using drugs . . . . That's a

---

* Not only is relevant evidence ignored in this example. There is also equivocation on the word 'China'.

25% drop in productivity right there, possibly. So, I think the autoworkers would appreciate a tough anti-drug program .... I'm not disparaging autoworkers. I'm just saying that in industry in general, that it is estimated by certain sources that about one out of every four workers is using some kind of an illicit substance. [*The Charlotte Observer*; 4 November 1987]

4. But the Liberals' discomfort pales in comparison to that of the NDP. What has them squirming is the firm declaration by several party elders that the next leader must be a woman. By all the tenets of NDP philosophy, she should be. After all, the NDP has had three leaders over the years, and none has been a woman. That's 0%. Whether you measure the female quotient in the population at large (51%), or of political candidates (33%), or of NDP MPs (12%) this is a clear statistical discrepancy, and you know what that means: systemic discrimination. The only remedy is mandatory quotas. [*The Financial Post*; 27 March 1989]

5. [God must have created the universe.] Have you ever noticed, no scientist or evolutionist has explained where the matter or the power involved in the "Big Bang" has come from. [*The Houston Post*; 7 January 1988]

6. Your comments on the so-called slasher movies available to kids on videocassettes ["100 Great Videos for Kids," January 22] understates the impact of this violence in daily entertainment fare. Repetitive TV violence is to society's future what chlorofluorocarbons are to the earth's ozone layer. There is sufficient research evidence now to show that the 10,000 acts of depicted violence that entertain a child before maturity generally causes harmful volatility in children's behavior. Can we afford to let such reckless exposure undermine our future well-being? The mounting prevalence of slasher movies on VCR, cable and local TV raises the stakes for all of us. Until now we have largely been able to avoid resorting to censorship or moral posturing. These latter choices unfortunately look more appealing. The violent challenge to our future requires new leadership of substantial statue. [*U.S. News and World Report*; February 1990]

7. In the context of examining a wide variety of sexual experience correlates, an hypothesis is tested that sexual experience helps bolster confidence and esteem. This is tested by predicting that the reported number of sexual partners is positively associated with self-esteem, attractiveness, and extraversion. Further associations are examined between the extent of sexual experience and background, sexual behavior, responsiveness, parent attitudes, social competency, and relationship attachment variables. [*Psychology*; No 2/3 (1986)]

8. I think the idea of having instant replay in baseball is ridiculous, as it is in football. If we keep making these changes in our national sports, within 20 years the games will be played and controlled by machines. Let's leave things the way they are and as they were meant to be. [*USA Today*; 7 October 1988]

9. Donna Gaetano did more than mourn after her daughter, Darlene, 6 was struck and killed by a school bus driven by a 17-year old student...."My daughter would be alive today if an adult had been behind the wheel," says Gaetano, 27, of Charleston, S.C..... In South Carolina, nine of the last ten fatal accidents involved under-18 drivers. [*USA Today*: 4 March 1988]

10. In the final analysis, the seeds of national restoration are within each American. But before these seeds may germinate and America may again flourish as a Christian Republic, the American people must turn back to God. For only a godly people may have a godly government. [*The New American*; 20 June 1988]

11. Five million Americans have diabetes and don't know it! These people are at risk of serious

complications if diagnosis and treatment are not sought in time. [*The Atlanta Constitution*, 31 October 1988]

12. Robertson's Iowa success could spell further trouble for Bush, who is vulnerable in the South to Robertson's potential as he begins to seem plausible as a candidate. Polls heavily favoring Bush in the South could crumble. Robertson's gains likely would be at Bush's expense. [*The Atlanta Constitution*, 10 February 1988]

13. Still, not seeing the aliens or their spacecraft causes far less consternation than the apparent lack of radio traffic. If the galaxy is truly filled with life, why do we not hear any communication? A lot of people are compelled...to conclude that there is no life elsewhere. [*The Saturday Evening Post*, September 1987]

14. [John] Ogbu's ethnographic studies of black and Hispanic schoolchildren in Stockton, CA, suggest that one reason today's inner-city children do poorly in tests is that "they do not bring to the test situation serious attitudes and do not persevere to maximize their scores." The fault lies neither with their intelligence, Ogbu argues, not with the absence of "quasi-academic training" that middle-class children experience at home. Rather, it is their lower caste status and the limited job prospects of their parents that lower their sights. [*Psychology Today*, September 1989]

15. Besides being the cleanest and least expensive method of generating electricity, nuclear power is also the safest. Other than Chernobyl in the USSR-where there was a serious and *predictable* accident, there has never been a fatality at a nuclear plant....Meanwhile, industry analysts tell us that America will become 50 to 70 percent dependent on foreign oil supplies during the 1990s. Our neck is being placed in a noose. The way to escape being strangled is to unleash the wonders of nuclear power. [*The New American*, 20 June 1988]

### Group B:

Present arguments for four claims you support. In each argument, use one of the fallacies discussed in Sections 13 through 16, using a different fallacy in each argument. Make these arguments as persuasive as possible. Next, construct a cogent argument for each of your original four claims. Test your arguments by having them criticized by members of your class.

### Group C:

Find an example of each of the four fallacies discussed in Sections 13 through 16 in newspapers, magazines, textbooks, or the like.

---

## 17.  REVIEW OF NEW TERMS

**Ambiguity fallacies:** Occur when a linguistic expression can be understood in two, or more, distinct ways, and there is no means to determine how that expression is to be understood within the context of an argument. Ambiguity can be either *syntactic* or *semantic*.

**Amphibole:** A sentence that is ambiguous because of faulty grammatical construction. See *syntactical ambiguity*.

**Appeal to Ignorance Fallacy:** Occurs when either a conclusion is said to be correct merely because there is no known evidence to establish that it is not, or when a conclusion is said to be incorrect merely because there is no known evidence to establish that it is correct. In both cases, this lack of evidence is appealed to in support of some conclusion.

**Appeal to Irrelevant Authority Fallacy:** Occurs when either (1) a recognized authority in one field is cited as supplying evidence for a conclusion in another field, or (2) when someone or something is assumed to be authoritative when not and as supplying evidence for some conclusion.

**Appeal to the Masses Fallacy:** Occurs when the beliefs of a group, large or small, about some claim are substituted for evidence for or against that claim, or appeals to emotions raised in a group by a claim are substituted for evidence for or against some claim.

**Appeal to Pity Fallacy:** Occurs to the extent that, instead of giving evidence to support a conclusion, an arguer appeals merely to the pity of the receiver to accept the conclusion.

**Appeal to Special Interests Fallacy:** Occurs when evidence for some conclusion is accepted, and hence also that conclusion, merely because of some special interests the receiver of the argument has.

**Cogent argument:** An argument in which (1) the premises logically support the conclusion; (2) the premises are rationally acceptable; and (3) only considerations relevant both to the justification and rejection of the conclusion are taken into account.

**Essentially used claim:** A claim in an argument that is either the conclusion or some premise without which the conclusion could not be justified or have the appearance of being justified.

**Equivocation Fallacy:** Occurs when justifying the conclusion of an argument depends on the meaning of a single ambiguous expression shifting between two or more claims, within the argument.

**Fake Precision Fallacy:** Occurs when a claim purporting to have a mathematical, or statistical, precision that is impossible, or very likely impossible, to have is used as evidence.

**Fallacious argument:** An argument which is not cogent.

**Fallacy:** An error that (1) occurs in an argument and (2) adversely affects the ability of the premises to support the conclusion.

**Hasty Conclusion Fallacy:** Occurs when a conclusion is drawn from premises that, while relevant to establishing the conclusion, are not sufficient to establish it.

**Neglect of Relevant Evidence Fallacy:** Occurs when considerations unfavorable to a conclusion are ignored or considered in a way less important to that conclusion than they are.

**Principle of Charity:** In making explicit any implicit claims of an argument, always state those claims that would make the argument as free from error as possible, given the surroundings of the argument, and always supply only the minimum number of claims required to complete the argument.

**Relative Words Fallacy:** Occurs when a distinct situation in which a word can be used appropriately is confused with another distinct but related situation in which that same word can be appropriately used in a different but related way.

**Semantic ambiguity:** Occurs when an expression has two or more distinct meanings and the context in which that expression is used does not clarify its use.

**Standard argument form:** The presentation of an argument in which each actually expressed premise is listed as a separate claim, and the conclusion, introduced by a conclusion flag word, is listed after all the premises.

**Syntactical ambiguity:** Occurs when different interpretations of a sentence result from unclear grammatical structure. See *amphibole.*

**Vagueness Fallacy:** Occurs either (1) when a vague premise is understood in an arbitrarily precise way while attempting to maintain an illusion of a broad meaning, in order to substantiate a specific conclusion, or (2) when a vague conclusion is understood in an arbitrarily precise way while attempting to maintain an illusion of a broad meaning, in order to be supported by some specific evidence.

# 15

# FALLACIES OF RATIONALITY

Fallacies of relevance are discussed in Chapter 14. Chapter 15 continues the discussion of fallacies. Each of the fallacies in this chapter breaks some guideline for being rationally acceptable. Thus, arguments that exhibit one of these fallacies cannot be used in rational thought to support a conclusion. Remember that an argument, if fallacious, might be flawed in more than one way. It is important, however, to recognize that something is wrong with an argument, and to be able to identify what is wrong and why it is a fallacy.

## 1. *AD HOMINEM*

One argument can be presented as a challenge to another. The purpose of the counterexample is to discredit the earlier one. This attempt to discredit can, itself, be fallacious. *Ad hominem* arguments are examples of abortive attempts to discredit other arguments.

> *Ad Hominem* ("Against the Man") *Fallacies* occur when an attempt is made to discredit an argument by bringing into question in some negative way the presenter of the argument instead of attacking the argument itself. There are two types of *ad hominem* fallacies; namely, *abusive ad hominem* and *circumstantial ad hominem.*

An *abusive ad hominem* attacks the personal character of the presenter of the original argument. A *circumstantial ad hominem* brings into question some particular condition or situation in which the presenter finds herself.

Imagine legislators debating whether capital punishment should be prohibited. The congresswoman from the ninth district argues for laws prohibiting capital punishment because there is no clear evidence that capital punishment reduces the crime rate while there is clear evidence that capital punishment is cruel and unusual punishment often unevenly handed out by the courts. The representative from the fifth district has a different view, however. Supporting capital punishment, he says,

**(1)**   The congresswoman from the ninth district suggests that we ought to pass laws prohibiting capital punishment. She talks about cruelty. Well, that's the sort of thing we can expect from an impractical and soft-hearted grandmother. I tell you, her position is both wrong and dangerous.

(1) is an instance of an *abusive ad hominem*. The phrase 'impractical and soft-hearted grandmother' creates an attack on the character of the congresswoman. This phrase is used to raise emotional ill-will against the congresswoman but is irrelevant to her argument. Even if it were true that the congresswoman is an impractical and soft-hearted grandmother, this would count neither for nor against her claims concerning capital punishment.

A *circumstantial ad hominem*, also called *"poisoning the well"*, cites some condition or situation of the presenter of an argument in an attack against the proposed argument. Often special or vested interests of the presenter are mentioned. Roy, a member of a Greek social fraternity, wants Michael to pledge. Roy argues that the Greek system is not perfect and not for everyone. Even so, it is a good way for many freshmen and sophomores to get to know new people and develop a network of supportive friends. Therefore, Roy claims that Michael should join. Michael, a freshman, dismisses these comments by saying,

**(2)**   Of course that's what you'd say, Roy. After all, you are a fraternity member.

That Roy is a fraternity member might be part of the circumstances motivating him to speak with Michael. But this is irrelevant to the cogency of his argument. His membership in a fraternity cannot be used as evidence that his argument is fallacious. Considerations of the circumstances of the presenter of an argument cannot replace criteria for determining whether that argument is cogent or not. To do so usually confuses giving an explanation with presenting evidence.

In general, *ad hominem* considerations cannot serve as grounds for attacking an argument. However, there are cases in which it is appropriate to question the character of a person, to inquire about her age and private background, to seek out her likes and dislikes, and to discover what vested interests she might have. One inquires into the circumstances of the presenter, in part, to discover whether she is likely to be telling the truth or not. Knowing the circumstances of the arguer, the receiver is also in a better position to look for possible flaws in the argument itself. A radical environmentalist might suggest exaggerated claims as evidence against single-hull oil tankers. That a person is a radical environmentalist cannot be reasonably used against her arguments. But knowing that she is a radical can put the receiver of the argument on guard against possible logical flaws motivated by the radical views of the presenter.

## 2.   *TU QUOQUE*

The *Tu Quoque* ("You, Too") *Fallacy* is a trick used to defend oneself against the criticism of someone else.

The *Tu Quoque Fallacy*, also called "*Two Wrongs Make a Right Fallacy*," occurs when (1) there is an attempt to defend an argument against attack by suggesting that the critic has done something very similar, if not the same thing, as what is being attacked, or (2) that the critic is presenting an argument as difficult to sustain as the argument under attack.

'You do it, too' or 'You believe the same thing' are frequently telltale signs of a *tu quoque*. Suppose parents were arguing with their child:

(1)   We don't care if most of your friends are using pot and practicing premarital sex. You are too young to handle either without getting into trouble, as well as the fact that both can be dangerous.

The child attempts to counter the argument in this way:

(2)   Come on! I know about the sixties, Woodstock, and all that stuff. The two of you were there when you were my age doing exactly what you say I can't.

In replying, the child is attempting to fault the argument of the parents in two ways. First, he is trying to absolve what they perceive as his guilt by pointing out that they are equally guilty of the same things. While this might make the child feel better, it does not count as evidence against the argument of the parents. Second, the child is challenging the cogency of the argument of the parents by suggesting an inconsistency between what they are saying and what they have done.*

An inconsistency between the actions and the argument of the presenter is seldom evidence counting against the cogency of that argument. This is even more likely when the incompatible action took place some time ago. It is possible that the parents "learned from their mistakes" and are now in a better position to argue for their present claims. Considerations of inconsistencies between what is said and what is done can be raised to question whether the presenter is telling the truth or not. This is especially the case when what is done and what is said occur within close temporal proximity. If it is discovered that the presenter is not telling the truth, the premises might be rejected. But to reject a premise because it is false should not be confused with an instance of the *tu quoque* fallacy.

## 3.   RED HERRING

The Red Herring Fallacy is used in attempting to counter another argument.

The *Red Herring Fallacy* occurs when an attempt to discredit an argument is made by interjecting considerations that, while broadly related to the original argument, are extraneous to the specific claims of that argument.

Suppose someone argues for the premise that 'Education in the United States is far behind Japan'. In opposition, the following is offered:

(1)   It is said that education in the United States is far behind Japan.

---

*See the discussion of pragmatic inconsistency in Section 14 of this chapter.

> This cannot be true, however. More people are finishing high
> school and going to college than ever before in the United States.
> The number of people in the professions is steadily increasing.
> None of this would be possible without increased education.

The opponent does not address the claim, 'Education in the United States is far behind Japan'. Rather, he introduces quantitative considerations concerning the numbers of people finishing various levels of schooling at the pre-college, undergraduate, and post-undergraduate levels. Nothing is said concerning the nature or quality of this instruction. What the opponent offers is a red herring. The challenge to the claim that education in the United States is far behind Japan might appear cogent, but it is not. The counterargument broadens the original argument in extraneous ways to maintain that the original argument is fallacious.

Here is another example of a red herring:

(2) Environmentalists in the United States and Canada are pressing for smoke-stack laws to reduce acid rain. They claim that acid rain is destructive to forests and fish. Their claims are wrong. The industrial complex of the United States is what has made this a great country. No other nation in the world provides the opportunities found here. This is obvious when you look at our standard of living and the number of foreigners seeking citizenship here each year. Our great traditions must be preserved. And that is why I oppose any legislation hindering American industry.

The issue in question is acid rain, its harmful effects on the environment, and legislation needed to bring these effects under control. Environmentalists do not argue for the closing of smokestack industries, the reduction of jobs, or the lowering of standards of living. They do argue for more efficient control of pollution created by these industries. Questions concerning the industrial strength of the United States, the number of foreigners seeking United States citizenship, and the American standard of living are red herrings used to divert attention from what is at stake in this argument.*

## 4.   STRAW MAN

The Straw Man Fallacy is yet another type of misguided attack on an argument.

> **The *Straw Man Fallacy* occurs when an attempt to discredit an argument is made by recasting it in a weak, exaggerated, or foolish way not intended by the arguer and, then, attacking that refashioned argument as if it were the original one.**

There are many ways to distort an argument. It is helpful to be aware of some more common types of distortion. An argument can be distorted by extending the scope of the conclusion beyond that intended by the arguer. An argument can be distorted by oversimplifying it to make it look ridiculous. Taking an argument in whole or part

---

*Furthermore, the truth of 'The industrial complex of the United States is what has made this a great country' is very questionable. Certainly, this industrial complex has *contributed* to the greatness of the United States. But that is another matter.

out of context can distort it. An argument can be distorted by introducing emotionally negative words or by replacing the definitions, intended by the arguer, of essentially used words with some other definitions. Consider the following examples.

In discussing abortion, Lucy presents a pro-choice position:

**(1)**    I contend that a woman has the moral right, under certain circumstances, to decide whether or not to have an abortion. Whether she does or does not actually have an abortion depends on many factors. I am only suggesting that having an abortion is morally permissable under certain circumstances. An abortion is the removal of a collection of human cells that have the potential to become a biologically self-sustaining person. Neither the zygote nor the fetus is yet an actual person. Because what is at issue is the removal of cells that have the potential to become a self-sustaining person, abortion is not to be taken lightly, and never used simply as a means of contraception. Abortion should always be viewed as a tragedy. Even so, it is morally permissable, under certain circumstances, for a woman to seek an abortion.

In countering this position, Sherrie, an anti-abortionist, says

**(2)**    I don't care how she puts it, Lucy is pro-abortion. She can talk all she wants to about zygotes and fetuses. They're still precious human babies, and when you kill one of those little defenseless babies, call it what you want, it is still murder. Next I suppose Lucy will defend euthanasia by pointing out that comatose persons are merely collections of human cells.

(2) is a distortion of (1). Lucy has argued only that abortion is morally permissible under certain circumstance. This is a pro-choice position; not a pro-abortion one. (2) also distorts (1) by glossing over an essential distinction between potentially being a person and actually being one. Perhaps this distinction is not well founded, but Sherrie should address that issue instead of ignoring it. Sherrie further distorts (1) by interjecting her definitions into the argument. The expressions 'the removal of' and 'the murder of' are not synonymous. Emotional uses of phrases such as 'defenseless babies' by Sherrie further distort the position of Lucy. These distortions permit Sherrie to take a final step in her attack on the position proposed by Lucy. Sherrie attempts to take the conclusion of Lucy far beyond its intended scope, applying it to cases of comatose people.

---

## EXERCISES

### Group A:

Consider each of the following examples. First determine which are arguments and which are not. Then, for those that are arguments, isolate, name, and explain any fallacy, or fallacies, that the arguments have. Remember, some arguments might be cogent.

1. Assuming excellent care for donors, and protection against exploitation by unscrupulous operators, what's wrong with trading an extra organ for salvation from the cruel realities of the impoverishment that afflicts major segments of humanity? . . . There is little in this

world, after all, that isn't for sale. So, why not kidneys and other body parts that can be sliced from the healthy and implanted in the medically needy who can pay the costs? [*Toronto Globe and Mail*; 29 March 1989]

2. The current crop of misfits who go schlepping about our streets thinking up new and ingenious ways to insult the flag deserve to be arrested, fined and locked up. . . . A pox on such punks. Who needs them? Are they the living embodiment of free speech? Flag burners deserve to have their heads broken. . . . Flag desecrator? There is nothing lower, nothing more disgusting, nothing more insulting and dishonorable—and we must not condone such impiety—not now, not ever. [*USA Today*; 22 March 1989]

3. Where have all you history buffs been? Many "good" presidents and a lot of "not so good" ones have had playmates on the side, only we did not find out about it until they were out of office or dead! [*The Houston Post*; 20 December 1987]

4. Gephardt won precisely because he was able to speak to the underlying issues of 1988 while Mr. Simon and Mr. Dukakis were stuck in a Democratic timewarp. [*The New York Times*; 11 February 1988]

5. "Jack Kemp—we have serious doubts about this man," read the flier. "Claims he opposes abortion. But does he deny that his own family was involved in an abortion?" [*The Atlanta Journal*; 12 February 1988]

6. [George Bush to Dan Rather] It's not fair to judge my whole career by a rehash of Iran. How would you like it if I judged your career by those seven minutes when you walked off the set in New York. [*New York Newsday*; 26 January 1988]

7. The liberal call to arms was proclaimed by Senator Ted Kennedy just hours after the nomination was announced. Said he: "Robert Bork's America is a land in which women would be forced into back-alley abortions, blacks would sit at segregated lunch counters, rogue police could break down citizens' doors in midnight raids, schoolchildren could not be taught about evolution, writers and artists would be censored at the whim of Government." [*Time Magazine*; 21 September 1987]

8. Liberal senators in this country have refused to confirm some of President Reagan's appointees to the court on the grounds that they were racist. But the most racist individuals in our country are these same liberals, who support the sangerian eugenists of Planned Parenthood. These eugenists were allied with the Nazis before World War II, and their primary goal of eliminating all so-called inferior races from the face of the earth hasn't changed. [*The New American*; 3 (17), 1987]

9. The Gorbachev regime's effort to appear more "open" is part of a two-step process designed to crush dissidents. The first step is to invite criticism with a sense of openness. The regime hopes that this appearance of openness will cause opponents of government to come forward. Once they are exposed, Gorbachev will "clean house"—meaning of course that firing squads, death camps, and "insane" asylums will be working at full speed. [*The American Sentinel*; 20 October 1986]

10. Recently, two doctors—in an opinion piece published in the *New England Journal of Medicine*—coldly stated, "Our proposal asserts that the anencephalic infant is not alive." . . . In one sentence, they seek to create a new class of humans, one not medically or morally equal to the rest of us. . . . This crude argument, if widely accepted, could set a dangerous precedent of arbitrarily judging the value of human life. [*USA Today*; 16 August 1989]

11. [It is nobody's business if an athlete uses anabolic steroids.] The dangers posed by steroids pale by the side of those posed by lye, for example, or by rubbing alcohol, either of which may be purchased in any supermarket by anyone, even by a child. . . . The dangers posed

by steroids are nothing by comparison with the dangers posed by driving on the roads and highways of the USA—or by attempting to walk across those roads and highways, even if one is an athlete. Yet no one advocates forbidding the use of cars or forbidding everyone to walk across the street. [*USA Today*; 11 April 1989]

12. There was corruption during my regime [said Ferdinand Marcos], but it's worse now. It's insidious and . . . involves both her and her brother. She is headed for disaster: Inflation is soaring; there is labor unrest, and 1½ million people have lost their jobs. [*U.S. News and World Report*; 3 August 1987]

13. In his first interview about the substance of allegations contained in a Sports Illustrated story last week, Rose questioned the credibility of sources named by the magazine. . . . "They talked with four guys: two of them go to jail, the other says he's a bookie, and the other one's my friend; they didn't say nothing about him," Rose said. [*St. Louis Post-Dispatch*; 26 March 1989]

14. What disturbs me is the selective criticism of hockey by the media while the more violent sports are considered sacred cows. . . . Football is like the Battle of Verdun compared to hockey, with about 1,000 deaths since 1930. Boxing has killed about 400 men since 1945. The National Hockey League, in comparison, has suffered only one fatality since 1917. It's obvious, at least to me, which sports are the real culprits. . . . But the constant condemnations of hockey won't have any validity until the other, deadlier sports receive their fair share of media criticism. [*The Sporting News*; 5 December 1988]

15. I read with dismay the Nov. 27 letter from Nathaniel Cobb. To say that the practice of removing the American flag from a veteran's casket as it enters a church for the funeral service is a "flagrant disrespect" shows Cobb's ignorance of most religious practices. For Roman Catholics, as the body enters the church it is draped with a white cloth. . . . For those of the Eastern Orthodox Christian churches, the casket is open throughout the divine liturgy and funeral service. [*The Boston Globe*; 8 December 1987]

**Group B:**

Present arguments for four claims you support. In each argument, use one of the fallacies discussed in Sections 1 through 4, using a different fallacy in each argument. Make these arguments as persuasive as possible. Next, construct a cogent argument for each of your original four claims. Test your arguments by having them criticized by members of your class.

**Group C:**

Find an example of each of the four fallacies discussed in Sections 1 through 4 in newspapers, magazines, textbooks, or the like.

---

## 5.   IS-OUGHT

**The *Is-Ought Fallacy* occurs when a conclusion asserting what ought to be the case is based solely on considerations of what is or has been the case. This fallacy also occurs in arguments asserting that something ought not to be the case solely because it is not nor has been the case.**

Granted, what is the case is sometimes what ought to be the case. Nevertheless, claims concerning what ought to be the case cannot, in general, be justified by appealing *solely* to considerations of what is in fact the case. For instance, it is an accepted historical fact that Nazi Germans killed vast numbers of people in concentration camps. It does not follow that these Nazis *ought* to have killed their victims.

There are seeming exceptions to the general supposition that what is the case can never be used as the sole justification for what ought to be the case. Someone might argue,

**(1)**    Child abuse ought not to be condoned because it is unnatural.

If by 'unnatural' is understood anything falling outside the bounds of the statistical norm, then child abuse, an I.Q. of over 100, being enrolled as a college student, or having green eyes and red hair are all statistically nonaverage conditions found in nature. These observations support nothing about what ought to be the case. On the other hand, by 'unnatural' the presenter might mean 'morally unacceptable'. Then another premise, 'If something is morally unacceptable, it ought not to be condoned', is needed to move to the conclusion. Now avoiding vicious circularity in terms of 'morally unacceptable' and 'not to be condoned' becomes problematic.

It is sometimes not clear whether an instance of an is-ought fallacy has been committed. Imagine overhearing this:

**(2)**    Julie ought to accept what the members of the sorority say because that's what is expected of pledges in this house.

As (2) stands it might display the is-ought fallacy by merely *appealing to the status quo* in an attempt to justify 'Julie ought to accept what the members of the sorority say'. Or (2) might be placed in this setting:

**(3)**    Part of the *status quo* of this sorority is that the pledges in the house are each expected to accept what the members say. If anyone is a pledge in this sorority and wants to be initiated, then she ought to follow the *status quo.* Julie is a pledge and she wants to be initiated. Therefore, Julie ought to accept what the members say.

Here appeals are made to factual claims in support of the conclusion. However, it is not *only* factual claims that are cited. The second premise introduces the conditional sense of 'ought'. *IF* a person desires to achieve certain goals, *THEN* that person ought to do other things. This is an assumption used in justifying claims about goal-oriented behavior. If, however, (2) is understood as an attempt to justify the claim 'Julie ought to accept what the members of the sorority say' *solely* by an appeal to the *status quo* of the sorority, an is-ought fallacy is committed. Care must be taken in reconstructing arguments concluding with an ought claim. What might first appear to be an is-ought fallacy can in some cases be treated as an enthymeme in which an ought premise is implicit in the argument.

Is-ought fallacies sometimes appeal to a sense of tradition. An is-ought fallacy merely *appealing to tradition* is different from one appealing to the *status quo*. Often claims concerning the traditions of a family, social organization, region of a country, or the nation carry with them powerful emotional overtones triggering deeply responsive feelings. These emotional overtones, and the responses to them, can make an instance of the is-ought fallacy very attractive. Consider this example:

> **(4)** A person ought always to put the nation ahead of personal desire because that is in keeping with our great and honored tradition of national prosperity.

(4) is packed with positive emotional overtones that are reinforced by 'great and honored'. Also note how vague the expression 'tradition of national prosperity' is. There are good *and* bad traditions of national prosperity. History indicates national tradition has not always brought about the best moral situations, or even what financially ought to have been done. The *mere* fact that something is traditional does not provide rationally acceptable evidence for an is-ought claim.

An instance of the is-ought fallacy can be reinforced by *appeals to guilt, ingratitude, or loyalty*. Louise is about to do something of which her mother disapproves. Her mother says this:

> **(5)** You ought not to do that after all the things your father and I've done for you.

Perhaps one person might say this to another:

> **(6)** You ought at least to do this for me after all the things I've gone out of my way to do for you.

A father might say this to his son:

> **(7)** You ought to be happy to register for the draft. After all we are loyal citizens of the United States.

It could be that Louise has parents who have sacrificed much for her. Or someone might have done a great deal for another person. In general, such considerations are, in themselves, not adequate justification for asserting that someone ought or ought not to do something. Factual claims would have to be combined with other premises, one of which contained an ought claim.

One such premise might be 'An individual ought to do whatever is asked by a close relative or friend who has done a great deal for her'. This premise is problematic, however. Suppose mother is an active alcoholic attempting to justify the claim that her daughter ought to bring some liquor to the house. Or imagine a person trying to justify the claim that he ought to be permitted to plagiarize the classwork of a friend. Evidence for such ought-claims has little to do with a sense of guilt, ingratitude, or loyalty. Such emotions often provide a strong motivation to act. But a strong motivation to act is not evidence for a claim that one ought to act in that way.

## 6.  DECEPTIVE ALTERNATIVES

> The *Fallacy of Deceptive Alternatives*, also called "*False Dilemma*," occurs when a disjunctive premise incorrectly suggests, explicitly or implicitly, that the alternatives mentioned by the disjunction are mutually exclusive and exhaust all possible alternatives relevant to the conclusion.

The argument is flawed when there are other alternatives that are ignored. Imagine a political candidate saying this:

(1)   The United States must stand fast and strengthen its commitments to those around the world fighting back the slavery imposed by communism. The United States either increases military spending and protects freedom around the globe or it allows the communists to enslave her allies.

In (1), a deceptive alternative is presented between the U. S. form of democracy and freedom, or communism and slavery. More than one form of government exists granting freedoms of expression, travel, and worship. More than one form of government guarantees rights to own property, select political candidates, and vote for political candidates. Further, not all communistic forms of government are identical. The communists of Spain and Italy are very different from those of North Vietnam.

The fallacy of deceptive alternatives presents two (sometimes more) conditions as if they were incompatible while also excluding any other possibilities. A "black or white" situation is posed. This suggestion can be wrong, ignoring other considerations relevant to the argument. Not all alternatives introduced into an argument are deceptive, however. There are clues indicating alternatives that are likely deceptive, flawing an argument. If the alternatives are prefaced with expressions such as 'it is obviously true', 'without doubt', or 'it is evident', be cautious of a deceptive alternative. When there is suspicion of a deceptive alternative, the best approach is to seek out other possible relevant alternatives that have been ignored. Finding such alternatives, ask if the conclusion is still justified.

## 7.   WISHFUL THINKING

The *Fallacy of Wishful Thinking,* or *Fallacy of Desire,* occurs when belief that some claim is correct (incorrect) is substituted for evidence for that claim being correct (incorrect).

Examples of wishful thinking are often found in the attitudes, positions, and comments of people who are deeply committed to some cause. Consider this example:

(1)   I'm going to be successful in business and happy in marriage.
      This is certain because I want both too much to be disappointed.

The only evidence the presenter gives is her desire for several things to be the case. This desire, however, is not rationally acceptable evidence for her conclusion. Too many people who desire to be successful in business are not, and too many people who want happy marriages have miserable ones.

Suppose someone says,

(2)   Surely God exists because I have complete belief that He does.

That one has complete belief about anything might fashion and direct the life of that person. But that life style coupled with the belief motivating it is not evidence for the existence of the object of belief. Many people throughout history have had profound belief in the existence of all sorts of things. Whether such things do exist or not is not merely a matter of belief.

Do not confuse the fallacy of wishful thinking with the phenomenon of self-fulfilling prophecy. A self-fulfilling prophecy such as, 'I am just certain no one will like me tonight at the party', can be a strong causal factor in bringing about the situation mentioned in the prophecy. Even so, such a self-fulfilling prophecy is not offered as *evidence* for the claim, 'No one will like me tonight at the party'. On the other hand, in the fallacy of wishful thinking, the belief of a person is presented as evidence for some claim.

## 8. NOVELTY

> The *Fallacy of Novelty* occurs when there is an attempt to substantiate some conclusion that one thing is better than another by appealing merely to the fact that something is new, modern, or the latest fad.

The appearance of cogency in arguments introducing this fallacy is often linked to the notion that progress is universal, inevitable, and good. But this assumption is highly questionable. Here are typical examples containing instances of the fallacy of novelty:

(1) Certainly my new hair style is the very best. After all it is the newest thing.

(2) While my old computer was perfectly satisfactory for what I have to do, the machine that I bought yesterday is much better. It is the latest thing in new technology.

(3) The new courses in *MIS* must be great. *MIS* is the newest area in computer management.

Merely because something is new does not, in general, provide evidence that it is in some way better. Similarly, simply because something is old does not, in general, supply evidence that it is worse. Appealing solely to novelty or age cannot generally be viewed as acceptable evidence in arguing that something is better or worse than something else.

---

## *EXERCISES*

### Group A:

Consider each of the following examples. First determine which are arguments and which are not. Then, for those that are arguments, isolate, name, and explain any fallacy, or fallacies, that the arguments have. Remember, some arguments might be cogent.

1. There are two directions in which you can go when facing a conflict; either you can fix the problem or you can fix the blame. If you make it your goal in a conflict to convince the other person that he or she is wrong (or bad), you will accomplish very little. It is more

productive to work on the problem by trying to get the person to change the negative behavior. [*Working Woman*; March 1988]

2. It is tragic anytime police must shoot and kill a fellow human being. I fail to see, however, why there is such an outcry about racism every time the victim of such a tragedy is a member of a minority group. York Regional Police shot and killed a white man in his apartment at around the same time as the Lester Donaldson shooting, yet hardly a protest was uttered. This shooting was similar to other police shootings and was equally tragic. Race did not play a part in any of them. I am confident that a jury will agree. [*MacLean's*; 6 February 1989]

3. Losers, who faced odds of 13 million-to-1, said they were disappointed but took the loss in stride. . . . "I just got one ticket [in the Illinois state lottery] because . . . if you're going to win, you'll win with one," said Lonny Taylor, a systems engineer from Chicago. [*The Houston Post*; 17 April 1989]

4. Abortions have always been commonplace. There has never been a time in the history of this country when women weren't having abortions. Now they are able to have them under safe and sanitary conditions. We believe that this is a right that women should never be denied. [*Seventeen*; January 1986]

5. Research on changing values points to the need to rethink our old rules, recognize emerging new rules, and spend time understanding people as human beings with the capacity for change. If our efforts to anticipate the future rely primarily on economics and technology, we could miss wonderful opportunities for a better world. [*The Futurist*; January–February 1989]

6. . . . he believed passionately in something, and he expressed far better than any of us in our administration . . . he expressed what was at stake in Central America. Freedom vs. Marxism. Freedom vs. Communism. . . . And Ollie North stood up there, took the heat, and the American people in every bar in Chicago and every bowling alley in Texas and every little home said, "Hey, this guy believes in something, and I can identify with it." And I [George Bush] feel that way about Ollie North. And so let the critics say what went wrong. He's admitted it. I've admitted it. But I respect somebody who feels passionately and strongly about values, about his country, his patriotism. [*U.S. News and World Report*; 14 December 1987]

7. My career path in the financial services industry will be in the continuing development of the latest technology, where I can be the first one to apply the new concept to light the brightest candle in the financial world. [*American Banker*; 10 March 1989]

8. With patience and a clear sense of our mutual interests and priorities, I believe that the U.S.–Japan partnership that has been forged with so much effort over the past 40 years will not falter. It will remain the force that assures the peace and prosperity of the Pacific region. [*Forbes*; 11 January 1988]

9. Beyond the impact on Canadian–U.S. relations, it [a vote for Mr. Turner or Mr. Broadbent in the 1988 Canadian race for prime minister] is also a refusal to face the new reality of a world economy of increasingly interdependent and thus vulnerable nations whose economic welfare is irrevocably tied to the nature and quality of their relationships with principle trading partners. An opportunity will have been missed to face up to this new reality and begin to grapple with it. The agreement is historic in the sense that it is a bold attempt to rework an already successful and huge trade relationship in such a way as to make it reflect the new and still evolving circumstances in which the modern industrial economics finds themselves. [*Toronto Globe and Mail*; 21 November 1988]

10. If you think that anybody believes a drug kingpin doesn't deserve to fry, then you are wrong. Or that a murderer, after all appeals are exhausted, shouldn't be burned. That's the way it is in the real world. [*USA Today*; 17 August 1988]

11. The debate over making English our official language is largely symbolic. English has been the de facto official language of the United States for 200 years. The real issue, however, is bilingual education. If we are truly concerned with providing the full benefits of citizenship to recent immigrants, we should be willing to spend millions of dollars to teach them English, but not a penny for bilingual education. Precisely because we are a nation of immigrants, it is essential that we all share a common language. The alternative is to become a modern Tower of Babel. [*Newsweek*; 20 March 1989]

12. Then, too, I saw how well the guys already on steroids were doing—maybe 30 of them at that time. There was also the fact that I was young and felt nothing bad could happen to me, combined with the fact that I was part of a drug-oriented society. In addition to all of that, I felt I had the coaches' encouragement. I'm told that Washburn says he opposes steroid use, but he told me, "Do what you have to do, take what you have to take." [*Sports Illustrated*; October 1988]

13. . . . we can have a Black man for president. I do not understand why whites are so afraid to have a Black man take over as leader of this so-called free country. They tell us and themselves that this is a color-blind country, but they certainly are not practicing what they preach. I think that we as Blacks should put all of our negative thinking about our own race behind us and vote for Rev. Jesse Jackson. A Black president can do no more damage to us than White presidents have and are still doing. We Blacks must stand together and let Whites know that we are not going to take it anymore; that for us, our equal justice means also putting a Black man in the White House. And we surely can put him there if we just get out and vote. [*Ebony Magazine*; June 1988]

14. The Civic has been winning small-car taste-offs for most of this decade, and the reason why is anything but a secret. Most car companies leave their cars in production for at least five years and as much as ten. Honda, however, insists on keeping its designs fresher than anyone else's; new models have only three years to thrive—four years at the outside—before giving way to replacements. [*Car and Driver*; November 1988]

15. Government has a degree of guardianship over the airwaves because they are assumed to be public property and to have limited availability. But the proliferation of technological means of delivering messages over the air has undercut this justification for government control. In this country, the normal thing is for people to be free to express their views without supervision from Washington. Dropping the intrusive Fairness Doctrine is a return to normality, not a reckless experiment. [*Conservative Digest*; October 1987]

## Group B:

Present arguments for four claims you support. In each argument, use one of the fallacies discussed in Sections 5 through 8, using a different fallacy in each argument. Make these arguments as persuasive as possible. Next, construct a cogent argument for each of your original four claims. Test your arguments by having them criticized by members of your class.

## Group C:

Find an example of each of the four fallacies discussed in Sections 5 through 8 in newspapers, magazines, textbooks, or the like.

## 9.   CONFUSING SUFFICIENT AND NECESSARY CONDITIONS

> The *Fallacy of Confusing Sufficient and Necessary Conditions* occurs when a
> necessary condition is presented as a sufficient one or a sufficient condi-
> tion is taken as a necessary one in supporting some conclusion.

To grasp this fallacy, one must first understand the use of 'sufficient condition' and
'necessary condition'.* Let '*A*' and '*B*' denote some event, object, or property
something might have. *A* is a sufficient condition for the occurrence of *B* if and only
if an occurrence of *A* guarantees an occurrence of *B*. *B* is a necessary condition for *A*
if and only if an absence of *B* guarantees an absence of *A*. Raining is a sufficient
condition for the ground being wet. Under normal circumstances, raining guarantees that the ground is wet. Suppose, on the other hand, that Maria observes that the
ground is wet. From this alone she is not able to assume that it has rained. A watering
system might have wet the ground. If the ground were *not* wet, however, Maria could
say that it had not rained. So, under normal circumstances, that the ground is wet is
a necessary condition for it having rained.

A particularly noticeable necessary condition might be taken for a sufficient one.
This oversimplifies the evidence given in support of some conclusion. Such oversim-
plification is not acceptable in rational thought. A person working in a chemistry
lab could say,

> (3)   If water is poured into sulfuric acid, there will be an explosion.
>        Hence, I better not pour water into this sulfuric acid.

This can be understood as,

> (4)   Pouring water into sulfuric acid is sufficient to cause an explo-
>        sion. I don't want to cause an explosion. Hence, I better not
>        pour water into this sulfuric acid.

Pouring water into sulfuric acid will not in itself cause an explosion. It is not the only
event that goes into making up the sufficient conditions for the explosion, although
it is the most noticeable one. Other conditions must also be met. For instance, the
acid has to be of a certain strength and oxygen must be present in the area where the
acid strikes the water. Unless these conditions exist, there will be no explosion.

Consider a politician arguing like this:

> (5)   To have social justice and fair opportunity for all, there is going
>        to be a redistribution of national wealth through a progressive
>        tax program. The increased tax dollars, obtained from those
>        who have more resources, will be used in social, health, and
>        educational programs. My supporters know I firmly support a
>        progressive tax program to fund these governmental functions.

---

*See Chapter 2, Section 9, for a review of the phrases 'necessary condition' and 'sufficient
condition'.

Consequently, the results of my political actions in the legislature will bring social justice and fair opportunity for all.

(5) can be restructured in this way:

**(6)**

1) If there a redistribution of nation wealth through a progressive tax program, then there will be social justice and fair opportunity for all.

2) I support a redistribution of national wealth through a progressive tax program.

3) Consequently, there will be social justice and equal opportunity for all.

Unfortunately, a redistribution of wealth is not a sufficient condition for social justice and fair opportunity for all. The end result can be, and in some cases has been, higher taxes, more government programs, graft and corruption, and continuing social injustice with lack of opportunity for many. A redistribution of wealth *may be* a necessary condition for social justice and equal opportunity. But suppose the national wealth were not redistributed through a progressive tax program. Would this guarantee that there would *not* be social justice and equal opportunity for all? No, for a great many social programs can be, and are, funded through private resources. Hence, the legislation suggested in (5) seems neither a sufficient nor a necessary condition for social justice and equal opportunity for all.

## 10. QUESTIONABLE CAUSES

A *Fallacy of Questionable Cause* occurs when (1) a phenomenon is claimed to be the cause of something when it is not or when a phenomenon is claimed to be the cause of something when there is poor evidence to support that it is and (2) this causal claim is offered as evidence for some conclusion.

The nature of causality is greatly debated. There is little agreement on how to characterize properly the cause-effect relation. However, there is agreement concerning what it is not. Following are several relations often mistaken for causal ones.

The **Post Hoc Fallacy** ('*post hoc ergo propter hoc*', or 'after that therefore because of that') occurs when it is assumed that merely because some event temporally proceeds another, there is a causal relation between these events. This fallacy assumes that temporal sequence is sufficient for establishing a causal relation. Following are two examples.

One sometimes hears on the obstetrics floor of a hospital,

**(1)** Since there's a full moon, there'll be more babies born this week.

It seems apparent to some hospital workers that more babies are born during or immediately after a full moon than at any other time of the month. It is assumed that some sort of relation holds between a full moon and an increased birth rate. But no causal relation is established between them by mere temporal priority. For even though temporal conditions might be considered a necessary condition for a causal relation, they are not sufficient. If they were, then any event temporally prior to another could correctly be cited as the cause of the later event.

The second example of a *post hoc* could be found in financial sections of newspapers in 1988:

(2)   Stock prices have given ground in the last year of every lame-duck president's second term since Andrew Jackson in 1836. Reagan is a lame-duck president. So, we can count on it happening again in 1988.

The temporal priority of lame-duck presidents and stock market activities might be an interesting coincidence. Admittedly, if enough investors *believe* that a causal relation exists between there being a lame-duck president and a decline in stock prices, there will likely be such a decline during the term of a lame-duck president. But then the causal factor is the belief of the investors and not some supposed causal relation holding between the sitting of a lame-duck president and the prices of stocks.

The **Simple Correlation Fallacy** wrongly suggests that correlation of phenomena is sufficient to establish a causal relation. A cause is always correlated with its effect. Yet not every correlation is a causal relation. A waiter is setting a table. Simultaneously, he puts down a fork with his left hand and a knife with his right. When the table setting is completed there is a perfect correlation of forks and knives. Nonetheless, it would be incorrect to say a causal relation holds between the forks and knives. Or it might be that every mental event such as a pain sensation or a thought is correlated with some specific brain activity. It does not follow simply from this correlation that these brain activities cause those mental events. Minimally, it would have to be shown that the mental events and brain events are independent activities related in terms of laws which themselves were a coherent part of contemporary science.

The **Statistical Correlation Fallacy** suggests that because phenomena are probably to be found together there is a causal relation between them. For some years, the U.S. advertising industry has been promoting "thin is beautiful." Many small companies promising quick and painless weight loss have come and gone. Here is an argument that many of them could have promoted:

(3)   *Fat Off* suppresses your appetite while giving you that marvelous after-a-meal satisfied feeling. Coupled with our easy to follow diet and exercise plan, over 80% of our customers have been happy with the wonderful and immediate results of *Fat Off.* You will be elated, too, as you watch the pounds melt away—or your money back.

Even though there might be a statistical correlation between using *Fat Off* and weight reduction, this is not sufficient to establish a causal relation. The cause of the weight loss might not be *Fat Off* but the "easy to follow diet and exercise plan." Indeed, several questionable points are found in (3). There is the overall positive emotional tone created by the use of 'marvelous', 'satisfied feeling', 'easy to follow', 'happy with', 'immediate results', 'elated', and 'pounds melt away'. And notice that 'easy to follow' is not synonymous with 'enjoyable to do'. In addition, it is unlikely that a firm selling a weight reduction product is going carefully to collect and compile statistical information concerning how pleased its customers are. Perhaps 20% of those purchasing *Fat Off* request a refund. This does not support the claim that 80% of those purchasing *Fat Off* were happy with it. Some might have thrown the product away and forgotten about any refund.

While neither temporal priority nor correlation establish causal relations, both can be cited in cogent arguments:

**(4)** There is a strong probability that both tobacco smoking and secondary tobacco smoke inhalation are a prime cause of lung cancer. After all, a high correlation between lung cancer and previous tobacco smoke inhalation has been found in a large percentage of cases of lung cancer both in human and laboratory animal populations.

(4) is not an example of a *post hoc* or correlation fallacy. The conclusions of a great part of the scientific and medical community concerning the relation between tobacco smoke inhalation and instances of lung cancer are based on the presence of tar in cigarette smoke and the well-established effects of tar on lungs. Those scientists who do not agree that tobacco smoke inhalation is a prime causal factor in lung cancer are, in many instances, hired by tobacco companies. And while the special circumstance of those researchers does not render their findings scientifically worthless, it does raise serious questions of bias and hasty conclusions.*

## 11.  SLIPPERY SLOPE

> The *Slippery Slope Fallacy*, also known as the "*Domino Fallacy*," occurs when it is asserted, without appropriate evidence, that one phenomenon will necessarily lead to another, and that this second will necessarily lead to still another in a chain of events until some final situation, usually unpleasant, is brought about.

Assume someone arguing,

**(1)** If we do not agree to the Russians' present disarmament proposals, we'll be in no position to agree to future ones. We need to act now and cut our conventional arms under their terms. Otherwise, they will distrust us and the result will be renewed mounting tension on both sides. We'll never be able to come together again under that situation to discuss other proposals and war will be the inevitable outcome. The destruction will be incalculable. We must work now with the Russians and sign those agreements to avoid catastrophic war.

Here is another example containing a slippery slope:

**(2)** I hear that Liz is into pot parties. That's really too bad. She'll be dead soon. It's only a matter of time before she'll start on the needle. Then to support her addiction she'll have to turn to prostitution. And she is bound to get *AIDS* either from dirty needles or her customers.

---

*One must guard against committing a circumstantial *ad hominem* here.

One hopes that Liz's fate is not as sealed as (2) suggests. The problem with this sort of reasoning is that no rationally acceptable evidence is given to support the claim that the first event necessarily leads to the second, the second to the third, the third to the fourth, and so on to the last. The explanations of why these proposed chains are persuasive and accepted might be clear enough in particular examples. A sense of fear or regret could be operative in many situations. Yet to explain why a fallacy is persuasive is not to turn a fallacious argument into a cogent one. Whenever an argument is presented in the form of a chain in which one situation necessarily leads to another, always demand rationally acceptable reasons justifying each supposed link in that chain. If at any one link justification cannot or will not be supplied, there is an example of the slippery slope fallacy.

## 12.  GAMBLER'S FALLACY

> The *Gambler's Fallacy* occurs when it is suggested as evidence for some conclusion that simply because a random event has had a certain run in the past it will have a different outcome in the future.

Imagine a person sitting in the acres of slot machines in Bally's Hotel in Reno. He has been playing for hours, winning nothing. His companion is bored. She says to him, "Come on, let's go," and he replies, "Not yet. I'm about to win big!" "What reason do you have to say that?" she asks. "I haven't won anything in nine hours. That means my luck is bound to change!" he replies. Under other circumstances, the conversation might go like this. The bored companion says, "Come on, let's go." "Not now," her friend replies. "Why not?" she says, "We've been here for nine hours doing the same thing." "Yes, and I've been consistently winning," he tells her. "That's just the point. You are bound to start losing big. So, you should leave now!" Both of these exchanges exhibit an instance of the gambler's fallacy.

Like all other fallacies, the gambler's fallacy draws its force from a similarity to cogent arguments that do supply statistical evidence for some claim. Such arguments have to be carefully constructed, however. Great attention must be paid to the selection of the evidence upon which a statistical conclusion is based. A sufficient number of observations must be made of a relatively stable group of individuals. And there must be reasons to suppose that this group is representative of the larger group about which the conclusion is being asserted. None of these considerations can be met, however, when talking about past random events. If some past events are random, then no consideration of them can supply evidence for concluding that the same type of event will or will not occur in the same way in the future.

---

## *EXERCISES*

### Group A:

Consider each of the following examples. First determine which are arguments and which are not. Then, for those that are arguments, isolate, name, and explain any fallacy, or fallacies, that the arguments have. Remember, some arguments might be cogent.

1. Since women entered the work force, family life has deteriorated, the number of divorces and broken homes has increased, children have become brazen and disrespectful, alcohol and drug abuse is on the rise, and dirty language is everywhere. [*The Atlanta Journal*; 15 March 1988]

2. The INF treaty is not the first with the claim that "an entire class of weapons has been scrapped." In 1922, Washington agreed to scrap capital warships along with the other naval powers. We did so, and supposedly too did the Japanese warlords. But in 1934 they ignored the treaty and built the armada which ultimately attacked Pearl Harbor in 1941. . . . The INF treaty is most dangerous in this regard, because it gives a false sense of security with an enemy who will eventually use our trusting nature to thrust us into another unnecessary war. [*The American Sentinel*; 25 January 1988]

3. India is "ambitious" to become a "regional superpower" from the Gulf to the coast of China, President Zia of Pakistan told us over lunch. That ambition makes a snug fit with the long Soviet effort to undermine Pakistan, India's archrival. Next to Turkey, Pakistan is America's strongest Asian ally, crucial in blocking a Soviet victory in Afghanistan. "Only two countries in south Asia—Turkey and Pakistan—have stood up to the Soviets," Zia said. "Take Pakistan out and the Soviets would become supreme from Turkey to Vietnam." [*The Washington Post*; 1 February 1988]

4. One of every 17 people in the District of Columbia are attorneys. Their number has jumped from 30,000 at the beginning of the Reagan Administration to 47,000 when the president stepped down last January. This figure is far above the national norm. It's also interesting to note that Washington has become the murder capital of the United States. Gunshots are heard in the streets every night, and we wonder if there is a connection between the disproportionately high number of attorneys and the extraordinary high level of crime. [*The American Sentinel*; 15 March 1989]

5. "A freak thing" is how Georgia coach Ray Goff described Jones' broken wrist, the implication being that it could've happened anyplace anytime. Alas, the reality is that it happened in a goofy game at the wrong time of year. Put it this way: A football player has only a finite number of collisions in him before he gets hurt. Why use up 1,000 of those in the spring? . . . Why have spring practice at all? [*The Atlanta Journal and Constitution*; 2 May 1989]

6. The recent terrorist attacks were just a preliminary salvo . . . As yet, terrorists have mostly left America herself alone. . . . *But the attacks here in America will come eventually*—unless we first take action. Soviet sponsored terrorism must be stopped *now*, before it reaches its desired goal—the complete disruption of everyday life in our free democracies. [*The American Sentinel*; 20 January 1986]

7. We're eating ourselves to death. . . . We eat too much fat. . . . We consume too many calories. And too often we don't even know they are in our food. Nutritional ignorance is the problem. Better labeling of food products is the solution. Congress should require it. [*USA Today*; 2 August 1988]

8. Age 6½ would be a good minimum age for entering first graders. But older would be better. . . . Several years ago I ranked the students in my class from strongest to weakest. Then I wrote in each child's age. It was an eye-opener! In almost every case, the oldest children were the strongest [academically] and the youngest were struggling. . . . Since then I have ranked my class like that every year and have noticed the same pattern. I would bet that every first grade would break down in roughly the same way, and the cut-off age between doing well and struggling is about 6½ years at entry. [*NEA Today*; December 1988]

9. The new law in California outlawing "assault" rifles should prove very effective in preventing someone who would never break the law from owning one. I think it will be somewhat less effective in preventing someone who would use such a gun to commit murder from getting one. As long as they are made, criminals will get them. [*The Atlanta Journal and Constitution*; 21 March 1989]

10. The record shows [in an argument for increasing the minimum wage level] that each time the minimum wage was increased since World War II, employment went up, except during the 1975 recession. [*Congressional Digest*; August–September 1987]

11. Tracy Lawrence and her husband, David Pelletier, knew when they bought their down-town condominium a few years ago that there was a homeless shelter nearby. But she was not prepared for what she found in her backyard this summer. . . . Lawrence was walking barefoot with her 4-year-old daughter, Sarah, in a small, fenced yard on Crombie Street when she noticed a syringe and hypodermic needle. She believes they were left by drug users from the shelter. . . . "When I found the needle, I said this is it. We will not tolerate heroin," said Lawrence, who hosts a radio talk show. . . . Since that discovery, Lawrence and her husband have started a campaign to close or relocate the shelter . . . [*The Boston Globe*; 15 August 1989]

12. Working in LSU's favor is another trend. The home team in this series hasn't won since 1980, the last time LSU played in Tuscaloosa. Since then, the Crimson Tide has been host in Birmingham. [*The Atlanta Journal and Constitution*; 5 November 1988]

13. The Democrats have come up with yet another scheme to advance the growth of federal power. Citing the very real need for the war on drugs, Democrats deleted some $475 million from the SDI research program to commit American armed forces to interdict drugs coming into the country. Of course drugs are a major problem here—but the Democrats are using our grave concern to achieve a long-cherished goal; a national police force. [*The American Sentinel*; 6 June 1988]

14. We are losing the drug war in the courts and on the streets. Right after the president's speech on the drug problem, the news programs were full of liberal professors who were worried about drug dealers' rights being violated. . . . These people are training our future attorneys and judges. We need long jail terms in miserable prisons and a return to good old-fashioned horsewhipping to win this one. [*The Houston Post*; 3 November 1989]

15. Individuals who smoke marijuana will eventually try cocaine because most narcotic addicts surveyed in Florida hospitals admitted to smoking marijuana before taking cocaine. [*The New York Times*; 12 February 1988]

## Group B:

Present arguments for four claims you support. In each argument, use one of the fallacies discussed in Sections 9 through 12, using a different fallacy in each argument. Make these arguments as persuasive as possible. Next, construct a cogent argument for each of your original four claims. Test your arguments by having them criticized by members of your class.

## Group C:

Find an example of each of the four fallacies discussed in Sections 9 through 12 in newspapers, magazines, textbooks, or the like.

## 13.  CIRCULAR ARGUMENT

> The *Circular Argument Fallacy,* or *Begging the Question,* occurs when the conclusion of an argument is a restatement, usually in different vocabulary or form, of one of the premises.

A circular argument is a verbal illusion. Some justification appears to be given for the conclusion. Yet if one of the premises asserts the same thing as the conclusion, that premise stands in as much need of justification as the conclusion. On the other hand, if the premise is rationally acceptable, the argument has no purpose because the conclusion is already accepted as one of the premises.

Circularity can occur in various ways. An argument can be circular because the conclusion is equivalent in meaning to one of the premises. Two sentences are equivalent in meaning if and only if they both assert the same thing in the same context:

> **(1)**   Craig throws the ball. Therefore, the ball is thrown by Craig.

Sentences can also be equivalent because of their logical forms:

> **(2)**   Neither *U2* nor *R.E.M.* is a punk group. This is obvious because *U2* is not punk, but neither is *R.E.M.*

(2) is circular. The premise and conclusion assert the same thing because their logical forms are equivalent. The following is a more complicated example of a circular argument based on an equivalence of logical form:

> **(3)**   Either there's more evidence that using crack is bad for me or I'm not going to worry about it. So, I'm not going to worry about using crack unless there's more evidence that it's bad for me since I can get it cheaply and I like it a lot.

Transforming (3) into standard argument form yields,

> **(4)**
>
> **1)** Either there's more evidence that using crack is bad for me or I'm not going to worry about it.
>
> **2)** I can get crack cheaply and I like it a lot.
>
> **3)** So, I'm not going to worry about using crack unless there's more evidence that it's bad for me.

The conclusion is a reassertion of the first premise. Not considering the second premise, the argument is valid, but not cogent because it is circular. If, however, the first premise is ignored to avoid circularity, the argument is still not cogent because the second premise is not sufficient to establish the conclusion.

Careless uses of definitions and synonyms can introduce vicious circularity into an argument.* In such cases, the conclusion of an argument can be a reassertion of a

---

*For a review of vicious circularity see Chapter 13, Section 4.

premise. Suppose someone said,

> **(5)**    Russell sleeps a great deal because he is somnolent most of the time.

(5) is put into standard form as

> **(6)**
>
> **1)**  Russell is somnolent most of the time.
>
> **2)**  So, Russell sleeps a great deal.

(6) is circular. 'Somnolent' means to sleep a great deal. (6) is valid, but not cogent.

## 14.   INCONSISTENCIES

> *Fallacies of Inconsistency* **occur when an argument contains contradictory claims, or when an arguer claims one thing at one time and its contradiction at another without providing reasons for this change of position.**

An inconsistent premise can never be rationally acceptable evidence in an argument.* It does not have to be known that a premise is true for it to be evidence in support of a conclusion. If, however, it is known that some premise is false, it generally cannot be accepted as evidence.† In a set of premises offered to substantiate a claim, if that premise set is known to be inconsistent, it might not be known precisely which premise is false. However, until it can be determined which one is unacceptable, the entire set of them must be held suspect.

A claim is inconsistent when there is no way to interpret it as true. Such inconsistency might be *syntactical* or *semantical*.‡ A claim is *syntactically inconsistent* when, because of its form, there is no way that it can be true. Two, or more, claims are syntactically inconsistent when, because of their forms, there is no way the conjunction of them can be true. It is not inconsistent to say, 'Wayne passed his Spanish course last fall' or 'Wayne didn't pass his Spanish course last fall'. It is inconsistent to say, 'Wayne both passed and didn't pass his Spanish course last fall'. Given standard uses of 'not' and 'and', it cannot be true that Wayne both passed and did not pass one particular Spanish course.

A claim is *semantically inconsistent* if it is used in an attempt to predicate two, or more, logically exclusive properties of the same thing at the same time. For instance, it is not inconsistent to say, 'This object is square'. Nor is it inconsistent to assert, 'This object is round'. It is, however, inconsistent to say of the same object at the same time, 'This object is both round and square'. Because of the definitions of 'round' and 'square', no single object can, at the same moment, be both round and square.

---

*For a review of consistency and inconsistency, see, for example, Chapter 3, Section 6, and Chapter 7, Section 3.

†Once more *reductio ad absurdum* arguments are exceptions. So are arguments in which a premise known to be false is assumed to see what conclusions it would entail if it were true.

‡See Chapter 13, Section 1, for a review of syntax and semantics.

A third type of inconsistency is *pragmatic inconsistency*.\* This type of inconsistency can take two forms. The first is seen when a person argues for some claim on one occasion and later argues its denial without giving any reasons for this change. Certainly a person might, for a variety of relevant and rational reasons, completely change his position on some issue. However, if he does this and is not prepared to give reasons for doing so, then he is being inconsistent. Assuming no relevant and rational reasons are given for this change, the premises of the separate arguments cannot be acceptable as supplying evidence for the conclusions. Within the contexts of the arguments there is no way to determine which, if either, of the two inconsistent arguments is acceptable.

The second type of pragmatic inconsistency is apparent when a person says one thing and does another. 'Your words are inconsistent with your actions' is commonly said to such a person.† This type of pragmatic inconsistency is not, generally, relevant to assessing the cogency of arguments. How a person acts, in general, does not count as supporting evidence for the acceptability, correctness, or the like, of what she claims to be the case. How a person acts often does count as evidence concerning whether she actually believes what she says and the trustworthiness of her claims. But even if her actions are consistent with what she believes and says, in general, personal beliefs do not supply rational acceptable evidence for a claim.

It can be difficult to spot instances of inconsistency. They are usually subtly hidden. To see inconsistencies requires a sense of the correct logical and grammatical structures of language and properly used vocabulary, as well as a grasp of what the arguer has said in the past. The sharper the sense of grammar and vocabulary a person has, coupled with a knowledge of the speaker, the more likely inconsistencies will be found if any are there. Inconsistencies are harder to discover when inconsistent claims are widely separated from one another. It may be that one of the claims is toward the beginning of a long article, speech, sermon, or lecture, and the other toward the end. Complicated and emotionally appealing language can camouflage inconsistencies. Definitions relative to a particular conclusion might not be explicitly mentioned in the argument. Inconsistent claims can occur in two different arguments offered at different times and places. Any of these situations makes it difficult to uncover inconsistencies in the presentation of evidence and conclusions supposedly supported by that evidence.

## 15.  FACTUAL CERTAINTY

> The *Fallacy of Factual Certainty*, or *Apriorism*, occurs when it is suggested, explicitly or implicitly, that a factual claim is absolutely beyond any doubt whatsoever; that no evidence can count against that claim.

Underlying the factual certainty fallacy is an ignored distinction between factual and *a priori* uses of declarative sentences.

---

\*For a review of pragmatics, see Chapter 13, Section 1.

†See Chapter 13, Section 2.

A declarative sentence is commonly used in an attempt to assert something true about particular things in the world. Such declarative sentences express factual claims. It is always at least possible, even when not very probable, that an attempt to assert something true might fail. The concept of *possibility* being invoked is *logical possibility*; namely, it would not be contradictory to claim something is the case. In many cases, something is logically possible even though it might be economically, politically, or technologically improbable. Hence, some *counterexample* to a factual claim is always possible even if highly improbable. Even the wildest claim counts as logically possible *counterevidence* provided that it is both relevant to the topic under discussion and not contradictory. So, if a person is making a legitimate **factual claim**, he must be willing to allow that his claim could be wrong and say, in general, what sort of logically possible evidence would count against his claim if that evidence were found.

On the other hand, **a priori claims** do not make any assertions about this or that particular thing, event, or action. An *a priori* claim is true or false because of considerations other than how particular things in the world might or might not be at some time. Some *a priori* sentences are necessarily true or false solely because of their logical form. Suppose someone says, 'It is either raining or it isn't'. No weather conditions are conceivable that could possibly make the claim false. Imagine a person suggesting, 'I'm both going to eat and not eat this steak at this very moment'. This claim cannot possibly be true. Such a possibility is precluded by the logical form of the claim. Other *a priori* claims are necessarily true or false because of the definitions of particular words used in them. 'All bachelors are unmarried men' is true because of the ways in which 'bachelor' and 'unmarried man' are presently defined. It is false that 'All balls are cubical' because of the definitions of 'ball' and 'cubical'. These claims are certain "by definition." They are not certain because of considerations of any particular thing, event or action in the world.

Serious errors occur when *a priori* claims are confused with factual ones. In a controversy concerning abortion, this might be heard:

> It is obviously the case that all self-induced abortions are nothing more
> than murders because all abortions are the willful killing of babies.

Is the conclusion, 'It is obviously the case that all self-induced abortions are nothing more than murders', a factual or *a priori* claim? If it is a factual assertion then, while accepted as true, it could have been false. Could the arguer describe a logically possible example of self-induced abortion that, at the same time, is not murder? If the arguer cannot or will not give such an example, then the conclusion is likely not a factual claim, but an *a priori* one. In that case, the conclusion is accepted as "obviously" true, not because of appeals to particular phenomena in the world, but because of some covert definitions of 'abortion' and 'murder'.

Because of what is meant by 'factual claim', factual claims about particular phenomena are not certain beyond any logically possible doubt. Indeed, it is contradictory, by definition, to say some claim is "an absolutely certain factual claim." Only when the distinction between factual and *a priori* claims is overlooked can there be the illusion of absolute factual certainty.

## 16.  QUESTION BEGGING

*Question Begging Fallacies* **occur in presenting an argument in ways suggesting a position on the conclusion without giving rationally acceptable evidence for that conclusion or giving only weak evidence.**

The purpose of an argument is to supply evidence in support of some claim. Question begging fallacies thwart this purpose.

Emotional or slanted language can introduce question begging fallacies into an argument. A salesperson argues that her product is better constructed than its competitors:

> **(1)**  The Super Doodad is obviously better constructed than its competitors. After all Super Doodad has superior parts and is indisputably assembled under the most advanced conditions.

Expressions such as 'obviously', 'indisputably', and 'it is obviously the case' can all be used to influence the receiver to accept the conclusion of an argument. And to use phrases such as 'superior parts' and 'advanced conditions' in arguments without defining them in any specific way is also to beg the question.

Definitions posing as factual claims can also be question begging. Suppose someone says,

> **(2)**  Genuine religion never leads to hypocrisy, conflict, hatred, or mutual distrust. Nonetheless, everything that goes or has gone under the name of 'religion' does this. Hence, there aren't any true religions now nor have there ever been any.

The conclusion in (2) is begged by an implicit definition of 'genuine religion' but presented as a factual claim in the first premise. But confusing a definition for a factual claim can never be acceptable in rational thought.*

---

## *EXERCISES*

**Group A:**

Consider each of the following examples. First determine which are arguments and which are not. Then, for those that are arguments, isolate, name, and explain any instance of a fallacy, or fallacies, that the arguments have. Remember, some arguments might be cogent.

1.  In Japan there is a general philosophy that government is the protector of the people and industries because of the vast dependence on the government. [*The Atlanta Constitution*; 2 November 1987]

2.  After years of complaining about Soviet interference in United Nations peace keeping efforts, particularly in the Middle East, the Administration flatly rejected recent Soviet

---

*See Chapter 13, Section 15.

offers of cooperation in arranging both a United Nations cease-fire in the Persian Gulf and a United Nations-sponsored Middle East peace parley. [*The New York Times*; 3 November 1987]

3. These roads must be expanded. And now is the time to plan and build roads that will be necessary to meet transportation needs in the next century. Some think the path from gridlock is found by divorcing Americans from their cars. They suggest that raising the federal gasoline tax by as much as 50 cents or $1 per gallon will force people to drive less and flock to mass transit. In fact, such an action would probably exacerbate the problem. [*USA Today*; 21 September 1988]

4. Pharmaceutical companies say they have no plans to seek Food and Drug Administration approval [of the new abortion-inducing drug, RU 486] that is necessary to sell abortion-inducing drugs in the United States. They say publicly that they are not cowed by the anti-abortion movement and that they had other reasons for not selling such drugs. . . . One company executive . . . said his company feared that if it sold such a drug, it would suffer greatly from a boycott by millions of members of National Right to Life and by "all the physicians, pharmacists and lay people who don't believe in abortions." [*The New York Times*; 22 February 1988]

5. It is ridiculous that the United States justice system uses murder as a tool of punishment. I don't feel that human beings have the right to judge whether another human being is to live or die. I feel that it is unfair to take this young lady's life when there are hundreds of people who have committed murders just as brutal and who are living it up in prison. [*Ebony Magazine*; September 1988]

6. Technically and tactically proficient sergeants and creative, demanding unit commanders make the difference between Reserve-force units that perform to Army standards and those that do not. . . . Quality leadership and a return to basic military discipline can go a long way toward alleviating the sad state of "weekend warriors." [*U.S. News and World Report*; 16 October 1989]

7. People who behave or act in unorthodox but perfectly logical ways aren't eccentrics. I call such people creative, forward-thinking professionals. You mention Dr. Patch Adams, who dresses like a clown and does not charge his patients any fees. He is simply acting out his philosophy and should not be considered an eccentric. The people who should be labeled that way are those whose behavior cannot be explained rationally. [*Time Magazine*; 4 July 1988]

8. I have been married 11 years and have been unable to have children. When I saw the picture of the L'Esperance quints, it stirred up feelings I thought I had dealt with long ago. I was reminded how much I really would have loved to have a baby. What I don't understand is how a couple married less than two years, with three healthy children between them, could ever be candidates for a test-tube pregnancy. Why couldn't they be content with what God blessed them with and let others have a chance. [*People Magazine*; 20 June 1988]

9. In Atlanta, 700 anti-abortionists have been arrested for non-violent direct action since July. Operation Rescue there serves as a training school for activists who return home to lead rescues at local abortion mills. Over 29 million abortions have been performed in the USA since 1973. Public awareness has been raised by the "body finds" of aborted children pulled out of garbage bins behind abortuaries. The shock and indignation from these finds often lead to an increase in activism. [*USA Today*; 14 September 1988]

10. Let's go back to a system where morals come first and the drive to make a quick buck is

second. There are too many people concerned only with how quickly they can make a million dollars. I think that attitude has got to go. What ever happened to the honest, hardworking American? . . . Let's see a return to education. Let's make teachers some of the highest paid professionals. . . . I guarantee that if a college student flipped on the television and saw that teachers were now being paid $150,000 a year and stockbrokers $35,000, he'd switch his course of study very quickly. [*American Banker*; 10 March 1989]

11. The Democrats are asking, "Where was George?" . . . Well, he was exactly where he belonged—standing in the shadow of his president. George Bush may or may not have the makings of a great leader, but he should not be judged harshly for doing what a good vice-president is supposed to do. [*Newsweek*; 29 August 1988]

12. [Concerning a flag amendment] I am appalled, shocked, and deeply saddened by Congress's failure to rise above politics and do what is clearly the decent thing to do. The message an amendment would send is not that "we are an insecure nation that cannot tolerate mindless expression by a few citizens," rather, the message would be that "we are a caring nation that holds the sacrifices of hundreds of thousands of Americans sacred." [*U. S. News and World Report*; 9 July 1990]

13. The controversy over whether homosexuals should be ordained as clergy and the demand for toleration toward gays [*Religion*. Nov. 13] are yet other sad indications that modern Christianity is decaying into little more that a high-minded social club. Those who are attempting to adapt church rules to their own lifestyles forget the underlying principle of Christianity. True Christianity is built on the unshakable foundation laid down by God, not man. God's laws cannot be modified to accommodate the whims of social conscience. [*Time*; 4 December 1989]

14. It is perilous to assess any president's legacy when he is still in office, and the final chapter has yet to be written on many of the administration's most important undertakings. But the promotion of free trade and controlled immigration, plus growing cooperation on drug enforcement within the hemisphere, are vital issues on which the Reagan administration has made some beginnings. There is much to be said for a "genuine North American Accord." [*The Atlanta Constitution*; 22 February 1988]

15. I don't care what the Glasnosters say—it is an absolute, carved-in-stone, 100% true fact, understood by every military leader on either side of the Iron Curtain, that the Soviets' military strategy boils down to two ferocious words: FIRST STRIKE! . . . Soviet military planners intend to hit us with everything in their arsenal, and they plan to do it before we can make a defensive move. What does it take to get that through the thick heads of some Americans? This is not some whispered speculation spread by "right wing nuts!" It is plain, simple, well-known truth. [*The American Sentinel*; 13 April 1987]

## Group B:

Present arguments for four claims you support. In each argument use one of the fallacies discussed in Sections 13 through 16, using a different fallacy in each argument. Make these arguments as persuasive as possible. Next, construct a cogent argument for each of your original four claims. Test your arguments by having them criticized by members of your class.

## Group C:

Find an example of each of the four fallacies discussed in Sections 13 through 16 in newspapers, magazines, textbooks, or the like.

**Group D:**

Find as many fallacies, and other poor features—bad definitions, emotional language—of rational thought, as you can in the following letter. Do not limit yourself to the particular fallacies discussed in this and the previous chapter. Fallacies, informal and formal, might occur for which you have no name. In such cases, describe the situation and then explain why you judge that a fallacious argument is being presented. Also mark all instances of emotive language that is given to persuade the reader to accept the views of Mr. Snodgrass. Explain why you mark the passages you do.

Dear Editor:

1    This is the first letter I've ever written to a newspaper. If certain things don't stop, it won't be my last. I am sick and tired of working hard only to pay more and more taxes so those stupid liberal folks in Washington can take my money to spend on supporting filth. When is anyone going to listen to us hard-working, decent, God-fearing folks? All you have to do is look around
5    at all the sin and corruption in the world and especially in our United States of America! One thing is for sure, if we decent folks aren't going to do something about it all, God is.

In fact, it is obvious today God is beginning really to publicly punish, and even wipe out, one of the very worst of all of them in His eyes. He is attacking and killing off all those queers who do awful unnatural things with one another. And isn't it about high time we follow His
10    commandments and examples, too? After all, we know very well from Holy Scripture that God punishes sinners. Everyone knows what happened to Sodom and Gomorrah and why God did what He did to those disgusting Sodomites! It's all there in *Genesis* 19: 1–25. Further St. Paul most clearly says in *Romans* 1:26–27 that homosexuality is unnatural and therefore is punishable by God. And who is a homosexual? He's a queer and a pervert. He's a man who
15    loves other men. People—that scum—who do such things, as St. Paul says in *Romans* 1:32, "are worthy of death."

And why should we go any easier on these queers than we do on rapists? At least rapists are doing something natural as far as sex goes. Rapists attack unprotected women, don't they? We want to protect our women who are, after all, too weak to protect themselves. We spend money
20    and make laws to protect our women and put rapists behind bars. (I think they should all be castrated the minute they're caught.) Why don't we spend money and make laws to protect our kids from perverts? Queers are to our kids just like rapists are to our women, only worse. Kids are more innocent and less suspecting than women. Even if a queer doesn't attack any kid, just him being around sets a bad example. Everybody knows what a pervert looks like. You
25    only have to turn on the TV to see thousands of them. Some try to hide like that Rock Hudson guy. But all you had to do was look in his eyes to know that he was one of them.

Us decent, God-fearing folks are getting pretty sick of all this. If we don't stop those queers, there's no telling how many of them we're going to have in the next ten years. Then what is going to happen to the human race? God said be fruitful and multiply. He didn't say be fruity.
30    And the only way queers can multiply is to seduce our kids. They're doing that all the time. Pretty soon there won't be any kids left to grow up and have normal families in our great country. Then the Communists will take over what's left of us. Anyway Communism is a queer government and that's why all those queers out there like red.

And just look at the way queers live. It's bad enough the way they dress, walk, and talk. It's
35    just plain disgusting to have to watch that in public. They have no sense of decency or shame. Like I say, this is bad enough. But how about all of those bath houses and gay bars you hear about? And what's so gay about them? It makes me, a decent, God-fearing person, just plain want to throw up when I imagine all the perversion those perverts do in them. If two of them would just stay stuck together. But they have to trade around all the time. I mean, I was in the

40   men's room last week in a real nice department store and one of them approached me. Let me tell you, I socked him right in the nose. Knocked him down. I think I broke his nose. It certainly was bleeding all over him. I did what the Lord wants any God fearing person to do. That's what my preacher said to me, too, when I told him about it.

The more I think about all this, the madder I get. God knows all those queers are sick.
45   They're all crazy. It's obvious to any moral person. You'd have to be crazy to be queer, and they're all just that—perverts. So it must be that they're all crazy. They are dangerous crazies. It's no telling what one of them would do if he could get his hands on you. They all need to be locked up in crazy houses. After all, that's what we do with other crazy folks. Lock them up. If we locked all those queers up together, we'd protect our kids, the human race, and the God-
50   given American way of life. Then when they're all locked up together, they can do whatever they want to with each other. If we're going to ever have a decent and moral life, we've got to get rid of all those crazy, unnatural queers. That's why I say let's get rid of them. Round them up. Lock them up. Then we'll all have a decent and moral life.

But those sinful politicians in Washington won't listen to us good folks out here. So God is
55   taking over. He's getting rid of the queers. Justice is Mine saith the Lord. And being queer is a sin worthy of death. So what do we see the good Lord doing? He's using *AIDS*, a vile disease ending in death, to kill off all those perverts. Of the millions of cases of *AIDS* in this great God fearing country of ours, almost all of them are queers. The rest are dirty drug pushers. So isn't it likely that all queers are going to get *AIDS* and die from it at the hand of God? God works in
60   strange and wondrous ways His powers to make known. Somebody is going to say that not everybody with *AIDS* is a pervert or dirty drug pusher. Well, I wonder about that. Even if it's true, it's the queers' fault they got *AIDS* and gave it to innocent folks. Nobody's making them be queers. It's their own free choice. Anyway in fighting in the holy army of God, some of His soldiers are going to get killed by the enemy. But they're going to a better life.

65   Those sinners in Washington are just about as bad as the perverts. Everybody knows God is using *AIDS* to fight the queers. Yet those liberals in Washington want to take my hard-earned money, and yours too, to find a cure for *AIDS*. They want to fight against God's divine plan and help queers get well. I tell you, I'm sick of my honest money being used to support the Devil and his works. Stop this *AIDS* research right now, I say, and let God do what He must. And
70   while they're at it they can also stop spending money on abortions to murder all of those babies. And stop letting liberal trash burn our American flag. And they can also stop trying to take away guns from us law-abiding folks. If somebody gets pregnant she ought to have the baby. If they don't stop all of this they are no better than the queers in the eyes of God.

I know my letter is long. A lot of folks won't like it either. But for our kids, country, and God's
75   sake I hope you print it. There're lots of us good folks out here who love God and our neighbors, and want to do what's right no matter what. It just makes us sick to see what is going on all around us.

Thank you,

Jimmie Snodgrass

In the next to last paragraph, Mr. Snodgrass suggests his views concerning abortion and federal spending in this area, as well as burning the American flag and gun control laws. Using his letter as a model, write a letter that would be acceptable to Mr. Snodgrass dealing with one of these topics. Use as many different types of fallacies, and other flaws in rational thought, as you can while also making your letter sound persuasive. You and your classmates might wish to exchange letters and critique each other's work.

## 17. REVIEW OF NEW TERMS

**Ad Hominem Fallacies:** Occur when an attempt is made to discredit an argument by bringing into question in some negative way the presenter of the argument instead of the argument itself. There are two types of *ad hominem* fallacies; namely, *abusive ad hominem* and *circumstantial ad hominem*; Against the Man.

**Ad Hominem Abusive:** Occurs when a person attempts to discredit an argument by attacking the character of the initiator of that argument.

**Ad Hominem Circumstantial:** Occurs when a person attempts to discredit an argument by attacking the personal surroundings, involvements, or interests of the initiator of the argument: *Poisoning the Well*.

**Against the Man:** See *Ad hominem Fallacies*.

**Apriorism Fallacy:** See *Factual Certainty Fallacy*.

**A priori claim:** A statement the truth or falsity of which does not depend on the existence or nonexistence of any particular phenomenon in the empirical world.

**Begging the Question Fallacy:** See *Circular Argument Fallacy*.

**Circular Argument Fallacy:** Occurs when the conclusion of an argument is a restatement, usually in different vocabulary or form, of one of the premises; *Begging the Question*.

**Confusing Necessary and Sufficient Conditions Fallacy:** Occurs when a necessary condition is presented as a sufficient one or a sufficient condition is taken as a necessary one in supporting some conclusion.

**Deceptive Alternatives Fallacy:** Occurs when a disjunctive premise incorrectly suggests, explicitly or implicitly, that the alternatives mentioned by the disjunction are mutually exclusive and exhaust all possible alternatives relevant to the conclusion; *False Dilemma*.

**Desire Fallacy:** See *Wishful Thinking Fallacy*.

**Domino Fallacy:** See *Slippery Slope Fallacy*.

**Factual claim:** A statement the truth or falsity of which depends on the existence or nonexistence of some particular phenomenon in the empirical world.

**Factual Certainty Fallacy:** Occurs when it is suggested, explicitly or implicitly, that a factual claim is absolutely beyond any doubt whatsoever; that no evidence can count against that claim; *Apriorism*.

**False Dilemma:** See *Deceptive Alternatives*.

**Gambler's Fallacy:** Occurs when it is suggested as evidence for some conclusion that simply because a random event has had a certain run in the past it will have a different outcome in the future.

**Inconsistency Fallacies:** Occur when an argument contains contradictory claims, or when an arguer claims one thing at one time and its contradiction at another without providing reasons for this change of position.

**Is-Ought Fallacy:** Occurs when a conclusion asserting what ought to be the case is based solely on considerations of what is or has been the case. This fallacy also occurs in arguments asserting that something ought not to be the case solely because it is not nor has been the case.

**Novelty Fallacy:** Occurs when there is an attempt to substantiate some conclusion by appealing simply to the fact that something is new, modern, or the latest fad.

**Poisoning the Well:** See *Ad Hominem Circumstantial*.

**Post Hoc Fallacy:** A specific Questionable Cause Fallacy that occurs within an argument when it is assumed that merely because some phenomenon always, or usually, temporally proceeds another, the former is the cause of the latter.

**Question Begging Fallacies:** Occur in presenting an argument in ways suggesting a position on the conclusion without giving rationally acceptable evidence for that conclusion or giving only weak evidence.

**Questionable Causes Fallacy:** Occurs when (1) a phenomenon is claimed to be the cause of something when it is not or when a phenomenon is claimed to be the cause of something when there is poor evidence to support that it is and (2) this causal claim is offered as evidence for some conclusion. Three specific types of Questionable Cause Fallacies are the *Post Hoc* Fallacy, the Simple Correlation Fallacy, and the Statistical Correlation Fallacy.

**Red Herring Fallacy:** Occurs when an attempt to discredit an argument is made by interjecting considerations that, while broadly related to the original argument, are extraneous to the specific claims of that argument.

**Simple Correlation Fallacy:** A specific Questionable Cause Fallacy that occurs within an argument when it is assumed that mere correlation between two phenomena is sufficient to establish a causal relation between those phenomena.

**Slippery Slope Fallacy:** Occurs when it is asserted without appropriate evidence that one phenomenon will necessarily lead to another, and that this second will necessarily lead to still another in a chain of events until some final situation, usually unpleasant, is brought about; *Domino Fallacy*.

**Statistical Correlation Fallacy:** A specific Questionable Cause Fallacy that occurs within an argument when it is assumed that the mere probable correlation between two phenomena is sufficient to establish a causal relation between those phenomena.

**Straw Man Fallacy:** Occurs when an attempt to discredit an argument is made by recasting it in a weak, exaggerated or foolish way not intended by the arguer and, then, attacking that refashioned argument as if it were the original one.

**Tu Quoque Fallacy:** Occurs when (1) there is an attempt to defend an argument against attack by suggesting that the critic has done something very similar, if not the same thing, as what is being attacked, or (2) that the critic is presenting an argument as difficult to sustain as the argument under attack; *Two Wrongs Make a Right*.

**Two Wrongs Make a Right:** See *Tu Quoque Fallacy*.

**Wishful Thinking Fallacy:** Occurs when desiring or believing that some claim is correct (incorrect) is substituted for evidence for that claim being correct (incorrect); *Wishful Thinking*.

UNIVERSITY OF BRISTOL

Department of Philosophy

9 Woodland Road
Bristol
BS8 1TB

# ANSWERS FOR
# SELECTED EXERCISES

Notations such as '6.4.D.' appear in the following. The first entry indicates the specific chapter in question. The second entry designates the section of that chapter. The capital letter, if there is one, indicates the group of exercises in that section. The page numbers of that section or group are enclosed in parentheses.

## CHAPTER 1

### 1.1. (3)

There are exercises in this book that require a student to give AND defend personal opinions concerning some topic. Here is one. When these exercises are done in class, they are good ice breakers. Students can become better acquainted with one another and the different opinions of their classmates.

### 1.1.A. (3)

Lively discussions, in class or out, can be generated by this exercise. On the surface most people would agree that it is reasonable to suppose that acting in accordance with true claims increases the likelihood of reaching desired goals and avoiding unpleasant situations. But, then, there is the issue of acting in accordance with a false claim—perhaps a lie—to one's own advantage regardless of the advantage of anyone else. Even dismissing the issue of lying, what is involved in being reasonable and what are rational standards to use in setting one's goals?

### 1.1.B. (3)

There are generally some local campus and town issues about which students, faculty, and administration have strong, and divided, opinions. Think about discussing some of these issues with the goal of both clarifying them and coming to some tentative resolution for which supportive reasons are given.

### 1.2. (8–9)

In having to reconstruct an argument in accordance with the Principle of Charity, there is often the possibility for legitimate differences of opinion of what is to be added and why. In the following, when a reconstruction is needed, whatever is added is clearly marked. There might be other acceptable possibilities.

**1.**

    **1)** The Razorbacks will win only if they play well.

    **2)** The Razorbacks play well.

    **3)** Therefore, the Razorbacks will win.

**3.**

    **1)** Murder is always morally wrong.

    **2)** *Abortion is a form of murder.* [added premise]

    **3)** So, abortion is always morally wrong.

**5.**

    **1)** A recent study of known carriers of the retrovirous, HTLV-3, shows that 53% are needle users.

    **2)** Needles are used by a sizable number of drug users.

    **3)** Hence, the majority of instances of contracting HTLV-3 now probably comes through intravenous drug use.

**7.**

    **1)** *The defining characteristic of 'sweatshop' is a place with non-functioning exits and sealed windows.* [added premise]

    **2)** This place has non-functioning exits and sealed windows.

    **3)** Accordingly, this place fits the definition of a sweatshop perfectly.

**9.**

    **1)** There has been a drop in the dollar against both the yen and the mark, coupled with a slow decrease in the national deficit.

    **2)** *A weak dollar and a high deficit is each an indicator of rising inflation.* [added premise]

    **3)** Thus, inflation can be expected to rise substantially over the next several years.

**11.**

    **1)** In a controlled study, volunteers with a family history of alcoholics, and a control group who didn't have alcoholics in their families, were given stress tests and then measured for the amount of adrenalin injected into their bloodstream.

    **2)** *Those with a history of alcoholism in their families tended to have low levels of adrenalin.* [added premise]

    **3)** So, people with low levels of adrenalin may be more susceptible to alcoholism.

**13.**

    **1)** More people in the United States have died in Toyotas than any other automobile.

    **2)** *Toyota is a Japanese made automobile.* [added premise]

    **3)** Thus, according to the American automotive industry, the Japanese are lagging behind in auto safety.

**15.**

    **1)** It is clearly the case that if there is less premarital sex among college students, there is less need for abortions within that group.

    **2)** It is equally as obvious that premarital sex will continue within that group at its current rate, if not increase in frequency.

    **3)** Accordingly, there will continue to be the need, among college students, for practicing abortion at the current rate or higher.

**1.3.A. (13–14)**

**1.** argument

**3.** explanation

**5.** argument

**7.** explanation

**9.** explanation

**11.** description

**13.** argument

**15.** description

**1.4. (19–20)**

**1.** deductive

**3.** inductive ('likely')

**5.** inductive ('probably')

**7.** deductive

**9.** deductive

**11.** inductive ('probably')

**13.** deductive

**15.** deductive

# CHAPTER 2

**2.3. (34)**

| | | | |
|---|---|---|---|
| **1.** ~D | **5.** ~R | **9.** ~A | **13.** ~S |
| **3.** L | **7.** I | **11.** I | **15.** ~A |

**2.4. (38–39)**

| | | | |
|---|---|---|---|
| **1.** P · K | **5.** ~K · P | **9.** ~R · A | **13.** I · P |
| **3.** S · ~L | **7.** C · F | **11.** V · P | **15.** C · R |

**2.5. (41–42)**

| | |
|---|---|
| **1.** P △ B | **9.** L ∨ C |
| **3.** ~S ∨ H | **11.** ~D △ ~C |
| **5.** ~P △ A | **13.** W ∨ Q |
| **7.** E ∨ A | **15.** W ∨ ~S |

**2.6. (45)**

| | |
|---|---|
| **1.** M ∨ ~G | **9.** ~[(J · L) · T] |
| **3.** ~(M ∨ ~G) | **11.** ~(I ∨ ~C) · T |
| **5.** (C ∨ A) ∨ ~F | **13.** (S · ~T) · E |
| **7.** ~(B · M) · R | **15.** ~{~T · ~[(E ∨ C) · (S ∨ Q)]} |

**2.7. (51)**

**1.**

| A | B | A · B | ~(A · B) |
|---|---|---|---|
| 1 | 1 | 1 | 0 |
| 1 | 0 | 0 | 1 |
| 0 | 1 | 0 | 1 |
| 0 | 0 | 0 | 1 |

**3.**

| A | B | A ∨ B | ~(A ∨ B) |
|---|---|---|---|
| 1 | 1 | 1 | 0 |
| 1 | 0 | 1 | 0 |
| 0 | 1 | 1 | 0 |
| 0 | 0 | 0 | 1 |

**5.**

| A | B | ~A | ~~A | ~B | ~~A • ~B |
|---|---|----|-----|----|----------|
| 1 | 1 | 0 | 1 | 0 | 0 |
| 1 | 0 | 0 | 1 | 1 | 1 |
| 0 | 1 | 1 | 0 | 0 | 0 |
| 0 | 0 | 1 | 0 | 1 | 0 |

**2.8.A.  (56–57)**

**7.**

| A | B | C | ~B | ~A | ~B Δ ~A | (~B Δ ~A) • C |
|---|---|---|----|----|---------|----------------|
| 1 | 1 | 1 | 0 | 0 | 0 | 0 |
| 1 | 1 | 0 | 0 | 0 | 0 | 0 |
| 1 | 0 | 1 | 1 | 0 | 1 | 0 |
| 0 | 1 | 1 | 0 | 1 | 1 | 1 |
| 0 | 1 | 0 | 0 | 1 | 1 | 0 |
| 0 | 0 | 1 | 1 | 1 | 0 | 0 |
| 0 | 0 | 0 | 1 | 1 | 0 | 0 |

**9.**

| A | B | C | ~C | ~A | ~C ∨ ~A | (~C ∨ ~A) Δ B |
|---|---|---|----|----|---------|----------------|
| 1 | 1 | 1 | 0 | 0 | 0 | 1 |
| 1 | 1 | 0 | 1 | 0 | 1 | 0 |
| 1 | 0 | 1 | 0 | 0 | 0 | 0 |
| 1 | 0 | 0 | 1 | 0 | 1 | 1 |
| 0 | 1 | 1 | 0 | 1 | 1 | 0 |
| 0 | 1 | 0 | 1 | 1 | 1 | 0 |
| 0 | 0 | 1 | 0 | 1 | 1 | 1 |
| 0 | 0 | 0 | 1 | 1 | 1 | 1 |

**2.8.A.  (56–57)**

**1.** ~F ⊃ B

**3.** F ⊃ D

**5.** P ⊃ M

**7.** (I ∨ A) ⊃ (I ⊃ D)

**9.** (P ⊃ W) • (W ⊃ F)

**11.** R ⊃ ~(W ∨ H)

**13.** ~{[S • ~(C ⊃ D)] • ~D}

**15.** T ⊃ [(~C • ~ ~ ~D) ∨ ~(B ∨ ~Y)]

**2.8.B.  (57)**

**1.**

| F | B | ~F | ~F ⊃ B |
|---|---|----|--------|
| 1 | 1 | 0 | 1 |
| 1 | 0 | 0 | 1 |
| 0 | 1 | 1 | 1 |
| 0 | 0 | 1 | 0 |

**3.**

| F | D | F ⊃ D |
|---|---|-------|
| 1 | 1 | 1 |
| 1 | 0 | 0 |
| 0 | 1 | 1 |
| 0 | 0 | 1 |

**5.**

| P | M | P ⊃ M |
|---|---|-------|
| 1 | 1 | 1 |
| 1 | 0 | 0 |
| 0 | 1 | 1 |
| 0 | 0 | 1 |

**7.**

| I | A | D | I ∨ A | I ⊃ D | (I ∨ A) ⊃ (I ⊃ D) |
|---|---|---|---|---|---|
| 1 | 1 | 1 | 1 | 1 | 1 |
| 1 | 1 | 0 | 1 | 0 | 0 |
| 1 | 0 | 1 | 1 | 1 | 1 |
| 1 | 0 | 0 | 1 | 0 | 0 |
| 0 | 1 | 1 | 1 | 1 | 1 |
| 0 | 1 | 0 | 1 | 1 | 1 |
| 0 | 0 | 1 | 0 | 1 | 1 |
| 0 | 0 | 0 | 0 | 1 | 1 |

**9.**

| P | W | F | P ⊃ W | W ⊃ F | (P ⊃ W) · (W ⊃ F) |
|---|---|---|---|---|---|
| 1 | 1 | 1 | 1 | 1 | 1 |
| 1 | 1 | 0 | 1 | 0 | 0 |
| 1 | 0 | 1 | 0 | 1 | 0 |
| 1 | 0 | 0 | 0 | 1 | 0 |
| 0 | 1 | 1 | 1 | 1 | 1 |
| 0 | 1 | 0 | 1 | 0 | 0 |
| 0 | 0 | 1 | 1 | 1 | 1 |
| 0 | 0 | 0 | 1 | 1 | 1 |

**2.9.A.  (60–61)**

**1.** S ≡ F

**3.** B ≡ C

**5.** (F ≡ O) ⊃ ~D

**7.** A ≡ ~(~S ∨ ~E)

**9.** (C Δ D) ≡ (L Δ N)

**11.** ~(A Δ B) ≡ (~W • ~P)

**13.** [(M • S) ⊃ P] ≡ (E · C)

**15.** ~(L ∨ P) ≡ [(S ∨ ~M) ⊃ (~W • ∨)]

**2.9.B.  (61)**

**1.**

| S | F | S ≡ F |
|---|---|---|
| 1 | 1 | 1 |
| 1 | 0 | 0 |
| 0 | 1 | 0 |
| 0 | 0 | 1 |

**3.**

| B | C | B ≡ C |
|---|---|---|
| 1 | 1 | 1 |
| 1 | 0 | 0 |
| 0 | 1 | 0 |
| 0 | 0 | 1 |

**5.**

| F | O | D | ~D | F ≡ O | (F ≡ O) ⊃ ~D |
|---|---|---|---|---|---|
| 1 | 1 | 1 | 0 | 1 | 0 |
| 1 | 1 | 0 | 1 | 1 | 1 |
| 1 | 0 | 1 | 0 | 0 | 1 |
| 1 | 0 | 0 | 1 | 0 | 1 |
| 0 | 1 | 1 | 0 | 0 | 1 |
| 0 | 1 | 0 | 1 | 0 | 1 |
| 0 | 0 | 1 | 0 | 1 | 0 |
| 0 | 0 | 0 | 1 | 1 | 1 |

**7.**

| A | S | E | ~S | ~E | ~S ∨ ~E | A ≡ (~S ∨ ~E) |
|---|---|---|---|---|---|---|
| 1 | 1 | 1 | 0 | 0 | 0 | 0 |
| 1 | 1 | 0 | 0 | 1 | 1 | 1 |
| 1 | 0 | 1 | 1 | 0 | 1 | 1 |
| 1 | 0 | 0 | 1 | 1 | 1 | 1 |
| 0 | 1 | 1 | 0 | 0 | 0 | 1 |
| 0 | 1 | 0 | 0 | 1 | 1 | 0 |
| 0 | 0 | 1 | 1 | 0 | 1 | 0 |
| 0 | 0 | 0 | 1 | 1 | 1 | 0 |

**11.**

| A | B | W | P | ~W | ~P | A △ B | ~(A △ B) | ~W · ~P | ~(A △ B) ≡ (~W · ~P) |
|---|---|---|---|---|---|---|---|---|---|
| 1 | 1 | 1 | 1 | 0 | 0 | 0 | 1 | 0 | 0 |
| 1 | 1 | 1 | 0 | 0 | 1 | 0 | 1 | 0 | 0 |
| 1 | 1 | 0 | 1 | 1 | 0 | 0 | 1 | 0 | 0 |
| 1 | 1 | 0 | 0 | 1 | 1 | 0 | 1 | 1 | 1 |
| 1 | 0 | 1 | 1 | 0 | 0 | 1 | 0 | 0 | 1 |
| 1 | 0 | 1 | 0 | 0 | 1 | 1 | 0 | 0 | 1 |
| 1 | 0 | 0 | 1 | 1 | 0 | 1 | 0 | 0 | 1 |
| 1 | 0 | 0 | 0 | 1 | 1 | 1 | 0 | 1 | 0 |
| 0 | 1 | 1 | 1 | 0 | 0 | 1 | 0 | 0 | 1 |
| 0 | 1 | 1 | 0 | 0 | 1 | 1 | 0 | 0 | 1 |
| 0 | 1 | 0 | 1 | 1 | 0 | 1 | 0 | 0 | 1 |
| 0 | 1 | 0 | 0 | 1 | 1 | 1 | 0 | 1 | 0 |
| 0 | 0 | 1 | 1 | 0 | 0 | 0 | 1 | 0 | 0 |
| 0 | 0 | 1 | 0 | 0 | 1 | 0 | 1 | 0 | 0 |
| 0 | 0 | 0 | 1 | 1 | 0 | 0 | 1 | 0 | 0 |
| 0 | 0 | 0 | 0 | 1 | 1 | 0 | 1 | 1 | 1 |

# CHAPTER 3

**3.1. (67–68)**

**1.** O · ~ N

```
1 0 0 1
1 1 1 0
0 0 0 1
0 0 1 0
  ⇑
```

**3.** ~ (B · ~ B)

```
1  1 0 01
1  0 0 10
⇑
```

**5.** ~ (G ∨ D)

```
0  1 1 1
0  1 1 0
0  0 1 1
1  0 0 0
⇑
```

**7.** (O · R) ⊃ (~ O ⊃ ~ R)

```
1 1 1 1  0 1 1 0 1
1 0 0 1  0 1 1 1 0
0 0 1 1  1 0 1 0 1
0 0 0 1  1 0 1 1 0
    ⇑
```

13. **[(W · N) ∨ (W · E)] ∨ ~ (W ∨ S)**

```
1 1 1  1    1 1 1    1  0 1  1 1
1 1 1  1    1 1 1    1  0 1  1 0
1 1 1  1    1 0 0    1  0 1  1 1
1 1 1  1    1 0 0    1  0 1  1 0
1 0 0  1    1 1 1    1  0 1  1 1
1 0 0  1    1 1 1    1  0 1  1 0
1 0 0  0    1 0 0    0  0 1  1 1
1 0 0  0    1 0 0    0  0 1  1 0
0 0 1  0    0 0 1    0  0 0  1 1
0 0 1  0    0 0 1    1  1 0  0 0
0 0 1  0    0 0 0    0  0 0  1 1
0 0 1  0    0 0 0    1  1 0  0 0
0 0 0  0    0 0 1    0  0 0  1 1
0 0 0  0    0 0 1    1  1 0  0 0
0 0 0  0    0 0 0    0  0 0  1 1
0 0 0  0    0 0 0    1  1 0  0 0
                     ⇑
```

### 3.2. (70–71)

**1.  S ∨ ~ S**

```
1 1 0 1
0 1 1 0
   ⇑
TAUTOLOGY
```

**3.  P ⊃ ~ Q**

```
1 0 0 1
1 1 1 0
1 0 0 1
0 1 1 0
   ⇑
CONTINGENT
```

**5.  ~ (A · L) ⊃ (~ L ∨ ~ A)**

```
0  1 1 1   0 1 0 0 1
1  1 0 0 1   1 0 1 0 1
1  0 0 1 1   0 1 1 1 0
1  0 0 0 1   1 0 1 1 0
        ⇑
      TAUTOLOGY
```

**7.  (K ∨ R) · (R ∨ B)**

```
1 1 1  1   1 1 1
1 1 1  1   1 1 0
1 1 0  1   0 1 1
1 1 0  0   0 0 0
0 1 1  1   1 1 1
0 1 1  1   1 1 0
0 0 0  0   0 1 1
0 0 0  0   0 0 0
      ⇑
 CONTINGENT
```

**9.  [L · (C ∨ W)] ⊃ [(L · C) ∨ (L · W)]**

```
1 1 1 1 1   1   1 1 1 1 1 1 1
1 1 1 1 0   1   1 1 1 1 1 0 0
1 1 0 1 1   1   1 0 0 1 1 1 1
1 0 0 0 0   1   1 0 0 0 1 0 0
0 0 1 1 1   1   0 0 1 0 0 0 1
0 0 1 1 0   1   0 0 1 0 0 0 0
0 0 0 1 1   1   0 0 0 0 0 0 1
0 0 0 0 0   1   0 0 0 0 0 0 0
            ⇑
        TAUTOLOGY
```

**13.** $[(E \lor N) \lor S] \equiv \sim W$

```
1 1 1  1 1 0 0 1
1 1 1  1 1 1 1 0
1 1 1  1 0 0 0 1
1 1 1  1 0 1 1 0
1 1 0  1 1 0 0 1
1 1 0  1 1 1 1 0
1 1 0  1 0 0 0 1
1 1 0  1 0 1 1 0
0 1 1  1 1 0 0 1
0 1 1  1 1 1 1 0
0 1 1  1 0 0 0 1
0 1 1  1 0 1 1 0
0 0 0  1 1 0 0 1
0 0 0  1 1 1 1 0
0 0 0  0 0 1 0 1
0 0 0  0 0 1 0 0
         ⇑
```
CONTINGENT

**3.3. (76–77)**

**1.**                /∴ ~ C

  **1)** C ∨ S   Pr

  **2)** S      Pr

  $\underline{[(C \lor S) \cdot S] \supset \sim C}$

```
1 1 1  1 1 0 0 1
1 1 0  0 0 1 0 1
0 1 1  1 1 1 1 0
0 0 0  0 0 1 1 0
        ⇑
```
CONTINGENT/INVALID

**3.**                /∴ ~ G

  **1)** ~R ⊃ G   Pr

  **2)** R        Pr

  $\underline{[(\sim R \supset G) \cdot R] \supset \sim G}$

```
0 1 1 1  1 1 0 0 1
0 1 1 0  1 1 1 1 0
1 0 1 1  0 0 1 0 1
1 0 0 0  0 0 1 1 0
          ⇑
```
CONTINGENT/INVALID

**5.**                 /∴ ~ (R · ~ L)

  **1)** R ∨ L   Pr
  **2)** ~ L     Pr

  $\underline{[(R \lor L) \cdot \sim L] \supset \sim (R \cdot \sim L)}$

```
1 1 1  0 0 1  1 1  1 0 0 1
1 1 0  1 1 0  0 0  1 1 1 0
0 1 1  0 0 1  1 1  0 0 0 1
0 0 0  0 1 0  1 1  0 0 1 0
              ⇑
```
CONTINGENT/INVALID

**7.**                 /∴ N △ M

  **1)** N △ S   Pr
  **2)** S ≡ M   Pr

  $\underline{[(N \bigtriangleup S) \cdot (S \equiv M)] \supset (N \bigtriangleup M)}$

```
1 0 1 0  1 1 1  1  1 0 1
1 0 1 0  1 0 0  1  1 1 0
1 1 0 0  0 0 1  1  1 0 1
1 1 0 1  0 1 0  1  1 1 0
0 1 1 1  1 1 1  1  0 1 1
0 1 1 0  1 0 0  1  0 0 0
0 0 0 0  0 0 1  1  0 1 1
0 0 0 0  1 0 1  1  0 0 0
                ⇑
```
TAUTOLOGY/VALID

**9.**                    /∴ F · S
   1) F · ~ A   Pr
   2) S △ A    Pr

[(F · ~ A) · (S △ A)] ⊃ (F · S)

```
1 0 01  0  1 0 1  1  1 1 1
1 0 01  0  0 1 1  1  1 0 0
1 1 10  1  1 1 0  1  1 1 1
1 1 10  0  0 0 0  1  1 0 0
0 0 01  0  1 0 1  1  0 0 1
0 0 01  0  0 1 1  1  0 0 0
0 0 10  0  1 1 0  1  0 0 1
0 0 10  0  0 0 0  1  0 0 0
                 ⇑
```
TAUTOLOGY/VALID

**11.**                    /∴ ~ S
   1) L ⊃ (R ⊃ S)   Pr
   2) ~ L            Pr
   3) L ∨ ~ R        Pr

({[L ⊃ (R ⊃ S)] · ~L} · (L ∨ ~ R)) ⊃ ~ S

```
1 1  1 1 1  0 0 1  0  1 1 0 1   1 0 1
1 0  1 0 0  0 0 1  0  1 1 0 1   1 1 0
1 1  0 1 1  0 0 1  0  1 1 1 0   1 0 1
1 1  0 1 0  0 0 1  0  1 1 1 0   1 1 0
0 1  1 1 1  1 1 0  0  0 0 0 1   1 0 1
0 1  1 0 0  1 1 0  0  0 0 0 1   1 1 0
0 1  0 1 1  1 1 0  1  0 1 1 0   0 0 1
0 1  0 1 0  1 1 0  1  0 1 1 0   1 1 0
                                 ⇑
```
CONTINGENT/INVALID

**17.**                              /∴ R △ B
   1) ~ A                     Pr
   2) (~ R · ~ B) ∨ A         Pr
   3) ~ A ≡ ~ (B · ~ R)       Pr

({~ A · [(~ R · ~ B) ∨ A]} · [~ A ≡ ~ (B · ~ R)]) ⊃ (R △ B)

```
0 1 0  0 1 0 0 1  1 1  0 0 1 0  1 1 0 0 1   1  1 0 1
0 1 0  0 1 0 1 0  1 1  0 0 1 0  1 0 0 0 1   1  1 1 0
0 1 0  1 0 0 0 1  1 1  0 0 1 1  0 1 1 1 0   1  0 1 1
0 1 0  1 0 1 1 0  1 1  0 0 1 0  1 0 0 1 0   1  0 0 0
1 0 0  0 1 0 0 1  0 0  0 1 0 1  1 1 0 0 1   1  1 0 1
1 0 0  0 1 0 1 0  0 0  0 1 0 1  1 0 0 0 1   1  1 1 0
1 0 0  1 0 0 0 1  0 0  0 1 0 0  0 1 1 1 0   1  0 1 1
1 0 1  1 0 1 1 0  1 0  1 1 0 0  1 0 0 1 0   0  0 0 0
                                            ⇑
```
CONTINGENT/INVALID

**3.4. (80–81)**

**1.**              /∴ S ⊃ C
   1) C · S   Pr

(C · S) · ~ (S ⊃ C)

```
1 1 1  0  0 1 1 1
1 0 0  0  0 0 1 1
0 0 1  0  1 1 0 0
0 0 0  0  0 0 1 0
       ⇑
```
CONTRADICTORY/VALID

**3.**                    /∴ ~ F
   1) F ∨ B   Pr
   2) B       Pr

[(F ∨ B) · B] · ~ ~F

```
1 1 1  1  1 1 1 0 1
1100 0 0 1 1 0 1
0111 1 0 0 0 1 0
0000 0 0 0 0 1 0
      ⇑
```

**5.**                    /∴ ~ R
   1) R △ I   Pr
   2) I       Pr

[(R △ I) · I] · ~ ~ R

```
1 0 1  0  1  0 1 0 1
1 1 0  0  0  0 1 0 1
0 1 1  1  1  0 0 1 0
0 0 0  0  0  0 0 1 0
             ⇑
```
CONTRADICTORY/VALID

**7.**                                    /∴ F
   **1)** (T · F) ⊃ P   Pr
   **2)** P            Pr

   {[(**T · F**) ⊃ **P**] · **P**} · ~ **F**

   1 1 1   1 1   1 1   0 0 1
   1 1 1   0 0   0 0   0 0 1
   1 0 0   1 1   1 1   1 1 0
   1 0 0   1 0   0 0   0 1 0
   0 0 1   1 1   1 1   0 0 1
   0 0 1   1 0   0 0   0 0 1
   0 0 0   1 1   1 1   1 1 0
   0 0 0   1 0   0 0   0 1 0
                 ⇑
   CONTINGENT/INVALID

**11.**                                  /∴ I · C
   **1)** I ≡ (C · E)   Pr
   **2)** C            Pr

   {[**I** ≡ (**C · E**)] · **C**} · ~ (**I · C**)

   1 1 1 1 1   1 1   0 0 1 1 1
   1 0 1 0 0   0 1   0 0 1 1 1
   1 0 0 0 0   0 0   0 1 1 0 0
   1 0 0 0 0   0 0   0 1 1 0 0
   0 0 1 1 1   0 1   0 1 0 0 1
   0 1 1 0 0   1 1   1 1 0 0 1
   0 1 0 0 1   0 0   0 1 0 0 0
   0 1 0 0 0   0 0   0 1 0 0 0
                 ⇑
   CONTINGENT/INVALID

**15.**                              /∴ ~ W ∨ P
   **1)** ~ (W · ~ H)   Pr
   **2)** ~ (~ P · H)   Pr

   [~ (**W** · ~ **H**) · ~ (~ **P** · **H**)] · ~ (~ **W** ∨ **P**)

   1   1 0 0 1   1 1   0 1 0 1   0   0 0 1 1 1
   1   1 0 0 1   0 0   1 0 1 1   0   1 0 1 0 0
   0   1 1 1 0   0 1   0 1 0 0   0   0 0 1 1 1
   0   1 1 1 0   0 1   1 0 0 0   0   1 0 1 0 0
   1   0 0 0 1   1 1   0 1 0 1   0   0 1 0 1 1
   1   0 0 0 1   0 0   1 0 1 1   0   0 1 0 1 0
   1   0 0 1 0   1 1   0 1 0 0   0   0 1 0 1 1
   1   0 0 1 0   1 1   1 0 0 0   0   0 1 0 1 0
                             ⇑
   CONTRADICTORY/VALID

**3.5. (85–86)**

**1.**       /∴ B ⊃ A            /∴ 1 ⊃ 0  = 0
   **1)** A            X 0          = 0

   **Interpretation**
   A = 0
   B = 1

   **VALID**

**3.**       /∴ B                /∴ 0  =  0
   **1)** (A ⊃ B) · A    X  (0 ⊃ 0) · 0      = 0

   **Interpretation**
   A = 0
   B = 0

   **VALID**

**5.**       /∴ B                /∴ 0  =  0
   **1)** (A ⊃ B) Δ A       (1 ⊃ 0) Δ 1      = 1

   **Interpretation**
   A = 1
   B = 0

   **INVALID**

**7.**                    /∴  C ∨ B              /∴  0 ∨ 0  = 0
**1)** (A ≡ B) ⊃ [C ∨ (A • B)]  X  (0 ≡ 0) ⊃ [0 ∨ (0 • 0)]  = 0
**2)** (A ⊃ C) • (C ⊃ B)             (0 ⊃ 0) •  (0 ⊃ 0)        = 1
**3)** (B ⊃ C) • (C ⊃ A)             (0 ⊃ 0) •  (0 ⊃ 0)        = 1

**Interpretation**

A = 0
B = 0
C = 0

**VALID**

**9.**              /∴  C Δ B        /∴  1 Δ 1  = 0
**1)** ~ [(B • ~ C) • ~ A]     ~ [(1 • ~ 1) • ~ 1]  = 1
**2)** ~ (A • ~ B)             ~ (1 • ~ 1)          = 1
**3)** ~ (~ C • ~ B)           ~ (~ 1 • ~ 1)        = 1

**Interpretation**

A = 1
B = 1
C = 1

**INVALID**

**15.**                   /∴  C ∨ ~ F                /∴  0 ∨ ~ 1 = 0
**1)** A ⊃ (B ⊃ C)               1 ⊃ (0 ⊃ 0)           = 1
**2)** ~ D ⊃ (E ⊃ ~ F)           ~ 1 ⊃ (1 ⊃ ~ 1)       = 1
**3)** ~ (A • D) ⊃ ~ (B ∨ E)     ~ (1 • 1) ⊃ ~ (0 ∨ 1) = 1
**4)** E ∨ B                     1 ∨ 0                 = 1

**Interpretation**

A = 1
B = 0
C = 0
D = 1
E = 1
F = 1

**INVALID**

**17.**             /∴  A ⊃ (B ≡ C)         /∴  1 ⊃ (0 ≡ 1) = 0
**1)** ~ (D • A)                 ~ (0 • 1)           = 1
**2)** A ⊃ (~ D ≡ ~B)            1 ⊃ (~ 0 ≡ ~ 1)     = 1
**3)** (D • A) ⊃ C               (0 • 1) ⊃ 0         = 1

**Interpretation**

A = 1
B = 0
C = 1
D = 0

**INVALID**

**3.6. (89–91)**

**1.**                    /∴ W ∨ C

  1) W ≡ C    Pr

| **W ≡ C** | **(W ≡ C) ⊃ (W ∨ C)** |
|---|---|
| 1 1 1 | 1 1 1  1  1 1 1 |
| 1 0 0 | 1 0 0  1  1 1 0 |
| 0 0 1 | 0 0 1  1  0 1 1 |
| 0 1 0 | 0 1 0  0  0 0 0 |
| ⇑ | ⇑ |
| CONSISTENT | INVALID |

**3.**                    /∴ P ⊃ Y

  1) P ∨ Y    Pr
  2) ~ Y      Pr

| **(P ∨ Y) · ~Y** | **[(P ∨ Y) · ~Y] ⊃ (P ⊃ Y)** |
|---|---|
| 1 1 1  0 0 1 | 1 1 1 0 0 1  1  1 1 1 |
| 1 1 0  1 1 0 | 1 1 0 1 1 0  0  1 0 0 |
| 0 1 1  0 0 1 | 0 1 1 0 0 1  1  0 1 1 |
| 0 0 0  0 1 0 | 0 0 0 0 1 0  1  0 1 0 |
| ⇑ | ⇑ |
| CONSISTENT | INVALID |

**5.**                    /∴ A ∨ J

  1) A ⊃ J        Pr
  2) ~ (A · J)    Pr
  3) ~ J          Pr

| **[(A ⊃ J) · ~ (A · J)] · ~ J** | **{[(A ⊃ J) · ~ (A · J)] · ~ J} ⊃ (A ∨ J)** |
|---|---|
| 1 1 1 0 0  1 1 1   0 0 1 | 1  1  1  0 0 1 1 1   0 0 1   1  1 1 1 |
| 1 0 0 0 1  1 0 0   0 1 0 | 1  0  0  0 1 1 0 0   0 1 0   1  1 1 0 |
| 0 1 1 1 1  0 0 1   0 0 1 | 0  1  1  1 1 0 0 1   0 0 1   1  0 1 1 |
| 0 1 0 1 1  0 0 0   1 1 0 | 0  1  0  1 1 0 0 0   1 1 0   0  0 0 0 |
| ⇑ | ⇑ |
| CONSISTENT | INVALID |

**7.**                        /∴ W ⊃ A

  1) (W · A) ⊃ S    Pr
  2) S ⊃ A          Pr

| **[(W · A) ⊃ S] · (S ⊃ A)** | **{[(W · A) ⊃ S] · (S ⊃ A)} ⊃ (W ⊃ A)** |
|---|---|
| 1 1 1  1 1  1 1 1 | 1 1 1  1 1  1 1 1   1   1 1 1 |
| 1 1 1  0 0  0 0 1 | 1 1 1  0 0  0 0 1   1   1 1 1 |
| 1 0 0  1 1  0 1 0 | 1 0 0  1 1  0 1 0   1   1 0 0 |
| 1 0 0  1 0  1 0 1 | 1 0 0  1 0  1 0 1   0   1 0 0 |
| 0 0 1  1 1  1 1 1 | 0 0 1  1 1  1 1 1   1   0 1 1 |
| 0 0 1  1 0  1 0 1 | 0 0 1  1 0  1 0 1   1   0 1 1 |
| 0 0 0  1 1  0 1 0 | 0 0 0  1 1  0 1 0   1   0 1 0 |
| 0 0 0  1 0  1 0 1 | 0 0 0  1 0  1 0 1   1   0 1 0 |
| ⇑ | ⇑ |
| CONSISTENT | INVALID |

**9.**                    /∴  P ⊃ ~ S

    **1)** ~ P ⊃ ~ W   Pr
    **2)** ~ (P ∨ ~ S)  Pr
    **3)** W ∨ ~ S    Pr

| [(~ **P** ⊃ ~ **W**) | • | ~ | (**P** | ∨ | ~ **S**)] | • | (**W** | ∨ | ~ **S**) |
|---|---|---|---|---|---|---|---|---|---|
| 0 1 1 0 1 | 0 | 0 1 | 1 | 0 1 | 0 | 1 | 1 0 1 |
| 0 1 1 0 1 | 0 | 0 1 | 1 | 1 0 | 0 | 1 | 1 1 0 |
| 0 1 1 1 0 | 0 | 0 1 | 1 | 0 1 | 0 | 0 | 0 0 1 |
| 0 1 1 1 0 | 0 | 0 1 | 1 | 1 0 | 0 | 0 | 1 1 0 |
| 1 0 0 0 1 | 0 | 1 0 | 0 | 0 1 | 0 | 1 | 1 0 1 |
| 1 0 0 0 1 | 0 | 0 0 | 1 | 1 0 | 0 | 1 | 1 1 0 |
| 1 0 1 1 0 | 1 | 1 0 | 0 | 0 1 | 0 | 0 | 0 0 1 |
| 1 0 1 1 0 | 0 | 0 0 | 1 | 1 0 | 0 | 0 | 1 1 0 |

⇑
INCONSISTENT

| {[(~ **P** ⊃ ~ **W**) | • | ~ | (**P** | ∨ | ~ **S**)] | • | (**W** | ∨ | ~ **S**)} | ⊃ | (**P** | ⊃ | ~ **S**) |
|---|---|---|---|---|---|---|---|---|---|---|---|---|---|
| 0 1 1 | 0 | 1 0 | 0 1 | 1 0 1 | 0 | 1 1 0 1 | 1 | 1 0 0 1 |
| 0 1 1 | 0 | 1 0 | 0 1 | 1 1 0 | 0 | 1 1 1 0 | 1 | 1 1 1 0 |
| 0 1 0 | 1 | 0 0 | 0 1 | 1 0 1 | 0 | 0 0 0 1 | 1 | 1 0 0 1 |
| 0 1 1 | 1 | 0 0 | 0 1 | 1 1 0 | 0 | 0 1 1 0 | 1 | 1 1 1 0 |
| 1 0 0 | 0 | 1 0 | 1 0 | 0 0 1 | 0 | 1 1 0 1 | 1 | 0 1 0 1 |
| 1 0 0 | 0 | 1 0 | 0 0 | 1 1 0 | 0 | 1 1 1 0 | 1 | 0 1 1 0 |
| 1 0 1 | 1 | 0 1 | 1 0 | 0 0 1 | 0 | 0 0 0 1 | 1 | 0 1 0 1 |
| 1 0 1 | 1 | 0 0 | 0 0 | 1 1 0 | 0 | 0 1 1 0 | 1 | 0 1 1 0 |

⇑
VALID

**3.7.  (93–95)**

**1.** B ≡ ~ ~ B

    1 1  1 0 1
    0 1  0 1 0
     ⇑
EQUIVALENT

**3.** (~ N ∨ Z) ≡ (~ N • Z)

    0 1 1 1  0  0 1 0 1
    0 1 0 0  1  0 1 0 0
    1 0 1 1  1  1 0 1 1
    1 0 0 0  0  1 0 0 0
          ⇑
NOT EQUIVALENT

**5.** ~ (~ C • ~ L) ≡ (L ∨ C)

    1 0 1 0 0 1  1  1 1 1
    1 0 1 0 1 0  1  1 0 1 1
    1 1 0 0 0 1  1  1 1 0
    0 1 0 1 1 0  1  1 0 0 0
          ⇑
EQUIVALENT

**7.** (R ∆ I) ≡ (~ R ≡ I)

    1 0 1 1  0 1 0 1
    1 1 0 1  0 1 1 0
    0 1 1 1  1 0 1 1
    0 0 0 1  1 0 0 0
       ⇑
EQUIVALENT

**9.** (R ⊃ S) ≡ (S ⊃ R)

    1 1 1  1 1 1 1
    1 0 0  0 0 1 1
    0 1 1  0 1 0 0
    0 1 0  1 0 1 0
       ⇑
NOT EQUIVALENT

15. $[(P \cdot A) \supset J] \equiv [(J \cdot P) \supset A]$

```
1 1 1 1 1 1   1 1 1   1 1
1 1 1 0 0 0   0 0 1   1 1
1 0 0 1 1 0   1 1 1   0 0
1 0 0 1 0 1   0 0 1   1 0
0 0 1 1 1 1   1 0 0   1 1
0 0 1 1 0 1   0 0 0   1 1
0 0 0 1 1 1   1 0 0   1 0
0 0 0 1 0 1   0 0 0   1 0
          ⇑
     NOT EQUIVALENT
```

17. $[F \supset (S \equiv A)] \equiv [(F \cdot A) \supset S]$

```
1 1  1 1 1   1   1 1 1   1 1
1 0  1 0 0   0   1 0 0   1 1
1 0  0 0 1   1   1 1 1   0 0
1 1  0 1 0   1   1 0 0   1 0
0 1  1 1 1   1   0 0 1   1 1
0 1  1 0 0   1   0 0 0   1 1
0 1  0 0 1   1   0 0 1   1 0
0 1  0 1 0   1   0 0 0   1 0
           ⇑
      NOT EQUIVALENT
```

# CHAPTER 4

## 4.1.A. (111)

**Exclusine Disjunction (ED)**

1) $p \triangle q$          ——

2) $(p \cdot \sim q) \lor (q \cdot \sim p)$   ✓   1, replacement

3) $p \cdot \sim q$     $q \cdot \sim p$   ✓   2, ID
4) $p$                    3, C
5) $\sim q$               3, C
6)            $q$         3, C
7)            $\sim p$    3, C

**Denial Conjunction (DC)**

1) $\sim (p \cdot q)$          ——

2) $\sim p \lor \sim q$   ✓   1, replacement

3) $\sim p$  $\sim q$     2, ID

**Denial Exclusive Disjunction (DED)**

1) $\sim (p \triangle q)$          ——

2) $(p \cdot q) \lor (\sim p \cdot \sim q)$   ✓   1, replacement

3) $p \cdot q$     $\sim p \cdot \sim q$   ✓   2, ID
4) $p$                    3, C
5) $q$                    3, C
6)            $\sim p$    3, C
7)            $\sim q$    3, C

Denial Material Equivalence (DME)

**1)** ~ (p ≡ q)     ————
**2)** (p • ~ q) ∨ (q • ~ p)   ✓   1, replacement

**3)** p • ~ q  ✓     q • ~ p  ✓     2, ID
**4)** p                            3, C
**5)** ~ q                          3, C
**6)**              q               3, C
**7)**              ~ p             3, C

## 4.1.B. (111–113)

**1.**                          /∴ P
1) P ⊃ W  ✓   Pr
2) W          Pr
3)       ~ P    Ap

4) ~ P    W    1, MI
          **INVALID**

**3.**                          /∴ L W
1) L ⊃ W  ✓   Pr
2) W          Pr
3)    ~ (L • W)  ✓   AP

4)  ~ L    ~ W    3, DC
              X
5) ~ L  W         1, MI
              **INVALID**

**5.**                          /∴ P ≡ A
1)  ~ (A ∨ P)  ✓   Pr
2)  ~ (P ≡ A)  ✓   AP
3)    ~ A          1, DID
4)    ~ P          1, DID

5)  P     A        2, DME
6) ~ A   ~ P       2, DME
     X     X            **VALID**

**7.**                          /∴ T ∨ S
1)  ~ S • (S ⊃ T)   Pr
2)  ~ (T ∨ S)       AP
3)    ~ T           2, DID
4)    ~ S           2, DID
5)    ~ S           1, C
6)   S ⊃ T          1, C

7) ~ S    T         6, MI
       X            **INVALID**

**9.**                          /∴ A    D
1)  (A Δ B) • A  ✓   Pr
2)  B ⊃ D  ✓         Pr
3)  ~ (A • D)  ✓     AP
4)    A Δ B          1, C
5)    A              1, C

6) ~ A    ~ D        3, DC
    X
7)     ~ B    D      2, MI
                X
8) A     B          4, ED
9) ~ B ~ A          4, ED
         X              **INVALID**

**15.**                         /∴ C • F
1) D • (U ⊃ F)  ✓    Pr
2) ~ (U ∨ ~ D)  ✓    Pr
3) D ⊃ C  ✓          Pr
4) ~ (C • F)  ✓      AP
5)    D              1, C
6)   U ⊃ F  ✓        1, C
7)    ~ U  ✓         2, DID
8)   ~ ~ D  ✓        2, DID
9)    D              8, DN

10) ~ D    C         3, MI
      X
11)  ~ C    ~ F      4, DC
      X
12)       ~ U    F   6, MI
              X          **INVALID**

**4.2. (115–118)**

**1.**                                         /∴ S
   **1)**   S ⊃ (F ⊃ S) ✓   Pr
   **2)**   F                     Pr

   **3)**  ~ S    F ⊃ S ✓   1, MI

   **4)**  ~ F          S      3, MI
          X                      CONSISTENT

**3.**                                         /∴ L ⊃ ~ R
   **1)** R ∨ L ✓          Pr
   **2)** ~ (~ L ⊃ R) ✓   Pr
   **3)**          ~ L       2, DMI
   **4)**          ~ R       2, DMI

   **5)**       R    L      1, ID
             X    X         INCONSISTENT

**5.**                                         /∴ ~ (S ∨ F)
   **1)**   ~ S • (F ⊃ S) ✓   Pr
   **2)**   S ∨ F ✓            Pr
   **3)**   ~ S                 1, C
   **4)**   F ⊃ S ✓            1, C

   **5)** ~ F    S             4, MI
         X                     X

   **6)** S   F                2, ID
         X   X                 INCONSISTENT

**7.**                                         /∴ L
   **1)** L ∨ (C ∨ N) ✓       Pr
   **2)** C ⊃ N ✓             Pr
   **3)** N                    Pr

   **4)**  ~ C          N       2, MI

   **5)** L  C ∨ N     L  C ∨ N ✓   1, ID

   **6)**   C   N       C   N    5, ID
         X                     CONSISTENT

**9.**                                                        /∴ ~ R ⊃ F

   **1)** F • ~ R ✓                      Pr
   **2)** (~ R • D) ⊃ ~ F ✓          Pr
   **3)** D                                   Pr
   **4)** F                                   1, C
   **5)** ~ R                                1, C

   **6)** ~ (~ R • D) ✓      ~ F      2, MI
                   X

   **7)** ~ ~ R    ~ D      X   6, DC
   **8)**     R                    7, DN
       X                        INCONSISTENT

**15.**                                                      /∴ ~ (D ∨ L) ∨ F

   **1)** (C ⊃ D) • (D ⊃ L) ✓      Pr
   **2)** C • F ✓                       Pr
   **3)** C ⊃ (L ⊃ ~ F) ✓            Pr
   **4)**   C                              2, C
   **5)**   F                              2, C
   **6)** C ⊃ D ✓                       1, C
   **7)** D ⊃ L ✓                       1, C

   **8)** ~ C    D                  6, MI
      X

   **9)**   ~ D      L               7, MI
      X

   **10)** ~ C      L ⊃ ~ F        3, MI
       X

   **11)**      ~ L      ~ F        10, MI
        X       X         INCONSISTENT

**4.3. (121–122)**

**1.**

   **1)** ~ (S ∨ B) • B ✓        ——
   **2)**   ~ (S ∨ B) ✓        1, C
   **3)**       B                   1, C
   **4)**     ~ S                 2, DID
   **5)**     ~ B                 2, DID
      X               CONTRADICTORY

**3.**

   **1)** (C • D) • (~ C ∨ ~ D) ✓    ——
   **2)**     C • D ✓             1, C
   **3)**   ~ C ∨ ~ D ✓         1, C
   **4)**       C                   2, C
   **5)**       D                   2, C

   **6)**   ~ C   ~ D            3, ID
      X    X         CONTRADICTORY

**5-a.**

1)  $(S \cdot I) \supset S$ ✓  —

2)  $\sim (S \cdot I)$ ✓   S   1, MI

3)  $\sim S$   $\sim I$   2, DC

**5-b.**

1)  $\sim [(S \cdot I) \supset S]$ ✓  —
2)  $S \cdot I$ ✓   1, DMI
3)  $\sim S$   1, DMI
4)  $S$   2, C
5)  $I$   2, C
    X   TAUTOLOGICAL

**7-a.**

1)  $(C \supset \sim F) \vee (C \cdot F)$ ✓  —

2)  $C \supset \sim F$ ✓   $C \cdot D$ ✓   1, ID
3)      $C$   2, C
4)      $D$   2, C
5)  $\sim C$   $\sim F$   2, MI

**7-b.**

1)  $\sim [(C \supset \sim F) \vee (C \cdot F)]$ ✓  —
2)  $\sim (C \supset \sim F)$ ✓   1, DID
3)  $\sim (C \cdot F)$ ✓   1, DID
4)  $C$   2, DMI
5)  $\sim \sim F$ ✓   2, DMI
6)  $F$   5, DN
7)  $\sim C$   $\sim F$   3, DC
    X   X   TAUTOLOGICAL

**9-a.**

1)  $[(A \supset C) \cdot \sim C] \supset (A \supset B)$ ✓  —

2)  $\sim [(A \supset C) \cdot \sim C]$ ✓   $A \supset B$ ✓   1, MI

3)  $\sim (A \supset C)$ ✓   $\sim \sim C$ ✓   2, DC
4)      $C$   3, DN
5)  $A$   3, DMI
6)  $\sim C$   3, DMI
7)      $\sim A$   $B$   2, MI

**9-b.**

1)  $\sim \{[(A \supset C) \cdot \sim C] \supset (A \supset B)\}$ ✓  —
2)  $(A \supset C) \cdot \sim C$ ✓   1, DMI
3)  $\sim (A \supset B)$ ✓   1, DMI
4)  $A \supset C$ ✓   2, C
5)  $\sim C$   2, C
6)  $A$   3, DMI
7)  $\sim B$   3, DMI
8)  $\sim A$   $C$   4, MI
    X   X   TAUTOLOGICAL

**15-a.**

1)   [(L ⊃ P) • (C ⊃ R)] ⊃ ~ [~ (L ∨ P) ∨ (C ∨ R)]  ✓   ——

2)  ~ [(L ⊃ P) • (C ⊃ R)]  ✓    ~ [~ (L ∨ P) ∨ (C ∨ R)]  ✓   1, MI

3) ~ (L ⊃ P)  ✓    ~ (C ⊃ R)  ✓                              2, DC
4)     L              C                                        3, DMI
5)    ~ P            ~ R                                       3, DMI
6)                              ~ ~ (L ∨ P) ✓                  2, DID
7)                              ~ (C ∨ R) ✓                    2, DID
8)                               L ∨ P ✓                       6, DN
9)                               ~ C                           7, DID
10)                              ~ R                           7, DID

11)                           L       P                        8, ID

**15-b.**

1)  ~ {[(L ⊃ P) • (C ⊃ R)] ⊃ ~ [~ (L ∨ P) ∨ (C ∨ R)]}  ✓   ——
2)            (L ⊃ P) • (C ⊃ R)  ✓                         1, DMI
3)           ~ ~ [~ (L ∨ P) ∨ (C ∨ R)]  ✓                  1, DMI
4)            ~ (L ∨ P) ∨ (C ∨ R)  ✓                       3, DN
5)                  L ⊃ P  ✓                               2, C
6)                  C ⊃ R  ✓                               2, C

7)    ~ (L ∨ P)  ✓          C ∨ R ✓                         4, ID
8)      ~ L                                                 7, DID
9)      ~ P                                                 7, DID
10)                   C              R                      7, ID

11)   ~ L    P    ~ L    P    ~ L    P                      5, MI
             X

12)  ~ C  R   ~ C  R  ~ C  R  ~ C  R  ~ C  R                7, ID
             X        X

CONTINGENT

**4.4. (125–126)**

**1.**

   **a)** W ∨ T
   **b)** ∼ (T · W)

**1)** ∼ [(W ∨ T) ≡ ∼ (T · W)]  ✓  ———

| | | | |
|---|---|---|---|
| **2)** | W ∨ T ✓ | ∼ (T · W) ✓ | 1, DME |
| **3)** | ∼ ∼ (T · W) ✓ | ∼ (W ∨ T) ✓ | 1, DME |
| **4)** | T · W ✓ | | 3, DN |
| **5)** | T | | 4, C |
| **6)** | W | | 4, C |
| **7)** | W   T | | 2, ID |
| **8)** | | ∼ W | 3, DID |
| **9)** | | ∼ T | 3, DID |
| **10)** | | ∼ T   ∼ W | 2, DC |

NOT LOGICALLY EQUIVALENT

**3.**

   **a)** ∼ B · ∼ C
   **b)** ∼ (B · C)

**1)** ∼ [(∼ B · ∼ C) ≡ ∼ (B · C)]  ✓  ———

| | | | | | |
|---|---|---|---|---|---|
| **2)** | ∼ B · ∼ C ✓ | ∼ (B · C) ✓ | | | 1, DME |
| **3)** | ∼ ∼ (B · C) ✓ | ∼ (∼ B · ∼ C) ✓ | | | 1, DME |
| **4)** | B · C ✓ | | | | 3, DN |
| **5)** | B | | | | 4, C |
| **6)** | C | | | | 4, C |
| **7)** | ∼ B | | | | 2, C |
| **8)** | ∼ C | | | | 2, C |
| | X | | | | |
| **9)** | | ∼ B | ∼ C | | 2, DC |
| **10)** | ∼ ∼ B ✓ | ∼ ∼ C ✓ | ∼ ∼ B ✓ | ∼ ∼ C ✓ | 3, DC |
| **11)** | B | C | B | C | 10, DN |
| | X | | | X | NOT LOGICALLY EQUIVALENT |

**5.**
   **a)** ~ (~ P • ~ T)
   **b)** P ∨ T

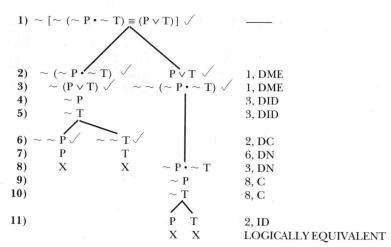

| | | | |
|---|---|---|---|
| **1)** | ~ [~ (~ P • ~ T) ≡ (P ∨ T)] ✓ | | —— |
| **2)** | ~ (~ P • ~ T) ✓ | P ∨ T ✓ | 1, DME |
| **3)** | ~ (P ∨ T) ✓ | ~ ~ (~ P • ~ T) ✓ | 1, DME |
| **4)** | ~ P | | 3, DID |
| **5)** | ~ T | | 3, DID |
| **6)** | ~ ~ P ✓    ~ ~ T ✓ | | 2, DC |
| **7)** | P      T | | 6, DN |
| **8)** | X      X | ~ P • ~ T | 3, DN |
| **9)** | | ~ P | 8, C |
| **10)** | | ~ T | 8, C |
| **11)** | | P    T | 2, ID |
| | | X    X | LOGICALLY EQUIVALENT |

**7.**
   **a)** F △ W
   **b)** F ≡ ~ W

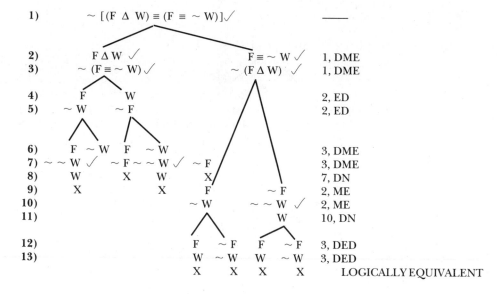

| | | | |
|---|---|---|---|
| **1)** | ~ [(F △ W) ≡ (F ≡ ~ W)] ✓ | | —— |
| **2)** | F △ W ✓ | F ≡ ~ W ✓ | 1, DME |
| **3)** | ~ (F ≡ ~ W) ✓ | ~ (F △ W) ✓ | 1, DME |
| **4)** | F    W | | 2, ED |
| **5)** | ~ W    ~ F | | 2, ED |
| **6)** | F ~ W   F ~ W | | 3, DME |
| **7)** | ~ ~ W ✓   ~ F ~ ~ W ✓   ~ F | | 3, DME |
| **8)** | W    X    W    X | | 7, DN |
| **9)** | X      X | F      ~ F | 2, ME |
| **10)** | | ~ W    ~ ~ W ✓ | 2, ME |
| **11)** | | W | 10, DN |
| **12)** | | F   ~ F   F   ~ F | 3, DED |
| **13)** | | W ~ W   W ~ W | 3, DED |
| | | X   X   X   X | LOGICALLY EQUIVALENT |

**9.**

**a)** R • P
**b)** ~ (~ P ∨ ~ R)

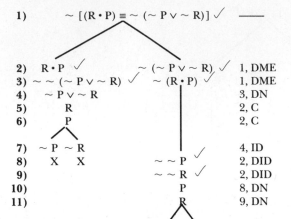

**1)**      ~ [(R • P) ≡ ~ (~ P ∨ ~ R)] ✓  ——

| | | | |
|---|---|---|---|
| **2)** | R • P ✓ | ~ (~ P ∨ ~ R) ✓ | 1, DME |
| **3)** | ~ ~ (~ P ∨ ~ R) ✓ | ~ (R • P) ✓ | 1, DME |
| **4)** | ~ P ∨ ~ R | | 3, DN |
| **5)** | R | | 2, C |
| **6)** | P | | 2, C |
| **7)** | ~ P   ~ R | | 4, ID |
| **8)** | X   X | ~ ~ P ✓ | 2, DID |
| **9)** | | ~ ~ R ✓ | 2, DID |
| **10)** | | P | 8, DN |
| **11)** | | R | 9, DN |
| **12)** | | ~ R   ~ P | 3, DC |
| | | X   X | LOGICALLY EQUIVALENT |

**15.**

**a)** (I ∨ M) • (C ∨ I)
**b)** (M • C) ∨ I

**1)** ~ {[(I ∨ M) • (C ∨ I)] ≡ [(M • C) ∨ I]} ✓   ——

| | | | |
|---|---|---|---|
| **2)** | (I ∨ M) • (C ∨ I) ✓ | (M • C) ∨ I ✓ | 1, DME |
| **3)** | ~ [(M • C) ∨ I] ✓ | ~ [(I ∨ M) • (C ∨ I)] ✓ | 1, DME |
| **4)** | I ∨ M ✓ | | 2, C |
| **5)** | C ∨ I ✓ | | 2, C |
| **6)** | ~ (M • C) ✓ | | 3, DID |
| **7)** | ~ I | | 3, DID |
| **8)** | I       M | | 4, ID |
| | X | | |
| **9)** | C       I | | 5, ID |
| | | X | |
| **10)** | ~ M   ~ C | | 6, DC |
| | X     X | | |
| **11)** | | ~ (I ∨ M) ✓   ~ (C ∨ I) ✓ | 3, DC |
| **12)** | | ~ I         ~ C | 11, DID |
| **13)** | | ~ M         ~ I | 11, DID |
| **14)** | | M • C ✓   I   M • C ✓   I | 2, ID |
| **15)** | | M       X   M       X | 14, C |
| **16)** | | C         C | 14, C |
| | | X         X | |
| | | | LOGICALLY EQUIVALENT |

In particular the "answers" to the following exercises are *only guides.* It must be remembered that *the great majority of arguments have several CORRECT proofs.* This is particularly the case as more rules are introduced for proof construction and premises become more complicated.

# CHAPTER 5

### 5.1. (132–133)

**1.**                          /∴  A
  1) A • (B • C)   Pr

**3.**                          /∴  B ⊃ C
  1) (A • B) ⊃ C   Pr

**5.**                          /∴  ~ A
  1) A ⊃ (B ⊃ C)   Pr
  2) ~ (B ⊃ C)   Pr

**7.**                          /∴  C • (A ⊃ B)
  1) (A ⊃ B) • C   Pr

**9.**                          /∴  ~ C ⊃ (B ⊃ A)
  1) A ⊃ B   Pr

**1.**                          /∴  A ∨ B
  1) (A ∨ B) • {~ (C ∨ D) • ~ [C ⊃ (D ⊃ B)]}   Pr

**3.**                          /∴  ~ (C ∨ D) ⊃ ~ [C ⊃ (D ⊃ B)]
  1) [(A ∨ B) • ~ (C ∨ D)] ⊃ ~ [C ⊃ (D ⊃ B)]   Pr

**5.**                          /∴  ~ (A ∨ B)
  1) [A ∨ B) ⊃ {~ (C ∨ D) ⊃ ~ [C ⊃ (D ⊃ B)]}   Pr
  2) ~{ ~ (C ∨ D) ⊃ ~ [C ⊃ (D ⊃ B)]}        Pr

**7.**                          /∴  ~ [C ⊃ (D ⊃ B)] • [(A ∨ B) ⊃ ~ (C ∨ D)]
  1) [A ∨ B) ⊃ ~ (C ∨ D)] • ~ [C ⊃ (D ⊃ B)]   Pr

**9.**                          /∴  ~ ~ [C ⊃ (D ⊃ B)] ⊃ [~ (C ∨ D) ⊃ (A ∨ B)]
  1) (A ∨ B) ⊃ ~ (C ∨ D)   Pr

### 5.2.A. (138–140)

| **1.** | **3.** | **5.** |
|---|---|---|
| 1) Pr | 1) Pr | 1) Pr |
| 2) /∴ 1, Simp | 2) 1, Com | 2) 1, Simp |
| | 3) 2, Simp | 3) 1, Com |
| | 4) /∴ 3, Simp | 4) 3, Simp |
| | | 5) 2, Com |
| | | 6) 5, Simp |
| | | 7) /∴ 6, 4, Conj |

**7.**

1) Pr
2) Pr
3) 2, Simp
4) 2, Com
5) 4, Simp
6) 3, Com
7) 6, Simp
8) 7, 5, Conj
9) /∴  8, 1, Conj

**9.**

1) Pr
2) 1, Simp
3) 1, Com
4) 3, Simp
5) 2, Simp
6) 2, Com
7) 6, Simp
8) 4, Simp
9) 4, Com
10) 9, Simp
11) 10, 7, Conj
12) 8, 5, Conj
13) /∴  11, 12, Conj

**5.2.B. (140)**

**1.**              /∴ A

1) A • B   Pr
2) /∴ A  1, Simp

**3.**              /∴ B

1) A • B   Pr
2) B • A   1, Com
3) /∴ B  2, Simp

**5.**              /∴ C • B

1) A • B        Pr
2) C            Pr
3) B • A        1, Com
4) B            3, Simp
5) /∴ C • B   2, 4, Conj

**7.**                      /∴  (C ∨D) • (A ∨ B)

1) (A ∨ B) • (C ∨ D)        Pr
2) /∴  (C ∨ D) • (A ∨ B)   1, Com

**9.**                      /∴  (B ⊃ C) • (C ⊃ D)

1) (A ⊃ B) • (B ⊃ C)        Pr
2) C ⊃ D                     Pr
3) (B ⊃ C) • (A ⊃ B)        1, Com
4) B ⊃ C                     3, Simp
5) /∴  (B ⊃ C) • (C ⊃ D)    4, 2, Conj

**5.2.C. (141)**

**1.**              /∴ T

1) T • N   Pr
2) /∴ T          1, Simp

**3.**              /∴ T • M

1) T        Pr
2) M        Pr
3) /∴  T • M  1, 2, Conj

**5.**                    $/\therefore\ D \cdot N$
1) $(T \cdot N) \cdot D$   Pr
2) $T \cdot N$   1, Simp
3) $N \cdot T$   2, Com
4) $N$   3, Simp
5) $D \cdot (T \cdot N)$   1, Conj
6) $D$   5, Simp
7) $/\therefore\ D \cdot N$   6, 4, Com

**7.**                    $/\therefore\ (S \cdot W) \cdot (E \cdot R)$
1) $(R \cdot S) \cdot (E \cdot W)$   Pr
2) $R \cdot S$   1, Simp
3) $R$   2, Simp
4) $S \cdot R$   2, Com
5) $S$   4, Simp
6) $(E \cdot W) \cdot (R \cdot S)$   1, Com
7) $E \cdot W$   6, Simp
8) $E$   7, Simp
9) $W \cdot E$   7, Com
10) $W$   9, Simp
11) $S \cdot W$   5, 10, Conj
12) $E \cdot R$   8, 3, Conj
13) $/\therefore\ (S \cdot W) \cdot (E \cdot R)$   11, 12, Conj

**5.3.A. (147–149)**

**1.**
1) Pr
2) Pr
3) 2, Com
4) $/\therefore$ 3, 1, DS

**3.**
1) Pr
2) 1, Simp
3) 1, Com
4) 3, Simp
5) 2, Com
6) $/\therefore$ 5, 4, DS

**5.**
1) Pr
2) Pr
3) 1, Simp
4) 1, Com
5) 4, Simp
6) 2, Com
7) 6, 3, DS
8) 5, Add
9) 8, Com
10) $/\therefore$ 9, 7, Conj

**7.**
1) Pr
2) Pr
3) 2, Simp
4) 2, Com
5) 4, Simp
6) 1, Com
7) 6, 5, DS
8) 7, Com
9) 8, 3, DS
10) 9, Add
11) 10, Add
12) 11, Com
13) 12, Add
14) $/\therefore$ 13, Com

**5.3.B. (150)**

**1.**                     /∴ B ∨ C
  1) A ∨ B    Pr
  2) /∴ B ∨ A  1, Com

**3.**                     /∴ A
  1) A ∨ B  Pr
  2) ∼ B  Pr
  3) B ∨ A  1, Com
  4) /∴ A  3, 2, DS

**5.**                     /∴ (C ∨ D) ∨ (B ∨ A)
  1) A ∨ B    Pr
  2) B ∨ A    1, Com
  3) (B ∨ A) ∨ (C ∨ D)  2, Add
  4) /∴ (C ∨ D) ∨ (B ∨ A)  3, Com

**7.**                     /∴ D ∨ C
  1) A ∨ [B ∨ (C ∨ D)]  Pr
  2) ∼ B • ∼ A  Pr
  3) ∼ B  2, Simp
  4) ∼ A • ∼B  2, Com
  5) ∼ A  4, Simp
  6) B ∨ (C ∨ D)  1, 5, DS
  7) C ∨ D  6, 3, DS
  8) /∴ D ∨ C  7, Com

**5.3.C. (150–151)**

**1.**                     /∴ A ∨ P
  1) P ∨ A  Pr
  2) /∴ A ∨ P  1, Com

**3.**                     /∴ L ∨ S
  1) (S ∨ E) • ∼ E  Pr
  2) S ∨ E  1, Simp
  3) ∼ E • (S ∨ E)  1, Com
  4) ∼ E  3, Simp
  5) E ∨ S  2, Com
  6) S  5, 4, DS
  7) S ∨ L  6, Add
  8) /∴ L ∨ S  7, Com

**5.**                     /∴ E ∨ D
  1) (∼ P • ∼ E) • (∼ A ∨ P)  Pr
  2) A ∨ D  Pr
  3) ∼ P • ∼ E  1, Simp
  4) ∼ P  3, Simp
  5) (∼ A ∨ P) • (∼ P ∨ ∼ E)  1, Com
  6) ∼ A ∨ P  5, Simp
  7) P ∨ ∼ A  6, Com
  8) ∼ A  7, 4, DS
  9) D  2, 8, DS
  10) D ∨ E  9, Add
  11) /∴ E ∨ D  10, Com

**7.**                                   $/\therefore \sim (P \cdot R) \vee (R \vee L)$

| | | |
|---|---|---|
| **1)** | $\sim P \vee (T \cdot R)$ | Pr |
| **2)** | $(R \vee L) \vee M$ | Pr |
| **3)** | $\sim (T \cdot R)$ | Pr |
| **4)** | $(\sim M \cdot \sim R) \vee P$ | Pr |
| **5)** | $(T \cdot R) \vee \sim P$ | 1, Com |
| **6)** | $\sim P$ | 5, 3, DS |
| **7)** | $P \vee (\sim M \cdot \sim R)$ | 4, Com |
| **8)** | $\sim M \cdot \sim R$ | 7, 6, DS |
| **9)** | $\sim M$ | 8, Simp |
| **10)** | $M \vee (R \vee L)$ | 2, Com |
| **11)** | $R \vee L$ | 10, 9, DS |
| **12)** | $(R \vee L) \vee \sim (P \cdot R)$ | 11, Add |
| **13)** | $/\therefore \sim (P \cdot R) \vee (R \vee L)$ | 14, Com |

### 5.4.B. (156–158)

**1.**
1) Pr
2) Pr
3) $/\therefore$ 1, 2, MP

**3.**
1) Pr
2) 1, Simp
3) 1, Com
4) 3, Simp
5) $/\therefore$ 4, 2, MP

**5.**
1) Pr
2) Pr
3) Pr
4) 1, Simp
5) 1, Com
6) 5, Simp
7) 4, 3, MP
8) 6, 7, MP
9) $/\therefore$ 2, 8, MP

**7.**
1) Pr
2) Pr
3) Pr
4) Pr
5) 2, Com
6) 5, 4, DS
7) 1, 6, MP
8) 3, 7, MP
9) 8, Add
10) $/\therefore$ 9, Com

### 5.4.C. (158–159)

**1.**                     $/\therefore C \cdot \sim A$

| | | |
|---|---|---|
| **1)** | $(A \supset B) \cdot C$ | Pr |
| **2)** | $\sim B$ | Pr |
| **3)** | $A \supset B$ | 1, Simp |
| **4)** | $C \cdot (A \supset B)$ | 1, Com |
| **5)** | $C$ | 4, Simp |
| **6)** | $\sim A$ | 3, 2, MT |
| **7)** | $/\therefore C \cdot \sim A$ | 5, 6, Conj |

**3.**                     $/\therefore D \vee C$

| | | |
|---|---|---|
| **1)** | $(A \vee B) \vee C$ | Pr |
| **2)** | $(A \vee B) \supset E$ | Pr |
| **3)** | $\sim E$ | Pr |
| **4)** | $\sim (A \vee B)$ | 2, 3, MT |
| **5)** | $C$ | 1, 4, DS |
| **6)** | $C \vee D$ | 5, Add |
| **7)** | $/\therefore D \vee C$ | 6, Com |

**5.**                           $/\therefore$   C

  **1)** $(A \cdot B) \supset C$      Pr
  **2)** $(D \supset A) \cdot (E \supset B)$      Pr
  **3)** $E \cdot D$      Pr
  **4)** $D \supset A$      2, Simp
  **5)** $(E \supset B) \cdot (D \supset A)$      2, Com
  **6)** $E \supset B$      5, Simp
  **7)** $E$      3, Simp
  **8)** $D \cdot E$      3, Com
  **9)** $D$      8, Simp
  **10)** $A$      4, 9, MP
  **11)** $B$      6, 7, MP
  **12)** $A \cdot B$      10, 11, Conj
  **13)** $/\therefore$  $C$      1, 12, MP

**7.**                           $/\therefore$   $(A \vee B) \cdot (A \cdot E)$

  **1)** $(A \vee \sim B) \supset \sim (C \vee D)$      Pr
  **2)** $(C \vee D) \vee (A \cdot E)$      Pr
  **3)** $(B \supset F) \cdot \sim F$      Pr
  **4)** $B \supset F$      3, Simp
  **5)** $\sim F \cdot (B \supset F)$      3, Com
  **6)** $\sim F$      5, Simp
  **7)** $\sim B$      4, 6, MT
  **8)** $\sim B \vee A$      7, Add
  **9)** $A \vee \sim B$      8, Com
  **10)** $\sim (C \vee D)$      1, 9, MP
  **11)** $A \cdot E$      2, 10, DS
  **12)** $A$      11, Simp
  **13)** $A \vee B$      12, Add
  **14)** $/\therefore$  $(A \vee B) \cdot (A \cdot E)$      13, 11, Conj

**5.4.D. (159–161)**

**1.**                        /∴ R

  **1)** I ⊃ R    Pr
  **2)** I        Pr
  **3)** /∴ R  1, 2, MP

**5.**                        /∴ D • F

  **1)** R • D              Pr
  **2)** (S ∨ R) ⊃ F    Pr
  **3)** R                  1, Simp
  **4)** D • R              1, Com
  **5)** D                  4, Simp
  **6)** R ∨ S              3, Add
  **7)** S ∨ R              6, Com
  **8)** F                  2, 7, MP
  **9)** /∴ D • F      5, 8, Conj

**7.**                        /∴ D • ~E

  **1)** (I ⊃ R) ⊃ ~ S              Pr
  **2)** (~ ~ S ∨ F) • (~ F ∨ E)    Pr
  **3)** ~ E                        Pr
  **4)** (I ⊃ R) ∨ D                Pr
  **5)** ~ ~ S ∨ F                  2, Simp
  **6)** (~ F ∨ E) • (~ ~ S ∨ F)    2, Com
  **7)** ~ F ∨ E                    6, Simp
  **8)** E ∨ ~ F                    7, Com
  **9)** ~ F                        8, 3, DS
  **10)** F ∨ ~ ~ S                 5, Com
  **11)** ~ ~ S                     10, 9, DS
  **12)** ~ (I ⊃ R)                 1, 11, MT
  **13)** D                         4, 12, DS
  **14)** /∴ D • ~ E             13, 3, Conj

**3.**                        /∴ E • A

  **1)** E ⊃ R          Pr
  **2)** R ⊃ S          Pr
  **3)** E • (S ⊃ A)    Pr
  **4)** E              3, Simp
  **5)** (S ⊃ A) • E    3, Com
  **6)** S ⊃ A          5, Simp
  **7)** R              1, 4, MP
  **8)** S              2, 7, MP
  **9)** A              6, 8, MP
  **10)** /∴ E • A    4, 9, Conj

**5.5.B.  (165–168)**

**1.**
  1) Pr
  2) Pr
  3) /∴ 2, 1, HS

**7.**
  1) Pr
  2) Pr
  3) Pr
  4) Pr
  5) 1, Simp
  6) 1, Com
  7) 6, Simp
  8) 2, 7, MP
  9) 3, 5, MP
  10) /∴ 8, 4, 9, CD

**3.**
  1) Pr
  2) Pr
  3) Pr
  4) 2, Simp
  5) 2, Com
  6) 5, Simp
  7) 3, 6, MP
  8) 1, 4, MP
  9) /∴ 7, 8, HS

**5.**
  1) Pr
  2) Pr
  3) Pr
  4) 1, Simp
  5) 1, Com
  6) 5, Simp
  7) 3, 2, HS
  8) 6, Add
  9) 7, 4, 8, CD
  10) /∴ 9, Com

**5.5.C.  (168–169)**

**1.**　　　　　/∴ B ∨ D
  1) A ⊃ B　　Pr
  2) C ⊃ D　　Pr
  3) A ∨ C　　Pr
  4) /∴ B ∨ D　1, 2, 3, CD

**3.**　　　　　/∴ D ∨ B
  1) A ⊃ B　　Pr
  2) A ∨ C　　Pr
  3) C ⊃ D　　Pr
  4) B ∨ D　　1, 3, 2, CD
  5) /∴ D ∨ B　4, Com

**5.**　　　　　/∴ C ∨ E
  1) (A ⊃ B) • (B ⊃ C)　　Pr
  2) D ⊃ E　　Pr
  3) D ∨ A　　Pr
  4) A ⊃ B　　1, Simp
  5) (B ⊃ C) • (A ⊃ B)　　1, Com
  6) B ⊃ C　　5, Simp
  7) A ⊃ C　　4, 6, HS
  8) E ∨ C　　2, 7, 3, CD
  9) /∴ C ∨ E　　8, Com

**7.**  $/\therefore\ (G \cdot H) \vee (G \vee H)$

| | | |
|---|---|---|
| **1)** | $[A \supset\ \sim (B \cdot \sim C)] \supset (D \vee E)$ | Pr |
| **2)** | $[A \supset (B \supset F)] \cdot [(B \supset F) \supset \sim (B \cdot \sim C)]$ | Pr |
| **3)** | $(D \vee E) \supset [(D \supset G) \cdot (E \supset H)]$ | Pr |
| **4)** | $A \supset (B \supset F)$ | 2, Simp |
| **5)** | $[(B \supset F) \supset\ \sim (B \cdot \sim C)] \cdot [A \supset (B \supset F)]$ | 2, Com |
| **6)** | $(B \supset F) \supset\ \sim (B \cdot \sim C)$ | 5, Simp |
| **7)** | $A \supset\ \sim (B \cdot \sim C)$ | 4, 6, HS |
| **8)** | $D \vee E$ | 1, 7, MP |
| **9)** | $(D \supset G) \cdot (E \supset H)$ | 3, 8, MP |
| **10)** | $D \supset G$ | 9, Simp |
| **11)** | $(E \supset H) \cdot (D \supset G)$ | 9, Com |
| **12)** | $E \supset H$ | 11, Simp |
| **13)** | $G \vee H$ | 10, 12, 8, CD |
| **14)** | $(G \vee H) \vee (G \cdot H)$ | 13, Add |
| **15)** | $/\therefore\ (G \cdot H) \vee (G \vee H)$ | 14, Com |

## 5.5.D.  (169–170)

**1.**  $/\therefore\ \sim (L \vee F) \vee (F \vee L)$

| | | |
|---|---|---|
| **1)** | $A \supset L$ | Pr |
| **2)** | $A \vee B$ | Pr |
| **3)** | $B \supset F$ | Pr |
| **4)** | $L \vee F$ | 1, 3, 2, CD |
| **5)** | $F \vee L$ | 4, Com |
| **6)** | $(F \vee L) \vee\ \sim (L \vee F)$ | 5, Add |
| **7)** | $/\therefore\ \sim (L \vee F) \vee (F \vee L)$ | 6, Com |

**3.** /∴ T ⊃ E

1) (T ⊃ S) • (S ⊃ F)     Pr
2) (F ⊃ M) • (M ⊃ E)     Pr
3) T ⊃ S     1, Simp
4) (S ⊃ F) • (T ⊃ S)     1, Com
5) S ⊃ F     4, Simp
6) F ⊃ M     2, Simp
7) (M ⊃ E) • (F ⊃ M)     2, Com
8) M ⊃ E     7, Simp
9) T ⊃ F     3, 5, HS
10) T ⊃ M     9, 6, HS
11) /∴ T ⊃ E     10, 8, HS

**5.** /∴ M ⊃ W

1) K ⊃ (T • C)     Pr
2) T ⊃ (M ⊃ P)     Pr
3) C ⊃ (P ⊃ W)     Pr
4) K     Pr
5) T • C     1, 4, MP
6) T     5, Simp
7) C • T     5, Com
8) C     7, Simp
9) M ⊃ P     2, 6, MP
10) P ⊃ W     3, 8, MP
11) /∴ M ⊃ W     9, 10, HS

**7.** /∴ U ∨ E

1) ~ (D • L) ⊃ (W ⊃ C)     Pr
2) (D • L) ⊃ U     Pr
3) ~ U • (P ∨ W)     Pr
4) (C ⊃ U) • (P ⊃ E)     Pr
5) ~ U     3, Simp
6) (P ∨ W) • ~ U     3, Com
7) P ∨ W     6, Simp
8) C ⊃ U     4, Simp
9) (P ⊃ E) • (C ⊃ U)     4, Com
10) P ⊃ E     9, Simp
11) ~ (D • L)     2, 5, MT
12) W ⊃ C     1, 11, MP
13) W ⊃ U     12, 8, HS
14) E ∨ U     10, 13, 7, CD
15) /∴ U ∨ E     14, Com

# CHAPTER 6

**6.1.A. (181–183)**

**1.**
  **1)** Pr
  **2)** 1, Assoc
  **3)** /∴ 2, Com

**3.**
  **1)** Pr
  **2)** 1, Assoc
  **3)** 2, Assoc
  **4)** 3, Com
  **5)** 4, Assoc
  **6)** /∴ 5, Com

**5.**
  **1)** Pr
  **2)** 1, Com
  **3)** 2, Assoc
  **4)** 3, Assoc
  **5)** 4, Com
  **6)** 5, Com
  **7)** 6, Assoc
  **8)** /∴ 7, Assoc

**7.**
  **1)** Pr
  **2)** 1, Assoc
  **3)** 2, Assoc
  **4)** 3, Com
  **5)** 4, Assoc
  **6)** 5, Assoc
  **7)** 6, Assoc
  **8)** 7, Assoc
  **9)** 8, Com
  **10)** /∴ 9, Assoc

**6.1.B. (183–184)**

**1.**                          /∴ B ∨ (C ∨ A)
  **1)** A ∨ (B ∨ C)        Pr
  **2)** (B ∨ C) ∨ A        1, Com
  **3)** /∴ B ∨ (C ∨ A)     2, Assoc

**3.**                          /∴ (D · A) · (B · C)
  **1)** (A · B) · (C · D)        Pr
  **2)** A · [B · (C · D)]        1, Assoc
  **3)** A · [(B · C) · D]        2, Assoc
  **4)** A · [D · (B · C)]        3, Com
  **5)** (A · D) · (B · C)        4, Assoc
  **6)** /∴ (D · A) · (B · C)     5, Com

**5.**                          /∴ [(C ⊃ D) ∨ (B ≡ C)] ∨ (B Δ ∼ A)
  **1)** [(∼ A Δ B) ∨ (C ≡ B)] ∨ (C ⊃ D)        Pr
  **2)** (C ⊃ D) ∨ [(∼ A Δ B) ∨ (C ≡ B)]        1, Com
  **3)** (C ⊃ D) ∨ [(C ≡ B) ∨ (∼ A Δ B)]        2, Com
  **4)** [(C ⊃ D) ∨ (C ≡ B)] ∨ (∼ A Δ B)        3, Assoc
  **5)** [(C ⊃ D) ∨ (B ≡ C)] ∨ (∼ A Δ B)        4, Com
  **6)** /∴ [(C ⊃ D) ∨ (B ≡ C)] ∨ (B Δ ∼ A)     5, Com

**7.**                          /∴ (F ∨ B) ∨ (D ∨ ∼ C)
  **1)** ∼ (A ≡ B)               Pr
  **2)** ∼ C ∨ (B ≡ A)          Pr
  **3)** (B ≡ A) ∨ ∼ C          2, Com
  **4)** ∼ (B ≡ A)               1, Com
  **5)** ∼ C                     3, 4, DS
  **6)** ∼ C ∨ D                 5, Add
  **7)** D ∨ ∼ C                 6, Com
  **8)** (D ∨ ∼ C) ∨ (F ∨ B)     7, Add
  **9)** /∴ (F ∨ B) ∨ (D ∨ ∼ C)  8, Com

**6.1.C.  (184–185)**

**1.**                              /∴  (S ∨ A) ∨ L     **5.**                              /∴  ~ L • ~ G

    **1)** A ∨ (S ∨ L)        Pr

    **2)** (A ∨ S) ∨ L        1, Assoc

    **3)** /∴  (S ∨ A) ∨ L    2, Com

    **1)** ~ (L ∨ S)           Pr

    **2)** (~ G ∨ S) ∨ G       Pr

    **3)** (R • W) ⊃ L         Pr

    **4)** ~ (R • W) ⊃ ~ L     Pr

**3.**                              /∴  P

    **1)** ~ (E • D)           Pr

    **2)** ~ L ⊃ (E • P)       Pr

    **3)** ~ L ∨ (D • E)       Pr

    **4)** (D • E) ∨ ~ L       3, Com

    **5)** ~ (D • E)           1, Com

    **6)** ~ L                 4, 5, DS

    **7)** E • P               2, 6, MP

    **8)** P • E               7, Com

    **9)** /∴  P               8, Simp

    **5)** ~ G ∨ (S ∨ L)       2, Assoc

    **6)** (S ∨ L) ∨ ~ G       5, Com

    **7)** ~ (S ∨ L)           1, Com

    **8)** ~ G                 6, 7, DS

    **9)** ~ (R • W)           3, 8, MT

    **10)** ~ L                4, 9, MP

    **11)** /∴  ~ L • ~ G      10, 8, Conj

**7.**                              /∴  E • P

    **1)** ~ (U ∨ T) ⊃ R              Pr

    **2)** ~ (T ∨ U)                  Pr

    **3)** R ⊃ (P • ~ T)              Pr

    **4)** E ∨ (T ∨ U)                Pr

    **5)** {~ T • [U ∨ (T ∨ E)]} ⊃ ~ U   Pr

    **6)** ~ (U ∨ T)                  2, Com

    **7)** R                          1, 6, MP

    **8)** P • ~ T                    3, 7, MP

    **9)** P                          8, Simp

    **10)** ~ T • P                   8, Com

    **11)** ~ T                       10, Simp

    **12)** (E ∨ T) ∨ U               4, Assoc

    **13)** U ∨ (E ∨ T)               12, Com

    **14)** U ∨ (T ∨ E)               13, Com

    **15)** ~ T • [U ∨ (T ∨ E)]       11, 14, Conj

    **16)** ~ U                       5, 15, MP

    **17)** T ∨ E                     14, 16, DS

    **18)** E                         17, 11, DS

    **19)** /∴  E • P                 18, 9, Conj

**6.2.A.  (190–193)**

**1.**                          **3.**                          **5.**                          **7.**

**1)** Pr                       **1)** Pr                       **1)** Pr                       **1)** Pr

**2)** Pr                       **2)** Pr                       **2)** Pr                       **2)** Pr

**3)** 2, Trans                 **3)** 1, Trans                 **3)** 2, Com                   **3)** Pr

**4)** 3, DN                    **4)** 3, 2, MP                 **4)** 3, Simp                  **4)** Pr

**5)** /∴  1, 4, HS             **5)** 4, Add                   **5)** 4, Add                   **5)** 1, Trans

                                **6)** /∴  5, Com               **6)** 5, Com                   **6)** 4, Trans

                                                                **7)** 6, DN                    **7)** 5, 3, MP

                                                                **8)** 1, 7, MT                 **8)** 7, Trans

                                                                **9)** 2, Simp                  **9)** 2, 3, MP

                                                                **10)** 9, Com                  **10)** 8, 9, HS

                                                                **11)** 10, 8, DS               **11)** 6, 3, MP

                                                                **12)** /∴  4, 11, Conj         **12)** 11, Trans

                                                                                               **13)** 12, DN

                                                                                               **14)** /∴  10, 13, HS

**6.2.B.  (193–194)**

**1.**                          /∴  B ⊃ ~ A

**1)** A ⊃ ~ B          Pr

**2)** ~ ~ B ⊃ ~ A      1, Trans

**3)** /∴  B ⊃ ~ A      2, DN

**3.**                                              /∴  [(A • B) • C] ⊃ ~ [D ⊃ (E ⊃F)}

**1)** [~ (~ F ⊃ ~ E) ⊃ ~ D] ⊃ ~ [(C • B) • A]          Pr

**2)** ~ ~ [(C • B) • A] ⊃ ~ [~ (~ F ⊃ ~ E) ⊃ ~ D]      1, Trans

**3)** [(C • B) • A] ⊃ ~ [~ (~ F ⊃ ~ E) ⊃ ~ D]          2, DN

**4)** [C • (B • A)] ⊃ ~ [~ (~ F ⊃ ~ E) ⊃ ~ D]          3, Assoc

**5)** [(B • A) • C] ⊃ ~ [~ (~ F ⊃ ~ E) ⊃ ~ D]          4, Com

**6)** [(A • B) • C] ⊃ ~ [~ (~ F ⊃ ~ E) ⊃ ~ D]          5, Com

**7)** [(A • B) • C} ⊃ ~ [D ⊃ (~ F ⊃ ~ E)]              6, Trans

**8)** /∴  [(A • B) • C] ⊃ ~ [D ⊃ (E ⊃ F)]              7, Trans

**5.**                  /∴ (H ∨ F) ⊃ G

1) B ⊃ ~ [A ∨ (C ∨ D)]      Pr
2) A • (~ B ⊃ D)          Pr
3) (A • D) ⊃ [~ G ⊃ ~ (F ∨ H)]      Pr
4) A          2, Simp
5) (~ B ⊃ D) • A          2, Com
6) ~ B ⊃ D          5, Simp
7) A ∨ (C ∨ D)          4, Add
8) ~ ~ [A ∨ (C ∨ D)]          7, DN
9) ~ B          1, 8, MT
10) D          6, 9, MP
11) A • D          4, 10, Conj
12) ~ G ⊃ ~ (F ∨ H)          3, 11, MP
13) (F ∨ H) ⊃ G          12, Trans
14) /∴ (H ∨ F) ⊃ G          13, Com

**7.**                  /∴ B ∨ D

1) (A ⊃ E) • (C ⊃ G)          Pr
2) (~ B ⊃ ~ E) • (~ D ⊃ ~ G)          Pr
3) ~ (A ⊃ B) ∨ (A ∨ C)          Pr
4) A ⊃ E          1, Simp
5) (C ⊃ G) • (A ⊃ E)          1, Com
6) C ⊃ G          5, Simp
7) ~ B ⊃ ~ E          2, Simp
8) (~ D ⊃ ~ G) • (~ B ⊃ ~ F)          2, Com
9) ~ D ⊃ ~ G          8, Simp
10) E ⊃ B          7, Trans
11) G ⊃ D          9, Trans
12) A ⊃ B          4, 10, HS
13) ~ ~ (A ⊃ B)          12, DN
14) A ∨ C          3, 13, DS
15) E ∨ G          4, 6, 14, CD
16) /∴ B ∨ D          10, 11, 15, CD

### 6.2.C. (194–195)

**1.**          /∴ S

1) ~ S ⊃ ~ A    Pr
2) A          Pr
3) A ⊃ S      1, Trans
4) /∴ S      3, 2, MP

**3.**                          /∴ P ⊃ Q

   **1)** ∼ (P ⊃ S) ⊃ D     Pr

   **2)** ∼ D • (∼ Q ⊃ ∼ S)   Pr

   **3)** ∼ D               2, Simp

   **4)** (∼ Q ⊃ ∼ S) • ∼ D  2, Com

   **5)** ∼ Q ⊃ ∼ S      4, Simp

   **6)** ∼ ∼ (P ⊃ S)     1, 3, MT

   **7)** P ⊃ S           6, DN

   **8)** S ⊃ Q           5, Trans

   **9)** /∴ P ⊃ Q      7, 8, HS

**5.**                          /∴ A ∨ I

   **1)** D ∨ [E ∨ (∼ I ⊃ ∼ B)]  Pr

   **2)** (D ⊃ E) • ∼E     Pr

   **3)** D ∨ (E ∨ B)     Pr

   **4)** D ⊃ E           2, Simp

   **5)** ∼ E • (D ⊃ E)    2, Com

   **6)** ∼ E             5, Simp

   **7)** ∼ D             4, 6, MT

   **8)** E ∨ (∼ I ⊃ ∼ B)  1, 7, DS

   **9)** ∼ I ⊃ ∼ B     8, 6, DS

   **10)** B ⊃ I          9, Trans

   **11)** E ∨ B         3, 7, DS

   **12)** B              11, 6, DS

   **13)** I              10, 12, MP

   **14)** I ∨ A        13, Add

   **15)** /∴ A ∨ I    14, Com

**7.**                          /∴ M ⊃ ∼ C

   **1)** ∼ (∼ A ⊃ D) ⊃ I    Pr

   **2)** (O ⊃ ∼ I) • (∼ O ⊃ ∼ M)  Pr

   **3)** (∼ D ⊃ A) ⊃ ∼ C   Pr

   **4)** O ⊃ ∼I          2, Simp

   **5)** (∼ O ⊃ ∼ M) • (O ⊃ ∼ I)  2, Com

   **6)** ∼ O ⊃ ∼ M     5, Simp

   **7)** M ⊃ O          6, Trans

   **8)** ∼ I ⊃ ∼ ∼ (∼ A ⊃ D)  1, Trans

   **9)** ∼ I ⊃ (∼ A ⊃ D)   8, DN

   **10)** O ⊃ (∼ A ⊃ D)    4, 9, HS

   **11)** M ⊃ (∼ A ⊃ D)    7, 10, HS

   **12)** M ⊃ (∼ D ⊃ ∼ ∼ A)  11, Trans

   **13)** M ⊃ (∼ D ⊃ A)    12, DN

   **14)** /∴ M ⊃ ∼ C    13, 3, HS

**6.3.A. (200–203)**

**1.**

1) Pr
2) Pr
3) 2, Com
4) 3, DeM
5) /∴  1, 4, MT

**3.**

1) Pr
2) Pr
3) 1, Com
4) 3, Dist
5) 4, Com
6) 5, Simp
7) 6, Com
8) /∴  7, 2, DS

**5.**

1) Pr
2) Pr
3) 1, Dist
4) 3, Simp
5) 4, Simp
6) 5, DeM
7) 2, Com
8) 7, 6, DS
9) 8, 4, Conj
10) 9, Dist
11) 10, DeM
12) /∴  11, DeM

**7.**

1) Pr
2) Pr
3) 1, Dist
4) 3, Simp
5) 4, DeM
6) 2, Simp
7) 6, Trans
8) 2, Com
9) 8, Simp
10) 9, Trans
11) 10, DN
12) 3, Com
13) 12, Simp
14) 7, 11, 13, CD
15) 14, DeM
16) /∴  5, 15, Conj

**6.3.B. (203–204)**

**1.**                                    /∴  ~ (B ∨ A)

1) ~ A • (A ∨ ~ B)      Pr
2) ~ A                          1, Simp
3) (A ∨ ~ B) • ~ A      1, Com
4) A ∨ ~ B                    3, Simp
5) ~ B                          4, 2, DS
6) ~ B • ~ A                5, 2, Conj
7) /∴  ~ (B ∨ A)          6, DeM

**3.**                    /∴  ~ A

1) (A • B) ⊃ C      Pr
2) ~ C • B             Pr
3) ~ C                   2, Simp
4) B • ~ C             2, Com
5) B                       4, Simp
6) ~ (A • B)          1, 3, MT
7) ~ A ∨ ~ B        6, DeM
8) ~ B ∨ ~ A        7, Com
9) ~ ~ B               5, DN
10) /∴  ~ A           8, 9, DS

**5.**                                    $/\therefore \sim (\sim D \vee \sim A)$

   **1)** $(A \cdot B) \vee (C \cdot A)$     Pr

   **2)** $(C \vee B) \supset D$     Pr

   **3)** $(A \cdot B) \vee (A \cdot C)$     1, Com

   **4)** $A \cdot (B \vee C)$     3, Dist

   **5)** $A$     4, Simp

   **6)** $(B \vee C) \cdot A$     4, Com

   **7)** $B \vee C$     6, Simp

   **8)** $C \vee B$     7, Com

   **9)** $D$     2, 8, MP

   **10)** $D \cdot A$     9, 5, Conj

   **11)** $\sim \sim (D \cdot A)$     10, DN

   **12)** $/\therefore \sim (\sim D \vee \sim A)$     11, DeM

**7.**                                    $/\therefore \sim (\sim E \cdot C) \cdot \sim (\sim C \cdot E)$

   **1)** $A \vee [(\sim C \cdot B) \vee (E \cdot D)]$     Pr

   **2)** $\sim A \cdot \sim (E \cdot \sim C)$     Pr

   **3)** $\sim A$     2, Simp

   **4)** $\sim (E \cdot \sim C) \cdot \sim A$     2, Com

   **5)** $\sim (E \cdot \sim C)$     4, Simp

   **6)** $\sim (\sim C \cdot E)$     5, Com

   **7)** $(\sim C \cdot B) \vee (E \cdot D)$     1, 3, DS

   **8)** $[(\sim C \cdot B) \vee E] \cdot [(\sim C \cdot B) \vee D]$     7, Dist

   **9)** $(\sim C \cdot B) \vee E$     8, Simp

   **10)** $E \vee (\sim C \cdot B)$     9, Com

   **11)** $(E \vee \sim C) \cdot (E \vee B)$     10, Dist

   **12)** $E \vee \sim C$     11, Simp

   **13)** $\sim \sim E \vee \sim C$     12, DN

   **14)** $\sim (\sim E \cdot C)$     13, DeM

   **15)** $/\therefore \sim (\sim E \cdot C) \cdot \sim (\sim C \cdot E)$     14, 6, Conj

**6.3.C.** (204–205)

**1.**                          $/\therefore \sim S$

   **1)** $S \supset (A \cdot U)$    Pr

   **2)** $\sim U$    Pr

   **3)** $\sim U \vee \sim A$    2, Add

   **4)** $\sim A \vee \sim U$    3, Com

   **5)** $\sim (A \cdot U)$    4, DeM

   **6)** $/\therefore \sim S$      1, 5, MT

**3.**                          $/\therefore \sim (\sim P \cdot O)$

   **1)** $\sim [\sim P \cdot (\sim H \vee O)]$    Pr

   **2)** $\sim \sim P \vee \sim (\sim H \vee O)$    1, DeM

   **3)** $\sim \sim P \vee (\sim \sim H \cdot \sim O)$    2, DeM

   **4)** $\sim \sim P \vee (\sim O \cdot \sim \sim H)$    3, Com

   **5)** $(\sim \sim P \vee \sim O) \cdot (\sim \sim P \vee \sim \sim H)$    4, Dist

   **6)** $\sim \sim P \vee \sim O$    5, Simp

   **7)** $/\therefore \sim (\sim P \cdot O)$    6, DeM

**5.**                                        /∴ S ∨ D
  **1)** (∼ D ⊃ ∼ F) • (M ⊃ S)        Pr
  **2)** (F • L) ∨ (U • M)            Pr
  **3)** ∼ D ⊃ ∼ F                    1, Simp
  **4)** (M ⊃ S) • (∼ D ⊃ ∼ F)        1, Com
  **5)** M ⊃ S                        4, Simp
  **6)** F ⊃ D                        3, Trans
  **7)** (F • L) ∨ (M • U)            2, Com
  **8)** [(F • L) ∨ M] • [(F • L) ∨ U]   7, Dist
  **9)** (F • L) ∨ M                  8, Simp
  **10)** M ∨ (F • L)                 9, Com
  **11)** (M ∨ F) • (M ∨ L)           10, Dist
  **12)** M ∨ F                       11, Simp
  **13)** /∴ S ∨ D                    5, 6, 12, CD

**7.**                                        /∴ B ∨ D
  **1)** ∼ [F • (∼ P ∨ ∼ O)]          Pr
  **2)** (∼ D ⊃ ∼ O) • (∼ B ⊃ F)       Pr
  **3)** ∼ D ⊃ ∼ O                     2, Simp
  **4)** (∼ B ⊃ F) • (∼ D ⊃ ∼ O)       2, Com
  **5)** ∼ B ⊃ F                       4, Simp
  **6)** ∼ F ⊃ ∼ ∼ B                   5, Trans
  **7)** ∼ F ⊃ B                       6, DN
  **8)** O ⊃ D                         3, Trans
  **9)** ∼ F ∨ ∼ (∼ P ∨ ∼ O)           1, DeM
  **10)** ∼ F ∨ ∼ ∼ (P • O)            9, DeM
  **11)** ∼ F ∨ (P • O)                10, DN
  **12)** ∼ F ∨ (O • P)                11, Com
  **13)** (∼ F ∨ O) • (∼ F ∨ P)        12, Dist
  **14)** ∼ F ∨ O                      13, Simp
  **15)** /∴ B ∨ D                     7, 8, 14, CD

## 6.4.A. (209–212)

**1.**
  **1)** Pr
  **2)** Pr
  **3)** 1, Com
  **4)** 3, Exp
  **5)** /∴ 4, 2, MP

**3.**
  **1)** Pr
  **2)** Pr
  **3)** 1, Trans
  **4)** 3, Exp
  **5)** 2, Com
  **6)** 5, Impl
  **7)** 6, Exp
  **8)** 7, 4, HS
  **9)** /∴ 8, Exp

**5.**
  **1)** Pr
  **2)** Pr
  **3)** Pr
  **4)** 1, Com
  **5)** 2, Add
  **6)** 5, DeM
  **7)** 4, 6, DS
  **8)** 3, Trans
  **9)** 8, Exp
  **10)** 9, 2, MT
  **11)** 10, DeM
  **12)** /∴ 11, 7, Conj

**7.**
  **1)** Pr
  **2)** Pr
  **3)** Pr
  **4)** Pr
  **5)** 4, Simp
  **6)** 4, Com
  **7)** 6, Simp
  **8)** 3, 7, MT
  **9)** 2, 8, DS
  **10)** 1, 9, MP
  **11)** 10, DeM
  **12)** 5, DN
  **13)** 11, 12, DS
  **14)** 13, Add
  **15)** 14, Impl

**6.4.B. (212)**

**1.**                              /∴ C

  **1)** (A ⊃ B) ⊃ C    Pr
  **2)** ~ A              Pr
  **3)** ~ A ∨ B          2, Add
  **4)** A ⊃ B            3, Impl
  **5)** /∴ C             1, 4, MP

**5.**                              /∴ G ⊃ C

  **1)** A ⊃ (~ C ⊃ ~ D)              Pr
  **2)** G ⊃ [A • (B • D)]            Pr
  **3)** G ⊃ [A • (D • B)]            2, Com
  **4)** G ⊃ [(A • D) • B]            3, Assoc
  **5)** ~ G ∨ [(A • D) • B]          4, Impl
  **6)** [~ G ∨ (A • D)] • (~ G ∨ B)  5, Dist
  **7)** ~ G ∨ (A • D)                6, Simp
  **8)** G ⊃ (A • D)                  7, Impl
  **9)** A ⊃ (D ⊃ C)                  1, Trans
  **10)** (A • D) ⊃ C                 9, Exp
  **11)** /∴ G ⊃ C                    8, 10, HS

**7.**                              /∴ (F • E) ⊃ (B ⊃ D)

  **1)** A ⊃ [B ⊃ (C ⊃ D)]      Pr
  **2)** (A ⊃ ~C) ⊃ ~ E         Pr
  **3)** A ⊃ [(B • C) ⊃ D]      1, Exp
  **4)** A ⊃ [(C • B) ⊃ D]      3, Com
  **5)** A ⊃ [C ⊃ (B ⊃ D)]      4, Exp
  **6)** (A • C) ⊃ (B ⊃ D)      5, Exp
  **7)** ~ ~ E ⊃ ~ (A ⊃ ~ C)    2, Trans
  **8)** E ⊃ ~ (A ⊃ ~ C)        7, DN
  **9)** E ⊃ ~ (~ A ∨ ~ C)      8, Impl
  **10)** E ⊃ ~ ~ (A • C)       9, DeM
  **11)** E ⊃ (A • C)           10, DN
  **12)** E ⊃ (B ⊃ D)           11, 6, HS
  **13)** [E ⊃ (B ⊃ D)] ∨ ~ F   12, Add
  **14)** ~ F ∨ [E ⊃ (B ⊃ D)]   13, Com
  **15)** F ⊃ [E ⊃ (B ⊃ D)]     14, Impl
  **16)** /∴ (F • E) ⊃ (B ⊃ D)  15, Exp

**3.**                              /∴ A ⊃ D

  **1)** A ⊃ (B • C)    Pr
  **2)** ~ B            Pr
  **3)** ~ B ∨ ~ C      2, Add
  **4)** ~ (B • C)      3, DeM
  **5)** ~A             1, 4, MT
  **6)** ~A ∨ D         5, Add
  **7)** /∴ A ⊃ D       6, Impl

**6.4.C.  (213–214)**

**1.**                                   /∴  M ⊃ D

   **1)**  M ⊃ (F ⊃ D)  Pr

   **2)**  F              Pr

   **3)**  (M · F) ⊃ D  1, Exp

   **4)**  (F · M) ⊃ D  3, Com

   **5)**  F ⊃ (M ⊃ D)  4, Exp

   **6)**  /∴  M ⊃ D)  5, 2, MP

**3.**                                   /∴  ~ (S ⊃ T)

   **1)**  (L · S) ∨ (T · L)  Pr

   **2)**  ~ T            Pr

   **3)**  (L · S) ∨ (L · T)  1, Com

   **4)**  L · (S ∨ T)  3, Dist

   **5)**  (S ∨ T) · L  4, Com

   **6)**  S ∨ T      5, Simp

   **7)**  T ∨ S      6, Com

   **8)**  S           7, 2, DS

   **9)**  S · ~ T    8, 2, Conj

  **10)**  ~ ~ (S · ~ T)  9, DN

  **11)**  ~ (~ S ∨ ~~ T)  10, DeM

  **12)**  ~ (~ S ∨ T)  11, DN

  **13)**  /∴  ~(S ⊃ T)  12, Impl

**5.**                                   /∴  T ⊃ (L ⊃ I)

   **1)**  T ⊃ (P ⊃ W)  Pr

   **2)**  (~ I ⊃ ~ W) · (L ⊃ P)  Pr

   **3)**  ~ I ⊃ ~ W  2, Simp

   **4)**  (L ⊃ P) · (~ I ⊃ ~ W)  2, Com

   **5)**  L ⊃ P     4, Simp

   **6)**  W ⊃ I     3, Trans

   **7)**  (T · P) ⊃ W  1, Exp

   **8)**  (T · P) ⊃ I  7, 6, HS

   **9)**  (P · T) ⊃ I  8, Com

  **10)**  P ⊃ (T ⊃ I)  9, Exp

  **11)**  L ⊃ (T ⊃ I)  5, 10, HS

  **12)**  (L · T) ⊃ I  11, Exp

  **13)**  (T · L) ⊃ I  12, Com

  **14)**  /∴  T ⊃ (L ⊃ I)  13, Exp

**7.**                           /∴  R ⊃ (~ W ⊃ ~ E)

    **1)**  ~ (E • ~ W) ∨ (D • E)   Pr

    **2)**  D ⊃ (E ⊃ ~ R)   Pr

    **3)**  (E • ~ W) ⊃ (D • E)   1, Impl

    **4)**  (D • E) ⊃ ~ R   2, Exp

    **5)**  (E • ~ W) ⊃ ~ R   3, 4, HS

    **6)**  ~ ~ R ⊃ ~ (E • ~ W)   5, Trans

    **7)**  R ⊃ ~ (E • ~ W)   6, DN

    **8)**  R ⊃ (~ E ∨ ~ ~ W)   7, DeM

    **9)**  R ⊃ (~ E ∨ W)   8, DN

    **10)**  R ⊃ (E ⊃ W)   9, Impl

    **11)**  /∴  R ⊃ (~W ⊃ ~E)   10, Trans

## 6.5.A. (219–222)

| **1.** | **3.** | **5.** | **7.** |
|---|---|---|---|
| **1)** Pr | **1)** Pr | **1)** Pr | **1)** Pr |
| **2)** Pr | **2)** Pr | **2)** Pr | **2)** Pr |
| **3)** 1, Trans | **3)** 1, Exp | **3)** 1, Simp | **3)** 2, Com |
| **4)** 3, Exp | **4)** 2, Com | **4)** 1, Com | **4)** 3, Simp |
| **5)** 2, 4, Hs | **5)** 4, Exp | **5)** 4, Simp | **5)** 4, Simp |
| **6)** 5, Impl | **6)** 3, 5, HS | **6)** 3, Exp | **6)** 1, 5, MP |
| **7)** 6, DN | **7)** 6, Exp | **7)** 2, Com | **7)** 2, Simp |
| **8)** /∴ 7, Taut | **8)** 7, Assoc | **8)** 7, Dist | **8)** 7, DeM |
|  | **9)** 8, Taut | **9)** 8, Simp | **9)** 8, DN |
|  | **10** /∴ 9, Exp | **10)** 6, 9, MP | **10)** 4, Com |
|  |  | **11)** 8, Com | **11)** 10, Simp |
|  |  | **12)** 11, Simp | **12)** 9, 11, DS |
|  |  | **13)** 10, 5, 12, CD | **13)** 6, Equiv |
|  |  | **14)** /∴ 13, Taut | **14)** 13, Simp |
|  |  |  | **15)** 14, Com |
|  |  |  | **16)** /∴ 15, 12, DS |

**6.5.B. (222)**

**1.**              /∴ A ⊃ C

  **1)** A ⊃ B         Pr
  **2)** (A • B) ⊃ C     Pr
  **3)** (B • A) ⊃ C     2, Com
  **4)** B ⊃ (A ⊃ C)     3, Exp
  **5)** A ⊃ (A ⊃ C)     1, 4, HS
  **6)** (A • A) ⊃ C     5, Exp
  **7)** /∴ A ⊃ C     6, Taut

**3.**              /∴ A ⊃ C

  **1)** A ≡ B         Pr
  **2)** C ∆ ∼ B     Pr
  **3)** (A ⊃ B) • (B ⊃ A)     1, Equiv
  **4)** (C ∨ ∼ B) • (∼C ∨ ∼ ∼ B)     2, Equiv
  **5)** A ⊃ B     3, Simp
  **6)** C ∨ ∼ B     4, Simp
  **7)** ∼ B ∨ C     6, Com
  **8)** B ⊃ C     7, Impl
  **9)** /∴ A ⊃ C     5, 8, HS

**5.**              /∴ ∼ A ≡ D

  **1)** ∼ (A • B) ⊃ (C • A)     Pr
  **2)** ∼ D ∨ ∼A     Pr
  **3)** ∼ ∼ (A • B) ∨ (C • A)     1, Impl
  **4)** (A • B) ∨ (C • A)     3, DN
  **5)** (A • B) ∨ (A • C)     4, Com
  **6)** A • (B ∨ C)     5, Dist
  **7)** A     6, Simp
  **8)** ∼ ∼ A     7, DN
  **9)** ∼ ∼ A ∨ D     8, Add
  **10)** ∼ A ⊃ D     9, Impl
  **11)** D ⊃ ∼ A     2, Impl
  **12)** (∼ A ⊃ D) • (D ⊃ ∼ A)     10, 11, Conj
  **13)** /∴ ∼ A ≡ D     12, Equiv

**7.**              /∴ C ⊃ D

  **1)** A ⊃ (B ⊃ D)     Pr
  **2)** C ⊃ (B ⊃ A)     Pr
  **3)** ∼ B ⊃ ∼ C     Pr
  **4)** (C • B) ⊃ A     2, Exp
  **5)** (C • B) ⊃ (B ⊃ D)     4, 1, HS
  **6)** [(C • B) • B] ⊃ D     5, Exp
  **7)** [C • (B • B)] ⊃ D     6, Assoc
  **8)** (C • B) ⊃ D     7, Taut
  **9)** (B • C) ⊃ D     8, Com
  **10)** B ⊃ (C ⊃ D)     9, Exp
  **11)** C ⊃ B     3, Trans
  **12)** C ⊃ (C ⊃ D)     11, 10, HS
  **13)** (C • C) ⊃ D     12, Exp
  **14)** /∴ C ⊃ D     13, Taut

**6.5.C. (223–224)**

**1.**              /∴ R ⊃ ∼ M

  **1)** ∼ D ≡ ∼ M     Pr
  **2)** R ≡ ∼ D     Pr
  **3)** (∼ D ⊃ ∼ M) • (∼ M ⊃ ∼ D)     1, Equiv
  **4)** (R ⊃ ∼ D) • (∼ D ⊃ R)     2, Equiv
  **5)** R ⊃ ∼ D     4, Simp
  **6)** ∼ D ⊃ ∼ M     3, Simp
  **7)** /∴ R ⊃ ∼ M     5, 6, HS

**3.**              /∴ V ⊃ P

  **1)** G ≡ V     Pr
  **2)** V ⊃ (G ⊃ P)     Pr
  **3)** (G ⊃ V) • (V ⊃ G)     1, Equiv
  **4)** (V ⊃ G) • (G ⊃ V)     3, Com
  **5)** V ⊃ G     4, Simp
  **6)** (V • G) ⊃ P     2, Exp
  **7)** (G • V) ⊃ P     6, Com
  **8)** G ⊃ (V ⊃ P)     7, Exp
  **9)** V ⊃ (V ⊃ P)     5, 8, HS
  **10)** (V • V) ⊃ P     9, Exp
  **11)** /∴ V ⊃ P     10, Taut

**5.**                          /∴ I ∨ R

1) I Δ D                         Pr
2) D Δ ~ R                    Pr
3) (I ∨ D) • (~ I ∨ ~ D)     1, Equiv
4) (D ∨ ~ R) • (~ D ∨ ~ ~ R)   2, Equiv
5) I ∨ D                      3, Simp
6) (~ D ∨ ~ ~ R) • (D • ~ R)   4, Com
7) ~ D ∨ ~ ~ R           6, Simp
8) ~ D ∨ R               7, DN
9) ~ ~ I ∨ D            5, DN
10) ~I ⊃ D              9, Impl
11) D ⊃ R               8, Impl
12) ~ I ⊃ R          10, 11, HS
13) ~ ~ I ∨ R         12, Impl
14) /∴ I ∨ R        13, DN

**7.**                          /∴ ~ (W ⊃ ~ A)

1) (D ⊃ W) • (L ⊃ W)     Pr
2) (A • D) ∨ (L • A)       Pr
3) D ⊃ W               1, Simp
4) (L ⊃ W) • (D ⊃ W)     1, Com
5) L ⊃ W               4, Simp
6) (A • D) ∨ (A • L)       2, Com
7) A • (D ∨ L)           6, Dist
8) A                      7, Simp
9) (D ∨ L) • A           7, Com
10) D ∨ L               9, Simp
11) W ∨ W            3, 5, 10, CD
12) W                    11, Taut
13) W • A              12, 8, Conj
14) ~ ~ (W • A)        13, DN
15) ~ (~ W ∨ ~ A)     14, DeM
16) /∴ ~ (W ⊃ ~ A)    15, Impl

# CHAPTER 7

### 7.1.B. (234–235)

**1.**                   /∴ A ⊃ E

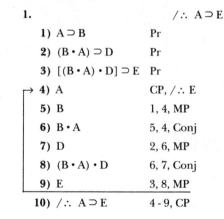

1) A ⊃ B           Pr
2) (B • A) ⊃ D      Pr
3) [(B • A) • D] ⊃ E  Pr
4) A                CP, /∴ E
5) B                1, 4, MP
6) B • A            5, 4, Conj
7) D                2, 6, MP
8) (B • A) • D      6, 7, Conj
9) E                3, 8, MP
10) /∴ A ⊃ E      4 - 9, CP

**3.**                                                    $/\therefore\ (A \lor B) \supset C$

    **1)** $[A \supset (B \cdot C)] \cdot [B \supset (D \cdot C)]$   Pr

    **2)** $A \supset (B \cdot C)$                      1, Simp

    **3)** $[B \supset (D \cdot C)] \cdot [A \supset (B \cdot C)]$   1, Com

    **4)** $B \supset (D \cdot C)$                      4, Simp

  → **5)** $A \lor B$                           CP, $/\therefore\ $ C

    **6)** $(B \cdot C) \lor (D \cdot C)$               2, 4, 5, CD

    **7)** $(C \cdot B) \lor (D \cdot C)$               6, Com

    **8)** $(C \cdot B) \lor (C \cdot D)$               7, Com

    **9)** $C \cdot (B \lor D)$                    8, Dist

  **10)** $C$                             9, Simp

  **11)** $/\therefore\ (A \lor B) \supset C$         5 - 10, CP

**5.**                                                    $/\therefore\ D \supset \sim A$

    **1)** $[A \supset (B \supset C)] \cdot [A \supset (C \supset B)]$   Pr

    **2)** $(C \equiv B) \supset \sim D$               Pr

    **3)** $[\sim A \lor (B \supset C)] \cdot [A \supset (C \supset B)]$   1, Impl

    **4)** $[\sim A \lor (B \supset C)] \cdot [\sim A \lor (C \supset B)]$   4, Impl

    **5)** $\sim A \lor [(B \supset C) \cdot (C \supset B)]$   5, Dist

    **6)** $\sim A \lor (B \equiv C)$              6, Equiv

    **7)** $A \supset (B \equiv C)$              7, Impl

    **8)** $A \supset (C \equiv B)$              8, Com

  → **9)** $D$                           CP, $/\therefore\ \sim A$

  **10)** $\sim \sim D$                       9, DN

  **11)** $\sim (C \equiv B)$               2, 10, MT

  **12)** $\sim A$                        8, 11, MT

  **13)** $/\therefore\ D \supset \sim A$         9 - 12, CP

**7.**                              $/\therefore\ \sim B \lor D$

1) $\sim (A \lor B) \lor C$            Pr
2) $C \supset D$                    Pr
3) $(\sim A \cdot \sim B) \lor C$       1, DeM
4) $C \lor (\sim A \cdot \sim B)$       3, Com
5) $C \lor (\sim B \cdot \sim A)$       4, Com
6) $(C \lor \sim B) \cdot (C \lor \sim A)$   5, Dist
7) $C \lor \sim B$                 6, Simp
8) $\sim B \lor C$                 7, Com
→ 9) $B$                        CP, $/\therefore\ D$
10) $\sim \sim B$                 9, DN
11) $C$                         8, 10, DS
12) $D$                         2, 11, MP
13) $B \supset D$                  9 - 12, CP
14) $/\therefore\ \sim B \lor D$          13, Impl

**7.1.C. (235–236)**

**1.**                              $/\therefore\ O \supset \sim E$

1) $\sim [\sim (\sim R \supset \sim D) \cdot \sim E]$   Pr
2) $\sim D$                      Pr
3) $O \supset (E \supset D)$            Pr
→ 4) $O$                        CP, $/\therefore\ \sim E$
5) $E \supset D$                   3, 4, MP
6) $\sim E$                      5, 2, MT
7) $/\therefore\ O \supset \sim E$          4 - 6, CP

**3.**                              $/\therefore\ (F \lor E) \supset M$

1) $[F \supset (M \cdot E)] \cdot [E \supset (C \cdot M)]$   Pr
2) $F \supset (M \cdot E)$             1, Simp
3) $[E \supset (C \cdot M)] \cdot [F \supset (M \cdot E)]$   1, Com
4) $E \supset (C \cdot M)$             4, Simp
→ 5) $F \lor E$                    CP, $/\therefore\ M$
6) $(M \cdot E) \lor (C \cdot M)$        2, 4, 5, CD
7) $(M \cdot E) \lor (M \cdot C)$        6, Com
8) $M \cdot (E \lor C)$              7, Dist
9) $M$                         8, Simp
10) $/\therefore\ (F \lor E) \supset M$       5 - 9, CP

**5.**                                        $/\therefore \ \sim K \supset \sim A$

| | | |
|---|---|---|
| **1)** | $\sim (I \cdot \sim K)$ | Pr |
| **2)** | $\sim (C \cdot \sim \sim A) \cdot \sim (\sim I \cdot \sim C)$ | Pr |
| **3)** | $\sim (C \cdot \sim \sim A)$ | 2, Simp |
| **4)** | $\sim (\sim I \cdot \sim C) \cdot \sim (C \cdot \sim \sim A)$ | 2, Com |
| **5)** | $\sim (\sim I \cdot \sim C)$ | 4, Simp |
| **6)** | $\sim I \vee \sim \sim K$ | 1, DeM |
| **7)** | $\sim I \vee K$ | 6, DN |
| **8)** | $I \supset K$ | 7, Impl |
| **9)** | $\sim (C \cdot A)$ | 3, DN |
| **10)** | $\sim C \vee \sim A$ | 9, DeM |
| **11)** | $C \supset \sim A$ | 10, Impl |
| **12)** | $\sim \sim (I \vee C)$ | 5, DeM |
| **13)** | $I \vee C$ | 12, DN |
| **14)** | $K \vee \sim A$ | 8, 11, 13, CD |
| →**15)** | $\sim K$ | CP, $/\therefore \ \sim A$ |
| **16)** | $\sim A$ | 15, 3, DS |
| **17)** | $/\therefore \ \sim K \supset \sim A$ | 15 - 16, CP |

**7.**                                        $/\therefore \ I \supset \sim C$

| | | |
|---|---|---|
| **1)** | $[I \supset (P \supset A)] \cdot [I \supset (A \supset P)]$ | Pr |
| **2)** | $(A \equiv P) \supset \sim C$ | Pr |
| **3)** | $I \supset (P \supset A)$ | 1, Simp |
| **4)** | $[I \supset (A \supset P)] \cdot [I \supset (P \supset A)]$ | 1, Com |
| **5)** | $I \supset (A \supset P)$ | 5, Simp |
| →**6)** | $I$ | CP, $/\therefore \ \sim C$ |
| **7)** | $A \supset P$ | 5, 6, MP |
| **8)** | $P \supset A$ | 3, 6, MP |
| **9)** | $(A \supset P) \cdot (P \supset A)$ | 7, 8, Conj |
| **10)** | $A \equiv P$ | 9, Equiv |
| **11)** | $\sim C$ | 2, 10, MP |
| **12)** | $/\therefore \ I \supset \sim C$ | 6 - 11, CP |

**7.2.A. (245)**

**1.**                    /∴ ~ E ⊃ ~ B

| | | |
|---|---|---|
| 1) | A ∨ (B ⊃ C) | Pr |
| 2) | C ⊃ E | Pr |
| 3) | ~ A | Pr |
| → 4) | ~ (~ E ⊃ ~ B) | IP |
| 5) | ~ (~ ~ E ∨ ~ B) | 4, Impl |
| 6) | ~ ~ (~ E • B) | 5, DeM |
| 7) | ~ E • B | 6, DN |
| 8) | B ⊃ C | 1, 3, DS |
| 9) | B ⊃ E | 8, 2, HS |
| 10) | ~ E | 7, Simp |
| 11) | ~ B | 9, 10, MT |
| 12) | B • ~ E | 7, Com |
| 13) | B | 12, Simp |
| 14) | B • ~ B | 13, 11, Conj |
| 15) | /∴ ~ E ⊃ ~ B | 4 - 14, IP |

**3.**                    /∴ ~ (~ D • C)

| | | |
|---|---|---|
| 1) | (A ∨ B) ⊃ ~ C | Pr |
| 2) | ~ D ⊃ (D ∨ A) | Pr |
| → 3) | ~ ~ (~ D • C) | IP |
| 4) | ~ D • C | 3, DN |
| 5) | ~ D | 4, Simp |
| 6) | C • ~ D | 4, Com |
| 7) | C | 6, Com |
| 8) | ~ ~ C | 7, DN |
| 9) | ~ (A ∨ B) | 1, 8, MT |
| 10) | ~ A • ~ B | 9, DeM |
| 11) | D ∨ A | 2, 5, MT |
| 12) | A | 11, 5, DS |
| 13) | ~ A | 10, Simp |
| 14) | A • ~ A | 12, 13, Conj |
| 15) | /∴ ~ (~ D • C) | 3 - 14, IP |

**5.**                    /∴ E ∨ D

| | | |
|---|---|---|
| 1) | A ≡ B | Pr |
| 2) | (C ∨ A) • ~ C | Pr |
| 3) | B ⊃ D | Pr |
| → 4) | ~ (E ∨ D) | IP |
| 5) | ~ E • ~ D | 4, DeM |
| 6) | ~ D • ~ E | 5, Com |
| 7) | ~ D | 6, Simp |
| 8) | ~ B | 3, 7, MT |
| 9) | (A ⊃ B) • (B ⊃ A) | 1, Equiv |
| 10) | A ⊃ B | 9, Simp |
| 11) | C ∨ A | 2, Simp |
| 12) | ~ C • (C ∨ A) | 2, Com |
| 13) | ~ C | 12, Simp |
| 14) | A | 11, 13, DS |
| 15) | B | 10, 14, MP |
| 16) | B • ~ B | 15, 8, Conj |
| 17) | /∴ E ∨ D | 4 - 16, IP |

**7.**                    /∴ D • A

| | | |
|---|---|---|
| 1) | (A ∨ B) • ~ C | Pr |
| 2) | ~ B • (C ∨ D) | Pr |
| → 3) | ~ (D • A) | IP |
| 4) | ~ D ∨ ~ A | 3, DeM |
| 5) | A ∨ B | 1, Simp |
| 6) | ~ C • (A ∨ B) | 1, Com |
| 7) | ~ C | 6, Simp |
| 8) | ~ B | 2, Simp |
| 9) | (C ∨ D) • ~ B | 2, Com |
| 10) | C ∨ D | 9, Simp |
| 11) | D | 10, 7, DS |
| 12) | ~ A ∨ ~ D | 4, Com |
| 13) | B ∨ A | 5, Com |
| 14) | A | 13, 8, DS |
| 15) | ~ ~ A | 14, DN |
| 16) | ~ D | 12, 15, DS |
| 17) | D • ~D | 11, 16, Conj |
| 18) | /∴ D • A | 3 - 17, IP |

**7.2.B.  (246–247)**

**1.**                                                    /∴  B • I

   **1)** (B • I) • (D • B)    Pr
   **2)** ∼ D                      Pr
→**3)** ∼ (B • I)                IP
   **4)** B • I                      1, Simp
   **5)** (B • I) • ∼ (B • I)   4, 3, Conj
   **6)** /∴  B • I              3 - 6. IP

**3.**                          /∴  L • D

  **1)** D ≡ T                    Pr
  **2)** T • L                     Pr
→ **3)** ∼ (L • D)              IP
  **4)** T                           2, Simp
  **5)** L • T                     2, Com
  **6)** L                           5, Simp
  **7)** ∼ L ∨ ∼ D           3, DeM
  **8)** ∼ ∼ L                   6, DN
  **9)** ∼ D                       7, 8, DS
 **10)** (D ⊃ T) • (T ⊃ D)   1, Equiv
 **11)** (T ⊃ D) • (D ⊃ T)   10, Com
 **12)** T ⊃ D                   11, Simp
 **13)** ∼ T                       12, 9, MT
 **14)** T • ∼ T                 4, 13, Conj
 **15)** /∴  L • D            3 - 14, IP

**5.**                                    /∴  ∼ (∼ C ∨ ∼ A)

  **1)** (A • W) • (D • A)        Pr
  **2)** (D ∨ W) ⊃ C             Pr
→ **3)** ∼ ∼ (∼ C ∨ ∼ A)     IP
  **4)** ∼ C ∨ ∼ A               3, DN
  **5)** (A • W) • (A • D)        1, Com
  **6)** A • (W ∨ D)             5, Dist
  **7)** A                             6, Simp
  **8)** (W ∨ D) • A             6, Com
  **9)** W ∨ D                     8, Simp
 **10)** ∼ A ∨ ∼ C               4, Com
 **11)** ∼ ∼ A                     7, DN
 **12)** ∼ C                         10, 11, DS
 **13)** D ∨ W                     9, Com
 **14)** C                             2, 13, MP
 **15)** C • ∼ C                   14, 12, Conj
 **16)** /∴  ∼ (∼ C ∨ ∼ A)   3 - 15, IP

**7.**                                                $/\therefore \ \sim F \equiv H$

   **1)** $\sim (F \cdot S) \supset (B \cdot F)$           Pr

   **2)** $\sim H \vee \sim F$                 Pr

  **→ 3)** $\sim (\sim F \equiv H)$               IP

   **4)** $\sim [(\sim F \cdot H) \vee (\sim \sim F \cdot \sim H)]$   3, Equiv

   **5)** $\sim (\sim F \cdot H) \cdot \sim (\sim \sim F \cdot \sim H)$   4, DeM

   **6)** $\sim (\sim \sim F \cdot \sim H) \cdot \sim (\sim F \cdot H)$   5, Com

   **7)** $\sim (\sim \sim F \cdot \sim H)$          6, Simp

   **8)** $\sim \sim (\sim F \vee H)$            7, DeM

   **9)** $\sim F \vee H$                  8, DN

  **10)** $\sim \sim (F \cdot S) \vee (B \cdot F)$     1, Impl

  **11)** $(F \cdot S) \vee (B \cdot F)$        10, DN

  **12)** $(F \cdot S) \vee (F \cdot B)$        11, Com

  **13)** $F \cdot (S \vee B)$            12, Dist

  **14)** $F$                      13, Simp

  **15)** $\sim \sim F$                14, DN

  **16)** $H$                    9, 15, DS

  **17)** $\sim F \vee \sim H$           2, Com

  **18)** $\sim H$               17, 15, DS

  **19)** $H \cdot \sim H$          16, 18, Conj

  **20)** $/\therefore \ \sim F \equiv H$      3 - 19, IP

    **7.2.C. (247–248)**

**1.**                                          $/\therefore \ C \supset (A \supset B)$

   **1)** $(A \supset B) \supset [C \supset (A \supset B)]$   Pr

   **2)** $\sim A \vee B$                Pr

  **→ 3)** $C$                  CP, $/\therefore \ A \supset B$

   **→ 4)** $A$                 CP, $/\therefore \ B$

   **→5)** $\sim B$                 IP

   **6)** $B \vee \sim A$             2, Com

   **7)** $\sim A$                 6, 5, DS

   **8)** $A \cdot \sim A$             4, 7, Conj

   **9)** $B$                    5 - 8, IP

  **10)** $A \supset B$             4 - 9, CP

  **11)** $/\therefore \ C \supset (A \supset B)$   3 - 10, CP

**3.**                                         $/\therefore \ D \supset [C \supset (B \supset A)]$

1) $[(\sim A \cdot B) \cdot C] \supset \sim D$   Pr
2) D   CP, $/\therefore$ C $\supset$ (B $\supset$ A)
3) C   CP, $/\therefore$ B $\supset$ A
4) B   CP, $/\therefore$ A
5) $\sim A$   IP
6) $\sim A \cdot B$   5, 4, Conj
7) $(\sim A \cdot B) \cdot C$   6, 3, Conj
8) $\sim D$   1, 7, MP
9) $D \cdot \sim D$   2, 8, Conj
10) A   5 - 9, IP
11) $B \supset A$   4 - 10, CP
12) $C \supset (B \supset A)$   3 - 11, CP
13) $/\therefore \ D \supset [C \supset (B \supset A)]$   2 - 12, CP

**5.**                          $/\therefore \ (B \supset \sim D) \supset \sim A$

1) $A \supset (B \cdot C)$   Pr
2) $A \supset (C \cdot D)$   Pr
3) $B \supset \sim D$   CP, $/\therefore \ \sim A$
4) $\sim \sim A$   IP
5) A   4, DN
6) $B \cdot C$   1, 5, MP
7) B   6, Simp
8) $\sim D$   3, 7, MP
9) $C \cdot D$   2, 5, MP
10) $D \cdot C$   9, Com
11) D   10, Simp
12) $D \cdot \sim D$   11, 8, Conj
13) $\sim A$   4 - 12, IP
14) $/\therefore \ (B \supset \sim D) \supset \sim A$   3 - 13, CP

**7.**                          $/\therefore \ A \vee B$

1) $\sim (A \vee B) \supset (C \cdot D)$   Pr
2) $C \supset (\sim B \supset \sim D)$   Pr
3) $\sim A$   CP, $/\therefore \ B$
4) $\sim B$   IP
5) $\sim A \cdot \sim B$   3, 4, Conj
6) $\sim (A \vee B)$   5, DeM
7) $C \cdot D$   1, 6, MP
8) C   7, Simp
9) $\sim B \supset \sim D$   2, 8, MP
10) $\sim D$   9, 4, MP
11) $D \cdot C$   7, Com
12) D   11, Simp
13) $D \cdot \sim D$   12, 10, Conj
14) B   4 - 13, IP
15) $\sim A \supset B$   3 - 14, CP
16) $\sim \sim A \vee B$   15, Impl
17) $/\therefore \ A \vee B$   16, DN

**7.2.D.  (248–249)**

**1.**                                  /∴  C ⊃ ~ E

    **1)**  (C ⊃ D) • (E ⊃ ~ D)   Pr

    **2)**  C ⊃ D                      1, Simp

    **3)**  (E ⊃ ~ D) • (C ⊃ D)   1, Com

    **4)**  E ⊃ ~ D                   3, Simp

→ **5)**  C                            CP, /∴  ~ E

  → **6)**  ~ ~ E                        IP

    **7)**  E                             6, DN

    **8)**  ~ D                          4, 7, MP

    **9)**  D                             2, 5, MP

    **10)** D • ~ D                    9, 8, Conj

  **11)** ~ E                          6 - 10, IP

    **12)** /∴  C ⊃ ~ E            5 - 11, CP

**3.**                                  /∴  (W • M) ⊃ S

    **1)**  (C Δ L) ⊃ S               Pr

    **2)**  ~ (L ≡ ~ C) ⊃ ~ W       Pr

→ **3)**  W • M                        CP, /∴  S

  → **4)**  ~ S                           IP

    **5)**  ~ (C Δ L)                   1, 4, MT

    **6)**  W                             3, Simp

    **7)**  ~ ~ W                        6, DN

    **8)**  ~ ~ (L ≡ ~ C)            2, 7, MT

    **9)**  L ≡ ~ C                     8, DN

    **10)** (L ⊃ ~ C) • (~ C ⊃ L)   9, Equiv

    **11)** (~ L ∨ ~ C) • (~ C ⊃ L)   10, Impl

    **12)** (~ L ∨ ~ C) • (~ ~ C ∨ L)   11, Impl

    **13)** (~ L ∨ ~ C) • (C ∨ L)   12, DN

    **14)** (C ∨ L) • (~ L ∨ ~ C)   13, Com

    **15)** (C ∨ L) • (~ C ∨ ~ L)   14, Com

    **16)** C Δ L                        15, Equiv

    **17)** (C Δ L) • ~ (C Δ L)     16, 5, Conj

  **18)** S                             4 - 17, IP

    **19)** /∴  (W • M) ⊃ S        3 - 18, CP

**5.**                                      /∴  (E • R) ⊃ W

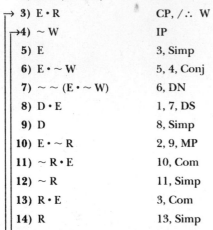

| | | |
|---|---|---|
| **1)** | ~ (E • ~ W) ∨ (D • E) | Pr |
| **2)** | D ⊃ (E • ~ R) | Pr |
| **3)** | E • R | CP, /∴  W |
| **4)** | ~ W | IP |
| **5)** | E | 3, Simp |
| **6)** | E • ~ W | 5, 4, Conj |
| **7)** | ~ ~ (E • ~ W) | 6, DN |
| **8)** | D • E | 1, 7, DS |
| **9)** | D | 8, Simp |
| **10)** | E • ~ R | 2, 9, MP |
| **11)** | ~ R • E | 10, Com |
| **12)** | ~ R | 11, Simp |
| **13)** | R • E | 3, Com |
| **14)** | R | 13, Simp |
| **15)** | R • ~ R | 14, 12, Conj |
| **16)** | W | 4 - 15, IP |
| **17)** | /∴  (E • R) ⊃ W | 3 - 16, CP |

**7.**                                      /∴  C ∨ T

| | | |
|---|---|---|
| **1)** | I ∨ [B ∨ (T ∨ C)] | Pr |
| **2)** | ~ (B ∨ I) | Pr |
| **3)** | (I ∨ B) ∨ (T ∨ C) | 1, Assoc |
| **4)** | ~ (I ∨ B) | 2, Com |
| **5)** | T ∨ C | 3, 4, DS |
| **6)** | ~ C | CP, /∴  T |
| **7)** | ~ T | IP |
| **8)** | C | 5, 7, DS |
| **9)** | C • ~ C | 8, 6, Conj |
| **10)** | T | 7 - 9, IP |
| **11)** | ~ C ⊃ T | 6 - 10, CP |
| **12)** | ~ ~ C ∨ T | 11, Impl |
| **13)** | /∴  C ∨ T | 12, DN |

### 7.3.A. (250)

**1.**                          /∴  ~ G ∨ P

| | | |
|---|---|---|
| **1)** | G △ E | Pr |
| **2)** | ~ (G • ~ E) | Pr |
| **3)** | ~ E ∨ G | Pr |
| **4)** | ~ G | Pr |
| **5)** | (G ∨ E) • (~ G ∨ ~ E) | 1, Equiv |
| **6)** | G ∨ E | 5, Simp |
| **7)** | E ∨ G | 6, Com |
| **8)** | G ∨ ~ E | 3, Com |
| **9)** | ~ E | 8, 4, DS |
| **10)** | G | 7, 9, DS |
| **11)** | G ∨ (~ G ∨ P) | 10, Add |
| **12)** | /∴  ~ G ∨ P | 11, 4, DS |

**7.3.B. (251)**

**1.**                    /∴  A • ~ B

   **1)** A ⊃ B          Pr

   **2)** ~ (~ B • ~ A)   Pr

   **3)** ~ B             Pr

   **4)** ~ ~ (B ∨ A)     2, DeM

   **5)** B ∨ A           4, DN

   **6)** A               5, 3, DS

   **7)** ~ A             1, 3, MT

   **8)** A • ~A          6, 7, Conj

**3.**                    /∴  ~ A ⊃ C

   **1)** (~ A • B) ⊃ C   Pr

   **2)** B               Pr

   **3)** ~ C • ~ A       Pr

   **4)** ~ C             3, Simp

   **5)** ~ (~ A • B)     1, 4, MT

   **6)** ~ ~ A ∨ ~ B     5, DeM

   **7)** A ∨ ~ B         6, DN

   **8)** ~ A • ~ C       3, Com

   **9)** ~ A             8, Simp

   **10)** ~ B            7, 9, DS

   **11)** B • ~ B        2, 10, Conj

**5.**                    /∴  B ≡ ~ A

   **1)** A ⊃ (~ B ⊃ ~ A)   Pr

   **2)** (B ⊃ ~ A) • A      Pr

   **3)** B ⊃ ~ A            2, Simp

   **4)** A • (B ⊃ ~ A)      2, Com

   **5)** A                  4, Simp

   **6)** ~ B ⊃ ~ A          1, 5, MP

   **7)** ~ ~ A              5, DN

   **8)** ~ B                3, 7, MT

   **9)** ~ A                6, 8, MP

   **10)** A • ~ A           5, 9, Conj

**7.**                    /∴  B Δ D

   **1)** (A • B) ∨ (C • D)           Pr

   **2)** (~ A • ~ D) ∨ (~ D • ~ B)   Pr

   **3)** (A • B) ∨ (D • C)           1, Com

   **4)** [(A • B) ∨ D] • [(A • B) ∨ C]   3, Dist

   **5)** (A • B) ∨ D                  4, Simp

   **6)** D ∨ (A • B)                  5, Com

   **7)** (D ∨ A) • (D ∨ B)            6, Dist

   **8)** D ∨ A                        7, Simp

   **9)** A ∨ D                        8, Com

   **10)** ~ ~ (A ∨ D)                 9, DN

   **11)** ~ (~ A • ~ D)               10, Dem

   **12)** ~ D • ~ B                   2, 11, DS

   **13)** (D ∨ B) • (D ∨ A)           7, Com

   **14)** D ∨ B                       13, Simp

   **15)** ~ D                         12, Simp

   **16)** B                           14, 15, DS

   **17)** ~ B • ~ D                   12, Com

   **18)** ~ B                         17, Simp

   **19)** B • ~ B                     16, 18, Conj

**7.3.C. (251–253)**

**1.**                                    /∴ O ∨ D

   **1)** L ∨ O                          Pr
   **2)** ~ (~ O ⊃ L)                  Pr
   **3)** ~ (~ ~ O ∨ L)              2, Impl
   **4)** ~ (O ∨ L)                     3, DN
   **5)** ~ O • ~ L                     4, DeM
   **6)** O ∨ L                           1, Com
   **7)** ~ O                              5, Simp
   **8)** L                                 6, 7, DS
   **9)** ~ L • ~ O                     5, Com
  **10)** ~ L                                 9, Simp
  **11)** L • ~ L                           8, 10, Conj

**5.**                                    /∴ ~L • (A ⊃ M)

   **1)** V ⊃ M                          Pr
   **2)** V • ~ A                         Pr
   **3)** L ⊃ ~ (V ⊃ A)               Pr
   **4)** M ⊃ A                          Pr
   **5)** V                                 2, Simp
   **6)** M                                1, 5, MP
   **7)** A                                 4, 6, MP
   **8)** ~ A • V                         2, Com
   **9)** ~ A                              8, Simp
  **10)** A • ~ A                           7, 9, Conj

**7.4.A. (256)**

**1.**

  →**1)** A                                CP, /∴ B ⊃ A
   **2)** A ∨ ~ B                       1, Add
   **3)** ~ B ∨ A                       2, Com
   **4)** B ⊃ A                          4, Impl
   **5)** A ⊃ (B ⊃ A)               1 - 4, CP

**3.**                                    /∴ L ⊃ ~ P

   **1)** (P Δ O) ∨ L                 Pr
   **2)** P • O                           Pr
   **3)** ~ L                              Pr
   **4)** L ∨ (P Δ O)                 1, Com
   **5)** P Δ O                           4, 3, DS
   **6)** (P ∨ O) • (~ P ∨ ~ O)   5, Equiv
   **7)** (~ P ∨ ~ O) • (P ∨ O)   6, Com
   **8)** ~ P ∨ ~ O                    7, Simp
   **9)** P                                 2, Simp
  **10)** ~ ~ P                              9, DN
  **11)** ~ O                                8, 10, DS
  **12)** O • P                              2, Com
  **13)** O                                   12, Simp
  **14)** O • ~O                             13, 11, Conj

**7.**                                    /∴ ~ E

   **1)** (P • ~ A) ⊃ S              Pr
   **2)** ~ (~ P • ~ S)              Pr
   **3)** ~ A • ~ S                     Pr
   **4)** S ⊃ ~ E                       Pr
   **5)** ~ ~ (P ∨ S)                 2, DeM
   **6)** P ∨ S                           5, DN
   **7)** S ∨ P                           6, Com
   **8)** ~ S • ~ A                     3, Com
   **9)** ~ S                              8, Simp
  **10)** P                                   7, 9, DS
  **11)** ~ (P • ~ A)                     1, 9, MT
  **12)** ~ P ∨ ~ ~ A                    11, DeM
  **13)** ~ P ∨ A                          12, DN
  **14)** A ∨ ~ P                          13, Com
  **15)** ~ A • ~ S                        8, Com
  **16)** ~ A                                15, Simp
  **17)** ~ P                                14, 16, DS
  **18)** P • ~ P                           10, 17, Conj

**3.**

| | | |
|---|---|---|
| 1) | $(A \supset B) \cdot (A \supset C)$ | CP, $/\therefore$ $A \supset (B \cdot C)$ |
| 2) | A | CP, $/\therefore$ $B \cdot C$ |
| 3) | $A \supset B$ | 1, Simp |
| 4) | $(A \supset C) \cdot (A \supset B)$ | 1, Com |
| 5) | $A \supset C$ | 4, Simp |
| 6) | B | 3, 2, MP |
| 7) | C | 5, 2, MP |
| 8) | $B \cdot C$ | 6, 7, Conj |
| 9) | $A \supset (B \cdot C)$ | 2 - 8, CP |
| 10) | $[(A \supset B) \cdot (A \supset C)] \supset [A \supset (B \cdot C)]$ | 1 - 9, CP |

**5.**

| | | |
|---|---|---|
| 1) | $\sim [(A \vee \sim B) \vee (B \vee \sim A)$ | IP |
| 2) | $\sim (A \vee \sim B) \cdot \sim (B \vee \sim A)$ | 1, DeM |
| 3) | $(\sim A \cdot \sim \sim B) \cdot \sim (B \vee \sim A)$ | 2, DeM |
| 4) | $(\sim A \cdot \sim \sim B) \cdot (\sim B \cdot \sim \sim A)$ | 3, DeM |
| 5) | $\sim A \cdot \sim \sim B$ | 4, Simp |
| 6) | $\sim A$ | 5, Simp |
| 7) | $(\sim B \cdot \sim \sim A) \cdot (\sim A \cdot \sim \sim B)$ | 4, Com |
| 8) | $\sim B \cdot \sim \sim A$ | 7, Simp |
| 9) | $\sim \sim A \cdot \sim B$ | 8, Com |
| 10) | $\sim \sim A$ | 9, Simp |
| 11) | $\sim A \cdot \sim \sim A$ | 6, 10, Conj |
| 12) | $(A \vee \sim B) \vee (B \vee \sim A)$ | 1 - 11, IP |

**7.4.B. (257–257)**

**1.**

| | | |
|---|---|---|
| 1) | $P \cdot E$ | CP, $/\therefore$ $(D \vee P) \cdot E$ |
| 2) | P | 1, Simp |
| 3) | $E \cdot P$ | 1, Com |
| 4) | E | 3, Simp |
| 5) | $P \vee D$ | 2, Add |
| 6) | $D \vee P$ | 5, Com |
| 7) | $(D \vee P) \cdot E$ | 6, 4, Conj |
| 8) | $(P \cdot E) \supset [(D \vee P)]$ | 1 - 7, CP |

**7.**

| | | |
|---|---|---|
| 1) | $\sim [(A \equiv B) \vee (\sim B \equiv A)]$ | IP |
| 2) | $\sim (A \equiv B) \cdot \sim (\sim B \equiv A)$ | 1, DeM |
| 3) | $\sim (A \equiv B)$ | 2, Simp |
| 4) | $\sim (\sim B \equiv A) \cdot \sim (A \equiv B)$ | 2, Com |
| 5) | $\sim (\sim B \equiv A)$ | 4, Simp |
| 6) | $\sim (A \equiv \sim B)$ | 5, Com |
| 7) | $\sim [(A \cdot \sim B) \vee (\sim A \cdot \sim \sim B)]$ | 6, Equiv |
| 8) | $\sim (A \cdot \sim B) \cdot \sim (\sim A \cdot \sim \sim B)$ | 7, DeM |
| 9) | $\sim (A \cdot \sim B) \cdot \sim (\sim A \cdot B)$ | 8, DN |
| 10) | $\sim (A \cdot \sim B) \cdot \sim (B \cdot \sim A)$ | 9, Com |
| 11) | $(\sim A \vee \sim \sim B) \cdot \sim (B \cdot \sim A)$ | 10, DeM |
| 12) | $(\sim A \vee B) \cdot \sim (B \cdot \sim A)$ | 11, DN |
| 13) | $(\sim A \vee B) \cdot (\sim B \vee \sim \sim A)$ | 12, DeM |
| 14) | $(\sim A \vee B) \cdot (\sim B \vee A)$ | 13, DN |
| 15) | $(A \supset B) \cdot (\sim B \vee A)$ | 14, Impl |
| 16) | $(A \supset B) \cdot (B \supset A)$ | 15, Impl |
| 17) | $A \equiv B$ | 16, Equiv |
| 18) | $(A \equiv B) \cdot \sim (A \equiv B)$ | 17, 3, Conj |
| 19) | $(A \equiv B) \vee (\sim B \equiv A)$ | 1 - 18, IP |

**3.**

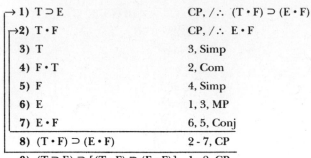

| | | |
|---|---|---|
| 1) | T ⊃ E | CP, /∴ (T · F) ⊃ (E · F) |
| 2) | T · F | CP, /∴ E · F |
| 3) | T | 3, Simp |
| 4) | F · T | 2, Com |
| 5) | F | 4, Simp |
| 6) | E | 1, 3, MP |
| 7) | E · F | 6, 5, Conj |
| 8) | (T · F) ⊃ (E · F) | 2 - 7, CP |
| 9) | (T ⊃ E) ⊃ [(T · F) ⊃ (E · F)] | 1 - 8, CP |

**5.**

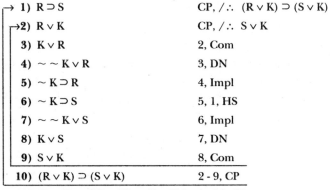

| | | |
|---|---|---|
| 1) | R ⊃ S | CP, /∴ (R ∨ K) ⊃ (S ∨ K) |
| 2) | R ∨ K | CP, /∴ S ∨ K |
| 3) | K ∨ R | 2, Com |
| 4) | ~ ~ K ∨ R | 3, DN |
| 5) | ~ K ⊃ R | 4, Impl |
| 6) | ~ K ⊃ S | 5, 1, HS |
| 7) | ~ ~ K ∨ S | 6, Impl |
| 8) | K ∨ S | 7, DN |
| 9) | S ∨ K | 8, Com |
| 10) | (R ∨ K) ⊃ (S ∨ K) | 2 - 9, CP |
| 11) | (R ⊃ S) ⊃ [(R ∨ K) ⊃ (S ∨ K)] | 1 - 10, CP |

**7.**

| | | |
|---|---|---|
| 1) | ~ [C ∨ (~ S ⊃ ~ C)] | IP |
| 2) | ~ C · ~ (~ S ⊃ ~ C) | 1, DeM |
| 3) | ~ C | 2, Simp |
| 4) | ~ (~ S ⊃ ~ C) · ~ C | 2, Com |
| 5) | ~ (~ S ⊃ ~ C) | 4, Simp |
| 6) | ~ (~ ~ S ∨ ~ C) | 5, Impl |
| 7) | ~ ~ (~ S · C) | 6, DeM |
| 8) | ~ S · C | 7, DN |
| 9) | C · ~ S | 8, Com |
| 10) | C | 9, Simp |
| 11) | C · ~ C | 10, 3, Conj |
| 12) | C ∨ (~ S ⊃ ~ C) | 1 - 11, IP |

**7.5.A. (260)**

**1.**

| | | |
|---|---|---|
| → **1)** | $\sim [(\sim A \vee \sim B) \equiv \sim (A \cdot B)]$ | IP |
| **2)** | $\sim [\sim (A \cdot B) \equiv \sim (A \cdot B)]$ | 1, DeM |
| **3)** | $\sim \{[\sim (A \cdot B) \cdot \sim (A \cdot B)] \vee [\sim \sim (A \cdot B) \cdot \sim \sim (A \cdot B)]\}$ | 2, Equiv |
| **4)** | $\sim \{\sim (A \cdot B) \vee [\sim \sim (A \cdot B) \cdot \sim \sim (A \cdot B)]\}$ | 3, Taut |
| **5)** | $\sim [\sim (A \cdot B) \vee \sim \sim (A \cdot B)]$ | 4, Taut |
| **6)** | $\sim \sim [(A \cdot B) \cdot \sim (A \cdot B)]$ | 5, DeM |
| **7)** | $(A \cdot B) \cdot \sim (A \cdot B)$ | 6, DN |
| **8)** | $(\sim A \vee \sim B) \equiv \sim (A \cdot B)$ | 1 - 7, IP |

**3.**

| | | |
|---|---|---|
| → **1)** | $\sim [(A \supset B) \equiv (\sim B \supset \sim A)]$ | IP |
| **2)** | $\sim [(A \supset B) \equiv (A \supset B)]$ | 1, Trans |
| **3)** | $\sim \{[(A \supset B) \cdot (A \supset B)] \vee [\sim (A \supset B) \cdot \sim (A \supset B)]\}$ | 2, Equiv |
| **4)** | $\sim \{(A \supset B) \vee [\sim (A \supset B) \cdot \sim (A \supset B)]\}$ | 3, Taut |
| **5)** | $\sim [(A \supset B) \vee \sim (A \supset B)]$ | 4, Taut |
| **6)** | $\sim (A \supset B) \cdot \sim \sim (A \supset B)$ | 5, DeM |
| **7)** | $(A \supset B) \equiv (\sim B \supset \sim A)$ | 1 - 6, IP |

**5.**

| | | |
|---|---|---|
| → **1)** | $\sim \{[A \vee (B \cdot C)] \equiv [(A \vee B) \cdot (A \vee C)]\}$ | IP |
| **2)** | $\sim \{[A \vee (B \cdot C)] \equiv [A \vee (B \cdot C)]\}$ | 1, Dist |
| **3)** | $\sim (\{[A \vee (B \cdot C)] \cdot [A \vee (B \cdot C)]\} \vee \{\sim [A \vee (B \cdot C)] \cdot \sim [A \vee (B \cdot C)]\})$ | 2, Equiv |
| **4)** | $\sim ([A \vee (B \cdot C)] \vee \{\sim [A \vee (B \cdot C)] \cdot \sim [A \vee (B \cdot C)]\})$ | 3, Taut |
| **5)** | $\sim \{[A \vee (B \cdot C)] \vee \sim [A \vee (B \cdot C)]\}$ | 4, Taut |
| **6)** | $\sim [A \vee (B \cdot C)] \cdot \sim \sim [A \vee (B \cdot C)]$ | 5, DeM |
| **7)** | $[A \vee (B \cdot C)] \equiv [(A \vee B) \cdot (A \vee C)]$ | 1 - 6, IP |

**7.**

| | | |
|---|---|---|
| → **1)** | $\sim \{(A \equiv B) \equiv [(A \supset B) \cdot (B \supset A)]\}$ | IP |
| **2)** | $\sim [(A \equiv B) \equiv (A \equiv B)]$ | 1, Equiv |
| **3)** | $\sim \{[(A \equiv B) \cdot (A \equiv B)] \vee [\sim (A \equiv B) \cdot \sim (A \equiv B)]\}$ | 2, Equiv |
| **4)** | $\sim \{(A \equiv B) \vee [\sim (A \equiv B) \cdot \sim (A \equiv B)]\}$ | 3, Taut |
| **5)** | $\sim [(A \equiv B) \vee \sim (A \equiv B)]$ | 4, Taut |
| **6)** | $\sim (A \equiv B) \cdot \sim \sim (A \equiv B)$ | 5, DeM |
| **7)** | $(A \equiv B) \equiv [(A \supset B) \cdot (B \supset A)]$ | 1 - 6, IP |

**9.**

| | | |
|---|---|---|
| 1) | ~ {(A Δ B) ≡ [(A ∨ B) • (~ A ∨ ~ B)]} | IP |
| 2) | ~ [(A Δ B) ≡ (A Δ B)] | 1, Equiv |
| 3) | ~ {[(A Δ B) • (A Δ B)] ∨ [~ (A Δ B) • ~ (A Δ B)]} | 2, Equiv |
| 4) | ~ {(A Δ B) ∨ [~ (A Δ B) • ~ (A Δ B)]} | 3, Taut |
| 5) | ~ [(A Δ B) ∨ ~ (A Δ B)] | 4, Taut |
| 6) | ~ (A Δ B) • ~ ~ (A Δ B) | 5, DeM |
| 7) | (A Δ B) ≡ [(A ∨ B) • (~ A ∨ ~ B)] | 1 - 6, IP |

**7.5.B. (260–261)**

**1.** /∴ L ⊃ (H ⊃ S)

| | | |
|---|---|---|
| 1) | H ⊃ (L ⊃ S) | Pr |
| 2) | (H • L) ⊃ S | 1, Exp |
| 3) | (L • H) ⊃ S | 2, Com |
| 4) | /∴ L ⊃ (H ⊃ S) | 3, Exp |

/∴ H ⊃ (L ⊃ S)

| | | |
|---|---|---|
| 1) | L ⊃ (H ⊃ S) | Pr |
| 2) | (L • H) ⊃ S | 1, Exp |
| 3) | (H • L) ⊃ S | 2, Com |
| 4) | /∴ H ⊃ (L ⊃ S) | 3, Exp |

**3.** /∴ (I • ~ M) ∨ (~ I • M)

| | | |
|---|---|---|
| 1) | ~ (I ≡ M) | Pr |
| 2) | ~ [(I ⊃ M) • (M ⊃ I)] | 1, Equiv |
| 3) | ~ (I ⊃ M) ∨ ~ (M ⊃ I) | 2, DeM |
| 4) | ~ (~ I ∨ M) ∨ ~ (M ⊃ I) | 3, Impl |
| 5) | ~ (~ I ∨ M) ∨ ~ (~ M ∨ I) | 4, Impl |
| 6) | (~ ~ I • ~ M) ∨ ~ (~ M ∨ I) | 5, DeM |
| 7) | (I • ~ M) ∨ ~ (~ M ∨ I) | 6, DN |
| 8) | (I • ~ M) ∨ (~ ~ M • ~ I) | 7, DeM |
| 9) | (I • ~ M) ∨ (M • ~ I) | 8, DN |
| 10) | /∴ (I • ~ M) ∨ (~ I • M) | 9, Com |

$/ \therefore \sim (I \equiv M)$

1) $(I \cdot \sim M) \vee (\sim I \cdot M)$       Pr
2) $\sim \sim [(I \cdot \sim M) \vee (\sim I \cdot M)]$       1, DN
3) $\sim [\sim (I \cdot \sim M) \cdot \sim (\sim I \cdot M)]$       2, DeM
4) $\sim [(\sim I \vee \sim \sim M) \cdot \sim (\sim I \cdot M)]$       3, DeM
5) $\sim [(\sim I \vee M) \cdot \sim (\sim I \cdot M)]$       4, DN
6) $\sim [(I \supset M) \cdot \sim (\sim I \cdot M))]$       5, Impl
7) $\sim [(I \supset M) \cdot \sim (M \cdot \sim I)]$       6, Com
8) $\sim [(I \supset M) \cdot (\sim M \vee \sim \sim I)]$       7, DeM
9) $\sim [(I \supset M) \cdot (\sim M \vee I)]$       8, DN
10) $\sim [(I \supset M) \cdot (M \supset I)]$       9, Impl
11) $/ \therefore \sim (I \equiv M)$       10, Equiv

**5.**       $/ \therefore (A \supset \sim M) \cdot (M \vee A)$

1) $(A \vee M) \cdot \sim (M \cdot A)$       Pr
2) $(A \vee M) \cdot (\sim M \vee \sim A)$       1, DeM
3) $(A \vee M) \cdot (\sim A \vee \sim M)$       2, Com
4) $(A \vee M) \cdot (A \supset \sim M)$       3, Impl
5) $(A \supset \sim M) \cdot (A \vee M)$       4, Com
6) $/ \therefore (A \supset \sim M) \cdot (M \vee A)$       5, Com

$/ \therefore (A \vee M) \cdot \sim (M \cdot A)$

1) $(A \supset \sim M) \cdot (M \vee A)$       Pr
2) $(M \vee A) \cdot (A \supset \sim M)$       1, Com
3) $(A \vee M) \cdot (A \supset \sim M)$       2, Com
4) $(A \vee M) \cdot (\sim A \vee \sim M)$       3, Impl
5) $(A \vee M) \cdot \sim (A \cdot M)$       4, DeM
6) $/ \therefore (A \vee M) \cdot \sim (M \cdot A)$       5, Com

**7.**       $/ \therefore \sim G \equiv \sim (P \cdot L)$

1) $G \equiv (P \cdot L)$       Pr
2) $[G \supset (P \cdot L)] \cdot [(P \cdot L) \supset G]$       1, Equiv
3) $[\sim (P \cdot L) \supset \sim G] \cdot [(P \cdot L) \supset G]$       2, Trans
4) $[\sim (P \cdot L) \supset \sim G] \cdot [\sim G \supset \sim (P \cdot L)]$       3, Trans
5) $\sim (P \cdot L) \equiv \sim G$       4, Equiv
6) $/ \therefore \sim G \equiv \sim (P \cdot L)$       5, Com

$/ \therefore G = (P \cdot L)$

1) $\sim G \equiv \sim (P \cdot L)$       Pr
2) $\sim (P \cdot L) \equiv \sim G$       1, Com
3) $[\sim (P \cdot L) \supset \sim G] \cdot [\sim G \supset \sim (P \cdot L)]$       2, Equiv
4) $[G \supset (P \cdot L)] \cdot [\sim G \supset \sim (P \cdot L)]$       3, Trans
5) $[G \supset (P \cdot L)] \cdot [(P \cdot L) \supset G)]$       4, Trans
6) $/ \therefore G \equiv (P \cdot L)$       5, Equiv

# CHAPTER 8

## 8.2. (274–275)

**1.** Some politicians are persons who are mendacious.

Some S are M.

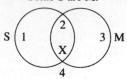

**3.** All cats are things that are grey in the dark.

All C are G.

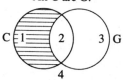

**5.** Some goals of life are things not obtainable by everyone.

Some G are not O.

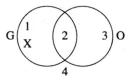

**7.** Some self-centered persons are persons who ruined the class.

Some S are R.

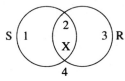

**9.** No persons who are ignorant are persons who are ever truly free.

No I are F.

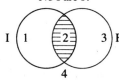

**13.** All persons who are rewarded are persons who are diligent.

All R are D.

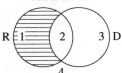

**17.** Some people are not persons belligerent toward their enemies.

Some P are not B.

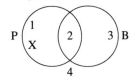

**21.** All friends who are understanding are friends valuable to have.

All U are V.

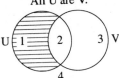

**25.** All things that are knowledge are things that are powerful.

All K are P.

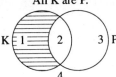

**29.** All things that are inside trading are things that become a Wall Street scandal in 1987.

All T are S.

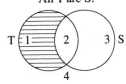

### 8.3.A. (281–282)

**1.** All Iraqis are persons who are mendacious.

All I are M.

Assuming the traditional square of opposition, if an *A* statement is assumed true, then the following hold:

*E* statements are false

*I* statements are true

*O* statements are false

Assuming the traditional square of opposition, if an *A* statement is assumed false, the following hold:

*E* statements are undetermined

*I* statements are undetermined

*O* statements are true

**3.** Some Americans are persons who exercise their privilege to vote.

Some A are E.

Assuming the traditional square of opposition, if an *I* statement is assumed true, then the following hold:

*A* statements are undetermined

*E* statements are false

*O* statements are undetermined

Assuming the traditional square of opposition, if an *I* statement is assumed false, then the following hold:

*A* statements are false

*E* statements are true

*O* statements are true

### 8.3.B. (282)

**1.** Some drug users are persons who will develop *AIDS*.

Some U are D.

Assuming the Boolean square of opposition, if an *I* statement is assumed true, then the following hold:

*A* statements are undetermined

*E* statements are false

*O* statements are undetermined

Assuming the Boolean square of opposition, if an *I* statement is assumed false, then the following hold:

*A* statements are undetermined

*E* statements are true

*O* statements are undetermined

**3.** Some STD's are things that are not successfully treatable.

Some S are not T.

Assuming the Boolean square of opposition, if an *O* statement is assumed true, then the following hold:

*A* statements are false

*E* statements are undetermined

*I* statements are undetermined

Assuming the Boolean square of opposition, if an O statement is assumed false, then the following hold:

*A* statements are true

*E* statements are undetermined

*I* statements are undetermined

## 8.4.A. (293)

**1.** Some chemical changes are things that are endothermic.

Some C are E.

Some E are C.

**3.** All heat-releasing chemical changes are things that are exothermic.

All C are E.

Some E are C. (by limitation)

**5.** All energies are the capabilities of a body to bring about changes in other bodies.

All E are C.

Some C are E (by limitation)

## 8.4.B. (293–294)

**1.** No persons who have *AIDS* are persons who are expected to live more than several years.

No A are L.

All A are non-L.

**3.** Some persons who are infected with *HTLV-3* are not persons who are inflicted with *AIDS*.

Some H are not A.

Some H are non-A.

**5.** All persons who are terminally ill are persons who deserve our compassion.

All I are C.

No I are non-C.

**8.4.C. (294)**

**1.** Some things that are non-taxable are things that are financial investments.

Some non-T are I.

NONE

**3.** No federal securities are things that are non-redeemable.

Non S are non-R.

Some R are non-S. (by limitation)

**5** Some junk stocks are not things that are sound investments.

Some S are not I.

Some non-I are not non-S.

**8.4.D. (294)**

**1.**                                        /∴ Some H are not non-C
  **1)** Some C are H          Pr
  **2)** Some H are C          1, Conversion
  **3)** Some H are not non-C   2, Obversion

**3.**                                        /∴ Some non-P are C
  **1)** No C are P            Pr
  **2)** Some non-P are not non-C   1, Contraposition by limitation
  **3)** Some non-P are C      2, Obversion

**5.**                                        /∴ Some S are not non-E
  **1)** All E are S           Pr
  **2)** Some S are E          1, Conversion by limitation
  **3)** Some S are not non-E  2, Obversion

# CHAPTER 9

**9.1.A. (302–303)**

**1.** No rock stars are jazz players.
Some jazz players are classically trained musicians.

So, some classically trained musicians are not rock stars.

No R are J
Some J are C

Some C are not R

EIO - 4

**3.** Some members of *U2* are non-dreamers.
All members of *U2* are Irish.

So, some Irish are not dreamers.

> Some M are non-D
> All M are I
>
> Some I are not D

This argument has four terms that must be reduced to three:

> Some M are not D  (obversion)
> All M are I
>
> Some I are not D

Some members of U2 are not dreamers.
All members of U2 are Irish.

So, some Irish are not dreamers.

OAO - 3

**5.** All lead guitarists in a famous rock band are persons with a great deal of money.
All persons who are identical to Paul Evans are persons who are lead guitarists in a famous rock band.

So, all persons who are identical to Paul Evans are persons who are wealthy.

> All L are M
> All E are L
>
> All E are W

This argument has four terms that must be reduced to three: 'wealthy' = def. 'a person with a great deal of money.'

> All L are W
> All E are L
>
> All E are W

All persons who are lead guitarists in a famous rock band are persons who are wealthy.
All persons who are identical to Paul Evans are persons who are lead guitarists in a famous rock band.

So, all persons who are identical to Paul Evans are persons who are wealthy.

AAA - 1

**7.** No notes backed by the federal government are speculative.
All treasury bonds are notes backed by the federal government.

So, no treasury bonds are speculative.

> No N are S
> All B are N
>
> No B are S

EAE - 1

**9.** Some financial news letters are not accurate market predictors.
All financial news letters are a relatively expensive business tool.

So, some expensive business tools are not accurate market predictors.

Some L are not P

All L are T

Some T are not P

OAO - 3

**13.** All things that are heroin are things that are dangerous to use.
All things that are heroin are things controlled by the FDA.

So, all things controlled by the FDA are things dangerous to use.

All H are D
All H are C

All C are D

AAA - 3

**9.2.A (316)**

**1.** EIO - 4

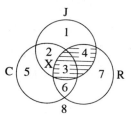

VALID

**3.** OAO - 3

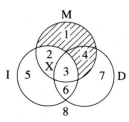

VALID

**5.** AAA - 1

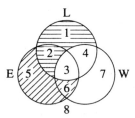

VALID

**7.** EAE - 1

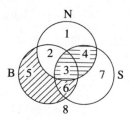

VALID

**9.** OAO - 3

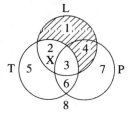

VALID

**15.** IAI - 4

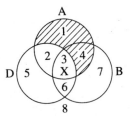

VALID

**9.2.B. (316–318)**

1. All persons pulling for the Buffalos are winners.
   Some persons betting on the Mets are not winners.
   _____

   So, some persons betting on the Mets are not persons pulling for the Buffalos.

   All P are W
   Some B are not W
   _____

   Some B are not P

   AOO - 2

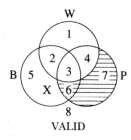

VALID

**3.** No Giant supporters are persons who root for Dallas.

Some Raider fans are persons who root for Dallas.

So, some Raider fans are not Giant supporters.

No G are D
Some R are D
───────────
Some R are not G

EIO - 2

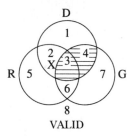

VALID

**5.** No sellers of political power are persons who are expected to be strictly honest in their operations.
Some diplomates are expected to be strictly honest in their operations.

So, some diplomates are not sellers of political power.

No S are H
Some D are H
───────────
Some D are not S

EIO - 2

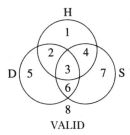

VALID

**7.** No particles explainable by the laws of quantum mechanics are things considered to be Newtonian atoms.
All Newtonian atoms are viewed as things completely located simultaneously in space and time.

Some things viewed as completely located simultaneously in space and time are not particles explainable by the laws of quantum mechanics.

No P are A
All A are L
───────────
Some L are not P

EAO - 4

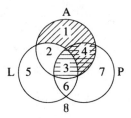

INVALID for Boolean interpretation

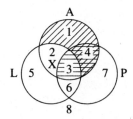

VALID if A's exist

**9.** All index arbitrages are very controversial forms of program trading on the stock market. Some index arbitrages are things that blamed for interjecting sudden price swings into stock purchase plans.

Some things blamed for interjecting sudden price swings into stock purchase plans are very controversial forms of program trading in the stock market.

All A are T
Some A are S
───────────
Some S are T

AII-3

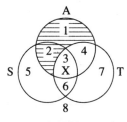

VALID

**15.** All non-pre-Gothic buildings are non-Norman structures.
   All ancient English cathedrals are non-pre-Gothic buildings.

So, some ancient English cathedrals are Norman structures.

> All non-G are non-N
> All E are non-G
> ———————————
> Some E are N

This argument has five terms that must be reduced to three:

> All N are G  (contraposition)
> No E are G  (obversion)
> ———————————
> Some E are N

All Norman structures are pre-Gothic buildings.
No ancient English cathedrals are pre-Gothic buildings.
———————————————————————
So, some ancient English cathedrals are Norman structures.

AEI - 2

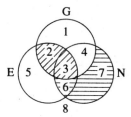

INVALID for Boolean interpretation

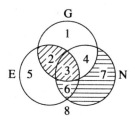

INVALID for any assumption of existence

**9.3.A.  (321)**

Invalid Arguments in *Group A* of *Section 1:*

**1.** *Exercise 3* in invalid under a Boolean interpretation, breaking Rule 5.  Hence, a fallacy of existential import appears in this argument.  However, if G is assumed to exist, 3 is valid.

**2.** *Exercise 5* is invalid.  Rule broken: #1; The middle term, F, is not distributed in the premises.  Hence, a fallacy of undistributed middle appears in this argument.

**3.** *Exercise 7* in invalid under a Boolean interpretation, breaking Rule 5.  Hence, a fallacy of existential import appears in this argument.  However, if D is assumed to exist, 7 is valid.

**4.** *Exercise 9* in invalid under a Boolean interpretation breaking Rule 5.  Hence, a fallacy of existential import appears in this argument.  However, if D is assumed to exist, 9 is valid.

Invalid Arguments of *Group B* of *Section 2:*

**1.** *Exercise* 7 in invalid under a Boolean interpretation, breaking Rule 5. Hence, a fallacy of existential import appears in this argument. However, if A is assumed to exist, 7 is valid.

### 9.3.B. (321–322)

**1.** Some hard acid musicians are musicians who use a great deal of metal.
No jazz musicians are musicians who use a great deal of metal.

Some jazz musicians are not hard acid musicians.

'hard acid musicians' = def. 'hard acid players'

> Some A are M
> No J are M
> _____
> Some J are not A

#### IEO - 2   INVALID

Rule broken: #2; A is distributed in the conclusion but not in the premises. Hence, a fallacy of illicit major appears in this argument.

**3.** No classical performers are funky entertainers.
Some punk players are funky entertainers.

Some non-funky entertainers are not non-classical performers.

> No C are F
> Some P are F
> _____
> Some non-P are not non-C

This argument has five terms that must be reduced to three:

> No C are F
> Some P are F
> _____
> Some C are not P  (contraposition)

Because C is now the minor term and P the major term in the conclusion, the premises need to be reordered:

> Some P are F
> No C are F
> _____
> Some C are not P

#### IEO-2   INVALID

Rule broken: #1; P is distributed in the conclusion but not in the premises. Hence, a fallacy of illicit major appears in this argument.

**5.** All organic growth processes are metabolic processes.
Some metabolic processes are not anabolic processes.

Some organic growth processes are not anabolic processes.

> All O are M
> Some M are not A
> _____
> Some O are not A

#### AOO - 4   INVALID

Rule broken: #1; the middle term, M, is not distributed in the premises. Hence, a fallacy of the undistributed middle appears in this argument.

7. Some conservatives are persons who support the international trade quotas to protect U. S. industries.
Some conservatives are persons who are hawks,

So, some persons who are hawks are persons who support the international trade quotas to protect U. S. industries.

Some C are S
Some C are H

Some H are S

III - 3   INVALID

Rule broken: #1; the middle term, C, is not distributed in the premises.
Hence, a fallacy of the undistributed middle appears in this argument.

9. No strong supporters of expanding federal government well-fare programs are persons who are non-liberals.
Some strong supporters of expanding federal government well-fare programs are Dixie Democrats.

So, some Dixie Democrats are persons who are political liberals.

No S are non-L
Some S are D

Some D are L

This argument has four terms that must be reduced to three:

All S are L  (obversion)
Some S are D

Some D are L

All strong supporters of expanding federal government well-fare programs are persons who are liberals.
Some strong supporters of expanding federal government well-fare programs are Dixie Democrats.

So, some Dixie Democrats are persons who are political liberals.

AII - 3   Valid

15. All seniors are persons hoping to find a good paying job.
All persons hoping to find a good paying job are persons eagerly awaiting graduation.

All persons eagerly awaiting graduation are seniors.

All S are J
All J are G

All G are S

AAA - 4   INVALID

Rule broken: #2; G is distributed in the conclusion but not in the premises.
Hence, a fallacy of illicit minor appears in this argument.

**9.4.A. (328–329)**

Discuss whether the supplied claims in the following are likely to be true or false, and reasons supporting your views of these claims.

1. All things that instill great fear of breaking the law are things that reduce crime.

   So, all things identical to the death penalty are things that reduce crime.

All I are R
...???...
———————
All D are R

All I are R
All D are I
———————
All D are R

All things that instill great fear of breaking the law are things that reduce crime.
All things identical to the death penalty are things that instill great fear of breaking the law.

So, all things identical to the death penalty are things that reduce crime.

AAA - 1    VALID

Is this argument likely to be sound? What of the acceptability of the supplied premise?

3. Some non-moral acts are acts that are non-punishable under civil law.

   So, some civil crimes are not non-moral acts.

Some non-M are non-P
...???...
———————————
Some C are not non-M

Some non-M are non-P
No C are non-P
———————————
Some C are not non-M

Some non-moral acts are acts that are non-punishable under civil law.
No civil crimes are non-punishable under civil law.

So, some civil crimes are not non-moral acts.

IEO - 2    INVALID

Rule broken: #2; non-M is distributed in the conclusion but not in the premises. Hence, a fallacy of illicit major appears in this argument.

Because the conclusion is negative, there must be a negative premise. But since the first premise is positive, the second premise must be negative. No syllogism can have two particular premises. Thus, the second premise must be universal.. Now, If the second premise were 'No non-P are C,' the argument would still be invalid because non-M would still be distributed in the conclusion but not in the premises.

5. All punk bands are bands that use violet lyrics.

   So, some bands that use violent lyrics are acid bands.

...???...
All P are V
———————
Some V are A

Some A are P
All P are V
_____

Some V are A

Some acid bands are punk bands.
All punk bands are bands that use violet lyrics.
_____

So, some bands that use violent lyrics are acid bands.

IAI - 4   VALID

**7.** All honest persons are straight-forward persons.
_____

No straight-forward persons are persons who thrive in politics.

...???...
All H are
_____

No S are T

No T are H
All H are S
_____

No S are T

No persons who thrive in politics are honest persons.
All honest persons are straight-forward persons.
_____

No straight-forward persons are persons who thrive in politics.

EAE - 4   INVALID

Rule broken: #2.  Hence, a fallacy of illicit minor appears in this argument.

**9.4.B.  (329–330)**

**1. (1)**

All person who can grasp the relation of evidence to assertions are persons who are assets in business.
All persons who read comprehensively are persons who can grasp the relations of evidence to assertions.
All persons who are assets in business are persons who are valuable employees.
_____

All persons who read comprehensively are persons who are valuable employees.

**(2)**

All G are A
All R are G
All A are V
_____

All R are V

All R are G
All G are A
All A are V
_____

All R are V

(3)

All R are G
All G are A
─────────
All R are A

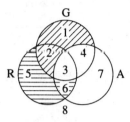

AAA - 4    VALID

All R are A
All A are V
─────────
All R are V

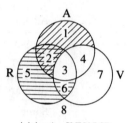

AAA - 4    INVALID

Since not every enthymeme making up the sorites is valid, the sorites is invalid.

**3. (1)**

All persons who are top managers are persons concerned with long term systems approaches to market conditions.
No persons who are business graduates are persons who will fail in the world of finance.
Some persons who are business graduates are not persons concerned with long term systems approaches to market conditions.
─────────
So, some persons who fail in the world of finance are persons who will not be successful top managers.

**(2)**

All M are A
No B are F
Some B are not A
─────────
Some F are not M

> No B are F
> Some B are not A
> All M are A
> _____
> Some F are not M

(3)

> No B are F
> Some B are not A
> _____
> ...???...

These premises cannot generate a valid argument since they are both negative. Rule 4 dictates that no valid syllogism can have two negative premises. The sorites of example 3 is invalid.

5. (1)

No tobacco products are healthy for humans.
Some tobacco products are causally linked to lung cancer.
All products conducive to a clean air environment are products healthy for humans.
_____
So, some products causally related to lung cancer are not conducive to a clean air environment.

(2)

> No T are H
> Some T are C
> All A are H
> _____
> Some C are not A
>
> Some T are C
> No T are H
> All A are H
> _____
> Some C are not A

(3)

> Some T are C
> No T are H
> _____
> Some C are not H

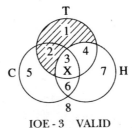

IOE - 3   VALID

Some C are not H
All A are H
_____
Some C are not A

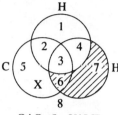

OAO - 2    VALID

Since every enthymeme making up the sorites is valid, the sorites is valid.

**7. (1)**

All ornamented musical compositions are musical compositions that are non-simple in musi-
cal design.
Some fugues are musical compositions that are simple in musical design.
No baroque musical compositions are non-ornamented musical compositions.
_____
Some fugues are not baroque musical compositions.

**(2)**

All O are non-S
Some F are S
No B are non-O
_____
Some F are not B

No O are S  (obversion)
Some F are S
No B are non-O
_____
Some F are not B

**(3)**

No O are S
Some F are S
_____
Some F are not O

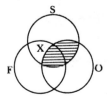

EIO - 2    VALID

No B are non-O
Some F are not F
───────────────
Some F are not B

All B are O  (obversion)
Some F are not O
───────────────
Some F are not B

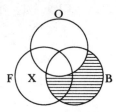

AOO - 2    VALID

Since every enthymeme making up the sorites is valid, the sorites is valid.

# CHAPTER 10

**10.1.  (336–337)**

1. Pa • ~ Da

3. Wr • Fl

5. Lt △ Dt

7. (We • Ae) • Te

9. (Fp • Fp) • Ap

11. Dt ≡ (Bt • Ct)

15. (Gl • ~ Bl) △ ~ Wl

19. (Bo • Eo) • (Ho • Ao)

23. (Dk • Ck) ⊃ (Rb • Gb)

27. [(Fr • Ir) • Pr] • (Ar ⊃ Ur)

**10.2.  (347–348)**

1. (∃x)(Mx • Lx)

3. (∃x)(Sx • ~ Px)

5. (∃x)(Fx • ~ Cx)

7. (∃x)[(Sx • Cx) • ~ Ex]

9. (∃x)[(Cx • Tx) • Ex]

11. (∃x)[(Px • Cx) • Sx]

15. (∃x)[Sx • (Px • Rx)]

19. (x){[Px • (Wx • Gx)] ⊃ ~ Sx}

23. (∃x){[Mx • (Hx ⊃ Rx)] • (Lx • Bx)}

27. (x){[Hx • Dx] ⊃ [~ Sx ⊃ ~ (Px • Mx)]}

**10.3. (353–355)**

1. ~ (x)(Wx ⊃ Jx)

3. Cg ∨ ~ (∃x)Qx

5. (x)(Qx ∆ Sx)

7. (Ee • Pe) ⊃ (∃x)(Px • Ex)

9. Ta ⊃ (x)(Sx ⊃ Px)

11. ~ (∃x)[(Vx • Cx) • ~ Hx]

15. (∃x)Rx ⊃ (∃x){Rx • (Ix • PX)}

19. (x)[Mx ⊃ (Lx ⊃ Bx)] ∆ (∃x)[(Mx • Lx) • ~ Bx]

23. (x){[(Mx ∨ Wx) ⊃ Ex] ≡ ~ ~ Cx}

27. (x)[(Sx • Gx) ⊃ ~ Bx] ∨ (x)[(Lx • Sx) ⊃ ~ Bx]

**10.4. (362–364)**

1. (x)Rxx

3. (∃x)(y)Rxy

5. (∃y)(x)Rxy

7. ~ (∃x)(y)Rxy

9. ~ (∃x)(∃y)Rxy

11. (x)(Nx ⊃ Sxa)

15. (x)(y)[(Ny • Sxy) ⊃ ~ Nx]

19. (x)[Dx ⊃ (∃y)(Ey • Fxy)]

23. (x)[(Lx • Px) ⊃ ~ (∃x)(Fy • Kxy)]

27. ~ (x){[Sx • (∃y)(Uy • Exy)] ⊃ (∃z)(Dz • Rxz)}

# CHAPTER 11

**11.1. (384–385)**

1.                                   /∴ Hh
| | | |
|---|---|---|
| **1)** | (∃x)(Ux • Hx) ✓ | Pr |
| **2)** | Uh | Pr |
| **3)** | ~ Hh | AP |
| **4)** | Uh • Hh ✓ | 1, EI |
| **5)** | Uh | 4, C |
| **6)** | Hh | 4, C |
| | X | VALID |

3.                                   /∴ ~ Sj
| | | |
|---|---|---|
| **1)** | ~ Uj | Pr |
| **2)** | (x)(Ux ⊃ Sx) | Pr |
| **3)** | ~ ~ Sj ✓ | AP |
| **4)** | Sj ✓ | 3, DN |
| **5)** | Uj ⊃ Sj | 1, UI |
| **6)** | ~ Uj    Sj | 5, MI |
| | | INVALID |

**5.**                                                            /∴  (∃x)(Ax • Mx)

    **1)**  (x)(Px ⊃ Mx)                    Pr
    **2)**  (∃x)(Ax • Px)  ✓               Pr
    **3)**  ~ (∃x)(Ax • Mx)  ✓             AP
    **4)**  (x)~ (Ax • Mx)                  3, QD
    **5)**      Aa • Pa  ✓                    2, EI
    **6)**      Aa                           5, C
    **7)**      Pa                           5, C
    **8)**      Pa ⊃ Ma  ✓                   1, UI

    **9)**    ~ Pa        Ma    8, MI
    **10)**    X   ~ (Ax • Mx) ✓      4, UI

    **11)**      ~ Aa   ~ Ma          10, DC
           X      X                 **VALID**

**7.**                                                      /∴  (x)[(Sx • Ax) ⊃ Mx]

    **1)**  (x)(Ax ⊃ Mx) ⊃ (x)(Mx ⊃ Sx)  ✓      Pr
    **2)**  (x)(Ax ⊃ Sx)                          Pr
    **3)**  ~ (x)[(Sx • Ax) ⊃ Mx]               AP
    **4)**  (∃x)~ [(Sx • Ax) ⊃ Mx]  ✓           3, QD
    **5)**    ~ [(Sa • Aa) ⊃ Ma]  ✓              4, EI
    **6)**          Sa • Aa  ✓                    5, DMI
    **7)**          ~ Ma                          5, DMI
    **8)**          Sa                            6, C
    **9)**          Aa                            6, C
    **10)**         Aa ⊃ Sa  ✓                    2, UI

    **11)**      ~ Aa        Sa                  10, MI
          X

    **12)**   ~ (x)(Ax ⊃ Mx)  ✓  (x)(Mx ⊃ Sx)   1, MI
    **13)**     (∃x)~ (Ax ⊃ Mx)  ✓                12, QD
    **14)**  ~ (Ab ⊃ Mb)  ✓                       13, EI
    **15)**      Ab                                14, DMI
    **16)**    ~ Mb                                14, DMI
    **17)**  Ab ⊃ Sb  ✓                           2, UI

    **18)** ~ Ab    Sb                            17, MI
    **19)**  X                      Ma ⊃ Sa  ✓    12. UI

    **20)**                        ~ Ma   Sa       19, MI

                             **INVALID**

**9.**                                                    /∴  (∃x)(Nx • Cx)

1) (x)[Nx ⊃ (Px ∨ Cx)]            Pr
2) (x)(Px ⊃ Rx)                   Pr
3) (∃x)(Nx • ~ Rx)    ✓           Pr
4) ~ (∃x)(Nx • Cx)               AP
5) (x)~ (Nx • Cx)                4, QD
6)          Na • ~ Ra    ✓        3, EI
7)          Na                    6, C
8)          ~ Ra                  6, C
9)          Pa ⊃ Ra    ✓          2, UI

10)   ~ Pa        Ra              9, MI
11) ~ (Nx • Cx)  ✓   X            5, UI

12) ~ Na    ~ Ca                  11, DC
13)   X     Na ⊃ (Pa ∨ Ca)  ✓     1, UI

14)      ~ Na      Pa ∨ Ca  ✓      13, MI
          X

15)              Pa    Ca          14, ID
                 X     X                        **VALID**

**15.**                                              /∴  (∃x)(Sx • Axx)

1) (∃x)[Sx • (y)(Sy ⊃ Ayx)]  ✓   Pr
2) ~ (∃x)(Sx • Axx)  ✓           AP
3) (x)~ (Sx • Axx)               2, QD
4) Sa • (y)(Sy ⊃ Aya)  ✓         1, EI
5)          Sa                    4, C
6)   (y)(Sy ⊃ Aya)                4, C
7)   ~ (Sa • Aaa)                 3, UI

8)  ~ Sa      ~ Aaa              7, DC
9)    X      Sa ⊃ Aaa  ✓          6, UI

10)      ~ Sa    Aaa             9, MI
          X      X                          **VALID**

**19.**                                        /∴ (x){Px ⊃ [(∃y)(Ly • Txy) ⊃ (∃z)(Fz • Txz)]}

1) (x)(Lx ⊃ Fx)                                                    Pr
2) ~ (x){Px ⊃ [(∃y)(Ly • Txy) ⊃ (∃z)(Fz • Txz)]} ✓   Pr
3) (∃x)~ {Px ⊃ [(∃y)(Ly • Txy) ⊃ (∃z)(Fz • Txz)]} ✓   2, QD
4) ~ {Pa ⊃ [(∃y)(Ly • Tay) ⊃ (∃z)(Fz • Taz)]} ✓       3, EI
5)                        Pa                                             4, DMI
6)      ~ [(∃y)(Ly • Tay) ⊃ (∃z)(Fz • Taz)] ✓          4, DMI
7)                  (∃y)(Ly • Tay) ✓                               6, DMI
8)               ~ (∃z)(Fz • Taz) ✓                               6, DMI
9)                    Lb • Tab ✓                                      7, EI
10)                      Lb                                               9, C
11)                     Tab                                              9, C
12)              (z)~ (Fz • Taz)                                    8, QD
13)                 ~ (Fb • Tab) ✓                               12, UI

14)            ~ Fb       ~ Tab                                    13, DC
15)          Lb ⊃ Fb  ✓  X                                       1, UI

16)          ~ Lb      Fb                                             15, MI
                X        X                                            **VALID**

**11.2.A. (388–389)**

**1.**                            /∴  (∃x)(Px ∨ ~ Mx)

1) (x)(Mx ⊃ Px)                Pr
2) (∃x)(~ Px • Mx) ✓          Pr
3) ~ Pa • Ma ✓                2, EI
4)    ~ Pa                          3, C
5)    Ma                           3, C
6)   Ma ⊃ Pa                    1, UI

7) ~ Ma       Pa                6, MI
       X          X                **INCONSISTENT**

**3.**                            /∴  (x)(Gx ⊃ Mx)

1)   (x)(Gx ⊃ Px)            Pr
2)   (x)(Mx ⊃ Px)            Pr
3)     Ga ⊃ Pa  ✓            1, UI
4)     Ma ⊃ Pa  ✓            2, UI

5)  ~ Ga       Pa              3, MI

6) ~ Ma Pa  ~ Ma Pa       4, MI

                **CONSISTENT**

**5.**                                              /∴ (∃x)(Dx • ~Cx)

  **1)** (x)(Cx ⊃ Dx)          Pr
  **2)** (x)(Hx ∨ ~ Dx)          Pr
  **3)** (∃x)(Dx • ~ Hx) ✓          Pr
  **4)**      Da • ~ Ha ✓          3, EI
  **5)**        Da          4, C
  **6)**       ~ Ha          4, C
  **7)**      Ha ∨ ~ Da ✓          2, UI

  **8)**    Ha    ~ Da          7, ID
       X      X          INCONSISTENT

**7.**                                              /∴ (x)[Cx ⊃ (Hx • Dx)]

  **1)** (x)[Cx ⊃ (Ix • Dx)]          Pr
  **2)** (x)[Dx ⊃ (Hx ⊃ Ix)]          Pr
  **3)**     Ca ⊃ (Ia • Da) ✓          1, UI
  **4)**     Da ⊃ (Ha ⊃ Ia) ✓          2, UI

  **5)** ~ Ca         Ia • Da ✓          3, MI
  **6)**              Ia          5, C
  **7)**             Da          5, C

  **8)** ~ Da   Ha ⊃ Ia ✓    ~ Da   Ha ⊃ Ia ✓          4, MI
                       X

  **9)**     ~ Ha   Ia      ~ Ha   Ia          9, MI

                                 CONSISTENT

**9.**                                              /∴ (∃x)[(Px • Sx) • ~ Dx]

  **1)** (∃x)[(Sx • ~ Px) • Dx] ✓          Pr
  **2)** (x)(Dx ⊃ Px)          Pr
  **3)**     (Sa • ~ Pa) • Da ✓          1, EI
  **4)**        Sa • ~ Pa ✓          3, C
  **5)**          Da          3, C
  **6)**          Sa          4, C
  **7)**        ~ Pa          4, C
  **8)**      Da ⊃ Pa ✓          2, UI

  **9)**     ~ Da    Pa          8, MI
           X      X          INCONSISTENT

**17.**                                                     /∴  (∃x)(∃y)[(Px • Bxy) • ~ Cx]

   **1)**  (x)[Px ⊃ (∃y)(Bxy ⊃ ~ Cx)]    Pr
   **2)**  (∃x)[(Px • Cx) • (y)Bxy]  ✓    Pr
   **3)**     (Pa • Ca) • (y)Bay  ✓    2, EI
   **4)**          Pa • Ca  ✓    3, C
   **5)**          (y)Bay    3, C
   **6)**            Pa    4, C
   **7)**            Ca    4, C
   **8)**   Pa ⊃ (∃y)(Bay ⊃ ~ Ca)  ✓    1, UI

   **9)**   ~Pa    (∃y)(Bay ⊃ ~ Ca)  ✓    8, MI
 **10)**    X      Bab ⊃ ~ Ca  ✓    9, EI

 **11)**      ~ Bab   ~ Ca    10. MI
 **12)**      Bab    X    5, UI
             X                **INCONSISTENT**

**11.2.B. (389)**

**3.**                                              /∴  (x)(Gx ⊃ Mx)

   **1)**  (x)(Gx ⊃ Px)    Pr
   **2)**  (x)(Mx ⊃ Px)    Pr
   **3)**  ~ (x)(Gx ⊃ Mx)    AP
   **4)**  (∃x)~ (Gx ⊃ Mx)  ✓    3, QD
   **5)**  ~ (Ga ⊃ Ma)  ✓    4, EI
   **6)**      Ga    5, MI
   **7)**    ~Ma    5, MI
   **8)**   Ga ⊃ Pa  ✓    1, UI
   **9)**   Ma ⊃ Pa  ✓    2, UI

 **19)**   ~ Ga  Pa    8, MI
          X
 **20)**    ~ Ma  Pa    9, MI
                     **INVALID**

**7.**                                                                      /∴  (x) [Cx • (Hx • Dx)]

1)  (x) [Cx ⊃ (Ix • Dx)]                                                           Pr
2)  (x) [Dx ⊃ (Hx ⊃ Ix)]                                                           Pr
3)  ~ (x) [Cx • (Hx • Dx)] ✓                                                       AP
4)  (∃x) ~ [Cx • (Hx • Dx)] ✓                                                      3, QD
5)  ~ [Ca • (Ha • Da)] ✓                                                           4, EI

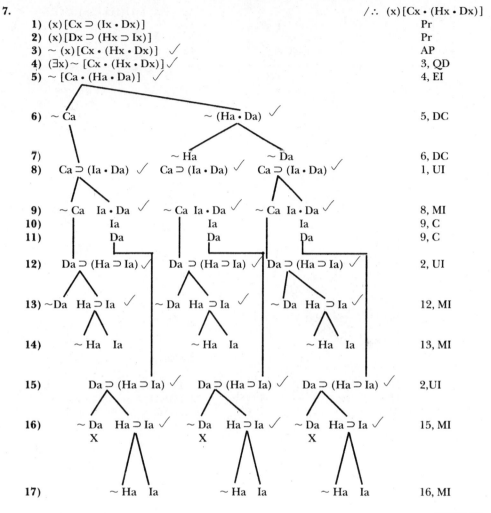

6)  ~ Ca                                 ~ (Ha • Da) ✓                             5, DC

7)                        ~ Ha                      ~ Da                           6, DC
8)  Ca ⊃ (Ia • Da) ✓   Ca ⊃ (Ia • Da) ✓   Ca ⊃ (Ia • Da) ✓                        1, UI

9)  ~ Ca  Ia • Da ✓    ~ Ca  Ia • Da ✓    ~ Ca  Ia • Da ✓                          8, MI
10)        Ia                  Ia                 Ia                               9, C
11)        Da                  Da                 Da                               9, C
12)  Da ⊃ (Ha ⊃ Ia) ✓  Da ⊃ (Ha ⊃ Ia) ✓  Da ⊃ (Ha ⊃ Ia) ✓                         2, UI

13) ~Da  Ha ⊃ Ia ✓   ~ Da  Ha ⊃ Ia ✓   ~ Da  Ha ⊃ Ia ✓                            12, MI

14)     ~ Ha  Ia          ~ Ha  Ia          ~ Ha  Ia                              13, MI

15)  Da ⊃ (Ha ⊃ Ia) ✓  Da ⊃ (Ha ⊃ Ia) ✓  Da ⊃ (Ha ⊃ Ia) ✓                         2,UI

16)  ~ Da  Ha ⊃ Ia ✓  ~ Da  Ha ⊃ Ia ✓  ~ Da  Ha ⊃ Ia ✓                             15, MI
      X                 X                 X

17)     ~ Ha  Ia          ~ Ha  Ia          ~ Ha  Ia                              16, MI

**INVALID**

**15.**                                                              $/ \therefore\ (x)[(Hx \cdot Sx) \supset Cx]$

| | | |
|---|---|---|
| **1)** | $(\exists x)[(Hx \cdot Sx) \cdot Ix]$  ✓ | Pr |
| **2)** | $(x)[(Sx \cdot Ix) \supset Rx]$ | Pr |
| **3)** | $(x)\ [(Sx \cdot Rx) \supset Cx]$ | Pr |
| **4)** | $\sim (x)[(Hx \cdot Sx) \supset Cx]$  ✓ | AP |
| **5)** | $(\exists x)\sim [(Hx \cdot Sx) \supset Cx]$  ✓ | 4, QD |
| **6)** | $(Ha \cdot Sa) \cdot Ia$  ✓ | 1, EI |
| **7)** | $Ha \cdot Sa$  ✓ | 6, C |
| **8)** | $Ia$ | 6, C |
| **9)** | $Ha$ | 7, C |
| **10)** | $Sa$ | 7, C |
| **11)** | $(Sa \cdot Ia) \supset Ra$  ✓ | 2, UI |

**12)**    $\sim (Sa \cdot Ia)$ ✓    $Ra$        11, MI

**13)**   $\sim Sa$    $\sim Ia$        12, DC
       X      X

**14)**      $(Sa \cdot Ra) \supset Ca$ ✓       3, UI

**15)**    $\sim (Sa \cdot Ra)$ ✓    $Ca$       14, MI

**16)**    $\sim Sa$    $\sim Ra$       15, DC
     X      X

| | | |
|---|---|---|
| **17)** | $\sim [(Hb \cdot Sb) \supset Cb]$  ✓ | 5, EI |
| **18)** | $Hb \cdot Sb$  ✓ | 17, DMI |
| **19)** | $\sim Cb$ | 17, DMI |
| **20)** | $Hb$ | 18, C |
| **21)** | $Sb$ | 18, C |

                                      **INVALID**

**11.3. (392–393)**

**1.**    $(x)Ex \supset (\exists y)Ey$

| | | |
|---|---|---|
| **1)** | $\sim [(x)Ex \supset (\exists y)Ey]$  ✓ | — |
| **2)** | $(x)Ex$ | 1, DMI |
| **3)** | $\sim (\exists y)Ey$  ✓ | 1, DMI |
| **4)** | $(y)\sim Ey$ | 3, QD |
| **5)** | $Ea$ | 2, UI |
| **6)** | $\sim Ea$ | 4, UI |
| | X | **LOGICALLY TRUE** |

**3.**    $(\exists x)[Ex \cdot \sim (\sim Cx \vee Ex)]$

| | | |
|---|---|---|
| **1)** | $(\exists x)[Ex \cdot \sim (\sim Cx \vee Ex)]$  ✓ | — |
| **2)** | $Ea \cdot \sim (\sim Ca \vee Ea)$  ✓ | 1, EI |
| **3)** | $Ea$ | 2, C |
| **4)** | $\sim (\sim Ca \vee Ea)$  ✓ | 2, C |
| **5)** | $\sim \sim Ca$  ✓ | 4, DID |
| **6)** | $\sim Ea$ | 4, DID |
| **7)** | $Ca$ | 5, DN |
| | X | **CONTRADICTION** |

**5.**   (x)(∃y)(Px ⊃ Wxy) ⊃ (∃x)(y)(Px • Wxy)

**a)**

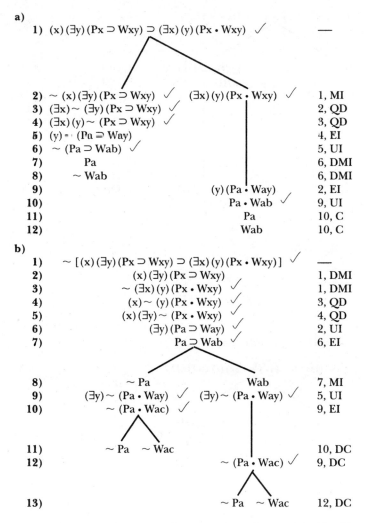

1)  (x)(∃y)(Px ⊃ Wxy) ⊃ (∃x)(y)(Px • Wxy)  ✓          —

| | | |
|---|---|---|
| **2)** | ~ (x)(∃y)(Px ⊃ Wxy) ✓ | (∃x)(y)(Px • Wxy) ✓ | 1, MI |
| **3)** | (∃x)~ (∃y)(Px ⊃ Wxy) ✓ | | 2, QD |
| **4)** | (∃x)(y)~ (Px ⊃ Wxy) ✓ | | 3, QD |
| **5)** | (y)~ (Pa ⊃ Way) | | 4, EI |
| **6)** | ~ (Pa ⊃ Wab) ✓ | | 5, UI |
| **7)** | Pa | | 6, DMI |
| **8)** | ~ Wab | | 6, DMI |
| **9)** | | (y)(Pa • Way) ✓ | 2, EI |
| **10)** | | Pa • Wab ✓ | 9, UI |
| **11)** | | Pa | 10, C |
| **12)** | | Wab | 10, C |

**b)**

| | | |
|---|---|---|
| **1)** | ~ [(x)(∃y)(Px ⊃ Wxy) ⊃ (∃x)(y)(Px • Wxy)] ✓ | — |
| **2)** | (x)(∃y)(Px ⊃ Wxy) | 1, DMI |
| **3)** | ~ (∃x)(y)(Px • Wxy) ✓ | 1, DMI |
| **4)** | (x)~ (y)(Px • Wxy) ✓ | 3, QD |
| **5)** | (x)(∃y)~ (Px • Wxy) ✓ | 4, QD |
| **6)** | (∃y)(Pa ⊃ Way) ✓ | 2, UI |
| **7)** | Pa ⊃ Wab ✓ | 6, EI |

| | | | |
|---|---|---|---|
| **8)** | ~ Pa | Wab | 7, MI |
| **9)** | (∃y)~ (Pa • Way) ✓   (∃y)~ (Pa • Way) ✓ | | 5, UI |
| **10)** | ~ (Pa • Wac) ✓ | | 9, EI |
| **11)** | ~ Pa    ~ Wac | | 10, DC |
| **12)** | | ~ (Pa • Wac) ✓ | 9, DC |
| **13)** | | ~ Pa    ~ Wac | 12, DC |

Since exercise 5 is neither contradictory nor logically true, it is CONTINGENT.

**7.**   (x)(Dx ⊃ Hx) Δ (∃x)(Dx • ~ Hx)

1)  ~ [(x)(Dx ⊃ Hx) Δ (∃x)(Dx • ~ Hx)] ✓    —

| | | |
|---|---|---|
| 2) | (x)(Dx ⊃ Hx)    ~ (x)(Dx ⊃ Hx) ✓ | 1, DED |
| 3) | (∃x)(Dx • ~ Hx)] ✓  ~ (∃x)(Dx • ~ Hx)] | 1, DED |
| 4) | Da • ~ Ha ✓ | 3, EI |
| 5) | Da | 4, C |
| 6) | ~ Ha ✓ | 4, C |
| 7) | Da ⊃ Ha ✓ | 2, UI |

| | | |
|---|---|---|
| 8) | ~ Da  Ha | 7, MI |
| 9) | X   X    (∃x)~ (Dx ⊃ Hx) ✓ | 2, QD |
| 10) | (x)~ (Dx • ~ Hx) ✓ | 3, QD |
| 11) | ~ (Da ⊃ Ha) ✓ | 9, EI |
| 12) | ~ (Da • ~ Ha) ✓ | 10, UI |
| 13) | Da | 11, DMI |
| 14) | ~ Ha | 11, DMI |

| | | |
|---|---|---|
| 15) | ~ Da   ~ ~ Ha ✓ | 12, DC |
| 16) | X    Ha | 15, DN |
| | X | **LOGICALLY TRUE** |

**9.**   ~ (x)(Dx ⊃ ~ Hx) ≡ (∃x)(Dx • Hx)

1)  ~ [~ (x)(Dx ⊃ ~ Hx) ≡ (∃x)(Dx • Hx)]    —

| | | |
|---|---|---|
| 2) | ~ (x)(Dx ⊃ ~ Hx) ✓  (∃x)(Dx • Hx) ✓ | 1, DME |
| 3) | ~ (∃x)(Dx • Hx) ✓  ~ ~ (x)(Dx ⊃ ~ Hx) ✓ | 1, DME |
| 4) | (∃x)~ (Dx ⊃ ~ Hx) ✓ | 2, QD |
| 5) | (x)~ (Dx • Hx) | 3, QD |
| 6) | ~ (Da ⊃ ~ Ha) ✓ | 4, EI |
| 7) | ~ (Da • Ha) ✓ | 5, UI |
| 8) | Da | 6, DMI |
| 9) | ~ ~ Ha | 6, DMI |
| 10) | Ha | 9, DN |

| | | |
|---|---|---|
| 11) | ~ Da  ~ Ha | 7, DC |
| 12) | X   X    Da • Ha ✓ | 2, EI |
| 13) | Da | 12, C |
| 14) | Ha | 12, C |
| 15) | (x)(Dx ⊃ ~ Hx) | 3, DN |
| 16) | Da ⊃ ~ Ha ✓ | 15, UI |

| | | |
|---|---|---|
| 17) | ~ Da  ~ Ha | 16, MI |
| | X   X | **LOGICALLY TRUE** |

**15.** (x) [Sx ⊃ (Ix Δ Lx)] • (∃x) [Sx • (~ Lx • ~ Ix)]

**1)** (x) [Sx ⊃ (Ix Δ Lx)] • (∃x) [Sx • (~ Lx • ~ Ix)] ✓    —
**2)**        (x) [Sx ⊃ (Ix Δ Lx)]       1, C
**3)**       (∃x) [Sx • (~ Lx • ~ Ix)] ✓    1, C
**4)**         Sa • (~ La • ~ Ia) ✓     3, EI
**5)**              Sa           4, C
**6)**          ~ La • ~ Ia ✓      4, C
**7)**            ~La          6, C
**8)**            ~Ia          6, C
**9)**       Sa ⊃ (Ia Δ La) ✓      2, UI

**10)**    ~ Sa      Ia Δ La ✓      9, MI
         X

**11)**          Ia    La        10, ED
**12)**        ~ La  ~ Ia     10, ED
           X     X          **CONTRADICTORY**

**17.** (x) [Sx ⊃ (∃y) (Gy • Mxy)] ∨ (∃x) [Sx • (y) (Gy ⊃ ~ Mxy)]

**1)** ~ {(x) [Sx ⊃ (∃y) (Gy • Mxy)] ∨ (∃x) [Sx • (y) (Gy ⊃ ~ Mxy)] ✓   —
**2)**         ~ (x) [Sx ⊃ (∃y) (Gy • Mxy)] ✓     1, DID
**3)**         ~ (∃x) [Sx • (y) (Gy ⊃ ~ Mxy)] ✓    1, DID
**4)**        (∃x) ~ [Sx ⊃ (∃y) (Gy • Mxy)] ✓     2, QD
**5)**        (x) ~ [Sx • (y) (Gy ⊃ ~ Mxy)]     3, QD
**6)**        ~ [Sa ⊃ (∃y) (Gy • May)] ✓     4, EI
**7)**               Sa            6, DMI
**8)**        ~ (∃y) (Gy • May) ✓      7, DMI
**9)**         (y) ~ (Gy • May)      8, QD
**10)**      ~ [Sa ⊃ (∃y) (Gy • May)] ✓    5, UI

**11)**    ~ Sa       ~ (y) (Gy ⊃ ~ May) ✓    10, DC
**12)**      X      (∃y) ~ (Gy ⊃ ~ May) ✓    11, QD
**13)**           ~ (Gb ⊃ ~ Mab) ✓     12, EI
**14)**               Gb          13, DMI
**15)**             ~ ~ Mab ✓      13, DMI
**16)**              Mab         15, DN
**17)**          ~ (Gb • Mab) ✓      9, UI

**18)**        ~ Gb    ~ Mab      17, DC
           X     X       **LOGICALLY TRUE**

**11.4. (394–395)**

**1.**

   **a)** (x)(Cx ⊃ Fx)
   **b)** ~ (∃x)(Cx • ~ Fx)

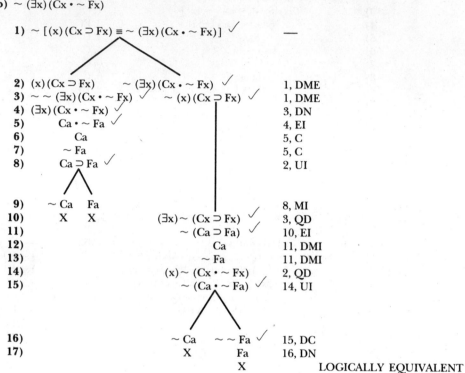

1)   ~ [(x)(Cx ⊃ Fx) ≡ ~ (∃x)(Cx • ~ Fx)] ✓     —

2)   (x)(Cx ⊃ Fx)    ~ (∃x)(Cx • ~ Fx) ✓     1, DME
3)   ~ ~ (∃x)(Cx • ~ Fx) ✓    ~ (x)(Cx ⊃ Fx) ✓     1, DME
4)   (∃x)(Cx • ~ Fx) ✓     3, DN
5)     Ca • ~ Fa ✓     4, EI
6)      Ca     5, C
7)      ~ Fa     5, C
8)     Ca ⊃ Fa ✓     2, UI

9)    ~ Ca    Fa     8, MI
10)    X    X    (∃x) ~ (Cx ⊃ Fx) ✓     3, QD
11)     ~ (Ca ⊃ Fa) ✓     10, EI
12)      Ca     11, DMI
13)      ~ Fa     11, DMI
14)     (x) ~ (Cx • ~ Fx)     2, QD
15)     ~ (Ca • ~ Fa) ✓     14, UI

16)    ~ Ca    ~ ~ Fa ✓     15, DC
17)     X     Fa     16, DN
         X     **LOGICALLY EQUIVALENT**

**3.**
   **a)** $(\exists x)(Fx \cdot Cx)$
   **b)** $(\exists x)Fx \cdot (\exists x)Cx$

| | | |
|---|---|---|
| **1)** | $\sim \{(\exists x)(Fx \cdot Cx) \equiv [(\exists x)Fx \cdot (\exists x)Cx]\}$ ✓ | — |
| **2)** | $(\exists x)(Fx \cdot Cx)$ ✓   $(\exists x)Fx \cdot (\exists x)Cx$ ✓ | 1, DME |
| **3)** | $\sim [(\exists x)Fx \cdot (\exists x)Cx]$ ✓  $\sim (\exists x)(Fx \cdot Cx)$ ✓ | 1, DME |
| **4)** | $Fa \cdot Ca$ ✓ | 2, EI |
| **5)** | $Fa$ | 4, C |
| **6)** | $Ca$ | 4, C |
| **7)** | $\sim (\exists x)Fx$ ✓   $\sim (\exists x)Cx$ ✓ | 3, DC |
| **8)** | $(x)\sim Fx$    $(x)\sim Cx$ | 7, QD |
| **9)** | $\sim Fa$    $\sim Ca$ | 8, UI |
| **10)** | X     X     $(\exists x)Fx$ ✓ | 2, C |
| **11)** | $(\exists x)Cx$ ✓ | 2, C |
| **12)** | $(x) \sim (Fx \cdot Cx)$ | 3, QD |
| **13)** | $Fa$ | 10, EI |
| **14)** | $Ca$ | 11, EI |
| **15)** | $\sim (Fa \cdot Ca)$ ✓ | 12, UI |
| **16)** | $\sim Fa$   $\sim Ca$ | 15, DC |
| | X | NOT LOGICALLY EQUIVALENT |

**5.**
   **a)** $(\exists x)(\sim Ix \cdot \sim Hx)$
   **b)** $\sim (x)(Hx \vee Ix)$

| | | |
|---|---|---|
| **1)** | $\sim [(\exists x)(\sim Ix \cdot \sim Hx) \equiv \sim (x)(Hx \vee Ix)]$ ✓ | — |
| **2)** | $(\exists x)(\sim Ix \cdot \sim Hx)$ ✓   $\sim (x)(Hx \vee Ix)$ ✓ | 1, DME |
| **3)** | $\sim \sim (x)(Hx \vee Ix)$ ✓  $\sim (\exists x)(\sim Ix \cdot \sim Hx)$ ✓ | 1, DME |
| **4)** | $\sim Ia \cdot \sim Ha$ ✓ | 2, EI |
| **5)** | $\sim Ia$ | 4, C |
| **6)** | $\sim Ha$ | 4, C |
| **7)** | $(x)(Hx \vee Ix)$ | 3, DN |
| **8)** | $Ha \vee Ia$ ✓ | 7, UI |
| **9)** | $Ha$   $Ia$ | 8, ID |
| **10)** | X   X   $(\exists x) \sim (Hx \vee Ix)$ ✓ | 2, QD |
| **11)** | $\sim (Ha \vee Ia)$ ✓ | 10, EI |
| **12)** | $\sim Ha$ | 11, DID |
| **13)** | $\sim Ia$ | 11, DID |
| **14)** | $(x)\sim (\sim Ix \cdot \sim Hx)$ | 3, QD |
| **15)** | $\sim (\sim Ia \cdot \sim Ha)$ ✓ | 14, UI |
| **17)** | $\sim \sim Ia$ ✓  $\sim \sim Ha$ ✓ | 15, DC |
| **18)** | $Ia$    $Ha$ | 17, DN |
| | X    X | LOGICALLY EQUIVALENT |

**7.**
   **a)**  ~ (x)(Ix ⊃ Dx)
   **b)**  (x)(Ix ⊃ ~Dx)

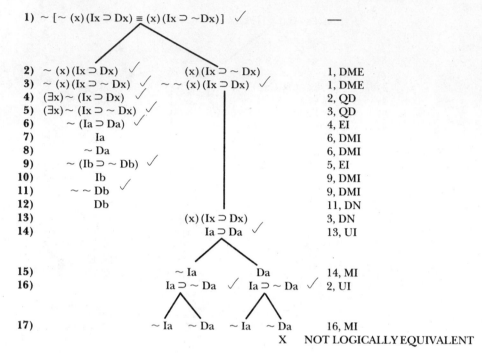

1)  ~ [~ (x)(Ix ⊃ Dx) ≡ (x)(Ix ⊃ ~Dx)]  ✓                    —

2)  ~ (x)(Ix ⊃ Dx)  ✓            (x)(Ix ⊃ ~ Dx)              1, DME
3)  ~ (x)(Ix ⊃ ~ Dx)  ✓    ~ ~ (x)(Ix ⊃ Dx)  ✓              1, DME
4)  (∃x)~ (Ix ⊃ Dx)  ✓                                        2, QD
5)  (∃x)~ (Ix ⊃ ~ Dx)  ✓                                      3, QD
6)      ~ (Ia ⊃ Da)  ✓                                        4, EI
7)          Ia                                                6, DMI
8)         ~ Da                                               6, DMI
9)      ~ (Ib ⊃ ~ Db)  ✓                                      5, EI
10)         Ib                                                9, DMI
11)        ~ ~ Db  ✓                                          9, DMI
12)         Db                                                11, DN
13)                            (x)(Ix ⊃ Dx)                   3, DN
14)                             Ia ⊃ Da  ✓                    13, UI

15)                  ~ Ia            Da                       14, MI
16)          Ia ⊃ ~ Da  ✓    Ia ⊃ ~ Da  ✓                    2, UI

17)              ~ Ia   ~ Da   ~ Ia   ~ Da                    16, MI
                    X      NOT LOGICALLY EQUIVALENT

**9.**
   **a)**  (x)(Sx ⊃ Tx)
   **b)**  (x)(Tx ⊃ Sx)

1)      ~ [(x)(Sx ⊃ Tx) ≡ (x)(Tx ⊃ Sx)]  ✓                   —

2)      (x)(Sx ⊃ Tx)           (x)(Tx ⊃ Sx)                   1, DME
3)   ~ (x)(Tx ⊃ Sx)  ✓      ~ (x)(Sx ⊃ Tx)  ✓                1, DME
4)   (∃x)~ (Tx ⊃ Sx)  ✓                                      3, QD
5)      ~ (Ta ⊃ Sa)  ✓                                       4, EI
6)          Ta                                               5, DMI
7)         ~ Sa                                              5, DMI
8)       Sa ⊃ Ta  ✓                                          2, UI

9)    ~ Sa    Ta                                             8, MI
10)                      (∃x)~ (Sx ⊃ Tx)  ✓                  3, QD
11)                         ~ (Sa ⊃ Ta)  ✓                   10, EI
12)                             Sa                           11, DMI
13)                            ~ Ta                          11, DMI
14)                          Ta ⊃ Sa  ✓                      2, UI

15)                        ~ Ta    Sa                        14, MI

                    NOT LOGICALLY EQUIVALENT

# CHAPTER 12

**12.2.A.** (406–408)

**1.**
1) Pr
2) Pr
3) 1, UI
4) 3, 2, MP

**3.**
1) Pr
2) Pr
3) 1, UI
4) 2, UI
5) 3, 4, HS

**5.**
1) Pr
2) Pr
3) 1, UI
4) 2, DN
5) 3, 4, MT
6) 5, DeM

**7.**
1) Pr
2) Pr
3) 1, Simp
4) 1, Com
5) 4, Simp
6) 5, UI
7) 3, UI
8) 2, UI
9) 6, 7, 8, CD
10) 9, Com
11) 10, UG

**9.**
1) Pr
2) Pr
3) 2, Simp
4) 2, Com
5) 4, Simp
6) 3, UI
7) 5, UI
8) 6, 7, HS
9) 8, UG
10) 1, 9, MP
11) 10, UI
12) 7, 11, HS
13) 12, UG
14) 6, 12, HS
15) 14, UG
16) 15, 13, Conj

**12.2.B.** (408)

**1.**                        /∴ Aa
1) ∼ Ba                    Pr
2) (x)(∼ Ax ⊃ Bx)    Pr
3) ∼ Aa ⊃ Ba          2, UI
4) ∼ ∼ Aa               3, 1, MT
5) /∴ Aa                 4, DN

**3.**                        /∴ Ca
1) (x)(Ax ⊃ ∼ Bx)    Pr
2) Aa                       Pr
3) (x)(Bx ∨ Cx)        Pr
4) Aa ⊃ ∼ Ba          1, UI
5) Ba ∨ Ca             3, UI
6) ∼ Ba                  4, 2, MP
7) /∴ Ca                 5, 6, DS

**5.**                                    /∴  (x)(Ax ⊃ Bx)

1)  (x)[(Ax • ~ Bx) ⊃ Cx]    Pr
2)  (x)(Cx ⊃ Bx)             Pr
3)  (Ax • ~ Bx) ⊃ Cx         1, UI
4)  Cx ⊃ Bx                  2, UI
5)  (Ax • ~ Bx) ⊃ Bx         3, 4, HS
6)  Ax ⊃ (~ Bx ⊃ Bx)         5, Exp
7)  Ax ⊃ (~ ~ Bx ∨ Bx)       6, Impl
8)  Ax ⊃ (Bx ∨ Bx)           7, DN
9)  Ax ⊃ Bx                  8, Taut
10) /∴  (x)(Ax ⊃ Bx)         9, UG

**7.**                                    /∴  ~ Ba

1)  (x)[(Ax • Bx) ≡ ~ Cx]                Pr
2)  Aa • Ca                               Pr
3)  (Aa • Ba) ≡ ~ Ca                      1, UI
4)  [(Aa • Ba) ⊃ ~ Ca] • [~ Ca ⊃ (Aa • Ba)]   3, Equiv
5)  (Aa • Ba) ⊃ ~ Ca                      4, Simp
6)  Aa                                    2, Simp
7)  Ca • Aa                               2, Com
8)  Ca                                    7, Simp
9)  ~ ~ Ca                                8, DN
10) ~ (Aa • Ba)                           5, 9, DN
11) ~ Aa ∨ ~ Ba                           10, DeM
12) ~ ~ Aa                                6, DN
13) /∴  ~ Ba                              11, 12, DS

**12.2.C. (409)**

**1.**              /∴  Sc

1)  (x)(Lx ⊃ Tx)    Pr
2)  (x)(Tx ⊃ Sx)    Pr
3)  Lc              Pr
4)  Lc ⊃ Tc         1, UI
5)  Tc ⊃ Sc         2, UI
6)  Tc              4, 3, MP
7)  /∴  Sc          5, 6, MP

**3.**                                    /∴  (x)(Mx ⊃ Cx)

1)  (x)(Bx ⊃ Mx) ⊃ (x)(Mx ⊃ Cx)    Pr
2)  (x)(Bx ⊃ Cx) • (x)(Cx ⊃ Mx)    Pr
3)  (x)(Bx ⊃ Cx)                    2, Simp
4)  (x)(Cx ⊃ Mx) • (x)(Bx ⊃ Cx)    2, Com
5)  (x)(Cx ⊃ Mx)                    4, Simp
6)  Bx ⊃ Cx                         3, UI
7)  Cx ⊃ Mx                         5, UI
8)  Bx ⊃ Mx                         6, 7, HS
9)  (x)(Bx ⊃ Mx)                    8, UG
10) /∴  (x)(Mx ⊃ Cx)                1, 9, MP

**5.**                                            /∴ ~ Ie

   **1)** (x){[Sx • (Ix • Cx)] ⊃ Px}    Pr

   **2)** Se • ~ Pe                      Pr

   **3)** Ce                            Pr

   **4)** [Se • (Ie • Ce)] ⊃ Pe          1, UI

   **5)** Se                            2, Simp

   **6)** ~ Pe • Se                      2, Com

   **7)** ~ Pe                           6, Simp

   **8)** ~ [(Se • (Ie • Ce)]            4, 7, MT

   **9)** ~ Se ∨ ~ (Ie • Ce)             8, DeM

  **10)** ~ ~ Se                             5, DN

  **11)** ~ (Ie • Ce)                         9, 10, DS

  **12)** ~ Ie ∨ ~ Ce                         11, DeM

  **13)** ~ Ce ∨ ~ Ie                         12, Com

  **14)** ~ ~ Ce                             3, DN

  **15)** /∴ ~ Ie                            13, 14, DS

**7.**                                            /∴ ~ (Fa ∨ Ta)

   **1)** (x)(Px ⊃ {[Ux • (Fx ∨ Ix)] ≡ ~ ~ Tx})    Pr

   **2)** Pm • ~ (Tm ∨ ~ Um)            Pr

   **3)** Pa ⊃ {[Um • (Fm ∨ Im)] ≡ ~ ~ Tm}    1, UI

   **4)** Pa                            2, Simp

   **5)** [Um • (Fm ∨ Im)] ≡ ~ ~ Tm     3, 4, MP

   **6)** ~ (Tm ∨ ~ Um) • Pm             2, Com

   **7)** ~ (Tm ∨ ~ Um)                  6, Simp

   **8)** ~ Tm • ~ ~ Um                  7, DeM

   **9)** [Um • (Fm ∨ Im)] ≡ Tm          5, DN

  **10)** {[Um • (Fm ∨ Im)] ⊃ Tm} • {Tm ⊃ [Um • (Fm ∨ Im)]}    9, Equiv

  **11)** [Um • (Fm ∨ Im)] ⊃ Tm              10, Simp

  **12)** ~ Tm                               8, Simp

  **13)** ~ [Um • (Fm ∨ Im)]                 11, 12, MT

  **14)** ~ Um ∨ ~ (Fm ∨ Im)                 13, DeM

  **15)** ~ ~ Um • ~ Tm                      8, Com

  **16)** ~ ~ Um                             15, Simp

  **17)** ~ (Fm ∨ Im)                        14, 16, DS

  **18)** ~ Fm • ~ Im                        17, DeM

  **19)** ~ Fm                               18, Simp

  **20)** ~ Fm • ~ Tm                        19, 12, Conj

  **21)** /∴ ~ (Fm ∨ Tm)                     20, DeM

**12.3.A.  (414–417)**

**1.**

1) Pr
2) 1, EI
3) 2, Simp
4) 3, Add
5) 2, Com
6) 5, Simp
7) 4, 6, Conj
8) 7, EG

**3.**

1) Pr
2) 1, Simp
3) 1, Com
4) 3, Simp
5) 4, EG
6) 2, UI
7) 5, Simp
8) 6, 7, MP
9) 5, Com
10) 9, Simp
11) 8, 10, Conj
12) 11, EG

**5.**

1) Pr
2) Pr
3) Pr
4) 2, EI
5) 1, UI
6) 3, UI
7) 4, Simp
8) 4, Com
9) 8, Simp
10) 5, 7, MT
11) 9, DN
12) 6, 11, MT
13) 12, 10, Conj
14) 13, DeM
15) 14, Eg

**7.**

1) Pr
2) Pr
3) Pr
4) 2, EI
5) 1, UI
6) 3, UI
7) 4, Simp
8) 4, Com
9) 8, Simp
10) 9, DN
11) 5, 10, MT
12) 11, DeM
13) 7, DN
14) 12, 13, DS
15) 7, 14, Conj
16) 6, 15, MP
17) 7, 16, Conj
18) 17, EG

**12.3.B.  (417–418)**

**1.**                                              / ∴  (∃x) ~ Ax

1) (x) [Ax ⊃ (Bx ∨ Cx)]        Pr
2) (∃x) (~ Cx • ~ Bx)          Pr
3) ~ Cx • ~ Bx                 2, EI
4) Ax ⊃ (Bx ∨ Cx)             1, UI
5) ~ Bx • ~ Cx                 3, Com
6) ~ (Bx ∨ ~ Cx)              5, DeM
7) ~ Ax                        4, 6, MT
8) / ∴  (∃x) ~ Ax             7, EG

**3.**                                              / ∴  (∃x) ~ Bx

1) (x) [(Ax • Bx) ⊃ Cx]       Pr
2) (x) (Cx ⊃ ~ Bx)            Pr
3) (∃x) Ax                     Pr
4) Ax                          3, EI
5) (Ax • Bx) ⊃ Cx             1, UI
6) Cx ⊃ ~ Bx                  2, UI
7) Ax ⊃ (Bx ⊃ Cx)            5, Exp
8) Bx ⊃ Cx                    7, 4, MP
9) Bx ⊃ ~ Bx                  8, 6, HS
10) ~ Bx ∨ ~ Bx               9, Impl
11) ~ Bx                       10, Taut
12) / ∴  (∃x) ~ Bx            11, EG

**5.**                                                                    $/\therefore$   $(\exists x)(Cx \lor Ax)$

  **1)** $[(\exists x)Ax \cdot (\exists x)Bx] \supset (\exists x)(Cx \lor Ax)$    Pr

  **2)** $(x)[Cx \supset (Ax \cdot Bx)]$    Pr

  **3)** $(x)(Dx \supset Cx)$    Pr

  **4)** $(\exists x)Dx$    Pr

  **5)** $Dx$    4, EI

  **6)** $Cx \supset (Ax \cdot Bx)$    2, UI

  **7)** $Dx \supset Cx$    3, UI

  **8)** $Cx$    7, 5, MΓ

  **9)** $Ax \cdot Bx$    6, 8, MP

  **10)** $Ax$    9, Simp

  **11)** $(\exists x)Ax$    10, EG

  **12)** $Bx \cdot Ax$    11, Com

  **13)** $Bx$    12, Simp

  **14)** $(\exists x)Bx$    13, EG

  **15)** $(\exists x)Ax \cdot (\exists x)Bx$    11, 14, Conj

  **16)** $/\therefore$   $(\exists x)(Gx \lor Hx)$    1, 15, MP

**7.**                                                                    $/\therefore$   $(\exists x)\sim (Dx \cdot Ax)$

  **1)** $(x)[(Ax \cdot Bx) \equiv \sim Cx]$    Pr

  **2)** $(\exists x)(Cx \cdot Bx)$    Pr

  **3)** $Cx \cdot Bx$    2, EI

  **4)** $(Ax \cdot Bx) \equiv \sim Cx$    1, UI

  **5)** $[(Ax \cdot Bx) \supset \sim Cx] \cdot [\sim Cx \supset (Ax \cdot Bx)]$    4, Equiv

  **6)** $(Ax \cdot Bx) \supset \sim Cx$    5, Simp

  **7)** $Cx$    3, Simp

  **8)** $\sim \sim Cx$    7, DN

  **9)** $\sim (Ax \cdot Bx)$    6, 8, MT

  **10)** $\sim Ax \lor \sim Bx$    9, DeM

  **11)** $\sim Bx \lor \sim Ax$    10, Com

  **12)** $Bx \cdot Cx$    3, Com

  **13)** $Bx$    12, Simp

  **14)** $\sim \sim Bx$    13, DN

  **15)** $\sim Ax$    11, 14, DS

  **16)** $\sim Ax \lor \sim Dx$    15, Add

  **17)** $\sim Dx \lor \sim Ax$    16, Com

  **18)** $\sim (Dx \cdot Ax)$    17, DeM

  **19)** $/\therefore$   $(\exists x)\sim (Dx \cdot Ax)$    18, EG

**12.3.C. (418–419)**

**1.**                                      /∴   (∃x)(Sx • Mx)

  **1)** (x)[Sx ⊃ (Mx • Cx)]   Pr

  **2)** (∃x)Sx                Pr

  **3)** Sx                     2, EI

  **4)** Sx ⊃ (Mx • Cx)        1, UI

  **5)** Mx • Cx               4, 3, MP

  **6)** Mx                     5, Simp

  **7)** Sx • Mx               3, 6, Conj

  **8)** /∴   (∃x)(Sx • Mx)    7, EG

**3.**                                      /∴   (∃x)Bx

  **1)** (∃x)(Ix ∨ Ux) ⊃ (x)(Ax ⊃ Bx)   Pr

  **2)** (∃x)(Ix • Ax)         Pr

  **3)** Ix • Ax               2, EI

  **4)** Ix                     3, Simp

  **5)** Ix ∨ Ux               4, Add

  **6)** (∃x)(Ix ∨ Ux)         5, EG

  **7)** (x)(Ax ⊃ Bx)          1, 6, MP

  **8)** Ax ⊃ Bx               7, UI

  **9)** Ax • Ix               3, Com

  **10)** Ax                    9, Simp

  **11)** Bx                    8, 10, MP

  **12)** /∴   (∃x)Bx          11, EG

**5.**                                      /∴   (∃x)[(Nx • Bx) • Dx]

  **1)** (x)[Nx ⊃ (Px ⊃ Bx)]   Pr

  **2)** (∃x)[(Px • Nx) • Dx]  Pr

  **3)** (Px • Nx) • Dx        2, EI

  **4)** Nx ⊃ (Px ⊃ Bx)        1, UI

  **5)** Px • Nx               3, Simp

  **6)** Px                     5, Simp

  **7)** Nx • Px               5, Com

  **8)** Nx                     7, Simp

  **9)** Px ⊃ Bx               4, 8, MP

  **10)** Bx                    9, 6, MP

  **11)** Dx • (Px • Nx)       3, Com

  **12)** Dx                    11, Simp

  **13)** Nx • Bx              8, 10, Conj

  **14)** (Nx • Bx) • Dx       13, 12, Conj

  **15)** /∴   (∃x)[(Nx • Bx) • Dx]   14, EG

**7.**                                      /∴   (∃x)∼(Gx ∨ Ix)

  **1)** (x)[(Sx ∨ Ix) ⊃ Dx]   Pr

  **2)** (x)[(Dx ∨ Gx) ⊃ Cx]   Pr

  **3)** (∃x)∼Cx               Pr

  **4)** ∼Cx                    3, EI

  **5)** (Sx ∨ Ix) ⊃ Dx        1, UI

  **6)** (Dx ∨ Gx) ⊃ Cx        2, UI

  **7)** ∼(Dx ∨ Gx)            6, 4, MT

  **8)** ∼Dx • ∼Gx             7, DeM

|        |                          |               |
|--------|--------------------------|---------------|
| **9)**  | ~ Dx                     | 8, Simp       |
| **10)** | ~ Gx • ~ Dx              | 8, Com        |
| **11)** | ~ Gx                     | 10, Simp      |
| **12)** | ~ (Sx ∨ Ix)              | 5, 9, MT      |
| **13)** | ~ Sx • ~ Ix              | 12, DeM       |
| **14)** | ~ Ix • ~ Sx              | 13, Com       |
| **15)** | ~ Ix                     | 14, Simp      |
| **16)** | ~ Gx • ~ Ix              | 11, 15, Conj  |
| **17)** | ~ (Gx ∨ Ix)              | 16, DeM       |
| **18)** | / ∴  (∃x) ~ (Gx ∨ Ix)    | 17, EG        |

**12.4.A. (423–427)**

**1.**

1) Pr
2) Pr
3) 1, QD
4) 3, DeM
5) 4, DN
6) 5, Impl
7) 1, Com
8) 7, 8, DS
9) 8, DeM
10) 9, Impl

**3.**

1) Pr
2) Pr
3) 1, QD
4) 3, EI
5) 2, UI
6) 4, Com
7) 6, Simp
8) 5, 7, MP
9) 8, EG

**5.**

1) Pr
2) Pr
3) 1, QD
4) 3, EI
5) 2, UI
6) 4, DeM
7) 6, Com
8) 7, Simp
9) 5, 8, MT
10) 9, 8, Conj
11) 10, DeM
12) 11, EG
13) 12, QD

**7.**

1) Pr
2) Pr
3) Pr
4) 3, QD
5) 4, EI
6) 5, Impl
7) 6, DeM
8) 7, DN
9) 2, UI
10) 8, Simp
11) 8, Com
12) 11, Simp
13) 9, 10, MP
14) 13, 12, Conj
15) 14, EG
16) 15, QD
17) 16, DeM
18) 17, DN
19) 18, Impl
20) 1, 19, MT
21) 20, QD
22) 21, Impl
23) 22, DeM
24) 23, DN

**12.4.B. (427–428)**

**1.**                               / ∴ (∃x) ∼ Ax

   **1)** ∼ (∃x)(Ax • ∼ Bx) • ∼ (x)Bx    Pr
   **2)** ∼ (∃x)(Ax • ∼ Bx)            1, Simp
   **3)** ∼ (x)Bx • ∼ (∃x)(Ax • ∼ Bx)   1, Com
   **4)** ∼ (x)Bx                   3, Simp
   **5)** (x) ∼ (Ax • ∼ Bx)           2, QD
   **6)** (∃x) ∼ Bx               4, QD
   **7)** ∼ Bx                    6, EI
   **8)** ∼ (Ax • ∼ Bx)              5, UI
   **9)** ∼ Ax ∨ ∼ ∼ Bx          8, DeM
 **10)** ∼ Ax ∨ Bx               9, DN
 **11)** Bx ∨ ∼ Ax              10, Com
 **12)** ∼ Ax                  11, 7, DS
 **13)** / ∴ (∃x) ∼ Ax        12, EG

**3.**                            / ∴ ∼ (x)(Cx ⊃ Ax)

   **1)** ∼ (∃x) ∼ (Ax ⊃ Bx)    Pr
   **2)** ∼ (x)(Cx ⊃ Bx)       Pr
   **3)** (x)(Ax ⊃ Bx)          1, QD
   **4)** (∃x) ∼ (Cx ⊃ Bx)     2, QD
   **5)** ∼ (Cx ⊃ Bx)         4, EG
   **6)** Ax ⊃ Bx            3, UI
   **7)** ∼ (∼ Cx ∨ Bx)      5, Impl
   **8)** ∼ ∼ Cx • ∼ Bx      7, DeM
   **9)** ∼ ∼ Cx            8, Simp
 **10)** ∼ Bx • ∼ ∼ Cx      8, Com
 **11)** ∼ Bx              10, Simp
 **12)** ∼ Ax              6, 11, MT
 **13)** ∼ ∼ Cx • ∼ Ax    9, 12, Conj
 **14)** ∼ (∼ Cx ∨ Ax)     13, DeM
 **15)** (∃x) ∼ (∼ Cx ∨ Ax)   14, EG
 **16)** ∼ (x)(∼ Cx ∨ Ax)    15, QD
 **17)** / ∴ ∼ (x)(Cx ⊃ Ax)   16, Impl

**5.**                     / ∴ ∼ (∃x)[Bx • (Ax • ∼ Dx)]

   **1)** ∼ (∃x)[(Ax • Bx) • ∼ Cx]    Pr
   **2)** (x)[Cx ⊃ (Ax ⊃ Dx)]       Pr
   **3)** (x) ∼ [(Ax • Bx) • ∼ Cx]    1, QD
   **4)** Cx ⊃ (Ax ⊃ Dx)         2, UI
   **5)** ∼ [(Ax • Bx) • ∼ Cx]     3, UI
   **6)** ∼ (Ax • Bx) ∨ ∼ ∼ Cx   5, DeM

**7)** $(Ax \cdot Bx) \supset \sim \sim Cx$      6, Impl

**8)** $(Ax \cdot Bx) \supset Cx$      7, DN

**9)** $(Ax \cdot Bx) \supset (Ax \supset Dx)$      8, 4, HS

**10)** $[(Ax \cdot Bx) \cdot Ax] \supset Dx$      9, Exp

**11)** $[Ax \cdot (Ax \cdot Bx)] \supset Dx$      10, Com

**12)** $[(Ax \cdot Ax) \cdot Bx] \supset Dx$      11, Assoc

**13)** $(Ax \cdot Bx) \supset Dx$      12, Taut

**14)** $\sim (Ax \cdot Bx) \vee Dx$      13, Impl

**15)** $(\sim Ax \vee \sim Bx) \vee Dx$      14, DeM

**16)** $(\sim Bx \vee \sim Ax) \vee Dx$      15, Com

**17)** $\sim Bx \vee (\sim Ax \vee Dx)$      16, Assoc

**18)** $\sim Bx \vee (\sim Ax \vee \sim \sim Dx)$      17, DN

**19)** $\sim Bx \vee \sim (Ax \cdot \sim Dx)$      18, DeM

**20)** $\sim [Bx \cdot (Ax \cdot \sim Dx)]$      19, DeM

**21)** $(x) \sim [Bx \cdot (Ax \cdot \sim Dx)]$      20, UG

**22)** $/ \therefore \ \sim (\exists x)[Bx \cdot (Ax \cdot \sim Dx)]$      21, QD

**7.**                               $(\exists x)(Cx \cdot Ax) \vee (\exists x)(Cx \cdot Dx)$

**1)** $\sim (\exists x)[\sim Ax \cdot (\sim Bx \cdot Cx)]$      Pr

**2)** $\sim (x)(Cx \supset Bx)$      Pr

**3)** $(x) \sim [\sim Ax \cdot (\sim Bx \cdot Cx)]$      1, QD

**4)** $(\exists x) \sim (Cx \supset Bx)$      2, QD

**5)** $\sim (Cx \supset Bx)$      4, EI

**6)** $\sim [\sim Ax \cdot (\sim Bx \cdot Cx)]$      3, UI

**7)** $\sim (\sim Cx \vee Bx)$      5, Impl

**8)** $\sim \sim Cx \cdot \sim Bx$      7, DeM

**9)** $\sim \sim Ax \vee \sim (\sim Bx \cdot Cx)$      6, DeM

**10)** $\sim \sim Ax \vee (\sim \sim Bx \vee \sim Cx)$      9, DeM

**11)** $Ax \vee (\sim \sim Bx \vee \sim Cx)$      10, DN

**12)** $Ax \vee (Bx \vee \sim Cx)$      11, DN

**13)** $(Bx \vee \sim Cx) \vee Ax$      12, Com

**14)** $Bx \vee (\sim Cx \vee Ax)$      13, Assoc

**15)** $\sim Bx \cdot \sim \sim Cx$      8, Com

**16)** $\sim Bx$      15, Simp

**17)** $\sim Cx \vee Ax$      14, 16, DS

**18)** $\sim \sim Cx$      8, Simp

**19)** $Ax$      17, 18, DS

**20)** $Cx$      18, DN

**21)** $Cx \cdot Ax$      20, 19, Conj

**22)** $(\exists x)(Cx \cdot Ax)$      21, EI

**23)** $/ \therefore \ (\exists x)(Cx \cdot Ax) \vee (\exists x)(Cx \cdot Dx)$      22, Add

12.4.C. (428–429)

**1.**                                          / ∴ (∃x)(Ax • ∼ Px)

    **1)** (x)(Ax ∨ Px) • ∼ (x)Px    Pr
    **2)** (x)(Ax ∨ Px)    1, Simp
    **3)** ∼ (x)Px • (x)(Ax ∨ Px)    1, Com
    **4)** ∼ (x)Px    3, Simp
    **5)** (∃x)∼ Px    4, QD
    **6)** ∼ Px    5, EI
    **7)** Ax ∨ Px    2, UI
    **8)** Px ∨ Ax    7, Com
    **9)** Ax    8, 6, DS
    **10)** Ax • ∼ Px    9, 6, Conj
    **11)** / ∴ (∃x)(Ax • ∼ Px)    10, EG

**3.**                                          / ∴ ∼ (∃x)(Ax • ∼ Ix)

    **1)** (x)(Ax ⊃ Tx)    Pr
    **2)** ∼ (∃x)[Tx • ∼ (Ix • Mx)]    Pr
    **3)** (x)∼ [Tx • ∼ (Ix ∼ Mx)]    2, QD
    **4)** Ax ⊃ Tx    1, UI
    **5)** ∼ [Tx • ∼ (Ix • Mx)]    3, UI
    **6)** ∼ Tx ∨ ∼ ∼ (Ix • Mx)    5, DeM
    **7)** ∼ Tx ∨ (Ix • Mx)    6, DN
    **8)** Tx ⊃ (Ix • Mx)    7, Impl
    **9)** Ax ⊃ (Ix • Mx)    4, 8, HS
    **10)** ∼ Ax ∨ (Ix • Mx)    9, Impl
    **11)** (∼ Ax ∨ Ix) • (∼ Ax ∨ Mx)    10, Dist
    **12)** ∼ Ax ∨ Ix    11, Simp
    **13)** ∼ ∼ (∼ Ax ∨ Ix)    12, DN
    **14)** ∼ (∼ ∼ Ax • ∼ Ix)    13, DeM
    **15)** ∼ (Ax • ∼ Ix)    14, DN
    **16)** (x)∼ (Ax • ∼ Ix)    15, UG
    **17)** / ∴ ∼ (∃x)(Ax • ∼ Ix)    16, QD

**5.**                                          / ∴ ∼ (x)(Ax ⊃ Hx)

    **1)** (x){Ax ⊃ [Gx ≡ ∼ (Sx ∨ Hx)]}    Pr
    **2)** (∃x)(Gx • Ax)    Pr
    **3)** Gx • Ax    2, EI
    **4)** Ax ⊃ [Gx ≡ ∼ (Sx ∨ Hx)]    1, UI
    **5)** Gx    3, Simp
    **6)** Ax • Gx    3, Com
    **7)** Ax    6, Simp
    **8)** Gx ≡ ∼ (Sx ∨ Hx)    4, 7, MP
    **9)** [Gx ⊃ ∼ (Sx ∨ Hx)] • [∼ (Sx ∨ Hx) ⊃ Gx]    8, Equiv

10) Gx ⊃ ~ (Sx ∨ Hx)                    9, Simp

11) ~ (Sx ∨ Hx)                         10, 5, MP

12) ~ Sx • ~ Hx                         11, DeM

13) ~ Hx • ~ Sx                         12, Com

14) ~ Hx                                13, Simp

15) Ax • ~ Hx                           7, 14, Conj

16) (∃x)(Ax • ~ Hx)                     15, EG

17) ~ (x)~ (Ax • ~ Hx)                  16, QD

18) ~ (x)(~ Ax ∨ ~ ~ Hx)               17, DeM

19)     (x)(~ Ax ∨ Hx)                  18, DN

20) /∴ ~ (x)(Ax ⊃ Hx)                   19, Impl

**7.**                                  /∴ (x)[Ax ⊃ (Vx ⊃ Hx)]

1) ~ (∃x)[Vx • (Ax • ~ Mx)]             Pr

2) ~ (∃x)[(Ax • Mx) • ~ (Hx • Cx)]      Pr

3) (x)~ [Vx • (Ax • ~ Mx)]              1, QD

4) (x)~ [(Ax • Mx) • ~ (Hx • Cx)]       2, QD

5) ~ [Vx • (Ax • ~ Mx)]                 3, UI

6) ~ [(Ax • Mx) • ~ (Hx • Cx)]          4, UI

7) ~ Vx ∨ ~ (Ax • ~ Mx)                 5, DeM

8) Vx ⊃ ~ (Ax • ~ Mx)                   7, Impl

9) Vx ⊃ (~ Ax ∨ ~ ~ Mx)                8, DeM

10) Vx ⊃ (~ Ax ∨ Mx)                    9, DN

11) Vx ⊃ (Ax ⊃ Mx)                      10, Impl

12) ~ (Ax • Mx) ∨ ~ ~ (Hx • Cx)         6, DeM

13) ~ (Ax • Mx) ∨ (Hx • Cx)             12, DN

14) (Ax • Mx) ⊃ (Hx • Cx)               13, Impl

15) (Vx • Ax) ⊃ Mx                      11, Exp

16) (Mx • Ax) ⊃ (Hx • Cx)               14, Com

17) Mx ⊃ [Ax ⊃ (Hx • Cx)]               16, Exp

18) (Vx • Ax) ⊃ [Ax ⊃ (Hx • Cx)]        15, 17, HS

19) [(Vx • Ax) • Ax] ⊃ (Hx • Cx)        18, Exp

20) [Vx • (Ax • Ax)] ⊃ (Hx • Cx)        19, Assoc

21) (Vx • Ax) ⊃ (Hx • Cx)               20, Taut

22) ~ (Vx • Ax) ∨ (Hx • Cx)             21, Impl

23) [~ (Vx • Ax) ∨ Hx] • [~ (Vx • Ax) ∨ Cx]    22, Dist

24) ~ (Vx • Ax) ∨ Hx                    23, Simp

25) (Vx • Ax) ⊃ Hx                      24, Impl

26) (Ax • Vx) ⊃ Hx                      25, Com

27) Ax ⊃ (Vx ⊃ Hx)                      26, Exp

28) /∴ (x)[Ax ⊃ (Vx ⊃ Hx)]              27, UG

**12.5.A. (433–434)**

**1.**                                      /∴ ~ (x)(Bx ⊃ ~ Cx)

| | | |
|---|---|---|
| **1)** | (x)(Ax ⊃ Bx) | Pr |
| **2)** | (∃x)(Ax • Cx) | Pr |
| **3)** | Ax • Cx | 2, EI |
| **4)** | Ax ⊃ Bx | 1, UI |
| **5)** | Ax | 3, Simp |
| **6)** | Cx • Ax | 3, Com |
| **7)** | Cx | 6, Simp |
| **8)** | Bx | 4, 5, MP |
| → **9)** | ~ ~ (x)(Bx ⊃ ~ Cx) | IP |
| **10)** | (x)(Bx ⊃ ~ Cx) | 9, DN |
| **11)** | Bx ⊃ ~ Cx | 10, UI |
| **12)** | ~ Cx | 11, 8, MP |
| **13)** | Cx • ~ Cx | 7, 12, Conj |
| **14)** | /∴ ~ (x)(Bx ⊃ ~ Cx) | 9 - 13, IP |

**3.**                                      /∴ (∃x)(Ax • Bx)

| | | |
|---|---|---|
| **1)** | (x)[Ax ⊃ (Bx • Cx)] | Pr |
| **2)** | (∃x)Ax | Pr |
| **3)** | Ax | 2, EI |
| **4)** | Ax ⊃ (Bx • Cx) | 1, UI |
| **5)** | Bx • Cx | 4, 3, MP |
| **6)** | Bx | 5, Simp |
| → **7)** | ~ (∃x)(Ax • Bx) | IP |
| **8)** | (x)~ (Ax • Bx) | 7, QD |
| **9)** | ~ (Ax • Bx) | 8, UI |
| **10)** | ~ Ax ∨ ~ Bx | 9, DeM |
| **11)** | ~ ~ Ax | 3, DN |
| **12)** | ~ Bx | 10, 11, DS |
| **13)** | Bx • ~ Bx | 6, 12, Conj |
| **14)** | /∴ (∃x)(Ax • Bx) | 7 - 13, IP |

**5.**                                    $/\therefore\ (\exists x)(Bx \cdot \sim Cx)$

  **1)** $(x)(Ax \supset Bx) \cdot (\exists x)(Ax \cdot \sim Cx)$ — Pr
  **2)** $(x)(Ax \supset Bx)$ — 1, Simp
  **3)** $(\exists x)(Ax \cdot \sim Cx) \cdot (x)(Ax \supset Bx)$ — 1, Com
  **4)** $(\exists x)(Ax \cdot \sim Cx)$ — 3, Simp
  **5)** $Ax \cdot \sim Cx$ — 4, EI
  **6)** $Ax \supset Bx$ — 2, UI
  **7)** $Ax$ — 5, Simp
  **8)** $\sim Cx \cdot Ax$ — 5, Com
  **9)** $\sim Cx$ — 8, Simp
  **10)** $Bx$ — 6, 7, MP
→**11)** $\sim (\exists x)(Bx \cdot \sim Cx)$ — IP
  **12)** $(x)\sim (Bx \cdot \sim Cx)$ — 11, QD
  **13)** $\sim (Bx \cdot \sim Cx)$ — 12, UI
  **14)** $\sim Bx \vee \sim \sim Cx$ — 13, DeM
  **15)** $\sim \sim Bx$ — 10, DN
  **16)** $\sim \sim Cx$ — 14, 15, DS
  **17)** $\sim Cx \cdot \sim \sim Cx$ — 9, 16, Conj
  **18)** $/\therefore\ (\exists x)(Bx \cdot \sim Cx)$ — 11-17, IP

**7.**                                    $/\therefore\ (\exists x)[(Ax \cdot Bx) \cdot (Ex \cdot Cx)]$

  **1)** $(\exists x)[(Ax \cdot Bx) \cdot (Cx \cdot Dx)]$ — Pr
  **2)** $(x)(Ax \supset Ex)$ — Pr
  **3)** $(Ax \cdot Bx) \cdot (Cx \cdot Dx)$ — 1, EI
  **4)** $Ax \supset Ex$ — 2, UI
  **5)** $Ax \cdot Bx$ — 3, Simp
  **6)** $Ax$ — 5, Simp
  **7)** $Ex$ — 4, 6, MP
  **8)** $(Cx \cdot Dx) \cdot (Ax \cdot Bx)$ — 3, Com
  **9)** $Cx \cdot Dx$ — 8, Simp
  **10)** $Cx$ — 9, Simp
→**11)** $\sim (\exists x)[(Ax \cdot Bx) \cdot (Ex \cdot Cx)]$ — IP
  **12)** $(x)\sim [(Ax \cdot Bx) \cdot (Ex \cdot Cx)]$ — 11, QD
  **13)** $\sim [(Ax \cdot Bx) \cdot (Ex \cdot Cx)]$ — 12, UI
  **14)** $\sim (Ax \cdot Bx) \vee \sim (Ex \cdot Cx)$ — 13, DeM
  **15)** $\sim \sim (Ax \cdot Bx)$ — 5, DN
  **16)** $\sim (Ex \cdot Cx)$ — 14, 15, DS
  **17)** $\sim Ex \vee \sim Cx$ — 16, DeM
  **18)** $\sim \sim Ex$ — 7, DN
  **19)** $\sim Cx$ — 17, 18, DS
  **20)** $Cx \cdot \sim Cx$ — 10, 19, Conj
  **21)** $/\therefore\ (\exists x)[(Ax \cdot Bx) \cdot (Ex \cdot Cx)]$ — 11-20, IP

**12.5.B. (434)**

1.                                              $/\therefore$  $(x)[(Fx \cdot Dx) \supset (Px \lor \sim Bx)]$

    **1)** $(x)\{(Dx \cdot Fx) \supset [\sim Px \supset \sim (Sx \lor Bx)]\}$   Pr

    **2)** $(Dx \cdot Fx) \supset [\sim Px \supset \sim (Sx \lor Bx)]$   1, UI

    **3)** $Fx \cdot Dx$   CP, $/\therefore$  $Px \lor \sim Bx$

    **4)** $Dx \cdot Fx$   3, Com

    **5)** $\sim Px \supset \sim (Sx \lor Bx)$   2, 4, MP

    **6)** $\sim \sim Px \lor \sim (Sx \lor Bx)$   5, Impl

    **7)** $Px \lor \sim (Sx \lor Bx)$   6, DN

    **8)** $Px \lor (\sim Sx \cdot \sim Bx)$   7, DeM

    **9)** $Px \lor (\sim Bx \cdot \sim Sx)$   8, Com

    **10)** $(Px \lor \sim Bx) \cdot (Px \lor \sim Sx)$   9, Dist

    **11)** $Px \lor \sim Bx$   10, Simp

    **12)** $(Fx \cdot Dx) \supset (Px \lor \sim Bx)$   3 - 11, CP

    **13)** $/\therefore$  $(x)[(Fx \cdot Dx) \supset (Px \lor \sim Bx)]$   12, UG

3.                                              $/\therefore$  $(x)[Bx \supset (Dx \cdot Ex)]$

    **1)** $(x)(Bx \supset Sx)$   Pr

    **2)** $(x)[(Bx \cdot Sx) \supset Ox]$   Pr

    **3)** $(x)\{(Sx \cdot Bx) \supset [Ox \supset (Dx \cdot Ex)]\}$   Pr

    **4)** $Bx \supset Sx$   1, UI

    **5)** $(Bx \cdot Sx) \supset Ox$   2, UI

    **6)** $(Sx \cdot Bx) \supset [Ox \supset (Dx \cdot Ex)]$   3, UI

    **7)** $Bx$   CP, $/\therefore$  $Dx \cdot Ex$

    **8)** $Sx$   4, 7, MP

    **9)** $Bx \cdot Sx$   7, 8, Conj

    **10)** $Ox$   5, 9, MP

    **11)** $Sx \cdot Bx$   9, Com

    **12)** $Ox \supset (Dx \cdot Ex)$   6, 11, MP

    **13)** $Dx \cdot Ex$   12, 10, MP

    **14)** $Bx \supset (Dx \cdot Ex)$   7 - 13, CP

    **15)** $/\therefore$  $(x)[Bx \supset (Dx \cdot Ex)]$   14, UG

**5.**                                              $/\therefore$ $(x)[(Px \cdot Sx) \supset (Rx \supset Ex)]$

   1) $(x)\{[Px \cdot (Sx \vee Tx)] \supset [Rx \supset (Ex \cdot Kx)]\}$    Pr

   2) $[Px \cdot (Sx \vee Tx)] \supset [Rx \supset (Ex \cdot Kx)]$    1, UI

   3) $Px \cdot Sx$    CP, $/\therefore$ $Rx \supset Ex$

   4) $Px$    3, Simp

   5) $Sx \cdot Px$    3, Com

   6) $Sx$    5, Simp

   7) $Sx \vee Tx$    6, Add

   8) $Px \cdot (Sx \vee Tx)$    4, 7, Conj

   9) $Rx \supset (Ex \cdot Kx)$    2, 8, MP

  10) $Rx$    CP, $/\therefore$ Ex

  11) $Ex \cdot Kx$    9, 10, MP

  12) $Ex$    11, Simp

  13) $Rx \supset Ex$    10 -12, CP

  14) $(Px \cdot Sx) \supset (Rx \supset Ex)$    3 - 14, CP

  15) $/\therefore$ $(x)[(Px \cdot Sx) \supset (Rx \supset Ex)]$    14, UG

**7.**                                              $/\therefore$ $(x)\{Vx \supset [(Cx \cdot Sx) \supset \sim Fx]\}$

   1) $(x)\{[(Rx \vee Fx) \cdot (Cx \cdot Sx)] \supset \sim Vx\}$    Pr

   2) $[(Rx \vee Fx) \cdot (Cx \cdot Sx)] \supset \sim Vx$    1, UI

   3) $Vx$    CP, $/\therefore$ $(Cx \cdot Sx) \supset \sim Fx$

   4) $\sim \sim Vx$    3, DN

   5) $\sim [(Rx \vee Fx) \cdot (Cx \cdot Sx)]$    2, 4, MT

   6) $\sim (Rx \vee Fx) \vee \sim (Cx \cdot Sx)$    5, DeM

   7) $\sim (Cx \cdot Sx) \vee \sim (Rx \vee Fx)$    6, Com

   8) $Cx \cdot Sx$    CP, $/\therefore$ $\sim Fx$

   9) $\sim \sim (Cx \cdot Sx)$    8, DN

  10) $\sim (Rx \vee Fx)$    7, 8, DS

  11) $\sim Rx \cdot \sim Fx$    10, DeM

  12) $\sim Fx \cdot \sim Rx$    11, Com

  13) $\sim Fx$    12, Simp

  14) $(Cx \cdot Sx) \supset \sim Fx$    8, 13, CP

  15) $Vx \supset [(Cx \cdot Sx) \supset \sim Fx]$    3 - 14, CP

  16) $/\therefore$ $(x)\{Vx \supset [(Cx \cdot Sx) \supset \sim Fx]\}$    15, UG

**12.6.A. (438–439)**

**1.**                                      /∴  ~ Bba

   **1)** Aab          Pr

   **2)** (x)(Bxa ⊃ ~ Aax)   Pr

   **3)** Bba ⊃ ~ Aab     2. UI

   **4)** ~ ~ Aab        1, DN

   **5)** /∴  ~ Bba      3, 4, MT

**3.**                                      /∴  (y)[Ay ⊃ (∃w)Cyw]

   **1)** (x)[Ax ⊃ (∃z)(Bz • Cxz)]   Pr

   **2)** Ay ⊃ (∃z)(Bz • Cyz)   1, UI

   **3)** Ay              CP, /∴  (∃w)Cyw

→ **4)** (∃z)(Bz • Cyz)     2, 3, MP

   **5)** Bw • Cyw       4, EI

   **6)** Cyw • Bw       5, Com

   **7)** Cyw          6, Simp

   **8)** (∃w)Cyw      7, EG

   **9)** Ay ⊃ (∃w)Cyw   3 -8, CP

  **10)** /∴  (y)[Ay ⊃ (∃w)Cyw]   9, UG

**5.**                                      /∴  (∃x)(y)(~ Cy ⊃ ~ By)

   **1)** (∃x)(y)[(Axy ⊃ By) ⊃ Cx]   Pr

   **2)** (y)[(Axy ⊃ By) ⊃ Cx]   1, EI

   **3)** (Axy ⊃ By) ⊃ Cx   2, UI

→ **4)** ~ Cx           CP, /∴  ~ By

   **5)** ~ (Axy ⊃ By)     3, 4, MT

   **6)** ~ (~ Axy ∨ By)    5, Impl

   **7)** ~ ~ Axy • ~ By    6, DeM

   **8)** ~ By • ~ ~ Axy    7, Com

   **9)** ~ By           8, Simp

  **10)** ~Cx ⊃ ~By      4 -9, CP

  **11)** (y)(~Cx ⊃ ~By)   10, UG

  **12)** /∴  (∃x)(y)(~Cx ⊃ ~By)   11, UG

**7.**                                                 $/ \therefore \ \sim (y)(Ay \supset Bxy)$

   **1)** $(x)\{[Ax \cdot (y)(Ay \supset Bxy)] \supset Bxx\}$    Pr

   **2)** $\sim (x)[Ax \supset (\exists y)Bxy]$    Pr

   **3)** $(\exists x)\sim [Ax \supset (\exists y)Bxy]$    2, QD

   **4)** $\sim [Ax \supset (\exists y)Bxy]$    3, EI

   **5)** $\sim [\sim Ax \vee (\exists y)Bxy]$    4, Impl

   **6)** $\sim \sim Ax \cdot \sim (\exists y)Bxy$    5, DeM

   **7)** $\sim \sim Ax$    6, Simp

   **8)** $\sim (\exists y)Bxy \cdot \sim \sim Ax$    6, Com

   **9)** $\sim (\exists y)Bxy$    8, Simp

   **10)** $(y)\sim Bxy$    9, QD

   **11)** $[Ax \cdot (y)(Ay \supset Bxy)] \supset Bxx$    1, UI

   **12)** $\sim Bxx$    10, UI

   **13)** $\sim [Ax \cdot (y)(Ay \supset Bxy)]$    11, 12, MT

   **14)** $\sim Ax \vee \sim (y)(Ay \supset Bxy)$    13, DeM

   **15)** $/ \therefore \ \sim (y)(Ay \supset Bxy)$    14, 7, DS

**12.6.B. (439–440)**

**1.**                               $/ \therefore \ Fpd$

   **1)** $(x)(Fxm \supset Fxd)$    Pr

   **2)** $Fpm$    Pr

   **3)** $Fpm \supset Fpd$    1, UI

   **4)** $/ \therefore \ Fpd$    3, 2, MP

**5.**                               $Tgw \supset \sim Hts$

   **1)** $(x)(Hxs \supset Axb)$    Pr

   **2)** $(x)(Txw \supset \sim Tbx)$    Pr

   **3)** $(x)(Atx \supset Txg)$    Pr

   **4)** $Hts \supset Atb$    1, UI

   **5)** $Tgw \supset \sim Tbg$    2, UI

   **6)** $Atb \supset Tbg$    3, UI

   **7)** $\sim Atb \supset \sim Hts$    4, Trans

   **8)** $\sim Tbg \supset \sim Atb$    6, Trans

   **9)** $\sim Tbg \supset \sim Hts$    8, 7, HS

   **10)** $/ \therefore \ Tgw \supset \sim Hts$    5, 9, HS

**3.**                               $/ \therefore \ \sim G_{73}$

   **1)** $(x)(y)(Gxy \supset \sim Gyx)$    Pr

   **2)** $G_{73}$    Pr

   **3)** $(y)(G_7y \supset \sim Gy_7)$    1, UI

   **4)** $G_{73} \supset \sim G_{37}$    3, UI

   **5)** $/ \therefore \ \sim G_{37}$    4, 2, MP

**7.**                                    /∴  (x){[Px • (y)(Py ⊃ Fxy)] ⊃ ~ Px}

    **1)** (x)(Px ⊃ ~ Fxx)                Pr
    **2)** Px ⊃ ~ Fxx                     1, UI
→  **3)** Px • (y)(Py ⊃ Fxy)             CP, /∴  ~ Px
    **4)** Px                             3, Simp
    **5)** (y)(Py ⊃ Fxy) • Px            3, Com
    **6)** (y)(Py ⊃ Fxy)                  5, Simp
    **7)** Px ⊃ Fxx                       6, UI
    **8)** Fxx                            4, 7, MP
    **9)** ~ ~ Fxx                        8, DN
    **10)** ~ Px                          2, 9, MT
    **11)** [Px • (y)(Py ⊃ Fxy)] ⊃ ~ Px   3 -10, CP
    **12)** /∴  (x){[Px • (y)(Py ⊃ Fxy)] ⊃ ~ Px}   11, UG

# CHAPTER 13

### 13.1.A. (444)

Develop your own position here.

### 13.1.B. (444–445)

Develop your own answers for this exercise. But be as creative as you can. The purpose of the exercise is for you to grasp how the meaning of a sentence can change given different contexts in which it is used. Compare and discuss your answers with your classmates.

### 13.2.A. (452)

1. All of the words in this exercise are English having standard meanings except 'wibbly'. The place of 'Wibbly' after the verb 'to wax', coupled with the '-ly' ending, suggests that 'wibbly'is an adverb modifying 'waxed'.

3. The '-ed' ending suggests that 'Tiddled' is a verb in the past tense. Following 'the', 'trik' is likely a noun. 'Tilley' appears to be a propername and the subject of the sentence. The combination, 'the tarry tuk', is the object of the English verb 'to toll'. In this phrase 'tuk' appears to be a noun modified by 'tarry'.

5. Following 'An', 'iglee iraa' is likely a noun phrase. The placement of 'iglee iraa' suggests that it is the subject of the sentence. 'Iglee' seems to be an adjective modifying 'iraa'. Coming after 'for the', 'boosic' appears to be a noun used as the object in the prepositional phrase modifying 'iraa'. The placement of 'coosta ceepa' after 'is a' suggests that it can be a predicate adjective modifying 'iraa'. 'Coosta' apparently is an adjective modifying 'ceepa'.

**13.2.B. (452)**

Use your own imagination and creative abilities here to concoct English sentences. Imagine that you are cracking a spy code. Compare and discuss your sentences with your classmates.

**13.2.C. (452)**

**1.** cat, mammal, animal, living organism

**3.** bachelor, male, adult, human

**5.** poem, epic, fiction, written work

**13.2.D. (452–453)**

1 and 7, 2 and 6, 3 and 8, 4 and 10, 5 and 9

**13.2.E. (453)**

**1.** 'Illegal drug' means a narcotic, often addictive, that is prohibited by law to be sold and/or used with the possible exception of being distributed through a prescription and used under the administration of a physician.

cocaine, crack, marijuana, morphine

**3.** 'Novel' means a long fictitious written piece, usually divided into smaller sections, such as chapters, typically having a plot disclosed through the speech and actions of various individuals appearing in the work.

*The Sound and the Fury, The Brothers Karamazov, The Castle, Don Quijote*

**5.** 'United States senator' means anyone who is a member of the United States senate either by election or appointment by a state governor.

Lloyd Bentsen, Dan Coata, Robert Dole, Sam Nunn

**7.** 'Communist government' means a form of classless society in which the materials and means of production, as well as the means of distribution of products, are owned by the government and not private citizens.

China, North Korea, USSR, Vietnam

**9.** 'Democratic government' means a form of society in which the materials and means of production, as well as the means of distribution of products, are owned by private citizens and not the government.

Canada, Great Britain, U.S.A., Germany

**13.2.F. (453)**

1) Barcelona is a city.
   Barcelona is a Spanish city.
   Barcelona is a Spanish port city.

2) Mike saw a human.
   Mike saw a woman.
   Mike saw Susie.

3) XYZ is a social organization.
   XYZ is a private club.
   XYZ is a college fraternity.

**13.2.G. (454)**

You are to develop your own answers here. However, refer to the relevant sections of this chapter in defending your opinions. Discuss your answers with your classmates.

### 13.2.H. (454)

You are to develop your own answers forthis exercise. However, refer to the relevant sections of this chapter in defending your opinions. Compare and discuss your answers with your classmates.

### 13.3.A. (465–466)

1. Enumerative, complete

3. Enumerative, complete

5. Definition by subclass, partial

7. Reforming

9. Synonymous

11. Enumerative, partial

15. Theoretical

19. Theoretical

23. Reforming

### 13.3.B. (466–467)

You are to develop your own answers for this exercise. However, refer to the relevant sections of this chapter in defending your opinions. Discuss your answers with your classmates.

### 13.4.A. (469–470)

1. No appropriate context. For instance, 'strike' is used not only in baseball but in talking about labor disputes.

3. Too broad. A canoe is not a ship but is a means of transportation through water.

5. Too narrow. A student can fear failing a test without having any bad feeling in the pit of his stomach.

7. Too broad. Whatever a homophlant is, it is not a cow or a horse.

9. Negative. Better to say that a parent is someone who has, or has had, a child.

11. Too narrow and too broad. Some religions, such as Hinduism, have no notion of God, whereas some religions, such as many Protestant groups, have no formalized worship.

15. Too broad. Typically in socialistic governments the principle means of manufacturing goods are also owned by the government.

### 13.4.B. (470)

You might wish to supply other precising definitions than the ones suggested here.

1. Anyone who can lift more than sixty pounds over his head and hold it there for five minutes.

3. Anyone who is five feet or less in height.

5. Anyone over 75 years of age.

### 13.4.C. (470)

1. Making a false statement with the intent to deceive. *False statement* is the genus and *intent to deceive* is the species.

**3.** Stealing someone else's intellectual property. *Stealing* is the genus and *intellectual property* the species.

**5.** A composition presented in verse. *Composition* is the genus and *presented in verse* the species.

### 13.4.D. (470)

You might wish to supply other operational definitions than the ones suggested here.

**1.** The density of an object is that amount of water displaced when the object is placed in a container of water.

**3.** The length of an object is the number of marks on a standard measuring device corresponding to that object when the measuring device is placed by the object such that the end of the measuring device is flush with one edge of the object.

**5.** The hunger of an organism is the rate of time taken to consume an amount of food appropriate to that organism.

### 13.4.E. (470–471)

**1.** Belize, Costa Rica, El Salvador, Guatemala, Honduras, Nicaragua, and Panama

**3.** Bulgaria, Czechoslovakia, Hungary, Poland, Romania, and the USSR

**5.** Harry Truman, Dwight Eisenhower, John Kennedy, Lyndon Johnson, Richard Nixon, Gerald Ford, Jimmy Carter, Ronald Reagan, and George Bush

### 13.4.F. (471)

You might wish to supply other operational definitions than the ones suggested here.

**1.** 'Contemporary popular music' means acid rock, hard rock, jazz, etc.

**3.** 'Motorized vehicle' means airplane, automobile, motorcycle, ship, etc.

**5.** 'Sexually transmitted disease' means *AIDS*, gonorrhea, syphilis, etc.

> In the following "answers" for Chapters 14 and 15, the name of the fallacy occurring in the exercise is given along with a brief comment about this fallacy in the particular example in which it occurs. The student might show more precisely where, and how, the named fallacy is found in each exercise. This could be done by putting the argument in standard form and then reconstructing it where necessary to supply missing premises or conclusions. Of course, if an example is not an argument, there can be no fallacy in it.

# CHAPTER 14

### Ambiguity, Equivocation, Vagueness, and Relative Words

### Pages 490–491, for Sections 5–8

**1.** *Vagueness* It is not clear what is meant by the expressions 'immaturity', 'verbal infelicity', and 'ignorance'. Each of these has a wide range of meanings. Not making his meanings clear, the author can also be rightly accused of using emotional language to persuade the reader to accept the conclusion that 'Mr. Quayle appears to be one of the least qualified candidates to appear on a national ticket in modern times'.

**3.** *Equivocation*: 'Guilt' is used in two different ways in the premises. Guilt as felt by a juror is an emotion of self-reproach for real or imagined transgressions of social, institutional, or legal standards. Used in the legal sense, 'guilt' means the establishment, by strict legal procedures, of sufficient evidence presented to indicate that a defendant has broken a law.

5. *Relative words*: The author is arguing that 'We should be responsible for only so much [financial] help for the elderly'. The word, 'bankrupt', appearing in the premises, is a relative word. A large institution, such as a government, might encounter serious cash flow problems, diminished bond ratings, and might have to raise taxes. But an individual who faces bankruptcy will likely have no sources of income capable of becoming solvent again, and might lose everything he owns.

7. This is not an argument, but a *description* of a specific use of 'rod'.

9. Ambiguity (syntactical): 'simple not' is syntactically ambiguous. It is not clear whether 'simply' is an adverb modifying the preceding verb, 'is', or an adjective modifying the noun 'difference'. Is apartheid simply not a difference of opinion, or not a simple difference of opinion but a complex one?

11. *Relative words*: 'Sick' is a relative word in that what constitutes a problem for professional sports might differ greatly from what constitutes a problem for the arguer's sport which is presumably an amateur one. Sickness in professional sports might involve greed by both owners and players, strikes and lockouts, illicit drug use by players, deliberate attempts to injure opponents, etc. The arguer is claiming that since his sport does not have the same types of problems that some professional sports do, his sport is not really sick. But his sport might have serious problems such as steroid use and point shaving.

15. *Equivocation*: The use of 'drug' in this argument shifts between two distinct meanings. The drug problem in high schools tends to involve the use of psychoactive, illegal drugs for unsupervised recreation. Much of the drug use cited by the arguer with respect to professional sports involves the enhancing or re-pairing of athletic function by experienced doctors and trainers using mostly legal drugs.

### Appeal to Irrelevant Authority, Appeal to Pity, Appeal to the Masses, and Appeal to Special Interests

### Pages 496–497, for Sections 9–12

1. *Appeal to pity*: Instead of providing reasons why Cooper should not be executed, the arguer tries to evoke the receiver's sympathy for Copper's situation. The exercise might also be seen as an instance of *appeal to special interests*. It is true that everyone makes mistakes, and so anyone might be interested in ensuring that mistakes are not too harshly punished.

3. This is not an argument, but a *report* of what the federal government has done in a certain situation.

5. *Appeal to irrelevant authority*: Indeed, Dr. James Naismith invented the game of basketball. Nonetheless, what he said about the game a half a century ago cannot be considered to have come from a relevant authority of the game as it is played today. Naismith knew basketball in its infancy, when it bore little resemblance to the present game of fast breaks, slam dunks, fancy pitch plays, college zone defenses, and seven-foot centers.

7. *Appeal to pity*: The joy and love that evidently surrounds the adopted granddaughter leads the receiver of the argument to pity those who lack these qualities.

11. *Appeal to special interests*: The arguer is appealing to the particular interests of single mothers and businesses to try to justify paying students, in many cases, less to do the same work as single mothers. No reasons are provided as to why one's social position is relevant to the amount that one should be paid to do a given job.

15. *Appeal to pity*: The arguer uses the severe abuse to which some infants are subjected to move the receiver to view abortion as preferable to such a life. But child abuse is a problem not directly connected with abortion, arising also in families that never even considered termination of pregnancy. No reason is given to think that lack of access to abortion is in any way connected to child abuse.

**Appeal to Ignorance, Fake Precision, Hasty Conclusion, and Neglect of Relevant Evidence**

**Pages 502–503, for Sections 13–15**

1. *Fake precision*: Undoubtedly some medical treatments provide no benefit to the patient, but how could the amount of such useless treatment ever be measured? For instance, a number of different treatments might be tried on a cancer patient. If the cancer goes into remission, could one determine which treatment or combination of treatments, *if any*, were causal in this remission? To say that thirty percent of what health care does has no apparent benefit is to use an exact percentage to bolster a dubious claim.

3. *Fake precision*: Since many people will not admit to [illegal] drug use, and since random testing is generally not done, it is difficult to see how the arguer determined that 25% of assembly line workers use drugs. An appeal to 'certain sources' only further clouds the legitimacy of the figures presents. In addition, it might also be an instance of the fallacy of fake precision to claim that 25% [illegal] drug use leads to a 25% decrease in productivity, since productivity is itself difficult to measure.

5. Appeal to ignorance: The argument claims that since no other satisfactory explanation has been found, the divine explanation must be the correct one. The arguer is requiring scientists to provide evidence and taking their failure to do so as evidence for her position, although she provides no evidence either.

7. This is not an argument, but a *description* of how a particular hypothesis is tested.

11. *Fake precision*: It is virtually impossible accurately to estimate the number of undetected cases of a disease.

15. *Hasty conclusion*: Although, with the exception of Chernobyl, there has never been a fatality at a nuclear power plant, only a small number of such plants have been in operation for only a relatively short period of time. Accidents are more likely to happen as the plants age and their systems become more likely to fail, and as plant operators are lulled into carelessness by years of safe operations.

# CHAPTER 15

**Ad Hominem, Tu Quoque, Red Herring, and Straw Man**

**Pages 509–511, for Sections 1–4**

1. *Red herring*: In this example the ethical issue at hand is whether or not human organs should be bought and sold. That there is little in this world that is not for sale is irrelevant to this issue in that human organs are not comparable to other sorts of things that are for sale. Furthermore, many things that are for sale, from an ethical viewpoint, ought not to be for sale. This example can also be read as containing a suggestion of *two wrongs make a right*. Many things are illegally sold and no one makes any great fuss over it. So what is wrong with selling human organs? Of course, such thinking is irrelevant to questions of ethics.

3. *Tu quoque*: The arguer claiming that since many 'good' presidents engaged in extramarital affairs, it is acceptable behavior for a current president or presidential candidate to do so.

But such *two wrongs make a right* type of thinking is not relevant to establishing the conclusion of an argument.

5. *Ad hominem (circumstantial)*: It is strongly suggested that Kemp is disqualified from opposing abortion because 'his own family was involved in an abortion'. However, rather than disqualify him, his family involvement and his relation to it might have provided him with a perspective on the issue that he would not otherwise have had.

7. *Straw man*: Kennedy's portrayal of Bork's vision of America is surely not accurate. Almost everyone would abhor an America like Kennedy describes here. Bork's vision is of free enterprise and an unobtrusive Supreme Court, not of totalitarianism.

9. *Straw man*: This argument assumes that Gorbachev's motives must be devious ones. But there is considerable reason to believe that he is trying peacefully to solve a number of extremely serious problems in his country. Indeed, events since the penning of this argument (1987) have shown how seriously flawed this way of thinking was and is.

13. *Ad hominem (circumstantial)*: Rose is claiming that those who provided evidence against him cannot be trusted because they have been involved in illegal activities. In effect, he is saying that anyone involved in crime is not capable of telling the truth. That a person has been involved in crime might be good reason to be especially on guard concerning any possible error in what that person is saying. This, however, is a different consideration and cannot be used to dismiss what a person is saying as, in fact, a lie.

### Is-ought Fallacy, Decptive Alternatives, Wishful Thinking, and Novelty

### Pages 515–517, for Sections 5–8

1. *Deceptive alternatives*: Contrary to this example, there are more than two directions in which one can go when facing a conflict. Other alternatives include backing away from the conflict, especially if the conflict is a trivial one. Or one could perhaps find a way of working around the conflict, allowing one to have her own way without addressing the conflict.

3. *Wishful thinking*: While it is true that having a single ticket might enable one to win a lottery, Taylor engages in wishful thinking by claiming that if you're going to win, then you're going to win, as if it is predestined who will win. Clearly one's probability of winning rises with the number of tickets held, although of course winning remains remote in any case. Any predestination might just as likely involve which *ticket* will win, rather than which *person* will win.

5. *Novelty*: It is not made clear why new values should be embraced. The argument provides no reason other than their very newness. Were one to take the arguer's advice, how long would it be before the receiver would hear the call once again to "update" his values?

7. This is not an argument but a *description* of what someone plans to accomplish.

11. *Deceptive alternatives*: It is not the case that the only alternatives are sharing a common language or being a tower of Babel. In many European countries, such as Switzerland, several languages are in wide use. This causes no appreciable problems and provides a degree of cultural diversity and enrichment.

15. *Is-ought*: To 'return to normality' by dropping the Fairness Doctrine is to return to the American tradition of government not interfering in the marketplace. This is an *appeal to tradition* because no reasons are given as to why a laissez-faire policy is the best one other than that it is 'normal', i.e., that it is traditional.

**Confusing Sufficient and Necessary Conditions, Questionable Causes, Slippery Slope, and Gambler's Fallacy**

**Pages 522–524, for Sections 9–12**

1. *Questionable cause:* No evidence is given that women entering the work force caused the problems cited, other than the claim that the problems arose after women began to work. Thus, this is an instance of the *post hoc fallacy.*

3. *Slippery slope:* It is claimed that if Pakistan falls to the Soviets, the Soviets will be able to obtain control over a wide sweep of countries. No reason is given as to why this must happen.

5. *Gambler's fallacy:* It is the case that each additional collision adds wear and tear to a athlete's body, but this does not account for a player's broken arm. As the coach correctly points out, a broken arm is a freak injury, resulting from a large amount of force being applied to the limb in just the right way. The probability of a player breaking a bone is the same on the 1000th play as it was on the first. Of course, the more plays in which a player participates, the higher the chance that he will sustain some freak injury during his career. But that a player has already participated in a large number of plays without injury does not affect the odds of a freak injury occurring on the next play. Unlike wear and tear injures, the probability of a freak injury occurring on the next play is independent of what happened during previous plays. So, the decision of the coach to allow Jones to play cannot be blamed for his broken arm.

7. *Confusion of necessary and sufficient conditions:* Better labeling of food products is necessary if one is to overcome nutritional ignorance, but it is certainly not sufficient. One must still be able to read this information and to interpret it properly. Further, people will have to be educated to put a high value on nutritional excellence and a lower value on convenience of food preparation.

9 *Confusion of necessary and sufficient conditions:* Banning assault rifles is a necessary condition for keeping them out of the hands of the public. But the arguer's complaint is that it is not a sufficient one. This is true, for as the arguer says, some criminals will manage to acquire them. There might be no set of sufficient conditions that will prevent *every* criminal from obtaining assault rifles. But there is also no certain way to prevent every murder. One should be satisfied to prevent the vast majority of such crimes. The arguer is assigning a goal that is impossible to attain and then complaining because the goal cannot be obtained by banning assault rifles.

13. *Slippery slope:* The claim is that increased drug interdiction by the federal government must inevitably lead to a national police force. However, no reason is given why this must be so.

**Circular Argument, Inconsistencies, Factual Certainty, and Question Begging**

**Pages 529–531, for Sections 13–16**

1. *Circular argument:* This argument is effect says that the Japanese depend on their government because they depend on their government.

3. *Factual certainty:* The final claim indicates that the arguer is not prepared to consider any evidence that might indicate that road expansion is not the best alternative. He dismisses increased gas taxes without either a thought or a trial.

5. *Question begging:* To refer to capital punishment as 'murder' is to beg the question against it. The arguer defines 'capital punishment' as murder while it might appear in the argument that she is presenting the results of her investigations. Here is also a *tu quoque* fallacy. Two wrongs do not make a right. The failure to execute those on death row, rather than providing reasons to spare the woman in question, might provide reason to execute her and many of them.

7. *Question begging:* Calling eccentrics 'creative, forward-thinking professionals' appears to be a factual claim. It, however, begs the question by defining 'eccentricity' in a very favorable way.

8. This is not an argument, but a *description* concerning the attitudes and feelings of a person towards having children.

9. This is not an argument, but a *description* concerning the attitudes of a person toward anti-abortion activities.

13. *Question begging*: The question is begged when the arguer introduces the notion of true Christianity in such a way as to preclude, by definition, any consideration of the ordination of homosexuals. There is also working in this argument an instance of *factual certainty* in what constitutes *true* Christianity.

———*Ad majorem glorium Dei*———

# INDEX

Numerals in *bold italics* indicate the page where an entry is first introduced and defined in the text. Numerals in brackets indicate the page where an entry is listed and defined at the end of a chapter.

$$\frac{(\alpha)\ \Phi\alpha}{/\therefore\ \Phi\beta}$$

### Universal Instantiation (UI)

where '$\beta$' stands either for (1) the name of an individual that occurs in '$\beta$' at all, and only those, places where '$\alpha$' is a free individual variable in '$\Phi\alpha$', or for (2) an individual variable that occurs free in '$\Phi\beta$' at all, and only those, places where '$\alpha$' is a free individual variable in '$\Phi\alpha$'.

$$\frac{(\exists\alpha)\ \Phi\alpha}{/\therefore\ \Phi\beta}$$

### Existential Instantiation (EI)

where (1) '$\beta$' stands for an individual variable that occurs free in '$\Phi\beta$' at all, and only those, places where '$\alpha$' is free in '$\Phi\alpha$', and (2) whatever individual variable '$\beta$' represents in the context of a particular proof, that individual variable cannot previously appear as a free variable in that proof.

$$\frac{\Phi\beta'}{/\therefore\ (\alpha)\Phi\alpha}$$

### Universal Generalization (UG)

where (1) '$\beta$' stands for an individual variable that occurs free in '$\Phi\beta$' at all, and only those, places where '$\alpha$' is an individual variable that occurs free in '$\Phi\alpha$'; (2) '$\beta$' does not occur free in any statement function, '$\Phi\beta$', obtained by Existential Instantiation; and (3), in a Conditional Proof, '$\beta$' is an individual variable that does not occur free in an assumption within whose scope '$\Phi\beta$' lies.

$$\frac{\Phi\beta}{/\therefore\ (\exists\alpha)\ \Phi\alpha}$$

### Existential Generalization (EG)

where (1) '$\beta$' represents either the name of an individual or an individual variable, and (2) '$\alpha$' represents a free individual variable in '$\Phi\alpha$' at all, and only those, places where '$\beta$' occurs in '$\Phi\beta$'.

$$(\exists\alpha)\ \Phi\alpha\ ::\ \sim(\alpha)\sim\Phi\alpha$$

$$(\exists\alpha)\sim\Phi\alpha\ ::\ \sim(\alpha)\ \Phi\alpha$$

$$\sim(\exists\alpha)\ \Phi\alpha\ ::\ (\alpha)\sim\Phi\alpha$$

$$\sim(\exists\alpha)\sim\Phi\alpha\ ::\ (\alpha)\ \Phi\alpha$$

### Quantificational Denial (QD)

# Truth Tree Rules

### Existential Instantiation (EI)

where (1) '$\beta$' occurs in '$\Phi\beta$' at all those places where '$\alpha$' occurs free in '$\Phi\alpha$', (2) '$\beta$' is an ambiguous name, (3) this name has not previously occurred in the branch in which '$\Phi\beta$' is appended, and (4) '$\Phi\beta$' is appended to every branch in which '$(\exists\alpha)\Phi\alpha$' previously appears.

### Universal Instantiation (UI)

where (1) '$\beta$' is the name of an individual that (2) occurs in '$\Phi\beta$' at all those places where '$\alpha$' occurs free in '$\Phi\alpha$'.

### Quantificational Denial